DR MUHAJIR

DR MUHAJIR

Hand of the Cause of God
Knight of Bahá'u'lláh

ÍRÁN FURÚTAN MUHÁJIR

Bahá'í
Publishing
Trust

Published by
The Bahá'í Publishing Trust
27 Rutland Gate
London SW7 1PD

Commemorative Edition

Published 28 May 1992, to commemorate the placing of the scroll bearing the Roll of Honour of the Knights of Bahá'u'lláh at the entrance door of the inner Sanctuary of the Most Holy Shrine.

British Library Cataloguing-in-Publication Data:

A catalogue record for this book is available from the British Library

ISBN 1 870989 25 2 (cased)
ISBN 1 870989 26 0 (paper)

FOR GISU

Dr Raḥmatu'lláh Muhájir, Hand of the Cause of God, Knight of Bahá'u'lláh (1923–1979).

May My praise, salutations, and greetings rest upon the stars of the heaven of Thy knowledge — the Hands of Thy Cause — they who circled round Thy Will, spoke not save after Thy leave, and clung not save unto Thy hem. They are servants whose mention and praise are recorded in the Holy Writ, Thy Books and Tablets, wherein are extolled their services, victories, and high resolve. Through them the standards of Thy oneness were raised in Thy cities and realms, and the banners of Thy sanctity were uplifted in Thy Kingdom. . . . Praise be to Thee, O my God, that Thou hast aided me to make mention of them and to praise them in their stations in Thy Cause and in Thy days.

Bahá'u'lláh

CONTENTS

Introduction xv

Foreword xix

1 A NOBLE SPIRITUAL HERITAGE 1
Ancestry; arrival at 'Akká; opposition to the new Faith; his parents; childhood; teenage years; with the pioneers; marriage; pilgrimage; intercontinental conference 1953; the determined pioneer.

2 A TRUE PIONEER 33
From Iran to Indonesia; our first miracle; by boat to the Mentawai Islands; welcomed by 'Mr Mayor'; the island store; Knights of Bahá'u'lláh; settling in Muarasiberut; the first Mentawai Bahá'í; doctor to the body — and the soul; a new way of life; communications from the Guardian; deepening the new believers; the Governor calls; conference and convention; Hand of the Cause of God; the passing of the beloved Guardian; a plea for caution; leaving the islands; praise and recognition; persecution in Indonesia.

3 A GLORIOUS FUTURE 91
From Africa to Asia; 'the pupil of the eye'; spiritual conquest of a continent; sending reinforcements; 'his heart was with the villagers'; intensive teaching projects; progressive teaching; consolidation and expansion; 'the lions of Bahá'u'lláh; exhaustion and enthusiasm; 'it depends on the teacher . . .'

4 AT ONE WITH THE MASSES 167
The Indian Subcontinent: India, Pakistan, Bangladesh, Nepal; Central Asia: Afghanistan, Turkey, Iran; South-East Asia: Burma, Laos, Malaysia, Philippines, Thailand, Vietnam, Cambodia; North-East Asia: Hong Kong, Japan, Korea, Taiwan, Macao.

5 IN THE MIDMOST HEART OF THE OCEAN 359
Australia; New Zealand; the Pacific region; Samoa; Fiji; Papua New Guinea; Guam; 1978 — his last visit.

6 MASS TEACHING IS POSSIBLE 401
Austria; Belgium; Cyprus; France; Germany; Greece; Iceland; Ireland; Italy; the Netherlands; Portugal; Scandinavia; Spain; Switzerland; the United Kingdom.

7 TEACHING NEEDS CERTITUDE 455
Hawaii; USA; Canada; his final visit; Caribbean.

8 ONLY HEAVEN IS HIGHER 495
His first visit: Bolivia, Paraguay, Brazil, Peru, Ecuador, Colombia, Panama, Costa Rica, Nicaragua, El Salvador, Guatemala; sharing the vision — Bolivia; ingenuity, patience, persistence — Brazil; unimaginable heights — Chile; 'Villa Raḥmat' — Colombia; rules for mass conversion — Ecuador; his restless soul.

9 THE OCEAN OF HIS MERCY 573
His passing; words of sympathy; Hands of the Cause of God; Bahá'í World Centre; Continental Boards of Counsellors; National Spiritual Assemblies; local Spiritual Assemblies; remembered around the world.

10 TIME IS SHORT 617
Travelling for the love of Bahá'u'lláh; never a moment's rest; father and family man; detachment and generosity; relations with Hands of the Cause; a friend to all; love and laughter; the power of prayer; at the World Centre; protection of the Faith; a life of dedication.

Appendix: Itinerary 665

Notes & References 674

ABOUT THE AUTHOR

Írán Furútan Muhájir was born 1933 into one of the most distinguished Bahá'í families of Persia, and married Raḥmatu'lláh Muhájir in 1951. In 1954 she pioneered with her husband to the Mentawai Islands, Indonesia, and attained the distinction of Knight of Bahá'u'lláh.

As well as ably assisting, and often travelling with, her husband after his appointment as a Hand of the Cause of God in 1957, Iran Muhájir has pursued an active life of service to the Bahá'í Faith in her own right. She has been a member of several national and local Spiritual Assemblies, and has served on a variety of Bahá'í institutions, including a period as manager of the Bahá'í Publishing Trust of India. She has compiled several popular Bahá'í books, including *The Mystery of God* (a portrait of 'Abdu'l-Bahá), and *Dawn of a New Day* (the collected letters of Shoghi Effendi to the Bahá'ís of India), and created a correspondence course used in many countries involved in mass teaching. She has travelled to more than 50 countries, and continues to work on many important international Bahá'í assignments.

She holds a Masters degree in Middle Eastern Studies from Harvard University, and makes her home in Washington D.C.

ACKNOWLEDGEMENTS

In the years of our pioneering in Indonesia and my husband's subsequent travels around the world, there were often extended periods when I was not with him. Although he often talked about his trips, I did not record the details, and our hectic lifestyle, constantly moving from country to country, meant that it was impossible to keep letters and documents. I therefore had to ask for the help and assistance of his many friends around the Bahá'í world in compiling the material for this book.

Hundreds responded. Friends sent notes of their personal memories and many national Spiritual Assemblies provided excerpts from their Bahá'í journals and newsletters, and from relevant assembly minutes. They all kindly gave me the freedom to use their words in whatever context I felt was needed, and the Persian friends allowed me to translate their letters. I am grateful to all of them. If any places in which Raḥmat served or events in which he was involved have been omitted, it has not been by design but simply for lack of information.

The Audio-Visual and Research Departments of the Universal House of Justice graciously supplied most of the photographs, and excerpts from Raḥmat's letters to the Bahá'í World Centre as well as his travel itineraries. I am indebted to Joseph Shinnik and to Dr Vahid Rafati for their assistance. I am particularly grateful to Janet Khan, who helped at the initial stages of this project, and who greatly encouraged me not to despair of the huge task I had to face. My special appreciation goes to Gordon Kerr for his dedication and assistance.

Finally I would like to express my thanks to Bahia and Faramarz Ettehadieh, and the staff of the United Kingdom Bahá'í Publishing Trust: Wendi Momen, George M. Ballentyne and Simin Yousefi.

INTRODUCTION

It has taken me nearly ten years of research to finish this book. Trying to collate all the materials about a man who spent most of his life continually travelling in the path of service to Bahá'u'lláh, proved almost an impossible task. For me personally, it has been a heart-rending experience, for Dr Muhájir, besides being a Hand of the Cause of God, was my beloved life-companion and I could not write about him dispassionately. It has taken time, but I have tried to make this an honest and balanced account, which will give a glimpse of his services to the Faith, provide an insight into his character and show something of the history and progress of the communities he visited.

It has not been my objective to write in detail about every aspect of his life. Rather, my aim has been to demonstrate the power of faith and share an example of how total dedication can succeed against all odds.

Dr Muhájir's mission was to take the glad tidings of the advent of Bahá'u'lláh to the masses of the world. He was one of the few in his generation to understand the urgency of the times, and the hunger of the millions of waiting souls who long for God's healing message of hope and unity. He has been described as perhaps the greatest mass teacher of the Faith, bringing thousands into the fold of Bahá'u'lláh. The philosophy behind his thoughts and actions, however, are not discussed here, as this is beyond my expertise. Dr Muhájir was moved more by his devotion to the beloved Guardian, and his conviction that service to the Faith was the most important thing in the world, than by any other belief. I have therefore focused on those aspects of his life which best illustrate this.

As a Hand of the Cause, he was also concerned with the protection of the Faith, and on behalf of the Universal House of Justice, had to take action to preserve the unity and integrity of the Cause. There were sometimes grave problems, which required firm measures, such as dealing with Covenant-breakers. I have tried to bypass mention of such events, as he would have wanted, and have instead focused on those activities which brought him joy in his often arduous life.

His constant movement from place to place in service to the Faith meant that much of his life had to be pieced together from secondary sources such as travel documents, Bahá'í news reports and personal letters and memoirs. The best insights, however, can be gained from his own diaries and notebooks, most of which have been reproduced here. I have faithfully translated these from the Persian to share the thoughts and concerns which motivated him during his globe-encircling journeys. Dr Muhájir's notes could be used as a manual for teaching, containing points on Bahá'í life and service, all of which are based on the Writings and the instructions of the beloved Guardian, as well as his own experience of the development and triumph of the Cause in many lands.

From his diaries and the accounts of others it will be seen that Dr Muhájir was a man of bold ideas and firm convictions. In some ways he was ahead of his time. His vision of the Cause was always on a grand scale, not readily understood by others, but most of his proposals have either come to pass or are now being implemented.

His itineraries were so complex and his records of some visits so brief, that the only way to present an intelligible account has been to group them systematically by continent: a chronological description of his life would have been impossible.

If some of the names and descriptions of places and people appear misspelled or inaccurate, this is entirely my fault. When there was doubt as to the meaning, a literal translation of what was in the diary has been given.

This work is by no means complete. Many other stories about Dr Muhájir will surely come to light, and future historians will no doubt write volumes about the effects of his labours. My intention has been to depict, as accurately as I could, the life of a man who lived only to serve Bahá'u'lláh, and who tried to carry out the instructions of the beloved Guardian to the best of his ability – a man who preferred to be called simply by his first name, 'Raḥmat', and whom Shoghi Effendi described as 'a true pioneer'.

I hope readers will look kindly on this humble effort.

5/192

v. Dorp 4568

DJAWATAN POS TELEGRAP- DAN TELEPON

99

Telegram No.

Diterima dari :

Tanggal : / 19

Djam :

Oleh :

LT = PAYMAN DJAKARTA INDONESIA

KANTOR: DJAKARTA

N. B. - Djawatan P.T.T. dan Kantor Telegrap partikulir tidak membajar kerugian disebabkan oleh tjatjat, tidak sampainja telegram dalam waktu jang tertentu atau hilangnja telegram.

Telegram dari :	Bilangan Kata	Tgl.	Djam.

PETUNDJUK DJABATAN

Via CW.

TAV201 EPAL425 TEHERAN 32 4 2000 =

BELOVED GUARDIAN CABLED QUOTE INFORM RAHMATULLAH MOHAJER ABULQASIM FAIZI THEIR ELEVATION RANK HAND CAUSE CONFIDENT NEW HONOUR WILL ENHANCE RECORD THEIR HISTORIC SERVICES UNQUOTE KINDLY INFORM MOHAJER IMMEDIATELY =

RAWHANI +

FOREWORD

How could we, a group of Bahá'í children in a certain neighbourhood of Ṭihrán, imagine that one among us was destined to play a significant role in the spiritual regeneration of the world? Raḥmat was a soft-spoken, hard-working, normal boy, unassuming and rather detached. I remember he was excellent at memorizing prayers and passages from the Writings, which he chanted in his sweet, mellow voice, and that he had a natural way of initiating a conversation about the Bahá'í Faith with friend and stranger alike. Looking back on those childhood days, I can see that Raḥmat was indeed 'a mine rich in gems of inestimable value'. His hidden treasure was revealed for all to see when he stepped into the arena of service with unique zeal and devotion, first as a Knight of Bahá'u'lláh, and later as a Hand of the Cause of God.

The Iranian Bahá'í community of the 1920s was mostly composed of believers who were born and raised in Bahá'í families, welded together over two or three generations by the ever-blazing fire of persecution. The children of those families, following in the footsteps of their parents, were always together, whether at school, at play, or in Bahá'í classes. Raḥmat and I became good friends.

After our school days we pursued our university studies at different faculties. We met again early in 1958, under greatly changed circumstances. Raḥmat had been with the other Hands of the Cause in the Holy Land for their first conclave after the funeral of the beloved Guardian. On his way back to Indonesia he stopped off to meet the friends in India. I was eager to see him again, not only because he was an old friend, but also because he was a Hand of the Cause, from whom I could seek comfort in the bewilderment of those ominous times, when the Bahá'ís of the world were grief-stricken and dazed by the sudden passing of Shoghi Effendi.

As we walked towards each other at the airport, I wondered how I should greet him? As a Hand of the Cause or as one of my old friends? How would he react? I was soon disarmed by his genuine humility and love, and by his unassuming manner. Although heartbroken at Shoghi Effendi's passing, he radiated confidence and determination. When we arrived at my home in New Delhi, the first thing he asked me was, 'How do you expect me to behave as a Hand of the Cause?' I had not expected such a direct question and found it difficult to reply. This question revealed the degree of his humility, and his conscientiousness to perform his allotted task as a Hand of the Cause of God. One can hardly imagine the weighty responsibilities which the Hands of the Cause had to bear in those days.

Many nations and peoples will be eternally indebted to Dr Muhájir for his guidance and encouragement in starting the process of mass teaching. As secretary of the National Spiritual Assembly of India at that time, I saw him set about his work in that country, which soon welcomed hundreds of thousands of believers into the Faith. This work was so blessed that it has now produced a beautiful House of Worship in the heart of the Indian sub- continent, which has itself proclaimed the Faith of Bahá'u'lláh to millions.

The next time Dr Muhájir came to India, he had already collected a number of quotations from the Bahá'í Writings about that country. He always sought guidance from the Writings, and wanted to delve into our national archives to find out what instructions the beloved Guardian had given the believers in India. He reminded us that 'Abdu'l-Bahá had said in one of His Tablets that the caravan of the Faith will make its camp in every corner of India. Raḥmat was preparing to convert us to the idea of mass teaching, the importance of which was not understood by most of the friends. He read a passage from the Writings of Bahá'u'lláh, which states that His Message was not intended to reach or benefit one country or one people only, but that 'mankind, in its entirety, must firmly adhere to whatsoever hath been revealed and vouchsafed unto it.' Dr Muhájir also reminded us that Shoghi Effendi, a few years before his passing, had stressed the importance of teaching the masses in India.

It was through Dr Muhájir's dynamic approach that a dormant Bahá'í community, which is what India was at the time, was suddenly electrified, speeding along a difficult terrain, labouring day and night without even feeling the hardships on the way. Whatever we were doing for the Cause in India, Dr Muhájir would always encourage us to do more; and when a trace of fatigue appeared among the friends, he used to come himself to cheer us up and lead the way.

Forsaking his own ease and comfort, he went places no pioneer wanted to go. Once he arrived at my home in New Delhi unannounced early in the morning, while we were having breakfast. He had come directly from mass teaching activities. I went to embrace him, as is the Persian custom, but he warned, 'Don't touch me! I'm full of lice!' Nothing could deter him from serving the Cause; for the sake of diffusing the Word of God, he would accept every difficulty.

Dr Muhájir seldom told stories about himself, but on his travels he would occasionally share some of his adventures as a way of encouraging the pioneers. One such adventure concerned a visit to a community of Indians in a remote mountainous area of South America. As night came on he was offered the 'place of honour', a hammock on the highest branch of the tree, so that he would be protected from predators during the night. This was a safe, cool and comfortable place until, in the middle of the night, the branch suddenly broke and Raḥmat fell onto a lower one which, luckily, held, and may have saved his life.

Dr Muhájir was a gentle, humble and unassuming soul, but when it came to the work of the Cause, he possessed a power of persuasion which I have not seen in anyone else. In 1961, when mass teaching was first seriously carried out in India, the National Spiritual Assembly was faced with many important decisions. I was ill in bed with fever when Raḥmat called to say that he would be attending the meeting of the National Spiritual Assembly that day. I explained that I could not come, as I was burning with fever and could not leave the house. He said nothing to me, but the next time I opened my eyes, there he was, with the eight other members of the National Spiritual Assembly sitting around my bed! It was a strange way to hold our meeting, but I am glad that we did, for it proved to be a significant one and we reached some very important decisions concerning the development of the Cause in India.

Dr Muhájir was always emphatic that Bahá'í communities, national or local, should be a mirror of unity. He used to quote Bahá'u'lláh's Tablet admonishing the Hands of the Cause of His time, that should they perceive any sign of disunity among the friends anywhere, they should not rest until the last trace of discord is dispelled, and harmony and love prevail once more. Dr Muhájir sought to unify the Bahá'ís by mobilizing them in the common task of teaching, assuring them that it would create harmony, even among those who could not see eye-to-eye on many issues.

His extensive practical experience in mass teaching makes his life a valuable guide for all those who wish to teach the Cause of God. As this book reveals, his wise counsels have been the reason for the expansion of the Faith in many parts of the world. His love and devotion to the Cause and to the beloved Guardian motivated him to hasten from country to country, from continent to continent, to proclaim the Faith, in many localities for the first time. He was a harbinger of the Light which will illumine the world.

Those who were close to him noticed his sense of urgency, as if he were acutely aware of the shortness of time he had to serve the Cause. Because of his wealth of knowledge and experience, his unique insights were of great assistance to the Universal House of Justice, particularly in the formulation of international and national teaching plans.

I recall how much Dr Muhájir relied on prayer in all his undertakings, how he would sometimes recite the well known passage from the Tablets of the Divine Plan, chanting with his beautiful voice, supplicating on behalf of the friends:

> O Thou incomparable God! O Thou Lord of the Kingdom! These souls are Thy heavenly army. Assist them and, with the cohorts of the Supreme Concourse, make them victorious . . . O God! Be Thou their supporter and their helper, and in the wilderness, the mountain, the valley, the forests the prairies and the seas, be Thou their confidant . . .

Among the quotations he usually carried with him was an excerpt from the Will and Testament of 'Abdu'l-Bahá. Whenever I read this beautiful passage I cannot help but remember dear Dr Muhájir. Raising the call of 'Yá-Bahá'u'l-Abhá!' all over the world, he bore aloft the standard placed in his hand by the beloved Guardian and carried out this injunction of the Master to the very end:

The disciples of Christ forgot themselves and all earthly things, forsook their cares and belongings, purged themselves of self and passion and with absolute detachment scattered far and wide and engaged in calling the peoples of the world to the Divine guidance, till at last they made the world another world, illumined the surface of the earth and even to their last hour proved self sacrificing in the pathway of that beloved one of God. Finally in various lands they suffered glorious martyrdom. Let them that are men of action follow in their footsteps!

Hushmand Fatheazam
Haifa

PREAMBLE

It was 'Muhájir Year': a year of mass teaching in South America. Hundreds had gathered at a conference in Quito, Ecuador, to dedicate themselves to a year of service in memory of Dr Muhájir. Inspired by his example, they would follow in his footsteps to teach the indigenous peoples throughout that vast continent, where he had sacrificed so much.

'Muhájir! Muhájir!' was the rallying cry of the pioneers and travel teachers, as they prepared for action. The stories of his remarkable travels, and of his total dedication to teaching, were legendary. On one occasion, when crossing the mountains of Bolivia on foot, a storm had blown up; Dr Muhájir recorded the incident in his diary:

> We had walked for half an hour when it started to rain. Large hailstones hit us. The hail was so fierce and the freezing cold so biting that we could not continue any further. I apologized to my companions and told them that I had only walked for two kilometres and was already in such bad shape that I simply could not envisage having the strength to continue. I was shattered and despondent. I sat there weeping because I couldn't walk a few kilometres in the path of God. I just sat there in the rain and wept. The weather was getting colder and the rain was worsening. . . . We walked from six a.m. to seven p.m. and accomplished nothing. . . . I have to take my ambitions to the Abhá kingdom.

He was, however, to walk many more hours and many more kilometres in the path of God.

Chapter 1

A NOBLE SPIRITUAL HERITAGE

Raḥmatu'lláh Muhájir was born on 4 April 1923, the fifth of seven children. His father, Ḥáfizu'lláh Khán, was descended from a long line of devoted Bahá'ís who had sacrificed their wealth and their lives for the sake of their Faith. The Muhájir family hailed from Dawlatábád, one of several villages in the vicinity of Iṣfahán. As far as can be determined, it was located in the tribal region of Bakhtiar. Áqá Mullá Muḥammad, the patriarch of the Muhájir family, was a wealthy and influential man who owned vast farmlands and kept large numbers of camels and mules to transport his merchandise from Iṣfahán. He traded in all kinds of household and farm goods, and his stores served most of the neighbouring villages. Mullá Muḥammad had four sons and three daughters. The youngest son, Mírzá Fatḥu'lláh, was Raḥmat's grandfather.

Every year during the holy month of Muḥarram, Mullá Muḥammad followed the Muslim custom and opened his house for the ten days of mourning preceding Ashurá, the day of the martyrdom of the Imám Ḥusayn. Among those who flocked to his house to be fed and entertained with Rawḍih, the traditional stories of the Imáms, were the mullás and the dervishes who came from far-off villages. The dervishes were treated with special attention and preference as it was a common belief that the curse of a dervish, invoked in the name of the Imám 'Alí, would bring bad luck to the recipient and his descendants for several generations. During the commemorations of Muḥarram in 1850, a dervish was so distraught and wept such bitter tears that Mullá Muḥammad, unseen by the other members of the family, felt compelled to take him to the living quarters of the house. The dervish could not be consoled and would not eat or drink. Mullá Muḥammad gently admonished him that, though weeping for the hardships endured by the Imám was a blessing, such extreme lamentation was unseemly for events which had occurred more than 1000 years ago. The dervish responded that he wailed not so much for that martyrdom of long ago, as for the Imám who had recently been martyred.

To the great astonishment of Mullá Muḥammad, the dervish, risking his life, confessed that he was a Bábí and talked about the teachings of the Báb to the family. He gave details of the martyrdom of the blessed Báb and equated it with the martyrdom of the Imám Ḥusayn. His confession led to lengthy and detailed discussions. After the dervish's departure, prominent Bábís from Iṣfahán came to Mullá Muḥammad's house to answer his questions and remove his doubts. Mullá Muḥammad's family was the first in Dawlatábád to convert to the Faith of the Báb.

The first Bahá'í teacher to visit Mullá Muḥammad's family was the erudite Ḥájí Mírzá Ḥaydar-'Alí-Iṣfahání. Bahá'u'lláh had instructed him to go to Dawlatábád and nourish the tender saplings which had taken root around the time of the martyrdom of the Báb. For many days Ḥájí Mírzá Ḥaydar-'Alí spoke about Bahá'u'lláh in relation to the guidance given by the Báb in the Bayán regarding 'the year nine' and 'He Whom God shall make manifest'. With the exception of one brother, Mírzá 'Abdu'lláh, all expressed their faith in the new religion and asked for Bahá'u'lláh's Writings. Ḥájí Mírzá Ḥaydar-'Alí had only one of Bahá'u'lláh's prayers with him: they memorized this and chanted it every day.

The conversion of the family was the cause of great opposition and upheaval in the village, which had dramatic consequences for the new believers. Through the help of Ḥájí Mírzá Ḥaydar-'Ali, the family had been granted permission to make a pilgrimage to 'Akká and attain the presence of Bahá'u'lláh. It was decided to leave Mírzá Fatḥu'lláh, the youngest brother, in charge of family affairs. Mírzá 'Abdu'lláh was persuaded to accompany the other two brothers on their journey. These three were given a festive send-off by the rest of the family, who defied the angry threats of Muslim fanatics and followed them to the outskirts of the village. The brothers, being experienced merchants, had planned well and had brought everything needed for their long and arduous journey.

However, God had another intention and sent them many trials and tribulations to test their faith and cleanse them of worldly desires, so that they would reach the threshold of their Beloved with pure hearts and with certitude.

A few miles outside the village they were set upon by highway robbers who stole all their money and belongings, and took their mounts and pack mules. The brothers, however, were determined not to turn back before attaining the presence of the Blessed Beauty. They continued on foot, undertaking menial jobs in the villages through which they passed to earn a little money for food. Sometimes, miraculously, they found help when they least expected it. On one occasion they found a few eggs under a bush, and a bag of flour which had fallen off a pack mule. They used the eggs and flour to make a kind of bread known as *talangi*, which fed them for days. Later, when they were so worn out that they felt unable to walk another mile, a caravan of pilgrims appeared on the road. The chief of the caravan approached them, saying that he had had a dream in which he was told that he would come across a few pilgrims on foot, and that, if he gave them a ride, the bounties of the Prophet would be showered upon him. The caravan chief fed the brothers and offered them mules to ride on. It took him some time to realize that the brothers were not going on the same pilgrimage as he was. They were thrown off the mules and the caravan went on without them. The brothers, however, were now rested, and continued cheerfully on their way.

ARRIVAL AT 'AKKÁ

They journeyed three-and-a-half months in this fashion until they reached the outskirts of 'Akká. Waiting under a tree for daylight to come so that they could enter the city, they were approached by a man bearing a parcel. He enquired if they were Bahá'ís, and welcomed them to 'Akká. He then told them that they were Bahá'u'lláh's guests, and that He had sent them a gift. The parcel contained saffron rice and turkey. The brothers ate this heavenly food, and, early the next morning, went to the house of Bahá'u'lláh. When the brothers arrived they were told that Bahá'u'lláh was unwell, and could not meet them until the next day. However, in the afternoon Bahá'u'lláh came to them and, while walking the length of the room, addressed them and the other pilgrims who were present.

Before leaving home, Mírzá 'Abdu'lláh had made a pact with his brothers that if Bahá'u'lláh singled him out and spoke to him directly, he would become a Bahá'í. Bahá'u'lláh told the brothers that He was with them throughout their sojourn. Although He was ill and could barely stand up, He had come because He wanted to see them. As He was leaving the room, Bahá'u'lláh paused in front of Mírzá 'Abdu'lláh, touched his shoulder and asked, 'What is your contention?' Mírzá 'Abdu'lláh fell down in a faint and was unconscious for a few hours. For several days he wept continuously and could not speak. He then declared his faith in Bahá'u'lláh, and repented of his past omissions and ignorance.

The newly confirmed brothers stayed for four months in the presence of the Blessed Beauty, before returning to Iran. 'Abdu'l-Bahá later assured them that this bounty, and hearing Bahá'u'lláh's revelation from His own lips, would remain with them forever. In a Tablet to the brothers, He wrote that the suffering they had endured would strengthen their spirits, and that they should now arise to do the bidding of their Lord. 'Abdu'l-Bahá addressed them as *Muhájirán* — 'Pioneers'. From that day forth 'Muhájir' was adopted as the family name.

OPPOSITION TO THE NEW FAITH

The brothers' return co-incided with that of the Muslim pilgrims from Mecca. When they were asked why they had not been seen in Mecca by their friends, they replied that they had gone to 'Akká. The mullás were furious. They shouted from their pulpits that anyone who went to 'Akká was a Bahá'í and a heretic. The brothers were given the choice of either recanting their Faith or losing their wealth: from that time on their lives were *halál* — legal for Muslims to take. The brothers chose to remain steadfast in their faith, and so their fields and cattle were plundered by the mob. Those who owed them money refused to pay and threatened to kill their wives and children if they tried to collect it. When the brothers decided to go to Iṣfahán to complain to the authorities, the chief mullá of the village informed the Imám-Jum'ih of Iṣfahán, a staunch enemy of the Faith, that these people were trying to convert all the villages to

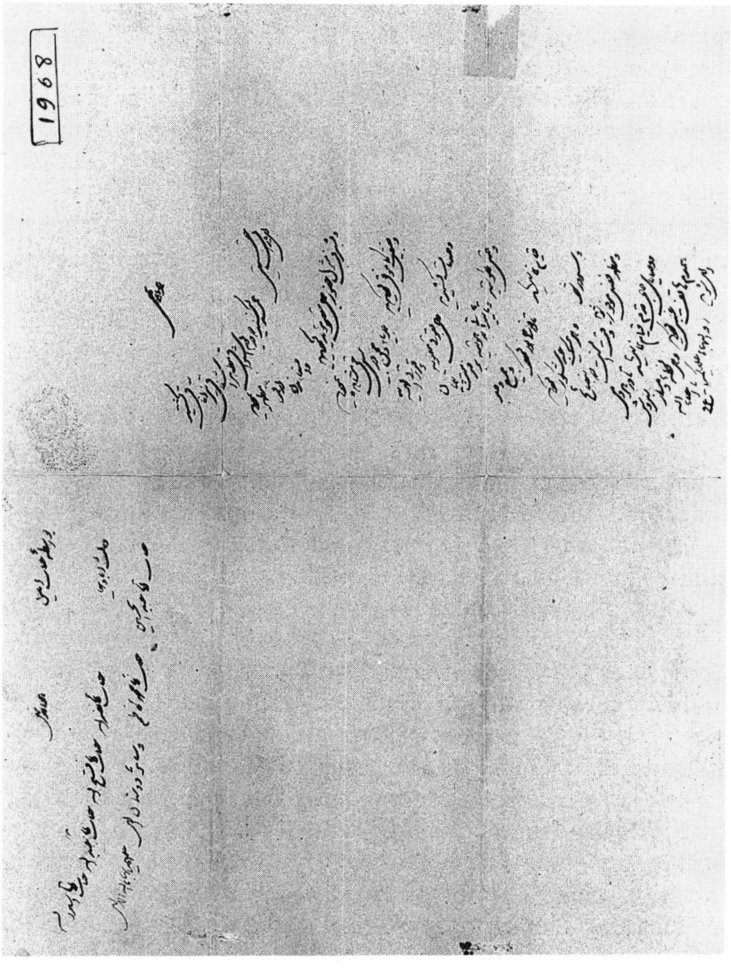

Facsimile of 'Abdu'l-Bahá's Tablet, in His own hand, to the Dawlatábádí brothers.

their heretical beliefs. The four brothers and other male members of the family, numbering 24 altogether, were arrested by the emissaries of the Imám-Jum'ih and taken to Iṣfahán. When they arrived at the Imám's house, they were bastinadoed, their clothing was removed and they were thrown into the basement of the outer house of the Imám's residence, dressed only in their thin underwear. It was decided that on the Friday of the following week, the group would be divided among the guilds of Iṣfahán so that each guild could have the bounty of killing a heretic. The men were given no food or water, or blankets to keep warm. Mrs Mehri Rowhani, Raḥmat's cousin, recalled an account of the prisoners' plight, told by her grandfather Mullá Muḥammad Baqír, a son-in-law of Mullá Muḥammad:

> One day while we were all sitting in jail awaiting execution, we heard a knock on the small basement window. We looked up and saw a stranger beckoning us. He asked what we were doing and we said we were praying, as we were Bahá'ís and were to be executed. He calmly asked, 'Why are you waiting like sheep to be slaughtered? Why aren't you trying to escape?' We replied that the door was locked and that there were guards in front of it. He said, 'There are no guards here now, and I can see the key hanging on a nail. I will open the door and you run as fast as you can.' I first went out to make certain that this was not a trap, but when I saw that the guard had mysteriously disappeared, we all ran out and hid in an alley under the roof of an abandoned house. We never found out the identity of our rescuer but we felt for certain that no Muslim would have risked his life to save us. We decided that I should go back to Dowlatabad and arrange the affairs of the women and children.
>
> I was authorized by the family to contact the Kad-khudá [headman] of the village, who was a friend, and offer him a hundred tumans, a handwoven Kashmir shawl and a gold laminated Qur'án so that he would look after our wives and children until we could arrange for their departure. We decided to leave in small groups, as we would easily be recognized. I left with my sons and two small nephews. As we were walking through the back alleys, a veiled woman approached us and

asked, 'Are you the Bábís who have fled from the Imám's jail?' I thought that we had been discovered and that our end had come. However, the woman assured us that she meant us no harm. Her employer, the wife of Mírzá Assadu'lláh Vazír,[1] had sent 24 pouches, each containing nine Qerans so that we could buy clothing and some food. I thanked her, left the boys in the alley, and went to buy some clothes with our share of the money. Because my first two sons had died in childhood, my grandmother, who was a Siyyid (a descendent of the Prophet), had made me promise always to wrap the green cloth, the mark of descent from the Prophet, around the waists of my surviving sons. With the money I therefore bought green cloth as well as clothes. I then returned. We put the new clothes on, wrapped the green shawls around the waists of each of my sons and went in search of food. When we saw any of our group we gave them their share of the money. We continued in this way until we reached Murchih Khurd, outside the city limits of Iṣfahán.

Night had fallen and the gates of the town were closed. I knocked on the door but the woman gatekeeper refused to let us in, telling us to wait until morning. However, when she saw, through the slits in the gate, the green belts worn by my sons, she immediately opened the gate and apologized for keeping the descendants of the Prophet in the cold. She invited us inside the house, gave us tea and asked where we were headed. When she learned we were fugitives from the Imám's prison, she became more helpful, as she had lost her own son to the tyranny of the Imám's officials. I left the boys with her to identify the rest of our clan as they arrived, and returned to Dowlatabad.

Once in Dawlatábád, I sneaked into my house and, with the help of my wife, hid in the barn. The Imám's servants were searching all of the houses in the village. They said that the Imám was furious with his guards for abandoning their posts and had vowed not to eat or sleep until all of the prisoners were recaptured. I hid in that barn for three days and nights. The Kad-khudá was contacted, and, after I got his agreement, I left the village in the middle of the night. When I arrived back in Murchih Khurd I learned that the rest of the party had passed through on their way to Ṭihrán. We thanked the old lady and started on our way.

Near the next town we discovered that the Imám's servants were guarding the gate and inspecting the identity of everyone who was entering the town on foot. We did not know what to do and were praying for God's help when a mule caravan appeared. The leader of the caravan asked what we were doing in the middle of the road. When I told him that we were going to Ṭihrán and were tired and ill, he offered to take us with him. He said that surely the Prophet would reward him in the next world for helping His descendants. By this miraculous incident we rode on the backs of four strong mules and escaped the servants of the Imám.

A few days later we arrived in Ṭihrán and stopped in a crowded caravanserai to await the arrival of the rest of our relatives. We shared two small rooms, and whoever had work shared his earnings with the rest. Although we were worn out and hungry, we were happy in the knowledge that we believed in the Manifestation of God. The local people would tell each other that we must be either millionaires or mad: 'They divide two pieces of bread among themselves, eat it, and then talk and laugh the whole night.' Little did they know that we were all listening to the stories of the pilgrimages of our relatives.[2]

The men were eventually joined by their wives and children, and each family found a home of their own. Raḥmat's grandfather, Mírzá Fatḥu'lláh, disliked city life, so he rented a small farm in a nearby village and opened a little store. His son, Ḥáfizu'lláh Khán (Raḥmat's father), went to the school of pharmacology which had just been opened and studied to become a pharmacist. He married Esmat Khánum at the end of his studies and established his pharmacy in the town of Sháh 'Abdu'l-'Azím.

HIS PARENTS

Although Sháh 'Abdu'l-'Aẓím was a Muslim religious centre with the most fanatical inhabitants, the honesty and philanthropy of Raḥmat's father won the hearts of one and all. He never charged those customers who could not afford to pay. Even the mullás would bring their business to him, as they could not trust the Muslim pharmacists. Ḥáfizu'lláh Khán would use these occasions to talk to the clergy about the Faith. His pharmacy was the centre of Bahá'í activity. Many Bahá'ís from neighbouring towns would come to him to hear the latest Bahá'í news.

Mírzá Fatḥu'lláh had been the only one of the brothers deprived of the bounty of pilgrimage to the threshold of the Blessed Beauty. However, his son Ḥáfizu'lláh Khán was able to go on pilgrimage to the Holy Land in 1924, and his grandson was destined to receive even greater honours. Visiting the Holy Shrines and meeting the beloved Guardian increased Ḥáfizu'lláh Khán's zeal in teaching the Cause, and he devoted the remainder of his life to the service of his Faith.

Iṣmat Khánum, Raḥmat's mother, came from the province of Káshán. Her family were well-known merchants who owned and operated several carpet factories in addition to their main business of trade in tobacco. The head of the family was Áqá Muḥammad Hashim Kisih-Porkon, a staunch Bahá'í who received many Tablets from Bahá'u'lláh. Iṣmat Khánum's father, Áqá Qulám Ḥusayn, a nephew of Áqá Muḥammad Hashim, had been introduced to the Faith by his uncle. In a Tablet addressed to him, 'Abdu'l-Bahá supplicates God on his behalf to assist and guide him so that he might diffuse the teachings of Bahá'u'lláh amongst the inhabitants of the whole world.

As the wealth of Áqá Muḥammad Hashim increased, so did the envy of those who wished harm on the followers of the new Faith. His fanatical adversaries incited the Islamic clerics to demand Áqá Muḥammad's disavowal of the Bahá'í religion. The families were thus forced to leave all they owned and flee to Ṭihrán. All their belongings were looted by the mob and the carpet factories and tobacco stores confiscated by the clergy. The family had purchased a small carpet shop in Ṭihrán and had begun to rebuild their lives when they were again faced with tragedy. A search party, which had been dispatched to Ṭihrán by the mullás of Káshán, kidnapped Áqá Qulám Ḥusayn. Despite their frantic searching his family could find no trace of him. It would fall upon Áqá Qulám's grandson to fulfil 'Abdu'l-Bahá's prayer. Raḥmatu'lláh Muhájir's single desire was that the message of Bahá'u'lláh be carried to the mass of humanity.

The Bahá'ís of South Ṭihrán, circa 1937. Raḥmat is standing in the top row, second from left. His father, Ḥáfizu'lláh Khán, is in the second row from the top, sixth from left. His mother, Iṣmat Khánum is in the fourth row from the top, second from left.

CHILDHOOD

Raḥmat's parents, custodians of such a noble heritage, continued the family tradition of service and dedication, and instilled the desire for sacrifice and devotion in the hearts of their children from an early age. In years to come Raḥmat would tell stories of his childhood to the Bahá'í children in the communities he visited. He always emphasized to parents the importance of teaching their children Bahá'í history and the Writings of the Faith while they were still young. He believed that children could not fully benefit from the knowledge, devotion and servitude of their parents if these were not imparted to them in their tender years.

Raḥmat was about nine years old when his family moved to Ṭihrán. His mother believed very strongly that her children should have the best possible education and training, and this was not available in Sháh 'Abdu'l-'Aẓim. She was prepared to sacrifice her own comfort and the security of having her husband always by her side in order that her children might progress. A spacious house was purchased and the large household settled in the capital. Raḥmat remembered this house with love and affection, and often talked about the Bahá'í activities that went on there. Although his father was away most of the time, Bahá'í meetings were regularly held at the house. The large living room doors were opened into the dining room and other adjoining rooms to accommodate as many people as possible. Nineteen Day Feasts, women's meetings, fund-raising activities and firesides were attended by large numbers of Bahá'ís. Prominent Bahá'í speakers conducted the meetings and very often all the guests were served dinner. The most popular event was the weekly fireside. Although the persecution of the Bahá'ís, especially in Ṭihrán during the 1930s, had considerably lessened, still the friends had to be prudent and cautious. The seekers were usually well-known to the Bahá'ís before they were brought to the firesides. Speakers were always invited weeks in advance and were well-versed in the Bahá'í Writings and Islamic traditions.

While still of tender years, Raḥmat used to sit quietly in a corner of the room listening to the discussions. Erudite Bahá'í teachers such as Mr Furútan, Mr Alavi and Mr Fazil would tackle difficult theological subjects. Raḥmat would dream of the day he could answer the seeker's questions. As he grew older, he began to bring his friends to these firesides. My father, Mr Furútan, remembers Raḥmat as a young boy constantly asking him questions about the Faith and bringing his friends to be taught by him. Once, when he could not find other seekers, Raḥmat coaxed the neighbourhood cobbler to attend a fireside by promising him a sumptuous dinner!

Attending a Bahá'í study class at the age of 14, third from right. Dr Mehdi Samandarí, Raḥmat's teacher, is in the front row, farthest right.

The seeds of devotion were thus sown in Raḥmat's heart at an early age. While attending high school, he was a member of both the local and national youth committees and spent every spare moment involved in Bahá'í activities. He continued his Bahá'í education every Friday at the Dars-i-Akhláq — Bahá'í classes — and by memorizing prayers and passages from the Writings. This is not to suggest that Raḥmat was a perfect child. He was like all children, occasionally playing pranks on his friends, but good humour would usually get him out of trouble. When he was very young he would kick stones along the street on his way home from school. His mother was none too pleased at the holes which kept appearing in his shoes as a result. He was fit and strong and enjoyed physical recreation and playing games. He was by nature very sociable, and was always very popular with his peers, many of whom remained his lifelong friends. He did well at school and gained the respect of his teachers for his diligence and polite manner.

TEENAGE YEARS

His first experience of pioneering was during the Iranian 45 Month Plan when his family left Ṭihrán to pioneer to Kalár-Dasht in the province of Mázindarán. The family stayed there for three years until the children became too ill with malaria. The women could not manage by themselves, so they had to return to Ṭihrán. When Raḥmat was fifteen, his father died of a heart attack. The family had to move to a smaller home, one of the two adjoining houses which his father had built to rent to others.

I remember Raḥmat as a teenager. He always had a lot of friends with him. He spent most of his time in Bahá'í activities, though he did enjoy going to the movies and to parties with his friends. He did not try to draw attention to himself in any way, but was always smart and tidy in appearance. He was constantly involved in helping organize youth activities, but did not try to conduct them himself. This was a characteristic which remained apparent all through his life. He always encouraged others to serve and to make presentations in Bahá'í meetings. On many occasions when, as a Hand of the Cause, Raḥmat was invited to give a talk, he would take one of the Bahá'í youth or an Auxiliary Board member with him. He would give a brief talk and then introduce his companion and ask him to speak. He always avoided confrontation and debate. He told me that when the Bahá'í teenagers would gather on the street corner for games and conversation, a friend of his would suggest to him, 'I will say there is no God and you say there is. Then we can have a debate proving our points of view.' Raḥmat never accepted that challenge. He did not believe in debating, and all his life counselled the Bahá'ís not to engage in it.

His love and enthusiasm for the Faith were infectious, and Raḥmat's house was always crowded with his friends, who often stayed overnight. His mother had to be on the alert and prepare extra food, as she knew that Raḥmat would very rarely come home without bringing his friends.

He was only sixteen years old when he began to make extensive trips around Iran. His travels took him to most of the provinces, but no trip was ever planned simply for pleasure or sightseeing. He visited all the Bahá'í holy places in Iran, from Máh-Kú to Núr, including nearly every site visited by the Báb and Bahá'u'lláh, and every city where a 'Dawn-Breaker' had been martyred. On these journeys he was sometimes accompanied by his close friends, including Hushmand Fatheazam (a future member of the Universal House of Justice), Dr Abbasian and Dr Naji (both of whom would be martyred in the Iranian persecutions of 1980), and Dr Ghadimi (who was to become a member of the National Assembly of Iran).

Friends remember Raḥmat's great sense of humour. He was a good companion who did not fuss about any of the discomforts of travel. He was always cheerful and smiling. They also remember the intensity of his devotion as he prayed and meditated at the sites of the Báb's prisons in Máh-Kú and Chihríq. Many times during our early pioneering days, when life seemed unbearable to me, Raḥmat would tell me stories of those trips. He described the beauty and comfort of the House of the Báb in Shíráz and the stark emptiness of the fortress at Máh-Kú. He reminded me of the majesty and splendour of Bahá'u'lláh's House in Ṭihrán and the pestilence of the Síyáh-Chál. If the Báb could live in the prison of Chíhríq without any candles, and Bahá'u'lláh could endure His days in the Síyáh-Chál, then we certainly could live without electricity and the comforts of a civilized world.

Mr Fatheazam recalls that during their travels, when they arrived late at a friend's home, or at a small rooming house where six of them had to share one room, exhausted from a day's hiking or climbing the mountains, the group just wanted to sleep. Not Raḥmat! He would urge them to read a few pages of *Nabíl's Narrative* to prepare for the next day's trip. The protests of his friends did not deter him from reading the passages aloud. After the others went to sleep, Raḥmat would quietly continue to read the history of those early events, as well as other writings, until the candle burned out in the small hours of the night.

In 1943, when he was only 19 years old, he organized a Bahá'í class and invited about 25 of his friends to attend. He thought it was time that all of them became familiar with the administrative order. Mr Furútan, 'Alí Nakhjavání and Miss Adelaide Sharp were invited to teach this class. The group of students was comprised of men only, as mixed meetings were not yet common in Iran. Raḥmat attended all of the classes, which were held in the modest home of one of the youth. Many of those who participated in those classes later pioneered in various parts of the world, most of them encouraged by their boyhood friend. Some were even accompanied by Raḥmat personally to their destinations, and were assisted by him to settle at their posts.

Early in 1943 he encouraged his friends to take a year off from their studies in order to visit and inspire the Bahá'ís around the country. This concept of a year of service, which he had conceived as a youth, was always dear to his heart. He shared this idea with the Bahá'í youth in many parts of the world and inspired many of them to rise to this service. When their parents objected, he would often go to meet with them and calm their fears by telling them of his own experiences. He believed that a year in the life of an 18-year old was only significant if it was spent in the service of the Faith. A youth could always go back to his or her studies, often with a much clearer understanding of the importance of education, but he or she could never recapture the opportunity to serve at a moment when it was needed.

In the autumn of 1944, though he had been admitted to the school of medicine at the University of Ṭihrán, Raḥmat decided to leave his studies and go to Rezaíyih, a city in the northern province of Ádhirbáyján. He is still remembered with love and affection in that area. He used his remarkable gift of planning and organization to initiate youth and children's classes, which he taught during the day. He held adult literacy classes in the afternoons, and his nights were spent in Bahá'í meetings and firesides. The celebration of the centenary of the Declaration of the Báb showed how Raḥmat would take affairs into his own hands. The celebration was to take place in a small hall on the ground floor of a house that the Báb had stayed in. It was in need of cleaning and complete renovation. Raḥmat organized a group of youth, and they all toiled day and night and prepared the house for the gathering of the friends. While in Rezaíyih he also travelled to other towns and villages to support their firesides and attend to their needs. It was two years before he was persuaded to return to Ṭihrán and resume his studies.

In Rezaíyih, 1944, on the celebration of the Centenary of the Declaration of the Báb, in front of the house visited by the Báb.

Medical school, with all its rigours, did not deter him from his Bahá'í activities. He even increased the level of his participation in Bahá'í meetings and firesides. His friends recall that when they admonished him to pay more attention to his studies, he would smile and say, 'Don't worry. Bahá'u'lláh can take better care of my studies.' He had a very sharp and logical mind. He was an honours student in maths and science, and often said that he had chosen medicine to be able better to serve the Faith. It was easier to find work as a physician in pioneering posts than other professions, and he had chosen his field of study accordingly.

WITH THE PIONEERS

In 1948 he was appointed to serve on the National Pioneering Committee. He had suddenly found his niche of service to the Faith. He threw himself wholeheartedly into the work of sending pioneers to both homefront goals and neighbouring countries. The idea of pioneering to foreign lands was still a new and strange one for the Iranian Bahá'ís at that time. For 20 years the Guardian had moulded the Bahá'í community in preparation for the day when they could rise to this act of service.

Relaxing with friends at a picnic, circa 1945. On the right is Hasan Afnán, person on left unknown.

The Bahá'í administration in Iran had grown from a few local Assemblies into one of the strongest national communities in the Bahá'í world, with a mature National Spiritual Assembly at its head. During the early ministry of the Guardian many of us had become familiar — and comfortable — with the idea of travelling within Iran to teach and visit other communities, even with moving our homes to areas which had few or no Bahá'ís. However, this new

Second year medical school, 1948. Raḥmat is in the second row, sixth from left.

45 Month Plan, from October 1946 to July 1950, was unique in that it called for pioneers to go to other countries. Raḥmat studied the Plan for days. He was particularly interested in the foreign goals. As the secretary of the Pioneering Committee, he used his utmost efforts to encourage the friends to pioneer, especially to Arabia. Anyone who volunteered to go was his guest at a lavish meal of chelo-kebab. This continued even after the completion of the Plan. A Bahá'í intending to pioneer to Arabia would call him and ask, 'What about my chelo-kebab?' and we would all go out and have an enjoyable evening together. Mr Golmuḥammadi, a long time pioneer to Arabia, recalls that before leaving, when he was having his chelo-kebab, he told Raḥmat that he wished he could have a copy of the Kitáb-i-Aqdas to take with him to Arabia. Editions of the Most Holy Book were very rare, the only copies being those which had been printed in Egypt many years before. On the day of Mr Golmaḥammadi's departure, one freezing winter dawn, Raḥmat met him at the bus-stop bearing a gift. It was his own copy

of the Kitáb-i-Aqdas, wrapped in a gold and green silk handkerchief, with his name embossed in gold lettering on the flyleaf. He told Mr Golmuḥammadi, 'You are a pioneer. You deserve this more than I do.'

Raḥmat considered pioneering a joyful event. Although we were all aware of the hardships of life in Arabia, whenever the volunteers were with him and listened to him he was so enthusiastic and envious of their achievements that it made them proud to be able to render this special service. Doctors, engineers, architects and youth from all walks of life contacted the Pioneering Committee. Raḥmat was engrossed in processing their applications and facilitating their departure. Those who left knew that they had to sacrifice their professions. If they were lucky they might be able to open a modest grocery or a bakery store. But this did not keep them from their task. Raḥmat himself longed for the day when he could join his friends. He was impatient to finish his studies, and on many occasions considered leaving school altogether, only to be dissuaded by his mother's pleas. The next best thing was for him to leave his studies for one semester and devote his whole time to the tasks of the Pioneering Committee. To the astonishment of everyone, this is exactly what he did. He spent all his time in the search for more pioneers to fulfil the goals of the Plan, working on their visas and passports and facilitating their moves.

MARRIAGE

Our marriage was in 1951. Raḥmat's parents and mine were old friends, and we had lived in adjoining houses for some years during my childhood. Raḥmat and I had seen each other in many youth meetings, and met once more in 1948 when I attended the Summer School in Karaj, near Ṭihrán, of which he, though only 25 years old, was director. In 1951 I had graduated from high school, and with the approval of the Guardian, was preparing to leave for England to continue my studies. When Raḥmat heard this, he immediately asked my father for permission to marry me. He told my father that two things had prompted him to seek permission to get married at this time. One was that he wanted to marry before he left to pioneer, and the other was that I was leaving Iran and he had no intention of spending the rest of his life with another girl. He later

Engagement photograph, 1951.

The day of our wedding, 15 October 1951.

told me that for some years he had prayed in front of the photograph of 'Abdu'l-Bahá to assist him in this marriage. I had always felt a great love for him since my childhood and it seemed the most natural thing for us to marry.

Our families met together several times, and, when all concerned had agreed to the possibility of the marriage, my father felt he had to seek the permission of the Guardian for any change in my plan to go to England. In answer to my father's letter concerning the proposed marriage, we received a telegram from Shoghi Effendi saying, 'Approve. Praying blessings.' Raḥmat and I were married on 15 October.

A few months after our marriage, Raḥmat graduated from medical school and promptly announced his decision to pioneer to Arabia. At that time I was in very poor health and my doctors strongly advised me against living in a hot climate. The solution would be for Raḥmat to go alone until such time as my health would allow me to join him. We finally decided humbly to seek the advice of the Guardian. In his loving reply Shoghi Effendi advised Raḥmat to stay in Iran until we could leave together.

The events of our future life made us realize that each adversity

Medical school graduation, 1952.

brought hidden bounties, and that submission to the Will of God brought greater harvests than could even remotely be imagined or anticipated. My illness, and the postponement of Raḥmat's cherished wish to pioneer, opened to him much greater arenas of service. He was quite prepared to give up his profession and pioneer to Arabia, where he could not teach the Faith at all, but in obeying the beloved Guardian he was rewarded with teaching thousands of souls around the world. Staying in Iran meant that Raḥmat had to begin practising as a physician. He took a job in Iṣfahán, at a hospital attached to the Point Four Marshal Plan. This position was coveted by many doctors, as it was a very prestigious job with a salary nearly four times that offered by other clinics.

PILGRIMAGE

In 1953 the gates of pilgrimage, which had been closed to the Iranian Bahá'ís since the war, were opened again by Shoghi Effendi. Raḥmat was amongst the first to seek permission, and we were among the second or third group of pilgrims to have the bounty of attaining the presence of the Guardian. Raḥmat was the only man in our group, and Shoghi Effendi received him at the gardens of the Shrine of the Báb, as was his custom. They walked in the gardens and visited the Shrines of the Báb and 'Abdu'l-Bahá, where the Guardian chanted the Tablet of Visitation. In later years, whenever he visited the holy Shrines, Raḥmat recalled those days of pilgrimage with great yearning. He said that when he walked in the gardens of the Shrine of the Báb he could feel the presence of the beloved Guardian and hear his melodious chanting. He would recall Shoghi Effendi talking about the Ten Year Crusade, and about pioneering to win the goals of the Plan. The Guardian spoke in a most thrilling manner about the Ten Year Crusade to Raḥmat, and to the group of Persian ladies who were admitted to his presence separately. He was so happy with this plan that we could feel the vibrations of his spirit. To Raḥmat, he spoke mostly about the goals in the vicinity of the Pacific, South-East Asia and, specifically, the Indonesian archipelago. He asked Raḥmat if he knew where Singapore was, then told him that the area was inhabited by the 'brown race' who were waiting to respond to the message of Bahá'u'lláh.

Remembering those days, I very often think that the reason for the great response to the Guardian's call for pioneers during the Ten Year Crusade, apart from the absolute love that everyone felt for him, was his own excitement and enthusiasm, which affected one and all. Every time the Guardian talked about the Crusade, or referred to the map he had drawn outlining the goals, his face would radiate joy, and his eyes would shine. He had such a beautiful smile.

In the presence of the Guardian, Raḥmat was transformed. At nights, when we all sat around the dining table of the Persian pilgrim house, we recounted the day's events. Raḥmat's love for the Guardian had increased a thousandfold. He was willing to give his life there and then if it would please his beloved. The guest book in the Mansion of Bahjí reflects this devotion in his words, 'I offer humble thanks to the threshold of the Beloved, who granted me the immense bounty to behold the beauty of the Báb, the majesty of Bahá'u'lláh and the kindness and hospitality of 'Abdu'l-Bahá in the countenance of the beloved Guardian. May the lives of his lovers be a sacrifice in his path.'

On Pilgrimage, with Raḥmat's mother, and Dr Luṭfu'lláh Ḥakím.

This pilgrimage was a watershed in Raḥmat's life of service to the Faith. All his efforts in the past now seemed insignificant. He spent hours on his knees praying at the Holy Shrines, supplicating Bahá'u'lláh to make him worthy of some small service in His path. When we returned to Iran, Raḥmat was on fire. He wanted to leave everything and go somewhere — anywhere — so long as it was one of the goals of the Ten Year Crusade. He had always loved the Guardian; now this love had become adoration. After a gruelling day of work at the hospital, followed by an evening spent at a meeting or a fireside, Raḥmat would come home and sit for hours praying that God would consider him worthy of participating in this Divine Plan. He believed that pioneering was a great bounty of which not everyone was worthy, and that only through prayer and supplication might God grant it. The habit of praying for hours at night continued throughout his life. He only prayed for spiritual things. When asked to pray for material objects his usual answer was that he did not have any desire to waste God's time by bothering Him with such nonsense. I was present on many occasions when, for the success of a teaching project, the purchase of a Bahá'í Centre, or the opening of a new area to the Faith in some remote corner of the world, he repeated the prayer of the Báb, 'Say: God sufficeth all things above all things . . .' 314 times,[3] chanting the Tablet of Aḥmad and the Fire Tablet after each hundredth repetition. He very seldom prayed on his own behalf, unless it was for success in his teaching work. After he was appointed a Hand of the Cause he said daily prayers to be worthy of this great bounty and to be able to serve the beloved Guardian; and he supplicated Bahá'u'lláh to give him humility and to safeguard him so that he would remain steadfast in His Covenant.

INTERCONTINENTAL CONFERENCE, 1953

Raḥmat's prayers were often answered in an unexpected fashion. The Intercontinental Conferences called at the instruction of the beloved Guardian prior to the commencement of the Ten Year Crusade were held throughout 1953. My father was appointed a Hand of the Cause with the first contingent in 1951, and was one of the Hands designated to participate in the Conference for Asia and Australasia, held in October that year in New Delhi. We decided that the best way to find a pioneering post would be to write to the Continental Pioneering Committee which held its sessions at the conference. Raḥmat wrote to them, volunteering us for any goal of the Ten Year Crusade which was in need of pioneers. The letter specified that the climate or living conditions of the pioneering post were immaterial and that we were ready to leave as soon as it was assigned to us.

Collis Featherstone, then a member of the National Spiritual Assembly of Australia and New Zealand, suggested that we go to the Mentawai Islands, which was a goal of that Assembly. The only visa that could be obtained for these islands, which were territories of Indonesia, was for a physician and Australia had no such qualified volunteers. Mr Featherstone suggested that we go to that goal, and Australia would fulfil a goal of the Iranian National Assembly. As such exchanges of pioneers had been suggested by the Guardian, the Continental Pioneering Committee approved Mr Featherstone's suggestion. The news was relayed to us when my parents returned to Iran from the conference. Raḥmat accepted this assignment immediately. As we had absolutely no idea where the Mentawai Islands were or what country claimed sovereignty over them, it took us a while to locate them on a map as three small dots in the Indian Ocean, to the West of Sumatra. We had no knowledge of the climate or culture of the islands. With the assistance of a Persian geography textbook, we discovered that Sumatra was a tropical island, part of Indonesia, with a Muslim population. The name 'Mentawai' did not appear anywhere in the text. Our knowledge of English and French was very limited and it never occurred to us to find out about Indonesia and its situation. If the Guardian had chosen the islands, we had to go. The climate or the economic circumstances were not important.

Raḥmat's only concession to the advice of well-meaning friends who wanted him to be more careful about uprooting himself was to write to Mr Khodarahm Payman, who lived in Jakarta, the capital of Indonesia. Raḥmat did not write to find out about the conditions of that country, but simply to inform Mr Payman about our pioneering plans. Mr Payman's business, exporting tea to Iran, had taken him to Indonesia from India. He was to become Raḥmat's close and dear friend in subsequent years. He assisted Raḥmat with much of the teaching work in that area, became his Auxiliary Board member and was later appointed a member of the Board of Counsellors in Asia. In answer to Raḥmat's letter, Mr Payman advised us not to be too optimistic about getting a visa or a job in Indonesia. However, he encouraged us to visit the country on a tourist visa so that on our return to Iran we would have a better idea of the situation and could make a more intelligent and informed decision.

The friends around the world who have known Raḥmat can attest to the fact that when he made up his mind, especially on a matter that concerned the Faith, he could seldom be persuaded to change it. This was even more the case in the early stages of his service to the Faith of Bahá'u'lláh. He simply did not find the living conditions of a country relevant to whether or not one should pioneer there. If one wanted to obey the directions of the Guardian, if one wanted to teach and spread the Faith, then the climate — hot or cold — or the people — poor or rich — made no difference.

When he travelled to various parts of the world as a Hand of the Cause, he often emphasized this point. In the early days of pioneering, data and graphs showing the price of potatoes, the amount of rainfall and the kinds of mosquitoes that prospered in different countries were non-existent. Raḥmat always encouraged the pioneers to be courageous and daring. It was possible that they would encounter hardships of all kinds, but the Faith of Bahá'u'lláh had always progressed through the sacrifice of His followers. If a volunteer waited until he knew every conceivable aspect of a goal and spent additional years acquiring higher educational degrees in the hope of getting a well-paid and secure job, the opportunity to pioneer would simply pass by. He often quoted these words of 'Abdu'l-Bahá:

> O that I could travel, even though on foot and in the utmost poverty, to these regions, and, raising the call of 'Yá Bahá'u'l-Abhá' in cities, villages, mountains, deserts and oceans, promote the Divine teachings! This, alas, I cannot do. How intensely I deplore it! Please God, ye may achieve it.[4]

When it was argued that some pioneers who had left on impulse and without proper preparation had been forced to return home and had often sustained material losses, Raḥmat's reply was that their stay in those countries, however short, had not been wasted. They had spearheaded the teaching of the Faith which would be carried on by those who followed. As for material loss, the Bahá'ís of the world were engaged on a spiritual crusade; material loss was part of that crusade. He said that when the Guardian compared the pioneers of the Ten Year Crusade to the Dawn-Breakers of the Heroic Age, it meant that courage and sacrifice were an essential part of their lives. Those who went to the fortress of Ṭabarsí to raise the banner of the Faith of the Báb had not surveyed the land prior to their departure. On the way they had shed their worldly possessions. Some had been forced to return home, and some had fallen to the bullets of their assailants. Many of them were not aware of the importance of their deeds. They were following Mullá Ḥusayn in devotion to their Beloved, the Báb. Their heroic sacrifices will be remembered for eternity.

This strong belief sometimes resulted in Raḥmat giving advice which seemed at variance with that of the different pioneering and goals committees. This was not his intention at all. He was always in a hurry and did not have the patience for detailed procedures. He worked closely with all the administrative bodies of the Faith but always urged them to follow the Guardian's instructions that nothing should hinder a pioneer in his appointed task. This quotation from the guidance of the Guardian is copied in many of Raḥmat's notebooks and has been underlined several times in his copies of the Guardian's letters:

> . . . each and every one of those enrolled in the Army of Light must seek no rest, take no thought of self, must sacrifice to the utmost, must allow nothing whatsoever to deflect him or her from meeting the pressing, the manifold, the paramount needs of this preeminent Crusade.[5]

THE DETERMINED PIONEER

Raḥmat's experience with the International Goals Committee of Iran may well have had a great effect on his convictions. As soon as we heard that our request to go to the Mentawai Islands had been approved at the conference in New Delhi, I left Iṣfahán to consult

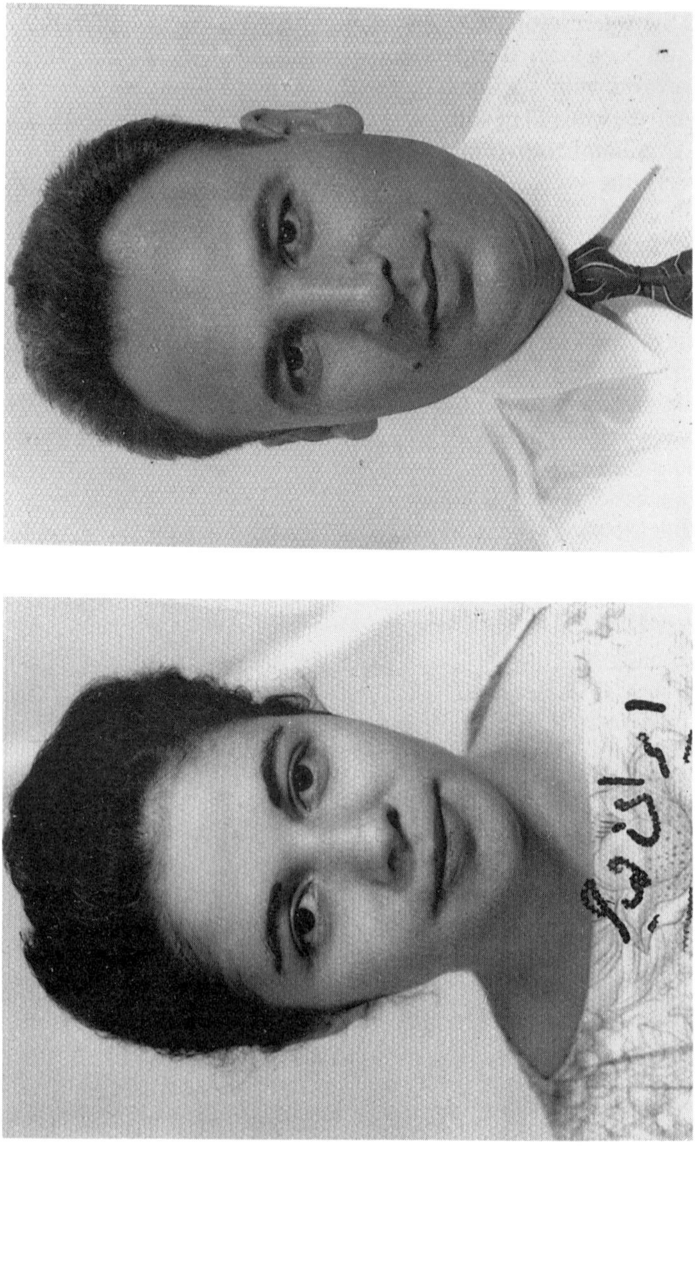

Preparing for pioneering. Passport photos, 1953.

with the International Goals Committee in Ṭihrán. This committee had just been formed and its members were struggling to familiarize themselves with the location of the goals. The members of the committee were all devoted, educated and experienced members of Bahá'í administrative institutions. Like the rest of us, they were tackling the intricacies of the Plan. We were probably the first volunteers to consult with them for pioneering to a goal of the Ten Year Crusade. I presented Raḥmat's letter asking how we should proceed to our goal. I was asked to sit in the waiting room while the committee consulted. Recalling that night, I still feel the bone-chilling nervousness which overcame me. I knew all the members of the committee, most of whom were close friends, among them our family doctor who had treated me since childhood; yet while answering their queries about our income and preparation for such a major step in our lives, I felt I had made a great mistake. I knew our limitations: lack of financial resources, our youth and lack of knowledge about the world outside Iran. Raḥmat had worked for only a few months and during that time we had been on pilgrimage, which had claimed a large chunk of our meagre savings. While the Secretary of the committee, whom I had always called 'uncle', kindly and affectionately talked to me, I wanted to run from the room in a panic. I wished with all my heart that I had not accepted this mission as Raḥmat's emissary and had left it to him to explain everything.

The committee's deliberations took about 45 minutes. They advised me that the members did not think we were the right people to go to those islands. Their explanation sounded completely logical to me: we were too young; we had been married for only a short time and had only just begun to settle down; Raḥmat had a good job in Iran; there was little prospect of a job for him as a physician in the Mentawai Islands. My friend the doctor lovingly explained that the greatest tragedy for a physician was not to be able to practise his profession. He was speaking from his own experience as a former pioneer to Afghanistan. The letter rejecting our application was to be mailed to Raḥmat in Iṣfahán.

I was so relieved to be free of the ordeal of sitting in the presence of the committee that I ran all the way home. At that time there were no direct telephone connections between Ṭihrán and the provinces. I briefly conveyed the committee's message to Raḥmat from a telephone office in downtown Ṭihrán. Late that night, Raḥmat arrived. He was absolutely livid. The Persian proverb 'Beware the wrath of a patient man' was especially true in this instance. He could not believe that a committee, which had received its mandate to facilitate the work of the pioneers direct from the Guardian himself, would reject volunteers willing to bear any hardship and face any eventuality.

We had not asked for financial assistance, so Raḥmat felt that the committee should not concern itself with our future financial stability. He asked to meet with the committee. Two of its members had been his university professors. His arguments did not persuade the committee to change its decision. Raḥmat, of course, was in no way deterred. He requested a meeting with the National Spiritual Assembly. Although my father was the Secretary of that sacred institution, nothing in the world could persuade me to go to that appointment alone.

That memorable day still lives in my mind. Mr Afnán, a member of the local Spiritual Assembly of Yazd, was also waiting to meet with the National Assembly. He told us about recent events in that city: the atrocities committed against the Bahá'ís by the fanatical mobs, the burning of Bahá'í homes, the desecration of the Bahá'í cemetery, and the beating of innocent men, women and children. We all wept. Raḥmat believed that this chance encounter with Mr Afnán, a relative of the blessed Báb, was a bounty which would bring blessings to our future as pioneers.

Our meeting with the National Assembly was quite different from our meeting with the International Goals Committee. All the members, which now included two Hands of the Cause, my father and Mr Valí'u'lláh Varqá, as well as two future Hands of the Cause, General 'Ala'í and Mr Khádem, greeted us with much love and kindness. The members of the National Spiritual Assembly understood the crucial importance of pioneering in relation to the goals of the Ten Year Crusade, and sought to encourage those willing to offer themselves for this service. My father had attended the New Delhi Conference, which had been such a decisive factor in our resolution to go to the Mentawai Islands. At that conference he had made a moving statement to the assembled friends, quoting from the words of 'Abdu'l-Bahá on the spiritual importance of pioneering. In the passages which had so stirred the hearts of those fortunate enough to attend that gathering, the beloved Master likened these early days of the Faith, when there was still the chance to render genuinely sacrificial services, to the time of the first Christians. The National Assembly approved our pioneering plans and assured us of its prayers.

Before going to the meeting of the National Spiritual Assembly, Raḥmat had a dream of Bahá'u'lláh. The Blessed Beauty was walking in the streets of Ṭihrán, carrying a very large rolled carpet on His shoulders. Raḥmat silently went behind Him and took up one end of the carpet. Bahá'u'lláh turned and smiled and expressed His delight that Raḥmat could help him with His burden.

Chapter 2

A TRUE PIONEER

Raḥmat did not want to waste a single day, and immediately submitted his resignation to the hospital. I stayed in Ṭihrán long enough to arrange our passports and secure a one month tourist visa for Indonesia. When I returned to Iṣfahán we sold nearly all our belongings, including most of my jewellery. Within a few days we were back in Ṭihrán. As our funds were very limited, we bought one way tickets to Jakarta via Karachi, Bangkok and Singapore. Although we could have borrowed the money to pay for round trip tickets — and all our friends advised us to — we did not do it. Raḥmat believed that Bahá'u'lláh would open all doors. Return tickets would have given us a sense of security which would induce us to leave at the slightest discomfort. We had about US$500 to cover our travel expenses. Raḥmat knew that after one month in Indonesia our finances would be in such a state that we would be unable to purchase return tickets. He wanted it that way. Many pioneers around the world remember him advising them never to think of leaving their pioneering posts. He knew that pioneering to a foreign and unfamiliar country was never easy. Whether in Europe, Africa, the Americas or Asia, pioneers were isolated, far from family and friends, in an unknown environment. It was simple human nature to want to go home. But perseverance and patience would bring their rewards: gradually the pioneers would come to know the people, and to love their pioneering post as their home.

We were finally ready to leave Iran. We still had no knowledge of the conditions of life or the climate of the place to which we were going. As far as I can remember, I never met anyone in Iran who had the slightest knowledge of Indonesia, and it did not occur to us to ask anyone at that country's embassy. Our visas were obtained through an agency, so we missed the opportunity to at least meet an Indonesian before leaving for that country. We knew that the Indonesian islands were tropical, but our concept of the tropics was simply that it had lots of rain and was sometimes hot. We each packed two suitcases, one containing summer clothes and books, one winter clothes and books. The contents of these four suitcases, two one-way tickets and US$500 was all our worldly wealth.

FROM IRAN TO INDONESIA

We left Ṭihrán for Karachi one bitterly cold afternoon in early January 1954. All our relatives were at the airport. Their good wishes and hugs mingled with tears and sorrow. No one was sure how to respond to this situation. Young people in Iran at that time just did not leave their home for far-off and unknown lands. Some of the pioneers had already left for Africa and Europe, but mostly they had gone with their families. My father was travelling in America at the time, on the instructions of the Guardian, but I still remember my mother, pale and bewildered, saying prayers for our protection on the journey. None of our relatives believed they would ever see us again, but they never tried to dissuade us from following this course. By contrast, Raḥmat was ecstatic. He was confident that in obeying the wishes of the beloved Guardian, we were submitting ourselves to the Will of Bahá'u'lláh and would be protected by Him. Although I was ten years Raḥmat's junior, my training also had prepared me to follow the will of the Guardian, but it was Raḥmat's confidence and inner tranquillity that was the deciding factor in helping me agree to this venture.

We arrived the next day in Karachi, and got our first taste of heat and humidity. At that moment we realized that the clothing in at least two of our suitcases was obsolete; the heat of Karachi, after the severe cold of the winter nights in Ṭihrán, was so scorching that it nearly burned our skin. Two days in Karachi revealed one more disturbing fact; we attended a conference addressed by a prominent Bahá'í speaker, but could not understand a word that was said. Our limited knowledge of English which consisted mostly of phrases learned from 'Essential English' books during the last two years of high school, did not help us. We had passed through 'customs' in

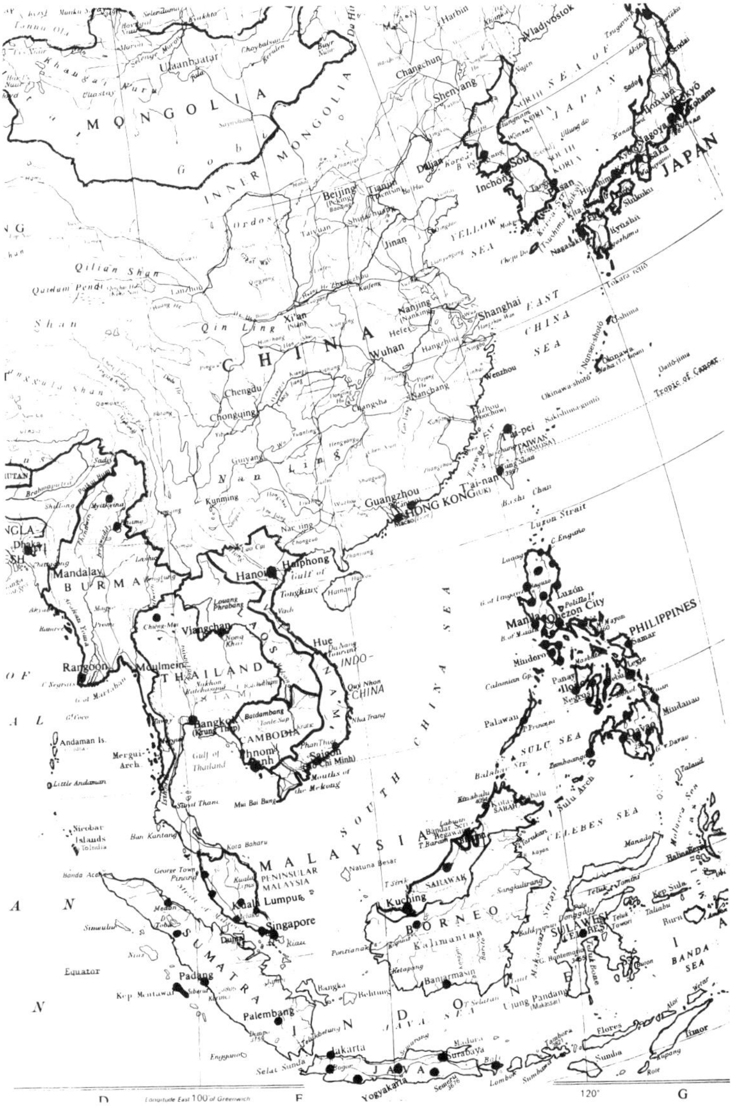

Our first pioneer post was in Indonesia. Asia was to be the arena of Raḥmat's greatest service to the Faith.

Karachi — an overturned wooden box used as a desk in the middle of an unpaved field with a single runway — by using those Persian words which speakers of Urdu could understand. Now we realized that we had a major problem. Even if the Indonesians had spọken English, our few phrases like, 'open the door', and 'shut the window,' would not take us too far.

Our next stop was Bangkok. We had thought Karachi was uncomfortable, but we had never experienced anything like the heat and humidity here. Our woollen clothes did not help matters. The KLM Dutch Airlines office had arranged a guided tour of the city; Raḥmat removed his coat and tie, rolled up his shirtsleeves and joined the crowd, but nothing in the world could persuade me to leave the bus. I had not eaten anything but bread and tea since we left Ṭihrán, had heat rash all over my skin and simply was in no mood to go among people who were walking around barefoot in short pants and sleeveless shirts. In the following years, we visited Bangkok many times. The beauty and splendour of that historic city are truly breath-taking. We loved the people and the food, and I very often wondered why I had been so scared that first night.

Raḥmat was always fascinated by new cultures and new faces. He walked around the city and did not find any of it threatening. He was at home right away. I believe that because of the intense love he felt for people everywhere, he was able to travel constantly for over 20 years and bear all the hardships and strains of those travels with tranquillity and resignation.

The torrential tropical rain that we had read about greeted us in full force upon arrival in Jakarta, capital of Indonesia. The combination of rain and heat was truly unbearable. Our only desire was to see a familiar face in the crowd. We had sent a telegram to Mr Payman a week before our departure. Although we had never met the Payman family, we were sure that we would recognize them. However, after two hours waiting at the airport we accepted the fact that no one was coming to greet us. Jakarta International Airport was small, with few attendants and no air conditioning. Our KLM flight was the last one of the day and the attendants were preparing to leave. The combination of Persian and Indonesian languages was somehow more of a barrier than a means of communication. We had not brought Mr Payman's letter with us, and, in our rushed preparations for departure, had not even copied out the address. All that we could communicate to the helpful airport official was that we needed a place to stay the night, and we managed that only by repeating the word 'hotel', over and over. The attendant shook his head and made us understand that there were no rooms to rent in Jakarta. Raḥmat finally wrote Mr Payman's cable address, 'Payman, Jakarta', and asked our friend if he could call him. His advice, which he conveyed to us with great difficulty, was that we should go to the main post office to find the phone number. He stored our luggage in a closet, found us a taxi (for which he paid, as we had no local currency), and sent us to the post office. By this time it was more than five hours after our arrival in Jakarta. Our clothes were soaked with rain and perspiration. I was so exhausted that my only thought was to sit in a corner and shut my eyes, in the hope that this whole scene would vanish.

We had been repeating the prayer of the Báb, 'Is there any Remover of difficulties save God' all afternoon, and we felt that Bahá'u'lláh had surely heard our prayer and would come to our rescue. He did. The clerk behind the counter at the post office, being a Muslim who had read the Qur'án, was familiar with Arabic. He would not give us Mr Payman's address, but kindly placed a call to his home. Within half-an-hour Mr Payman was with us. The cable had not reached him, so our arrival was as much a surprise to him as it was to the bemused airport and postal attendants. Looking back on that day, I can imagine what a strange spectacle the two of us must have presented. Clad in woollen clothing in a tropical city, with no hotel reservations in a capital known for its scarcity of hotels, and speaking no language that anyone else could understand. We did not resemble the primarily European tourists with whom the Indonesians were familiar, and we had not even once mentioned the island of Bali, the first destination of any tourist. Perhaps our helplessness was the reason for their kindness.

I cannot remember a happier moment than when we heard Mr Payman's greeting of 'Alláh'u'Abhá!' Soon we forgot how exhausted and famished we were, and started to take an interest in our surroundings. Jakarta was a charming city. On the way to his home, Mr Payman expressed his astonishment that we had decided to leave Iran without a firm offer of a job. However, he assured

Raḥmat that he would help all he possibly could to secure a permanent visa for us. Mr and Mrs Payman did their utmost to make our first night very comfortable. Our luggage was still at the airport, so we had to borrow clothes from them. That night, which was the start of our long years of pioneering, is one of the most memorable and cherished events in our lives. I can still remember the feel of the cool air from the ceiling fan, the taste of the delicious food and the tea from the samovar, and the pleasant conversation we had with the Payman family, who were to become our dearest and closest friends.

With the Payman family, Jakarta, circa 1964.

OUR FIRST MIRACLE

Early next morning, despite objections from Mr Payman, Raḥmat insisted that he wanted to search for a job. Mr Payman's argument sounded reasonable to the rest of us. He suggested that Raḥmat should spend the month allowed on our tourist visas to learn Indonesian, and become familiar with the health care system of the country. Raḥmat's view was that his primary purpose in coming to Indonesia was to open the Mentawai Islands to the Faith. This was a goal of the Ten Year Crusade and the Guardian wanted all these goals settled in the first year. Time was short, and there were only four months left before the deadline. Raḥmat did not care about the type of work he could find, as long as it took us to the Mentawai Islands. Mr Payman finally surrendered, though it was not clear just where to start looking for a job. Raḥmat's opinion was that they should start with the Ministry of Health and work their way down. To humour him, Mr Payman agreed. I willingly stayed at home and waited for our luggage to arrive from the airport.

That day was the start of an extended and glorious spiritual journey for Raḥmat. None of us could imagine that this eager, intense young man, who so urgently looked for any sort of job which would enable him to pioneer to his given goal, would be instrumental in bringing the Faith of Bahá'u'lláh to thousands among the masses of humanity.

When Raḥmat and Mr Payman returned home that evening, Raḥmat's face was radiant with happiness and Mr Payman repeated over and over, 'It is undeniably a miracle!' When the receptionist at the Ministry of Health was told that Raḥmat was a doctor, he was immediately conducted to the office of the Deputy Minister. There was a great shortage of physicians in Indonesia at that time. The Dutch colonization had come to an end in 1945, and the newly-formed Republic of Indonesia was in the process of rebuilding the country. Doctors were desperately needed but there were not many who were able or willing to apply, especially since they had to pay their own way to enter the country. The Deputy Minister had kept Raḥmat and Mr Payman with him the entire day. He had asked for maps, examined them for some time, and chose Bukittinggi on the island of Sumatra as a post for Raḥmat. This is a beautiful city on a hilltop, with cool and crisp air. During Dutch rule, Bukittinggi had been a vacation spot for the elite. The Minister, learning that Raḥmat was accompanied by his young wife, had chosen it so that we could live in comfort. A house and servants, as well as a car and driver, came with the job. Raḥmat would work for the State hospital in the mornings and have his own clinic in the afternoon.

This offer would have been ideal for anyone whose purpose was to accumulate wealth and live a comfortable life. Raḥmat had another purpose. Bukittinggi is situated in the west of Sumatra, a few hundred miles from the Mentawai Islands. When Raḥmat asked the Minister if he could work on those islands instead of Bukittinggi, the minister treated his request as a joke. Bukittinggi, with a population of around 500,000, was without a doctor. The population of the Mentawai Islands was only about 25,000. The Minister had not even noticed the existence of these islands before Raḥmat pointed them out to him. They discussed the matter for the rest of the day, and the Minister finally agreed that we could go to the Mentawai Islands on a trial basis. Years later, when we had become friends, the Minister told us that he still could not understand how that agreement had been reached. Saying goodbye to Raḥmat, the Minister expressed his opinion that, even if *he* survived the conditions of those islands on his altruistic beliefs, a white, nineteen-year old woman would not, and could not, endure them. Raḥmat signed a three-year contract with the Ministry of Health on the spot, the Mentawai Islands his designated post. His salary was Rs. 400 (about US$25) a month, and he was to pick up the air tickets for Padang, capital of Sumatra, next morning.

What Mr Payman considered a miracle was not how swiftly the contract had gone through, but that of all the hundreds of islands in the Indonesian Archipelago, the Minister had chosen Sumatra. Any other island would not have given Raḥmat the opportunity to fulfil the goal of pioneering to the Mentawai Islands.

BY BOAT TO THE MENTAWAI ISLANDS

We had to go to Padang to board the boat for the Mentawai Islands. A few days later we left Jakarta. Our luggage was much lighter now, as we had disposed of all our woollen clothes. Our days in Padang were mostly spent trying to learn the basics of the Indonesian

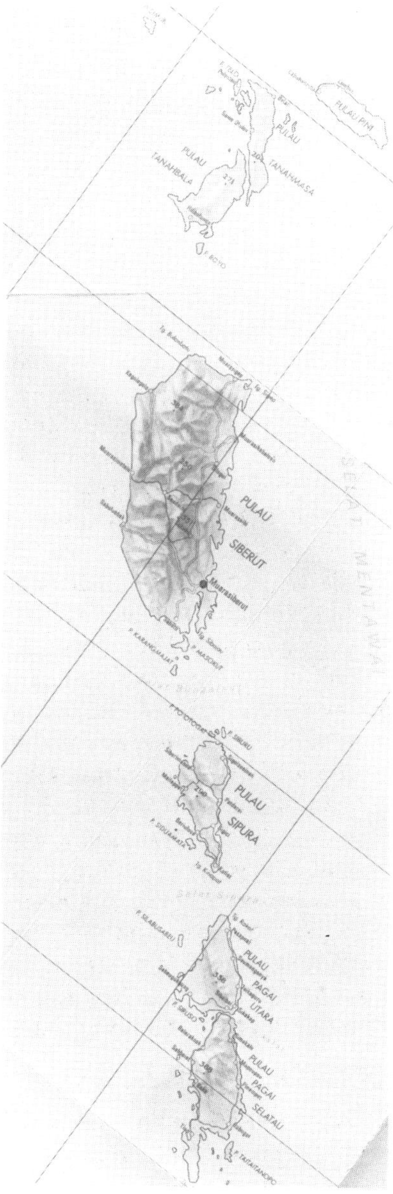

Map of the Mentawai Islands.

language. We were informed that the only means of transportation to the Mentawai Islands was a small State-owned cargo boat named the *Beo*, or 'Mina Bird'. It followed no fixed schedule and set sail every few months, whenever there was sufficient cargo to warrant the expense. We had to wait two weeks before we were told we could leave. Arrangements had been made by the Governor of Sumatra for the boat to make a special trip, to take the doctor to his post. The boat took 40 hours to cover the 100 miles or so that separated the Mentawai Islands from the mainland of Sumatra.

This was our first experience of sea travel. The closest I had ever come to an ocean was in the North of Iran, when we had gone for a few days' rest to a beach on the Caspian Sea. To be tossed about for a night and a day on the rough waves of the Indian Ocean in this small vessel was not something that we had bargained for. There were no passenger cabins on this boat, but the captain had very courteously relinquished his quarters for our use. I slept on a small bunk for the duration of the journey.

Raḥmat was seasick most of the time, and developed a severe headache which no amount of pain-killer could alleviate. In later years, whenever he visited pioneers on islands which could be reached only by boat, he would often tell me that he wished the friends knew how much he suffered to get there: then they might treat his suggestions more kindly.

Nothing in our life had prepared us for the Mentawai Islands. We certainly had not seen anything like them in Iran, and the four cities we had visited on our way to Indonesia were not remotely comparable to what confronted us at the moment of our arrival. The turbulent sea and heavy rain had continued throughout our voyage from Padang.

The boat had to drop anchor a long way from shore, and we were told to climb down a rope ladder, hanging at the side of the boat. Then we had to board a rowing boat, crewed by two men who appeared to be completely naked. My first thought was to run back to the cabin and hide, until the *Beo* returned to civilization. However, my hand was held firmly by Raḥmat, who was quietly chanting the Tablet of Aḥmad, oblivious to what was going on around us.

Raḥmat had a unique attitude to spiritual challenges. His only feeling on arrival in the Mentawai Islands was exhilaration that a goal assigned by the beloved Guardian had been achieved. His first thought was that we should pray constantly that we would be worthy of this great honour bestowed upon us by Bahá'u'lláh.

Our final destination was Muarasiberut, the main settlement on Siberut Selatan, one of the four islands of Mentawai. The residents of Muarasiberut were natives of Sumatra, mostly Muslims, who had lived on the islands since the time of the Dutch colonization. The Mentawai Islands had been used as a penal colony by the Dutch authorities; hardened criminals were exiled there, then practically forgotten. Malaria, combined with all kinds of skin diseases and other illnesses, the tropical heat and lack of medical attention, resulted in an extremely high mortality rate. The independence of Indonesia and the departure of the Dutch left the small number of Sumatrans on the islands without jobs or a source of income; so they turned to trading with the native tribal people of Mentawai.

The indigenous Mentawais lived in scattered hamlets, far from

A view of Muarasiberut and the bay in 1991:
a more modern village today.

Muarasiberut. The main crop of the island was coconuts, which they bartered for the poorest quality and cheapest tobacco that the mainlanders could buy. They had never received money, and did not know its value. I saw this place as wilderness, far from the comforts of civilization: Raḥmat saw a beautiful, green tropical island with indigenous inhabitants whose pure hearts and minds were ready to receive the Message of Bahá'u'lláh. He never equated lack of formal education, and what most of us consider 'civilization', with lack of intelligence or understanding.

Prayers — and the assistance of the assembled crew — helped us slide down the side of the ship into the rowing boat. Our suitcases were lowered, and the two natives, mystified by our manner and appearance, rowed us to the shore. Word had already reached the

A Mentawai, in traditional loin cloth, tattooed from head to toe.

village about us, and every one of the two hundred residents — men, women and children — had gathered to view the spectacle of our arrival. Mixed with the mainland residents greeting us were a few native men and women, clad only in very narrow loincloths, their bodies covered from forehead to ankle in tattoos of the most ornate and fascinating designs. Everyone was wading through mud, covering their heads with what I later came to know were banana leaves, to protect them from the downpour. Raḥmat and I were, of course, soaked to the bone. The rain and humidity posed no threat to our luggage, however, which had already fallen into the sea while being transferred from the boat.

A narrow plank was thrown over the lake of mud for our benefit. Raḥmat just waded into the mud while holding my hand and helping me manoeuvre down the slippery, wobbly plank. My patent-leather high heels were not designed for this sort of thing and, after a few steps, I was flat on my back struggling with the mounds of wet slippery leaves, which were mixed in with the black smelly mud. The facade of bravery that I had carried with me suddenly evaporated. I just lay there and burst into tears. This broke the ice. Suddenly, all those who had come to stare were transformed into sympathetic hosts. I was pulled out and taken to a nearby stall where the ladies helped me wipe off the mud. Raḥmat, meanwhile, kept reminding me that we were pioneers of Bahá'u'lláh, and that we had to maintain our decorum. My first purchase in the Mentawai Islands was a pair of rubber sandals to replace the high heels that I had lost to the mud.

With our few words of Indonesian we tried to thank them for their kindness. It was then that we found the two men who were to become our translators in the following months. One was Eddie, a very pale and emaciated young man, a Protestant who had studied English for a few years at the mission school in Padang, the other was named Kamaluddin ('Luddin' to everyone), a man of about 30, clad in a sarong with a traditional Indonesian black hat, who had studied the Qur'án and understood Arabic.

Three final blasts of the boat's siren heralded its departure. It would not return for at least another three months.

WELCOMED BY 'MR MAYOR'

Under the direction of the village chief, 'Abdu'lláh, the Mentawais had paved the paths with small stones, only to lose them in the first storm. 'Mr Mayor' —*Tuan Chamat*— tried his best to persuade us to stay on his island. Once he was assured that we would stay, he had to decide what to do with us. Chamat was appointed by the government, and disliked by the majority of the population. He occupied the lowest rank within the government system, which started at '2a' and rose to '6c'. The rank of Chamat, or assistant *wedana*, was '2a'. Being a physician, Raḥmat was automatically entitled to the rank of '6b'. According to Chamat 'Abdu'lláh, the only other person he had known of such high rank was a long-departed Dutch Colonel, who, of course, had never actually needed or wanted to find accommodation in Muarasiberut.

Chamat was to prove a good and reliable friend to us in the years that we spent in Mentawai, and helped us through many a hardship. His tall tales were a source of relief and entertainment during many lonely days, and he tolerated Raḥmat's teasing with good humour. Often, when he mentioned that he had been offered the governorship of Sumatra but had refused it, Raḥmat, with a straight face, would encourage him to accept the position for the good of the people of Mentawai. On one occasion, Chamat ran to our house with great excitement to inform us of the sighting of an 'enemy plane'. No plane had ever passed over the Mentawai Islands: that one was sighted was proof of its hostility. Raḥmat assured Chamat that, with his wisdom and bravery to lead us, we could face any onslaught. Chamat agreed, and told us how he had hunted lions with the Dutch Colonel, and how he had saved him from one lion's attack. We knew by this time that the jungles of the Mentawai Islands did not harbour lions, but still we did not question his claim. He left happy in the knowledge that the doctor would be available to tend the wounded if the islands were attacked.

As the months passed and we became more familiar with conditions in the village, we understood the nature of Chamat's dilemma at our first encounter. However, on that first day I could not understand why he was not prepared to offer us hospitality in his home. What Chamat did do was to gather the other government officials, eleven altogether, one of whom was the owner of the stall to which we had been led, to consult about our accommodation. The only vacant place in the village was an abandoned building with three rooms which had been the residence of the Dutch Warden. It seemed a plausible solution. With Chamat in front and the whole village following, we went to inspect the proposed dwelling. We had to walk single file through the passage made in the tall wild grass, holding the hand of the person in front so that we would not slip. I still thank God for our ignorance on that day. Had I known what lived in the shrubbery, I would have preferred to stay where we were, rather than risk being bitten by the snakes and centipedes abounding in the grass and mud. The whole venture, however, proved futile. The house assigned to us had been built some 30 years before on wooden planks with walls of tree bark and a thatched roof. It had been abandoned to the ravages of nature for more than ten years. The roof had gaping holes, the walls were rotten, and termites were feasting on the remaining wood. A few goats had

With Chamat ('Mr Mayor') first on the left, in front of our simple village home.

occupied the doorless rooms, and chickens were nesting in the corners among the pieces of thatch that had fallen from the roof.

Although Chamat assured us that the water snakes, which had been flooded out of the brook in front of the house and were now slithering around us, were completely harmless, I had no intention of finding out for myself. Huge rats were running about, some sitting on their hind legs and observing us with curiosity. Raḥmat's attempts to calm me down, by saying that we could just sweep a corner and wait till better accommodation was found, did not have its usual effect. I preferred to go back to the shore and wait out the three months for the return of the *Beo*. My Persian protestations were somehow understood by Chamat. The village council gathered under their banana leaves, and after a while informed us that the village schoolmaster had generously agreed to give us temporary shelter in his house — for a small remuneration. The congregation followed us to the schoolhouse on the other side of the village. It consisted of two small rooms and a smaller shed which served as the kitchen. The room facing the ocean had a window which caught the breeze, and was quite pleasant. The back room stored bails of tobacco, which the schoolmaster bartered with the natives, as a sideline business. Its only opening was the entrance door. This was offered to us for the two months that the school was in recess. The ceiling was low and Raḥmat had difficulty standing up. However, there were no rats visible, as the smell of tobacco drove them away. I thanked God profusely for this great bounty: the whole village sighed with relief.

It was now about six hours since our arrival. It was getting dark and the rain had become much stronger. The villagers had lost interest in our affairs, and, one by one, had left the scene. The house had no bathroom facilities. Eddie explained that we should wrap ourselves in sarongs, collect rainwater in a pail, and take our bath in front of the house. This was what everyone else did. The schoolmaster's wife, a portly and kind middle-aged lady, took my hand and guided me through the tall grass, over a slippery wooden plank, to a brook about 30 yards from the house. Two planks were thrown over the muddy water, which abounded with water snakes and bullfrogs. To my amazement, she smilingly demonstrated its use as a toilet facility.

A small kerosene lamp was lent to us. Chamat brought us a bowl of boiled rice and some dried fish smothered in ground hot chilies, and bade us good night. Had I known that this was to be our only meal for the next two days I would have forgone my apprehension of eating dry goldfish, and would have tried to get accustomed to chili. In time I learned to follow Raḥmat's advice to eat whatever was available. However, on that first night I was too exhausted to think about the future, and made do with a few mouthfuls of rice. The room was so small that we could not close the door; the smell of tobacco was very strong. We made a bed out of our clothing and tried to rest. The open door and the lack of a mosquito net was an open invitation to all the bugs of the village to make a feast of these two unknowing foreigners.

THE ISLAND STORE

The next morning, Chamat, Luddin and Eddie visited us to discuss Raḥmat's work. My questions about getting some basic household goods were greeted with tolerant smiles. There was nothing in the village to be bought or borrowed. The only store belonged to a Chinese expatriate, Si Temeh, who bartered tobacco for coconuts and bananas, and who sometimes sold rice and matches. Si Temeh, a kind elderly man, became a very good friend of ours in the ensuing years. He would order goods from Padang, then sell these to me at very inflated prices. However, his store was the only place with a battery-operated radio, so it became a haven for us. Once a week he would turn on his radio in our honour and allow us to listen, without charging us for his precious water battery. Although he tried his best to accommodate our needs, we had to make do with what he had. If we asked for soap he would reply, 'I have no soap, but I have something else: matches.' This was a regular feature of our trips to the store, and we were often offered soap when we needed salt, and candles when we needed soap. Raḥmat called him *Si La'in* — 'Mr Something Else': Si Temeh grinned toothlessly and offered green tea to *Tuan Doktor*. A few years after our departure Raḥmat returned to visit the island and found that Si Temeh had passed away. His wife lamented that Raḥmat had not been there to tend to her husband, and said, 'Si Temeh's illness was something, but the medication given to him was for something else.' We often prayed for Si Temeh's soul, but Raḥmat could not keep a straight face, remembering how the old man had kept his habit to his last breath.

Chamat advised us that the only way to buy anything was to wait for the boat and order goods from Padang. The only problem with this suggestion was that the boat would not come for another three months, and with the usual postponements and delays, it would be about ten months before we could meet our basic needs. The village council was convened again, and we were informed that some of the villagers were ready to lend us the necessary materials — for a small monetary compensation. By that evening two chairs, two plates, two tin cups and a few cooking utensils were brought to us. Although most of them were chipped and broken, we were very grateful. Our landlady cheerfully took it upon herself to teach me how to cook on firewood, though it took her a while to realize that I could not cook at all. However she persevered in teaching me how to collect firewood, and how to make a wood stove with mud and stones, sheltering it with banana leaves. In the following years I realized how helpful this skill was and what a debt of gratitude I owed that kind lady. Drinking water was another problem. We were told that in the months of the monsoon we could collect water in pails for washing and cooking, and drinking water in hollow bamboo sticks by leaning them against a tree trunk. However, when the long months of the dry season arrived, with temperatures above 45°C, I had to walk to a spring about two miles away, and carry water in a pail.

Raḥmat was already planning his first visits to the natives of Mentawai. Despite Chamat's efforts to convince him that these people were not worthy of a doctor, Raḥmat prepared to leave in a few days. The only medication available in the village was the few pills Raḥmat had brought with him. A small wooden box containing the village's medical supplies proved completely useless. A few bottles of penicillin had long passed their expiry date, and many of the pills were mixed together and could not be identified. It took many months before the Ministry of Health could fill Raḥmat's orders and send appropriate supplies to the Mentawai Islands. By that time both of us had contracted the severest kind of tropical malaria. Every two days we went through a sequence of chills and blinding fever, and extreme fatigue and weakness followed each attack. We were not much comforted by our landlady's story about a Dutch military man who had suffered from the same kind of malaria, had gone quite mad and had to be sent home in a strait-jacket! By the time we obtained a supply of quinine tablets the disease's grip on us was so strong that, although it did not occur so frequently as in that first year, we suffered from it throughout our five years in the Mentawai Islands.

KNIGHTS OF BAHÁ'U'LLÁH

Five days after our arrival, accompanied by Luddin as his translator, Raḥmat set out in a small canoe rowed by five Mentawai men. This marked the culmination of many months of prayer and preparation to fulfil the wishes of the beloved Guardian. At this time my father was on pilgrimage and the Guardian was anxiously awaiting news of the opening of the Mentawai Islands to the Faith. One day he happily announced the receipt of a cable from the National Spiritual Assembly of India, which supervised the affairs of the Faith in Indonesia, informing him of our arrival in the Mentawai Islands. He gave my father a cable, to be sent from Turkey to Iran, that another virgin territory had been opened on 4 February 1954. It was a long time, however, before we were informed that the Guardian had announced our names to the Bahá'í world as Knights of Bahá'u'lláh.

From his first encounter with the indigenous people, Raḥmat established a systematic routine, the foundation of his mass teaching methods throughout his service to the Faith. The Mentawais were a simple people, with primitive traditions based on animistic beliefs. They had great respect for their ancestors but did not have formal rituals of worship. When someone died, the corpse was wrapped in banana leaves and bark, and was lifted to the top of a tree growing on a river bed. Every so often the corpse was washed in the river and the remains re-wrapped. When the bones were completely clean, the relatives of the deceased took them to their home and hung them from the rafters of the ceiling. On one of our first visits to a hut, I was hit on the head by one of these hanging bones. It was not till months later that I realized that the bones were not ornaments, but the remains of the host's father.

SETTLING IN MUARASIBERUT

Raḥmat's trips upriver took a few days. To reach the farthest hamlets he had to walk through thick jungle, sometimes for days on end. He and his Mentawai guides carried machetes to cut a passage through the tree branches and undergrowth. They had to repeat this every time they passed the same way, as the shrubbery grew so fast that within a few days it covered the path they had cleared. On his first trip Raḥmat was gone for about two weeks: I had to start life in the small village of Muarasiberut on my own. We had brought with us a book from which to learn Indonesian, and I started to study the language. For the first time I understood the importance of Bahá'u'lláh's teaching about a universal language. Learning Indonesian was not very difficult, since I had nothing else to do. I had been warned by the Sumatran villagers not to leave our room when Raḥmat was away, as I might be attacked by the Mentawais, who had not seen a white woman before. Although Chamat emphasized that he would severely punish anyone who dared cut off my head, I felt it more prudent to heed the advice of the villagers and not venture out of the room unless absolutely necessary. Such notions about the natives were, of course, completely erroneous. As we became more familiar with them, we found the Mentawais to be the most friendly and gentle people we had ever known. In the early days, however, I locked the door of the little room, and studied Indonesian from sunrise to sunset. In a few months I had no trouble with the language, and could comfortably communicate with the villagers. I felt a great deal less lonely and helpless.

Time had no meaning any more. We had no calendar and our only timepiece, a small delicate wristwatch given to me as a wedding gift, stopped working after a few days. I never discovered the cause of its demise, although Chamat suggested that it could have been the extreme heat. We started fasting on a day that we thought was 2 March. I have never been so happy at the approach of the fasting period as I was then. I did not have to think about food, which was not available anyway. We opened our fast with boiled rice and the juice of lemons which grew wildly on the island, and Raḥmat, while travelling, ate coconuts and bananas. It was only by accident that we realized we had continued fasting for 22 days. My despair on missing the Naw-Rúz feast was so funny to Raḥmat that I decided it was better to forget the whole thing. He couldn't understand what I would have done differently on Naw-Rúz, as we said the same prayers and ate the same meal every day.

THE FIRST MENTAWAI BAHÁ'Í

In the first months of his travels Raḥmat tried to study the customs and habits of the Mentawais and learn their language. Although he told them about the Faith through Luddin, he did not expect them to become Bahá'ís. He wanted them to get to know and trust him first. He also wanted to talk to them directly in their own language. He tried to help them with the limited amount of medical supplies that he had, visiting the villages several times within a few months. Skin diseases, malaria, tuberculosis and many other ailments were rampant. Shamans were the only ones who tended the sick.

On one of these frequent trips, in the middle of 1954, he was going to Si Pai Pajet, the farthest village in Siberut. One of the men rowing the canoe was an elder of that village by the name of Amata Sinanga. During the week that they spent travelling, Raḥmat talked to him in the Mentawai language, which he had mastered by this time, telling him about Bahá'u'lláh and His teachings. Amata Sinanga explained that the Mentawai natives never accepted anything unless it was done collectively, and with the approval of the village elders. On arrival in Si Pai Pajet, Amata Sinanga called a meeting of the elders and asked Raḥmat to talk to them about the Faith. After a few hours they took a vote and all agreed that what they had heard was good. Amata Sinanga declared that all of them had decided to be Bahá'ís. These 25 elders formed the nucleus of a community of thousands who were to accept the Faith in those islands. Amata Sinanga was the first Bahá'í of the Mentawai Islands, and Si Pai Pajet the first Bahá'í village.

Chamat and his helpers, meanwhile, were busy repairing the former warden's house for our occupation. After about four months the council proudly asked us to inspect their handiwork. The school had already started, as had the dry season, and life in our small room, with the growing bails of tobacco and bundles of banana and coconut, had become intolerable. By the mercy of God, the forty or so children at the school tried to keep the noise to a minimum until

Mentawai homes and children.

Raḥmat sometimes travelled by canoe – a popular form of transport among the Mentawai.

the two intruders could vacate their premises. Although we were paying for the room, the schoolmaster was also anxious to get rid of us, as our occupation of his trading office hampered his barter business. One room of the old building had been repaired. Despite lack of materials, the council had patched the holes as best they could. Old and yellowed Dutch newspapers were used as wallpaper. The paste, a mixture of sago flour and water, seeped through the thin newsprint and left light brown patches. For a while, just looking at the room gave us a sensation of dizziness not unlike sea-sickness. However, we had no choice. We thanked the village council for all the trouble to which they had gone, and moved our suitcases to our new abode.

We lived for more than four years in that room, and I gradually became well versed in all the words and pictures of our wallpaper. I could quote whole paragraphs without knowing the meaning of a single word. The holes in the ceiling were merely covered by the paper, and with the first monsoon rains they reappeared, and remained for the duration of our stay. During the torrential tropical rains, which were practically continuous, it was much safer and more convenient for us to stand outside in the open. After each rainfall, we swept out the water and waited for the next downpour. There was no fear of damage to our belongings: we simply did not have any, except the second-hand stuff which had been given to us on our arrival.

The most exciting event connected with the room happened a few weeks after our move. I could hear loud thumping noises from the attic, which could not be attributed merely to rats. My complaints were ignored for a while, but after I flatly refused to spend one more night under the gaping hole, horrified at the prospect of some creature falling on me, Raḥmat approached Chamat, who sent two Mentawai men to investigate the alleged noise. After a vigorous chase around the attic, they climbed down carrying a live, three-foot long lizard which they promptly roasted over a fire in front of our room, making quite a feast of it. Seeing the creature consumed by them, and Raḥmat's sworn statement that this was the only culprit, gave me considerable peace of mind and made our single room feel a little more like home.

DOCTOR TO THE BODY — AND THE SOUL

We settled into a routine and started planning our work in the islands. Raḥmat's trips, only a few days long at first, became more extended as he tried to reach more villages, keeping him away, for up to 40 days, teaching the Faith and tending to the physical ills of the natives. His visits brought joy to the people. His love for them was so great and so obvious, that they immediately felt and responded to it. Amata Sinanga related that when the doctor even approached their village, people felt it, and their health improved.

The Mentawais lived in widely separated villages, in small clannish groups. Each group had claim to a few coconut and banana trees and did not intrude on the property of others. Their longhouses were raised wooden platforms with thatched roofs but no walls. The smoke from damp lighted grass could not drive away the bugs and mosquitoes. At night the only light came from a little wick floating in coconut oil. A rag dipped in coconut oil and wrapped around a bamboo stick served as a torch when one had to walk in the pitch dark of the jungle. Their chickens and pigs were housed under the platform, and the extended family lived above them. The Mentawais were monogamous, and their marriage rituals very simple. Gifts were exchanged between the two families and the groom moved to the bride's house. Children were taken care of, collectively, by all members of the clan. There was strict equality of labour and social status between men and women, and they shared in all chores, including cooking, child-rearing, rowing and fishing. The Mentawais of Siberut did not consume alcohol; their main refreshment was a drink made from coconut juice, bananas and cane sugar. They did not eat chillies, and the only seasoning they used was sea water salt. Meals were eaten with most of the group gathered together. Raḥmat often shared their meals, and never refused anything. Only once did he decline to eat a special delicacy offered to him; it consisted of live large red ants, cultivated in special hollow bamboos under the damp earth. If the ants had been cooked he would have eaten them without hesitation.

The acceptance of the Faith by the 25 council elders of Si Pai Pajet paved the way for the rest of the villages. Hearing about the Faith and Raḥmat's kindness, the other villagers sought his advice and treated him as their brother. They loved him dearly, and called

A happy Mentawai couple.

him *Si Lottoro* — 'Mr Doctor'. Raḥmat's first act as their physician was to examine methodically every member of each village group, and make medical charts for them. The most visible and prevalent of their ailments, besides malaria, was a skin disease called framboesia, a bleeding wound which ate into their flesh, was very contagious and caused deformity of the limbs. Raḥmat had to wait for months before the required medicine could be sent from Padang. After months of experiment, he found out that framboesia could be treated with penicillin injections. Raḥmat started a systematic programme of treatment which achieved great results. The disease was completely eradicated leaving only scars as a reminder of the hideous ulcers which the islanders had suffered for generations.

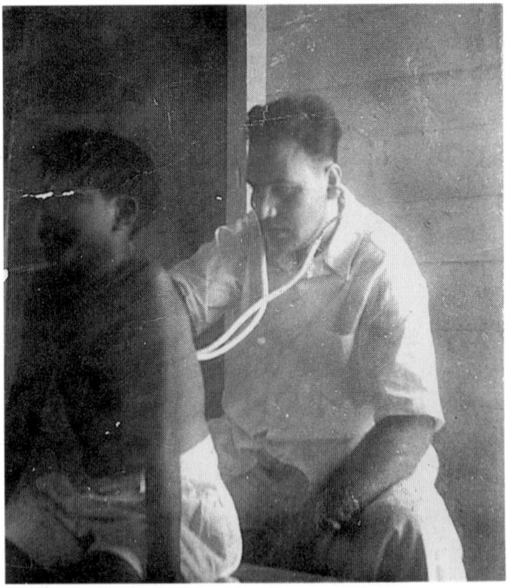

All Mentawai children were examined and vaccinated by Raḥmat.

A rare viral disease called *penjakit babi* — 'pig's disease' — indiscriminately affected people of all ages on the islands. It had similar symptoms to mumps, attacking the glands of the ears and the neck and causing a very painful swelling which gradually blocked the throat. It was invariably fatal. During one of Raḥmat's long absences I noticed a small swelling below my jaw which, unaware of *penjakit babi*, I thought to be a tooth infection. As the swelling rapidly grew, and all the cold and hot compresses did not help, I asked for aid from *Njonja Wali Negri* — 'Mrs Assistant Chamat' — an old lady who had had no schooling at all, and who had been the village midwife before Raḥmat's arrival. She immediately quarantined me in our room, painted my neck with blue ink and covered it with a very hot poultice made of boiling rice. She advised me that I should pray to whoever I believed in, and then she left. I did not see her again for a long time. The hot poultice burned my thin swollen skin, and blisters appeared over my neck and face. In addition to saying prayers, I took all the antibiotics available in the house and prepared penicillin injections which I asked passing villagers to administer on the spot to which I pointed. Nothing helped. The massive doses of antibiotics, lack of food, regular bouts of malaria and the severe pain of the glands had made me so weak that I could only sit on the wooden plank that served as our bed and pray to Bahá'u'lláh to come to my rescue.

Raḥmat could not be contacted, as I had no idea which direction he had taken. Even if I had, no one would approach the house whom I could ask to help find him. At last, some days later, the old midwife came to the door and advised me to pay some of the villagers to go look for my husband. I gratefully accepted her suggestion, and paid the required amount. The same night Raḥmat arrived. He had been in Si Pai Pajet, when he suddenly had felt that he should return. It had taken him about ten days to reach home. On arrival, he was very surprised to notice the strange glances of the people. Finally Luddin had told him that the villagers believed his wife was on the verge of death.

Although Raḥmat's presence was a great mental support, the disease continued to get worse. There was no way to have tests. Raḥmat said prayers continuously, and I took the antibiotics. Another week passed before we suddenly noticed that the swelling was down and the fever was dropping. It was nearly a month before I was able to leave the room and take a short walk, assisted by Raḥmat. We had a small flashlight with a very weak battery, which we had to use sparingly. While we were walking, Raḥmat suddenly stopped and told me not to move. A deadly poisonous snake, a few metres long with black and white markings, wound its way under our feet. It seemed an eternity before the snake disappeared into the shrubbery. Now it was Raḥmat's turn to collapse. The thought of having to watch his wife die from snake bite, and not be able to do anything about it, was too much for him. News of my recovery, and my escape from the deadly snake, spread around the village: everyone considered it a miracle performed by *Si Lottoro*. His prestige among the local population increased enormously, and people started to come to him instead of the old midwife. As far as I know, however, no one else afflicted with 'pig's disease' was ever cured with antibiotics, and it persisted as a fatal illness for as long as we remained in Siberut.

The old midwife started to visit me regularly and, although she was a staunch Muslim, asked me about the Faith. Raḥmat treated her as a colleague, and, with loving patience, taught her a more hygienic way to deliver babies. After we had left the islands, she called the Bahá'í school teacher to her death-bed, confessed her belief in Bahá'u'lláh, and asked him to tell Raḥmat.

I relate these incidents in detail as a reminder that Bahá'u'lláh always protects those who arise in His path — no matter how insignificant the service. It is my belief that Bahá'u'lláh's love for Raḥmat protected me from any serious illness. If I had needed an operation, even for something like appendicitis, I surely would have died. For a doctor to have to stand by helplessly and watch his wife die would have been an agonizing experience. I never even thought about what I would do if Raḥmat were to fall seriously ill.

Two local customs gave us great concern because of their effects on the natives' health. Tattooing began in childhood, and continued till the mid-20s. Beautiful, intricate patterns covered almost the entire body, and varied for each individual with distinctive features for each Mentawai tribe. The tattoos, however, often brought about painful infection and severe fever, and the ministrations of the shaman were not always helpful. Raḥmat did not try to prevent them from continuing this cultural tradition, but rather taught them to sterilize their needles: this lessened infection to a great degree. Antibiotics took care of those who still became infected.

Sharpening the front teeth, by filing them with a piece of iron, was also considered a thing of beauty by the natives. However, this practice often caused them to lose their teeth at an early age. As this custom was definitely harmful to their health, Raḥmat insisted that it stop. He introduced dental hygiene by making toothbrushes out of coconut husks, and taught them how to brush their teeth, using salt for toothpaste. For months he used the same method himself until the Mentawais became accustomed to it. He thanked God that in later years he did not have to extract teeth as much as he had done in those early days. Being the only physician, he had to perform the duties of a dentist without any kind of anaesthetic, which made it almost as painful for him as for the poor patients.

Malaria was systematically eradicated by the spraying of the marshes and distribution of quinine tablets. Raḥmat's revolutionary achievements were unique in Indonesia, and became a model for social and environmental development work in that country.

A NEW WAY OF LIFE

By the time a few months had passed, our life before Mentawai faded to a distant existence, of no significance in our present environment. The *Beo* finally brought us some goods from Padang. As there was no electricity and no cooling facility, we could only order dry goods, and these in small quantities. Humidity was so strong that even rice would mould after a few weeks. Little by little we learned to survive on bananas, rice and fish. Although fish was the staple food of the expatriates, it was not available every day. It took me about a year before I could eat dry chillied fish, the smell of which hung heavily around the village. My friend the midwife taught me how to distinguish between *kangkung*, an edible wild vegetable which grew everywhere, and other, poisonous, plants. *Kangkung* boiled in coconut milk and chili became — and remained — one of our favourite foods. Years after leaving Indonesia, while visiting Holland for a conference, Raḥmat and I searched a whole afternoon for an Indonesian restaurant, and ordered rice and *kangkung*, to the great bemusement of the owner. Another source of greens was the leaves of the sago plant, which had to be boiled and strained several times before its bitter taste was lessened. I gradually mastered the cooking tricks of our Sumatran neighbours, and could get by with whatever was available at a given time.

Raḥmat had started training the Mentawais in social matters, while tending to their physical health. He taught them to value their goods and not barter them for tobacco. The Bahá'ís in the villages knew that we would only exchange useful materials such as soap, clothing and household items for their goods. As they had no idea how to use soap, Raḥmat spent many hours teaching the villagers how to bathe and wash their clothes. He waded into the streams and rivers, washing himself and his clothing, encouraging them to imitate his methods. After a while the natives loved the aroma of Lux soap so much that they would rub it on their skin as a perfume.

The natives had no clothing as such in their natural habitat, only a narrow loincloth made of soft tree bark. When they visited the village of Muarasiberut, the men wore short pants, and the women wrapped an apron made of banana leaves around their waist. Raḥmat never forced them to wear conventional western clothes. He believed that the native customs of Bahá'ís should not be tampered with, as long as they were not against the laws of Bahá'u'lláh.

The new method of barter introduced by Raḥmat, while enraging the expatriates, was of great benefit to the natives. They started demanding food, clothing, soap and other materials in exchange for their bananas and copra. They no longer accepted the cheap tobacco which had been given to them for generations, and said that *Si Lottoro* had advised them to ask for the best of everything. Although Raḥmat preferred them not to smoke at all, he knew he could not stop them. The cheap tobacco was so foul that it virtually guaranteed an early death for the natives, many of whom were already afflicted with tuberculosis. In the years that we spent in Mentawai, Raḥmat used his authority as a government physician to make smoking below the age of 18 illegal. Although this could not be strictly enforced, many Mentawai parents did stop their children from smoking.

The Mentawais learned from Raḥmat that, although they were Bahá'ís, they could not expect to receive free gifts from us, and should contribute to their own village fund. They understood this principle and accepted it without hesitation. A few years later, when the Catholic church opened a mission in Siberut and offered free clothing and tobacco in exchange for attendance at Mass, many of the Bahá'ís were able to resist this temptation. In this new environment the natives started bringing us chickens and fruit from their villages. Although the bananas rotted and the coconuts were returned to them for some chore that Raḥmat invented, he always bought everything they brought, so that they would not be tempted to exchange their goods for tobacco. On Raḥmat's advice I started a chicken farm, which kept me occupied on those days I had to spend alone. This occupation did not actually help our food situation, as I absolutely refused to slaughter any of our chickens, and left the eggs to hatch. Only at such times when I was delirious with malaria was Raḥmat able to sacrifice one of them to feed us. I remember on one occasion, Amata Sinanga sent us a large white rooster. His son told me that his father, as a good Bahá'í, did not want to give a free gift, and he was sure that *Si Lottoro*'s wife, also as a good Bahá'í, would send him three bars of soap instead of two. He received his three bars only through Raḥmat's intervention, as I believed in keeping to the barter rate, and did not like bargaining.

Raḥmat gradually taught the natives the value of money and encouraged them, while keeping the barter system in their villages, to sell their goods to the Sumatrans for money. This brought to an end years of exploitation of the natives of the Mentawai Islands by the expatriates.

COMMUNICATIONS FROM THE GUARDIAN

Our only contact with the outside world was when the *Beo* arrived every six months. Its appearance, always unannounced, was received with great joy, and generated new life in the village. Shouts of 'Kapal tiba' — 'the boat has arrived' — rang from every home. The village mina birds, ours included, had learned these words and shouted them every day from their cages. As the *Beo* appeared on the horizon, people would flock to their boats, loading them with bananas, copra, dry fish and coconuts, and row out to exchange them for rice, salt, matches, candles, kerosene and other goods. We waited at the door of our room, daytime or midnight, scorching heat or pouring rain, for the ship's orderly to bring the mail. No one else received any letters, and the few government communications were easily distinguishable in their brown paper wrapping. Sacks of mail, their number depending on the amount of letters we received, would be brought to our dwelling, and the contents dumped in our room. We sat for hours, sorting through the letters and occasional magazines by their dates, which would range over six months. We awaited our mail with special anticipation, as it often contained messages from the Guardian. Whenever there was a communication from the Holy Land our spirits soared, hardships were forgotten and homesickness seemed trivial. Often pilgrims wrote to tell us that the Guardian had made inquiries about us, and had praised Raḥmat for his services.

On one occasion we found a box containing 1000 calcium tablets in the mail bag. My father's note said that these were sent by the Guardian for me, with the instruction that I take them every day. After the passing of the beloved Guardian, Amatu'l-Bahá Rúḥíyyih Khánum told me the story behind this gift. A Persian pilgrim had been asked by the Guardian about us, and she had mentioned that I had written to my parents that, for some unknown reason, my teeth were chipping. When they were alone, the Guardian had told Amatu'l-Bahá that the reason was lack of calcium, and had asked her to send one box of her own calcium pills to my father, so he could forward it to me. I took the pills regularly following the instructions of the Guardian, and to this day have had very few problems with my teeth. This is just one example of the way in which the love of the Guardian surrounded and sustained us during all the years of our pioneering in the Mentawai Islands.

DEVELOPMENT OF THE BAHÁ'Í COMMUNITY

As the number of Bahá'ís grew, Raḥmat spent more time with them in the villages. He taught them the Faith in a simple language that they could understand and commit to memory, and taught their children Bahá'í songs which he composed in Mentawai and Indonesian. He taught them prayers in Arabic and Persian, as none had yet been translated in their own language. Many children learned their prayers by imitating Raḥmat's style of chanting. By the middle of 1955 there were 400 Bahá'ís on the island of Siberut Selatan.

In one of his reports to the National Assembly of India about our work in the Mentawai Islands, Raḥmat stated that the natives, though declaring their belief in Bahá'u'lláh, knew very little about the Faith, and since they had no concept of God, much time and patience was needed before they could grasp the significance of the religion they had accepted. The news of these enrolments had been conveyed to the Guardian by the National Assembly. Years later, we found out that he had announced this as a major victory to the Bahá'í world. Following Raḥmat's report my father had received a letter from Dr Hakim written on behalf of the Guardian asking him to, 'assure Dr Muhájir and his wife that the Guardian prays for them and their services to the Faith. The outstanding services that he and his wife have rendered have brought much joy to the Guardian's heart.' This letter, dated 18 July 1955, was accompanied by a cable dated 20 March 1955, sent by the Guardian in answer to our cable supplicating his prayers. His cable read 'Loving remembrance Shrines.' Receipt of these two communications was welcome confirmation that Raḥmat was following the right path in teaching and enrolling the natives. In thanksgiving he composed a song in Indonesian in praise of Bahá'u'lláh, and taught all the children to sing it:

Marila kita bersama-sama,
Meminta doa kepada Bahá,
Bahá'u'lláh jang maha kuasa,
Alláh'u'Abhá, Alláh'u'Abhá.

Kita Bahá'í dimana-mana,
Puti dan hitam bersama sama,
Berseru dengan satu suara,
Alláh'u'Abhá, Alláh'u'Abhá.

Kesatuan umat manusia,
Inilah Bahá'í bertjita tjita,
Prsodaan dan perdamajan,
Alláh'u'Abhá, Alláh'u'Abhá.

Come let us all supplicate prayers from Bahá'u'lláh,
the All-Powerful,
We are Bahá'ís everywhere,
White and black all are the same,
With the same voice we all sing,
Alláh'u'Abhá, Alláh'u'Abhá.

> Oneness of mankind is what Bahá'ís cherish,
> Brotherhood and peace,
> Alláh'u'Abhá, Alláh'u'Abhá.

After a few months not only the children, but also men and women in all the villages had memorized this song.

The number of Bahá'ís was rapidly increasing, and by 1956 had reached more than 1000. This was announced to the Bahá'í world in the Guardian's message of April 1957:

> A special tribute, I feel, should be paid . . . to the heroic band of pioneers, and particularly to the company of the Knights of Bahá'u'lláh, who, as a result of their indomitable spirit, courage, steadfastness, and self-abnegation, have achieved in the course of four brief years, in so many of the virgin territories newly opened to His Faith, a measure of success far exceeding the most sanguine expectations . . .
>
> To Uganda, opened on the eve of the Global Crusade, where the number of the avowed adherents of the Faith has now passed the eleven hundred mark . . . must be added Mentawai Islands, where adult Bahá'ís now number over eleven hundred . . .[1]

Malaria had seriously sapped Raḥmat's strength, but he continued to trek through jungles, wade in marshes, and travel by canoe on the rivers and ocean, through searing heat and torrential rain. I was often left behind. We would have had to travel in separate canoes, and did not consider it worth the risk — despite Chamat's assurances that he would hold the oarsmen responsible if anything happened to me. Raḥmat always returned from his travels exhausted, his clothes soaked in blood from the bites of leeches which still clung to his body. He dismissed my worries, and said that this was God's providence, as the blood-letting prevented him from having high blood pressure.

THE BAHÁ'Í VILLAGES

The Mentawai people, young or old, whether Bahá'í or not, loved and respected Raḥmat. They were so attached to him that they would follow him anywhere, and do whatever he asked of them.

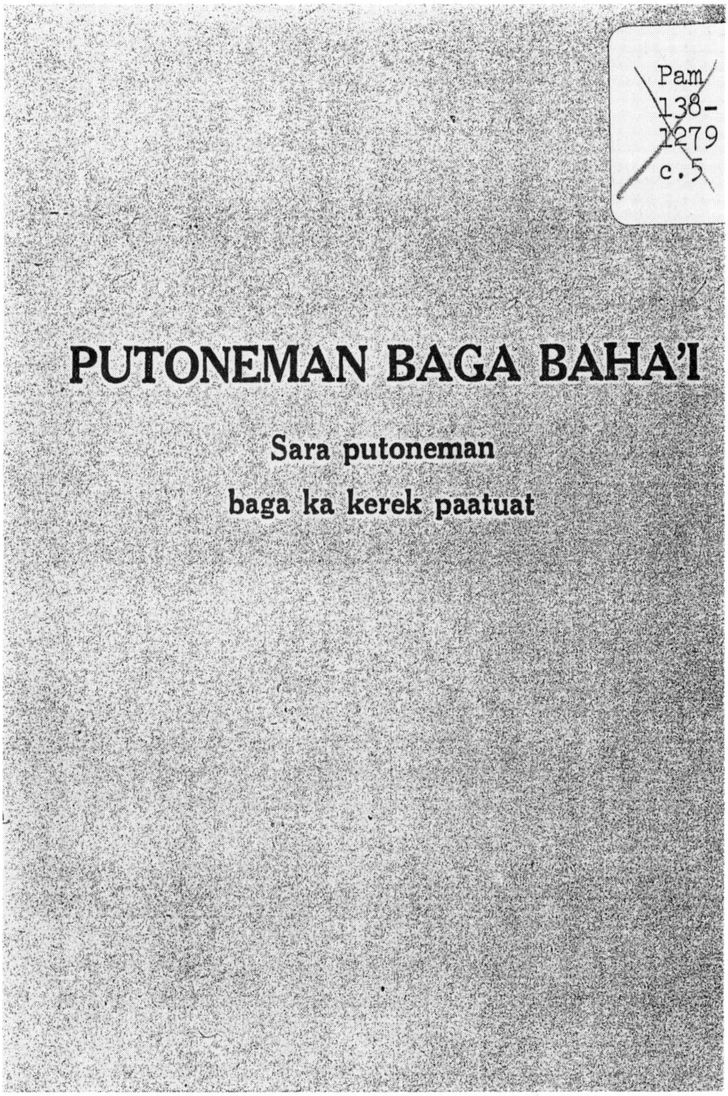

Cover of the Mentawai translation of The Bahá'í Message.

Now he wanted to establish schools for the children in remote areas. In classes that he organized in the villages, children and adults learned the alphabet, and to write words and simple sentences in Mentawai and Indonesian. The Ten Year Crusade called for translation of Bahá'í material into Mentawai, which up till then had only been a spoken language. With Luddin's help we were able to translate the leaflet *Bahá'í Message* into Mentawai: *Putunuman Baga Bahá'í* became the first ever publication in the Mentawai language.

Our schools had to be directed in Indonesian, therefore we had to wait until the Faith had progressed sufficiently in Indonesia for Bahá'í teachers to come from there and live in the Mentawai Islands. The first step, however, was the construction of schoolhouses. Raḥmat visited three of the most deepened villages — Si Pai Pajet, Simatalu Ulu and Simatalu Saibi — gathered the elders, and consulted with them how to achieve this goal. The suggested solution was to move the whole village to a better and larger site, and build new houses, which would include a Ḥaẓíratu'l-Quds and a schoolhouse. Raḥmat wholeheartedly agreed with this project, and, using the Tablet of 'Abdu'l-Bahá to the Local Assembly of Bombay as a guide, planned whole new villages for them. In this Tablet the Master gave instructions regarding the shape of the Bahá'í cemeteries which should, in outward appearance, resemble a palace. He wrote that four large avenues in the shape of a cross should be constructed in the middle of the land, with a pool of water in the middle of the crossing. Each grave should have a flower-bed one yard wide around it, and trees should be planted all over the land.The three villages were built in this fashion, on land adjoining their old settlements. The villagers supplied the wood and labour; Raḥmat gave them the necessary tools for the work. In three months' time the new villages were ready for occupation, each with a schoolhouse and Bahá'í Centre. The move to the new sites was made with great ceremony and festivity. The old dwellings were kept to house the livestock. The greatest achievement of this move was the establishment of a Bahá'í cemetery in the old land. The Mentawai Bahá'ís showed their true allegiance to the Faith by agreeing to bury their dead according to Bahá'í laws. For a while Raḥmat presided over the burials, showed them how to wash and shroud the remains, and how to make wooden caskets. In later years the schoolteachers undertook this duty. All those villages which were not Bahá'í had to follow suit, as the government had accepted Raḥmat's recommendation and banned the practice of leaving dead bodies in trees.

Raḥmat showed his respect for Mentawai customs by his participation in their pre-burial ceremonies. The body would be placed in a sitting position, surrounded with banana leaves and wild orchids, its face painted black and white. All the villagers paid their respect by touching the face of the deceased. The village shaman, called *Si Kerei* — 'the Seer' — in full regalia of banana leaves and feathers, his face painted red, white and black, danced and sang, while another man played a mouth xylophone. Raḥmat, who by now was accepted by *Si Kerei* as an equal, put feathers in his hair and allowed them to paint his face. He participated in the chanting and dancing, and touched the face of the dead person. This respectful attitude toward their traditions and customs made the natives so happy that they easily agreed to the burial of their dead according to Bahá'í law. Raḥmat's willingness to participate in the traditional ceremonies and celebrations of indigenous people was one of his outstanding characteristics, and one reason for his success in dealing with native peoples throughout his travels. He loved and encouraged local traditions, believing them to be a thousandfold better than the customs prevalent in the so-called 'civilized' world. Unless a custom contradicted the Bahá'í teachings, he would accept it, appreciate it and share in it with the people he was teaching.

FRIENDS AND MISSIONARIES

In the middle of 1955 we had to make a trip to Jakarta, on the instructions of the Guardian. Despite his many cables to expedite the purchase of the Ḥaẓíratu'l-Quds in Jakarta, the friends had not been able to find a suitable place, and the Guardian had instructed Raḥmat to assist in this project. This was the first time that we had left the Mentawai Islands for any length of time. Raḥmat was determined to complete the purchase as soon as possible, and return to his pioneering post. The task was accomplished in a few days, a cable was sent to the Guardian, and we left Jakarta at the first opportunity. On our return we were informed that the Catholic

Church was in the process of establishing a mission in Muarasiberut. Although Protestant missionaries had arrived in the southern Mentawai islands of Sipora and Pageh in 1901, and Christianity had flourished there, the Catholic Church focused its attention on Siberut after hearing about the great number of Bahá'ís on that island. They considered opposition to the Protestant Church futile, but regarded the Bahá'í work as insignificant, and dismissed the idea of a Persian doctor as a religious teacher.

We enjoyed a very cordial relationship with the Protestant pastor, Pastor Klappert, and his wife. They were German missionaries who had done very good work among the Mentawais of Sipora. They once visited us for a few days, and the Pastor travelled to some Bahá'í villages with Raḥmat. In 1968 a Persian Bahá'í friend told me that he had asked a German girl, who was not a Bahá'í, to marry him. She had consulted her uncle — Pastor Klappert — who had immediately agreed to the marriage, and told her that if her young man was anything like Dr Muhájir she would be very lucky indeed.

Within a few months of the first appearance of the Catholic priests, two special cargo ships brought building materials for a church, a school and a clinic. Chamat gladly sold them a choice piece of beautiful land on top of the highest hill in Muarasiberut, and informed us regularly about the progress of the construction work. Although I was ready to drop Chamat's name from our list of friends, Raḥmat continued his friendship with him, and scolded me for not having enough faith, and for thinking that a few priests could hinder the progress of the Faith of Bahá'u'lláh.

As the people of Muarasiberut were Muslim, the work of building the church had to be done by the Mentawais. These natives were the real focus of the missionaries' attentions, and they began their attempts at conversion by offering clothing and other gifts, so that the natives would participate in weekly Mass. As construction of the church neared completion, two special motorboats arrived for the priests to use on their journeys to the villages. The Bahá'ís were their first target. In addition to the motorboats, they also received monthly deliveries of canned foods and other supplies for the four priests and two nuns who were managing the affairs of the mission.

I never visited the church, but regular reports were given to me by *Njonja Wali Negri* and others, about the wealth and splendour of the priests and their residence. We continued living in our humble room, and Raḥmat continued to travel on foot and by canoe. After a month the priest at the head of the mission, an Italian sent from Rome, visited us and informed us in perfect Indonesian that he was a threat to the Bahá'í Faith: 'Saja Bahaja untuk Bahá'í.' This did not disturb Raḥmat at all. He asked the priest about his methods of teaching, offered help in their medical needs and wished him well. Raḥmat's hospitality encouraged the priest to visit us more often. His main purpose was to guide me to the 'right path' as he believed that I, being so young, was only following my husband's religion because I had no choice. The priest's visits became a source of comic entertainment for Raḥmat, and he encouraged me not to rebuff him. He often sat in on the Bible lessons that the priest imposed on me, and believed that these lessons would be of great benefit to me in teaching Christians. I was, however, growing angrier with each encounter, and took advantage of one of Raḥmat's absences to tell the priest in no uncertain terms that I was a fourth-generation Bahá'í and had no intention of converting to Catholicism. The priest's only consolation was that as I professed great love for Christ, He might one day guide me aright. From that time he ceased his weekly missions of mercy to our house, despite Raḥmat's repeated invitations.

The priests stepped up their visits to Bahá'í villages, hoping to convert the Bahá'ís, who, since they were now aware of the existence of God, were easier to teach. Some of the Bahá'ís gave in to the temptations of clothing and cigarettes, and left the Faith. Amata Sinanga sent urgent messages for Raḥmat to visit Si Pai Pajet. This was the time that I felt I had to pray for the removal of this 'danger'. I thought that the only way was for me to say all the prayers I knew, plus the Tablet of Aḥmad for 40 days, and beg Bahá'u'lláh to free us from this hardship.

Twelve days later, the priest's houseboy came to our place very late at night to ask for Raḥmat's help. The head priest was desperately ill with typhoid. The ministrations of the nuns, who gave him aspirin and fried bananas, had brought him to the verge of death. Raḥmat was in Si Pai Pajet, and it took about a week to bring him back by motorboat. For nearly six weeks after he came back Raḥmat visited the priest every day, sitting by his bedside, monitoring his fever and supervising his medication. All this time I had to make soup for the priest from my precious chickens. Raḥmat pointed out that since the poor priest's illness was due to my hostile prayers, I had better compensate for it.

News of the priest's illness and near demise prompted the Vatican to recall him to Rome. A special boat was sent for him and, as soon as Raḥmat permitted, he was taken away. Before leaving he sent us a note containing Rs. 400 and said, 'I hope you will accept this moderate fee. I have never seen the love and kindness you showed me, even from my parents. I am truly sorry for any trouble I might have caused you and hope that you will forgive me.' Raḥmat returned the money and told the priest that he had no hard feelings towards him, and was sorry to see him leave. On the day of his departure the priest visited us for the last time. He brought with him four white geese which he begged me to accept as a gift. He said he was sure that the minute he left, the geese would be butchered by the other priests and he simply could not tolerate the thought. He embraced Raḥmat and assured him that he would never again oppose the Bahá'í Faith. The priest left and the geese multiplied. When we left the islands we gave a pair to each of the Bahá'í villages. On his last visit to the Mentawai Islands, Raḥmat saw flocks of geese running in the villages.

The three junior priests did not have the zeal or drive of their leader. They left the Bahá'ís alone, and tried to have a good relationship with us. They often caused inadvertent offence to the local population, and Raḥmat had to intervene to calm things down. Once when a cow which had strayed on to church land was wounded by a machete thrown by a gatekeeper, there was a riot in the village. Providentially, Raḥmat was at home, and was able to prevent a mob attack on the church. After this incident, the priests seldom ventured into the village. They tried to show their appreciation by sending us a box full of canned foods: the *Beo* was some months overdue, and they were aware that everyone was short of provisions. Raḥmat was away, and although our food stocks were very low I felt duty-bound to return their gift. It was a matter of honour.

Two days later the shouts of 'Kapal tiba' woke the whole village at midnight. At the knock on our door I went to receive the mail, and, to my great astonishment, saw Mr Rustam Payman standing outside. I was so delighted and surprised that I dropped the candle and had to grope about in the dark to search for a match. Rustam was a young cousin of Khodarahm Payman, who had decided to visit us for 'a few weeks'. When the first hours of happy conversation about the outside world had passed, Rustam realized that if he stayed it would not be for a few weeks; it might be months before he would be able to leave. This jolted him back to reality. Dawn had arrived and he could see the state of the room and the village. He decided that he had shown enough kindness, and started to get ready to leave on the same boat. Only my appeals that he should wait for Raḥmat's return persuaded him to remain.

Rustam stayed on the Mentawai Islands for nearly a year. He visited native villages, at first accompanied by Raḥmat and later on his own, and was instrumental in bringing hundreds of Mentawais under the banner of Bahá'u'lláh. He suffered many a hardship, including a bout of typhoid, and left the islands with great regret only when his business affairs demanded. During this year, although it was not a goal of the Ten Year Crusade, Raḥmat purchased a few acres of land in the name of the Faith on a beautiful hilly spot. For the first time in the history of the islands, the deed was sent to Padang and registered. The Guardian announced this achievement in his message of April 1956:

> Nor should mention be omitted in this brief survey of Bahá'í victories and achievements in the course of the closing year of the second phase of the Ten Year Plan . . . of the purchase in an island near Muara Siberut [sic], Mentawai Islands, of a plot supplementing the Bahá'í endowment established in Jakarta, the Indonesian capital.[2]

The beloved Guardian's encouragement continued. In his talks with the pilgrims he often mentioned the Mentawai Islands and Raḥmat's services to the Faith. Once he had likened Raḥmat to Hand of the Cause Banání, and called him a true pioneer. Raḥmat was living up to his family name: Muhájir — 'Pioneer'.

DEEPENING THE NEW BELIEVERS

Raḥmat's activities intensified throughout 1956. The schools had started functioning, and needed constant supervision. Raḥmat was away for much longer periods, and I had to fill the days as best I could. I had already mastered Indonesian, and now decided to learn English, memorizing words from the only dictionary we had brought with us. In the middle of that year we received three messages from the Guardian, all in the same batch of mail. They had been written by Dr Hakim to my father: these energizing words sustained us for many more months.

> *5 February 1956*: The Guardian appreciates the services of Dr Muhájir and his wife. He is a true pioneer. He prays for them both to become more successful each day.
>
> *15 March 1956*: Assure them the Guardian remembers them all the time and prays for them.
>
> *18 May 1956*: [Inform them about] the Guardian's appreciation of Dr Muhájir, who is a true pioneer, and also his wife.

The Mentawai Bahá'ís were now very much at ease with Raḥmat, and our one-roomed abode was of great interest to them. Another of the rooms in the building had been cleaned and wallpapered with newsprint for Rustam, and this clearly gave the house greater prestige in the eyes of the natives. Those who were familiar with the surroundings brought their friends on a tour and, despite my objections, Raḥmat never stopped them. On one occasion I was sleeping on the wooden bed, recovering from an attack of malaria, when I was awakened by one of the Bahá'ís showing a friend our belongings with casual informality. He pointed out *Si Lottoro*'s chairs, table, bed, suitcases and, in passing, pointed to me and said, 'and that is his wife'. My screams brought Raḥmat to the room. Doubled up with laughter, he persuaded the touring party to leave. He considered the natives innocent children, and saw nothing unpleasant in their behaviour. Although our room had a door which was nearly always left ajar, the Bahá'ís would often enter the room by jumping through the open window. Sometimes I would ask them to jump back out and come through the door. Raḥmat considered this an unnecessary discipline, as the Mentawais had no doors and windows in their homes and did not distinguish between them. However, to humour me he would ask them to do as I wanted. They usually jumped out with great laughter and shouts of amusement.

When the Bahá'ís came to our house it was usually for deepening sessions with Raḥmat. He spent hours patiently explaining the history and teachings of the Faith, with simple stories and examples. He taught them prayers, repeating each sentence many times so that they could memorize them. At fixed intervals he would offer them bananas, and allow them to have their cigarettes. Both lunch and dinner consisted of sago and fish, which they cooked in a large pot over a wood fire in front of our house. Raḥmat always shared these meals, joking and laughing as one of them. Such sessions were the foundation of the Bahá'í Institutes which were later established all over Indonesia with great success. Always before they left I would hand them a broom and ask them to sweep up the cigarette ash that had fallen on the floor. They did it with good humour but told their friends, 'Si Kelabai Maghulu' — 'his wife is bad tempered'!

As I look back on those days, I realize how much Raḥmat was able to accomplish purely through his intuition. He had no experience of mass teaching, yet became a champion in that field. His blueprints for success were the instructions of the Guardian, who had asked for entry by troops among the 'brown race', and it was our duty to accomplish it. There were no committees, no minutes of meetings, no picture books and no prescribed methods. He went to the people, told them about Bahá'u'lláh, and, if they agreed with what he said, he considered them Bahá'ís. He would visit the same village over and over, and deepen the new Bahá'ís one word at a time. When they visited us, he welcomed them with open arms, offered them hospitality and shared whatever was available as a meal. All Mentawais, whether Bahá'í or not, were like his children, and he loved them all. This love was the magnet that attracted the natives first to him, and eventually to the Faith. He did not demand anything of them, and if they learned a few words of a prayer over a period of six months he was happy.

Although he later refined these methods to suit different nationalities, his basic concept remained the same. Mass teaching among indigenous people was effective when conducted in a simple and direct manner, with repeated visits to the same village, so that all the villagers became Bahá'ís.

THE GOVERNOR CALLS

As Raḥmat's efforts in the field of social and health development began to produce results, the Governor of Sumatra made an unannounced trip to the islands. He arrived in a special boat, accompanied by an entourage of nearly 30 ministers and bureaucrats. We thought it was an early arrival of the *Beo* and were waiting for the mail, when Chamat knocked on the door, breathless and trembling, to inform us that the Governor was asking for us. The Governor's first question was 'What is Alláh'u'Abhá?' He had been greeted with this phrase by all the natives, and when they were asked what it meant he was referred to *Si Lottoro*. This resulted in lengthy discussion about the Faith. The Governor became a good friend, and remained so for the remainder of his term of office.

The Governor's biggest surprise was that a young white woman had actually been able to survive in Mentawai. As a reward he announced his decision to build a new house for us and a hospital for Raḥmat. To my great regret, Raḥmat recommended that this task be entrusted to Chamat. It was as if he had discovered a gold-mine, and was in no hurry to finish the work. It took more than a year before we were able to move to the new building, which was made according to his instructions.

It was now four years since our arrival in Mentawai. The number of Bahá'ís had grown to nearly seven thousand and we had five Bahá'í schools. It was also in this year that Raḥmat nearly lost his life. On a trip to Si Pai Pajet, torrential rains had swollen the river and the canoe had overturned. Raḥmat had tried to swim to the shore against the onrushing waters, but had finally given up. As he was drowning, a tree trunk hit him in the back, and clinging to it, he finally reached the side. His four Mentawai companions were also safe, and had been looking for him all along the bank. They continued on foot, reaching the village two days later. For many

South-East Asia Conference 1956. Hand of the Cause General 'Alá'í is in the centre, Raḥmat is seated second from right.

Regional Spiritual Assembly of the Bahá'ís of South East Asia, May 1957. Hand of the Cause Furútan is first on the left, Raḥmat first on the right.

In Jakarta, May 1957.

months the natives related this incident and considered themselves lucky that their *Si Lottoro* had not drowned.

The effect of Raḥmat's work was quite evident by now. The Mentawais had become self-assured and confident that they were not inferior to the Sumatrans. The children attending the Bahá'í schools knew prayers, and as they chanted them their parents learned and repeated them in their homes. Raḥmat's regular visits to the villages had resulted in better standards of health, cleanliness and education for the entire population. Mentawai Bahá'ís were quite distinct from the other people of the islands. Men kept their hair short and clean; women wore clean clothes, and had wild orchids in their hair. Many adults, as well as their children, were literate and could hold their own with the expatriates, many of whom could neither read nor write. Lice and fleas had lessened considerably, and soap had become a regular item in village homes.

CONFERENCE AND CONVENTION

On the Guardian's instructions, the South-East Asian Regional Conference was held in Jakarta in October 1956, with Hand of the Cause of God Mr 'Alá'í participating. Although Raḥmat was very reluctant to leave the islands, we attended the conference, accompanied by twelve of the Mentawai Bahá'ís. Amata Sinanga, our first Bahá'í, gave a brilliant speech in one of the sessions. I can still see Raḥmat's face, beaming with pleasure like a father listening to the valedictory address of his child.

The Regional Convention of South-East Asia was held in Jakarta in April 1957. My father, Hand of the Cause of God Mr Furútan, represented the beloved Guardian. Again the friends from the Mentawai Islands were the shining stars of this gathering. Completely unaware that they were the focus of attention, they humbly and happily attended the meetings, said prayers, prepared their own food in the garden of the Bahá'í Centre just as they did in their own villages, and offered to share it with the rest of us. The Mentawai Bahá'ís were later among those indigenous believers represented at the first Bahá'í World Congress — the 'Most Great Jubilee' — in London in 1963.

Raḥmat was elected to the Regional Spiritual Assembly. He did not feel happy about this at all, since it meant that he would have to leave the Mentawai Islands every so often to attend the meetings. However, he did not resign, but submitted to the will of the majority, as was his manner. The Regional Assembly made Raḥmat responsible for purchasing a temple site in Jakarta. We left for that city in September 1957. Raḥmat immediately embarked on a search for a suitable property, and, whenever he had free time, went to the surrounding towns and villages to teach the Faith.

HAND OF THE CAUSE OF GOD

We were still in Jakarta in the first week of October, when a letter arrived from the Hands of the Cause of God for Asia, appointing Raḥmat to the Auxiliary Board. He had been offered this position several times, but had declined, as he did not want to leave the Mentawai Islands, even for short periods. He was on one of his teaching trips to the villages, still wondering how to decline this appointment once again, when a cable was received from the National Assembly of Iran relaying the telegram of the beloved Guardian elevating him to the rank of Hand of the Cause of God. The cable read:

> ROWHANI CARE KHADEM TEHERAN, INFORM RAHMATULLAH MUHAJIR ABULQASIM FAIZI THEIR ELEVATION RANK HAND CAUSE CONFIDENT NEW HONOUR WILL ENHANCE RECORD THEIR HISTORIC SERVICES STOP

It took me two days to locate Raḥmat and convey to him the cable's contents. He came back to Jakarta immediately. His first reaction was absolute perplexity. He shut himself in a room for hours and wept constantly. It took two days of continuous prayer before he could emerge, pale and wan, to cable his obedience to the beloved Guardian.

The Bahá'ís of Jakarta urged him to remain in the city to meet the friends, but he just wanted to go home. Although he was aware that he now had other more pressing duties, he wanted to return to his pioneering post to meditate and await the Guardian's instructions. On arrival in Padang we were informed that the *Beo* had engine trouble again, and that it would be more than a month before we could leave for Siberut. A week passed before we heard that a fishing sampan was leaving for the Mentawai Islands, and that we could go with it if we wanted. We were on board for less than five hours when a severe storm hit the boat. So as not to endanger the lives of a foreign doctor and his wife, the fishermen decided to return to Padang. After another few frightening hours we put ashore. On arrival at the hotel we were told that there had been frantic phone calls from Jakarta: the Bahá'ís had left urgent messages that we contact them. The date was 5 November 1957.

THE PASSING OF THE BELOVED GUARDIAN

Many Bahá'ís around the world remember the exact moment that they heard the horrifying news of the passing of the beloved of our hearts. I can vividly see the small office of the hotel manager, and Raḥmat's ashen face as he listened on the phone, moaning in disbelief. He asked me also to talk to the Secretary of the Regional Assembly, to ascertain if he had heard him correctly. To our great distress we were told that they had received a cable from the Holy Land regarding the ascension of the Guardian to the Abhá Kingdom. Raḥmat was asked to leave immediately for London.

We spent that night in prayer and torment. We had suddenly lost the core of our existence. We were paralysed. Our beloved Guardian, for whom we were willing to give our lives, was gone. The Sign of God on earth, our only refuge, whose love and care had sustained us through all the hardships of the past five years, was not with us any more. We felt lost and aimless. There seemed no reason to go back to the Mentawai Islands — or, for that matter, to do anything else. Raḥmat, however, had to leave for the funeral, and we had to find a way for him to get to London. We drew on our friendship with the Governor to find seats on the plane to Jakarta, and the next day Raḥmat was on his way.

That day changed Raḥmat's life and manner forever. His overflowing humour gave way to a quiet gentleness. The smile so well remembered by his friends was now accompanied by deep sadness in the eyes. His exuberant optimism gave way to contemplative hope. The spontaneous moments of joyful banter, which had been a great source of relief in our often stressful years in the Mentawai Islands, were gone forever. The passing of the Guardian had transformed him into another personality. To the outside

With his mother in Ṭihrán, after returning from the Holy Land, December 1957.

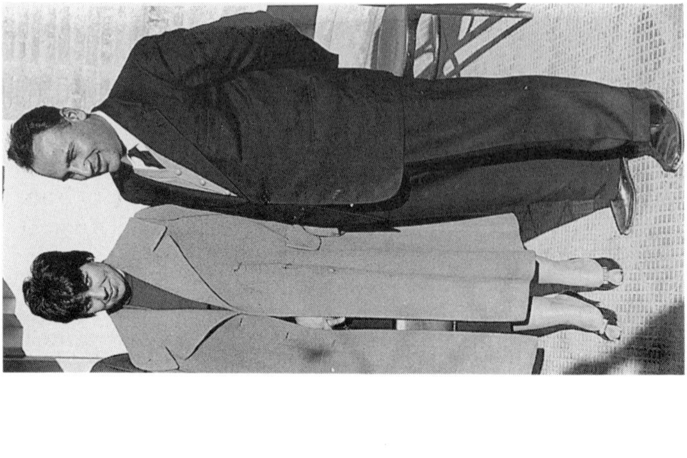

With his sister Lamieh, Ṭihrán, December 1957.

world, he appeared calm and relaxed, but inwardly he never overcame the sadness of the loss of his Guardian.

Raḥmat's sense of humour and joy of life had been my salvation, and had enabled me to deal with every hardship. I remember on one occasion, when a particularly severe bout of malaria had made me so weak that I thought I would not survive, his funny stories and jokes kept me occupied for hours while he fed me soup he had made. Often, when I felt homesick, he would sing Persian songs, accompanying himself on a tin box. He told me that if we were in Iran I would be listening to the radio, to singers who did not have as good a voice as he. The spectacle of his pounding on the rusty tin box, in a room with no furniture or light, rain-water dripping from the ceiling and the walls, was so funny that we would laugh and I would forget my sadness. Although he loved music, he never sang again, and the only occasions on which we heard his melodious voice was when he chanted prayers. To the end of his life, whenever he chanted one of the Guardian's prayers, tears poured down his face. Despite his great sense of loss and grief, his only thought was to return to the Mentawai Islands and continue the work that had pleased the Guardian. After participating in the first conclave of the Hands of the Cause in the Holy Land, he was asked to visit Iran for a few weeks, and explain to the friends about the end of the Guardianship and the start of a new era in the Faith of Bahá'u'lláh. He told me that when the friends were asking about another Guardian they thought that it would be the same person; they wanted the Guardian to come back. However, he believed that after some time they would realize that their beloved Guardian would not be returning, and they would settle down to carry out Shoghi Effendi's wishes and instructions. With the exception of a few rare cases, Raḥmat's prediction proved right.

We went back to the Mentawai Islands. Repeated letters from the Hands of the Cause in the Holy Land suggesting that Raḥmat reside in a more accessible city did not persuade him to leave.

A PLEA FOR CAUTION

The Intercontinental Conference for Asia, planned by the Guardian, was to be held in Jakarta in September 1958. We were asked to help in the preliminary preparations for the conference, and left the islands for Jakarta during July. Work progressed smoothly. Permits were issued by the government, and the venue, a large and beautiful hall, was booked. Raḥmat warned all of us on the organizing committee against excessive publicity. The conference was for the Bahá'ís, not for proclamation of the Faith in a country which had just awakened to Muslim fundamentalism. Although freedom of religion was one of the articles of the Indonesian Constitution and the Faith had been officially recognized as an independent religion, Raḥmat felt that it was not the time for widespread publicity.

Raḥmat was engaged on a teaching trip when a member of the Regional Assembly, and another Bahá'í (who was a professional media consultant), arrived in Jakarta. Pleas for caution were rejected and a media blitz started. News of the conference, and of the imminent arrival of hundreds of Bahá'ís was headlined in all major newspapers. Contacts and interviews with government ministers were arranged, and many people of high office were invited to attend a public meeting during the course of the conference. It was only a matter of days before the storm broke. The permit for the conference was revoked, and no amount of contact with the friends of the Faith could persuade the government officials to reverse their decision. Raḥmat was hastily recalled to Jakarta, and he immediately put a stop to the publicity activities of the two friends. Although he and Mr Payman tried, through their personal contacts, to obtain another permit for the conference, they did not succeed.

Raḥmat did not reprimand anyone. In all the years of his service he never blamed others, even in private, when something went wrong. His philosophy was that dwelling on the past was useless, and he tried to find remedies for whatever had happened. He always said that Bahá'u'lláh was most forgiving, and did not watch His followers all the time to find faults with them. On this occasion, however, when he was told by the two gentlemen that he was too cautious and did not realize the value of publicity, he firmly told them not to interfere any more, and assured everyone that this was the Will of God and that someday we would realize its significance. The Hands of the Cause of God Samandarí, 'Ala'í, Featherstone and Ioas (who was to represent the Holy Land at the conference), were now in Jakarta. They decided that rather than make further efforts to save the situation, the conference should be moved to Singapore.

Though this achieved great publicity among the Chinese population of Singapore — with positive results — the cancellation of the conference in Jakarta was the start of severe repression of the Faith in Indonesia, which led eventually to the Faith being banned.

Intercontinental Conference, Singapore, 1958. Hand of the Cause Leroy Ioas (the Guardian's representative) on the right, Daud Tweq, member of the NSA of Iraq second from right, Mrs Ioas seated on the left.

LEAVING THE ISLANDS

This incident made it clear to Raḥmat that he had to be accessible in case of emergency. His duties as a Hand of the Cause outweighed his work as a pioneer. He had been entrusted with the protection and propagation of the Faith throughout that whole region: now he had to think of leaving the beloved friends of the Mentawai Islands. We had lived on those islands for nearly fivc years. It was our home, and its people were our friends and family.

Raḥmat was offered a very profitable job in Jakarta which he flatly refused. He did not want to live anywhere that had a large number of Bahá'ís. To the astonishment of the government health authorities, he opted for a small hospital in a town called Pacitan.

He returned to the Mentawai Islands, visited the friends in all the villages, and took his leave of them with great sorrow. There were nearly nine thousand Bahá'ís and eight schools, which he left to the care of the Bahá'í teachers.

The clinic in Pacitan had no doctor. Raḥmat was the first physician there, and stayed there a little under two years. Raḥmat charged his patients only what they could afford to pay — which was often nothing. Once, when a tribal man who had come some distance asked how much he had to pay, Raḥmat asked him how much he could afford. He opened his handkerchief, which contained a few rupees. Raḥmat took one and gave him some medicine. He had gone a few yards when Raḥmat called his nurse and asked him to run after the man, and give him back the money, plus some more which he had added. Despite Raḥmat's charity and free treatments, the clinic was still lucrative. As our years on the Mentawai Islands had left us without the habit of spending, the paper rupees remained stacked, with a rubber band around them, in the drawer of his desk. Before we left Indonesia in 1958, Raḥmat contributed most of his earnings for the purchase of a Bahá'í Centre on another island.

Raḥmat was a good and experienced physician with a gentle and loving manner. He often sat at the bedside of a patient in his white overall and chanted the Healing Prayer. Although Muslims, the patients swore that his chanting made them feel better. He seldom lost a patient. During all his years of medical practice, his rapport with those he treated went beyond the mere relationship of a physician and patient. People simply gravitated to him, and he liked all of them. While in Siberut, a young man lost his senses, and had to be restrained until he could be sent to Padang. He was kept in a cell of the former prison. No one dared even pass the road in front of that room. Just seeing people made him so violent that he could endanger his own life. Food and water were left for him outside the bars on the end of a long bamboo pole. Raḥmat, however, would go inside the cell to sit with him and comfort him. I once watched from a safe distance. For the 15 minutes that Raḥmat was with him, the young man acted perfectly normally, talked and smiled and was very pleasant. When Raḥmat stood up to leave he begged him to stay longer and tried to kiss his hand. Raḥmat had to promise that he would return, or else he would not allow him to leave. The moment Raḥmat left the cell, the man's screams began again. Raḥmat shrugged this off and said that the young man felt an affinity with him because he was just as crazy. The truth was, that the rest of us did not show as much compassion as Raḥmat to this unfortunate young man.

PRAISE AND RECOGNITION

In 1960 a delegation of Indonesian government officials and lecturers from the University of Padang visited Mentawai. In their 115 page report, entitled *Research News*, Mr Sihombing, lecturer, and Mr Slamet Suradisastra, Dean of the College of Law at the University of Padang, made the following observations:

> [The] Bahá'í religion started to spread in Siberut in the year 1955. This religion has its root in Iran and its promoter came from a very prominent and rich family. His name was Bahá'u'lláh. The teachers of this religion are mostly educated people who are Persian and teach their Faith wherever they are. Almost in every corner of the world there are followers of Bahá'u'lláh who are called Bahá'ís, although they are not many in number. Since the Bahá'ís are rich people, periodically the leaders organize conferences in different countries of the world. These conferences are vitally important as the reports of the progress and different activities in the world are given . . .
>
> The progress of the Bahá'í religion in Siberut can be explained as follows: In the year 1955 [sic] a Persian doctor came to Siberut. His name was Muhájir, Raḥmatu'lláh, a government doctor who assisted and worked for the health of the people. At the same time he was very active in spreading the Bahá'í Faith. He went to different villages deep into the island, going through very difficult and dangerous circumstances. Facing death he distributed medicines and other things for free. This work brought in great results. In a short time many Bahá'ís were registered. Until now [1960] in Siberut Selatan 2500 followers exist and the number is increasing . . .
>
> The Bahá'í way of teaching is very special, unique and interesting. To attract the heart of the people they have much

> more patience than the other missionaries who were present in Mentawai. They meet at the houses of the people, drink and eat with them, and live months and months in the middle of the jungle with the people. In short there is no movement that can compare itself with the Bahá'ís in Siberut, specially in their courage, perseverance and purity of motive.

PERSECUTION IN INDONESIA

The restrictions on the Faith in Indonesia increased and finally reached a point when the Bahá'ís were being deliberately persecuted. The Bahá'ís of the Mentawai Islands were subjected to imprisonment and beatings. The authorities sought to compel them to recant their Faith: some succumbed, many more refused to give up their beliefs. Some had been in prison for years. Raḥmat returned in 1964, to assist the National Spiritual Assembly determine the appropriate response to this development. He went to Padang to ask the Governor to intercede and through his friendship with government officials helped lessen the persecutions of the Mentawai Bahá'ís to a great degree.

Through these difficult times, the Bahá'í children of the Mentawai Islands continued to study in the Bahá'í schools, which numbered 20 by this time. On a visit to Indonesia in 1970, Raḥmat suggested the establishment of a Bahá'í *Asrama* (boarding school), for the Mentawai children. The Faith had been officially banned in 1962 and Raḥmat did not want the persecution, coupled with the increased activities of the Church, to cause the children to drift away. This proposal was approved by the Universal House of Justice, and a small house was rented in Padang. Dr and Mrs Astani, long-time pioneers, took over the duty of visits to the Mentawai Islands and helped with the establishment of the *Asrama*. Raḥmat asked Manuchehr Tahmasbian, a young man who wanted to pioneer to Thailand, to go to Padang and help. Mrs Iṣmat Vahdat, also a long-time pioneer in Indonesia, who had visited us in the Mentawai Islands for a few months and had come to love the natives, volunteered her services as manager of the *Asrama*.

Mentawai Youth at the Asrama in Padang.

Manuchehr visited Siberut and other islands of Mentawai many times, accompanied by Surip Sukiman, one of the Javanese teachers, and brought some of the children with him to Padang. Another Bahá'í, Pa Karim, who had been sent to the Mentawai Islands as a vaccinator also assisted in this venture. He was a staunch Muslim who had accepted the Faith through Raḥmat, and had 'BAHAI' tattooed on his arm.

The children of the *Asrama*, now about 20 in number, were all able to attend high school, and some have graduated from university. Many of their parents still remember the gentle and kind man whom they called *Si Lottoro*, who sat on the damp and dirty ground, teaching the alphabet by drawing letters in the shapes of different birds and animals. They also remember him holding their children on his knee and teaching them prayers.

Raḥmat was able to visit the Mentawai Islands on two further occasions. His final visit to Padang was in April 1979. On this trip he had a dream which made him very happy: years before he had asked Hand of the Cause Samandari that if he were to go to the Abhá Kingdom first, he should mention his name in the presence of Bahá'u'lláh. In Padang he dreamt that Mr Samandari came to him and said 'Raḥmatján, I have fulfilled my promise.'

Some of the locations visited by Dr Muhájir on his trips to Africa.

Chapter 3

A GLORIOUS FUTURE

The two years at Pacitan were not easy for Raḥmat. Trying to teach the Muslim population there was a different challenge from teaching the indigenous people of the Mentawai Islands. Sadly, there was very little response. Although they liked 'the Doctor', who was so different to any other foreigner they had encountered, his religion was of no great interest to them.

The final chapter of the Ten Year Crusade was about to open, and the Hands of the Cause residing in the Holy Land appealed to Raḥmat to leave Indonesia, as his services were more urgently needed in other countries. In October 1960 we left Indonesia for the Holy Land, Raḥmat to attend the Conclave of the Hands of the Cause (held annually during the five years of their stewardship of the Faith), I to visit my parents. This trip marked the end of the most cherished period of our life together, a time which Raḥmat looked upon with great nostalgia.

During those years, thousands had been enrolled in the Cause, the beloved Guardian had dubbed us 'Knights of Bahá'u'lláh', and had bestowed on Raḥmat — at the age of only 34 — the mantle of 'Hand of the Cause of God'. Although Raḥmat was leaving one arena of service, he stood on the threshold of another, the results of which would astonish even his closest friends. Our lives were never to be the same again.

The Guardian had appointed four Hands of the Cause for Africa: Músá Banání, William Sears, Enoch Olinga and John Robarts. At the October 1960 Conclave, John Robarts, for many years a pioneer in Africa, announced his decision to return to Canada shortly. The Conclave suggested that Raḥmat replace him. This request came as a shock. The Guardian had appointed him a Hand of the Cause for South-East Asia, and he wanted to live in that region and keep his assignment to the end of his life. For many days we visited the holy Shrines to seek guidance. Although Raḥmat was heart-broken at the thought of leaving his post in Indonesia, he finally acceded to the request of the Hands, on condition that he also continue his services in South-East Asia.

We left directly for Africa, with the one suitcase that we had brought for our short stay in the Holy Land. We asked Mr Payman to sell our meagre belongings in Pacitan. The journey reminded us of the time we first left Iran for Indonesia. Once again we were going to a place completely unknown to us, and were totally unprepared — we would have to rely on Bahá'u'lláh's help.

Our first stop was Nairobi, a beautiful and very modern city. The wide roads lined with flowers, the high-rise buildings, the hustle and bustle of traffic and pedestrians were a stark contrast to the muddy pathways and thatched huts we had been used to in Muarasiberut. The next day we left Nairobi in a single-engine plane carrying mail to Kampala, Uganda, which was to be our home and Raḥmat's base. We were the only passengers. The landscape of Africa was breathtakingly magnificent. The plane landed in several villages to deliver the mail, and the smiling faces of the Africans who would surround us when we touched down won Raḥmat's heart. This relaxed him tremendously, and he immediately began to think about how he could travel over the entire continent to teach the native peoples so admired by Shoghi Effendi. Raḥmat's love affair with Africa had begun.

On our arrival in Kampala we were taken to the home of Hand of the Cause Músá Banání. The Kampala friends were busy preparing for the dedication of the first Bahá'í temple in Africa. Final touches were being applied to the 'Mother Temple', and everywhere there was an air of great excitement. The dedication ceremonies were to be performed in the presence of Amatu'l-Bahá Rúḥíyyih Khánum, and hundreds of African Bahá'ís and friends from around the world were to arrive in Kampala in just a few weeks. Raḥmat did not let these activities distract him from his chief intention, which was to teach in the villages. Only two days after our arrival he left Kampala for the interior of Uganda and to visit the neighbouring countries of Tanganyika, Kenya and Northern Rhodesia.

His move to Africa was announced in the *Bahá'í News* of Uganda: 'To replace Mr Robarts, we welcome HOC Raḥmatu'lláh Muhájir, formerly a pioneer to Indonesia, who will travel both in Africa and in South-East Asia.'

The extent of the change to our lives was just beginning to dawn on me. Although we had spent many days apart in Mentawai, it was only a small island and, although it may have taken him several days to return from some of the furthest villages, I could always reach Raḥmat in an emergency. Now I was left behind in a completely strange environment with no hope of having him by my side should need arise. Little did I know that this was to be our way of life for the next 20 years. On the day of Raḥmat's departure I moved to temporary accomodation at the YWCA, hoping soon to find a place for us to live. I was the only non-African in the hostel. Although everyone was kind, I did not speak the local language, Swahili, and the unfamiliar food and conditions reminded me of those first days in Muarasiberut. I felt ill and could not eat. Bouts of malaria coupled with loneliness compounded my misery. The director of the YWCA finally recommended that I see a physician and I was taken to a hospital where Africans were treated. The sympathetic doctor smilingly informed me that I was expecting a baby. He said that unless I could afford to go to the expatriate's hospital I had better leave Kampala: my pregnancy was complicated by anaemia brought on by malaria, and he could not treat me. I had nowhere to go. Cables were sent to Raḥmat, and after a few days he appeared at the door of my room at the hostel, with the matron of the YWCA frantically chasing after him. She sternly told him that no men were allowed in the building. We were given only enough time to pack my bag before moving to a hotel.

After a few days it became clear that, if I was to survive, I would have to get proper medical attention. After much consultation we decided that the best solution was for me to go to my uncle in Germany where I could get the care I needed. After consulting Mr Banání and Mr Robarts, we decided that it was important for Raḥmat to stay for the temple inauguration ceremonies, so I left Kampala by myself. Seeing me leave so distressed Raḥmat that he left his bag containing his passport, tickets and other documents at the airport. Thankfully, the police were able to retrieve it and return it to him after several days.

It was Raḥmat's firm conviction that if a venture was not in accordance with the Will of God, it would not succeed, no matter how hard one tried. The transfer to Africa seemed to be one such instance. I had to stay in Germany for the duration of my pregnancy and could not return to Africa, therefore the question of Raḥmat living permanently on that continent did not arise again. From that time on we were to have no permanent home. Over the next twenty-five years our family home moved to eight different countries spread across four continents.

Dedication of the 'Mother Temple' of Africa. Kampala, Uganda, 14 January 1961.

In the weeks prior to the dedication of the temple, Raḥmat visited many villages and communities, sometimes in the company of Hand of the Cause John Robarts and Mr 'Alí Nakhjavání, who was then serving as an Auxiliary Board member. The Ugandan *Bahá'í News* reported 'Our Region is greatly blessed to have been the scene of this unusual and highly fruitful tour by two of the revered Hands of the Cause simultaneously . . . It is primarily with peoples of that Pacific area that we are competing for the final victory in carrying the Faith to the masses.' This last comment referred to the Guardian's message of April 1957 in which he had noted that, 'In the Pacific area . . . Bahá'í exploits bid fair to outshine the feats achieved in any other ocean, and indeed in every continent of the globe, now competing for the palm of victory with the African continent itself . . .'[1]

FROM AFRICA TO ASIA

In January 1961 Raḥmat attended the dedication ceremony and conferences held at the Kampala temple, then left Uganda for Asia and South America. His diary reflects:

> *20 January*: I am leaving Kampala for Nairobi and a trip around the world. I am writing these notes in the plane. I humbly beseech God to have mercy on my soul. 'Although my sins would fill a myriad ships, yet His compassion fills the oceans.' I spent two months in Africa. What I had desired all my life came to pass. I met the beautiful people of Africa and witnessed the wonderful progress of the work of the Bahá'í institutions. What is certain is that the flame of this continent will set ablaze the whole world. This continent has been blessed with the beloved Guardian's presence.
>
> *23 January*: I am leaving Africa for Asia. I left Nairobi at 11 a.m. for Pakistan. I wrote a detailed letter to the Hands in the Holy Land about co-operation among the four Regional Spiritual Assemblies in Africa. As the National Assembly of the British Isles is responsible for this area, it should collect and publish the letters of the Guardian to Africa. Perhaps the Hands in Africa should have specific regions so that they could have more direct supervision over the affairs of the Faith.

'THE PUPIL OF THE EYE'

Raḥmat's next extended visit to that continent was to West Africa in 1969, when he travelled to Senegal, the Gambia, Ghana, Nigeria, Dahomey, and Togo. He also visited Gabon, Congo, Central African Republic and Zambia. His priority on·these trips was to visit those villages in the interior which seldom received visitors, though this did not prevent him from undertaking other activities. He represented the Universal House of Justice at conventions and conferences, gave radio and television interviews, had audiences with Heads of State, addressed large meetings, and lectured at universities and gatherings of physicians.

His happiest moments were, however, spent among the native Africans at home in their villages. When teaching those pure souls Raḥmat would remember how Bahá'u'lláh compared the Africans to the black pupil of the eye, through which 'the light of the spirit shineth forth'.[2] He would often say that Bahá'u'lláh gave the Hands of the Cause the direct duty to teach his Faith, and that his greatest regret since leaving the Mentawai Islands was that he seldom had time to do this. Africa gave him that opportunity, and whenever some of the villagers accepted the Faith he would be positively radiant. Once he visited a village in Monrovia where about 30 tribal people became Bahá'ís. His great joy at this is reflected in his notes. Although on the same trip he appeared twice on television with Hand of the Cause Olinga, met with officials and dignitaries and gave talks at meetings in the cities, he did not consider these to be of real importance and did not record anything about them. Everywhere he visited, Raḥmat reminded the friends about the victories achieved in the years of the 'spiritual conquest of Africa' and appealed to them not to slacken in their zeal.

SPIRITUAL CONQUEST OF A CONTINENT

For some time Raḥmat had been considering how African countries could best co-ordinate their teaching efforts in the border areas, as was done in Asia. When he returned to Africa in 1971 he conceived and presented the believers with 'The Lake Victoria Plan'. This joint venture among the National Spiritual Assemblies of Uganda, Kenya, Tanzania and Burundi was designed to carry the Faith to all

Leroy Ioas Teacher Training Institute, Swaziland, 1971.

Attending the Indian Ocean Conference, Rose Hill, Mauritius, 14–16 August 1970.

the peoples and tribes living within Africa's largest lake basin. Such co-operation among neighbouring countries was something he always strongly advocated, and helped to implement in many parts of the world. Throughout this trip he also encouraged the friends to pursue their goal to establish new National Spiritual Assemblies of Chad, Central African Republic and Gabon. He urged them not to be discouraged by a seeming lack of progress, but to try and visualize that glorious day, and redouble their efforts. His next visit to this region took place after these National Spiritual Assemblies had been established. When he arrived in Central African Republic he simply waved his yellow transit card to the friends waiting to meet him and told them he had decided to go directly to Chad. He had been informed by a member of the Universal House of Justice that the friends in Central African Republic were doing very well, so he decided not to stop there.

His letters to various National Assemblies in Africa not only urged them to extend their efforts on all fronts but also offered

Malagasy Republic, Tenanarive: First National Convention, 1972.

practical suggestions on how to achieve their goals. Most of the Assemblies followed his advice and acted on his suggestions. One of them, Rhodesia, reported,

> . . . teacher-training institutes were held for training additional teachers so that by the time the Hand of the Cause Raḥmatu'llah Muhájir first visited Rhodesia, urging the acceleration of the process of mass teaching, a group of five trained teachers was available. All five of these teachers were sent to the Gokwe area where five hundred new Bahá'ís were enrolled, including the paramount chief Nemangwe. Teachers based in this area also established contact with the remote Batonga tribes and soon established a Local Spiritual Assembly among them.

Raḥmat did visit the Central African Republic later. Jan Mughrabi, who was a pioneer in Bangui, recalled his visit:

> My husband went to town to collect our mail and found a note in the slit of our post box saying that Dr Muhájir was staying at the Hotel Minerva. We were greatly surprised. The previous day we had been on a teaching trip, our first [since the Bahá'ís had been cleared of the false charge of plotting against the government and had been released from detention]. We had stopped in Trangue where three people had shown interest in the Faith. One of them had given us a large pineapple which we shared with Dr Muhájir. He commented, 'He is a good man. Any time someone gives you something freely from his heart like this you must teach him the Faith, because his heart is pure.' Later we did as he advised and Joseph became a Bahá'í.
>
> Dr Muhájir asked us about the goals received from the Universal House of Justice. Among them was the important goal of acquiring a National Ḥaẓíratu'l-Quds. Dr Muhájir asked what we had found. We had four possible locations and he came to see them with us. When he reached the third building he said, 'This is the place. I will pray that Bahá'u'lláh will assist you to purchase this property.' He got out of the car and, turning towards the building, chanted prayers for some time. We did not even look at the fourth place. His prayers were answered. That building is the present National Ḥaẓíratu'l-Quds.

In the evening we shared a meal in a small restaurant in the centre of Bangui. I asked him why sometimes it is so difficult to achieve the tasks entrusted to us. For some years we had been trying to obtain the recognition of the Faith to no avail. Dr Muhájir answered, 'We do not always understand the timing of these things. Rely on Bahá'u'lláh. Do your best, and if it seems the doors are closed, leave it for a while and then go back to it and try again. Eventually the doors will open.'

When we obtained the recognition of the Faith a few months later, it became clear that there was a very good reason for the doors to have been closed to us: the goal had to be achieved spectacularly with the assistance of Dr Aziz Navidi.

In January 1971, Raḥmat represented the Universal House of Justice at the Continental Conference held in Monrovia, Liberia. In his talk to the conference he said:

> Africa is rapidly developing. African societies are beginning to shape themselves. There is a purity and a youthfulness here. When a tree is small it can be made to grow straight. When it is old, can you straighten it? In Africa 41 countries and 22 territories are opened to the Faith. Africa has been deprived of material civilization. God has protected it for Himself. The Bahá'í civilization must start in Africa. We have gathered here to consult on how to conquer, spiritually, this continent. The result of this conference is mass conversion in every country. What is mass conversion? There is no secret to it, no one method. One idea: people in a village have the same life, they live together, work together. They are one unit. How do you teach one person ? You show him love and win his trust. If you teach only the ideas, your job is not finished. You must go back again and again. Sometimes we spread seeds and run away. Let us focus. Let us start in one nearby area, teach one area! Complete that area! Then go to another area. Which people? All types. In Africa we must go to the tribes. Also to talented people who will assume responsibility for the Faith. Teach young people before they get involved in politics. You also have 51 universities in Africa. Teach there too.

SENDING REINFORCEMENTS

In 1972 it became apparent that the friends in Africa needed extra help to win the goals of the Nine Year Plan. Raḥmat consulted the Universal House of Justice, and a plan was developed which resulted in great victories for many of the African countries. It was decided that Raḥmat would personally visit Persia, India, Malaysia and the Philippines, and call for believers who would assist their brethren in the three East African territories, as well as in Swaziland, Chad and the Cameroon Republic. The *Bahá'í International News Service* reported:

> Forty teachers have arisen since the call was made in Persia and have reached Africa, to spread out to whatever posts are assigned to them. All have volunteered to go wherever they are needed, without any preferences. Twenty-one more volunteers arose from other countries, eleven from India, six from Malaysia, and four from the Philippines. Shortly after the beloved Hand of the Cause visited India, Sankaran Nair Vasudevan, member of the Board of Counsellors in western Asia, arose and led the way, blazing a path which sets an example for the entire Bahá'í world. The National Spiritual Assembly of Malaysia received one letter from the National Assembly of Swaziland which read, '. . . We are all so excited and happy about this . . . We have purchased tents to enable some of the teachers to go to remote areas . . . We hope some of your dear people will be able to enjoy this method of teaching, as we find it most successful.
>
> Six believers volunteered to go to Africa from Malaysia, creating a need for a by-election, as three of the six were members of the National Spiritual Assembly.
>
> The believers in the Philippines arose to send four devoted teachers, one a member of the National Assembly and another an Auxiliary Board member.

Silan Nadarajan, then a member of the National Assembly of Malaysia and who, at Raḥmat's behest pioneered to New Guinea, told me,

> We had received a cable from Dr Muhájir about sending travel teachers to Africa. We had many youth who were eager to go.

> We thought this was an easy task and cabled him that many had volunteered. A few days later Dr Muhájir arrived. He expressed his delight at the enthusiasm of the young people of Malaysia and praised the National Assembly for its quick and decisive action. He then smiled and said, 'Which of you are going to accompany the youth and guide them in their tasks?' We were stunned. After a few minutes of silence, three of the members volunteered! He smiled happily and said, 'Now call the following Auxiliary Board members and tell them from me to be ready to leave for Africa with the members of the National Assembly.' Within a few days three Auxiliary Board members and three members of the National Assembly were in Africa. This was a unique way of getting volunteers!

Many youthful teachers and pioneers have similar stories to tell: 'I was walking around the gardens in the Holy Land', or, 'I was on my way to India when Dr Muhájir tapped me on the shoulder, and here I am.' One such pioneer was Parviz Hatami, who later went to serve in the Holy Land. He relates that he had arranged all his affairs, including a visa for a European country which was a goal of Iran. Two nights before his departure he went to say goodbye to the International Pioneering Committee in Ṭihrán. Raḥmat was there and asked him why he wanted to go to Europe. Parviz replied that the country he was going to needed pioneers, and he would also be able to continue his studies there. Raḥmat smiled and said, 'If you are pioneering for yourself, this plan is very good. If you are going for Bahá'u'lláh, go to Africa.' Although he had to go to a great deal of trouble to change all his plans, Mr Hatami did pioneer to Africa.

Another friend relates that for many weeks he had approached the Pioneering Committee about a particular pioneer goal. The necessary information was not available, and he was advised to wait. Finally one night he decided in frustration that this was the last time he was going to meet with the committee. If it did not have an answer for him, he would abandon his plan to pioneer. At the meeting was a man whom he had not met before. This man gave him detailed information about every country in Africa and suggested cities to which he could go, and the types of jobs he could get. The friend was so happy at this unexpected occurrence that he praised the newcomer and said, 'The National Assembly should have made you a member of this committee much earlier.' The gentleman smiled and said he wished someone would recommend him to the Assembly. Months later in Africa the young man realized who his mentor had been!

Fuad Khuzain was 17 when his path crossed Raḥmat's. His older sister had already volunteered to pioneer and he could only look with envy at her preparations to leave Iran. He went to Raḥmat about some matter connected with his sister's pioneering. He told me,

> [Dr Muhájir] was very tired and said he had been away from his family for a long time. That day was his daughter's birthday and he missed her very much. I realized then that serving the Faith was not an easy matter. As I was relating my sister's questions, the Hand asked me why I did not volunteer myself. I replied that I was only 17 and that my father would not agree. He said, 'Talk to your father.'

It took some days of consultation and Raḥmat's intervention before Fuad was given permission to pioneer to Africa, but his wish was granted. Fuad saw Raḥmat once more in Kenya, laughing and joking as he gave him news of his parents and relatives.

Raḥmat accompanied the youth, many of whom had never experienced the thrill of mass teaching, and guided them step by step. He advised them to travel in groups, to say prayers together and, on arrival in their chosen village, to visit the Chief to pay their respects. They should first explain to him the purpose of their visit before they began to teach the villagers. He told them that they all were teachers and lovers of Bahá'u'lláh, and that if they just moved and persevered they would reap unprecedented victories. He gave them a few guidelines which he followed in his own teaching work, and which bear repeating here:

> Never consider yourself an important instrument, but just a tool in the Hands of Bahá'u'lláh.

> Never entertain reasons why the work cannot be done, but accept the ways that it could be achieved.

> Realize that we Bahá'ís are not the best people in the world but we are the luckiest.
>
> The first time you visit an area, teach. The second time you visit, teach again. This teaching is, in itself, deepening.
>
> It is good to ask one of the visitors to preside at public meetings.
>
> When youth accept the Faith, it is good if their parents are visited so that the Faith can be explained to them. If they are angry, do not worry. Once they learn about the Faith they will not mind their children being Bahá'ís.
>
> Everywhere that there are new Bahá'ís, organize children's classes, prepare a programme of Bahá'í education, help the Bahá'ís learn how to conduct an Assembly meeting, assist them to build a centre and visit their homes to say prayers.
>
> When you visit the homes of new believers, avoid giving speeches. Talk to them and listen to them.

To augment the work of these pioneers, Raḥmat approached some of his friends and asked them to purchase books and pamphlets from the Bahá'í Publishing Trust of India. More than 50,000 copies of various publications flooded the continent of Africa. The arrival of these devoted youth in Africa, called the 'Rescue Squad' by the local believers, coupled with the influx of Bahá'í literature, infused such energy that the success of the Nine Year Plan was assured.

By now Raḥmat was travelling regularly to Africa, and he had become widely known to the African Bahá'ís. Many of the pioneers were friends he had encouraged to go to Africa, and he considered it his obligation to visit them, even though they lived in remote and inaccessible places. Two Filipino pioneers recall his visits as the sustaining element in their difficult and lonely existence. In all the years that they were at their post they had no other visitor but him. He would arrive, tired and worn out after travelling for more than eighteen hours on trucks and buses, to spend a day or two in their town. He would bring them news of their families whom he had

In Nigeria with Vilma Villasenor, dedicated pioneer from the Philippines.

With one of the Persian pioneers in Gambia.

visited in the Philippines, help them financially if they needed it, and deliver gifts sent by their relatives. Then, having cheered their hearts, he would leave them with a promise to visit in a few months. Raḥmat's purpose in visiting the pioneers was not to discuss profound and complicated subjects, or to find out whether they had followed his suggestions. He simply wanted to cheer their hearts and assist them in their work for the Faith. 'If I can bring joy to the hearts of the Bahá'ís,' he said, 'give them some suggestions to help them in their work and meanwhile teach a few people myself, I have fulfilled my heart's desire.'

'HIS HEART WAS WITH THE VILLAGERS'

In 1973 he again took a long journey throughout Africa. In Botswana, a project to teach the masses was developed in consultation with the National Spiritual Assembly, which reported;

> Through his guidance, pioneers and local Bahá'ís converged on Selebi-Pikwe for a three week period, divided into teaching teams, conducted public meetings and tried to reach as many people as possible. This was highly successful: more than 300 people accepted the Faith at that time, contacts were made with government officials and well-attended public meetings were conducted at schools and at the local Bahá'í Centre.
>
> The Faith became very well known in Selebi-Pikwe and in surrounding areas. The effects of the project were far-reaching: many of the new believers were in transit or soon after returned to their villages, and in this way the Faith spread to many other villages.

In September of that year, with Raḥmat's help, a new Six month Plan was launched in Zambia. One report stated, 'The project which lasted from 20 October 1973 to 21 April 1974 resulted in the enrolment of 1500 new Bahá'ís in the northern area of Zambia at the beginning of the Five Year Plan.'

After a long and tedious journey he arrived in Accra, the capital of Ghana. As so often happened, the friends hadn't received his cable, so no programme had been planned for him. The *Bahá'í News* of Ghana for October 1973 reported, 'Hand of the Cause Dr

Muhájir, accompanied by Mr Ardekani, member of the Continental Board of Counsellors, stopped in Accra en route to Togo, Dahomey, Nigeria and Kenya.' Raḥmat noted in his diary,

> After my travels . . . accompanied by Mr Ardekani I arrived in Dakar on 23 August 1973. The letter of the Universal House of Justice was awaiting me. With God's assistance, I will go to as many of the African countries as possible.
>
> A few young Africans came to see me. They are simple and wonderful souls. If we can establish a Bahá'í Institute in this country like the one we had in the Bahá'í Centre of Jakarta, hundreds of young students from nearby towns can be deepened in the Faith. They can study for one week and then take the Faith to their own villages. Particularly in the countries of West Africa like Ghana, the Gambia and Liberia this project can easily be implemented.
>
> This can bring thousands to the Faith. God should assist us to be able to reach all these pure and receptive souls. Perhaps these institutes can be supported by the Bahá'ís of Iran and the Bahá'í youth of Iran can be the teachers. We can easily teach the masses in West Africa and bring them together with those in the East; this will happen a thousand times sooner than we can imagine. We need Bahá'u'lláh's bounties.

Mrs Behin Newport, a pioneer in Zaire, remembers Raḥmat's visit to Lubumbashi:

> The first time that our beloved Dr Muhájir visited our home in Lubumbashi was in the summer of 1973. He had waited a long time at the airport, not knowing where to go, when two cars carrying the local Bahá'ís and friends arrived. He had sent a cable about his arrival but we were so busy preparing the house for him and so many were eager to go to meet him that we were delayed.
>
> The Bahá'ís surrounded him, singing and shouting 'Alláh'u'Abhá'. How much he loved them, and how they reciprocated this love. He arrived at our house exhausted, but sat with the friends and chanted the Prayer of Visitation of 'Abdu'l-

> Bahá, answered all their questions and showed love and kindness to all.
>
> He had a problem with his visa in Zaire, as he had overstayed. We were all worried and wanted to consult about it. However, he said, 'Don't worry about it. Bahá'u'lláh will take care of everything.' He proved to be right.

Ola Pavlowska, a pioneer of many years in Zaire, has recorded more details of Raḥmat's travels in the Bukavu region.

> Kavivira and Uvira were always the first stop before entering the narrow road by the lake along which the Local Assemblies were strung like beads on a necklace. There was an excellent meeting in Kavivira one night in the Bahá'í Centre, a small mud and wattle construction packed with Bahá'ís. Dr Muhájir loved village Bahá'ís and they loved him in return. A rapport was always immediately established. He would say: 'Friends, I was born in a mud hut like you. My grandfather was poor but wanted to give a university education to his children. He wrote to 'Abdu'l-Bahá and asked what to do. 'Abdu'l-Bahá replied, 'Contribute to the Fund.' He obeyed and all of us got a university education.' Of course the friends loved it.
>
> There were several subjects on which Dr Muhájir would speak. One of them was the education of children. On this particular evening he explained that education has to be both spiritual and academic. He stressed the responsibility of parents to teach children by example and by word. 'Mother teacher, father teacher.' He said that he woke up as a child to the sound of his mother chanting prayers. He stressed that waking up a child should be done gently. He was very explicit about not beating children. There were objections from the women present. He compared the children to tender plants which are easily bruised. He called for a flower. A pink hibiscus was brought in. He gave it a slap. The delicate petal was immediately bruised. He said that this is like a child who is easily wounded. The wounds of childhood are difficult to heal. Sometimes they never heal. The young plant under the care of the gardener can grow straight or crooked according to his will, but when the plant is old, it is not

pliable and can break. He asked the women present not to beat their children, explaining that a child will start lying to avoid punishment, and that lies are difficult to uproot.

Years later in the Bukavu Bahá'í Centre during the Sunday meeting there was a talk about children's education. I asked one of the women from Fizi who had been present that evening if she beat her children. She recalled, almost verbatim, the words of the Hand of the Cause and said that she followed them, but the mother must have a great deal of self-discipline and patience not to slap a child.

On this first trip to South Kivu Dr Muhájir spoke in eight localities to an audience of more than 1800, where 77 local Assemblies were represented.

When he returned to Bukavu, the Hand of the Cause decided to go to Kinshasa and I was allowed to accompany him. During the meeting with the National Assembly of Zaire, Dr Muhájir was asked to go to Mbuji-Maya in Kasai Oriental, as there was a serious problem with a leader of a [Christian] sect . . . The meeting with the man was not a pleasant one . . . Dr Muhájir was patient but very firm. There was not a glimpse of spirituality in the man. The usually radiant face of Dr Muhájir was clouded. His smile would disappear when he was dealing with insincere people. One would do anything to bring this radiance again to his face so that it would shine . . . We were staying in a miserable hotel in the city, the food was bad, there was no water and it was very hot. Dr Muhájir wanted some cheese but there was none to be found . . . On the return trip to Kananga we stayed in the Atlanta Hotel. Dr Muhájir sent a hotel clerk to bring a big chunk of cheese and three loaves of bread. He told me, 'Ola, you can go to the restaurant, but I will eat bread and cheese while we are here . . . please make me some tea.' He drank great quantities of tea which I made on a small camping gas stove during our travels.

There was no time to go to the villages in Kasai. Dr Muhájir did not like cities. His heart was with the villagers. We proceeded to Lubumbashi in Shaba where he met the pioneers and Bahá'ís. He also spoke to the university youth. Then he went alone to Zambia and Kitwe where there were many declarations.

It was on this trip that Raḥmat went to South Africa for the first time, where he lovingly awakened the friends to the many teaching possibilities in the region. He stayed in a hotel which was used by the black South Africans and which foreigners scarcely frequented. He was taken in the dead of night to see the South African friends, and was delighted that the political situation in that country had not deprived him of visiting them.

Raḥmat's diary for this period gives an indication of how intensive his travels were in his resolve to 'go to as many of the African countries as possible'.

> On August 25 we arrived in Bathurst, the Gambia. In the evening some of the friends were met and then we left for Freetown. We stayed for two days and met some of the friends. Ms Sanchez and Shidan Kouchekzadeh are the pioneers. We consulted about teaching in all the regions of the country and left after two days for Monrovia.
>
> This is the third time that I have come to this country [Liberia]. We had a meeting with the Teaching Committee and I had an interview on TV. They showed the photograph of the Master and the 25-minute interview was very useful.
>
> In the evening we had a wonderful meeting with about 20 seekers. Monrovia is doing a very good job.
>
> Arrived in Abidjan, Ivory Coast, on 30 August. Mr Navidi had met with the Prime Minister and given him, in a conference in which 2000 had been present, the Bahá'í peace plan. The next day the complete text was printed in the papers.
>
> I arrived in South Africa on 4 September, visited Lesotho on the seventh and had meetings with the friends and the National Assembly. On the tenth went to Swaziland. We had long consultations on teaching for three nights. They devised a new plan to have 1500 new Bahá'ís in 17 border towns and decided to establish a teaching institute in the South.
>
> Returned to Johannesburg on 13 September. Had meetings with the NSA and the NTC. A six-month plan was formulated to have

Launch of the Five Year Plan at Kenyan National Conference, May 1974.

Lunch queue at National Conference, Nairobi, May 1974.

six teaching programmes for six areas of South Africa. The Bahá'í Centre in Cape Town will be the teaching institute and they will have a correspondence course committee to strengthen the Bahá'ís through lessons.

22 September: I left Africa for Rome. I spent two months in African countries. My heart and soul is overflowing with joy and gratitude for the bounties of Bahá'u'lláh. I will never forget the memory of this trip. How can I ever thank Him?

INTENSIVE TEACHING PROJECTS

The launch of the Five Year Plan in 1974 was the main reason for Raḥmat's visits to Africa that year. He said that the friends tend to leave the achievement of the goals of the Plans to the last year. This time he wanted to urge the Bahá'ís everywhere to finish every goal in the first two years and spend the last three strengthening the communities, possibly even achieving new goals. His diary entries for spring 1974 demonstrate how he worked closely with the friends to develop local teaching programmes which could bring such early success, and show his exhausting schedule.

His first stop en route to Africa was Mauritius. Whenever he could, Raḥmat would arrange his tickets to start his journey in India, because this was where the lowest airfares could be obtained. Flying from India he was able to visit the island communities of the Indian Ocean off the west coast of Africa. In Mauritius, Raḥmat helped the friends prepare a six-month intensive teaching project, and a series of activities aimed at fulfilling the goals of the Five Year Plan. The project was enthusiastically received when launched at a meeting attended by approximately 200 friends.

6 May: Arrived in Réunion, Indian Ocean, and that night we had a very good meeting with a few seekers. The same night I went to Saint-Pierre and stayed at Joseph's house. He is a Canadian pioneer. The next morning I transferred to the hotel. I met the Assembly and we devised a six-month plan consisting of a ten-day teaching campaign every month. All the teachers are to gather and concentrate in one place, then the next month go to another area. We chose the six cities.

I talked to them about having an oceanic collective teaching enterprise — one teaching campaign in each of the Indian Ocean islands for three months. All of the islands would assist each other. Start in December '74 in Madagascar, then '75 in Reunion, '76 in Mauritius, '77 in Seychelles, and so on. All the communities should co-operate and send teachers and youth to all areas.

9 May, Madagascar: They had good meetings. I met the NSA, the NTC and the Youth Committee. We divided the teaching plans between the Teaching Committee and the Youth Committee. They had a very successful public meeting. The Minister of Industry attended. They had invited a large audience and had very good publicity.

13 May, Nairobi, Kenya: I arrived at 1.30 a.m. and went to the Ambassador Hotel. In the afternoon the Counsellors came to see me and brought me the good news from the Holy Land that the youth project had been approved. The project was to encourage the youth to go travel teaching and pioneering with the NSAs assisting and supporting them. In this way the joint projects could be fulfilled.

15 May, Dar es Salaam, Tanzania: Had a meeting with the NSA and studied their plan. They have 13,000 Bahá'ís, more than 4000 in the west of Tanzania and the rest in the East and the North. We finally came to the conclusion that the NSA would appoint two teaching committees and give a third of the goals to the West, and the rest to the East. They would also appoint local teaching committees to concentrate on teaching and proclamation, and on teaching in colleges and universities. I met the friends on the 16th and 17th and attended a conference which had participants from all over the country.

18 May, Nairobi, Kenya: I participated in the NSA meeting. They plan to have two teaching committees. There are more Bahá'ís in the West of Kenya than in the East. Teaching committees were appointed to contact prominent people and to develop teaching campaigns in each city.

One person from Tanzania came to correct the translation of *Paris Talks*, and went to Nakuru with Dr Malakuti. All were happy and active and much was achieved. God will send them His bounty and assistance.

20-4 May, Kampala, Uganda: I was beloved Olinga's guest for four days. He is such a trustworthy man. He is humble, spiritual and loving. Unity is engraved on his soul. We had long consultations and he decided to go to the West of Africa, particularly Zaire, for a few months. He is the conqueror of those regions and is the Father of Victories.

We had several prayer sessions in the temple and for 24 hours all the Bahá'ís had continuous prayers. I was at dear Banání's house, which now belongs to Olinga. These days were full of happiness and spirituality.

24 May, Kigali, Rwanda: A group of Bahá'ís came from far- off villages. We met in the evening and the next day. Their intelligence and understanding of subjects is astonishing. They ask questions and learn and remember. They speak French and Swahili and are mostly young. Dr Ta'eed has been a pioneer here in Rwanda for nine years. Mrs Ta'eed has many classes and has educated these people. Now they have about 5000 Bahá'ís. What a bounty!

25 May, Bukavu, Zaire: I came to the border in a very old car. The driver and two other passengers were very kind and helpful. I asked one of them if he had heard about the Faith. He had not, but the other passenger said 'Alláh'u'Abhá'! He was a Bahá'í from Kigali and had met Mr Naḥvi on his trip. I gave him a Greatest Name ring and a picture to remember me by. This is how the Faith has progressed in Africa! In every corner Bahá'ís can be found.

At the border a German gentleman gave me a ride and took me to a hotel. Later I went to the Bahá'í Centre and left a note. In the evening a young American Bahá'í, Timothy, came to see me.

I met with the National Assembly at the home of Dr Jazzab for three nights. We formulated a vast teaching programme for

Zaire. A separate Teaching Committee was appointed for Bukavu and we discussed the goals of the Five Year Plan. They will form 550 Assemblies in Bukavu, 110 centres and 95 endowments will be purchased. On each endowment they will plant fruit trees.

Early next morning I met the Regional Teaching Committee and consulted for about an hour. They plan to have a conference for the Swahili-speaking friends of these areas in November '74 . They will have a joint effort on the border of Uganda and Zaire and will try to form ten Assemblies in each zone.

They decided to have a separate teaching programme for Kisangani, which has been visited by the beloved Guardian. They plan to increase the number of believers in their region to at least 25,000 and have 300 Assemblies, 60 Bahá'í Centres and 50 Bahá'í endowments. They will start this in August. They have invited French-speaking youth from Canada, Europe and Iran to participate in this project. A project in Lubumbashi will commence in January '75.

Altogether we can have tens of teaching projects for Africa. For instance, all areas blessed by the visit of the beloved Guardian can have their own projects. Each tribe, each lake area, each river bank, each university, each capital, each border area can have its own plans. The Divine Plan clearly shows that each should have its own projects and then send groups of teachers to other areas.

After meeting with the Regional Teaching Committee I left for Kisangani. The beloved Guardian visited this city for a few days. It was my ardent desire to see it and the Hotel Kisangani, where he had stayed. This is the heart of the heart of Africa.

5 June, Lagos, Nigeria (Hotel Carlton): We can have conferences for the French-speaking areas: for instance, in October, '75 a conference in Abidjan for the friends of Mauritania, Senegal, Niger, Upper Volta, Togo and Dahomey and a conference in Yaounde for Central Africa, Chad, Zaire, Cameroon, Gabon and Congo. If by the Grace of God we can have these sorts of conferences, we will have to prepare for at least one year and then launch them.

In Dahomey, Raḥmat met with the National Spiritual Assembly to consult about winning the goals of the Plan in Niger, Togo and Dahomey. Plans were made to establish the Faith for the first time in the northern provinces of Dahomey. He later met with the Minister of Information and was interviewed for an article in the magazine *Horizons Nouveaux*, and also met with the communities of Borgu province and Porto Novo. As always, when he was in one country he thought about the affairs of another. From Dahomey he wrote to the Universal House of Justice:

> Nigeria is one of the most populous countries in Africa. The latest census indicates the population is 80 million. It is one of the most receptive areas for teaching the Faith. Up to now the number of the Bahá'ís is only 2500, which is the same as Botswana, Swaziland and Lesotho, each of which has less than a million people.
>
> In consultation it was decided to have five or six teaching projects for the regions that have a pioneer or strong local Assemblies. In the first year each of these centres will increase the number of the Bahá'ís to one thousand . . . I think the friends of Ireland, who are mostly youth and are eager to enter the arena of international service, will be very valuable in serving the Faith in Nigeria, even if it is only for one or two years. I have written a letter to the National Assembly of Ireland asking it to write to the Supreme Body to give its opinion on this matter, and if approved this important task can be pursued . . .

While in Cameroon, also in June 1974, Raḥmat wrote to the Universal House of Justice asking it to instruct the Bahá'í Publishing Trust in Uganda to print 30,000 copies of *The New Garden* instead of the 15,000 they had planned.

Charles Lerche recalls meeting Dr Mahájir in Lomé, the capital of Togo, in June 1974:

> We went teaching in a village on the outskirts of Ile-Ife, the spiritual centre of the Yuroba people. Dr Muhájir took particular interest in a man who came late to our meeting. This man, who claimed to be a Jehovah's Witness, was very sceptical. He

First National Convention, Togo, 1975.

became angry and shouted at the Bahá'ís. Dr Muhájir went over to him, spoke to him quietly for a time, came back to the Bahá'ís, smiled, and said, 'You think he's a bad man: he's not a bad man.' He taught us that one has to be very gentle, considerate, and not judgemental when teaching village people.

Dr Muhájir seemed almost able to smell spiritual potential. He would close his eyes and somehow sense which direction to take. He would just go off on his own somewhere, on a bus, and, wherever he went, a few months or a few years later we would have mass declarations in that area.

After his short visit to Togo, Raḥmat arrived in Ghana. Unlike his first visit, this time the friends were ready for him. Meetings had been arranged and he was interviewed on national television. His diary for this period shows how he took advantage of every situation and used it for teaching. Even a story heard in passing would suggest to him a way to aid the progress of the Faith:

11 June: Left Lomé in a taxi for Accra. I am staying in the Bahá'í Centre. I met a young man who became a Bahá'í in Kumasi. His friend had told him that he had heard about the Bahá'í Faith in England, and that if he were to accept a religion it would be that. His friend had given him *Christ and Bahá'u'lláh* to read. The young man had become so interested that he had written off for more books. In this way he had come into contact with the National Assembly of Ghana, and had become a Bahá'í. His friend is not yet a Bahá'í as he works with Christian organizations and it is difficult for him.

Christ and Bahá'u'lláh is the book the beloved Guardian said has defined the relationship between the Faith and Christianity in the best possible manner. I think they should use this book to teach the Africans in England. If the Bahá'ís there would present this book to each African, the Africans will then spread the Faith in their own countries. The beloved Guardian has said that the United Kingdom will have a great effect on the proclamation of the Faith in the Commonwealth countries. They will have a great role to play in this field. Maybe this can be part of a plan for their youth.

> The British can publicize *Christ and Bahá'u'lláh* in the African language newspapers in England, and have an information centre which will respond to their enquiries and invite them to meetings. . . . Perhaps the Persian Bahá'ís could participate in this project. We should have a European teaching plan for the Africans in Europe.

While in Accra, Raḥmat asked the National Assembly of Ghana to consider teaching the Faith to whole families. He didn't remind them that he made the same proposal in 1973, and didn't ask if they had acted on it. This was typical of Raḥmat. He would give his ideas and suggestions to various communities, and leave it to them to accept or reject. He wasn't offended if, on his return to a community he found that his suggestions had been ignored. He would simply offer them again and leave it until the next time.

Amatu'l-Bahá Rúḥíyyih Khánum, also a frequent and experienced traveller in Africa, was involved in one episode which served to illustrate this personal characteristic which Raḥmat possessed. On a trip to an African country, Amatu'l-Bahá visited a village in the middle of a vast desert. The village was comprised of a few huts and a small water-hole, and had a large number of Bahá'ís. The chief conducted Amatu'l-Bahá to a spot in the surrounding countryside. He pointed to a corner and said, 'This is where Dr Muhájir has asked us to build our Bahá'í Centre.' Amatu'l-Bahá replied that surely he did not mean this exact spot. 'You can build it anywhere suitable which is near the village,' she suggested. The chief shook his head and said, 'No. He pointed exactly to this spot and this is where we are going to build it! He will be back soon, so we had better do what he said and build the Centre here.'

PROGRESSIVE TEACHING

In 1975 his African itinerary took him to twelve countries in four months. Although he often began diaries only to abandon them after a few days, this trip was an exception. He noted most of the events, from 14 May to 26 July. This record of his sojourn is an insight into the way he travelled in Africa. He describes in a matter-of-fact fashion his mode of travel, and his submission to the Will of God in painful and sometimes unbearable conditions.

This is my eighth trip to Africa. I left England on 7 April and went to Paris to obtain a visa for Mali. I found a cheap hotel near the air terminal and was so tired that I had to rest the whole afternoon. On the eighth I was able to get the visa for Mali, and on the ninth went to the airport. After hours of waiting I was unable to get a seat. All stand-by passengers left the air terminal. I changed my ticket for one to Abidjan. The plane had been delayed for four hours and was just departing. Thank God I could get on it. At Freetown I sent messages with some departing passengers for the Bahá'í friends. They have elected their National Assembly this April.

Arrived in Abidjan at 11 p.m. Contacted one of the friends who took me to the Centre. We talked for an hour. Met the National Assembly on 11 April and discussed their mass teaching efforts.

Some time ago I sent a suggestion to the Holy Land about progressive teaching: To concentrate in one area, teach 1000 people, train 100 youth and 100 children and the next year add to the number of pioneers and literature and expand the teaching to 2000 people. The National Assembly of the Ivory Coast adopted this plan and chose Daloa as their target. Daloa is near Abidjan and close to the areas where the Bahá'ís are concentrated, so by travelling only a few kilometres they can reach them. It was a blessed meeting. After a few days I heard that the chairman of the National Assembly had personally gone to Daloa, taught a group and elected a local Assembly. Two Persian pioneers have volunteered to go to that area to start mass teaching.

14 April, Abidjan: Had a meeting in town with 20 seekers. One medical student accepted the Faith. In the evening met with the National Assembly and suggested a one-year plan to be presented to the Convention. In the Ivory Coast the northeners are Muslims and the South is Christian. The central part of the country is relatively free of religious influences and is ready to receive the Faith. This belt starts from Danane in the West, which has 12 local Assemblies, reaches Daloa, which is the goal for mass teaching, and then Yamussaukro, where Dr Sadiqzadih pioneers. It continues through Dimbokro and on to Abengourou in the East and the border of Ghana. It was decided to include the last two cities in the mass teaching plan. Fortunately these areas have good roads. Bouake also should be a goal as it is the second largest city after Abidjan. If the Faith progresses in this central area we can easily penetrate the North and the South. Bahá'u'lláh's blessings and the efforts of the friends are needed.

The National Assembly's report of his visit states:

As a result of [Dr Muhájir's] consultations with the National Assembly of the Ivory Coast, Mali and Upper Volta, a model mass teaching project was launched in Daloa, a recently opened region near the centre of the Ivory Coast. The results were unprecedented: in less than a year more than 16 local Spiritual Assemblies were formed and the new believers had assumed responsibility for teaching, forming new local Assemblies, holding children's classes, Nineteen Day Feasts and Holy Day observances, and propagating the Faith throughout the region.

Raḥmat's diary continues:

17 April, Togo: Spent a week in Ivory Coast, and came to Togo. They are electing their first National Spiritual Assembly. From the airport I called Dr Khelghati. He and Marere were waiting at the University Hotel when I got there. I spent some time with them and then took a rest. On the 18th and 19th, the Convention was in session. I read the message of the Universal House of Justice. Each goal was discussed.

We talked about the endowments donated by four or five villages, and local Assemblies, Bahá'í Centres, and mass teaching. We chose 14 localities, including Lomé, as targets, to teach hundreds, elect Assemblies and form children's classes. The National Assembly was elected in the afternoon. I offered the delegates the attar of roses which Mr Rahmani had sent for me when I was in the Holy Land, so that each time they inhaled its fragrance they would remember this first election.

This is the first National Assembly of Togo. I met with it at eight p.m. They had been meeting since five a.m. This Assembly

Consultation with the friends in Cameroon.

With some of the friends in Cameroon.

is very capable, united and spiritual. Its members come from all important regions of the country. An eighteen-month programme was drawn up to fulfil all the goals of the remaining four years of the Plan before the Nairobi conference. They announced this to the Convention and sent a cable to the Universal House of Justice to this effect. It brought immense joy to all hearts. I am sure they will achieve much more than they have planned.

Two nights later I again met with the National Assembly and the Teaching Committee and consulted about the 18-month plan. An initial six-month plan to go to three areas for mass teaching was drawn up. They decided to invite the National Assemblies of Dahomey and Ghana and also Counsellors Ekpe and Kazemi to meet them on the 24th and 25th of May to formulate plans for the July youth conference and to decide how to utilize youth services for teaching, consolidation and Bahá'í education. Spent one week in Togo.

24 April, Upper Volta: Early morning, went to Abidjan to leave for Upper Volta. Dr Khelghati and other friends were at the airport. Spent a happy hour with them and left for Ouagadougou. Dear Sobhani, his wife and sister were waiting to take me to their home. The heat was unbearable but the house was cool and comfortable. Spent two days with them. They showed me much love and hospitality and invited other pioneers and friends to meet me.

In the evening we consulted with the friends. They decided to send five of their youth to Upper Volta after the Lomé conference. One of the fertile areas in Upper Volta is Gaoua, the home of the Luly tribe, who are neither Muslim nor Christian. There are already two Bahá'ís there. The town of Bobo [Dioulasso] has good and faithful Bahá'ís. Best of all is the city of Ouagadougou and its surrounding areas. The National Assembly of Niger also has decided to help Upper Volta and establish local Assemblies in Gaurmanche and Diapaga. Stayed two days and left for Niamey.

26 April, Niamey, Niger: Went with Mr Kazemi to Niamey. Dear Amini and later Mr Joneidi joined us. We had a meeting with the beloved pioneers at the Sahel Hotel. These dear souls have spent ten sacrificial years in this country and now they have witnessed the election of their first National Assembly. Blessed are those who can see the result of their services, though it be in its infant stages. God willing, one day these countries will have Bahá'ís all over their lands who will forever remember the sacrifices of these wonderful servants of Bahá'u'lláh.

The weather is extremely hot and sometimes passes 41°C. Amini said that when they were on the way to the airport it had been 65°C. I said that this was impossible, but he insisted that in the sunshine it really is that hot. This kind of heat, which is so hard to bear even for two days, has been tolerated by them for ten years and they still serve and work and joke and laugh and show hospitality to dozens of Bahá'ís and non-Bahá'ís.

In the evening the friends gathered at Mr Joneidi's house. The next day we all went to the teaching institute. We had prayers for two hours and consulted on all aspects of the work of the Faith. In the afternoon the convention was opened and the National Assembly elected. Most of the members are youth of the highest calibre. In the evening they had a show about the Dawn-Breakers. The next day the National Assembly met in room 31 of the Sahel Hotel, and we consulted on how to help Upper Volta, the youth movement, the purchase of Bahá'í Centres, etc. We made plans which are to be implemented.

In the evening, participated in the wedding ceremony of Mr Amini and Doris, which was a fitting finale for the convention.

The last day of my stay in Niamey was spent locating a proper house for the Ḥaẓíratu'l-Quds. Finally we chose a modern new house which they had seen before, and which everybody liked. The same night the down-payment was made, and this great task accomplished. This is all through the grace of God. Spent one week in Niamey.

The weather was so hot that I hesitated going to northern Nigeria. I even reserved a seat to go to Zaire. However, finally decided to rely on God and in whatever way possible travel to Nigeria. The plains of Niger as seen from the air for the whole two hours, were bone dry. Once in a while a small body of water would come into view with a few huts around it.

On arrival at the Maradi airport I asked a gentleman who was travelling alone to allow me to go in his car to Kano. He said that going to Kano was useless and drove me to the border. He advised me to ask the passing cars to take me over the border. He introduced me to a border guard who was his friend and left. I had to wait for two hours . The heat was so intense that I had to pour water over my head all the time. Noon was approaching and I felt that I could not tolerate the heat any longer, when suddenly a truck stopped. The driver was reluctant to take me as he was not going the same way. However, after a lot of persuasion, he agreed to take me to Jibia, a border town just inside Nigeria.

In Jibia an army officer who spoke English took pity on me and came to my rescue. He promised to accompany me all the way to Kano. To my great delight he found a taxi out of nowhere, and the rest of the way we were happy and comfortable. However, outside the taxi it was so hot that we preferred to keep the windows closed.

We stopped in Katsina and some other towns to douse ourselves with water and to rest. I bought a piece of bread and shared it with other passengers.

After four hours we arrived in Kano and the taxi driver took me to the Central Hotel. The rooms were $50 a night. I asked for a cheaper room, but was told that the cheaper rooms were not air-conditioned and were very hot. Finally they gave me a room which was less than half-price. When I entered the room I found out it was air-conditioned and cool. All the toils of the trip vanished. I took a shower and rested a while.

The friends were supposed to come to the hotel to see me. I waited in the lobby all evening but no one showed up. The next morning at nine a.m. I left for Zaria.

I travelled in a station wagon with seven others. On the way we had a flat tyre and had to spend more than an hour in the intense heat on the road. As there was no jack, the passengers helped lift the car. They were so united in this work, as if they were all brothers. Finally we arrived in Zaria.

By now it was 1 May. I knew that Dr Seddiq lived in Zaria but I did not have his address. A man took me in his car to a guest house, and said he would return in the afternoon to see if I had found my friends. Finally I was able to call the university and find Dr Seddiq's address. I went to his home by taxi.

These dear people were the first Bahá'ís I had seen in Nigeria. I was confident that things would go right from that day onwards. The Bahá'ís came for two nights and we visited Kadima, which has a good Bahá'í community.

The next day we visited Jos. It is a beautiful town, the weather is cool and there are beautiful trees and flowers. The whole town is like a garden. This is a mountainous region and the centre of the tribes, which makes it the best place for mass teaching.

The next day we took a full day's bus ride to reach Gboko, and then visited Yandev to see Mr Khayltash and his family. They showered us with love and hospitality. Their beautiful daughter, Gul, although only two-and-a half years old, has memorized many prayers which she chants. In the afternoons Mrs Khayltash goes teaching from house to house. They have brought in 30 Bahá'ís at Hihu which is 22 miles from their town. They have a local Assembly. They love all the people and the people love them.

The next morning Dr Seddiq accompanied me for about 40 miles until I could find a car to take me to Ogoja. On the way we had a flat tyre and had to spend several hours under a tree in the desert. Finally a truck came by and gave me a ride to Gakem.

It was market-day and a huge crowd was roaming the streets. Some were drunk and the rest busy with their buying and selling. The truck driver kindly took my suitcase to a taxi which would take me to Ogoja. He advised me to go to the Christian school and find a room for the night as there was no place to stay in town. The principal of the school, an Irish Catholic, very kindly gave me a room in his own apartment and, although he was invited out for dinner, prepared some food for me. Early next morning he brought me breakfast and drove me to the bus stop.

I left for Ikom and Calabar. The truck I rode in was named *Glory* and the driver, a nice humble man, drove very fast on the potholed roads. On the way we found that the bridge had collapsed and we had to wade across the water, carrying our luggage. On the other side of the river we took a taxi to Ikom, on the border with Cameroon. There are a few Bahá'ís in Ikom, but I could not find them.

I rested for an hour or so while waiting for transportation. A clean, new bus arrived and we left for Calabar. The roads were wide and well paved, and after riding for 217 kilometres we reached Calabar in the evening. This is the southernmost town in Nigeria.

I went to the Capital Hotel where the friends were supposed to be waiting for me. No one was there. It seems that my cable, sent to them more than a week before, had not reached them. I got a room and sent someone to inform Counsellor Ekpe of my arrival. He and his wife came and I was delighted to see them.

This area has hundreds of Bahá'ís. I have come all this way just to visit these radiant and wonderful souls.

We left for the villages the next day. The first one was Ikot Uba. Stayed at Joseph's house. He is well-off and has a big house. Olinga and others have been his guests. Joseph has two wives and a few children, and works day and night. His father had been the village chief, and he is very well respected. For three days I had meetings with the Bahá'ís. In this village they have a good teaching institute and Joseph has donated a piece of land in the next village. This area has 36,000 Bahá'ís and 15 local Assemblies.

There are only two elementary schools, one with four classes and one with six. There are no high schools. It was decided to use two acres of the institute land for a high school. The first year they will build two rooms and ask the government to establish a high school in their village. There are 300 Bahá'í children in this area alone who cannot continue their studies after the fourth and sixth grades in their village. The nearest schools are 25 kilometres away and it is too far and too expensive for them, and so many remain without further education. If the National Assembly supplies the corrugated roofing and the local Bahá'ís build the two rooms and then next year add another two rooms, in four years they will have a high school which will attract the bounties of God to this area.

Maybe Mr Ekpe can employ two English-speaking youth in his school in Calabar. They could teach there for two days and use five days for the Bahá'í children in this area. I advised them to use their houses and Bahá'í Centres to plant fruit trees and flowers to be of use to the children.

A committee of five was appointed to do the work of the building. We have sent these suggestions to the National Assembly. It is now up to them to approve and implement them.

On 10 May, accompanied by Oscar and Mrs Ekpe, I went on the road to Mamfe. There are almost 1000 Bahá'ís along this road. Those we met were young, educated and enthusiastic. This area is inhabited by the Ejacham tribe. Many of them are Bahá'ís. There are hundreds of thousands of this tribal people with the capacity to accept the Faith. We visited Akor, Orem, Ntebachot, Nyaje and Qwom. The last village is large and has about 100 Bahá'ís. We spent the night in Nyaje and met a large number of people. The emphasis of our talks was on the establishment of Bahá'í classes for children. It is now 20 years since the Faith has come to this area, and there is a dire need for Bahá'í education.

I returned to Calabar on 11 May and stayed at the Taj Mahal Hotel, room ten. I had thought of going to Mamfe by car, but I really do not have the strength to change cars so many times, so decided to go to Douala by plane.

Today is 14 May. I have made a comprehensive plan from the result of my consultation with Counsellor Ekpe, Oscar, Dr Seddiq and others. This plan calls for a vast teaching project in Nigeria. The following is a summary:

The Nigeria Plan

1. Important places where there should be a Local Assembly, mostly centres of regions: Benin City, Onitsha, Oyo, Oshogbo, Ijebu-Ode, Maiduguri, Ibrin, Abakaliki, Kontagoara, Sokoto, Makurdi, Gusau, Ogoja, Kano, Baclu.

2. Areas in need of education and teachers: Calabar, Mamfe Road, Agbaja, Akpabuyo.

3. Areas where mass teaching is possible: Jos — using teachers from Ireland; North — teachers from Iran and East Africa;

South-East — English-speaking teachers with knowledge of Christianity.

4. Pioneering needs: Port Harcourt — physicians; Kano — Persian physicians and teachers; Aba — teachers, students; Kabba — teachers; Ibadan — students; Jos — agricultural engineers; Benin City — students, teachers; Nsukka (university city) — teachers, students.

5. Need for travel teachers: Central East — June to December, teaching Christians; West — teaching Christians all year; South-East — teaching Christians and education programmes, June to December.

I have suggested to the Universal House of Justice that Mr Navidi be sent to Nigeria to negotiate with the immigration office and pave the way for about 20 Bahá'ís from all over the world to come as pioneers. This will open the way for both pioneers and travel teachers.

Raḥmat's letter of 12 May to the Universal House of Justice gives details of his proposals to the National Assembly:

Around Calabar in an area called Ikang, we have a community of about 600 voting members and more than 1000 Bahá'í children. In the whole area we have only two small elementary schools . . . they do not have a high school for a region of more that 36,000 inhabitants . . . The institute has ten acres of land, two of which are used, and the rest have become a wild jungle. It would be a great opportunity for the Cause if two acres of this wasteland could be earmarked for a high school . . . Please pray that the need for a little material help will not hinder the Assembly from approving this project . . . I have no words to thank God for the wonderful times that He has granted me in meeting with the Bahá'ís of this area.

With Counsellor Ardekani and an African friend, Gambia.

With Auxiliary Board Member Muḥammad Al-Salihi and some members of the Gambian NSA.

He continues the story of his travels:

> Went to the airport on the 14th and waited a long time for the plane. However it did not land in Calabar. It had gone directly to Douala from Lagos. I took a car to Ikon, arrived at eight p.m., and took a room in a hotel. It was very hot so I slept in the courtyard where it was cooler: the sky was beautiful with shining stars. Early in the morning it started to rain and I had to get up. Left at seven a.m. for the border of Nigeria and Cameroon. Around ten a.m., we arrived in Cameroon. The roads were very good and red in colour, rivers were wide and flowing. The real Africa in its natural beauty and simple ways and the serene and kind natives greeted us on our arrival.
>
> The immigration officer was Olinga's friend and showed me much courtesy. He said that half of the inhabitants of his village were Bahá'ís. Finally a taxi came along and I left for Mamfe.
>
> Arrived 3.30 p.m. at Ayamba's house. His wife and children were home, and in the evening we had a meeting with the friends. Early next morning we went to the village of Kenlio. One by one the Bahá'ís gathered and we were able to have a good meeting with about 15 of them.
>
> A few youth who were present heard about the Faith. After a simple lunch we returned to Mamfe and at four p.m. went to Tinto. They have a beautiful teaching institute there. We had a good meeting and stayed for the night. The next morning at six a.m., left for Kumba. Mrs Vajiheh Iqani returned to Mamfe and the rest of us went to Kumba.

From Kumba Raḥmat left for Douala, Cameroon and stayed a few days in that country. The Cameroon *Bahá'í News* carried an enthusiastic report of Raḥmat's visit there:

> Within this short space of time [15-23 May], he met with the National Spiritual Assembly twice . . . he met the Bahá'ís in Mamfe, Kembong, Tinto, Kumba, Buea, Victoria, Douala and Yaounde, where he had a radio interview in English. [He] speaks in such a loving gentle way, radiating kindness; but, suddenly, we find ourselves swept off our feet and pledged to fulfil a

tremendous plan . . . In order to achieve it we must try to emulate Dr Muhájir's energy and concentration in pursuing a matter.

He urged us not to waste time, not to let opportunities slip from our grasp. Some opportunities will never come to us again — once lost, they are lost forever. Others may be lucky enough to seize opportunities that we are missing. New opportunities will come, but we should not miss any.

Dr Muhájir's picture of universal participation makes all goals seem possible. Everyone should teach. When we go to a village, we should go to the first house and teach the whole family, make it a Bahá'í home. Then each Bahá'í home should become a Bahá'í temple, a Bahá'í school, a Bahá'í teaching institute.

It was at this meeting that he first outlined the 'Concentrated Programme', which was later worked out in consultation with the National Assembly.

Raḥmat's diary recorded the details of this programme and his subsequent activities:

In Victoria, in consultation with the National Assembly, the following small teaching plan was made:

1. Mass teaching in three areas: Kumba, 500; Bamenda, 100; Yaoundé, 400.

2. Education of children in Mamfe. Two Persian pioneers who have come for this purpose will be sent to establish children's classes in Tinto and Kimbo and other places with Bahá'í children.

19 May: Visited a high school in Victoria to teach the Faith. There were ten students in the meeting which was quite wonderful. The next day had lunch with the NSA members and in the evening had a meeting in Buea. Twenty friends were present and I talked about the Universal House of Justice and its station. Next day left for Yaoundé with Iraj Yeganeh and his dear family.

21 May: Local Assembly of Yaoundé at Iraj's home. The meeting lasted till 1.30 a.m. Mass teaching was discussed and we drafted a plan to have six public meetings in a year, and four book exhibitions, to teach university students from tribal backgrounds, and to form a teaching committee for high schools.

22 May: Public meeting in Yaounde.

23 May: Returned to Douala by plane to participate in the NSA meeting at Baskaran's home. Teaching of the area between Yaounde and Douala was the topic of consultation. It was decided to teach at least 3000 in that area. This project is to start from the day of the anniversary of Bahá'u'lláh's Ascension and continue for 18 months until 4 October 1976. I hope with the grace of God an international conference can be held on that day with the participation of Nigeria along with the Bahá'ís of Mamfe, Yaoundé and Douala. Bahá'u'lláh will assist His friends and the servants of His Cause.

25 May (Zaire): The Hotel Albert is now called the Globe. This is where the beloved Guardian stayed when he passed through Lubumbashi.

I am meeting with the NSA of Zaire. All nine members and ABM Paul are present.

I don't know how the tasks of this vast country can be accomplished and the goals achieved. Some of the pioneers have left and some are in the process of departing. There are no prospective pioneers. Bahá'u'lláh should assist us to have a new vigour and zeal to serve His Cause in this country.

What we can do: Co-operation in teaching and conferences between neighbouring countries; education of the 15,000 Bahá'ís and 10,000 children in Kivu; have plans for pioneering, teaching and education. There are three teaching institutes in Katanga, Kisangani and Bukavu where they have pioneers and can educate local teachers.

An educational team should travel around West Africa. There should be a census of Kivu children. Two pioneers should come from Kibenge and Brazzaville. If a few trusted and dedicated Bahá'ís prepare themselves for the education of Bahá'í children and travel from village to village and establish Bahá'í classes, they will render a great service.

> I wish people in Africa would realize the importance of Bahá'í education, and that the Bahá'í institutions would pay attention to it and prepare the tools for it. I wish they would encourage those who know French and English to come to these areas and help with the education of Bahá'í children. Maybe I should write to the Universal House of Justice and the NSA of Iran. Hopefully a way will be opened.
>
> I was the guest of Dr Jazzab and his family in Kinshasa for six days. It was a restful time. I met the NSA several times and teaching and educational plans were formulated. It is all in God's hands.

On 28 May Raḥmat went to Lubumbashi again. The friends were excited to receive a cable that he was coming to visit. Once more, as in 1973, because they were busy fixing and cleaning the Bahá'í Centre for his arrival, they were late getting to the airport. Raḥmat arrived at the Centre by taxi and said with a smile, 'So you forgot to fetch me again!'

That night they made plans for the next day. Three days before his arrival a reporter who had passed the Bahá'í Centre had become interested in the word 'Bahá'í' and had asked the friends for an interview. He was invited to meet Raḥmat. He was so impressed that he wrote a long article and brought it for Raḥmat's approval before publication. In the evening he had a meeting with about 100 university students.

In a meeting with the National Teaching committee, he pointed out the importance of teaching whole families and entire villages. A pioneer who was with Raḥmat at this time said,

> He always listened to every suggestion and never opposed any of them. He would not allow long discussions and opposing views. He was very sympathetic to the opinions of local believers and when the pioneers disagreed with what the local believers wanted, he would always tell them, 'Do what *they* want.'

Raḥmat's diary continues:

> Today is 29 May. Last night was the Ascension of Bahá'u'lláh. Spent the night in humble prayers and meditation. Early

morning prepared my bag to leave for Kisangani. I am writing this in the plane. At the airport I wrote a detailed letter about Bahá'í education to the Universal House of Justice and hope to mail it. Thank God with the help and kindness of the friends things move smoothly and God's blessings surround us.

31 May: Stayed in Kisangani for two days. Dear Kristoph, a young man from Kenya, is the pioneer there. He is a dedicated and active Bahá'í who knows English and Swahili and has enrolled 80 members of the pygmy tribe in the Faith. He is now the caretaker of the Ḥaẓíratu'l-Quds, and teaches the Faith in the city. I stayed for two nights at the Ḥaẓíra and had two meetings with about twenty of the friends and two seekers.

Last night I dreamt I asked the beloved Guardian about his travels in Africa. He looked very young and had a grey suit on. He told me about the route and said he had met one of his relatives. I was wondering who that relative could be when someone said, 'He means one of Amatu'l-Bahá's relatives.' I woke up, and despite the stifling heat, felt happy and elated. When I fell asleep again I dreamt the Guardian was present in a meeting of the youth and pioneers. Michelle from Togo was also there. The Guardian asked for a prayer and one of the ladies started to chant the prayer for the Hands of the Cause. I was astonished that she did that in the presence of the beloved Guardian, so I started chanting from the Will and Testament of 'Abdu'l-Bahá about the Guardian:

> After the passing away of this wronged one, it is incumbent upon the Aghṣán, the Afnán of the Sacred Lote-Tree, the Hands of the Cause of God and the loved ones of the Abhá Beauty to turn unto Shoghi Effendi — the youthful branch branched from the two hallowed and sacred Lote-Trees and the fruit grown from the union of the two offshoots of the Tree of Holiness — as he is the sign of God, the chosen branch, the guardian of the Cause of God . . .[3]

I woke up still chanting.

> Kisangani is the heart of Africa. It has been blessed with the presence of the beloved Guardian for a few days. The present Ḥaẓíra is a few blocks from the Kisangani Hotel where he stayed. The Ḥaẓíra is large and strong. I hope it will become a centre of Bahá'í meetings where myriads of new Bahá'ís can come to serve the Faith.
>
> I hitched a ride with a gentleman who was going to Bukavu. At the hotel they gave me a nice large room with a view of the lake. This is one of the most beautiful spots I have seen. Went to the Bahá'í Centre at five p.m. Tim was there. Stayed there for about an hour, and then, together with Tim, went to the American Consulate to meet Ola [Pawloska] who was going there to see a movie. Dear Ola was, as usual, radiant and the movie was good.
>
> Early next morning changed my hotel to the Belvue, which is much cheaper, and went to the Centre to meet two seekers. At three p.m., more than forty Bahá'ís gathered and for a few hours we talked about the importance of the teachings of the Faith. There were a few non-Bahá'ís.

According to Ola Pawloska, six meetings were held in the zones of Uvira, Fizi and Walungu. One particularly memorable meeting took place in the small community of Kibungu Nyamutiri, in the Balfulero. They gathered in an unfinished Bahá'í Centre, in the middle of a field covered with stubble. The walls of stick were not yet plastered with mud and the blue sky could be seen through the unfinished roof, but it protected them from the sun. Raḥmat spoke about the Báb, and about sacrifice and the power which it releases. In the question period somebody asked, 'What were the words that the Báb spoke to Mullá Ḥusayn at the time of His declaration of the Faith?' Raḥmat, smiling, turned to Ola and said, 'Ola, I have been perhaps four times around the world but nobody asks questions as the Kivu Bahá'ís do. All right, I will chant for you the opening verses of the Qayyúmu'l-Asmá', but you must repeat after me and chant with me.' Ola recalls,

> In the stillness of the noon hour, with only the chirping of the cicadas as a background, rose the clear, warm, beautiful voice of the Hand of the Cause chanting the sacred verses. Yes, the Bahá'ís, so musically gifted, repeated the chant after him.

The teaching of Dr Muhájir inspired the friends and they composed songs that served as illustrations of the dramatic events of the Faith. The beautiful song 'Amani, Peace' about the sufferings of Bahá'u'lláh which He bore so that peace would be established in the world, was composed then. Another, about the martyrdom of the Báb, and Mullá Ḥusayn, 'Imani ya Bahá'í', was composed on our next stop in Kaberagule on the plain of Ruzizi.

It was cotton-picking time. The friends from neighbouring Assemblies came for the meeting. As the Centre was small we met outside, but there was no tree to give shade. After the meeting he looked around and saw a kind of large cage made of bamboo slats in which freshly-picked cotton was stored. It was half full. He instructed me to put a sheet over it and stretch a mosquito net across, and that is how he slept.

In Kabimba there was an excellent talk on progressive revelation in which the Hand of the Cause compared God to a tree — the tree of life in paradise — and the different Manifestations to the trunk, the branches, buds, flowers and fruits of that tree, starting with Adam and ending with Bahá'u'lláh. Bahá'u'lláh was like the fruit, like an olive, which was crushed by suffering in prison to give oil for the light of the world. This simile was easily understood and accepted as an explanation of the universal oneness of the Manifestations. Years later I saw a Bahá'í using a young banana tree to demonstrate this concept to a spellbound audience.

Raḥmat's diary continues:

2 June: Early morning, Tim came to my hotel and we drafted a questionnaire about Bahá'í education. We spent the rest of the day in consultation with Ola.

3 June: Tim typed the questionnaire and I wrote a few pages about progressive teaching. We put the finishing touches to both.

4 June: Early morning, left for Uvira. We had to pass through Rwanda to reach the other side of Zaire. Immigration and customs were no problem. The first village we visited was Kbungu. The chairman of the LSA, an African woman, is a very dedicated Bahá'í who has been instrumental in forming 12 LSAs. About 30 people had gathered from all over. It was a most inspiring and spiritual gathering. They asked about the words the Báb spoke to Mullá Ḥusayn on the first night of their meeting, so I chanted a few verses from the Qayyúmu'l-Asmá' and asked them to repeat it with me: 'All praise be to God Who hath, through the power of Truth, sent down this Book unto His servant, that it may serve as a shining light for all mankind . . .'[4]

I made this trip specifically to emphasize the importance of the education of children. I read many of the Writings on this subject to them. Representatives of other LSAs promised that on their return they would establish Bahá'í classes in their villages. We were there for four hours.

In the afternoon, went to Kaberagule. From eight p.m. we had a meeting of hundreds of Bahá'ís. Spent the night there.

5 June: It was the Nineteen Day Feast and we had meetings from eight a.m. to lunch-time, and again from three p.m. until evening. As there were many seekers Ola and others talked about the fundamentals of the Faith. One person enrolled. Spent the night there.

6 June: Had dawn prayers and left for Kaminvira. There are many Bahá'ís in this village and they have a children's class with 80 pupils. The village is on the seashore. The Bahá'ís are very spiritual and wonderful. We had a large gathering at one p.m. I talked about the importance of Bahá'í education and explained the role of the parents with simple stories and examples. Members of 11 LSAs were there — most have Bahá'í classes.

7 June: We had a good meeting from eight a.m. Many prayers were said and we again talked about Bahá'í education for children. They all promised to give this important matter priority. There are hundreds of intelligent Bahá'í children. If they receive Bahá'í training the face of Africa will change. We will have thousands of teachers and educators for the future of the Faith to ensure the establishment of the Golden Age of Bahá'u'lláh.

A significant impediment to their providing education is their inability to pay for the children's transportation. We consulted about this matter and suggested ways and means to help them. They are determined to find answers to this question. Bahá'u'lláh's bounties are needed.

I very often think about Africa these days. This vast and beautiful continent is ready to embrace the Teachings. How can we harness this energy and channel it for the education of thousands of children? I wish this unworthy soul could stay in this continent for many years, and serve and educate these beloved children. I wish I could give my life for them. May God grant my desire. I have spent many years in talk but with no deeds. I wish God would aid me to do something of substance.

Between Bukavu and Fizi there are thousands of Bahá'ís, and hundreds of Bahá'í villages. We can teach, we can consolidate, we can educate. Everything is possible. We can establish thousands of Bahá'í homes and educate their children. How many possibilities exist! We have to have a map of these areas, write down the names of the villages and mark those towns which have LSAs. We need a census of Bahá'í families and children and must develop teaching and education plans, and implement them in each Bahá'í and non-Bahá'í home.

I visited three villages on my way — Kamimba, Rumingo and Nigamarge. There were more than 400 Bahá'ís in Kamimba, gathered from about 12 LSA areas. The Bahá'í Centre is clean and full of flowers, and the friends very intelligent, spiritual and gifted. Dermot and his wife are in Rumingo with the Peace Corps. About 40 Bahá'ís were there and some had attended other conferences. It is a united and active community.

11 June: Nigamarge, in western Bukavu, is a far-off village in the middle of tea plantations. There were more than 200 Bahá'ís at the meeting, representing about 15 LSAs. They have a very active committee. The meeting lasted for four hours.

This was my first time in western Bukavu. I have spent 15 days in this area.

CONSOLIDATION AND EXPANSION

On the first of two journeys to Africa in 1976, Raḥmat concerned himself mostly with teaching whole families. The June issue of *Nairobi Bahá'í News* reports that when he visited the community he 'shared his ideas of a progressive teaching plan which aims at teaching families, house by house, and thus building a unit of community. This ensures that consolidation and expansion go together.' He also urged the Bahá'ís to teach the children, as one way to get their parents interested. He explained that these methods had been tried in West Africa with great success.

He encouraged those friends who had used such methods in other countries to travel and pioneer to Africa. He also encouraged the Iranian Bahá'ís to pioneer there.

I remember a group of pioneers from the Philippines who passed through New Delhi on their way to Africa. Most had become Bahá'ís when we had been pioneers in Manila between 1963 and 1968. They arrived on a day when a large teaching conference was being held to consult on the goals of the Five Year Plan. Raḥmat greeted them and took them to the rooms which he had arranged for them in the Bahá'í Centre. He instructed them to 'take a shower, rest a while and come and join in the consultation.' He made them feel at ease and at one with the Indian Bahá'ís. It was quite a sight to see these wonderful and dear friends following him around, telling him with great excitement about the achievements of the Bahá'ís in the Philippines.

He had arranged for their tickets and had asked permission for them to go on pilgrimage to the Holy Land. The next day he accompanied them to the airport and told them that he would be in Africa before they arrived! These pioneers, some of whom are still at their posts, recall that on their arrival in Kenya, the first person to greet them was Raḥmat. He took each pioneer to their assigned post, took them on teaching trips with him, and familiarized them with the local conditions.

In this year, during his third visit to Bukavu, Zaire, they held a meeting under a huge mango tree. The beautiful teachings were explained by using a plant — with its roots, leaves and flowers — as an example of the human world. Raḥmat spoke of the hard work of

On the road again. Leaving Gambia, August 1976.

Building a Bahá'í Centre at a village in Kenya, 1977.

the roots, digging in the dark earth in search of moisture and nourishment, not knowing what the result of their efforts would be. He explained that the roots have no inkling of the world above the surface, of the glory of the sun and rain, the beautiful sky, even of their own flowers and fruit. In the same way, we are living in the world of matter and cannot imagine the bounties of the spiritual world. Yet these bounties can be gained only through our efforts on this physical plane.

He encouraged the Bahá'ís, where the local Assemblies were close to one another, to have five or six Assemblies band together and construct a Centre which would serve for larger gatherings. South Kivu is still dotted with these local Ḥaẓíratu'l-Quds.

On the way to Lubumbashi Raḥmat's thoughts were concentrated on how to accelerate the progress of the Faith in Africa. He wrote:

> To greatly advance the Faith in Africa and to conquer the hearts and souls of the people as happened during the lifetime of the beloved Guardian, perhaps we should keep in mind the following:
>
> 1. We should realize that the spiritual revival of Africa will be achieved by the indigenous peoples of Africa. Whatever assistance is given from outside should only be to deepen the Bahá'ís, to strengthen the Bahá'í administration and to make the Faith self-supporting here. The pioneers, teachers, students and literature from non-African countries should be used solely for these purposes.
>
> 2. The NSAs in Africa should increase their co-operation over teaching projects. Countries which have the same language and the same tribes should have joint teaching projects along their borders. If each NSA would start teaching along the borders of its own country, the projects would spill over to nearby villages in the neighbouring country. A good example of this is the community of Bojomburo which came into existence as the result of teaching in Kivu in the East of Zaire. In the same manner, teaching on the border of Angola and

Zaire will strengthen the Faith in Angola. Teaching in the West and North of Liberia has resulted in the entry of the people in Guing.

We have to assign these borders as part of a teaching plan, as the basis of a vast effort to make Africa one spiritual entity. Hopefully this plan could be accomplished in the next five years. It is very easy and can be done. Examples to consider are:

a) Senegal: from Ziguinchor to S. Domingo to Suzana to Wareia to Farini to Tanafe to Colinado to Boindan to Kaundara, etc.

b) Sierra Leone: Yana to Kambia to Falaba.

c) Liberia: Voinjama to Zorzor to Ganta to Suakoko to Sanniquellie.

d) Ivory Coast: Odienne which is situated near the border of Ivory Coast, Guinea and Mali, and also Toulia near the border of Guinea.

There are 1,000,000 Angolan refugees in Zaire in the border towns of Sangololo. We could teach from there to Matadi to Dilolo to Tshikapa to Kahemba to Kolwezi to Luashi and Mutshatsha which is on the border of Zaire with Zambia.

3. The national plans of each country should consist of:

a) Educational plans for areas with strong communities.

b) Mass teaching plans for areas with a strong capacity and readiness to accept the Faith.

c) Pioneering plans for areas that have no Bahá'ís.

4. Regional and international teaching plans.

> Unfortunately, many indigenous Africans, for financial reasons, cannot participate in the continental conferences. A few regional conferences will result in the spiritual deepening of the people from these regions. If the Hands of the Cause can visit this continent more often it will greatly benefit the teaching effort and increase the knowledge of the friends about the Faith.

On 21 June, while he was in Zambia, Raḥmat received a cable from the Universal House of Justice advising him not to let the work in Africa prevent him from visiting his ailing mother in Iran. He recorded in his diary,

> The same day I went to Nairobi and had to wait for two days to catch the plane for the Holy Land. Went to Dar es Salaam for those days and met with the NSA and the friends. Returned to Nairobi and went to the Holy Land. I spent two wonderful days in Haifa, visited the holy Shrines and went to Ṭihrán. Spent four weeks in Ṭihrán . . . Thank Bahá'u'lláh, mother is well now.
>
> *26 July*: I am leaving for London and home.* This trip took four months, during which I visited 12 countries.

Raḥmat returned to Africa in October that year, although this visit was destined to be cut short. In Zaire, Raḥmat was being driven by one of the pioneers as he returned from a teaching trip. It was a very dark night and the roads were bumpy and unlit. Suddenly they came upon a stationary lorry. They were going at a high speed, and the driver could not stop. They hit the back of the lorry, which was carrying long steel rods. One of the rods went through the windscreen and hit Raḥmat on the forehead. He bled profusely and could not see anything. He was taken to a hospital, where bits of glass were removed from his face and hands. He was scheduled to go on to Cameroon and other countries, but had to cancel his plans and return to London. He asked the friends not to tell anyone about this accident, and did not talk about it to me. When I enquired

* We had moved to London from India in 1972.

about his injuries the reply was that he had fallen while walking in a village and had bumped his head on a rock. It was months later, when he was planning another journey to Africa and we were waiting in an African embassy for his visa, that he eventually told me the full story. The only report of the incident appeared in *The Bahá'í World*, which merely stated, 'An extensive autumn journey to Africa was cut short in Cameroon.'

Letters were sent to the Universal House of Justice by some African National Asemblies, with copies to Raḥmat, complaining about the cancellation of his trip. I tried to convince him to answer and explain, but he would not agree. His policy was never to defend himself. He said, 'If I write and explain, I will prove the friends wrong and they will feel bad. It is better if they think I was wrong to put them through the trouble of cancelling their programmes at the last minute. The next time I go there I will apologize and everything will be forgotten.' True to his word, Raḥmat kept Africa uppermost in his mind. In the months that he spent in London recuperating, he wrote letters and sent cables to many different African countries asking about the progress of the Faith and their teaching needs.

In a letter to the Universal House of Justice, he said that he had visited such West African countries as Sierra Leone, Togo, Liberia and Zaire. He expressed his delight that in Sierra Leone three Bahá'í villages had been established, and an additional three in Togo. He observed that the educated youth from Iran, the United States and Canada who had pioneered to some countries, were not being used as well as they might, and suggested that some of them could go to countries which issued religious visas, Liberia and Sierra Leone, for instance. They could then travel and teach in those countries and help the friends, who were looking forward to receiving travelling teachers from other continents. As these pioneers were now familiar with Africa, some speaking French and Swahili, their assistance would be invaluable in establishing local Assemblies and achieving the goals of the Plan.

In an address to the International Teaching Conference held in Nairobi, he spoke about the 'world-wide teaching efforts', and again stressed the importance of teaching whole families and having all-Bahá'í villages. He said that the Bahá'ís of one village should go to another and teach. He reminded the friends that the teaching of families, which had started in India, had met with tremendous success, and should be copied in other mass teaching countries.

'THE LIONS OF BAHÁ'U'LLÁH'

Exactly one year later, in a letter to the Universal House of Justice dated 18 October 1977, Raḥmat wrote, 'Tomorrow, God willing, I will leave for Africa. I intend to visit all the African countries from East to West and South.' He ended the letter by writing, 'I beg the supreme infallible Body to pray for me so that I will not waste this marvellous opportunity for humble service that God has granted me in His infinite bounty.'

February 1979, dancing with Bahá'ís in front of the Bahá'í Centre of Sugar Bush, Transkei.

On 26 and 27 November Raḥmat attended the National Teaching Conference in Nairobi, where he addressed the friends several times. Extracts of his talks appeared in Kenya's *Bahá'í News*:

> The secret of progress in Africa is teaching people to become teachers. But teaching is not enough. Teaching without administration and administration without teaching will not work. Local Assemblies must make and carry out teaching plans or

> they will die. Individual believers must be connected to the administration like a leaf to a stem or they will wither and fall away from the Faith of Bahá'u'lláh. Bahá'u'lláh says that to be patient is very good, except when it comes to teaching.

He remarked on the marvellous spirit so apparent in the Bahá'í children of Kenya, and said,

> Encourage them to read *Nabil's Narrative* and *The New Garden.* Then encourage them to share what they have learned so as to show their understanding. Children must be taught the Faith the same way that others are taught, and when going out teaching, children should be taken along. This is how they learn to be teachers themselves . . . Teach whole villages and families, teach everyone, so that all people are represented within the Bahá'í community and we can build a solid foundation for the unity of mankind.
>
> Why is the revelation of Bahá'u'lláh of such great significance? Bahá'u'lláh initiated the period of the collective evolution of mankind. Previous Manifestations brought teachings for the evolution of the individual man, but Bahá'u'lláh teaches us how to work and live together as the family of man. In the future, the Bahá'í institutions and the individual believers will work together in absolute unity. Consultation, as taught by Bahá'u'lláh, is the key to working in groups.
>
> Shoghi Effendi paid special attention to the work in Africa. Imagine how happy he must be in the Abhá Kingdom witnessing the achievements of the Bahá'ís of this continent. 'Abdu'l-Bahá said that Africa will roar like a lion. If you notice, in the game parks, wherever there is a lion, all the other animals are gazing in its direction, keeping track of its movements. You are the lions of Bahá'u'lláh. The work you are doing today is only the beginning of much, much greater work in the future.

He then went on to visit Zambia, Malawi, Madagascar, Botswana, South Africa, Lesotho, Transkei, Swaziland, Rhodesia and Zaire. He spent three or four days in each country, visiting as many centres and Bahá'ís as he could.

EXHAUSTION AND ENTHUSIASM

Despite his extreme fatigue, Raḥmat's letters to the Universal House of Justice in 1978 were cheerful and full of good news about Africa:

> *5 January*: Now that my trips to the South and southwest Africa are over, I would like to share some of my observations with the Supreme Body: In South-West Africa a group of very zealous and sacrificial pioneers are serving the Faith. Teaching has accelerated . . . with the help of the friends of Germany they have bought a large and beautiful Ḥaẓíratu'l-Quds. I visited Umtata, the capital of Transkei, for one day and met a few of the wonderful Bahá'ís. In the north of Transkei they have 32 Local Assemblies, and now they have started to teach in the South . . . Transkei is a paradise for teaching the Faith and can surpass many other countries . . . Today I am leaving for Malawi and Zambia. On the 24th I will be in Lubumbashi, on 10 January in Central Africa, and, God willing, in Cameroon on 14 January.

Raḥmat was in Cameroon sooner than he expected. The Cameroon *Bahá'í News* reported his arrival on 9 January, stating that although 'he was exhausted from his non-stop travels', he stayed in Douala for two nights and then went to Yaoundé. In several meetings he talked to the friends, as well as giving an address at the university, where one girl accepted the Faith.

He then went on to Victoria to meet about 50 newly-declared Bahá'ís. He again emphasised the importance of Bahá'í education of children. He stressed that the children should be treated with love and kindness, and that parents should encourage their children to strive for higher education. The *Bahá'í News* noted, 'No one could imagine from the enthusiastic way he spoke how exhausted this beloved Hand of the Cause was. He left next morning for England, where we hope and pray he [will recover] his strength and [enjoy] the rare chance of being with his family.' After the meetings, he often spent hours long into the night jotting down his thoughts and recommendations about the work in Africa:

1. Teaching in the large cities in Africa should start with the universities. It is easy for Bahá'í lecturers and students to teach their peers and in turn they will bring the Faith to their cities.

2. Each National Assembly should have a special plan for teaching in universities. At least 20 per cent of the believers in each country should be educated youth.

3. Special attention should be given to the teaching of young girls. On the whole, in many of these countries the majority of the Bahá'ís are men. Maybe if we teach educated girls they can in turn bring many women to the Faith.

4. The young pioneers are very effective. It is very important that the National Assemblies of their countries of origin and their host countries use them in the best possible way.

5. Travel teachers with university degrees should come to Africa, and their visits should be methodical and on a permanent basis. For instance, each year ten teachers from England and Ireland should visit the commonwealth countries in Africa. The programme should be devised in such a way that the youth could return another time.

6. The presentation of books to the libraries of the universities started at the time of the beloved Guardian. Some of the National Assemblies should be responsible for sending Bahá'í books in different languages to the libraries.

7. There should be joint conferences all over Africa so that many of the indigenous Africans can participate. The aim should be to inform all the heads of African countries about the Faith, proclaim the Faith all over the continent, and teach in such a way as will be a reminder of the early sacrifices made on this continent.

8. In each tribe we should have at least one all-Bahá'í village so that it will become the fountainhead for teaching in other villages.

9. In the tribal areas where the Faith has progressed, we should try to have an all-Bahá'í tribe.

10. We need a special teaching committee for the tribes to consider the translation of Bahá'í prayers, the education of children, and teaching. Gradually we can have sub-committees for each tribe.

'IT DEPENDS ON THE TEACHER . . . '

Raḥmat challenged educated Bahá'ís to travel extensively in Africa. One person who took up that challenge was Dr Faramarz Ettehadieh. He recalls how, in 1979,

> Dr Muhájir cabled me to go to West Africa to teach for a few months. We were supposed to meet in Senegal. By the time I arrived he'd left. I continued my travels, but on arrival in Cameroon I was ill and had to go to hospital. The next day, Dr Muhájir arrived at my bedside, made me dress and leave the hospital.
>
> After a few days we went to Togo. I was refused entry but the customs officer allowed Dr Muhájir to enter, saying that as he was Irish there was no problem! Dr Muhájir insisted that he was Iranian but the man just waved him in. I had lost my suitcase and wanted to wait for it. Dr Muhájir told me that his suitcase was also lost but that he had told the airline simply to return it to London, as he did not consider it worth waiting for. In the end we just went our separate ways.
>
> We met again in South Africa. He was supposed to go to Namibia but asked me to replace him. He said he was exhausted and besides he wanted to visit Hand of the Cause Olinga in Kampala, and then go back to London for his daughter's graduation.
>
> My protests were to no avail. He told me, 'If they ask you why you have come in my place, tell them you are better than nothing. Consider me as nothing.'
>
> He brought his tea and sat with me on the steps of the Bahá'í Centre, encouraging me to continue my travels and to trust in God. He said, 'If I die now, I have no regrets. I have done all I could.' With these words he said farewell and left for Kenya.

Although all the reports of his summer of 1979 visit comment on his extreme exhaustion, Raḥmat continued his travels in buses, lorries and old broken-down taxis. On this, his last trip to Africa, he visited the friends in the Cape Verde islands, Dakar, Banjul, Gaberone, Freetown, Monrovia, Abidjan, Accra, Lomé, Cotonou, Lagos, Calabar, Douala, Kinshasa, Kisangani, Bukavu, Goma, Kigali and Nairobi. He repeatedly told them that everyone should rely only on the Will of God, as there was a reason for everything, and that Bahá'ís should endeavour to their last breath to serve Bahá'u'lláh.

After visiting Burundi, Tanzania and Kenya, accompanied by Counsellor Isobel Sabri, he went on to Togo and the Gambia, to help and encourage the friends to achieve the goals of the Five Year Plan. He urged the pioneers to submit to the wishes of the indigenous Africans in planning events, and to be flexible with the new believers. Kenya's *Bahá'í News* gave a brief report:

February 1979. Ha-Talimo village, Bu Bothe District, Lesotho, where 16 people embraced the Faith and the LSA was formed.

He inspired the friends and deepened their understanding of the important topic of detachment. Dr Muhájir pointed out that the minimum level of detachment is to give of our material possessions such as our *shambas* [farms] or our money. Real detachment is to be detached from our own wills, wishes, ideas, ways of thinking, and to take the ideas of the Faith for ourselves. In discussing prayer, Dr Muhájir stressed that prayers must be followed by action. The bounty of God is like rain — it comes to all, but it comes in the shape of our desires. The believers must be busy with the work of the Faith and not with their [own affairs].

Detachment and movement are needed. Marvellous results can occur. Only two people opened Malaysia, India and Burma [to the Faith].

Now is the time when the Faith must be spread all over Kenya. We must have LSAs in big towns. Receptive areas need to be explored. The shift from more LSAs to more believers must be made.

When questioned on how to carry out teaching in the towns, Dr Muhájir presented a plan of a 21-day 'crusade'. He suggested that the Bahá'ís of Nairobi make a mighty effort to personally invite seekers to the Centre, where meetings were to be held every night for 21 days.

This crusade started on 2 August and went on until 22. Many seekers attended and besides being a successful teaching campaign, it was a great deepening programme for the Bahá'ís. Each night a topic of the Faith was discussed. The participation of a large number of visitors and travelling teachers greatly enriched the spirit of the 'crusade'. At the end, the friends who had participated unanimously agreed that more crusades should be held in the future.

While in Nigeria Raḥmat travelled extensively, under very difficult conditions, to visit as many villages as possible. Friends remember his frustration at the Bahá'ís' lack of enthusiasm for teaching. He would travel for miles under the scorching sun, usually in a crowded old bus or truck. Once he joked, 'At least I can say I have seen all the roads, if not all the Bahá'ís.'

He arrived in Jos late one afternoon and that night attended the Feast. His journey through the villages had been long and tiring and he had not eaten; yet he stayed with the friends until very late. At one a.m. he asked his hostess if he could have something to eat. He just stood in the kitchen eating bread and cheese and then went to bed. The next morning he was awake at 5.30, calling the friends to get up for their next trip. They offered him breakfast but he declined and just took some bread and cheese with him. They still remember him chanting 'Yá Iláha'l-Mustag͟háth' [O God, He Who is invoked (for help)] for hours on end during that trip. He travelled from village to village for days, with only bread and onions for food. Once, when the friends arrived in a town after many days of travelling and while everyone else rested, Raḥmat attended to the washing of his one and only suit, which then had to be dried in front of a fan to be ready for his next day's departure for Cameroon.

Raḥmat usually went to bed at one a.m., and was up before anyone else, at five-thirty. Friends remember him chanting prayers for the progress of the Faith first thing in the morning. One day, after saying many prayers, he lamented that the friends had become so busy that they had less and less time to give to the Faith. He suggested that the Bahá'í communities should hold 21 days of continuous firesides, with the aim of having as many new Bahá'ís as possible.

He left Nigeria for Cameroon and spent a few days there visiting many areas. Once again he stressed the importance of the education of children, and their being familiar with the teachings. When children disturbed the meetings he would prevent the parents from taking them away.

His nephew, Dr Farzin Davachi, who, with his family, had pioneered to Africa in 1975, tried to slow him down, but without success. Farzin recalls his uncle's trips to Zaire and Nigeria:

> The progress of the Faith in Nigeria remained slow until December 1970, when, one afternoon, I found Dr Muhájir standing at our door. My wife Nancy had gone to the United States and I was alone in Port Harcourt. My delight at seeing my uncle was beyond description. With ten years difference in age, he had been like an older brother to me.

His visit was timely, as we were desperate because of the Faith's lack of progress and the magnitude of the goals before us. He brought both hope and vision which were truly God-sent. He made some very practical suggestions on how to accomplish the goals of the Nine Year Plan. From that point on, the doors began to open. We registered the first declaration in Port Harcourt and began to receive news of declarations in Aba.

Dr Muhájir recommended that we have full-time local travel teachers, as the pioneers were restricted in the chaotic post-war atmosphere. He advised us that having travel teachers was no guarantee of success, unless regular reports of contacts and declarations were made. This, he said, would enable the National Teaching Committee to contact these people directly. We acted in this way, and in the remaining few months of the Nine Year Plan we began receiving the names and addresses of new contacts. By Riḍván we had more than 80 Assemblies, surpassing the goals of the Plan.

Dr Muhájir believed that the purpose of pioneers was not just to implant the Faith in a new region, but to train the local believers in Bahá'í principles and Bahá'í administration. He felt that this was particularly important in Africa, as the people were spiritually receptive, but had great need for organizational skills. His motto was to teach, teach, teach. He never stopped teaching for one minute and the whole time that he was visiting us he lovingly encouraged us to teach.

After his visit to Port Harcourt, we attended the International Bahá'í Conference in Monrovia, where he represented the Universal House of Justice. It was a time of great exhilaration and thanksgiving, as Amatu'l-Bahá Rúḥíyyih Khánum and hundreds of Bahá'ís came from Africa and from many parts of the world. I cannot adequately describe his great love for the Africans. He often told me that he believed that God had protected the Africans from materialism to keep them for Himself. He had heard from the Guardian that Africa would be the first continent to become spiritualized.

The next time I saw Dr Muhájir was in 1976 at the International Bahá'í Conference in Paris. I explained to him the challenges we faced in Zaire, the second most populous country in black Africa. He agreed to come to Zaire to consult with the National Assembly. After our return to Kinshasa one morning the telephone rang at six a.m. It was Dr Muhájir calling from a hotel in town saying that he had arrived at one a.m., but, not wishing to disturb us or to spend money on a room, he had sat in the hotel lobby all night. I picked him up at the hotel and brought him home for breakfast. He was visibly exhausted after a 12-hour flight, and I suggested he rest while I went to work at the hospital for a few hours. He insisted that his time was short and he wanted to visit the Bahá'ís in the province of Bas Zaire, located next to Kinshasa. Recognizing his state of exhaustion I insisted that he rest. However, he said that if I didn't go with him, he would go by public transport. We packed a lunch and I drove him to Bas Zaire. That day we visited four different towns, where Dr Muhájir spoke to the Bahá'í communities about the Five Year Plan and the importance of teaching and consolidation. We returned the same day, having gone more than 400 kilometres.

I accompanied him to Kivu, in the eastern part of the country, some 2000 miles from Kinshasa. In one village he called the people to dawn prayers at six a.m. We continued to pray and talk, teaching and deepening until late in the evening. Every 30 minutes he would ask them to stand up and sing, thus enabling them to be attentive for many hours. At night, the village was pitch black: there were no lights, not even a candle. They led us to a small hut in absolute darkness where we slept on a wooden bed with a grass mat, and a piece of wood for our pillow. To my surprise, my dear uncle seemed very familiar with the conditions; he asked me not to complain, and to rest as much as I could.

The Hand of the Cause knew many of the villagers personally, and expressed a great admiration for their ability to turn Bahá'í history and Bahá'í teachings into song. This delighted him, as he realized that it was the most effective way for an illiterate population to learn the Faith. One day, as he was teaching in a village, many small children were rolling in the sand and throwing it at each other. He turned to me and said, 'You must have teaching programmes for these children. Bahá'í education is the most important issue and these children need spiritual education and must learn to read and write.' Upon returning to

> Kinshasa plans were made to organize schools in that region. Dr Muhájir envisioned the day when the Bahá'ís of the world would make great contributions to the education of children in remote and poor areas of the globe.
>
> He continually emphasized the vital importance of unity among the members of a village. He was, therefore, very keen on a whole village becoming Bahá'í together. He believed that the Bahá'ís, in God's own time, would become more progressive and prominent, and that the spiritual and material gap between them and the rest of the population would become greater. He told me, 'A spiritual person is the person who loves everyone.'

In January 1979 Raḥmat was back in Zaire. The friends had gone to a public meeting, and at ten p.m. a messenger came to tell them that Dr Muhájir had been waiting for three hours. He seemed very tired. The next day he told his hosts, 'Last night was very strange. Lately I very often feel like this. I started to say a prayer and when I woke up in the morning I was still chanting the same prayer. It seems the whole night I had been saying that prayer.'

They had a meeting of 120 university students the next day, then a committee meeting, a large public meeting in the nearby Kisushi village, and a meeting at a home of one of the believers, where many friends came to see him, and stayed till very late at night. That same day he had also had a meeting with a group of twelve physicians who became fascinated with the teachings. Many of them are now in high positions and are still friends of the Faith.

The local Bahá'ís were in the process of building a large hall at the site of their Centre. Due to lack of funds they had not put in any windows. Raḥmat had one look and said that the place was suffocating and needed windows. He gave the pioneers the necessary money to do it. He was expected back in Lumumbashi in December 1979, but instead they received the news of his passing. Lumumbashi now has a large hall added to the Centre, which is dedicated to his memory.

Ola Pawloska recalls Raḥmat's fourth visit to Kivu:

> I was in Kabimba, sick with malaria. I received a note signed 'Farzin', saying that they were in Uvira and that I should fetch

them there . . . by the time I got there Dr Muhájir and Dr Farzin Davachi were almost half way to Kabimba on foot.

The Hand of the Cause visited the friends of the Walungu zone, where 230 came for the meeting. After the excellent meeting and many songs, they took him to a spare room which was filled with gifts. I counted ten chickens, three large stalks of bananas, a heap of pineapples, and necklaces of eggs, which they wrap like beads in banana fibre. The Hand of the Cause thanked them, took one pineapple and taught them how to contribute to the Fund by bringing their produce to the Feasts if they were short of cash.

Gordon Kerr, a travel teacher from Scotland, recalled Raḥmat's visit to Botswana:

My wife and I reached Gaberone the same day as he was due to arrive, and drove with a member of the NSA to meet him at the airport. As we approached the airport a bus passed us and I saw Dr Muhájir sitting by one of the windows. The plane had landed early, and although we arrived before the scheduled time, Dr Muhájir had not waited around for our welcoming party, but had jumped on the first bus into town. So anxious was he to get on with the teaching work that every second counted.

Dr Muhájir's first task was to arrange a meeting that very night in the National Centre. He first listened very intently to a discourse by a member of the National Assembly who explained the goals and plans for teaching. Dr Muhájir then spoke very briefly about the need for prayer and sacrifice, and the importance of teaching in the villages. He then suggested that we pray together for the success of the teaching work. It was hot and sticky and Dr Muhájir must have been exhausted from his journeys, but he knelt in that crowded Centre, and prayed for some considerable time. I think everyone was uncomfortable at first, but I remember how his determination and sense of urgency gradually communicated itself to us. Those prayers were hard. Dr Muhájir was genuinely loving and gracious, but his eyes and manner also had that steely quality which said quite clearly to me, 'Stop messing around and get out there and teach!' We all looked at each other, heads bowed in silent acknowledgement of this truth.

The morning after his arrival we set off to teach in the villages. We assembled at dawn. Most of us were still half asleep, but this time we all got down on our knees to pray with Dr Muhájir. There were about twelve of us in two cars, and after prayers Dr Muhájir hustled us along like a sergeant-major. The time for formalities was past, the sleeves were up, this was work — we set off.

Our first stop was a new village where an American pioneer was working as a teacher at a local school. Dr Muhájir asked to see the headmaster, and an interview was hastily arranged. The headmaster was not courteous. Dr Muhájir was, but he very directly told the headmaster that God had sent a new messenger whose name was Bahá'u'lláh, whose teachings were for the whole world and that all people must know about it. He left some books and instructed the headmaster to read them and to share this important news with the students in his school. He said that the Bahá'ís would come back next month to see if he had done this.

We stopped at one or two villages where the Faith was well-known, but Dr Muhájir was not really interested in hanging around to meet the Bahá'ís. He was anxious to press on to areas where there were no Assemblies. Late that morning we arrived at a large village which was, as usual at that time of day, more or less deserted. Many people were at work in the fields, which were often miles apart — many of the men were at the cattle stations even further away. Outside a simple shop, which also served as a bar, one young man wearing a rather loud shirt and carrying an even louder transistor radio laconically observed us from a less than upright position. When asked for some information he let it be known that 'white missionaries' were not welcome in his village. He spoke excellent English and seemed well-educated, but his contempt for us was scarcely concealed. We asked to see the chief but were advised that he was still 'indisposed' from the night before. Dr Muhájir instructed a passing villager to gather the people together and we sat down beneath the shade of a large tree and waited. It struck me later how Dr Muhájir exuded natural authority, not in an officious way — for he was genuinely humble — but people everywhere seemed instinctively to recognize his spiritual stature without even knowing who he was. He was a lion for the Cause in Africa.

It took about an hour for the people to gather. We prayed silently and arranged some logs to sit on. About 200 people, mostly women, some with young children, huddled in the shade. Dr Muhájir sat on a dining room chair, mopping his brow. He raised his hand for silence. He very firmly ordered the young man in the loud shirt to stand beside him, which he did — reluctantly. He then even more firmly told the young man that he was to translate precisely everything he said which, remarkably, he did. That young man was later to become a firm Bahá'í. Dr Muhájir announced that a prayer would be read and asked one of the Bahá'ís present to read a Bahá'í prayer in Setswana.

I waited excitedly. Now I would learn how to teach in the villages. Dr Muhájir turned, pointed to me and said loudly, 'Teach them the Faith'. I was completely taken aback. I did not know what to say. He continued to look at me intently, so I began to speak. After about two minutes he said, 'Enough', and pointed to the next person and then to the next, until four or five of us had spoken. He was teaching us, not them.

We were now completely focused on Dr Muhájir, rather than on the villagers, as he reached up and took down a leaf from the tree above. Dr Muhájir very simply and slowly explained that he had good news. God had sent us His messenger to tell us that now was the time for all the peoples of the world to gather under the shade of one tree and to build the Kingdom of God. Using the leaf, which had three portions, he said that there was only one God, that all religions were one and that all people were one. The messenger's name was 'Bahá'u'lláh' — which meant the 'Glory of God' — and His followers were called 'Bahá'ís'. He said that the message of Bahá'u'lláh would unite all the people of the world. He spoke about the suffering of Bahá'u'lláh and the love which He brought. The people watched, listened, understood and felt his love for Bahá'u'lláh. So short, simple and true. I remember weeping.

Dr Muhájir then invited questions. Several villagers asked questions related to Christian theology, for instance, do Bahá'ís believe in Christ, the holy Trinity, life after death, baptism, etc. To my amazement Dr Muhájir answered 'yes' to all these questions.

It was hot and someone humbly offered a china cup of water to Dr Muhájir while an enamel pail of water was passed around for the villagers. Dr Muhájir did not drink from his cup but instead stood up and presented it courteously to a young nursing mother. He then asked for, and drank from, the communal pail in an act of solidarity which was immediately understood and appreciated. We then formed lines and shook hands with everyone, and all the villagers shook hands with each other in turn saying 'Allah'u'Abha', as he had shown them.

Afterwards I asked Dr Muhájir about the finer points of his Bahá'í theology. 'None of that matters,' he said. 'All that will come later. People must know that Bahá'u'lláh has come, that Bahá'u'lláh is from God, and that He loves us all. When the people of the world know that and feel that, then we can worry about theology.'

He was not dismissive of others' beliefs; indeed he had a deep knowledge of Christian and Islamic theology. He always listened carefully to the opinions of others, and never argued about religious matters, but above all he understood the cultural context in which he was operating. In this village setting, Dr Muhájir knew that to pursue such matters would only lead down a blind alley and destroy the spirit of the occasion. Dr Muhájir understood people because he genuinely loved them, especially the pure-hearted village people all over the world. His heart was open to them, and they felt the sincerity of his love, and, through him, learned of the love of Bahá'u'lláh.

Raḥmat had grown to know Africa so well that he learned to immediately recognize the different nationalities and tribal origins of the Africans he met. However, he always regarded Africans as a single people whom he longed to embrace, and to introduce to the Faith. He travelled from city to city, and country to country, without noticing borders and boundaries. The respective countries and their border guards, however, did not share this perspective and he very often had to spend days or weeks obtaining visas from very unco-operative consulates. Sometimes, for no apparent reason, the visa would be denied, and no amount of pleading would soften the heart of the official in charge. I cannot remember a single occasion when Raḥmat acquired a visa for an African country without having to face some kind of problem.

Once, when we had been sitting in the Chad Consulate in London for more than an hour waiting to be seen by the First Secretary, Raḥmat said a prayer and told me that this was just the first step in the process of getting a visa for only one of the fifteen countries he had to visit. Some of these countries did not have consulates in London and he would have to apply for the visas in other countries, which would make things even more difficult. 'All my travels are like this,' he said. 'After going through the exhausting process of getting visas and plane reservations, I have to go through hours of delays in airports, then ride on dilapidated trucks and buses to get to my destination. When I arrive the friends complain that I am not on time!'

His complaints were, however, very rare. Raḥmat had infinite trust in the grace of Bahá'u'lláh, and faced all the hardships which dogged his steps with great fortitude.

When he consulted with the Bahá'í institutions, he repeatedly spoke about the vital need for the friends to take seriously the responsibility which should be borne by each individual Bahá'í. He quoted the beloved Guardian:

> The preeminent task of teaching the Faith to the multitudes who consciously or unconsciously thirst after the healing Word of God in this day — . . . primarily involving and challenging every single individual; the bed-rock on which the solidity and the stability of the multiplying institutions of a rising Order must rest — such a task must . . . be accorded priority over every other Bahá'í activity.[5]

He said that plans, teaching conferences and consultations among institutions, though of paramount importance, would not be successful unless each individual Bahá'í realized his or her personal responsibility and commitment to the Faith. The specific tasks entrusted to the members of the Bahá'í Administration did not absolve them from their spiritual obligations, which weighed upon the shoulder of each and every one of us. He said that the Writings tell us clearly that the believers should not consider the name 'Bahá'í' merely to be a title which automatically carries privileges and blessings. We have to strive for those privileges.

He often reiterated that the teachings of Bahá'u'lláh are so superlative that if Bahá'ís would only do their duty and give a little more of their time, the Faith would engulf the planet in a short span of time. He frequently accompanied the pioneers on teaching trips and demonstrated to them his methods of mass teaching. He expressed the belief that if the friends aspired to teach only two people then they would achieve only that goal. If, however, their vision was to conquer the world, and they realized that they had the power of Bahá'u'lláh with them, they would conquer the hearts of all humanity. His maxim was: 'It depends on the teacher not the student.'

He gave special importance to bringing whole families and villages into the Faith, a process which would be a source of unity to the community. He told the friends in one meeting, 'I was teaching in a village once. One half wanted to become Bahá'ís and the other half wanted to remain pagan. I said that was wrong, as it would divide the village. The village was a pagan village, but united. Did Bahá'u'lláh come to disunite? I said no. All must remain united. Later the villagers came and said, 'We are now united in wanting to be Bahá'ís.' The friends in the Philippines and in South America pursued the goal of bringing whole families and villages into the Faith, using Raḥmat's mass teaching methods, and gained impressive results. He encouraged the African believers to copy these activities, certain that Africa could surpass the efforts of the rest of the Bahá'í world. Raḥmat asked the friends in Africa to visit the villages in groups, as their diversity, and the love and harmony manifested in their actions, would by itself be immensely attractive.

One of his unique qualities was his willingness to get involved in all aspects of the teaching and consolidation work at local and national levels. He never felt superior to, or detached from, the work of the country in which he was: the work of the friends was his work too. He was familiar with minute details of the plans and requirements of each country, and willingly participated in the fulfilment of their goals. He helped the local friends to choose properties for their Bahá'í Centres, endowments and institutes, and facilitated their purchase by arranging financial help from individuals and Bahá'í institutions. Many times in his notes about Africa he reminded himself to write to the Universal House of Justice or the National Assembly of Iran or such and such an individual to request assistance for the purchase of a property in some part of the continent.

He was always gentle and patient with the Africans. His talks with them were simple, and filled with stories and examples. In a village in Togo he was asked, 'When will the Bahá'ís have schools?' He pointed to a sapling and said, 'Look at this plant. It is going to take years for it to grow and become a strong sheltering tree. The Bahá'í Faith is the same. You have to work and toil and learn and educate your children for the time being. You might not see any results yourself but your children will.'

He never promised a happy and comfortable life to people just so that they would accept the Faith. He stressed that what they were accepting was a religion for their spiritual well-being, but if this also resulted in material comfort, so much the better. He believed that new Bahá'ís should not be forced to follow the Bahá'í laws all at once. His method was to introduce and explain just one of the laws to the villagers. If the next time that he visited them they still remembered it, he was quite happy. He said that it had taken Bahá'ís like him more than 100 years to reach this stage of development; given the same period of Bahá'í education, the indigenous people of the world would become angels.

On one occasion the friends took him to a village and asked him to be with them for a deepening course which they were conducting. He sat with them for some time and saw that the villagers were finding it difficult to understand what was going on. He asked to be allowed to try. He said a few words of a Persian prayer beginning, 'O God, my God' and asked the gathering to repeat them. There was no response. He shortened the sentence, but again there was no response. Eventually he said, 'All right, just repeat after me 'O God, my God'. Again, no response. He smiled and said, 'All of you repeat with me 'O'. Everyone shouted 'O'! Raḥmat applauded them and said it was very good. He then turned to the friends and said he would do more deepening on his next trip. Now he wanted to teach. And that is what he did.

If the villagers made plans which were not implemented, Raḥmat would modify the plans on his next visit and ask them to try again. However, he could not understand why deepened Bahá'ís would leave things undone, or say they would do them the next day or week or month. He simply had no patience with such friends. Once, while discussing a teaching plan in Togo, Raḥmat said that there was no 'tomorrow' in his vocabulary. He did not know what 'tomorrow' was. 'We are here now. Let us have a great teaching effort today — we will do it again "tomorrow".' Once when he was in Cameroon the friends happily informed him about their plan to have 100 new believers within a month. He thought about it and then said, 'It is wonderful. Do it within 20 days.'

Although he was always in a hurry, he had infinite patience when it came to difficulties encountered on his trips. Very often he had to deal with border guards who did not understand his language, and simply refused him entry because his visa had expired. He would stand there for a long time trying to reason with them. A friend who accompanied him on one of his trips remembers that after hours of pleading with a guard at a crossing, Raḥmat asked the man why he refused to stamp his passport. The answer came that it was against the rules and therefore impossible. Raḥmat told him, 'No, it is not impossible. Let me show you.' He then took the man's hand with the stamp in it, stamped his passport and said, 'See how easy it was?' He then passed the border, with the guard looking on in astonishment. His decisiveness and sense of humour often took officials by surprise and helped him out of potentially difficult situations.

For the occasional traveller to Africa, the experience is a unique and wonderful one. For Raḥmat it meant often having to stand for hours in the heat by the roadside, praying and hoping for a car to pass and give him a ride. As soon as he arrived at his destination, however, he was anxious to get to work and meet the friends. After a while he would just lie down on a cot or on the floor, rest for half-an-hour, then get up, refreshed, and carry on.

On one trip he went to his hotel and, as often happened, no one came to meet him. He went to the Bahá'í Centre only to be told that the Bahá'ís had moved and no one knew where they had gone. He told me that he just walked the streets, praying that someone would tell him the whereabouts of the Bahá'ís. As he walked he saw a young man sitting on the ground in an alley, painting something on a piece of wood. Raḥmat stood and watched the man. He noticed that the painter had already written 'BA' and was adding an 'H'. He asked the man if he was painting a sign for the Bahá'í Centre. The man could not believe that this was Dr Muhájir standing in front of him. The Bahá'í Centre was right there, and the friends were busy preparing it for his arrival! Raḥmat said that incidents like these were the reason that he never despaired. He knew that Bahá'u'lláh was watching over His servants.

On these trips he ate simply, usually just bread and cheese. He told me that such food was cheap, nutritious and the safest that could be carried for several days in hot weather. Raḥmat's frugality caused him many sleepless nights in cheap hotels. On one occasion, after days of backbreaking travel, he arrived in a town and registered in a good hotel and was given a room with a beautiful view. The next day he moved to a much cheaper hotel.

He struggled to send pioneers to Africa, helped in the teaching and consolidation work, and wrote detailed letters to the Universal House of Justice and many National Assemblies around the world suggesting ways to help that continent. More than ten times he travelled throughout Africa, yet he never considered he had done enough, and always wished that he could do more.

One of his most ardent desires was for the Bahá'í children of Africa to receive both Bahá'í and general education. He persistently championed this cause and finally succeeded in obtaining the approval of the National Assembly of Iran to send teachers for the Bahá'í education of African children. A special national committee was formed with the sole responsibility of sending teachers to Africa for Bahá'í classes.

His wish that educational institutions be established is now being gradually fulfilled. With funds donated in his memory, two large schools have been established in Africa. The 'Muhájir, Banání and Olinga School' in Tanzania, and the 'Muhájir Educational and

Agricultural Institute' in Zaire provide education for hundreds of rural African children. Many thousands more attend tutorial schools in Bahá'í Centres and institutes which Raḥmat helped establish. The children of Africa were always in his heart. As he said 'If they receive Bahá'í training the face of Africa will change. We will have thousands of teachers and educators for the future of the Faith to ensure the establishment of the Golden Age of Bahá'u'lláh . . . I wish I could give my life for them.'

Chapter 4

AT ONE WITH THE MASSES

Nearly three years after leaving Indonesia we found ourselves back in Asia. The Philippines offered Raḥmat a base from which he could more readily visit the other parts of a continent which contained nearly half the world's population. We moved our home there in 1963, although Raḥmat's extensive travels throughout Asia had begun long before this. In 1961 his visits to many Asian countries were instrumental in the tremendous progress of the Faith. At the end of this trip he made a country-by-country evaluation of the region:

> It is now time for me to write some brief observations about Asia. May God guide and assist me. There is no need for profound thoughts. May He give me a grain of sincerity which is better than a thousand logical thoughts. I beseech God to make me pure so that I may burn like a candle in His path and not leave even ashes as a reminder of my existence.
>
> With regard to Asia: Pakistan is still asleep . . . it needs to be re-awakened through a few sincere and active pioneers. India is already awake and is becoming more alert than any other nation. Ceylon needs a great deal of help . . . maybe the dear pioneers can do something. Malaysia is on the way to maturity and pretty soon will distinguish itself among the communities of the world. The Guardian's instructions that we should concentrate our efforts in one place and gradually expand to other areas is what they are practising.
>
> The work in Indonesia is only half done, and friends are not concentrating on important matters. The Philippines are like a

> huge ship which has set its sails and will soon run a magnificent race. Hong Kong needs the patience of Job. Japan needs perseverance and new blood. I have great hopes for this country. Although judgement is not easy and I have been there only a short time, I feel that the work for the yellow race has not been as assiduously pursued as with the black and brown races. Do the beloved pioneers spend their time teaching? Do they have systematic teaching plans? I don't know. I only know that we can achieve a lot in this country. This is only the beginning. I wish it was possible for me to live there, and together with the friends, serve those wonderful people.
>
> I am thinking how we can speed up the work in each country. I think each National Assembly should have a bulletin to record the progress of their work and the plans they have devised. This bulletin should be given to the Hands, the Counsellors and other National Assemblies. This will encourage the Bahá'ís and will also inform each country how to emulate the work of others. It is not a 'Bahá'í News', but a bulletin of facts for Bahá'í administrators.

In 1963 Raḥmat set out to fulfil his own predictions, by visiting every country in Asia.

THE INDIAN SUB-CONTINENT

INDIA

The dust of India was in Raḥmat's blood. Although he travelled to all parts of the world and was closely concerned with innumerable teaching and consolidation plans, wherever he went, he constantly thought, planned and prayed for the progress of the Faith in India. Such love between one man and a people is very rare, especially when the man is not a native. He was happiest of all when teaching in the remote rural villages of India, where he joined the villagers in their singing and dancing, and slept on their wooden cots. India showed so much potential and its gentle, courteous and kind people were so ready for the teachings of the Faith. Raḥmat believed that if the Bahá'ís in India followed the instructions of the Guardian and exerted a little more effort, millions would enter under the banner of Bahá'u'lláh in a very short time.

His first trip to India was in December 1957, on his way back to Indonesia from the Holy Land after the passing of the Guardian. He stopped in New Delhi for a few days and spent time in the company of his lifelong friend, Hushmand Fatheazam and his family, who were pioneers in India. Hushmand, who was Secretary of the National Spiritual Assembly, arranged a meeting with the Bahá'ís of New Delhi, who were few in number at that time, so that Raḥmat could talk to them about the passing of Shoghi Effendi.

Raḥmat also attended the Summer School in Deolali, where he talked of his experience in mass teaching in the Mentawai Islands. He explained to the Bahá'ís how the village schools functioned in Mentawai, and encouraged the assembled friends to start similar village schools in those places where mass teaching had begun. He reminded them that the Guardian had many times urged the friends in India, mostly Persian expatriates, to concentrate on teaching the Indian masses:

> He would also appeal to all the friends to lend full and continued support to the Cause of teaching throughout India. He would suggest that those believers who have the means and the necessary physical requirements, to settle in those locations where the light of the Cause has not yet penetrated, with the view of establishing a new group. This, he feels, is a very effective way of spreading the Cause in a vast and exceptionally varied country like India.[1]

By 1957, the year of the Guardian's passing, most of the teaching was still concentrated in large cities, and no great strides forward had yet been made. Raḥmat was determined to carry out the Guardian's wishes, and, even though his first visit to India was brief, it triggered a deep and abiding interest in that land. On his return to Indonesia he started to read and collect extracts from the Writings of 'Abdu'l-Bahá and Shoghi Effendi about India's great future, and pondered ways to implement their instructions. In his notebook, into which he copied Writings and prayers, and which he carried with him at all times, he wrote in very bold letters 'Must ask Mr and Mrs Muḥammad 'Alí Faizí to visit India.' This trend of jotting down reminders about India continued throughout his life, even when he

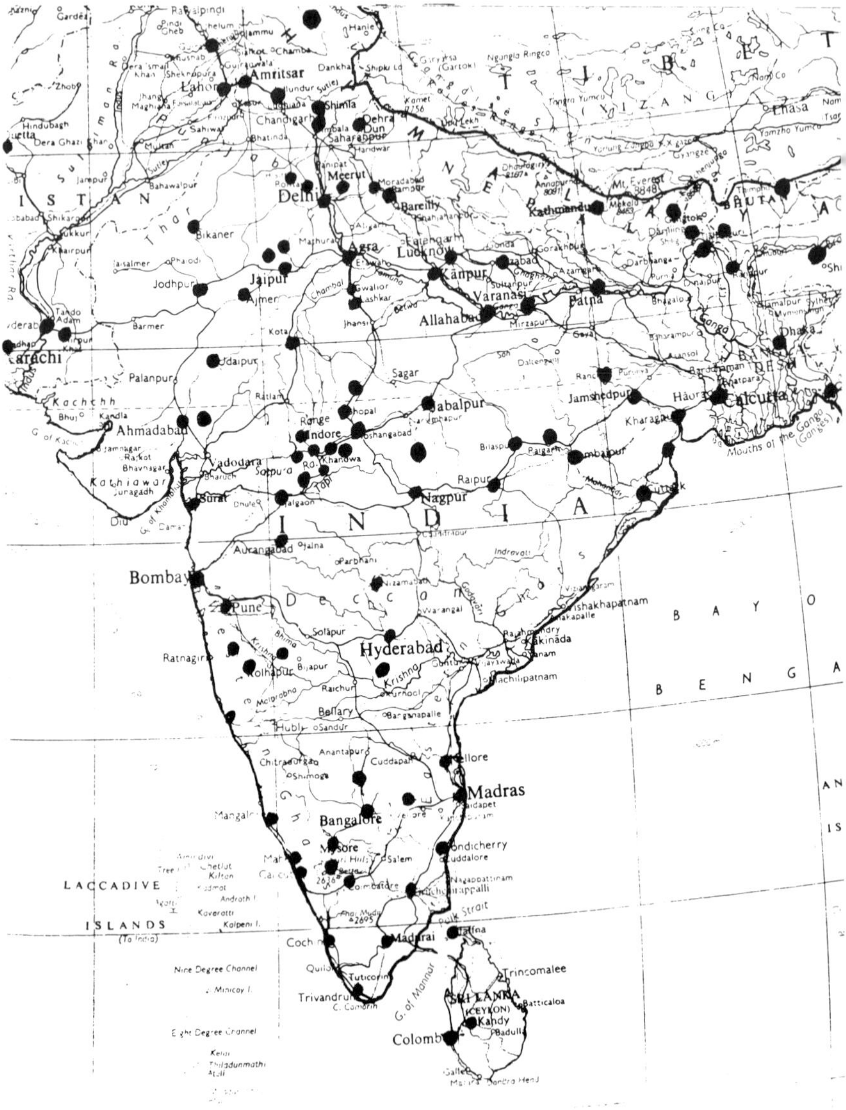

Raḥmat travelled the length and breadth of India, visiting hundreds of villages in addition to the towns and cities shown here.

was far away, in Africa or South America. In 1973, he had thoughts about India while writing about teaching possibilities in Europe: he wrote (and highlighted), 'Bahá'í books should be translated into 15 Indian languages. Any book that is ready should be immediately published with 5000 copies. Must ask the assistance of the NSA of Iran.' Then, his mind at rest about India, he finished the sentence about the work in Europe.

Raḥmat's absolute obedience to, and immense love for the Guardian were the real reasons for his preoccupation with India. He felt he had to do all he could, even if it required giving his own life. In June 1960, he wrote to the National Spiritual Assembly about his intended visit in October of that year, and asked them about the possibility of arranging a visit for him to the tribal regions. This might have been the first such request. The National Spritual Assembly graciously replied that they would try their utmost to arrange such a programme and 'if circumstances permit' they would organize a Summer School to coincide with his visit. Today, with the hundreds of Summer and Winter Schools and national, regional and international conferences which have been held in India, it is hard to imagine that there was a time when it was difficult to arrange just one Summer School.

In October 1960 Raḥmat visited India again. He met with the National Spiritual Assembly and reviewed the details of the Ten Year Crusade. Many of the goals had been accomplished. Raḥmat urged that the remaining goals be completed within the next year, so that India could show the rest of the Bahá'í world that they were not falling behind Africa in service to their beloved Faith.

The Guardian had designated the fourth phase of the Ten Year Crusade for entry by troops. All agreed that this was the time to start mass teaching in India. Raḥmat spoke of the importance of the remote regions and villages, and reminded the friends that most of the ancestors of the present day Bahá'ís of Iran had themselves come from hamlets and villages. This agreement proved to be a historic occasion in the annals of the Faith in India. It was decided to target five areas of the sub-continent for entry by troops: Shamshirpur, Shajahanpur, the Indore area, Sikkim and Nepal. Plans were formulated to hold conferences, and distribute pamphlets and simple literature. The National Assembly decided to appeal immediately for the Rs. 30,000 necessary for this campaign. Mr and Mrs Muḥammad 'Alí Faizí were invited to visit India and participate in this project.

In January 1961 Raḥmat was back in India. His notes state:

> With Shahriar Nuryazdan, Bahram Ayadi and Khosrow Azordegan, I went to Indore. Indore is the heart of India, it is the very centre of Central India. Mr and Mrs Irani and Mrs Bahram were at the airport, and presented me with beautiful and fragrant garlands, as is the custom in this country. Mr and Mrs Faizí and Shírín Khánum Boman and Mr Sháh joined us.
>
> Went to Ujjain in the evening, where Mr Vajdi is pioneering and they have one LSA. I met a new Bahá'í, Sharmaji, who is on fire with the desire to teach the Faith. He asked if it would be possible for him to go to Africa to teach. I told him to teach here as, God willing, this area, the heart of India, will become ablaze and will spread the Faith of Bahá'u'lláh to the whole of India.

During this trip Raḥmat first met Dayaram, a new believer, and the only Bahá'í in the village of Harsudan, near Ujjain. Dayaram was a simple but pure-hearted soul, a farmer and member of the council of village chiefs. His name had the same meaning as 'Raḥmatu'lláh' — literally, 'the bounty of God'. This Indian farmer and the Persian physician, who just happened to be a Hand of the Cause of God, immediately felt at ease with one another, and a kinship developed which was to last all their lives. In later years Dayaram was often asked by Raḥmat to visit remote areas to teach the Faith, and he always rose to the occasion magnificently. Though a tiny man, he had a gigantic spirit, and, with Raḥmat's encouragement, became instrumental in bringing thousands of men and women to the Faith. He had a powerful memory and had learned many of the Bahá'í prayers, including the Tablet of Aḥmad. He also composed beautiful Bahá'í songs, many of which are copied in Raḥmat's notes, which are now sung all over India. What was remarkable about this relationship was that, although Dayaram spoke only Hindi and Raḥmat did not, often the two of them would be seen together, happy and smiling. Whatever language they were using they certainly seemed to understand each other — they were one in their faith, and in their love for Bahá'u'lláh. Thinking of them calls to mind a passage from the Arabian poem quoted by Bahá'u'lláh in *The Seven Valleys*: '. . . only heart to heart can speak the bliss of mystic knowers'.[2]

Raḥmat's diary entry for this historic period says:

> *30 January [1961]*: Three months ago in the meeting with the NSA it was decided to appoint five centres for mass teaching; one is Shajahanpur, where we are today. How can I thank Bahá'u'lláh for this great bounty. Mrs Boman and Dorothy Baker have previously been to this area. I hope we can reap the harvest of their services. We rode in a jeep for 12 miles and realized we were lost. Suddenly a small boy appeared, said 'Alláh'u'Abhá', bowed, and guided us to the village of Samgimanda. A group of men and women had gathered. They had cleaned their village and greeted us with much love. These are the children of Bahá'u'lláh. They took us to the schoolhouse which they had built four months ago. It was clean and simple and beautiful. I remembered the schools in Mentawai and wept. How pleased the beloved Guardian must be with the friends in India for this accomplishment. There were about 60 people present. They sang their wonderful and melodious songs, which they had memorized from the *Bahá'í News* sent to them from Delhi, and we all had a wonderful time. Some have come from as far as one hundred kilometres away.

In this gathering the villagers performed their songs and native dances. When some of the city friends wanted to stop them — as they believed it was improper to dance in the presence of a Hand of the Cause — Raḥmat asked them not to interfere, and joined in the singing and dancing himself! This so much endeared him to the villagers that they never forgot the occasion, and many times related the story.

His diary continues:

> *31 January*: Last night 15 people had come from a nearby village, and invited us to visit them. We thought they had left, but this morning five of them were still here to take us to their village.

> How fast the Faith is spreading. The Guardian was so insistent that we teach the Indians. In all his letters and cables he emphasized the importance of teaching the natives of India. God willing, His bounties are still with this country and will help us to carry out His Will. Everything is in the hands of the Indians. They teach, they sing Bahá'í songs and they encourage the rest of us. It is a wonderful scene. We have now 95 new believers from several villages. About 300 people from 17 villages were present in the conference.
>
> We then went to Shoghipur in a bullock cart. All the way we talked about the beloved Guardian. It was a most inspiring and wonderful time. We arrived in Kotapani, where the first person who started the teaching was Dr Barghava. He became a Bahá'í when he was 18, and heard about the Faith from Mr Saberan in Khánighayn, Iraq. This is the fruit of the sacrifice of the dear pioneers to Iraq, which was thought to have produced nothing. More than 100 have accepted the Faith and this is just the beginning.

Raḥmat always advised the friends not to be rigid. While plans were very important, flexibility in their implementation was also needed. Very often, plans did not coincide with existing conditions, and it was necessary to rely on Bahá'u'lláh and abide by His Will. Raḥmat always followed this principle of flexibility in his own life. If obstacles arose and, after some persistence, did not disappear, he would change his plans. In this trip, while going to the village of Shoghipur, the friends lost their way. After hours of circling around, Raḥmat said that this was the Will of God: they should go to another village. The friends were uncomfortable with this suggestion and wanted to stick to the original plan, as they had informed the villagers they were coming and did not want them to become anxious and worried. Finally, they agreed with Raḥmat's suggestion and went to Kotapani. A few days later, news was received that the fanatics of Shoghipur had learned that the name of the head of the Bahá'í Faith was 'Shoghi' and had become agitated. They had decided to petition the government to change the ancient name of the village. Had the teachers gone there as originally planned, they would have faced a reception of *lhatis* (bamboo sticks) and rocks which the angry mob had prepared for them. At a later date Bahá'í teachers did visit Shoghipur, which is still called by that name, and many of its inhabitants accepted the Faith.

His diary continues:

> There is a wonderful Bahá'í in this area called Sadru'lláh. At the time of the partition of India he was a policeman. In a house destroyed by fire he had found a half-burnt copy of *Bahá'u'lláh and the New Era*, and, after reading it, decided to be a Bahá'í. He did not meet any other Bahá'ís for some years until one day, when filling out a routine job application for another man, he wrote down 'Muslim' for religion. The man explained that he was not a Muslim, but a Bahá'í. Sadru'lláh wept, saying that he was a Bahá'í also. Now he is teaching in this area. It is the miracle of God that one person finds the Faith in the middle of a river, one in a barber's shop, and one in a burning house.
>
> The gathering in Kotapani was singing in Hindi:
>
> The world is shrouded in darkness,
> O God send us light!
> The world is engulfed by huge waves,
> O God send us a boat!
> A high flying bird has fallen to the earth
> and is being stifled by its poisonous foul air,
> O God rescue her!
>
> We all wept. Many, with great difficulty, had come from Harsudan and 19 each were enrolled. This is the same village where, until three days ago, dear Dayaram was the only Bahá'í. Now it is on fire. It was decided to send Sharmaji and Ṭáhirih Vajdi every Sunday to visit them.
>
> While in Africa I dreamt that the beloved Guardian told me that if I had gone to a certain place, in two months I could have had two hundred new Bahá'ís. When I woke up I could not remember the name of the place. I think he meant this conference, because within a few days 95 people have become Bahá'ís. These dear souls were waiting in line till midnight to be registered as Bahá'ís.

In order to get to the mass teaching areas, which, like most Indian villages, were far apart from each other, open jeeps and bullock carts were used. On this trip Raḥmat rode on a bullock cart and his navy blue suit was completely covered with grey dust. He laughingly told the concerned friends that if dust, which is the lowest form of existence, can have such power to turn everything its own colour, imagine how powerful the Bahá'ís are, who have the might of Bahá'u'lláh with them.

On the way to Samgimanda, and the start of mass teaching in India, 1961, Raḥmat in dark glasses.

A report by Hushmand Fatheazam, published in the October 1961 issue of the American *Bahá'í News* gives details of Raḥmat's trips:

> All of a sudden we received news that revered Hand of the Cause Dr Muhájir, whose encouragement and guidance had previously made the National Spiritual Assembly lay stress on the importance of teaching the masses, was coming to Bombay . . . When the Bahá'ís started for Samgimanda on foot and in bullock carts,

they did not know what was awaiting them. The approach to the mud huts of the village was decorated with simple coloured papers. A number of villagers came out several times to receive the guests. By firing their guns in the air they proclaimed in their traditional way that important and respected guests were coming to the village. Women, in groups, were chanting welcome songs and hymns. Amid the beating of drums, booming of guns and devotional songs, cries of 'Alláh'u'Abhá' and 'Bahá'u'lláh ki Jai' were heard. Children of the Bahá'í school, over 60 in number, lined up to receive the Hand of the Cause.

Dr Muhájir was brought in a hired jeep by Mr Vajdi. In a simple and direct presentation Dr Muhájir invited the villagers to embrace the Cause if they believed in Bahá'u'lláh. All those present . . . wanted to declare as Bahá'ís. The group brought out some paper and took signatures and (mostly) thumb prints under a statement that they accepted Bahá'u'lláh as the Manifestation of God for the age. In that faraway village, amidst mud huts sat Dr Muhájir in a rough chair with a broken table in front of him and two friends on either side, receiving declarations. An ink pad was used to make thumb impressions. Over 100 declared that day.

The conference was publicized within a few hours and attracted over 300 people. Despite the severe cold, this conference continued well past midnight. Nobody wanted to leave. The Message of God was so attractive, soul stirring, and inspiring that they sat spellbound. Representatives from neighbouring villages did not leave the people till they were assured by the Bahá'ís that they would send somebody to their places to give to the people the assuring and hope-fostering Message of God.

A group of Bahá'ís, organized by Dr Muhájir, was then despatched to various villages. After a few days, while the NSA was in session in the presence of Dr Muhájir in Bombay, news came that about 300 people had enrolled as Bahá'ís. So, from the beginning of February a chain reaction has begun. Every few days a conference would be organized by the new believers in their villages. The number of participants in each conference would range between 300 and 800 people; the result of each conference would be between 100 and 200 declarations.

> Again each newly declared Bahá'í on returning to his home village, wanted another conference for the benefit of his own area.
>
> This was how the process of entry by troops began under the guidance of our beloved Dr Muhájir.
>
> It was Shoghi Effendi, our beloved Guardian, who in his last message to the Bahá'í world, promised that the last phase of the Crusade 'will witness an upsurge of enthusiasm and concentration before which every single as well as collective exploit associated with any of the three previous phases will pale.'
>
> Within two years between February 1961 and February 1963 the number of believers rose from 850 to 65,355.

After a few days in Madhya Pradesh, Raḥmat and some friends went to Bombay, and then to Nasik. On his previous trip, Raḥmat had asked Mr A. K. Furudi to pioneer to Nasik. He was delighted to find Mr Furudi, Mr Mobed Zadeh and Mrs Zena Sorabjee waiting for him. It was winter, and Mr Furudi was shivering in the cold. Raḥmat removed his jacket and, despite Mr Furudi's objections, gave it to him and did not take it back.

The first village they went to was Shamshirpur, which had no Bahá'ís. They had to take shelter in the ruins of an old temple, which was filthy and full of bugs. Raḥmat's face and arms were badly bitten and covered with blisters. Some nights he would walk till dawn and say prayers, rather than stay in the shelter. Despite the hardships his notes cheerfully relate:

> Nine people came to hear about the Faith . . . One of them from Akola said, 'The Indian people are firmly grounded in their beliefs and customs. They should be taught like children so that they can learn to forget their dogmas. A large river does not come into existence all at once, many small brooks have to merge to form it. The Faith should train people one by one so that they can merge and create a large community.' The Nasik Conference was very successful. One person, named Nili, became a Bahá'í. It was only two days that he had heard about the Faith. He told me, 'as soon as I am able to render some service to the Faith I will write you.'

With the leaders of the villages of Saitpalaya, Karianpalaya and Hennur, 1961.

Last night I talked to Dayaram about the need for a Bahá'í Centre in that area. He said he would donate a piece of land, and, if we wanted, he would donate a house. I told him we would talk in the morning. Early this morning Mrs Boman told me that Dayaram had not slept the whole night and cried because his offer had not been accepted. He said he had 100 acres of land, and wanted to give it to the Faith. I had to reassure him that his offer had not been rejected, but he should wait until we consult with the National Spiritual Assembly. Meanwhile he should continue to teach and increase the number of Bahá'ís. This is the extent of the love and devotion of these spiritual people.

It was on this trip that Raḥmat offered his proposals to the National Assembly for a systematic plan of mass teaching in India. Some of these proposals are indicated in his notes:

> Purchase of Bahá'í Centres; printing of easy and simple pamphlets for mass distribution; education plans for children and youth; employment of teachers and travel teachers; Mrs Boman to travel regularly; tutorial schools to be established in different localities; translation of Bahá'í writings and history into Marathi; teachers to travel for three weeks and stay in one place for one week to deepen the new believers; all-Bahá'í villages; mass teaching should not receive publicity.

In a corner of one page of his diary, Raḥmat wrote in capital letters, 'MUST PURCHASE A BICYCLE FOR MR BAHRAM.'

One of Raḥmat's proposals was for a group of travel teachers to be employed full-time, so that they could go teaching from village to village. He did not think that conventional means of travel between Indian villages, whether by bullock cart or on foot, should be abandoned, but those who had to go greater distances should be provided with jeeps and bicycles.

From the earliest days of mass teaching in India, Raḥmat was concerned with the education and deepening of the new believers. He had followed this rule in the Mentawai Islands, and always quoted the beloved Guardian's instruction that teaching and consolidation should go hand in hand:

> The nuclei that are now being formed, and the groups that are beginning to emerge, must be speedily and systematically reinforced, not only through the dispatch and settlement of pioneers and the visits paid them by itinerant teachers, but also through the progressive development of the teaching work which the pioneers themselves must initiate and foster among the native population in those countries. Any artificially created assembly, consisting of settlers from abroad, can at best be considered as temporary and insecure, and should . . . be supplanted by broad-based, securely grounded, efficiently functioning assemblies, composed primarily of the peoples of the

> countries themselves, who are firm in faith, unimpeachable in their loyalty and whole-hearted in their support of the Administrative Order of the Faith.[3]

Although Raḥmat was ecstatic about the rapid progress of the teaching work in India, he cautioned the friends that teaching should be done in a very careful manner so that the new believers would not confuse the Bahá'ís with missionaries. He stressed that no promises of a material nature should be given. Entry of the masses was a process that was to continue for many years and should be started in a correct and spiritual manner.

After the Nasik Conference, Raḥmat, revived in spirit by the arrival of 'dear Hushmand', proceeded to Bombay to meet with the National Spiritual Assembly. That historic meeting was recorded in the Assembly's minutes:

> Revered Hand of the Cause Dr Muhájir addressed the meeting and narrated the extraordinary achievements in Africa, saying that the beloved Guardian's personal interest in Africa was chiefly responsible for the victories there. Therefore the Bahá'í world has much to learn from the African campaign in the spiritual crusade.
>
> The beloved Guardian had written so many letters to the National Spiritual Assemblies in Africa as well as to individual pioneers and believers in that continent that, if collected, will be a source of guidance for all, specially in the field of mass teaching.
>
> Dr Muhájir informed us of his wonderful experience which he had a few days ago at the village of Samgimanda, in the central State of India, Madhya Pradesh. He said that although notice for the conference was given to the villagers less than 24 hours before, 300 people from 20 villages gathered, and received the Bahá'ís with such enthusiasm and manifest love that was quite heartening. This congregation was attended by women who are usually reserved and do not attend public gatherings. During the course of the conference one could see groups of villagers arriving from many directions and very politely and quietly taking their seats.

Dr Muhájir expressed his opinion that the masses in India . . . had some spiritual background and had adopted a pure and clean life for themselves which is far more advanced than the way of life which masses in many other parts of the world have pursued. These loving souls have inherent devotion, therefore we should develop this spiritual feeling of the masses and gladden their hearts with the message of Bahá'u'lláh.

He said that the beloved Guardian advised the Bahá'ís that any person [who accepts Bahá'u'lláh as the Manifestation of God] should be welcomed, and none of these pure souls should be prevented from becoming a Bahá'í. We should not discourage people who, with great hope, come to us and acknowledge the divine origin of the Faith. By refusing them, merely because we expect too much of them from the beginning, we cut them off from the source of the spiritual life that [they seek]. There are two open gates in the Cause . . . Everyone is welcome to enter and everyone is also free to leave if he desires. Our job is not to impose restrictions on the people who want to enter under the Tabernacle of Bahá'u'lláh. We have to welcome them and develop their potential.

Dr Muhájir said the Guardian had said that there are those who accept the Faith through their mind and those who accept with their hearts. The masses are in the second category. Their mere faith in Bahá'u'lláh creates an unexpressable joy [in their hearts]. When the masses accept Him, we should gradually develop their knowledge about the Cause through pictures, stories from the history of the Faith and the progress of the Faith in other countries.

When the majority of the people of a village accept the Faith, build a small Ḥaẓírat'ul-Quds for them: that would be dear to their hearts. Do not involve them too much in administration in the beginning.

He advised that believers, pioneers and local Assemblies must allow the flame to burn all over, and help the masses to enter the Cause. Older Bahá'ís should know that their individual mistakes in teaching the masses may retard the progress of the Faith for years to come. The major mistakes . . . were having doubts about [new believers and] their being Bahá'ís and looking down on them and suspecting their motives . . . and having too much expectation from them in their administrative duties and personal lives as Bahá'ís. We should remember that in the beginning of the Cause in Iran [many of those who gave their lives for the Faith] had only been blessed with the love of the Báb and Bahá'u'lláh and had no knowledge about the purpose of God or World Order of Bahá'u'lláh. Therefore whenever these simple-hearted people come to us as Bahá'ís, we should welcome them amongst us and even give them a certificate [stating that they are] Bahá'ís. This will make them very happy and increase their sense of belonging. We should treat them as schoolchildren. We do not expect a child to be a graduate first and then enter the school. We accept him in the school knowing that he does not know anything, and step by step guide him to higher grades. Even experienced [Bahá'í] teachers can make mistakes and stop the progress of welcoming the masses to our fold.

When the masses come to us, personal laws should not be imposed on them right away, first we have to create a Bahá'í spirit among them. We can teach them prayers. Their habits and customs which are not in accordance with the teachings of the Cause should be modified very gradually after they become [deepened] Bahá'ís. In other words, their abandoning of their customs should not be a condition for their becoming a Bahá'í.

Dr Muhájir, citing his experiences, said that the aim of teaching the masses should preferably not be to increase merely the number of centres. It is much better that a village in its entirety or majority become Bahá'ís than to have ten or twelve persons in one village and a few in another. [If a few persons become Bahá'ís in a village and there is a lapse of time before the second visit to that village] the rest of the people will not become Bahá'ís so easily. It is much easier to deal with the Bahá'ís in great number in fewer centres, than with a few Bahá'ís in many centres. Let us concentrate on one village and turn the whole population of that village into Bahá'ís.

As our aim is to guide the masses, and not merely establish Assemblies, the important matter is not to give any material temptation to the people to become Bahá'ís. [Material temptation] is very dangerous. It mars the purity of motives. Let them

> come by themselves and serve themselves. Let them build their own schools and Ḥaẓíras. When this spirit is created then necessary moderate assistance may be given by the National Assembly.
>
> He informed us that some of the new believers had offered pieces of land to the Bahá'ís for building of Ḥaẓíratu'l-Quds. He advised that nine Ḥaẓíratu'l-Quds may be built for the time being in the villages which have become Bahá'ís. Four thousand rupees had been pledged in the Deolali conference for this purpose. It was decided to call these buildings 'Bahá'í Bhawans' [Bahá'í Houses]. Each should not cost more than Rs. 1500. The construction of three such Bahá'í Houses, including one in Samgimanda is to start immediately.

At this time I was in Germany awaiting the birth of our daughter. I'd had to go there to wait out my pregnancy because of complications, for which medical facilities were not available in Uganda, where we had been trying to settle. By August 1961, Raḥmat had been away from home for eight months. The Hands of the Cause in the Holy Land asked him to go to Germany to spend a few weeks for the expected birth. He, however, decided to remain in India, as he believed that if he left at that crucial time, when mass teaching was in its early days, the friends might lose heart and the impetus would be gone. I agreed with this decision, and he informed the Hands of the Cause that he would continue his work in India. Gisu was born on 13 August. We never regretted this decision. To both of us it was obvious that Raḥmat's teaching in the villages of India would bring greater bounties for his daughter than his pacing the corridors of the hospital.

By September, the number of Bahá'ís in India had increased enormously, and it was time to plan for deepening and consolidation of the new believers. Raḥmat believed that the method of mass teaching in India was the best in the world, and that the people of India were the most spiritual. He advised the field workers that while teaching should not stop, deepening should start immediately. The purchase and construction of village 'Bahá'í Bhawans' did not meet the growing need for places to train and educate the large numbers who would flock to the Faith. Early each morning while in Indore, Raḥmat would rise before everyone else, say his prayers and ask Shírín Khánum and Mr Bahram to go with him and search for a suitable house that could be bought for a Bahá'í Institute. Every day they covered miles in each direction, before they finally found the house which was to be the first Bahá'í Institute in India.

The building was far from the city proper, and was for rent only. Raḥmat felt certain that if it was the Will of God, the way would open so that the Bahá'ís could buy it. Being outside the city limits made the house cheaper. The Boman family, through their contacts with relatives of the owner, finally succeeded in persuading him to sell the property. Today the city has grown and has surrounded the Institute and made it one of the most valuable pieces of real estate in that area.

Raḥmat asked Ramnik Sháh to stay in the Institute, and immediately start deepening and training classes for the new Bahá'ís. Mr Sháh, despite many difficulties, accepted this task, left his work in Bombay and stayed in Indore for six months. The Institute was by this time a gathering place for the masses, and the course of its future was set. Years later, Raḥmat asked the National Spiritual Assembly to name the Indore property after Hand of the Cause 'Abu'l-Qásim Faizi. The Faizi Institute has since been the training ground for hundreds of Bahá'í teachers, who, in turn, have taught and deepened thousands in Madhya Pradesh.

It was also in 1961, in New Delhi, that Raḥmat asked Mrs Boman to travel in the mass teaching areas, to conduct and co-ordinate the activities of the teachers. To her surprise Raḥmat also asked her not to delay her trip by going home to make any preparations. She agreed, and proceeded directly to the teaching areas. On the same day that one of the Indian believers contributed Rs. 1000 for the teaching projects, news was received that 1000 new believers had joined the ranks of the followers of Bahá'u'lláh.

Shírín Khánum recalls that in those days Raḥmat would often pray and say, 'O Bahá'u'lláh, give us Your hand in assistance and we will conquer the world in Your name.' He felt that the Cause of God was triumphantly progressing, and that no one could stop it.

By December 1961, the National Spiritual Assembly had completed the purchase of the Indore Institute and many mass teaching

With the members of the National Spiritual Assembly of India, outside the National Bahá'í Centre, New Delhi, 1962.

conferences were being held all over India. The most significant of these was the Dhar conference. This was the first 'All India' mass teaching conference. The National Spiritual Assembly reported that,

> A *dharamshala* [meeting hall] was hired. Many village Bahá'ís as well as friends from Bombay, Poona, Bangalore, the States of Gujarat, Kerala, Uttar Pradesh, etc., came to this place, some 20 miles from Indore. An unseasonal rain marked the conference. It was wet and cold but the conference was memorable — those who came from the cities were grouped together and went with the villagers from Madhya Pradesh to teach in the countryside,

some for a few days, others for weeks. In this conference, mass teaching was carried on to other states. Soon the masses responded in Sholapur, Mysore, Dang, Bangalore, Gwalior, Rewa, Satna, Nasik and Deolali.

Raḥmat's notes record his travels to most of the mass teaching centres:

6 January, [1962]: In this span of time I have visited the villages around Nasik, Deolali, Indore, Ujjain and Gwalior. I don't remember any of their names.

From 26 to 31 December I attended the Indore conference. It was wonderful. India is on its way. The progress is so rapid that it is going to surpass the rest of the world. I wish I could spend more time here. Except for Asia, this subcontinent has a larger population than any other continent. What a potential exists here.

Now we can see her potential . . . The conference was truly historic and unprecedented in India. Nearly 275 people from 71 villages participated. Two hundred were new believers and the rest Bahá'ís from the cities. All were gathered in love and harmony and unity. This conference was unique. It was convened in the Indore Institute, which, by the grace of God, has just been purchased. Friends were united and enthusiastic. What a great bounty! We were not tenants any more, but had unfurled the tent of love and service in our own property.

This gathering is the harbinger of thousands of conferences to be convened in future years and decades and centuries . . . this will be the Mother Institute, especially as its acquisition is the result of the instruction of the beloved Guardian in his letter to the National Assembly. He wrote that,

> . . . the adoption and enforcement of whatever measures are required to increase the number of Indian and Muslim converts to the Faith, on whom its ultimate triumph and recognition must depend; the steady consolidation and expansion of newly-established institutions, such as the Summer School, the hostel and the local Ḥaẓíras . . . these stand out as

> the primary duties and obligations of both the participants of the Plan and of those who conduct its operation.[4]

May my life be sacrificed for him.

At this conference the Ten Year Plan was again studied and reviewed, and decisions were made to send pioneers to Andaman and Dio, Goa, the Maldive Islands and Nicobar. Extra languages will be translated . . . most important were decisions about mass conversion in Indore and other areas, and the allocation of the budgets. When I look at this conference and the enthusiasm of the friends, I remember the letter of 'Abdu'l-Bahá to the first convention in India in which he assured the friends that Bahá'u'lláh would be with them at their sacred meeting.

On 31 January it will be exactly one year since the first teaching conference in Samgimanda. Maybe with the help of the friends who have enthusiastically dispersed all over the country, we can have 19,000 Bahá'ís soon and have a real celebration of the anniversary of mass teaching in India.

Raḥmat's travels in India continued under very difficult conditions. Shírín Khánum, whose name is synonymous with mass teaching in the Indian subcontinent, was a dear friend and collaborator who often travelled with Raḥmat throughout India. She remembers the many times they had to cover hundreds of miles in a third class compartment on the Indian railway. The train would stop only for a few minutes, and, as there were no reserved seats, hundreds of people would rush to get on: 'Often we would throw our luggage on the train only to be unable to get on ourselves, and many times we would hurl ourselves on the train, but our luggage would be left behind!'

The compartments were so crowded that even a slight movement was impossible. Raḥmat would stand for hours in the aisles and just lean on the wall. At night, Shírín Khánum would ask some of the passengers to take pity on the foreign gentleman, so that he might sit on his small suitcase near the window and lean his head on the window sill. The windows had no glass, and the dust of the deserts, combined with the soot of the train, the extreme heat of summer — or the biting cold of winter — and the smell of breath and perspiration, created a stifling atmosphere which even the natives could not bear. She remembers Raḥmat would stand serenely, fanning himself with a notebook, while chanting prayers and Indian songs.

Raḥmat would eat only bananas and dry coconut on these journeys. On those which took place in March, he fasted. Once S͟hírín K͟hánum reminded him that travellers are not obliged to fast. He replied, 'But I travel all the time, when do you suggest I should fast?' During their train journeys Raḥmat would urge S͟hírín K͟hánum not to waste time. He would say, 'I will pray and you teach. Where else will we find such a captive audience?'

Once, on arrival in a village at night, the friends assigned Raḥmat a bamboo cot, and a pail of water for his morning bath. He was up at dawn the next morning. S͟hírín K͟hánum remembers, 'I inquired if he had slept well. Like a child who was having his first camping adventure, he said, "You are asking if I slept well? The moment I sat on the cot, down it came, Dr Muhájir and all!" He laughed as if this was the funniest thing that had ever happened to him!'

On another occasion they were travelling by jeep through the villages, and had been on the road the whole day. They stopped at one village around three o'clock in the afternoon. There was nowhere to have lunch. They went to a hut and asked the owner if she would prepare a little rice which they could buy. She had only lentils. She boiled some lentils, poured them into bowls, and spread some sugar over it. When asked why she had not used salt, she replied, 'I did not have sugar, but I sent someone to the next village to get some. We have noble guests, how could we let you leave without sweetening your mouths?' Raḥmat said that this was the best meal he had ever tasted.

Sometimes, when he returned home from these trips, Raḥmat suffered from asthma attacks and severe skin rashes, which were diagnosed as the results of exposure to dust and extreme heat. He would play down my concern, and say, 'I might have had these problems anyway. At least now I can tell God that I got them in His path.'

In 1967, Mrs Boman was involved in a car crash while on a teaching trip, resulting in the paralysis of her left side. Cables were sent to Manila about the accident, which I had to relay to

Raḥmat, who was in South America. He immediately left for India. Shírín Khánum relates,

> He came to Gwalior to my bedside, sat beside me and chanted many prayers. I wept and said I was finished. If I could not move to teach the Faith it was better to be dead. He laughed and said, 'Your tongue is all right and you certainly can move your mouth. You can still teach.' I said I wanted to be able to sit. He admonished me to remember the Tablet of Aḥmad wherein Bahá'u'lláh says, 'If thou art overtaken by affliction in My path, or degradation for My sake, be not thou troubled thereby.' We chanted the Tablet of Aḥmad together. He then put his hand on my back and made me stand up. In response to the objections of my daughter, Dr Perin Olyai, he laughed and urged me to try to walk. With his help I was dragged a few steps. He then brought me back to bed and said we will try again. That was the beginning of my healing. Perin and other doctors were astonished at how fast and completely my paralysis vanished.

Many stories are fondly related by the friends about her constant reminders of the wishes of Dr Muhájir. Once I asked Raḥmat about a suggestion attributed to him by Shírín Khánum. He smiled and said that he could not remember it, but if Shírín Khánum said he'd said it, then it was alright with him. She knew India much better than he, and if he had not made that suggestion, he should have. Once, in Mrs Boman's presence, he jokingly told the National Assembly of India that 'if Shírín Khánum tells you I have suggested some venues for teaching, or where to purchase Bahá'í Centres, accept it as my word. For the rest of my suggestions — check with me first.'

Shírín Khánum regarded Raḥmat as the son she never had, and consulted with him in all matters, whether a family affair or related to the Faith. Raḥmat, in turn, loved the Boman family as his own. He often asked the family members to serve in specific areas and without any hesitation they always complied. The one he most often called on was Mrs Ṭáhirih Vajdi. A Ph.D. in economics and professor at Ujjain University, Ṭáhirih had to take leave from her job every time Raḥmat visited India. He would call her and say, 'Are you still wasting your time in that college?' and she would know the time had come to take her vacation. Raḥmat believed that Ṭáhirih had the capacity to bring thousands to the Faith, and he proved to be right. She was the first person to be asked to remain in the mass teaching villages in 1960, a request which she accepted immediately. For the next 19 years she was always in the vanguard of teaching and deepening. At Raḥmat's request, for many years she conducted the deepening classes at the Faizi Institute, in addition to travel teaching and attending National Assembly meetings. Every time he arrived back in New Delhi he would immediately call Mr Sháh, Secretary of the National Assembly, and request him to send an urgent cable to Shírín Khánum and Ṭáhirih to come to Delhi for consultation. I do not remember a single time when Ṭáhirih did not accept his invitation.

Though the first years of mass teaching in India were gloriously successful and made Raḥmat extremely grateful and happy, they also exhausted him. His diary reflects his fatigue.

> *27 January [1962]*: My work in India is finished. Tomorrow I will go to East Pakistan. How can I lift my head in the presence of God? I have not rendered any valuable service in His path. I need a few days to meditate and pray so that I'll be cleansed of my sins and shortcomings to continue in my endless journey, and reach my desired abode, which is not accessible except in the Abhá Kingdom.

In February 1962, Raḥmat finally was able to leave India for the Holy Land to spend a few weeks with his family. We had left Cologne, where Gisu had been born, for Haifa. There we awaited Raḥmat's return, so that we could decide where to set up home. Gisu was five months old when she was introduced to her father. He had been away for more than a year.

We decided that, for the time being, Gisu and I would stay in Haifa, where my parents were. Raḥmat left the Holy Land after a few weeks. By May 1962 he had passed through Asia and some of the Pacific islands, and had arrived in New Hebrides. India, however, was still on his mind.

> *5 May, New Hebrides*: I feel I have to return to India as soon as possible. Last night I dreamt that ten Bahá'ís from Bombay had

> volunteered to go on teaching trips. India has so many possibilities. I wish we could take advantage of them. There are many things to be done, teaching of the 30,000,000 tribal people, strengthening of the Bahá'í community, and administration needs great attention. We have to train all new local Assemblies how to function and even how to keep minutes. This is the task of the National Assembly, to devise a method to make it very easy for them. This could be a programme of the Indore Institute.

He returned to India in the autumn of 1962. Mrs Boman recalls his trip to Gwalior:

> When we gave him the news of the progress of the Faith in India, his eyes gleamed. He often said that the States of India should vie with each other and surpass each other's achievements. He reminded us that there was no more time left to wait. The time was now and we should endeavour to open all regions of India to the Faith of Bahá'u'lláh.
>
> When he was told that the area around Gwalior was infested with highway robbers, he advised us to teach them, rather than avoid the villages. The friends tried it and visited those areas and had many good results.
>
> We thought that we had achieved a great deal and that Dr Muhájir would be immensely pleased with our efforts. He asked us how many all-Bahá'í villages we had in our area. The answer was many. He was very pleased, but immediately said 'Why don't you purchase an Institute in Gwalior, hold more frequent conferences and deepening classes with the sole aim of having more all-Bahá'í villages?' With his help we pursued this goal.

The property chosen for the institute belonged to the Maharani of Gwalior, and was located in Susera, an isolated area outside Gwalior. It was priced at Rs. 50,000. There were no funds, and Mr and Mrs Boman were seeking Raḥmat's advice before approaching the National Spiritual Assembly. He calmly told them to rely on Bahá'u'lláh, and a way would be found. A few prayers were said, and then Raḥmat said that the problem was solved: the Bomans would contribute Rs. 20,000, the Olyais and the Vajdis would each contribute Rs. 10,000 and the National Assembly would be asked for the remaining amount. The Olyais and the Vajdis, daughters of Shírín Khánum and their husbands, were not present, but they gladly complied with the decision. Thus was the Gwalior property purchased.

At Raḥmat's suggestion, this property was later converted into a boarding hostel solely for Indian children. He helped the friends transform the boarding hostel into a school, and named it the 'Rabbani School', which is now an accredited agricultural school with many Indian and tribal students.

The autumn weather in northern India is quite chilly, with a biting wind. Others crawled under quilts and sleeping bags to keep warm, but Raḥmat would sit on the ground around the fire with the villagers long into the night, singing songs and trying to communicate with them in the few Hindi words he had learned. Mr A. K. Furudi, one of the teachers present, remembers:

> Dayaram, Mrs Boman, Sohrabkhani, Firoozeh Yeganegi, Ne'mat Yeganegi and a few others were with him. We went to one of the big villages and were faced with opposition. No one came to the meeting. After some time we found the situation changed and many people gathered. Dr Muhájir, while talking to one of the villagers, had presented him with a small vial of Persian attar of roses. That man was like a humble brother to him from then onwards. He went around telling the rest of the village that Dr Muhájir is like Ram* and his friends are all good people. This made the villagers curious, and they decided to come and hear us. Many months later, when I was visiting the friends in that village, this man still remembered Dr Muhájir with reverence and love. He took me to his house and showed me the vial of attar of Roses which he had placed beside the images of Sita and Ram.

Raḥmat's genuine affection for the pure-hearted villagers of India was not dependent on their being Bahá'ís. He loved them for

---

* *Ram*, or *Rama*, virtuous hero of the Indian epic poem, *The Ramayana*.

themselves, and was certain that whatever they worshipped, they were under the protection of Bahá'u'lláh.

During this trip he asked Mr Fatheazam to write a book, simple in language and content, to be used as a basic teaching manual for the masses in India. Thus *The New Garden* was born. This comprehensive book, which contains Bahá'í history, principles and teachings, is, to date, the most effective teaching tool in all mass teaching countries, and has been translated into more than 90 languages.

When he was away from India, Raḥmat would write detailed letters to the National Spiritual Assembly, giving suggestions for all aspects of the teaching work. He felt it was his duty to express his opinions about the work in India, and believed that this had nothing to do with his being a Hand of the Cause. His close and cordial relationship with the National Spiritual Assembly made him feel at one with them. It was sometimes hard to remember that he was neither an Indian nor a member of the National Assembly, such was his passion and concern for the progress of the Cause in that country. He would sit with that National Assembly for days, ironing out difficulties. He never tried to impose his will, but continued to discuss every point until all were comfortable, and a unanimous decision was reached.

Between February 1962 and February 1963, Raḥmat wrote five detailed letters to the National Assembly about the Centenary celebrations. The National Assembly kept in constant touch with him and consulted on every aspect of the celebrations. His ideas were sometimes very advanced and futuristic, which made them a difficult responsibility for those who had to carry them out. When he promised to help in any way he could, those working in the field would take the chance to implement his ideas, and were never disappointed at the results.

He was back in New Delhi in May 1963, to participate in the National Convention. Mass teaching was progressing quite successfully and his thoughts were now concentrated on consolidation and deepening of the new believers. He asked the National Assembly to consider the purchase of an Institute in Mysore. When his recommendation was approved he went to Mysore himself to help the friends find a suitable property — and to take part in the village teaching. A house was found, and the Mysore Teaching Institute purchased. He later helped in the selection and purchase of the Institutes of Susera, Deolali and Sholapur. He believed that these properties would not only facilitate the holding of deepening classes and conferences but also would enhance the wealth of the Faith. Programmes were devised to train village travel teachers, so that they could teach more effectively in their own villages. These programmes are still the basis of the teaching institutes all over India.

By this time a pattern had been set. Raḥmat visited India every year, sometimes more than once, to assist however he could. When he was not in India, he was still thinking of ways to help in the progress and consolidation of the Faith there. He felt no reserve in approaching his friends in India, and often wrote to individual Bahá'ís asking them to contribute to the purchase of properties and other projects. They never refused.

In the span of a few years Bahá'í Centres and Institutes were purchased all over India, from Leh to Kanyakumari and Manikpur to Udaipur. Raḥmat was directly involved in choosing locations and raising funds for many of them including those in Madras, Cochin, Trivandrum, Cannanore, Mangalore, Bangalore, Susera, Belgaum, Sholapur, Deolali, Jaipur, Patna, Bhubaneshwa, Chandigarh, Srinagar, Kathmandu, Gangtok, Calcutta, Mysore, Gwalior, Indore, Ujjain, Hyderabad, Vijayawada, Rajnipur and Broach. He was also instrumental in the establishment of hundreds of village Bahá'í Centres.

After living in Haifa for nearly two years, we left the Holy Land in 1963 to pioneer to the Philippines. Our first stop was New Delhi, where Raḥmat was to attend the National Convention in May. I had never experienced the sultry, scorching weather that greeted us in New Delhi. Although we had an air-conditioned room, Gisu had to have a cold shower every few hours. Raḥmat had frequently been in India in the hot season, sometimes in Calcutta where the climate is unbearable, even for its native inhabitants. While we tried to stay indoors as much as we could, he happily attended the Convention sessions. During our stay of more than a week, he invited the National Assembly members and other guests to have dinner in our

On the way to Manila from the Holy Land, 1963. Our first stop was New Delhi, where Raḥmat attended the National Convention.

room where their consultations sometimes lasted till the early hours of the morning.

It was now two years since the inception of mass teaching in India. The Ten Year Crusade had come to a successful conclusion. The Universal House of Justice was now at the helm of the Faith, and we were all excitedly anticipating the announcement of further plans — plans in which Raḥmat believed India would have a glorious part to play.

He was in India again in August and November 1964, emphasizing the importance of training the local Assemblies and Area Teaching Committees to carry the burden of the goals of the new Nine Year Plan. In a gathering of the Auxiliary Board members and the National Assembly, he pointed out that 40 per cent of the goals of the plan were given to India, and it was incumbent on the Bahá'í

National Bahá'í Convention, New Delhi, 1966. Hand of the Cause Samandarí, holding the Greatest Name, is seated next to Raḥmat.

institutions there to see that the Plan was implemented as soon as possible.

With regard to the importance of literature in teaching, the following recommendation had been written on behalf of the Guardian to the Bahá'ís of India: '. . . books can do infinitely more work than teachers. Sitting in a chair in a solitary corner one is infinitely more receptive to truth than in a lecture hall or in a discussion group. The public has learned the habit of reading. It is through that channel therefore that we have to approach them.'[5] Raḥmat suggested that a pocket-book of prayers in Hindi be printed immediately, and that Bahá'í Writings be translated into all major languages of India.

I remember him reading the Guardian's letters and cables to India every night till dawn, jotting down Shoghi Effendi's specific

Intercontinental Conference, New Delhi, 1967: Mrs Boman and Dr Munje.

Receiving a garland of honour at a conference in New Delhi, 1967.

With Bahá'ís of New Delhi and Hand of the Cause Furútan, 1968.

With more friends in New Delhi, 1968.

instructions. He said that these letters tell us everything we have to do, and lamented that those instructions had not been carried out when first given. His ardent wish that the letters of the beloved Guardian to India be made widely available to the friends was fulfilled some years later, when a compilation of the letters of Shoghi Effendi was published as *Dawn of a New Day* in 1970.

Raḥmat constantly sought the assistance of the National Assembly of Iran for the work in India. One year it was for jeeps to be used by the teaching teams, the next, for money to purchase Bahá'í Centres. While in Bombay he would encourage the friends to contribute funds and manpower: the friends would respond with enthusiasm and sacrifice.

His diary notes of his regular visits to the Holy Land indicate how often he consulted with the Universal House of Justice and the Hands of the Cause regarding Bahá'í affairs in India. He repeatedly prayed in the holy Shrines solely for the progress of the teaching in India. He suggested that the National Assembly invite Amatu'l-Bahá Rúḥíyyih Khánum and other Hands of the Cause to visit India. These invitations were accepted, and, in 1967, Amatu'l-Bahá and Mr Furútan visited India. These were the first of numerous visits made by Hands of the Cause of God to the subcontinent.

In autumn 1967, the Universal House of Justice asked Raḥmat to spend a few months in India, to guide and direct the consolidation and proclamation efforts prior to the Intercontinental Conference, to be held on 7-8 October. He invited many people, myself included, to go to New Delhi to help with preparations. He sent several letters and cables asking me to go to India. Gisu was in kindergarten, and I wanted to wait for the close of the school year. Raḥmat's final cable said, 'Your presence is urgently needed. Do not worry about Gisu's college!' We left Manila within a few days.

For two months Raḥmat travelled all over India, frequently returning to New Delhi to assist with all aspects of the conference — venue, budget, speakers, and transportation of hundreds of village Bahá'ís who were to attend the conference. At this time he also introduced the idea of collaboration with other countries for mass teaching in India. In Malaysia he encouraged the friends to pioneer to India, especially to the South. As a result, a few Bahá'ís of Indian descent volunteered, opening a new phase of service and activity in

India. The services of the Malaysian Bahá'ís in India was so impressive and their contribution to teaching work so vital that those who had come for only a short spell were persuaded to stay on.

During the course of the conference Raḥmat was up and about for 18 hours each day. He met with the members of National Assemblies from different countries, explained the various needs of India and how they could assist. He worked with those who volunteered to pioneer, and advised them where to go. He consulted with individuals on contributions to various funds. He visited the villagers in their tents, dined with them, and participated in their special programmes. He seemed to have an endless reservoir of energy. Whereas most of us were nearly collapsing from exhaustion and could have slept for a week, he would sit from dusk until dawn collating and formulating the suggestions made at the conference into a comprehensive plan of action.

This conference, the first occasion for the villagers of India to come into contact with Bahá'ís from other parts of their country and the world, opened a floodgate of new opportunities for the expansion of the Faith. It generated opportunities for broader proclamation in India. A special seminar for the press was arranged — the first of its kind — which proved very successful. A systematic programme of nationwide teaching in colleges and universities was also launched after the conference. This yielded great results.

Raḥmat suggested that the time had come for nationwide proclamation. He reminded them that the Guardian had said that the name of the Faith should be heard by every individual in India. This goal was pursued so determinedly — with Raḥmat's assistance and perseverance — that by the end of 1969 all Indian States were inundated with posters, newspaper advertisements and billboards proclaiming the Faith. Personal and direct mailing of Bahá'í literature to all strata of society was undertaken on a grand scale. At every conference, Summer School and Winter School, he would urge the participants to scatter about the area and talk to the people in the streets, restaurants and coffee shops. He accompanied a group of youth to a coffee shop, and did not allow them to sit together. He asked each Bahá'í youth to sit with someone and talk to them about the Faith. He told them that if Bahá'ís gathered together and did no more than give speeches and talk to each other, it would be a waste of time and resources.

The most significant of these proclamation efforts was the publication by the Bahá'í Publishing Trust of India in 1969 of an eight page folder, presenting the basic tenets of the Faith and inviting the recipient to attend a local fireside. This was mailed to hundreds of thousands in India. Raḥmat took samples of this folder to other National Assemblies. It was copied and used all over the world, and 100,000 copies were distributed at the Sapporo World Fair in Japan. It is still one of the most effective proclamation tools used in India.

In 1968, after a great deal of soul searching, we decided to transfer our pioneering post to India. Our changes of residence were determined mainly by where we thought I could do most to serve the Faith. All countries were the same to Raḥmat: Gisu and I were the pioneers. By that time the Philippines had gained a lot of experience in mass teaching. Indigenous Bahá'ís were active in the field and could take care of the affairs of the Faith. India had a large number of new believers and was in need of assistance. We therefore decided to move to New Delhi. Raḥmat spent a few days with us, then left it to me to find a place to live. As soon as we established our new home I sent the address to him.

Raḥmat arrived at the door one day, at dawn, unannounced. He was laughing so hard that it was difficult for him to stand up. He said, 'I had lost the address you had sent me. I only remembered "Golf Links", so I told the cab driver to bring me to this neighbourhood. I had to peer through many windows before I saw a *Bahá'í News* on the coffee table. I told myself this must be my house. Can you imagine what would have happened if it had been another Bahá'í home and Dr Muhájir rang their bell at dawn?'

In 1968 mass teaching in India was at its highest pitch, but the consolidation and deepening of new believers being pursued in the teaching institutes did not progress as rapidly. Raḥmat's saddest moments were when some of the friends and local Assemblies criticized mass teaching and doubted the validity of the names collected on registration forms. In all these years he had never had the slightest doubt that all who said they accepted Bahá'u'lláh meant it. I remember how often he tried to overcome the scepticism

Pioneering to New Delhi, 1968.

of various committees about the validity of the enrolments. I saw him weep for the villagers who were bypassed by the friends. Once, in a committee meeting, after hours of deliberation, one of the friends still was not happy, and suggested that only Dr Muhájir believed that anybody who says he is a Bahá'í means it. This was one of the few times that I saw Raḥmat really furious. He could not believe that any Bahá'í could even contemplate measuring another person's faith in Bahá'u'lláh.

As the numbers increased, those who thought impossible the management of the Bahá'ís at this high rate of enrolment became more and more vociferous. Raḥmat, however, insisted that the answer was not to stop teaching, but to mobilize the Bahá'ís and the administration, and to strengthen the local Spiritual Assemblies to be able to deal with the increasing number of new believers.

The first step was the re-establishment of the Bahá'í Publishing Trust. This duty fell on my shoulders. We all knew the importance of Bahá'í literature in the teaching work in India, but the vision that Raḥmat had for the Publishing Trust was quite different. He believed that the Indian Publishing Trust should be able to disseminate affordable books to the mass teaching regions all over the world. He gave his support to the Publishing Trust so that it would grow and expand. He brought samples of teaching literature from Africa and Colombia to be translated into local Indian languages. In his travels he asked Bahá'í authors to send their manuscripts to be published. He asked the friends of Arabia for financial assistance for specific books. Thus, with his help and guidance, within three years the Indian Publishing Trust became a viable and profitable enterprise. It exported thousands of inexpensive Bahá'í books, particularly to Africa. One African friend, when encouraged by Raḥmat to buy books from India, wondered if it was to help India or Africa. Raḥmat smilingly replied that his business was the business of the Faith. He was a salesman for India, but the profit went to Africa.

A Bahá'í correspondence course, developed in the Philippines with Raḥmat's help and encouragement was now introduced in India, to augment the process of consolidation and deepening. It proved a very successful project. Thousands, from Kashmir in the North, to Kaniakumari in the South, received the course of 24 lessons, and responded to the questions. In addition to deepening the Bahá'ís, this course led hundreds to accept the Faith, amongst them professional people such as physicians and engineers.

Raḥmat's efforts for the Indian Publishing Trust continued to the last days of his life. Helen Hornby recalls that on his final trip to Quito, Ecuador, he asked if he could take her compilation, 'Lights of Guidance', to his hotel room to read. The next day he passed away. However, he had given the manuscript to Counsellor Raul Pavon and asked him to return it to Helen with the request that she send it to India to be published. This valuable reference book, widely used by Bahá'ís throughout the world, was Raḥmat's last gift to the Indian National Spiritual Assembly.

In 1969, he proposed that a Bahá'í Education Fund be established, with capital contributed by the friends in Iran, Arabia and the cities of India. He believed that without such a fund, children of the new believers would never have the opportunity to obtain higher education. He single-mindedly pursued this goal, convinced the friends of its importance, and sought the guidance of the Universal House of Justice. The Bahá'í Education Trust was later incorporated in the plan for India. It is now a prime source of income for various educational projects there.

It was also in 1969 that he encouraged the Bahá'í youth of Iran to pioneer to India and continue their studies in the universities and colleges there. He spent many weeks in Iran personally reviewing the résumés and transcripts of the youth, and guiding them in their choice of locations. That year we were busy the whole Summer trying to get the many students who had decided to come to India accepted in various colleges. On one occasion a group of ten youth had arrived at the Bahá'í Centre. They wanted to visit us, and took a taxi asking the driver if he knew the house of Írán Muhájir. He nodded, and took them directly to the Iranian embassy! The Ambassador, a friend of ours, directed them to our house. He later told me 'It seems your business is progressing much better than ours!'

This was the start of a wonderful enterprise which was to bring hundreds of young and enthusiastic Bahá'ís to India, who were instrumental in establishing the Faith in many virgin areas. The following accounts provide an illustration of the work that was accomplished by these youthful pioneers.

Shahnaz Parnian, who served in India for many years, relates:

> In October 1968, I went to see Dr Muhájir in Ṭihrán, to inform him about my desire to pioneer to India. This made him very happy and he encouraged me to travel by road, so I would be able to visit Bahá'ís in various cities, and at the same time become familiar with the Hindi and Urdu languages. He told me that his family was also pioneering to India and we would soon see each other there. I was heartened to know he would be there to guide me in my new pioneering post.
>
> Dr Muhájir's house in New Delhi became a sanctuary for the pioneers. If we became tired or depressed we would take refuge in his house and be restored with love and affection. I stayed for

With National Assembly of India, 1969.

With the friends in Rajasthan, 1969.

eight months in Chandigarh, the centre of the State of Punjab. Dr Muhájir then directed me to go to Jaipur, the capital of Rajasthan, to help establish its local Assembly. He told me Jaipur and its surroundings had a population of 10,000,000 and I was appointed to teach 1,000,000 of them. He said, 'Go as soon as you can, you will be successful. There are five roads leading from Jaipur. Take one road and go to each village on both sides of the road. On the way back visit all of them again.' Nasrin Buroumand and Rizvan Rahimi were also sent to Jaipur by Dr Muhájir, and the three of us followed his plan, with the help of some local believers. Within four months we had taught in 600 villages and had nearly 6000 new believers.

Dr Muhájir visited us and spent a whole day in Jaipur. He said 'What the three of you have done is unique in the Bahá'í world. Now is the time for you to visit the villagers again and again and deepen them in the Faith.' He accompanied us to some of the villages and talked to the new Bahá'ís; only then did he leave us.

In 1971, during the Asian Youth Conference, he encouraged all of us to teach in colleges and universities and very often accompanied us. When the conference was over, I went to bid him farewell. He said, 'You must stay here until the number of new believers reaches 2000.' My sister had just arrived and I was worried about her enrolment in college. Dr Muhájir said, 'God is great. His bounties will be with you. Take your sister with you. This is the time to teach, do not let this opportunity pass you by.' We remained for another ten days in New Delhi and continued to go to colleges to teach the students. On Sundays, Dr Muhájir accompanied us to different locations to help and guide us. He told us first to try to attract the people to the Faith by giving them the history and the principles of the Faith. He said 'You should accept all who want to become Bahá'ís, later you can deepen them in the laws and requirements of the Faith. No one can read another person's mind and heart. We have to invite all and accept all.'

He believed that all the inhabitants of the world were potential Bahá'ís. It was up to us to find them. He made teaching look so easy that we would all volunteer to go with him. He talked to the seeker with such calm, and in such a simple and direct manner, that anybody who came in contact with him wanted to declare.

After a few years he asked me to go to the Punjab again. I travelled for ten days in that State, and many became Bahá'ís. A few days after my return the war between India and Pakistan over the Punjab broke out and no one could go to teach there.

He encouraged us to go to the university city of Pilani. No one wanted to go there, because we thought the intellectuals would not gather to listen to us. However he insisted that the teachings of Bahá'u'lláh were for all humanity and we should not be scared. After the National Convention he urged a group of the youth to travel to Pilani. He said that Pilani had only 10,000 inhabitants, and that it would be very easy to make it a Bahá'í city. He chanted the Prayer of Visitation of 'Abdu'l-Bahá and started us on our way. In ten days more than six hundred students, teachers and others accepted the Faith. This success was unprecedented, and we all felt that it was the result of his prayers.

He was always with us — his guidance, hospitality, jokes and advice kept us willing to do whatever he asked of us. After his family had left India, we could all see that he suffered during the long separations from them. Once, when a member of the NSA had come accompanied by his daughter, Dr Muhájir said, 'How lucky you are to be with your daughter. I wish I could at least talk to mine.' He then tried for hours to book a call to London and talk to his family. In the afternoon he looked much happier. He had been able to talk to them.

On his last trip to Delhi, he advised me to pioneer to Tanzania, and said that my husband and I were needed much more there. I said I had become familiar with India and preferred to stay there, but he again insisted, and said many people will come to India, but not everyone can go to Tanzania. I invited him to dinner. He said, 'Go to Tanzania and I'll come to dinner there.' We left for Tanzania in September 1979. We were so eager to see him in our new pioneering post and seek his guidance. His radiant soul is with us, and we are trying to follow his instructions.

Another early pioneer to India, Mrs Nasrin Boroumand recalls the challenges which Raḥmat set the friends:

> He had come just to meet us — two Persian girls who had pioneered to Rajasthan at his instruction. He talked to us with compassion and humility and told us how to teach. I had short hair and dressed in European style. He told me to get a wig that was in the style of the Indian women, wear a cotton sari, and go to the villages to teach. He said, 'Go and stay with them. Clean their houses, wash their children, give them first aid if needed, and meanwhile teach them Bahá'í prayers. Let them learn the names of Bahá'u'lláh and 'Abdu'l-Bahá. If you achieve this, it is a great victory.'
>
> He advised us always to hurry. There was no time to be wasted. If we needed books we should go to Delhi ourselves and get them. Correspondence and waiting for mail and train parcels was a waste of time.
>
> Once he asked us why we did not have all- Bahá'í villages. We had to answer frankly that it had never occurred to us. He patiently explained the methods and means for this project and then said, 'Can you form 5000 local Assemblies?' We gasped with shock. He laughed and said, 'All right how about 300?' This number seemed to be much more attainable and we nodded our agreement. The next time he visited us we could only give the report of 180 local Spiritual Assemblies and seven all-Bahá'í villages. He was delighted. His eyes shone with joy and he told us that we had performed miracles and should praise God for this great bounty.
>
> His next visit was for our unit convention. He came with his family and we all went to the village where we were supposed to have the convention. No one was there. Dr Muhájir smiled and said, 'look at the crowd', pointing to a few farmers who were resting under a tree. Fortunately the *Sarpanch* [village chief], who knew us, greeted him with a garland of flowers and invited us to his house. One of the local friends who had accompanied us went to gather the Bahá'ís, and by noon the meeting started. Delegates from 12 villages arrived and, little by little, 100 Bahá'ís gathered. They had erected a throne-like seat for Dr Muhájir.

Ujjain Summer School, June 1968.

With Hand of the Cause Furútan and the Vice-President of India, second from left, 1969.

He refused to sit there, and sat on the dirt floor with the rest of them.

Like a loving parent he embraced and greeted all of them, and talked to them with real love and understanding. When the chairman asked for volunteers for travel teaching, his was the first hand to be raised.

On the way back he again talked about teaching, and that we should always rely on Bahá'u'lláh and never become discouraged. He advised us to go to the villages, 'Sit with them. If they are in the fields, go to the fields, if they are gathered around a fire join them, if they sit on the floor, sit on the floor. Do what they do and be one of them.'

With his guidance the National Youth Committee organized groups to visit North and East India. He Knew the map of India so well that he was able to dictate names of the cities to be visited which none of us had heard about. Under this plan, Orissa, Calcutta, Darjeeling, Kalimpang, Assam, Meghalaya, Simla, Kulu, Manali and others were visited. That was the start of the formation of local Assemblies and later settlement of pioneers in those areas.

Except for Calcutta and Bhubaneshwar, there were no pioneers in East India. He instructed me to pioneer to Calcutta and promised to send student pioneers, travel teachers and literature to help me. I went to Calcutta, and Dr Muhájir kept his promise. Groups of Iranian students settled in Orissa, Bihar, Darjeeling and West Bengal. He himself visited us often and helped in the teaching.

He was always anxious about the progress of the Five Year Plan. Once he asked me what I would do if I had only five years to make the whole world Bahá'í. I said, 'But Dr Muhájir, what if these multitudes cannot withstand the tempests of tests and tribulations?' With a stern look he said, 'How do you know that tests and trials will not make them firmer in the Faith?' As the years have passed I have realized how right he was. The new believers in many areas, when opposed by the clergy or government officials, have shown unbelievable steadfastness. His fourth and last visit to Bihar was in April 1979, when we proudly invited him to the new Ḥaẓíratu'l-Quds.

Raḥmat frequently visited Bombay, the central city of the State of Maharashtra, which had the greatest concentration of Bahá'ís before the onset of mass teaching, and was the earliest Bahá'í community in India. He participated in conferences and meetings there, and consulted with the experienced Bahá'ís about the great work of teaching in India. Many of his talks in Bombay shows the sense of urgency that he felt about all actions in that land:

> For the Faith to spread around the world, the greatest power is the power of movement, i.e., action. Only when we are a part of this movement will the bounty of Bahá'u'lláh be with us. Prayer is essential, but simply sitting at home and saying prayers, when one has the ability to move, is not enough. We must move. Sincerity and action are the two qualities needed for success in the promotion of the Faith. If one is sincere and makes mistakes, then he will be helped to correct them. But if one is not sincere and makes mistakes, then such actions will bring their own punishments. In this world, the greatest bounty is teaching the Cause and love for mankind. In the spiritual world the greatest bounty is the presence of Bahá'u'lláh. Sincerity means to work with no axe to grind. This type of sincerity will surely draw forth the bounty of God.
>
> The moment you are detached you can be successful. Bahá'u'lláh has said so. Bahá'u'lláh says 'In My Kingdom I have lions of detachment. If I release them they will conquer the world for Me.' Be one of those lions. The only thing necessary is — detachment. Whether you are working in banks or offices, taking care of your future, all these things can be postponed for three months, or six months. You can take your vacation with pay, or without pay, anything. Just think that if the Five Year Plan is not finished what will happen to all of us? This is what the beloved Guardian says — ultimately the success of all the plans depends on individual Bahá'ís. If each individual will not take it as their own personal responsibility, it will not work.
>
> If a large group of Bahá'ís from one village goes to another village [for teaching], we do not need any travel teachers, we do not need any arrangements, organization, any planning, because if we learn to go with our children and women from one village to

Lucknow Youth Conference, 1970.

> another village, it will be deepening, consolidation, child education, women's progress, anything that you want. We have no fear of failure. We Bahá'ís know that Bahá'u'lláh is going to help us, we will not fail. Why are we afraid of success? Success should not create fear in your hearts. There is no limits to the bounties of Bahá'u'lláh.
>
> This is the second phase of mass teaching in India. Our first phase was in tribal areas and villages. The second phase is the coming of educated youth into the Faith. Now we are going to perfect our mass teaching in India. I beg you, I beg all institutions, the National Spiritual Assembly, local Spiritual Assemblies, Counsellors, State Teaching Committees, Board members, let us be united in this one idea. Let us not say, 'Do not repeat past mistakes.' Let us positively, unitedly, work together and approach educated youth. We must still go to the villages, we must still go to tribes but now there is an additional dimension — *youth* — and also — *women*. Women can teach other women. They can go to their neighbours and, as 'Abdu'l-Bahá said, encourage them to investigate. When you cannot see the President, the Prime Minister and others — except in your country, the Prime Minister is a woman — you can see their wives. When you cannot see the head of a bank because he is so busy, you can arrange to see his wife. We should have a national plan to reach the women at every level — village level, town level, educated level. The Guardian said Bombay will be the fountainhead of Divine Mysteries. Do you know what is the condition for that? Don't stay in Bombay.

In the final stages of the Nine Year Plan, Raḥmat's concentration on the goals of India increased. He assiduously devised means and plans to accomplish the remaining goals as speedily as possible. He brought to the attention of the friends in India the Guardian's call for the urgent teaching of the masses: 'There is no time to lose. The masses, greatly tried by the calamities of the age, restless, disappointed, and eager to obtain real and complete relief in their hour of trial, hunger for the Message of the new Day . . .'[6]

In 1971, Raḥmat proposed holding youth conferences in the South of India, and in New Delhi. Both were very successful. The

Addressing joint meeting of Regional Teaching Committees August 1972.

A year before leaving India for London.

youth visited many colleges, and as a result, large groups of young people accepted the Faith. So that they could be deepened, he asked the Publishing Trust to introduce a new line of literature specifically geared to college and university audiences. Bahá'í literature published for this purpose carried the emblem, 'Service to Universities' and was widely used and welcomed by the youth. The National Youth Committee reported,

> At the recent Youth conference held in New Delhi in the presence of Hand of the Cause of God, Dr Muhájir, a youth project was chalked out for the summer vacation of all the youth of India. India has been divided into 31 areas, to which the youth will travel in order to teach and proclaim the message of God . . . More than 25 youth, most of them being Iranian pioneers, have volunteered to teach the Faith in Bihar, Orissa, West Bengal, Punjab, Kashmir, Haryana, Himachal, and Assam for two months.

The pressure and pace of the teaching work, the duties of managing the Publishing Trust, and many other projects for which I had responsibility, had completely exhausted me. After months of deliberation, we finally decided to move our home to London. With heavy hearts we left our beloved India at the completion of the Nine Year Plan in 1972. However, Raḥmat's close association with India did not diminish. Due to his busy schedule in other parts of the world, he could not visit India as often as he liked, but he communicated his thoughts and suggestions through frequent letters and cables.

In 1973, Raḥmat met the National Spiritual Assembly of Iran at the International Convention, and asked it to purchase ten Bahá'í Centres, one in each Indian State capital, and to support fifty youth to travel and teach in India for a period of two years. In May 1973 he was in India to help organize and implement these projects. In 1974 he visited many parts of the country and held detailed consultations with the Indian National Assembly. As usual he was involved in all aspects of the work. The Bahá'í Publishing Trust needed a manager, so Raḥmat interviewed applicants wherever he went to find a qualified person. His final choice was approved by the

National Assembly, and the individual chosen served in that position for many years. Raḥmat's notes for that period are subdued and lack his usual exuberance:

> *26 January*: Came to Delhi and Kathmandu . . . On 1 February went to Calcutta and Patna and then to Delhi and Gwalior. Met the NSA on the ninth and tenth. Had detailed discussions on Bahá'í education and other aspects of the Plan. An Education Committee was appointed to be convened in Panchgani. I went to Bombay and then to Panchgani to meet the committee. We prepared a few Bahá'í lessons, 35 of which will soon be translated and published to be sent to local committees for the education of the Bahá'í children. Went back again to Delhi for consultation with the NSA. All aspects of proclamation and translation and publication of literature were discussed and plans were made. I left for Bangkok on 1 March.

In the years 1974-5, mass teaching in India was at a low ebb: a state of affairs which wounded Raḥmat's heart. He could not understand how such great momentum had been slackened for administrative reasons. He prayed at the Guardian's Resting Place in London for the revival of teaching in India. He wrote letters and made phone calls trying to recreate the zeal for teaching. However, the friends were bent on deepening the existing Bahá'ís before teaching on a large scale again. Raḥmat grieved for this lost opportunity. He said that he could not understand how the Bahá'ís in India were going to deepen the hundreds of thousands of villagers with their small manpower — according to what they thought 'deepening' meant. He knew it was only teaching that attracted the bounties of Bahá'u'lláh, and it was only teaching that could lead to deepening. In the words of Shoghi Effendi:

> . . . it should be constantly borne in mind — and this applies to all communities without exception participating in this World Crusade — that the twofold task of extension and consolidation must be supplemented by continuous and strenuous efforts to increase speedily not only the number of the avowed followers of the Faith in both the virgin and opened territories and islands

> included within the scope of the Ten Year Plan, but also to swell the ranks of its active supporters who will consecrate their time, resources and energy to the effectual spread of its teachings and the multiplication and consolidation of its administrative institutions.[7]

Raḥmat kept quiet, as was his custom when his efforts did not succeed. Despite his great love for the subcontinent, he simply could not bring himself to go there while the administration and communities were busy with matters other than teaching.

In June 1975, the National Assembly of India recorded in its minutes the decision to write to Raḥmat and remind him that, 'It was more than 15 months that he had not visited India and the Indian Bahá'í community would be greatly encouraged if he could visit us at his earliest convenience.' Raḥmat's notes of 21 September 1975 say:

> This afternoon I had the bounty of meeting with the Supreme Body. Teaching in India was discussed and it was decided to restart mass teaching in villages which has been stopped for some time. The Universal House of Justice gave their approval for me to study all aspects of the work in India and then present my ideas to the National Assembly. I have to concentrate on this matter and have consultations with others so that with God's grace and assistance we can accomplish His Will.
>
> On Thursday, in the presence of the Universal House of Justice, I will visit the Shrine of the Báb to pray for India.
>
> *26 September*: It is six a.m. I am flying by El Al to Ṭihrán. I stayed two weeks in the Holy Land, which revived and refreshed my soul . . . The House of Justice made significant decisions regarding India and South-East Asia. They have given instructions to restart teaching in villages and have assigned budgets for translation and publication of books for children's education in local languages. Yesterday we had prayers for India at the holy Shrine of the Báb. Amoz [Gibson] chanted the Tablet of Aḥmad and Hushmand [Fatheazam] said the special teaching prayer. We all prayed that teaching would resume in India, and once more

make that country an example for the rest of the world. It was a very special occasion and affected us all very deeply.

I want to propose the following suggestions for the approval of the NSA:

A small simple booklet should be prepared to show the importance of the local Assemblies. Quotations from Writings and photos should be included. This should be translated in all Indian languages and distributed to all the villages. It should be shown how consultation increases the power of the Bahá'ís, what Bahá'í consultation is, why members of the LSA should say prayers before they start the meeting.

There should be a Bahá'í Centre in each village, even if it is in someone's house. This will give the villagers a point of gathering and belonging. Plastic signs saying, 'Bahá'í Bhawan', should be prepared in New Delhi and given to all the villages.

A Bahá'í Fund should be established in all the villages to be used primarily for the education of children.

Establishment of children's classes.

Small prayer books in large lettering be printed and given to Bahá'ís.

Ten lessons be devised on the manner of teaching the Faith so that the Bahá'í teachers study them before their travels.

Five hundred LSAs be designated to teach first in their villages and expand it to other areas.

Concentrate on teaching all households in the village.

Have dawn prayers every morning.

Choose one area that has a few hundred Bahá'ís, with villages at walking distance, and during a teaching campaign bring the number to 1000. There should be two full-time teachers. At least ten per cent of the children should attend Bahá'í classes. In the second year the number of the Bahá'ís should reach 2000 and the number of teachers should increase to four. The villagers should donate a Bahá'í Centre for each 1000 new believers.

Most of the Bahá'í conferences should be held in these areas.

We should train 100 teachers to teach Bahá'í Sunday classes. These teachers should travel to the villages, stay for a while, establish Bahá'í classes and train local teachers.

Resume teaching in tribal areas and universities. Resume proclamation and increase the output of the Publishing Trust.

We should request the NSA of Iran to assist the Publishing Trust financially, establish the Educational Trust, and have a joint education plan specifically for Iranian Bahá'í women to assist in teaching the children in the villages. They should undergo an initial orientation on how to dress and work in Indian villages.

Pioneers be sent to large cities.

Auxiliary Board members to manage each of the teaching institutes and also concentrate on cities like Sholapur, Indore, Kanpur, Madras, Bangalore , Ujjain, Mysore, etc.

The two states of Maharashtra and Mysore should surpass Madhya Pradesh.

Ten teachers to travel in each state.

Teachers from Malaysia, Philippines and Ceylon be invited to assist in the South.

Auxiliary Board members concentrate on these two States.

Panchgani Bahá'ís assist in the projects.

Education of children.

Teaching in villages.

Establishment of State Teaching Committees.

Conquering of universities through youth activities.

Iranian students should be utilized.

If it meets the approval of the House of Justice, funds should be collected in the 1976 conference for a Ḥaẓíra in each State.

In October 1975 Raḥmat returned to India.

> *28 October*: I have come to India after 18 months . . . attended meetings and conferences. May God shower His Bounties on this land.

Another 18 months passed before he could go to India once more. On the instructions of the Universal House of Justice, Raḥmat went to New Delhi in January 1977, to consult with the National Assembly and to send 'realistic recommendations' to the Supreme Body for the acceleration of teaching activities in India. His concern was the accomplishment of the goals of the Five Year Plan, and he asked that each State Teaching Committee double the number of their local Assemblies by Riḍván 1979. He recommended that the educated Bahá'í women be encouraged to teach and take part in all Bahá'í activities, and give the message of Bahá'u'lláh to prominent women of India. He also suggested that permission be sought from the Universal House of Justice for a three-day 'All Asia Women's Conference', to be held in New Delhi in October 1977, and that Amatu'l-Bahá Ruḥíyyih Khánum be invited to grace the conference with her presence.

On 29 January 1977, he cabled the National Assembly with this challenge: FINAL FULFILMENT GOALS ALMOST IMPOSSIBLE UNLESS RAISING NUMBER ASSEMBLIES FIVE THOUSAND THIS APRIL.

He followed up his letters and cables by going to India in April 1977. This time he was focusing on a programme for women to coincide with the October conference, which had been approved by the Universal House of Justice. Amatu'l-Bahá attended the conference, and hundreds of women from all over Asia participated. Raḥmat suggested that Amatu'l-Bahá be requested to lay the foundation stone of the Indian temple. Mr Sháh, Secretary of the National Spiritual Assembly recalls,

> We were very reluctant and apprehensive to do this. Our permit for the temple land had been revoked by the government and we were fighting this in the courts. We were certain that the land would not be given to us. Dr Muhájir, however, insisted and said that Bahá'u'lláh would take care of His own. We should not fear, and should continue with our plans. We finally agreed and Amatu'l-Bahá graciously accepted our request, and the foundation stone was laid in a very spiritual and heart-warming ceremony.

Raḥmat continued to send letters and cables to India. His suggestions for an Institute of Higher Education for women in Panchgani, a three-year publication plan for regional languages, and immediate commencement of a teaching campaign in South India were approved by the National Assembly and implemented.

South India held a special attraction for Raḥmat, as some of his dearest friends, the Yeganegi family, had lived there since his first visit to India. He had a close relationship with them, and they always sought and followed his advice in their personal affairs. Mr Yeganegi has recollections of Raḥmat's visits to Bangalore and Mysore:

> The first time that he came to Bangalore was in 1961. He went with us to many villages to show us the methods of mass teaching. The LSA of Mysore had invited him to go there but he had replied that he would only go there if they had mass teaching. The Mysore friends — together with some from Bangalore — started to teach, resulting in several new Bahá'ís. The next time that Dr Muhájir visited us he asked us to drive him to Mysore to

participate in the mass teaching. On this trip he was accompanied by Vasu Devan and Sabapathy, two youths from Malaysia. He said, 'I have brought you two wonderful souls to start a fire in the South.' Sabapathy later married my daughter and on the instructions of Dr Muhájir they pioneered to Africa and are now in Mozambique.

My son, Atapur, had graduated, and planned to go to Arabia. Dr Muhájir told him to forget about that and pioneer to Bhutan to be with his brother. He agreed; it was the best possible thing for him. Another of our sons, Faiz, graduated from college the same day that Dr Muhájir arrived. He asked Faiz if he was ready to go pioneering. Faiz replied that he was. Dr Muhájir told him to get his transcripts and immediately come to Delhi. On arrival in Delhi Dr Muhájir was waiting for him. He gave Faiz a ticket and $20, and told him that his destination was Laos. Faiz left the next day. Dr Muhájir had arranged for a Bahá'í friend to meet Faiz in Bangkok airport and direct him to Laos. Faiz is still in Laos. He has a Laotian wife and is the only foreign Bahá'í allowed to remain. All through his pioneering years Dr Muhájir visited him and advised him how to run his business. Thank Bahá'u'lláh he is doing very well.

He asked my daughter Tuba and my son-in-law Mohan to pioneer to Nepal. They immediately followed his instructions.

Dr Muhájir was the link between us and our children, whom he had sent around the world. He was like a father to all of them and like a son to me.

On a teaching trip with Mrs Boman, our jeep was involved in a bad accident. Mrs Boman was half paralysed and I suffered several broken ribs. After visiting Mrs Boman, Dr Muhájir came to see me. He sat by my bed for hours, said prayers, and gave me news of the children. While he was there I could not feel any pain.

Raḥmat's next sojourn in India was in August 1978. He had three days of intensive and detailed consultation with the National Assembly on all aspects of the work of the Faith. His suggestions for a stronger National Teaching Committee and the launch of a teaching project for East India were approved, and means of implementation were provided with his help. His notes record:

> *15 August*: I have to go to Calcutta, the plane is delayed and I can't make the connection to Dacca. I wonder what God's Will is. Maybe it is better if I stay in India for a longer time and go to the Holy Land at the end of September.
>
> I am finally in Calcutta. I talked to Ramnik at three a.m. There is an NSA meeting on the 18th. I will go to New Delhi to meet with them.
>
> *17 August*: I met with the West Bengal Teaching Committee. God willing we will formulate a teaching plan for East India.

The pages that follow these diary entries contain detailed proposals for a vast teaching plan for East India. After meeting with the National Assembly he visited Chandigarh, Haryana, Himachal, Kashmir, Kerala, Orissa, Tripura, Rajasthan, Gujarat, Bihar, and many other areas.

> *1 September*: I have covered areas from Thailand to Indore. After Kashmir I went to Delhi to meet the NTC and consulted on teaching projects with them. Then visited Gwalior and the Rabbani School. I was delighted to see the young people so happy. We also went to three villages to teach. My soul was truly elated. We had consultations with the State Teaching Committee and the Regional Teaching Committee and then participated in a two-day conference in Indore. We decided to establish the hostel for tribal and village girls in Indore Institute. They promised to restart mass teaching and have all-Bahá'í villages with fifty teachers, and each have six Bahá'í classes for children. My trust is in God and His Blessings.

On the same day he met the National Youth Committee in Bombay. The Committee's report states,

> Dr Muhájir very lovingly greeted each member of the committee, saying a word of praise and love to all. He explained that it

was not the right time to hold a West Asia Youth Conference, since Iran and other countries could not attend. We should hold . . . regional youth conferences and conduct them in local languages. He also advised us to ask the consent of the NSA to send a youth group on pilgrimage to the Holy Land.

He said the youth should aim for the moon and they will be able to catch the eagle. If they aimed for the eagle they would catch the rock. He said the more remote an area the more receptivity. The tribes share our ideas of unity. We must think that one year is one month. Some countries say they phase the plans. In fact they are postponing it. In His Writings, Bahá'u'lláh says people do not realize the value of time. If we miss a moment we cannot regain it in centuries to come. The Báb says it is better for you if a man accepts the Faith one ninth of one ninth of one tenth of one tenth of an instant sooner. Our work is never finished. Even the people who die have not finished their tasks.

Raḥmat's diary continues:

2 September, Kerala: It is my first visit here. In 1971 they had one regional committee operating in Mangalore, now they have 8000 Bahá'ís . . . On 14 September I went to Sikkim and visited Gantok, Darjeeling and Kalimpong. This was my first visit.

17 September: I am in Calcutta. With the blessings of Bahá'u'lláh the Eastern Teaching Project will start today. From the 18th to the 23rd I visited Assam, Gauhati, Orissa, and Bangladesh. On the 24th I will meet the NSA to discuss the projects for Bahá'í Centres, deepening, proclamation and children's education

Mrs Boman was with him on most of this trip and remembers,

He expressed a wish to visit the friends in Sikkim. We — as usual — said that it was impossible, that it would require at least three months to go through the red tape at Delhi to obtain a permit. We were all at a meeting in Delhi when a phone call was received from the Ministry informing us that Dr Muhájir had a permit to go to Sikkim, and his visa could be collected in Darjeeling.

From Sikkim he went to Kalimpong. He urged the friends to immediately buy a property for the Bahá'í Centre. He felt that this beautiful little town on the border of the Himalayas would one day hold a very strategic importance and would be a glorious gate to Tibet and Bhutan. He asked about the names of the Knights of Bahá'u'lláh for Bhutan, and asked them to contribute funds for the purchase of the Ḥaẓiratu'l-Quds in Kalimpong. This was done without any delay.

The National Assembly's report said:

> Dr Muhájir . . . informed us that the East India project had started on 17 September, and many local friends had offered to join the project, and also to pioneer to some of the eastern States. Dr Vasudevan would be holding deepening institutes for the volunteers, and the Project will be started at six different places aimed at enroling believers from every strata of society.
>
> In Orissa two simultaneous projects had been started, one in the North, the other in the South. Similarly, in Assam he found many capable local Bahá'ís. Dr Muhájir further said that, according to his understanding, the East India Teaching Project is one of the most important and significant teaching campaigns and it has already started making a great impact on the Bahá'ís.

The report goes on to outline Raḥmat's efforts to locate venues for Bahá'í Centres in Gauhati, Udaipur, Kalimpong, Mandsaur, and Shajahanpur, and how the National Spiritual Assembly consulted with him regarding raising the funds needed for the purchase of those properties.

Raḥmat approached his friends and relatives and urged them to assist in those projects in any way they could. I was present during many of these conversations, and was sometimes concerned that his friends might feel uncomfortable. He dismissed my concerns, and said that a businessman always thought of his business, 'My business is the business of the Faith. I am not asking anything for myself. I am suggesting that they buy stock in a conglomerate that belongs to Bahá'u'lláh. If they are smart they'll do it, and if they are not there is no coercion.'

He asked his sisters to contribute towards the cost of Bahá'í Centres and jeeps for India. One of his sisters, Mrs Heshmat Adlparvar, who was always very close to him, was the one he approached most often. The balance of the amount needed for the purchase of the Centre in Kalimpong was contributed by her at his request. He also asked her to travel extensively in India. Her love, kindness and cheerful demeanour are still remembered by all those who met her. Many jeeps, Bahá'í Centres and publications were acquired with her assistance. The minutes of one National Assembly meeting states: 'Mrs H. Adlparvar, member of the NSA of Kuwait, was invited to the meeting. She offered her services to the National Assembly in acquiring Ḥaẓíratu'l-Quds by visiting the concerned cities and assisting the local friends in finalizing the negotiations for the purchase of properties.' Afterwards she travelled to most of the states and helped to find and purchase many of the Ḥaẓíras.

Heshmat Khánum pioneered to Sudan a few months after the passing of her beloved brother, where she gave her life in the path of Bahá'u'lláh. After only a few weeks at her pioneering post she succumbed to a particulary deadly strain of malaria, falling into a coma, from which she never recovered.

During this penultimate visit to India in 1978, Raḥmat's thoughts were centred on devising specific teaching campaigns for all regions. The South India Teaching Project had been so enormously successful that the time had now come to imitate it elsewhere. The *Bahá'í News* of India reported in its May-August issue:

> Encouraged by the wonderful and exciting results of the South India Teaching Project, a similar plan for East India has been prepared in consultation with the Hand of the Cause Dr Muhájir . . . One of the objectives of this teaching programme is to train teachers and pioneers for eastern States.
>
> Nine more teaching Projects covering many states will be finalised in the next meeting of the NSA . . . when Dr Muhájir will be present after visiting Gwalior, Indore, Bombay, Cochin, Coimbatore, Sulur, the base of South India Teaching Project, Bangalore, Madras and Hyderabad.

> Dr Muhájir reached Cochin and attended the evening session of the Conference called forth by the [State Teaching Committee] . . . the next day after attending the morning session of the Conference he left for Sulur where he participated in the day-long conference . . . the next two days were spent in consultation with the members of the South India Project . . . on the fourth evening a village programme including a public talk was arranged for the beloved Hand . . . Dr Muhájir reached the Bahá'í Centre (in Assam), where about nineteen garlands were offered to [him] . . . All the friends who had come from outside Gauhati to have *darshan* [the honour of meeting] of the beloved guest were much influenced by his talk. Anybody could see the expression of joy and wonderment on the faces of new believers who were greatly touched by Dr Muhájir's simplicity, compassion and love.

In 1979 Raḥmat's letters and cables to his adopted country were largely concerned with the speedy achievement of the goals of the Seven Year Plan:

> REACHING BOMBAY THIRD WEEK MARCH HOPE VAST CONSULTATIONS ALL INSTITUTIONS LAUNCHING GLORIOUS SEVEN YEAR PLAN STOP SUGGEST EXPEDITE BOLDLY PRAYERFULLY PURCHASE REMAINING CENTRES EAST SOUTH HIMACHAL ANDHRA FOUNDATION FUTURE UNPRECEDENTED ACTIVITIES DEEPEST LOVE

In March 1979 he met with the National Assembly, Counsellors and Auxiliary Board members to work out the details of implementing the Plan. He toured many of the southern and eastern States to assist in planning their teaching projects. In the jumble of his notes about the goals, in one corner he wrote, 'Today is 9 April. The Seven Year Plan has arrived. I am extremely happy.'

The *Bahá'í News* reported in 1980,

> In March 1979 he was in India again and undertook extensive tours of the projects in the South and other parts, reaching Calcutta in April. He was worn out. Daily he used to phone

> Delhi to see if the Seven Year Plan had been received. He convened an NSA meeting immediately on receipt of the document and as he read through the Plan he was a changed man — full of energy and vitality. Then he helped the NSA formulate its own implementation plan and left eastward to Bangladesh and the Far East.
>
> On the second day of the last National Convention [1979], the entire gathering was electrified to see Dr Muhájir suddenly appear at the Convention. He called on the friends from every State to formulate their own projects for a new effort at consolidation and expansion. In the afternoons, seated in groups under trees and in corners of the *shamiana* [tent] they worked.
>
> Immediately after the Convention the Counsellors had convened a meeting . . . to study the Seven Year Plan . . . the Hand presented the Teaching Projects worked out by the representatives of the provinces. In two blessed hours, there was explanation and encouragement . . .

Mrs Boman recalls that on that trip Raḥmat was very often exhausted, and sometimes he could not get up from his chair. Often his neck and shoulders had to be massaged. When asked where his radiant smile had gone, he replied that he was worried about the Plan and how the friends would carry out its goals. This was to be his last trip to India.

On 24 October, he cabled the National Assembly, suggesting that they invite Amatu'l-Bahá to visit India for a few months. He regularly contacted the Secretary of the National Assembly to ask about the teaching progress. Three days before his passing he called Mr Sháh to inquire about the details of teaching work, and then Mr Sahba, the architect, to ask about progress on the construction of the temple, which was in its first stages. Raḥmat's association with this particular project had started 20 years before. During our stay in India we often went to the temple land and said prayers. In the uncertain years when Bahá'í ownership of the land was disputed by the government, Raḥmat said special prayers at the Shrines for the removal of obstacles. However, he never doubted that the Faith would finally be triumphant: miraculously, ownership of the land was returned to the National Assembly, and the construction of the temple was incorporated into the goals of the Five Year Plan. Most developments of the Faith in India were usually in some way connected to Raḥmat's initiative. The finding of an architect for the temple was no exception. Mr Sahba relates:

> At the time I was an associate of Mr Amanat, and we had just finished the work on the plans for the Seat of the Universal House Of Justice. Dr Muhájir, during one of his visits to Ṭihrán, asked me if I had submitted a plan to the Universal House of Justice in response to their call for designs for the temple of India. The thought had never even occurred to me. I was very young and thought there were many more experienced architects in the world to tackle this project.
>
> But he insisted and I said I would try. A few months later he was back in Ṭihrán and again asked if I had started the project. I had not. Again I gave him all my reasons for not doing this work and again he insisted and said he was returning to Ṭihrán in a few months and I should have the plans ready so that he could carry them to the Holy land. A few months later he called me from Ṭihrán airport and asked me to bring the plans to him. Of course I had not done anything. This time just to make him happy I made a firm promise to draw a preliminary plan and submit it for the consideration of the Universal House of Justice. I did and the rest, of course, is history.

Many Bahá'ís in India wear Bahá'í rings that once belonged to Raḥmat. His worldly belongings were very few, but whatever he had, whether his coat, Bahá'í ring, pen, or even a notebook, he shared with the friends. He laughed with them, ate their food, danced their dances and sang their songs. At the dedication of the Bahá'í temple, while I was guiding the masses of participants, a gentleman who had come from one of the remote towns of South India read my name tag, stared for a while and asked if he could talk to me. He took a small, worn calendar from his pocket, pointed to the date of 29 December, and said, 'This is the day of the passing of Dr. Muhájir. I want you to know that every year I fast on this day in his memory.' He left without introducing himself.

When the temple was inaugurated the National Assembly, with the approval of the Universal House of Justice, named the beautiful

Dedication of the 'Muhájir Gate' by Amatu'l-Bahá Rúḥíyyih Kh͟ánum, December 1986.

Official opening.

With Gisu.

The Muhájir Gate, with Hands of the Cause, Amatu'l-Bahá, William Sears, Collis Featherstone. Mr Sears leaned on the Gate and said, 'It's as solid and strong as Raḥmat was'.

entrance gate in Raḥmat's honour. The 'Muhájir Gate' was dedicated by Amatu'l-Bahá in the presence of other Hands of the Cause, Counsellors and National Assembly members from all parts of the world. India's future generations, while passing through the 'Muhájir Gate', will surely remember the servant who loved them so deeply.

India and her adopted son were now parted. He had first arrived one sultry day when there was only a handful of Bahá'í communities, and less than 1000 believers. On his last visit, some 22 years later, India had thousands of communities and over 1,000,000 devoted Bahá'ís. Tickets found in his suitcase after his passing included two stops in India which he had planned for 1980.

Although in his lifetime Raḥmat would not allow anything to be named after him, after his passing the National Spiritual Assembly of India decided to dedicate the teaching Institutes in Deolali, the Bahá'í Centres of Trivandrum, Kerala, and Shimla, and a dormitory complex of the New Era School in Panchgani in his name. The cornerstone of the Muhájir Teaching Institute was laid by Amatu'l-Bahá in Bhagwatipin, near Patna, capital of Bihar. These locations, together with the 'Muhájir Gate', at the Mother Temple of India, represent all parts of the subcontinent. In the words of the Secretary of the Indian National Assembly, 'Countless institutes, centres and projects also draw inspiration and succour from association with his name.'

PAKISTAN

Raḥmat often stopped in Pakistan on his way to India. Unfortunately, there are few records of his time in that country, and I was unable to accompany him there. One useful account of the condition of the friends in Pakistan is contained in a letter he wrote to the Universal House of Justice following his last visit, in November 1975.

> I am very happy that I was able to visit Pakistan after many years, and to travel in villages and participate in teaching. I was delighted to see that many pure souls have accepted the Faith. The children have Bahá'í classes, women chant prayers by heart, and the men are on fire to teach the Faith. The National

> Assembly has young and active members, and, under its direction, all kinds of progress in this country are possible. Thanks be to Bahá'u'lláh. I consulted the National Spiritual Assembly about Mirpur, which is on the border with India. They are to increase the number of the believers and combine teaching and consolidation work. The people have great receptivity. I am sure that the Supreme Body has offered prayers for the progress of the Faith in this country. Thank God that a new happy spirit has appeared here.

BANGLADESH

Although so near to India, Dacca was not very accessible. Not many planes flew there and the political situation was often in turmoil. Raḥmat, however, made an effort to visit Bangladesh whenever possible, and encouraged many of the Persian youth to pioneer and study there. In his letter of 3 November 1975 to the Universal House of Justice, he wrote:

> I have now been in Bangladesh for a few days and am meeting the beloved friends. If the number of pioneers could be increased, gates to a new campaign can be opened. In particular, many youth can come here to study in the universities. Already the majority of the pioneers are youth. My humble suggestion is to give extra teaching goals in Bangladesh to the Bahá'ís of Iran so that it generates enthusiasm for their pioneering. Unlike many other countries, foreign students are still accepted in these colleges and doors are still open. Many of those who are reluctant to go to African countries such as Angola and Mozambique, or to Laos, Vietnam and other countries can easily come here. At least ten people can come from Australia, New Zealand, Malaysia, and the Philippines. The youth can come to study or get jobs in the volunteer organizations which foreign countries have begun to operate.
>
> I hope to discuss teaching of the tribes and others with the National Assembly tonight.
>
> P.S. Today is the ninth. I had to spend these days in Dacca as the roads were closed and I could not leave. I need your prayers and your infallible instructions.

By 1978 there were 26 young pioneers from Iran in Bangladesh, many of whom are still there and have degrees in medicine, engineering and education.

On his last trip, Raḥmat arrived at the National Ḥaẓíratu'l-Quds on the evening of 21 September 1978. He had been given the wrong address of the Centre by his hotel and had to look for hours before he found it. As Mr Sabour, the Secretary of the National Assembly remembers, 'He humbly but majestically arrived into our hearts. As I rushed to greet him, he said he did not want to trouble anyone to meet him at the airport. He said he had been to Dacca several times and could find his way.'

In the evening all 26 of the Iranian pioneers, together with those from Malaysia, India, Pakistan, Iraq and the local Bahá'ís, gathered to meet him. Raḥmat spoke in Persian and asked the newly-arrived Iranian pioneers about the earthquake in Iran which had recently occurred. He then talked about the Five Year Plan:

> This plan has achieved in five years what previously would have taken fifty years to complete. I was in India two years ago and went to Madhya Pradesh, Indore and Gwalior. You cannot compare the India of today with two years ago. There are now many villages which are completely Bahá'í. Thank God the Faith is now in their own hands. The travelling teachers are all Indians and the work is not in the hands of Persians or Americans. They have 72 teaching committees. You now have five teaching committees. Three years ago you had ten local Assemblies and now one hundred. In Malaysia and the Pacific they have achieved all their goals. Twelve teachers have gone from Malaysia to South India and have taught 7000 people and elected 400 new local Assemblies.
>
> I went to the conference in Kerala. It was mostly the youth who had done all the work. These are not only numbers. There is quality also. The Faith of Bahá'u'lláh is amazing. It has its own dynamics. After the ascension of the beloved Guardian, the effect of his soul made the Faith progress even faster. It is always like this.
>
> The Guardian's passing shook the Bahá'ís. Instead of complaining about each other they read his writings and derive power

> from him. Do not be too hard on the native people. In one country they happily told me that they had refused to enrol 2000 sweepers ['untouchables', members of the lowest caste]. Why? To be a Bahá'í has nothing to do with education and caste. It depends on the heart. It is not for us to decide. God knows the heart of the people. The Persians especially should not be critical. Teach their children, teach them 'Alláh'u'Abhá', teach them to say ''Abdu'l-Bahá'. If a person . . . has an idol in his house, or if he is a Bahá'í and his wife is not, do not criticize them. Do something for these people. If they are poor, help them; find them some work, give them a few chickens and show them how to have a chicken farm. Help the people. Be their friends.

One day two youths, who were not Bahá'ís, were passing the Centre and came in. Raḥmat talked to them for a long time and explained the Bahá'í teachings. He told them,

> Nothing in this world is accidental. In Bolivia they put a sign on the door of the Bahá'í Centre which said, 'Unity of Mankind. Please ring if you want to know more.' Two men rang and came in. That night they heard about the Bahá'í Faith for the first time. For three days they studied and then they said, 'We are Bahá'ís.' They walked over the mountains of Bolivia from house to house teaching the Bahá'í Faith. Now one in every fifty Bolivians is a Bahá'í. You two may have a mission also.

That night in the meeting of the friends he again talked about unity.

> Don't criticize others. Don't be hard on people. You cannot force a banana tree to grow just by giving it a lot of water. As to consolidation, you should know that the people's capability varies. You must be like a breeze. A typhoon uproots all trees. Give them time to think, do not push them. They are like olive trees. An olive tree needs 200 years to bear fruit. Be patient and loving to the new plants. At the time of Bahá'u'lláh and 'Abdu'l-Bahá, Jamál Effendi came to India and taught the Nizam of Hyderabad. In Calcutta, Mullá Muṣṭafá Rúmí became a Bahá'í

> through Jamál Effendi, and later became a Hand of the Cause. These two men went to Indonesia and travelled in Java, Bali, Celebes and Parepare, where the ruler accepted the Faith. Only two people did so much. Imagine, if two hundred Bahá'ís had come out of Persia, all the world would be Bahá'ís.

Raḥmat then asked for volunteers at that meeting and encouraged the friends to follow the path that India was taking. He told them to go to the remote parts of Bangladesh, to start from the town centre and teach nine of the surrounding villages. Mr Sabour recalls,

> Dr Muhájir's face was red, and he looked as if he was burning from the heat. We gave him some iced water. He wrapped his fingers around the glass and put it to his head. Then he said, 'Would anyone who does *not* want to volunteer, please raise your hand.' Twenty-eight people volunteered to go teaching in Rajshahi, Mymensingh, Jessore and Chittagong.
>
> The next morning at 6.30 the friends gathered to have dawn prayers with him. He told them that they should always be happy: 'In every adversity there is some hidden victory. In the history of the Faith each negative event has produced a positive result. The Síyáh-Chál and the banishment of Bahá'u'lláh resulted in the fulfilment of prophecy. Obstacles in one place inevitably led to opportunities in another.
>
> He explained that the 'NO!' of Indonesia [where the Faith was banned in 1958] was the 'YES!' of Vietnam, Malaysia and the Philippines [Refering to the mass teaching opportunities and victories]. 'Be happy. Be positive. Be dead to the "No's". If you want to go teaching, do not leave it until tomorrow and do not worry about yesterday. Yesterday is gone forever. I always think as if my life has begun today. The Knight of Bahá'u'lláh is in the past. What do I want to do today? If you want to teach that village, do it today. Teach both in towns and villages; have a "City Project" and a "Village Project". We have manpower enough for both. Give the message to all strata of society. You need the root of the tree if you want the fruit. If you make your teaching conditional, you will not be successful. People are different from one another, we all have good and bad points. I

> was once travelling in a country and was very tired. People criticised me saying "Dr Muhájir has not tied his shoe-laces". In Bangladesh you too might catch me out. My faults are international!'

On 23 September everyone gathered at the airport to bid him farewell. Raḥmat talked to each of the friends and listened to their problems for the last time. He said,

> In India they decided to have dawn prayers for nineteen days for the success of the last year of the Five Year Plan. You can do the same. Read the Tablets of Bahá'u'lláh. Memorize them and chant them, if not at the Ḥaẓíratu'l-Quds, then in your hostels. I suggest the youth go to West Bengal to experience teaching. These days will not return, days of youth and study.

NEPAL

Although the Bahá'í community of Nepal was founded in the 1920s, the Faith made slow progress. It had to rely on occasional travel teachers sent by the National Spiritual Assembly of India, which was responsible for the affairs of the Faith there.

As mass teaching began to flourish in India, its bordering countries, including Nepal, reaped the fruits. For the first time Raḥmat visited Kathmandu and became aware of its needs. Nepal had no pioneers and, as it had no universities to attract the youth, it was not possible to send Persian pioneers there.

It was in 1968 that Raḥmat, while on a visit to Calcutta, found the perfect pioneer family for Nepal. Tuba and Mohan Munje were children of Raḥmat's old friends in India. Tuba was the daughter of Mr Yeganegi, who would do anything Raḥmat asked. Mohan was the son of Dr Munje, a member of the National Assembly of India who was involved in mass teaching and had travelled widely in India at Raḥmat's request.

The scenario was perfect. The only problem was how to approach Mohan. Raḥmat decided on the direct path. While at dinner he quietly asked Mohan about his job. Mohan recalls, 'I proudly recounted all the wonderful things that were happening in the corporation that I worked for, and how I was in line for a major promotion. He listened carefully and said, "Mohan, I think you should pioneer to Nepal." '

All Mohan's objections were to no avail. His office had no branch in Nepal; his children were at school; he had responsibilities in the office that he could not leave. Raḥmat just smiled and said that he should rely on God and go. Finally, to appease him, Mohan promised to think about it and consult his wife. 'All right,' Raḥmat said, 'think as much as you like. Give me your answer tomorrow. The next morning Raḥmat called him to inquire about his decision and said, 'Mohan did you resign from your job?' Mohan told me,

> I was flabbergasted. However, in all the years of our family's association with Dr Muhájir we had always followed his suggestions and always reaped the benefits. So I asked him if he was really serious. He said he had never been more serious. I consulted with Tuba, who said her father had always told all his children to obey Dr Muhájir's guidance and instructions. In 1961 he had asked her brother Enayat Yeganegi to pioneer to Nepal, but when Enayat arrived in New Delhi, Dr Muhájir was there and told him that Bhutan was more important. Enayat left for Bhutan, married a local girl, and established a local Assembly. Although Bhutan was a restricted country, through Enayat many Bahá'ís could go there.
>
> The next day Dr Muhájir again said, 'Mohan did you resign? Are you ready to leave?' That day I went to my boss and submitted my resignation. We left for Kathmandu two weeks late. Dr Muhájir promised to come and visit us, and help us in the teaching work. On arrival in Kathmandu I started to look for work. A large hotel chain was looking for a manager for their luxury hotel in Kathmandu, and I was employed within a couple of days. Dr Muhájir kept his promise and visited us a few months later. He came to our large and comfortable house, said prayers and commented, 'Is this not a thousand times better than those cramped quarters you had in Calcutta?' I said that the only inconvenience was that I did not have a car of my own. He said, 'You go on with the teaching work, leave the car to me. I will pray for you that the next time I come here you will have a car, so that you will not complain any more.' In a few months he was

with us again. I had received a bonus and bought a car. I went to the airport to fetch him. He was the first guest to ride in our car.

The Munjes were the first family to pioneer to Nepal. A few more pioneers followed them. Martha Tebyani, a pioneer in India, was asked by Raḥmat to go to Kathmandu. Keith Defolo, an American pioneer in India was sent to Nepal, and the teaching work started to grow.

Raḥmat visited Kathmandu frequently to help the pioneers in their endeavour. He knew the importance of Nepal and Sikkim, not only for their own sake, but because of their proximity to China. As in other countries, Raḥmat encouraged cross-border co-operation between Nepal and India. Professor Rai, a knowledgable and devoted Bahá'í, settled in a town in Nepal near the border of India and was instrumental in teaching and deepening hundreds of Bahá'ís.

Once, when we were accompanying Raḥmat on one of his visits to Nepal, I could see that he had no intention of just being a tourist. Keith Defolo and the Munjes would sit with him and talk the whole day. Mahshid Ighani, a young Persian who had pioneered to the Philippines, was now in Kathmandu. I asked her if Raḥmat had seen the city. She didn't know. When I asked Raḥmat himself, he laughed and said that he was not interested in sightseeing. He had seen one of the Hindu temples, and knew what they looked like. He was more interested in the people than their monuments. I was astonished. People from all over the world came to Kathmandu just to see the temples. Raḥmat had been there more than ten times and had not gone to see anything. At my insistence he took one day off and we went to see the city. Still he told me, in no uncertain terms, that if he accompanied me to all the sights I wanted to see he would never get any work done. But all this did not dissuade me from visiting the house of the 'Living Goddess'.

We were taken to the gate of a large house, and had to wait outside for about 40 minutes in the hot sunshine. Finally the gate opened, and after paying for tickets we were taken into the courtyard. A child of about five years in a beautiful red dress was standing serenely on a balcony, surrounded by a group of women, looking down at us. No one said anything or explained anything.

After a few minutes we were simply ushered out. I thought I would never live this incident down and would have to suffer Raḥmat's jokes. He, however, took pity on me, and only inquired if I had been much enlightened by my sightseeing. He used this experience to ponder how such firm faith could cause these people to worship a young child as a 'Living Goddess'. He said that this was the kind of feeling we had to instill in the hearts of Bahá'ís.

This was the end of our sightseeing days together. If Raḥmat did not want to see monuments in other cities and countries, I did not insist.

On this trip, he spent hours with the pioneers, planning for teaching and consolidation of the local Assemblies prior to formation of the National Assembly of Nepal. By 1972 Nepal had 19 local Spiritual Assemblies, which was the criterion set by the Universal House of Justice for the formation of their National Spiritual Assembly. Of course, the fact that these goals had been achieved did not stop Raḥmat making further proposals:

> *9 April 1973*: I am at Motel Makalu, which is the name of a mountain on the north east of Nepal. I had dinner with Mohán and Tubat, and Mahshid and her husband. I told them than they should teach the Faith freely and without fear. Now is the time to teach the tribes, simply and easily.
>
> I understand that in Birganj and Biratnagar, many youth have accepted the Faith. We can choose from amongst them to teach the tribes. We have to have teachers from India, and send students to study art and economics in the Nepalese colleges.
>
> There is a very good plot of land in front of the University which overlooks the river and the mountainous area of Nepal. This is very good for the temple land.
>
> There are 64 tribes in Nepal which are accessible. There is still no activity in the western part, which needs teachers and pioneers.

Raḥmat's only visit to Sikkim was in September 1978. He wrote in his diary,

14 September: I visited Sikkim for the first time and stayed for two days. I went to Gangtok, Darjeeling and Kalimpong. It was most enjoyable.

CENTRAL ASIA

AFGHANISTAN

Raḥmat went to Kabul twice in the late 1960s, although conditions in the country meant it was not prudent to openly visit the handful of Bahá'ís in Afghanistan. On a postcard sent to me from Kabul, in the Autumn of 1967, he expressed his admiration for the simple and kind Afghan people, and his wish that we could all live there and bring the Faith of Bahá'u'lláh to those wonderful souls.

He was in Kabul for three days, and spent only a few hours with the sole pioneer to Afghanistan in his small appliance store. He then cancelled his plane reservation to Tihrán and hitched a ride to Mas͟hhad with an oil tanker. He later told me that he could not bear to go to another airport or board another plane. He preferred to travel by truck, even though it meant a gruelling 20-hour ride on uneven and dusty roads.

Gisu and I were with him on his next trip to Kabul in 1970. We found it a charming city, just as Raḥmat had said. The unpaved roads, the colourful bazaars, the manner of dress and the Persian spoken with a provincial accent, all reminded us of the Iran of times past. It was Thursday and people were getting ready for their prayers at the mosques the next day. Verses from the Qur'án were being broadcast from loudspeakers located in Kabul's central park. It was not wise for us, as a family, to visit our pioneer friend. Raḥmat felt that the next best thing would be to visit a kebab house whose owner had become friendly with him during his previous trip. The owner greeted us with much happiness and called Raḥmat, 'Dr. Bahá'í', in a whisper.

The stall was small with two wooden benches and one long table. A torn curtain divided the kitchen and customer areas. The aroma of barbecued meat and smoke filled the whole stall. The elderly man, draped in an 'abâ and white turban told me, 'The last time

A postcard sent by Raḥmat from Kabul, Afghanistan, July 1967.

your husband was here I was in trouble and very sad. He spoke to me about his religion and gave me a book of poetry. Now whenever I am sad, I remember "Dr Bahá'í", go to the back of my cafe and read a few of the poems. Then I become happy and my troubles vanish.' The book he referred to was the compilation of poems of Na'ím, the great Bahá'í poet.

The old gentleman then put pieces of newspaper on the bare table to serve as plates for us. The raw kebabs which lay prepared on their metal rods were covered with flies. He assured us, however that the flames of the coal fire would kill all germs. Raḥmat advised me not to eat any of the kebabs and not to give anything from the stall to Gisu. He ate a few morsels himself, thanked his friend and promised not to forget him.

Although there were clean and modern restaurants catering to Europeans, Raḥmat chose this dingy stall so that he could give the message of Bahá'u'lláh to at least one soul in Kabul. For him the essential thing was the pure-hearted man, not the cleanliness of the restaurant or the taste of the food. He said every time that this kind and noble man mentioned the word 'Bahá'í' he risked his life; everytime that he hid in the back of his stall and read the poems of Na'ím, he was in danger; nevertheless he did both. Raḥmat considered the stall keeper a true lover of Bahá'u'lláh. I have visited many places around the world but the image of that kebab house and the old turbaned man in his long 'abá, whispering to Raḥmat about the wonderful gift of a book of poetry remains most vividly in my memory.

TURKEY

As with so many other countries, Raḥmat's visits to Turkey were mostly unannounced. He would arrive there and then call the friends and ask them for a meeting. On one trip he arrived in Istanbul to find the friends had all gone to the Summer School at a nearby town, Yalova. He did not know where the Summer School was being held, and did not consider it prudent to ask its whereabouts from non-Bahá'ís: but, relying on Bahá'u'lláh, he went there. Late at night he reached Ankara and checked into a hotel so that the next day he could look for the friends. At dawn he heard prayers being chanted in Persian, and realized that the Summer School was being held in a house next door to the hotel! He joined the meeting of the friends without their knowledge. They told me later that they were all chanting prayers and suddenly heard the Tablet of Visitation of 'Abdu'l-Bahá being chanted by someone imitating Dr Muhájir's style. It was only at the end of the prayer session that they realized the voice indeed belonged to Dr Muhájir himself!

In 1973 we travelled to Turkey together. In consultation with Counsellor Doktoroghlu, a small plan was devised to initiate widespread teaching in Turkey. Many pioneers and some local Bahá'ís gathered to meet Raḥmat. During this trip we were able to make a pilgrimage to the House of Bahá'u'lláh ('Izzat Áqá) in Edirne. We travelled together with a group of pioneers in a rented van, and spent a beautiful day there. We were received by the custodians, Mr and Mrs Ghadimi, a devoted couple who prepared a delicious Persian meal for us. We said many prayers and Raḥmat chanted the Tablet of Visitation. Here we could feel the presence of the Holy family and were reminded of the hardships and sufferings of Bahá'u'lláh. It was a sad but glorious occasion.

The bridge between Turkey and Europe which was being built at that time was near completion. All the friends hoped that this new connection between two continents might be the beginning of a new era, which would give more freedom to the followers of the Faith of Bahá'u'lláh.

Raḥmat's last trip to Turkey was in October 1976. He spent about two weeks there and visited Istanbul, Izmir, Adana, Antakya, Gazi Antep, and Ankara. He had a close working relationship with the National Assembly and the Counsellors in Turkey. His diary contains his thoughts about the possibility of teaching the Alavis [Shí'í] of Turkey.

IRAN

Raḥmat's Persian heritage profoundly affected every aspect of his life and service to the Cause. No amount of detail could adequately illustrate his close and continuous relationship with the land of his birth, particularly with its Bahá'í institutions. He visited his homeland frequently, and was always cordially assisted in all his ventures by the National Spiritual Assembly of Iran. It is possible to offer only a glimpse of the lifelong work he carried out in the cradle of God's Faith.

Raḥmat's association with Iran's Bahá'í Administration started early in his youth. In 1947 he became a member of the Youth Committee, and was elected its Chairman. He was very conscientious in his duties, had a vast knowledge of the Writings, and demonstrated a strong and determined will. These personal characteristics were to stand him in good stead for the rest of his life.

During the two decades of his service as a Hand of the Cause, he maintained a strong and loving association with the National Spiritual Assembly, and frequently called on the assistance of the Bahá'ís of Iran in the advancement of the Faith in the rest of the world. In his letters to the Universal House of Justice and to the National Assembly of Iran he always praised the Iranian friends for their services to the Bahá'í world:

A relaxed Dr Muhájir with Hand of the Cause Furútan, surrounded by Bahá'í youth in Iran.

> The dear Iranian friends, since the inception of the Faith in the continent of Africa, have had a great share in the establishment of Bahá'í institutions and have been in the forefront of service in the entire world. They have adorned the pages of the Faith's history with their service, sacrifice and sincerity over the past twenty years.
>
> With the grace of God the present generation will also continue these great undertakings with their bodies and souls and will trod in the path paved by Ḥájí-Mírzá-Ḥaydar-'Alí and Jináb-i-Banání . . .
>
> Today is the day that the beloved pioneers from the Cradle of the Faith and other countries should rush to this continent to have a share in the creation of a new Africa . . . When Persian pioneers first went to Arabia it was not much more than an arid sand dune. The economy was limited and material comforts were scarce. The situation, however, changed rapidly. Because the Bahá'ís were already settled there, they were able to be closely involved with the economic development of the region and become, like the warp and the woof of a tapestry, an integral part of a new nation. They were able to firmly establish themselves and so gradually provide the means to facilitate the arrival of other pioneers.
>
> We have to go to the Iranian Conference in Europe with a positive spirit and exciting practical plans and many copies of the Writings, so that the continent of Europe which is bereft of spirituality and is immersed in endless sufferings and hopelessness on the one hand, and is receptive and eager on the other, could be awakened with the 'Most Mighty Bell'.

Raḥmat undertook many of his trips to Iran at the request of the Universal House of Justice :

> The Hand of the Cause of God Dr Muhájir who has just made propitious journeys throughout Africa . . . is now on his way to Iran. He has been requested to consult with that Assembly on various subjects, specifically sending of pioneers, and the ways they could be sent, especially those who can be helpful in the field of education.

> He is to counsel that Assembly and the various committees, especially the local Assembly of Ṭihrán. The speedy departure of pioneers from Iran, in accordance with the goals of the Five Year Plan, as pointed out several times before, is of utmost importance.
>
> The presence of the Hand of the Cause of God [Muhájir] in Iran is the best opportunity for that Assembly to accomplish this noble service in the best and quickest manner.

Raḥmat collaborated with the National Spiritual Assembly of Iran on the most cordial terms. He would sit with the Assembly for hours to find ways to meet the needs of various countries. Their letters in response to his requests were always in the affirmative: 'After consultations of this Assembly, at the Intercontinental Conference of New Delhi, we are hopeful of fulfilling all your requests for help according to the list you had given us.'

On two occasions, in 1967 and 1978, he travelled extensively throughout Iran, visiting many of the provinces to assist the National Assembly in their home front goals. As a friend said, 'He had time for everyone and everything. He never refused to meet the friends because he was tired or busy. Everyone who went to see him had a problem, but when they left him they were happy and their burden greatly lessened.'

While he was travelling in the provinces of Á<u>dh</u>irbáyján in 1967, a huge landslide occurred. We in the Philippines heard the news on television. Hundreds had perished and many cars had been buried under the mud. It was a few anxious days before we could contact Iran and ask about Raḥmat's well-being. He had passed the road the day before the landslide and was safe in Ṭihrán.

After this trip he wrote a 13-page letter to the Universal House of Justice. He elaborated his ideas on the purchase of properties which had any connection with the Central Figures of the Faith, and listed suggestions on preparing the youth of Iran for pioneering to other countries. Raḥmat wrote this letter while in Malaysia, but in the end did not feel it necessary to send it to the Universal House of Justice. Although he never kept letters, he did preserve this one.

Friends remember the simple and straightforward manner in which he undertook these trips. On his visit to the province of

Mázindarán, Raḥmat was driven around by local Bahá'ís. In Bábúl he spent the night at the house of Quddús in prayer and meditation. His food consisted of bread and cheese, bought at the local market. Most of the time that was all he ate. He met with the friends in Bábúl, and other cities and towns of Mázindarán, and was then taken to Ṭihrán. There was a gathering of representatives of the National Assembly and national committees, which he had to attend.

He went to Khurásán to advise the Spiritual Assembly of Mashhad, which was responsible for the whole province, about the teaching work in that city and the goals in various parts of their province. He expressed a strong wish to spend the night alone in the Bábíyyih.*

Despite their fears for his safety, the Spiritual Assembly agreed with his wish. Certain precautions were taken and Raḥmat stayed there by himself. The next day the Assembly met him there and found him still in prayer.

He was told that the Spiritual Assembly was doing extensive repairs to the Bábíyyih. He reacted with surprise: 'Why are you doing this work now? How do you know that this building will not be attacked and demolished by the enemies of the Faith? Don't you think that now is the time to teach? Repairs will be done by the future generation in a much better way. It is our assignment to teach for the future generation!' The Spiritual Assembly was baffled by his words. It had expected praise for the meritorious service it was rendering, rather than a rebuke. They went ahead with the repairs. A few years later the Bábíyyih was confiscated and demolished during the upheavals against the Faith.

In one meeting, after speaking to the youth with some enthusiasm, he was worried about them as they did not seem very happy. He was told the reason for their sadness was that they felt as if they were shackled in chains. The local Spiritual Assembly had cautioned the youth to be prudent and careful, and did not allow them to vent their enthusiasm and zeal for teaching. Raḥmat advised the

---

* The house built by Mullá Ḥusayn, in which Quddús received many new believers into the Bábí Faith. See *The Dawn-Breakers*, pp. 189-90.

Assembly to send the youth pioneering to other countries. The Faith was free in other countries and the youth of Iran could be of great help in teaching and in winning the goals.

At this time the Bahá'í children had started a campaign to give the message of Bahá'u'lláh to their school friends, gradually and tactfully. This had brought a new spirit to the Bahá'í community of Mashhad. Raḥmat was delighted with the children's activities and said that he had sent a cable to the organizers of the Paris Conference suggesting that they include a special programme on the importance of Bahá'í children and their contribution to teaching the Faith.

While he was helping the local Assembly with home front goals, he did not forget international commitments. He would encourage all those who expressed their wish to pioneer to go to goals in foreign countries. On one occasion a friend asked to drive him to Níshápúr. They were just setting out, when Raḥmat found out that this person spoke French and was willing to pioneer to one of the French-speaking African countries. Raḥmat asked the driver to stop the car and told him, 'My dear, there is no need for you to go with me to Níshápúr. It was very kind of you to offer and I thank you. But it is much better if you go home and start preparing to leave for Africa immediately.' The gentleman left the car to go home. After a short time he pioneered to Africa.

In this trip Raḥmat visited Níshápúr, Ghuchán, Bujnúrd, Gurgán, Sabzevar and Gunbad-e-Kavus. Despite the difficulties and the opposition from the lcoal populace, the friends in each community gathered in crowds to meet and listen to him. In each community he spoke according to the needs of that place. In Bujnúrd there was a rose on the table. He spoke about the beauty and freshness of that rose and compared it to the teachings of Bahá'u'lláh. Just as the rose made everyone feel happy and fresh, so did Bahá'u'lláh's teachings.

Raḥmat was very uncomfortable when chairmen of meetings praised him or his services to the Faith, or spoke about the station of the Hands of the Cause. He said that although the beloved Guardian had appointed a few of the servants of Bahá'u'lláh as Hands of the Cause to render special services, 'Abdu'l-Bahá had explained that 'The Hands of the Cause are the Hands of God.

Hence whosoever is the servant and the promoter of the Word of God, he is the Hand of God. The object is the spirit and not the letters or words. The more self-effacing one is, the more he is assisted in the Cause of God; and the more meek and humble, the nearer is he to God.'[8]

During these trips, Raḥmat would talk about the situation of the Faith in each town and village through which he passed. He took short naps in the car, his only rest of the day. He would ask the driver to stop by a shop and would buy some bread and cheese and sometimes grapes, and would ask all to share in this simple meal. Once when his companions wanted to stop so that they could wash the grapes, he said 'Don't bother. We will eat them just like this. Don't worry. Nothing will happen.' One of the friends once told him, 'Dr Muhájir, you are a very easy Hand of the Cause to travel with.' He laughed and said that all the Hands were the same.

Once he was asked whether he was going to write his biography. He shrugged his shoulders and said, 'The story of my life is not important. What is significant are the events of the Faith and the stories of what the friends have achieved to help its progress.'

Although Raḥmat was always on the move, he didn't neglect his study of the Writings and history of the Bahá'í Faith, and those of other religions. He always carried books and notes with him in his briefcase. The knowledge he gained in this manner helped him develop his pioneering ideas for Iran's Bahá'ís. Dr Iraj Ayman recalls how Raḥmat's deep knowledge and concern about the education of children in the developing countries led him to suggest using Iranian Bahá'í educators in 21 African countries. This was incorporated in the Five Year Plan. To implement this programme, a special International Education Fund was created in Iran, for the assistance of education plans in developing countries. Its capital remained as a trust fund under the jurisdiction of the Universal House of Justice. At the same time the Universal House of Justice appointed an International Education Committee in Iran to work under the auspices of Hand of the Cause of God Dr Varqa.

A publication which particularly attracted Raḥmat's interest was *Study Abroad*, issued annually by the United Nations. He read it from cover to cover, and sat for hours with Bahá'í youth in Iran, advising them on obtaining grants, and on countries and universities to which they could apply. Opportunities for enrolment in Iranian universities were very limited. Dr Ayman, who was involved in the implementation of these projects, believes that, with Raḥmat's help and guidance, some 1000 young Bahá'ís left Iran to study abroad. He opened new horizons to a whole generation of youth, which led them to many countries engaged in mass teaching. Many other Persian students followed the example of their Bahá'í friends, and took advantage of this facility to study overseas. A considerable number went to countries such as the Philippines and India, which Raḥmat had singled out for pioneering purposes!

When Raḥmat met with the National Assembly of Iran he shared his vast knowledge about the teaching work in Africa, Latin America, Asia and other parts of the world, and asked the Assembly to encourage the youth to pioneer to those places. Invariably he succeeded in persuading them to go in large numbers. He believed that although Bahá'ís were few in number and had limited means, they could reach their spiritual goals provided they did not waste time, and they used all their energy and resources to the best advantage. As always, Raḥmat referred to the instructions of the Guardian:

> 1. Every individual who has offered to pioneer, must be encouraged in every way by the National Assembly.
>
> 2. The National Assembly should assist each pioneer, so they may be placed in their post just as quickly as possible.
>
> 3. The handling of each application for pioneering service, must be expedited, and not allowed to be bogged down for any reason, or in the hands of Committees.[9]

Raḥmat stressed that the purpose of the Administration was to facilitate the progress of the Faith. When it did not do so, he would take it on himself to accomplish the task. He took any criticism for such action willingly, but would not abandon what he saw as his spiritual responsibility. At a meeting of the Pioneering Committee, he was told that they were going to reject the application of one of the pioneers. This man had completed the committee's questionnaire, which indicated that he was not a suitable candidate for pioneering. He did not have sufficient funds and was not a college graduate. He had no specific skills and could not speak any foreign language, nor was he much versed in Bahá'í literature. His only asset was his burning desire to pioneer. Raḥmat had always abhorred the use of questionnaires to select pioneers. He believed the committees should spend time talking to the prospective pioneers. This young man reminded him of himself, and his own rejection by the pioneering committee many years before. He tried to change the mind of the committee, but with all due respect to a Hand of the Cause, they felt that they were right. Raḥmat finally asked them, 'What is the most difficult pioneering post you have which no one will accept?' They named a place. The young man was called in, and immediately agreed to go there. He is still serving with distinction at his post.

Raḥmat's personal credo for pioneering was taken from the Guardian's instruction that,

> All must participate [in pioneering], however humble their origin, however limited their experience, however restricted their means, however deficient their education, however pressing their cares and preoccupations, however unfavourable the environment in which they live . . .
>
> How often . . . have the lowliest adherents of the Faith, unschooled and utterly inexperienced, and with no standing whatever, and in some cases devoid of intelligence, been capable of winning victories for their Cause, before which the most brilliant achievements of the learned, the wise, and the experienced have paled.[10]

As a friend records,

> Dr Muhájir was the essence of humility and power, of calm and action. He had the uncanny ability to use an individual in just the right way. A devoted Bahá'í who may have become a stumbling block in his own community, would often become a tower of strength in another community, sometimes in another country, by responding to Dr Muhájir's loving encouragement to render a unique service.

Dr Cyrus 'Alá'í, a member of the National Assembly of Iran, recollects that, as a result of Raḥmat's visit, many of those who were assigned to home front pioneer goals changed their minds and left for international posts. This caused consternation for the Home Front Goals Committee, which voiced its concerns directly to Raḥmat. He smiled serenely and said, 'Every time you send a pioneer abroad he can bring hundreds of people under the banner of the Faith. The result of their activities in Iran is negligible. The priority is pioneering to Africa, to India, to South East Asia, and to South America.' This did not make the Home Front Goals Committee any happier, but events were to prove him right.

The International Goals Committee had to face its own dilemma each time Raḥmat went to Ṭihrán. He always wanted three times the number of teachers and pioneers that the committee had planned. He asked them to meet every single day so that they could clear the backlog of interviews and applications. One of the members relates, 'Not only did we have lucrative jobs that we were loathe to leave in order to meet every day, but our wives were also unhappy with what he proposed.' So a compromise was reached, and for the duration of Raḥmat's stay a sub-committee met, rotating members so that all would not have to be there every day. Raḥmat attended all their meetings and personally talked to all prospective pioneers.

Despite their pleas that they could not produce the number of pioneers he was asking for, Raḥmat continued to write to the Pioneering Committee, asking for increased effort to encourage pioneering from Iran:

> Regarding teaching and pioneering needs in the next three years, ten thousand new Bahá'í localities should be added in Africa. To establish these 10,000 centres at least 200,000 adult Bahá'ís are needed. If all the friends arise for this service, it is certain that not only the Bahá'í community but the whole of humanity will benefit. We will have a great victory which will influence the future of mankind for generations to come.
>
> The beloved pioneers need pure intention and great sacrifice to rise to this momentous task. They have to follow the footsteps of Christ, and the saints, and the Knights of Bahá'u'lláh.

Raḥmat was travelling in Africa in 1978 when his mother became ill in Ṭihrán. It took me a few days to locate him and convey the message sent by his family. He left immediately for Iran, bypassing London and home, to arrive in Ṭihrán as soon as possible. His mother, Iṣmat Khánum, was in a coma and did not recognize him. Raḥmat sat by her bed every day for many hours, chanting prayers and reading the Writings aloud.

He stayed in Iran for two months and met with the National Spiritual Assembly, the Counsellors and the Pioneering Committee repeatedly to consult on international pioneering and teaching goals. He talked to the Spiritual Assembly of Ṭihrán, and asked for a special meeting to find 90 pioneers to leave Iran before Naw-Rúz. Selected Bahá'ís were invited by telephone. Raḥmat spoke about the importance of pioneering and the dangers of ignoring the Guardian's warnings that the friends should disperse and leave Ṭihrán.

From that day onwards he sat in a room in the Garden of Tejeh, the meeting place of the Bahá'ís of Ṭihrán, and met with all those who had volunteered to pioneer. He consulted with every one. He seldom accepted offers of hospitality from the friends, and on the rare occasions that he did go to dinner, he was always exhausted and left early.

He spoke at every opportunity about the futility of striving for material gain, and often quoted the beloved Guardian's message to the Bahá'ís of America as applying equally to the friends in Iran:

> It is therefore imperative for the individual . . . believer, and particularly for the affluent, the independent, the comfort-loving, and those obsessed by material pursuits, to step forward, and dedicate their resources, their time, their very lives to a Cause of such transcendence that no human eye can even dimly perceive its glory.[11]

This was at the height of the Iranian industrial revolution, a period of rapid economic growth, and many people, Bahá'ís included, were practically reaping money. Only a few families took Raḥmat's pleading to heart.

This was his last visit to his native land. He stayed on until his mother passed to the Abhá Kingdom, remaining for her funeral and memorial meetings before leaving for London. The Universal House of Justice, in their letter of 5 March 1978, wrote to him:

> Your letter which contained wonderful spiritual glad tidings gave the hearts of these suppliant souls great joy. Thank God that, through the bounty of your presence, a group of dedicated and spiritual youth have arisen to go to Japan. We hope that you will continue these meritorious and praiseworthy efforts and meet with the National Assembly and its committees to guide and encourage them to fulfil their pioneering obligations as soon as possible, even in the next few weeks . . . We assure you of our ardent prayers on behalf of your esteemed mother. We also beseech confirmations for the efforts of that warrior of the field of faithfulness.

SOUTH-EAST ASIA

BURMA

The gentle, dedicated and steadfast Bahá'ís of Burma were a source of inspiration to Raḥmat. Each time he went there, he visited the Bahá'í village of Daidahnaw, known as 'the village of 'Abdu'l-Bahá', where the sarcophagus of the Báb had been carved, and from where it had been sent to the Holy Land. Raḥmat said that he went to Burma to gain spirituality from the friends there.

The only available records of his travels in Burma relate to his first and last trips. In 1958, the *Indian Bahá'í Newsletter* reported:

> Dr Muhájir visited in a state of great veneration the tomb of the late revered Hand of the Cause of God, Jinab-e-Seyed Mustapha Rumi [sic] and spent the night at the Ḥaẓíratu'l-Quds of Daidahnaw addressing the Bahá'í friends on the importance of pioneering to distant virgin places and admonishing them to serve the Cause with greater resourcefulness and loyalty.

Raḥmat's diary contains the following notes of his last trip to Burma in 1978:

> *10 August*: I consulted with the National Assembly and we arranged a good teaching programme. Eleven teaching teams

With the Bahá'í youth of Mandalay, Burma.

With Deepening Committee at National Ḥaẓíratu'l-Quds, Rangoon, 7 March 1973.

were formed all of which will participate. If the Auxiliary Board members and their assistants and the women begin to work they will be very successful.

11 August: I am writing these notes in North Burma. This is the place that U Soe Tin, the Auxiliary Board member lives. The son of Siyyid 'Abdu'l-Ḥusayn Shírází and another teacher are pioneers here. We had a good meeting last night. There were a few educated youth, women, and also a medical doctor. They all have pure souls and with the bounties of God they will become Bahá'ís. There is a slum area near the town. We must teach there. This town is in the heart of the tribes. We can teach many of the tribal people.

12 August: I came by plane to Mandalay. The whole day from eleven in the morning to five in the afternoon people came to see me. We had continuous consultation. They were all happy and ready to go on teaching trips. This work should be pursued.

In the evening we had a large meeting with the Bahá'ís of Mandalay. Perhaps there were more than 100 present. There were many seekers, mostly educated and young. I spoke about the teachings of Bahá'u'lláh. They all agreed with what I said. After my talk we divided the meeting among the Bahá'í youth and they spent many hours with the guests.

13 August: I stayed in Mandalay for one night and left for Rangoon. Today is my beloved Gisu's birthday. I miss her very much.

LAOS

Raḥmat first visited Laos as early as 1958, when only Dr Ta'eed and his family were there, struggling to establish the Faith. In later years he visited repeatedly, sent pioneers, undertook teaching trips in the interior, and involved himself in all aspects of the various plans. Sometimes he had to tolerate the disapproval of some believers in a neighbouring country who considered themselves in charge of Bahá'í affairs in Laos, and felt that their authority was being usurped. Raḥmat, as was his custom, continued his efforts and avoided confrontation. He told me that it was good that the friends should feel so strongly about serving the Faith; perhaps this would make them actually go to Laos and serve there.

The Ta'eed family had to leave in 1961, and it was apparent that Laos was in dire need of pioneers. However, it was not well-known in Iran and not attractive to prospective pioneers: Raḥmat could not find people to settle there.

It was in 1963 that a young man crossed Raḥmat's path in Thailand, and was persuaded to go to Laos. Firaydún Missaghian went to Ban Ham Ton, a remote village, where he was later joined by Bijan and Manijeh Bayzai. These two had been asked by Raḥmat to go to Laos from Thailand and the Philippines respectively. In later years Raḥmat arranged for a few young Filipinos to pioneer to Laos, and Faiz Yeganegi, at his behest, arrived from India.

Ban Ham Ton was home to the Mong people in the region of Sayabury, in the northern province of Laos. The village was about eight hours from the town of Sayabury. One of the few pleasures that the young pioneers enjoyed was to walk into town and relax in a small coffee shop. Although there was no electricity, cinema, entertainment or social facilities, to the pioneers this was a taste of home. Sitting in these familiar surroundings, they could feel at ease, read their mail and talk with people. On one of these occasions the pioneers received a letter from Raḥmat, containing $200 in travellers' cheques. The letter said he was very happy to hear of the progress of the Faith in Sayabury province, and that now it was time for the formation of local Spiritual Assemblies so that, God willing, next year Laos could be ready to form its National Assembly.

This came as a shock to the pioneers. All the native Bahá'ís were from tribal areas, and had little or no knowledge of Bahá'í administration. The pioneers were not well-versed in Laotian dialects; those who knew the language did not know how to teach the new believers the fundamentals of running a local Spiritual Assembly.

In a letter to Raḥmat, Firaydún expressed the thanks of the pioneers for the travellers' cheques, as they were down to their last penny, but voiced their astonishment about Raḥmat's suggestion to form Assemblies. The pioneers firmly believed that it was impossible to establish local Spiritual Assemblies that year, or a National Spiritual Assembly within the next five years. They did, however, pledge to continue teaching, and informed him of the enrolment of 200 new believers and the opening of additional villages.

Raḥmat's response was to come to Laos himself. In the long and detailed consultations he held with the pioneers it was resolved that a National Teaching Committee be appointed to manage the affairs of the Faith until they could have their National Spiritual Assembly. Formation of the National Assembly was a goal of the Nine Year Plan, and the friends felt that they had time enough to fulfil it. As Firaydún says, they had not reckoned with Dr Muhájir! The Universal House of Justice approved the formation of the National Teaching Committee and it came directly under the supervision of the Supreme Body.

Bijan Bayzai recalls Raḥmat's 1965 visit as being particularly significant. Raḥmat was determined that the National Assembly be formed by the pioneers conquering new frontiers, rather than continuing with a small number of believers scattered around a few towns. He spent four days in Laos, revitalizing the pioneers, helping them understand the significance of mass teaching, the long-term importance of teaching the tribes, and the value of the education of their children.

I remember Raḥmat proposing a plan for Firaydún to travel around Laos and teach. Firaydún was reluctant to leave his job as an electrician with USAID. He had pioneered at an early age and had not finished his college studies, so relied heavily on his natural skills. After some discussion Raḥmat askd him, 'What are you reluctant to leave behind? Your screwdriver? You can take that with you wherever you go.' The matter was decided. Firaydún remembers,

> He himself sent a cable to the World Centre and requested a sum of $50 a month from the International Deputization Fund for me and he put me on the road. I was fully engaged in travel teaching for several years. Once or twice a year when the farmers were busy with their plantation, I would go back to work for a month or two. This gave me a chance to reinforce the strength of the communities in the cities. Besides being a good source of

> income, this became a way of relaxation for me. Dr Muhájir and the Bahá'í administrative bodies knew about it and approved. Although I had asked them not to send me funds for those months, they continued to arrive and so gave me the chance to contribute some of it to the Fund. In this manner I never felt needy during my pioneering years. Leaving my job for several years not only did not make me poor, it spiritually enriched me and had a tremendously positive impact on my life.

In 1965 Raḥmat decided to appoint an Auxiliary Board member for Laos. He consulted with the pioneers and asked who they would recommend for this position. He felt the most important consideration for the progress of the Faith was the unity of the pioneers, and did not want the appointment of a Board member to disrupt the harmony that existed among them. Bijan and Firaydún each recommended the other. Firaydún recalls,

> One morning I went to [Dr Muhájir's] room very early. He opened the door smilingly and let me in. He had been praying and asked me to say a few prayers from his prayer book. It was wrapped in an olive-coloured silk cover. After our prayers he handed the book to me and said, 'This is for you.'
>
> He was explaining the duties of the Auxiliary Board members when he suddenly stopped and said, 'Let's go for breakfast.' We went to a small Chinese coffee shop. He again said, 'Who do you think is good for this position? Bijan, Manijeh, or you?' I thought for a few minutes and said, 'Bijan, of course'. He asked me what my reasons were. I told him that Bijan was thoughtful and more knowledgable, and was not impulsive like me. He asked, 'How is your relationship with him?'I replied that we had a perfect relationship. 'That is good', he said. We then went to see the Bahá'í endowment land. He rode with me on my motor cycle and reminded me to ride carefully or I would be hit on the head. I tried my best.
>
> A month later we received a cable from him appointing Bijan an Auxiliary Board member.

Bijan was responsible for Laos, Thailand and Cambodia. He was often asked by Raḥmat to travel in the interior of Laos and to other

Thahkek village, Laos; with Yan Kee Leong and Giselle, 1967.

With Yan Kee Leong, Firaydún Missaghian and Giselle, 1967.

countries for teaching the masses. Raḥmat asked other Board members in the region to go to Laos and stay for some weeks to help in teaching and strengthening the new believers. Dr Sorraya was sent from Indonesia, and Orpha Daugherty from the Philippines.

The most influential person to help the mass teaching work was Yan Kee Leong, an Auxiliary Board member from Malaysia. Yan Kee was an experienced mass teacher, and his loving and mild manner attracted one and all to him. He initially went for three weeks, but, at Raḥmat's request, stayed for six months.

The war-torn Laotian populace, deprived of spiritual bounties for almost four years, was very receptive and the friends had begun to give systematic and vigilant help for the spiritual and educational needs of the people of Laos. The roots of the Faith of God were growing stronger within the hearts of the native inhabitants, which in turn enabled the Bahá'í Administration to develop, thus helping the friends there achieve the status of a genuinely 'national' community.

When, in 1966, Raḥmat returned to Laos, ten months after his previous visit, the results of the teaching work were astonishing. Bijan writes,

> Dr Muhájir, whom we had known earlier as a most informal, down-to-earth, yet very powerful figure who had changed our entire outlook, was now concerned with every detail of the development of the Cause in Laos, whether the steady and uninterrupted expansion of the Faith, or deepening and consolidation; he was also very sensitive about having correct publicity to promote the Faith. In short, he looked like a man whose business it was to help create the National Bahá'í community of Laos.
>
> His stay was short, three days, during which he met with the National Teaching Committee, which was the embryo of the first National Spiritual Assembly. He made sure that the development of the Cause was leading towards a successful National Convention, and he also ensured that the remaining steps towards the formation of the National Assembly were firmly and wisely taken.

On this trip Raḥmat did not neglect his travels to the remote areas. His main love was teaching, and he wanted to experience it himself as often as possible. Firaydún, who was in Thakhek, 300 kilometres South of Vientiane, comments,

> The only way to reach it was by a dusty dirt road, built by the French in the early 1900s. What made it important was its location. It was in the middle of several hundred villages, close to the border of Thailand, along the shores of the Mekong river. Its single road connected it with the rest of Laos, and went on to the South China Sea through Vietnam.

Firaydún had been assigned to this town by the National Teaching Committee, and his efforts had brought thousands to the Faith of Bahá'u'lláh. Raḥmat, accompanied by a few of the pioneers, travelled for eight hours in an open truck with only wooden planks for seats, arriving on a dry hot afternoon. Everyone was covered in a thick layer of red dust. Raḥmat stayed for two nights to meet the Bahá'ís. He told them stories to encourage them in their work and said that at Riḍván 1967 the National Spiritual Assembly of Laos would be elected. Firaydún relates how,

> We said we were worried as our believers were not deepened enough and it seemed too early to have a National Assembly. He assured us that our National Assembly would be one of the best in the Bahá'í world. He mentioned that the Universal House of Justice had not planned to form our National Assembly so early. However, as we had grown considerably, both in size and in the number of our activities, the Supreme Body had decided that we were ready.

Accompanied by Firaydún, Raḥmat left on a pick-up truck across the river to Thailand, where he was to catch a bus to Bangkok. All they had to eat were a few pieces of barbecued chicken which Firaydún had bought at a roadside stall. As he was leaving their country, Raḥmat told the Bahá'ís that he would take the red dust of Laos, which had penetrated his clothes and suitcase, to the Holy Land, and that he would pray for the success of their teaching work.

In one of the early entries in his diary, Raḥmat noted that he wished that an increasing number of teachers and Hands of the Cause would visit those areas to help the pioneers and deepen the friends. He knew the value of these travels, and often tried to convince his fellow Hands to undertake such journeys. Some accepted, and great results were achieved. In December 1966, Hand of the Cause Mr Samandarí visited Laos at Raḥmat's invitation. He was elated with the spirit of the friends and considered his week there as one of his happiest times. Mr Samandarí's presence, his stirring tales about Bahá'u'lláh, and his kindness and love for the Laotian Bahá'ís revived the spirit of dedication and sacrifice in the friends.

At the end of his travels in South-East Asia, Mr Samandarí wrote a brief note to Raḥmat:

> O essence of allegiance and spirituality, devoted Hand of the Cause of Bahá'u'lláh. May my life, my soul and my existence be sacrificed for you. Right now we are leaving and I am extremely tired. Forgive me. Your letter reached me in Colombo and gave me a new spirit. I am extremely happy to hear about your travels. I am grateful for all your help and attention.

Two months before the National Convention, Raḥmat returned to Laos as the representative of the Universal House of Justice for the election of the first National Assembly. He worked with the National Teaching Committee and the pioneers to iron out the last details of the Convention. Firaydún recalls,

> Dr Muhájir helped us draw up a simple plan for wide expansion of the Faith. Volunteers were called for, and many delegates arose to teach. When the Convention was over he met the newly-elected National Assembly and suggested that we gradually adopt a number of full-time Bahá'í teachers to teach and consolidate the new communities. He told me to leave my job at USAID, which I had just started again. [Bijan] Bayzai also was told to leave his job at the Book Centre. Bijan and Manijeh were now married, and had a small son. However, we all accepted Dr Muhájir's advice. Our Plan had been given by the Universal House of Justice and had to be fulfilled, despite our weaknesses.

First National Convention, Laos, 1967.

First National Spiritual Assembly of Laos, 1967.

> In the evening we saw him at his hotel. He spoke about mass teaching, how it had happened in Africa, in the Pacific, in Indonesia and in Sarawak. He said that now it must happen in Laos. He gave me a book about the development of the lifestyle and economy of hundreds of villages along the Mekong River on both sides of Laos and Thailand. He asked me to read it and hoped that one day we could buy a boat to conquer the Mekong.
>
> His words went deep into our hearts and became the prime motivation for our teaching of the masses. It was due to his persuasion, and his continuous visits and support that by the end of 1972 we had about ten thousand believers in Laos, four per cent of the total population. It was, at that time, the country with the highest percentage of believers.

It was very easy for Raḥmat to persuade those whom he felt to be great mass teachers to give up their jobs and devote their time to enrolling new souls. He had no qualms about it, as he had done it himself. I once talked to him specifically about Firaydún. I told him that Firaydún wanted to get married sometime, but no girl would marry him if he had no means of livelihood and lived the life of a gypsy. This, of course, had no effect on Raḥmat. He said,

> I went to school for 25 years. I am a physician and gave it up. I am married and I have a child. I am sure Firaydún won't miss anything by not fixing light bulbs at the American base. Look what he can do for the Faith! When the time comes he is resilient enough to find another job. He will convince someone that he is an excellent engineer.

Within a few years, Firaydún, after bringing thousands under the banner of the Faith in Laos, India, Thailand and other countries, married a beautiful young girl in Iran, and gained a degree in engineering by correspondence while working in a lucrative job in Laos maintaining aeroplane engines at the American air base. Raḥmat always joked with Firaydún about his job, and told him how grateful he was to God that Firaydún was not working on the planes on which we travelled. Once, going to New Delhi from Manila, our plane developed engine trouble and we had to return to

Saigon. Raḥmat reassured us and said, 'Don't worry, this is Saigon, not Vientiane. Firaydún has nothing to do with fixing this engine, we'll be safe!'

Raḥmat returned to Laos in autumn 1967 and called together the pioneers and teachers in Vientiane to consult about the teaching work, within Laos and countries nearby. He asked some of the pioneers to participate in the Intercontinental Teaching Conference in New Delhi. Their help resulted in the enrolment of the first Bahá'ís of Tibet.

The National Assembly of Laos functioned in a mature and united manner, as Raḥmat knew it would. But this newly-established community was not without its share of problems. In 1968 the National Assembly had to be re-elected because of an irregularity in procedure. On the instruction of the Universal House of Justice, Raḥmat went there and stayed for two weeks. It was a very difficult time for him. He told me that he could not bear to see disunity among these people who had, with so much dedication and joy, worked so hard to achieve so much. His presence there, however, defused the situation. The National Spiritual Assembly was re-elected according to the proper procedure, with the approval of the Universal House of Justice.

In spring 1969 Raḥmat helped the friends in Laos draw up a plan to translate and publish Bahá'í literature. While they wanted to print only 1000 copies of each publication, he urged them to print no less than 10,000. He helped the friends in planning for a proper National Office and in purchasing its equipment. Teaching plans were made and conferences organized.

It was a few years before Raḥmat could go to Laos again. In 1973 he visited the refugee camps in Vientiane. Mass teaching had reached its peak, but then had stopped. Travelling teachers had become engrossed in collecting statistics, and others were trying to find ways of deepening new believers. Raḥmat's goal was to re-activate mass ṭeaching in Laos. He was convinced that, since Laos had 100,000 Bahá'ís, they could certainly reach several hundred thousand more. He believed that time was short and opportunities would be lost. The only entry in Raḥmat's diaries for any of his visits to Laos was made on 15 February 1973:

In the village of Bon Nom Pod, Laos, 100 miles North of Vientiane, February 1973. All the villagers had just become Bahá'ís.

12 February: I got visas for Laos and Burma, and left for Vientiane. I rested the next day, and this morning, went to some villages. Maybe tonight I can meet the National Assembly.

There is great receptivity among the refugees, but they need systematic teaching. The bounties of Bahá'u'lláh will open all doors. These refugees are kind, intelligent and clean people. The chief of the village is a full-time Bahá'í teacher. He said that they'd gone to several villages, about 3000 families are now Bahá'ís — 21,000 altogether, 4000 of whom have attended meetings. It reminded me of Mentawai.

Tonight we had a meeting with the friends and they decided to teach at least 200 villages in the next year, specially among the refugees. They said that 90 per cent of the refugees accept the Faith immediately, and only 10 per cent want to read and spend

> some time before accepting. There is a great readiness for the Faith. In one year 20,000 have enrolled. There are about 800,000 refugees here. Some will remain, but the majority will return to their homes. Most of them are literate.

This was Raḥmat's last trip to Laos. The political situation did not allow him to visit the friends and the country whose Bahá'í community he had helped to shape. His sadness about the stagnation of mass teaching is quite apparent from his unusually restrained notes.

> On the way and in all gatherings I talked about the importance of teaching and about the plans of South America and Colombia; they seemed to like it. It is in God's hands. TODAY THEY SIGNED THE CEASE-FIRE TREATY IN LAOS.

Although mass teaching did begin again, it did not go far. One by one, the pioneers were forced to leave. Faiz Yeganegi and Pol Antipolo, the Filipino pioneer, were the only ones able to remain there. Faiz, through his good relations with the authorities, has been able to continue teaching and deepening the Bahá'ís. The Bahá'í school has a large number of non-Bahá'í pupils, many of whom are children of Laotian officials.

A large number of Laotian Bahá'ís are among the refugees in Thailand and the United States. Bijan Bayzai, who now lives in Chicago, is in constant contact with the Laotian friends who come to the meetings and participate in Bahá'í activities. Naser and Maliheh J'afari, pioneers in Thailand, report that many Laotian Bahá'ís are in Chiang Mai and are deepened in the Faith.

MALAYSIA

Had Raḥmat been asked to name a community which he considered a jewel amongst all others, he would certainly have named Malaysia. He frequently spoke of the Malaysian Bahá'ís and praised their unity, their absolute devotion to the Faith, their unwavering obedience to the instructions of the Universal House of Justice, their presence of mind and their understanding of the urgency of teaching and of fulfilling the goals. He said that the potential of their community was so great that they could accomplish a hundred times more than they were then achieving. When he travelled to Malaysia he went eagerly; he said that he could rest there, as he could not tell the friends anything that they did not already know.

His high regard for the friends in Malaysia encouraged him to undertake more with them than with any other community. He was never surprised with their victories. The more that was asked of them the more they achieved. He once told me that the Malaysian community was like a child who is always awarded A+ at school. After a time the parents expect this result, and it becomes routine, whereas they have to pay more attention to the child with a D average. Raḥmat was always proud of the Malaysian community and mentioned and praised them wherever he went.

His first association with the Bahá'ís of Malaysia was in 1961, while we were still in Indonesia. He met Malaysian Bahá'ís during the South-East Asian Conferences and on the occasional trips that we made to Singapore. The first mention in his diary of the Malaysian community appears in the entry for 13 February 1961. On that date he wrote one sentence: 'Malaya has a well developed community capable of managing all teaching campaigns.' He was in Malacca to attend a Teaching Conference and noted:

> The two days of the conference proceeded with great love and unity. On the 12th we went to Alor Gaja to inaugurate their Ḥaẓíratu'l-Quds. A group from Seremban, Penang and Kuala Lumpur were also there. It is a simple and attractive Bahá'í Centre, located in a beautiful spot overlooking a valley. God willing, it will become the focus of all their teaching activities. The same night we visited Mesjid Tanah to invite the friends to gather the next day. A few of them were eagerly and lovingly waiting for us. I will go to see all of them this afternoon.
>
> This morning the youth came to see me. They are wonderful. One had come to say goodbye as he was leaving for Australia; one wants to pioneer to Guam. I hope Bahá'u'lláh will assist them all to be steadfast and serve the Faith.
>
> I long to visit all the villages and towns, to meet the friends and give them the glad tidings that the spiritual springtime has come and that it is time to teach all over the world.

The Faith spread to the rest of Malaysia chiefly from Malacca. Raḥmat encouraged the Bahá'ís to approach the Aslis, the indigenous people of Malaysia. He guided them to go to the 'Estates' — rubber plantations — where they attained the largest single concentration of new believers. Counsellor Shanta Sundram paid tribute to the inspirational role which Raḥmat had played in all these campaigns: 'He pushed them over the southern border and into Singapore, and over the northern border into Thailand, over the mountains into the East Coast region and over the sea into the Malaysian longhouses of Sarawak and Brunei.'

After this initial visit Raḥmat spent a few days in Indonesia and returned to Malaysia . His diary records:

> On 23 February 1961 I arrived in Singapore. This is a special day in my spiritual life. This is the anniversary of our arrival in Mentawai, and of the day that we left Indonesia after seven years, in 1960. Now I am free to travel and I hope Bahá'u'lláh, in His compassion, may enable me to travel continuously until 1963 and the end of the Ten Year Crusade. I do not want to rest, even for a second. I hope this tired and broken body will be able to bear it.
>
> *29 February*: I am once again in Malacca, to travel in Malaysia for four days. I was supposed to go to Brunei today but the air ticket costs $200 Malayan. This is too much to spend for only one night, so I changed my plans. I had just arrived here when they gave me the wonderful news that teaching in the villages had begun, and that in one of them there are 25 new Bahá'ís. In Alor Setar, where dear Theresa lives, eight people have declared their Faith in Bahá'u'lláh. Two youth from Seremban have gone to the villages to teach. This is just the first of the good news. This is just the beginning.

When Raḥmat went to Malaysia for the first time, Yan Kee Leong accompanied him to Seremban, Malacca, and Kuala Lumpur. He became a close and trusted colleague, and worked with Raḥmat for two decades, for much of that time as his Auxiliary Board member. Yan Kee was much older than Raḥmat, and thought of him as a son.

Just a few months before he passed to the Abhá Kingdom, Yan Kee (who was appointed a Counsellor) wrote to me about those wonderful days when all the Bahá'ís in Malaysia were ablaze with the desire to teach the masses. He particularly recalled visiting the Aslis, at Raḥmat's request:

> I went to a place called Sangai Mangkuang, and two natives accepted the Faith, who later became travel teachers. Then the whole village accepted the Faith, adults and children; they totalled 80. A school was organized for the children of the village and the teacher was supported by the Regional Teaching Committee.
>
> Every morning Dr Muhájir prayed alone for at least an hour. I remember one day we went teaching in the East Coast of Malaya, he came back very exhausted. He started to wash his shirt but was so tired that he left it half done and went to sleep. I finished the washing for him.

In the early days, when Raḥmat informed the Malaysian National Assembly about the need for Chinese-speaking pioneers and teachers in Hong Kong and Taiwan, Yan Kee was the first to volunteer. Years later, many youth followed his example, and Malaysian Bahá'ís conquered many hearts and souls for Bahá'u'lláh in those two countries. Though small in stature, humble and unassuming, Yan Kee Leong was such an effective teacher that he had no rival. He always smiled, and never said no when his services were required. When a Chinese-speaking teacher was needed, Raḥmat called on Yan Kee more often than anyone else.

Yan Kee Leong was asked by Raḥmat to go to many countries, usually a year or so before a new National Spiritual Assembly was to be formed. Yan Kee would stay in each country, visit all the Bahá'ís personally, and prepare them for the formation of their National Assembly. He did this in Taiwan, Laos, Brunei, Singapore and Hong Kong. Once, having been in Laos for six weeks, Yan Kee was preparing to leave when he fell ill and had to postpone his departure for one day. The next day there was a cable from Raḥmat asking him to go to Taiwan for another six months. A short while after that the National Assembly of Taiwan was formed.

In the Bahá'í Centre, Kuala Lumpur.

Yan Kee said that people consented to Raḥmat's requests so willingly for the simple reason that he himself did what he asked of them. 'No matter how exhausted, he always went teaching when it was needed'.

Raḥmat's travels took him from Malacca to Pegoh where 17 people accepted the Faith, and back to Alor Gaja. He recorded,

> *25 February*: Seven people accepted the Faith tonight. There are now 35 Bahá'ís in this town. The beloved Guardian has said that in the fourth phase of the Plan the progress of the Faith must overshadow all other efforts. This rapid progress in teaching is because of his bounty.

On the 26th there were a few gatherings in Seremban. Of one of these Raḥmat wrote:

> There was a special meeting for Major Charles, as he wanted to enrol in the Faith. The Malacca Conference greatly affected him: the same day he had stopped drinking alcohol and started reading Bahá'í books.
>
> He is a wonderful, knowledgable and humble soul. He was so excited about his registration as a Bahá'í that he could not eat dinner. He was afraid to lose his sense of exhilaration and delight if he ate.

Raḥmat spent the next day meeting the youth, and planning methods of teaching in the villages. He was very happy and praised the enthusiasm and unity of the youth. 'This is the start of great victories in Malaya' he noted.

After meeting the youth and visiting some villages he returned alone to Malacca. He arrived at 1.30 in the afternoon and went to the house of Auxiliary Board member Leong Tat Chee. I received a letter from him saying that he was writing while sitting on the pavement outside the house as he did not want to knock and wake the family from their siesta. His diary entry for that day was written in similar fashion:

> I am writing this outside Leong Tat Chee's house. I don't want to disturb them. It is now 1.30. At three, the youth are supposed to come here, so I will wait and see what happens.

Years later, Leong Tat Chee told me how sad they had been when they found out that Raḥmat had waited for more than two hours in the afternoon heat outside their house, despite his fatigue. This was not unusual for Raḥmat. He never wanted to be a burden to anyone, and tried to avoid situations which obliged the friends to look after his comfort.

Leong Tat Chee was a kind and humble man, lovingly called 'Uncle Leong' by all the Malaysian Bahá'ís, who greatly admired him. Like his close friend Yan Kee Leong, he was always available for teaching in Malaysia, but unlike Yan Kee, he was unable to devote all his time to serving the Faith. For some months in 1966, Leong Tat Chee struggled with the notion of leaving his job and devoting himslf completely to teaching. He turned to Raḥmat for help in reaching his decision. 'The only way out for me,' he wrote in a letter, 'is to retire, then I have to invest my Provident Fund wisely so that I would not be a heavy burden on the International Fund. It is always good and fruitful if one can assist the Cause and I am entirely under your direction. Please help me to solve this most important problem . . .'. A few months later he wrote: 'I definitely will be going on the proposed trip. My bosses may grant me two or three months leave, part of which is without pay . . .'. Another month later he wrote again,

> I have now found a way of investing my Provident Fund, if I retire, that can give me a steady income to finance my domestic teaching trips for years . . . Please advise me whether I should retire from Municipal service and man the fort in Malaysia. As a Bahá'í I have done my best to project the image of what a Bahá'í should be, as was witnessed by the bestowal of a meritorious medal to me by His Excellency the Governor of Malacca on his birthday. My dear beloved Hand of the Cause, if you feel that I should retire and serve Lord Bahá'u'lláh entirely, please advise me to do so.

Raḥmat loved and respected Leong Tat Chee dearly, and was well aware of his family obligations. However, to ask Raḥmat to choose between full-time service to the Faith and commercial work was like asking a child whether he preferred to buy a chocolate bar now or keep the money for some other time. Raḥmat made the obvious choice.

In November 1967, Yan Kee Leong wrote to Raḥmat,

> Leong Tat Chee has just returned on the ninth. Our teaching programme will be: one round trip of Malaya and Singapore; after that we will be prepared to go to Taiwan. Leong Tat Chee will pay his own expenses. We will try to get at least a six-month visa. Leong says his trip to Ceylon was successful, with some declarations.

'Uncle' Leong served the Faith with great distinction for many more years.

At the home of the Sundrams. Leong Tat Chee is first on left.

In 1965, the friends in Kuala Lumpur were hurriedly called together to meet Raḥmat when he unexpectedly arrived in their city. According to the *Malaysian Bahá'í News*, the friends were 'thrilled with the exciting ideas put forward in his usual spiritual and dynamic way. His ideas covered a vast field of activity ranging from new angles on immediate teaching plans to public relations in connection with mass proclamation of the Faith.'

Although some members of the NSA could not be present in this meeting, nevertheless the Assembly announced, '[We] will be soon releasing to every local Assembly a practical plan for implementing Dr Muhájir's inspired suggestions for greater activity.'

In June 1966, in a lengthy meeting with the National Assembly, Raḥmat proposed an 18-month programme to implement the goals of the Nine Year Plan. His proposals included increasing the number of Bahá'ís to 5000, officially registering local Assemblies, purchasing a temple site, proclaiming the Faith to all strata of society, translating Bahá'í books into aboriginal languages, and giving greater attention to the Bahá'í education of children. The plan also required members of the National Assembly to accompany teachers to different parts of the country.

By the end of the meeting, the National Spiritual Assembly had formulated the details of the programme, called the 'Muhájir-Inspired 18-Month Plan', and was ready to announce it to the community. The friends in Malaysia never put off any Bahá'í activity for the next day! The *Malaysian Bahá'í News* reported:

> Just as we Malayans were happily patting ourselves on the back for having achieved 93 LSAs when the Nine Year Plan called for only 60, Dr Muhájir, while congratulating us, has quietly proposed that we raise the figure to 135! Likewise the localities to be raised to 350 and the number of believers to 5000. Another scheme was that we should have a minimum of 1000 firesides and 1000 teaching trips during this period. When Dr Muhájir suggests a plan in his quiet humble way, things begin to happen almost immediately. Already wheels have been set in motion around the country and soon reports will be pouring in from all corners of Malaya.

In this same year Raḥmat appealed to the Malaysian community for pioneers to neighbouring countries, as well as to India and Africa. He wrote to the National Assembly about the needs of various countries, informing them of job possibilities, and how to obtain visas. The response of the Malaysian friends was beyond even Raḥmat's expectations. Members of the National Assembly and the National Teaching Committee, as well as many others, arose to pioneer. The *Malaysian Bahá'í News* of March 1967 reported,

> Today we are happy to record the wonderful news that nine Malayan friends have arisen to pioneer to the countries around us that have called for help — Sabah, Sarawak, Taiwan, Laos and Ceylon. A wave of joy and pride and gratitude sweeps throughout the country, as the news is flashed to all communities . . . Beloved Dr Muhájir was the Hand behind it all . . . It is amazing how much power that gentle Hand can exert. We in

> Malaya are deeply grateful to Dr Muhájir for the trust he has in us.

The Malaysian pioneers and travelling teachers, many of whom are still serving in their posts, are among the best teachers in the Bahá'í world. They have helped various communities in their teaching activities, with the education of their children, and with administrative duties.

Before leaving Malaysia, Raḥmat met with a large group of youth — 'potential pioneers' he called them — and told them stories of experiences which he and other pioneers had gone through. He told them that,

> For the Faith to spread around the world, the greatest power is the power of movement and action. Only when we are a part of this movement will the bounty of Bahá'u'lláh be with us. Prayer is essential but simply sitting at home and saying prayers when one has the ability to move is not enough. We must move. Sincerity and action are the two qualities needed for success in the promotion of the Faith. If one is sincere and makes a mistake then he will be helped to correct it, but if one is not sincere and makes mistakes then such actions will bring their own punishments.
>
> Devotion is sincerity put into practice. To accept the Faith is not enough. To believe sincerely in the Manifestation and then do nothing more about it is not enough. One must be devoted and act accordingly. One must sacrifice personal interests for the Cause.

During this stay Raḥmat travelled to many teaching areas, gave speeches in colleges and schools, and attended conferences and farewell parties for the pioneers. At one such meeting he was asked, 'How can a Bahá'í be different from others?', to which he replied,

> Lack of prejudice should be his distinguishing feature. Every individual should review his own set of prejudices and gradually eliminate them. This is by no means an easy process, but it could be a wonderfully rewarding one. The secret is that each one

> should constantly bear in mind the fact that he is, before anything else, a Bahá'í. When we stop thinking of ourselves as Chinese, Indian, Christian, Buddhist or Hindu Bahá'ís, and simply remember that we are Bahá'ís, we will be happy to share our talents with the rest of mankind. In this way, we will build up a Bahá'í civilization which will incorporate the best of all worlds. What a glorious privilege.

Although Raḥmat was unable to attend the Malaysian National Convention in 1969, he suggested a six-month plan of activity to the National Assembly which was approved and presented to the Convention.

The 1971 National Convention was supposed to be a relatively low-key affair. A small hall, accommodating 50 people had been reserved, and all the plans had been made. Then Raḥmat told the organizers that he was coming. The hall was packed with 200 delegates and observers. Raḥmat told stories of the Master, and accounts of what was happening in the rest of the Bahá'í world. The European Bahá'í youth were planning a teaching conference for 1972, with the aim of gathering 500 youth together. They planned to repeat this conference in successive years, but with increased number of participants, won to the Faith by teaching. They wanted 1000 in 1973 and 2000 in 1974.

Raḥmat then called their attention to the Guardian's instructions regarding deepening one's knowledge of the Faith by studying the writings:

> To deepen in the Cause means to read the Writings of Bahá'u'lláh and the Master so thoroughly as to be able to give it to others in its pure form . . . There is no limit to the study of the Cause. The more we read the writings the more truths we can find in them and the more we will see that our previous notions were erroneous.[12]

Raḥmat empahasized the importance of the youth, and challenged them to bring the message of Bahá'u'lláh to every village, town and *kampong* in Malaysia by the end of the Nine Year Plan. 'Movement, just movement of Bahá'ís from place to place exerts a

Attending a fireside at the Bahá'í Centre, Penang, 1969.

spiritual impact,' he said. 'MOVE! PIONEER! The further you go the greater the reward. Ride! Run! Walk on every road in Malaysia! Sail to all the inhabited off-shore islands! Fly to Hong Kong, Saigon, Rangoon. Arise and go forth armed with the power of the Greatest Name. Awaken and quicken the world. Bring the Chinese into the Faith in troops.'

In less than a month this plan was being put into action. All over Malaysia and Singapore, teaching conferences were held. 'Every mile of the road' was 'assigned for opening to the Faith.'

In June 1972 Raḥmat sent a telegram to the National Assembly asking them to convene a teaching conference and to appeal for volunteers to pioneer to Africa. The response was immediate. Raḥmat and Counsellor Payman attended the conference. The *Malaysian Bahá'í News* reported, 'Hand of the Cause Dr Muhájir arrived in Malaysia and personally appealed for travel teachers. He went off smiling happily with six volunteers all set to go to Africa, three of them members of the National Spiritual Assembly.'

The launch of the Five Year Plan brought Raḥmat back to Malaysia. Although he was aware of most of the provisions of the Plans (since he assisted in their formulation), Raḥmat was always exhilarated when the final version was received from the Universal House of Justice. He did not look at plans as mere numbers and figures, but as divinely-inspired guidance which was to transform the world. His excitement and happiness were so great and genuine that they would rub off on everyone in his presence. For him, each plan was a new entity, not merely a repetition of the previous ones.

The Malaysian community always grasped the moment of opportunity and carried it through the whole year. Its strong and loving National Spiritual Assembly constantly guided the friends and conveyed the wishes of the Universal House of Justice in numerous conferences and communications without allowing a moment to be wasted. The Five Year Plan was no exception. The *Malaysian Bahá'í News* reported,

> Malaysia was one of the earliest ports of call on Hand of the Cause Dr Muhájir's current orbit around Earth. Mission: Five Year Plan . . . As the global Plan had not arrived yet, he recommended that a draft plan be made in anticipation, and he particularly stressed the need to eliminate a social delay between receiving the plan and the beginning of ACTION. Then he left for his next port of call.
>
> After a few days, the long-awaited Five Year Plan arrived. Dr Muhájir who was then in Indonesia turned right around and met with the NSA again. His constructive suggestions were all carefully noted and immediate plans were made to be presented to the community.

As I record the achievements of the friends in Malaysia and remember Raḥmat's love and admiration for them, I recall his letters and phone calls to us conveying, on the one hand, his delight at the progress of the Faith and, on the other, his tiredness and loneliness.

The mail and telephone systems of Singapore and Malaysia, being the best in the region, enabled him to contact us regularly. By this time we were living in London, and Raḥmat's absences were becoming lengthier. He was seldom in Europe, and it was impossible for him to return home from such far-off places as Singapore whenever he wished. He always arranged for around the world tickets, not because he particularly wanted to go round the world, but because it was the cheapest form of air travel.

In Malaysia he told the friends how much he missed his family and how sorry he was that he could not see his daughter grow up. But he knew that the only thing that could stop him from serving the Cause was this love for his family, and he did not want to put that spiritual burden on his child's shoulders.

He once wrote to me from Singapore that on a particular night, after he had been dropped at his hotel following a meeting with the friends, he found he simply could not face going to his room and being alone again. He went to the hotel garden, which faced the sea, and sat on a bench the whole night. 'I said a lot of prayers that night,' he wrote, 'I wanted to be with my family and have my child by my side. In the morning I decided to go to a book store and buy some books. That evening I went to a silly movie and the next day left for Thailand.'

I mention this episode to show that Raḥmat's service entailed great personal sacrifice, and brought him a soul-wrenching loneliness. When all the excitement was over and the meetings ended, the friends returned to their families and the comforts of home; Raḥmat, however, went alone to a cheap hotel room with little comfort and few amenities.

Throughout the Five Year Plan he repeatedly visited Malaysia, and encouraged the friends to achieve their goals as swiftly as they could. They did. In November 1975, the National Assembly, in consultation with Raḥmat, decided to accomplish all their goals by Riḍván 1976. A detailed plan of action was drawn up, and the friends immediately went to work. In their letter of November 1976 the Universal House of Justice praised their efforts and said,

> We are delighted to note through a letter received from the Hand of the Cause of God Dr Muhájir the rewarding activities of your National Spiritual Assembly and the wonderful spirit emanating from the vigorous Bahá'í community in Malaysia.

> The decision to fulfil all your goals within twelve months in order to compensate for the losses which may occur in South Asia because of political circumstances in some countries is indeed praiseworthy.

Like a proud father who wanted everyone to be aware of the achievements of his children, Raḥmat had not waited for the National Assembly's report to the Supreme Body; he had written himself immediately after the conferences and his meeting with the National Assembly.

On 17 November 1976, he wrote a detailed letter to the Universal House of Justice, in which he again praised the Malaysian community for its rapid growth and for fulfilling most of the important goals of its Plan. In consultation with the National Assembly, Raḥmat had devised another six-month plan and announced that the Malaysian community had attained the maturity to begin mass teaching on a large scale. He stated that Malaysia had a unique position in the Faith because of its excellent administration. The secret of its success was that every believer pulled their weight in teaching the cause.

For the first time, however, some of the friends became hesitant. Although teaching had been going on steadily since 1961, the friends needed time to get used to the concept of entry by troops. Raḥmat explained that entry by troops had its foundation in the writings of Bahá'u'lláh. He had written to Náṣiri'd-Dín Shāh, saying that by closing Him up in prison the Sháh had opened the gates for the people of the world to enter the Cause of God in troops.The National Assembly distributed the plan to the community, and the work started. The results were spectacular. Yan Kee Leong wrote, 'Dr Muhájir asked me to teach the tribes in Malaysia. It was successful beyond our expectation. Village after village came in, and finally by troops. Now thousands of these pure souls have accepted the Faith of Bahá'u'lláh.'

In his letter to the Universal House of Justice, Raḥmat strongly recommended that the friends in Malaysia be specially utilized for teaching in Hong Kong and Taiwan, and that they start to train and prepare for the day that they could serve the Faith in mainland China.

Dr Muhájir shaking hands with Dr Sreenivasan. Jeffrey Koh in background.

During a two-day meeting with the National Assembly in June 1976, he recommended that that year be dedicated to the education of women and children. This was approved and detailed plans made in the same meeting for its implementation. It was decided to increase the number of Bahá'í classes for children, to translate materials for children into Tamil, to initiate a three-year educational programme in collabortion with India, to educate mothers and children together, and to use the Bangalore Institute in India for training women.

At the 1977 national Summer School, at Port Dickson, nearly 1000 Bahá'ís gathered, 100 of them aboriginal Bahá'ís who had entered the Faith during the previous year. Raḥmat talked there about the effect of persecutions, although there was then no sign of the upheavals which were to happen in Iran two years later.

> It is very strange that the Faith always grows when there is opposition to it. Perhaps half of the teaching work in the world is done by the Bahá'ís and the other half by the enemies of the

Faith. I think maybe they have done a greater share of the work! When in the beginning of the Faith the Mullás shouted from the pulpits that this new heresy was destroying Islám and its followers should be annihilated, Bahá'u'lláh said these people are proclaiming the Faith and they do not realize it. 'Abdu'l-Bahá says that when an idea is opposed it starts to grow and take root and become stronger. He said that when they started to kill the Bahá'ís, out of each person martyred, a hundred new souls grew. God has His own way.

There is a well established Bahá'í family in Iran, called Sarvestani, who are scattered all over the country. I asked one of them how the family had accepted the Faith. He said, 'One Naw-Rúz Day, my father had his new suit on and left the house to see his friends. He saw in the market that they were going to execute a man. He asked who he was, and was told that he was a Bábí. My father stood to watch. When they severed the man's head, one drop of his blood fell on my father's shoe. That shook my father. He started to enquire about the Faith and became a Bahá'í.' That drop of the blood of the martyrs caused a whole family to become Bahá'ís, and now they are pioneers all over the world.

Another young man in Iṣfahán, only 12 years old, went to the market and witnessed the execution of a young Bahá'í. This martyrdom had a strange effect on him. He went home and told his father about it. The father beat him up and said did he want to be known as a Bahá'í by talking such blasphemy? The boy shouted back that, yes, he wanted to be a Bahá'í and he ran away from home never to return. Do you know who he was? The grandfather of Firuz Kazemzadeh, the chairman of the National Assembly of the United States, and the grandfather of Farzam Arbáb, who is now a pioneer in Colombia. Two great families became Bahá'ís as a result of that one martyrdom. The Faith progresses with opposition.

Shoghi Effendi says that the life-giving water for the growth of the Faith is the blood of the martyrs. Now think of the martyrs of Persia a hundred years ago. What happened? They said they were good believers and they were killed. What had they seen of the greatness of the Faith? Nothing. They only said they believed, and were martyred. Is their blood wasted? Where has it gone ? It has come here. Their blood flows in your veins. It is in you. The blood of the martyrs is flowing in the world, from nation to nation, from strength to strength. It is still pulsating. All blood dies except the blood of the martyrs. It is alive, it is moving, it is pushing. The blood of the martyrs is the Universal House of Justice. The blood of the martyrs is in the heroes of the Faith. It is not wasted. Put your hand on your pulse, if it is beating it is the blood of the martyrs which has changed your blood.

The Faith will grow with opposition. We are talking about mass conversion, entry by troops. The beloved Guardian has said the Faith will grow a thousandfold, materially and spiritually. If we are one thousand we will be one million. If we are one million we will be one thousand million. How? The Guardian said in three stages: establishment of the Faith, spread of the Faith and opposition to the Faith, which will lead to proclamation of the Faith and entry by troops. Proclamation is linked to opposition, and without opposition we will not have large proclamation.

The Guardian has talked about Europe, and said first we must try to spread the Faith all across Europe. We can make a map of the areas he mentioned. Southern Germany, Italy, Greece and the Mediterranean islands. He said this will cause the established religions to awaken and come out of their lethargy. This is the word he used — 'lethargy'. They will awaken, and oppose the Faith. They will proclaim the Faith in a way that we can never do. It is out of our power to proclaim the Faith the way they will do. After their opposition the Faith will emerge out of obscurity. When they say, 'do not listen to these so-and-so Bahá'ís', everybody will want to know about the Bahá'í Faith. 'Abdu'l-Bahá has said that movement of the Bahá'ís from place to place will result in people talking about the Faith, after that they will investigate and then they will accept the Faith.

What happened at the time of the martyrdom of the early believers will again happen in the whole world. 'Abdu'l-Bahá said that all religions, with all their might, materially, physically and spiritually will rise to quell the Faith. That will be the cause of proclamation of the Faith and entry by troops.

Bahá'í Summer School, East Coast, July, 1978.

When opposition starts what will happen to the Faith? The Bahá'ís will become better Bahá'ís. This is necessary for us. It is necessary that we test our own Faith. How steadfast are we? 'Abdu'l-Bahá says that in springtime everybody is a friend. However, if at times of hardship someone remains a friend then it is real friendship. Our faith must be tested. The Qur'án says 'Do you expect a man to say "I believe" yet not be tested'? The Guardian says tests are necessary to separate the true believers from the shaky ones. Unfortunately tests are needed for individual believers. This Faith is the Faith of God, and will only grow through sincere believers.

Another result of opposition will be the independence of the Faith and the announcement that it is a separate religion. The way we look at events and the way 'Abdu'l-Bahá and Shoghi Effendi look at them are quite different. In Egypt the friends had some difficulties with the Muslims about their burial ground. The Muslim court ruled against the Faith, and announced that the Bahá'í Faith was as different from Islám as Islám was from Christianity: it had its own book and laws. The Bahá'ís appealed

and the Muslim higher court ruled the same way. It condemned the Bahá'ís, called them heretics and a separate entity from Islám. The Bahá'ís were despondent and did not know what to do.

But look at Shoghi Effendi. This edict was the greatest document in his hand. I think that, after the Writings, Shoghi Effendi loved this document the most. He made such great publicity with it. He said an Islamic court has recognized the Bahá'í Faith as an independent religion. The Egyptian court of appeals is the greatest Islamic court in the world. It pronounced the Bahá'í Faith an independent religion.

The Guardian said that the Faith grows in cycles — crisis and victory, crisis and victory. If you read *The Promised Day is Come* you will find this is the theme. First it describes the Declaration of the Báb and opposition to it. The result of His banishment from Shíráz to Iṣfahán was the acceptance of the Faith by [Manúchíhr Khán] Mu'tamidu'd-Dawlih, the governor [of Iṣfahán]. He was the first official to believe in the Báb. 'Abdu'l-Bahá says that whoever prays at Mu'tamid's grave, God will grant them all their wishes. ‘Abdu’l-Bahá said that the Hands of the Cause and others should visit Mu‘tamid’s grave on His behalf.

Opposition has its results. When they banished the Báb to Á<u>dh</u>irbáyján, and Prince Náṣiri’d-Dín questioned Him, the Báb clearly announced for the first time that He was the promised Mahdí for whom they had been waiting. Before then He had only said that He was ‘the Báb’ — ‘the Gate’.

The result of the martyrdom of the Báb was the imprisonment of Bahá’u’lláh in the Síyáh-<u>Ch</u>ál of Ṭihrán. In the darkest hour of the Faith, God imparted His revelation to Bahá’u’lláh. The Guardian says the Faith of God is like a tree. Its fruit was the Báb; when He was martyred that fruit was crushed and turned into oil which, when lit, illumined the whole world.

Do you have any doubts about what is going to happen? Tests are for the whole world and for every individual. ‘Abdu’l-Bahá said His bones burnt from the weight of tests. The Báb says ‘. . . I swear by God: everything is tested in everything, from everything, towards everything, itself in itself.’* Once I prayed to God not to make others a test for me. For a while I was happy. Then I realized that not only were others tests for me — I was a test for others. So I started praying that God would not make *me* a test for others. Then I read this saying of the Báb, which made me realize that I am a test for myself! Many people are tested unnecessarily by themselves. Now I pray to God not to make me a test for myself. Sometimes I say this verse of the Báb for two hours, and beg God to protect me from tests.

In the Writings we read about certitude. What does it mean, that at the times of tests we should remain steadfast? Bahá’u’lláh, in the Book of Aqdas, talks about great certitude. He has made it very simple. You must believe whatever is revealed by the Pen of Bahá’u’lláh. If He says heaven is earth and earth is heaven we must believe it. Don’t bring your ideas and judgements into the Word of God. Whatever is revealed by the Pen of Bahá’u’lláh is right. Whatever. Before you become a

---

* This abridged transcript of Dr Muhajir’s talk contains his own paraphrases of passages from the Writings.

Bahá'í you are free to question and search, but after that you must have absolute obedience to the Word of God.

Bahá'u'lláh says that His Faith is great and simple. Its greatness is that it is revealed only once in every 500,000 years, its simplicity is that everything should be seen with God's eyes and not our own. This is another way to say 'certitude'. Bahá'u'lláh says that if you reach this stage you'll be exempted from tests.

Shoghi Effendi says the amount of the bounties of God equals the amount of the opposition to and oppression of the Faith. The more difficulties we have, the more successful we will be. Some do not understand this, but it is very clear. When there is persecution and oppression in one corner of the world, the Faith progresses in another. Bahá'u'lláh says if people extinguish the light of the Faith on land it will rise in the sea and will shout 'I am the life-giver of the world'. Opposition in one place gives courage and incentive to others to work more. This is because our Faith is one Faith, and we are all one people.

The victories of the Ten Year Crusade are because of the persecutions of Iran. In 1955 they martyred eight people in Iran. the result was great progress of the Faith in other parts of the world. Mass conversion in West Africa, in Gilbert, in Mentawai started in 1955. This is what Bahá'u'lláh has promised. The light of this Faith cannot be extinguished. Shoghi Effendi says every set-back is the cause of further progress. When he gave the Two Year Plan of Africa to the Bahá'ís of the United Kingdom, he told them they should know from the start that they would have set-backs. Not everything would go smoothly, but every set-back would be the cause of great progress. He said, often in difficulties we try and we pray and our problems do not seem to be solved. We should not be discouraged as our prayers will be answered in some other manner. We should not think it is easy to change the world. It is all in the Hands of Bahá'u'lláh. He is the owner of His Faith and He knows when and where and how to help it.

We must now see everything with the eyes of the Universal House of Justice and not our own eyes. We must put its instructions first. We must know that whatever happens, in the end victory is ours.

It was reported to the conference that the Aslis made up the highest single ethnic grouping of Bahá'ís in Malaysia, and their contribution to the national Bahá'í Fund constituted the highest proportion. Raḥmat had a special session with them. He sat on the floor and, to their great delight, spoke to them in Malay. While speaking about tests and difficulties, tears suddenly started rolling down his face. No one had seen him like that before. After the meeting he stood up and shook hands with them, hugged them all and said goodbye.

In August 1978, Raḥmat was again in Malaysia, reviewing details of the Five Year Plan with the National Assembly. His diary states,

> In the Summer School [In Kuala Lumpur] I met a large group of the friends. I had long consultations with Counsellor Nagaratnam and others. Four regions were chosen in the West and East of Malaysia for them to concentrate on teaching. It means that full time teachers will be used in the same way as South India.

The last mention of Malaysia in his diary is the entry of 18 April 1979. There are several pages listing names of Bahá'ís and areas in Malaysia, and notes proposing certain people who should be asked to help in teaching. Most of his thoughts are about Chinese teaching, the number of Chinese-speaking regions and the people who could assist in the work. On the last page of his notes on Malaysia he wrote: 'I had a dream about saturation of the Faith in the cities and also dreamt that 'Abdu'l-Bahá was very happy, and told me that there were 4000 new Bahá'ís in the area between Uganda and another city.'

Yin Hong Shuen, Chairman of the Malaysian National Assembly, sums up Raḥmat's services to Malaysia and express the feelings of the friends of that country:

> Dr Muhájir was the essence of humility and kindness. He was natural and comfortable in his relationship with others. If we failed to perform our duty he would lovingly scold us, something not easy to describe but most effective.
>
> If there was a negative remark about a discussion, he changed his stance on the subject without appearing to be flustered or let down in any way. He developed us through his example and not

with words. He was a positive motivator. He was receptive, he listened. He asked for our views and we felt involved.

Every time we met our goals or responded to his call — whether it was sending pioneers to the most undreamt of places, like Africa, or teaching campaigns in very tough areas — he would smile and say how wonderful it was. Before we knew it, he was at it again. It was like climbing mountains with him: each time we reached the summit of a hill and heaved a sigh of relief, he pointed out the next peak and said, 'Let's go there.' He never quit, and though we were tired and weary we wanted to do as he directed because of his love.

He was never sharp with his words. He used simple analogies and through them we could see the vision of the growing new order the beloved Guardian and the Universal House of Justice were building.

If any one were to ask me what was instrumental in the making of the Malaysian community's growth in the last 30 years, it was this: Dr Muhájir was the conductor of the symphony orchestra in which we as a group and individual players were lovingly trained and developed to play our part in relation to others in unity.

PHILIPPINES

The Philippines are geographically close to Indonesia, where we had lived for eight years. However, the culture, people and language were so different, that the purpose of Raḥmat's first trip there in 1961 was to explore the possibilities of teaching and to familiarize himself with the local customs.

The first Bahá'í teacher to visit the Philippines was Martha Root. After a visit to Hong Kong in 1924, she stopped in Manila and gave a lecture which was published in Manila newspapers. A young Filipino, Felix Maddela, who had searched for a long time for a religion which could satisfy his soul, came across the Faith when he purchased some cheese wrapped in a newspaper in which Martha Root's article was printed. This was the beginning of the Bahá'í Faith in the Philippines. Felix Maddela and his whole family became Bahá'ís. The first time that they met another Bahá'í was in 1945 when Alvin Blum, an American soldier, visited them in Solano.

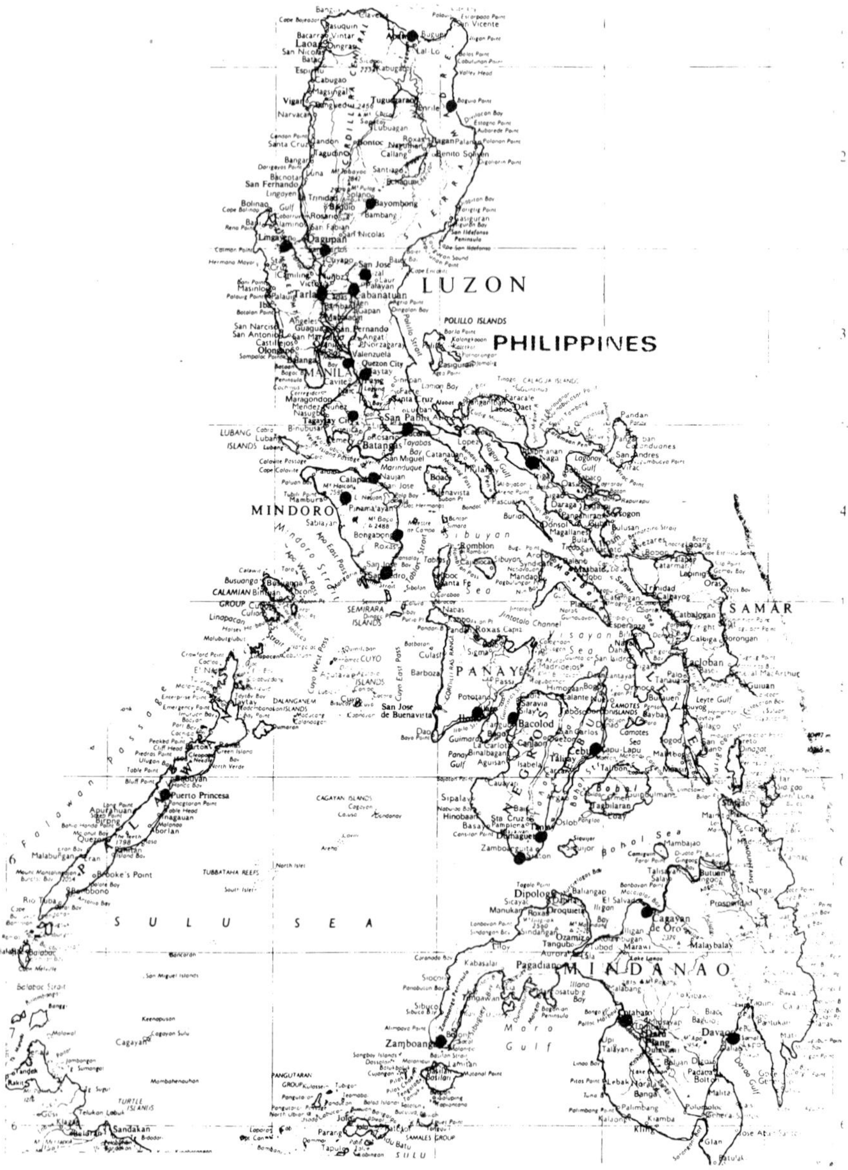

Raḥmat encouraged the pioneers to the Philippines to travel to all the islands of the archipelago and open them to the Faith. He led the way, visiting the remotest tribes and villages.

When Raḥmat arrived in Manila in March 1961, the Philippines had two local Spiritual Assemblies and about two hundred Bahá'ís. He recorded this trip in his diary:

> I arrived in Manila on 3 March. Mrs Gomez, Bill Allison and Orpha Daugherty, a pioneer to Cebu, were at the airport. There was a meeting of the Bahá'ís and we visited the Philippines University which has 14000 students.
>
> *4 March*: After starting the Fast we left for Santiago at 6.30 a.m. We were on the way the whole day. Bill Allison was with me. He told me that he was soon leaving for Mindanao on an assignment from his job. This was most welcome news. This will be the start of the mass teaching among the tribes of the Philippines. We talked all the time about teaching the tribes. We arrived in Santiago at 7.30 p.m.
>
> *5 March*: After dawn prayers and beginning the Fast we left to meet the friends at the Bahá'í Centre. These are wonderful Bahá'ís. We stayed with them till noon and consulted about all aspects of the Faith, and the teaching work in that area. I was informed that there were many tribes in that area, and it was very easy to contact them. The Chairman and Vice-Chairman of the local Assembly, both of whom are well-off and have time, decided to visit some of the tribes for a week and later continue these trips.
>
> The Bahá'ís offered to pay half their expenses. We established a Bahá'í Fund and asked all the friends to contribute as much as they could. We collected 42 Pesos. They only needed 10 Pesos, but they contributed 42. My heart overflowed with happiness. I could see many strong and self-sacrificing Bahá'ís scattered throughout these lands, walking the terrain, climbing the mountains and spreading the teachings of Bahá'u'lláh.
>
> Today is a day of fasting. This day seven years ago, while fasting, I was walking in the jungles of Mentawai. It took me three days to reach Sirareket Ulu. That was my first journey in Mentawai. Now I am visiting similar hamlets once more, this time in the Philippines. I wish all 19 months were fasting months and I was travelling to teach in the tribal areas.

> There is an aura and a special quality in this small village of Santiago that gives light to one's soul. I am certain that these wonderful Bahá'ís will carry the Faith to all parts of these islands.
>
> At noon we left for Solano to the home of Mr Maddela's son. Mr Maddela was the first Bahá'í of the Philippines. We broke our fast there and left for Manila. We arrived in Manila at four a.m. and went to the home of Mrs Gomez. I left Manila for Hong Kong the next day.

Raḥmat's next trip to the Philippines was in March 1962. On this trip he encouraged the American pioneers — Orpha Daugherty, Jack Davis and Bill Allison — to leave Manila and try to establish their residences in other islands. Orpha was at the time in Cebu and she continued to teach and travel on that island. Jack accepted Raḥmat's suggestion, and transferred his residence to Santiago.

It was also on this trip that a young Filipino school teacher who had been studying the Faith for less than a month declared as a Bahá'í at a meeting held for Raḥmat. Vicente (Vic) Samaniego, went on to teach thousands of people, to become a member of the National Assembly, to serve as an Auxiliary Board Member and eventually be appointed a Counsellor for Asia by the Universal House of Justice. Vic recalls,

> In that year Dr Muhájir began leading teaching teams into areas of Isabela and Nueva Vizcaya for mass teaching. The first team, consisting of some older Bahá'ís and some American pioneers, had to learn from Dr Muhájir how to overcome their shyness and give the message to one and all, and not to hesitate in enrolling the new believers on the spot. From then on, each trip to the Philippines found Dr Muhájir proceeding with a group of believers directly to mass teaching areas. Believers from Manila, Solano, and Santiago arose to assist him, and in this manner thousands accepted the Faith.

Raḥmat returned to the Philippines several times that year. Baltazar Mariano, who went on to serve in the Holy Land, accepted the Faith on one of those trips. Later he accompanied Raḥmat and other pioneers travel teaching in many parts of the Philippines.

Manila, 1965. Fred Santiago first on the right. He pioneered to Africa at Raḥmat's request, and is still there.

Baltazar and Vic Samaniego were with Raḥmat when he visited Diffuncian in Nueva Vizcaya, a small village at the foot of a mountain. Rain was pouring, and as they were getting ready to sleep, they heard loud noises from the adjoining house. Raḥmat was told that the next-door neighbours were members of the Igorot tribe on their way to the mountains and that they would be leaving early in the morning. He asked Baltazar to go to them immediately and make friends.

Early next morning, Raḥmat and his companions found themselves hiking up the mountain with their new Igorot friends. After five hours they reached the Igorot village, and, exhausted, stayed at the first house they came to. The house had a raised bamboo floor supported by four posts with no walls. The newly arrived Igorots started telling other members of their tribe about the newcomers and very soon many of them arrived to see the Bahá'ís. Raḥmat spoke in a simple manner, and one of the Santiago Bahá'ís,

Dominador Anuncacion, translated his words into Ilocano: 'We are all like fingers of one hand. We are not so different from each other. We are all the same. We all have two eyes and two ears and one nose. There is one God and He has created all of us.' Raḥmat then asked others to speak to the Igorots, and show them a pictorial presentation which they had carried with them. Raḥmat then said 'Ask them if they want to become Bahá'ís.' During all this time a very shy young man, Joseph Domingo, was tending the fire, cooking rice and dry fish. When they asked the question he immediately said that he wanted to be a Bahá'í. He then took some of the visitors to other houses.

Raḥmat remained behind to say prayers for them. Everyone in the other houses became Bahá'ís, and later accompanied Joseph down the mountain to Santiago. Raḥmat was awake well into the early morning, listening to the Ilocano voices answering questions. From that time onwards, Joseph devoted himself full-time to teaching the Faith. He was later asked to serve as a member of the Auxiliary Board. Within a week hundreds had accepted the Faith. Mass teaching in the Philippines was underway.

During his next visit later that year, Raḥmat told the Bahá'í teachers that it was time to bring the Faith of Bahá'u'lláh to other areas of the Philippines besides the island of Luzon. He asked each of them to go to islands where they had friends and relatives. In that week Tarlac, Pangasinan, Nueva Ecija, Zambales, and the Benguet Mountains were all opened to the Faith. Raḥmat remained in Santiago to keep an eye on activities and to deepen the friends through stories from the history of the Faith and explanations of Bahá'u'lláh's teachings. There was no Bahá'í literature in local languages. The few English Bahá'í books were also inadequate to satisfy the needs of the large number of new believers. Vic Samaniego recalls,

> After about a week the teachers returned one by one to Santiago to be greeted by a beaming Dr Muhájir who somehow knew that these individuals had been successful in their efforts. When one of them said, 'I have only a few enrolments,' he said, 'But this is already too much!' He ordered fruit and food for everyone. One

teacher still remembers the taste of the fresh, cool watermelon he had that day.

In one of the villages an entire Catholic family became Bahá'ís, and each member was given a Bahá'í pin by a delighted Dr Muhájir. On his next visit Dr Muhájir noticed that the pins were gracing the dress of the image of the Virgin Mary in the altar nook of the house.

Dr Muhájir had so much understanding and kindness in his dealings with people.

In the few remaining months before the end of the Ten Year Crusade, Raḥmat asked Mr Payman, Dr Surraya and Dr Astani — his friends from Indonesia who were familiar with mass teaching methods — to visit the Philippines. With their help many people from the head-hunting Ilongot tribe, the Ifugao, and other tribes accepted the Faith. Raḥmat emphasized that these teaching efforts should go hand-in-hand with deepening and consolidation. Many Filipino and American pioneers volunteered for this task and settled in the newly opened areas.

By the end of the Ten Year Crusade the number of the Bahá'ís in the Philippines had risen from less than 200 to more than 20,000. The number of local Assemblies had increased from 4 to 150, and the number of localities opened to the Faith from 8 to 946.

A few months before the Nine Year Plan was announced in 1963, Raḥmat, Baltazar Mariano and a few other friends travelled to Mindanao to open that island to the Faith. Raḥmat first approached the Commission of National Integration in Davao to find out about the tribes, of which there are many on Mindanao. While there, he met Datu Eloy Epa, the chief of the Bilaan tribe. The Datu invited him to his home.

Together with the representative of the Commission, Raḥmat and Baltazar accompanied the Datu to his village. On arrival in Talambato, two men brought horses to take them to the villages. But horse riding through steep and narrow passes was not for Raḥmat. They hiked for a whole day to reach Datu Eloy's home. He and his family greeted the visitors graciously and told them, 'Your visit to our village is a bounty of God because nobody has ever visited our home. You have brought light to our dark world. I am very grateful to Dr Muhájir for bringing us the light of God, and hope that my people will be enlightened.'

Datu Eloy was the first Chief to accept the Faith in the Philippines. Fifteen of his people followed his example. Raḥmat suggested that they build their Bahá'í Centre in an elevated place; the Datu promised to do so, and to finish it within six months.

These tribal people are still Bahá'ís and their numbers have greatly increased. Vic remembers that on one of Raḥmat's visits to Davao City, Datu Eloy came to visit him. In honour of the occasion the Datu had decided to wear shoes — which made him very uncomfortable and tired. On arrival in Raḥmat's room he stretched out on Raḥmat's bed and went to sleep. Raḥmat prevented the friends from removing Datu Eloy's shoes and asked them to let him rest. He said, 'I know what it is to be tired after a long journey.' Datu Eloy called Raḥmat 'Humajir'. Raḥmat loved this new title and called himself 'Dr Humajir' when he was with Datu Eloy. He treated the Datu like a brother and showered love and affection on him. Datu Eloy also considered Raḥmat a member of his family and treated him accordingly.

Raḥmat and Baltazar travelled all over the Mindanao Islands, and brought the first members of the Manobo tribe to the Faith. From 1961 to 1963, Gisu and I lived in the Holy Land. Raḥmat, en route to different continents, would come to Haifa for short periods. We had no fixed home, and stayed in my parents' house. After attending the Bahá'í World Congress in London in 1963, we decided to pioneer to the Philippines. We arrived in Manila a few months before the first National Convention of the Philippines was to be held in that city. Raḥmat was glad of the opportunity to spend more time in the Philippines. He cherished the people of those islands. They reciprocated with enthusiasm, and tried to make him happy by carrying out all his proposals.

In the many years of my association with the friends of the Philippines, I cannot remember a single instance when they resisted Raḥmat's suggestions. He always said that the Filipino Bahá'ís were a good example of the fact that mass conversion worked: it was not an illusion. Many who became Bahá'ís in those early days are still active, and their families and relatives are also Bahá'ís.

First National Spiritual Assembly of the Philippines, 1964.

Our house became the centre of Bahá'í activities in Manila. It was home to all the friends who came to see Raḥmat, whose hospitality and love made them feel very much at ease. Those were days of great activity as the Bahá'ís prepared for the election of their first National Spiritual Assembly. Vic relates,

> It was now time for the Hand of the Cause of God to prepare his adopted community for the great responsibilities of conducting a National Convention. He helped the friends to appoint a Convention Committee, with the task of ensuring maximum attendance. The Convention was a rousing success. Dr Muhájir was present at all sessions as the representative of the Universal House of Justice. On his instruction, plans were made for all the delegates and guests to pass through different communities, give the news of the Convention and hold teaching conferences. We still use this method for all conferences and conventions.

Raḥmat attended the first meeting of the National Assembly of the Philippines, and helped them formulate new teaching plans. The National Assembly reported,

> When we felt overwhelmed by the magnitude of our tasks and responsibilities he would smile and reassure us that he would always be there to help. This made us confident to attempt greater goals. The reliance on his love was a great source of joy and comfort. We wanted to achieve as much as we could so that when he came back to us we could make him proud.

The first Convention was an occasion of great happiness and pride for Raḥmat. Three of the delegates were Datus from the tribes of Bilaan, Bagobo and Manobo. One of them was appointed a teller. Raḥmat's joy knew no bounds. It was as if his own children had grown up and were serving the Faith.

A few days after the Convention, Raḥmat decided to go teaching on the island of Palawan. Terrible turbulence nearly caused the plane to crash, and forced it to land in San Jose, Mindoro. Raḥmat later told me that he thought they had arrived in Palawan, and proceeded into town. When he realized he was in Mindoro, he decided to stay for a few days. He went to the Municipal Office and asked about the location of the tribes on that island. He found a farmer to accompany him and walked for eight hours through the mountains to reach the tribal area of the Mangyans. There was immediate response to him and enthusiasm for the Faith. As Raḥmat had no registration cards with him he wrote the names of the new believers on a sheet of paper and had each of them sign against their names. This sheet is kept in the archives of the National Assembly of the Philippines.

On that trip one of the tribal chiefs, Lauriano Onella, accepted the Faith. Shortly after this, his son, Rogelio, began using a room in his house to teach his fellow tribesmen the fundamentals of the Faith so that they could perform Bahá'í elections. This small class developed into the 'Rogelio Onella Memorial School', in Occidental Mindoro, and was the nucleus for four tutorial schools which now exist on that island.

Raḥmat visited the Mangyan area repeatedly, and many more embraced the Faith. American pioneers Toni Mantel McCants and

Tyson Clark, together with Filipino teachers — in particular Fe Samaniego — continued the work until the tender young sapling of the Bahá'í community grew into a sturdy and sheltering tree. A cable sent in December 1977 to the Universal House of Justice testifies to this growth:

> TWO ADDITIONAL TUTORIAL SCHOOLS BENGUET AND MANGYAN TRIBE ORIENTAL MINDORO ESTABLISHED STOP FIRST BAHAI TRIBAL CONFERENCE TO BE HELD JANUARY SEVEN TO NINE TABLONGAN TUTORIAL SCHOOL ONE THOUSAND MANGYAN PARTICIPANTS EXPECTED INVITING HAND MUHAJIR ATTEND . . .

The 'Muhájir Project' was another achievement of this period. It involved the long-term goal of establishing an agricultural and vocational school, serving the Mangyan tribal believers. In 1980 the National Spiritual Assembly purchased 13 hectares of land for this purpose, with contributions donated in Raḥmat's name. The Muhájir Institute, as it became known, began its work by training 19 young Mangyans to teach the tribal children.

Raḥmat was involved in every aspect of the work and the growth of the Faith in the Philippines. Whether he was in the country or in some other part of the world, he was kept informed by the National Assembly, which often requested his counsel.

The Philippines was now home to Gisu and me, and the Filipinos were like our family. Raḥmat often referred duties to me, expecting them to be carried out immediately. My first task was the translation of Bahá'í literature into local languages. I had, of course, no knowledge at all about the many languages of the Philippines. Raḥmat did not consider this an obstacle. He took me and a Filipino Bahá'í to the Centre for Translation in Manila where we could easily find good translators for our books. The translated works were then thoroughly checked by a committee of Bahá'ís before being passed for publication. Raḥmat helped find publishing houses and negotiated good prices with them. Many books were translated and printed during that period. On his travels to Iran he asked the National Spiritual Assembly there for contributions for literature in the Philippines.

The increase in the number of Bahá'ís and the need for a national office necessitated the purchase of a Bahá'í Centre. Although this was a goal of the Nine Year Plan, our endeavour to build a Centre was not successful. Real estate prices were so high that our budget simply could not afford it. At this time, Raḥmat was spending a few months in Manila prior to an extended trip to Latin America. He decided to study Spanish so that he could communicate with the people of that region. A teacher was found through an advertisement in the paper. After a few lessons, which were conducted in our house, Raḥmat happily announced that our predicament about the Bahá'í Centre was over.

His teacher had a beautiful house located in a very convenient and central part of Manila which she wanted to sell immediately. The asking price was exactly what had been budgeted by the National Assembly. The Centre was bought and the goal achieved. Two years later the house was demolished and much larger premises built on the same land. The Centre was renovated in 1988 and is now one of the finest in the Bahá'í world. Raḥmat remarked that if his Spanish had progressed as quickly as the purchase of the Centre he would have had no complaints. He had to abandon his studies due to pressure of work.

Every year he suggested a new idea to the National Assembly, which was immediately adopted and carried out. In 1965 he proposed teaching in prisons. The first person to arise for this service was Mrs Luisa Mapa Gomez, fondly known as 'Momsu'. She was an aristocratic lady who was then 73-years old. She had accepted the Faith in 1953 and was the first Bahá'í of Manila. Her vast and splendid house by the sea-shore was known as one of the best residences in Manila and was always open to the Bahá'ís. Many pioneers spent months in her house, and all visitors were her guests.

Her relationship with Raḥmat was extraordinary. She told me that the first time she had seen him in Manila airport, she knew that she would love him forever. Her daughter, Neva Gomez Dulay recalls:

> Momsu adored Dr Muhájir. She called him her 'son-in-law' because she loved Írán like her own daughter. If you wanted to see Momsu get excited, which was not often, all she had to hear

With Mrs Luisa Mapa Gomez, the first Bahá'í of Manila, 1964.

> was 'Dr Muhájir is coming!' One time she had the room upstairs completely repainted and new drapes made just for him. I know Dr Muhájir returned her feelings. He never failed to visit her. Once, in 1977, the last time that they were to see each other, he asked a group of youth to go to Momsu's house to serenade her with their guitars and singing, which mother enjoyed very much. Dr Muhájir was very loving and thoughtful and so appreciative of people.

When this dear and wonderful lady arose to visit the prisoners, many others followed suit. The first visit, however, was made by Momsu, Raḥmat, Neva and Rose Mangapis. Rose was a Bahá'í of a few years standing, who had declared her Faith in a meeting at which Raḥmat was present. She became a devoted Bahá'í, and always accepted Raḥmat's requests. Despite her advanced years and poor health, she pioneered to Nicaragua, where she served for several years.

The Muntinlupa National Penitentiary, whose director was a friend of Momsu, was chosen for their first prison teaching venture. Neva relates,

> The first and only teaching trip I made with Dr Muhájir was to Death Row in Muntinlupa prison. I was not a Bahá'í then, but just went to accompany Momsu. Since mother knew the director, we were given permission to visit the group that was serving life imprisonment. We met our former mayor of La Castellana who was there for life, and he greeted Momsu with great affection. I translated Dr Muhájir's talk into Tagalog and Visayan, and he was the only one who applauded my effort.

The prison visits continued: Raḥmat accompanied the teachers whenever he was in Manila. Within a few months there were many Bahá'ís in the penitentiary. They all learned prayers and many kept the Fast. Using their own funds they established a Bahá'í Centre, and observed Bahá'í Holy Days. After Muntinlupa, other prisons were also opened, and large groups accepted the Faith in Rizal, Sablayan, Occidental Mindoro and Davao penitentiaries.

Momsu often spoke about Raḥmat's compassion for the prisoners, and marvelled that a foreigner could express so much understanding for these hardened Filipino criminals. She told me that every night before she went to sleep she said the Tablet of Aḥmad for Raḥmat, and asked Bahá'u'lláh to safeguard him.

Momsu passed to the Abhá Kingdom in September 1977. Despite her great wealth, her most cherished possession was a copy of *Selections from the Writings of the Báb*, presented to her by Raḥmat in which he had inscribed: 'To dearest Momsu, my greatest love and respect.'

By 1966 the Philippines had a large community. Raḥmat invited the Hands of the Cause to visit the Philippines so that the new flourishing Bahá'í community could receive nourishment and encouragement from their presence. The first ones to accept his invitation were Hands of the Cause Agnes Alexander and Mr Samandarí.

Arrival in Manila, with Hand of the Cause Samandarí.

Miss Alexander came to the Philippines several times, visiting a number of the islands. Raḥmat paid special attention to details of her travels so that they would not prove tiring for her. He accompanied her on some of her trips, and took her to Muntinlupa to meet the prisoners. In her letter of 14 December 1966, she wrote to Raḥmat, 'I always think, with pleasure, of my trips to the Philippines and especially I remember the prisoners. Please give my love to all the Bahá'ís. If God so wills, I hope that I might again meet them all. My love to your wife and dear little daughter and especially my loving wishes to you in your wonderful work.'

Hand of the Cause Samandarí graced our home in 1966 for about two months, and went with Raḥmat to the island of Mindanao, to meet the believers, many of whom travelled there from remote communities. Hand of the Cause Samandarí's stories of his pilgrimage to the threshold of Bahá'u'lláh are still remembered by the Filipino friends.

In later years, at Raḥmat's urging, the National Assembly invited many other Hands of the Cause to the Philippines. Amatu'l-Bahá Rúḥíyyih Khánum, Mr Furútan, Mr Khádem, Mr Olinga, Mr Robarts, Mr Featherstone, and Mr Faizí all accepted the invitation. Their visits galvanized the Bahá'ís of the Philippines, and revitalized the spirit of the community. Vic recalls,

> When beloved Hand of the Cause Olinga visited the Philippines, Dr Muhájir gave careful instructions to the National Spiritual Assembly that Mr Olinga was to be booked into the best hotel and his expenses paid by the National Assembly. He told us that wherever Mr Olinga visited there was a tremendous effect on all the people, and we found out the truth of these words.
>
> While he provided superlative care for these fellow Hands, Dr Muhájir himself demanded and received no special attention. Until his own family arrived he always stayed in a little room in a small hotel facing Luneta, Manila's beautiful Rizal Park. He loved to eat at the little cafe in the park operated by the deaf and dumb, and appreciated them and their service. Often after meetings he would invite the friends there and we would have refreshments together.

In the course of his travels to Iran, Raḥmat had been told that many of the Bahá'í youth were unable to gain admittance into university because of shortage of places. He thought of opportunities in other countries. The beloved Guardian had praised the American youth for their pioneering and teaching work, presenting them as a model for young Bahá'ís everywhere. In a letter written on his behalf, the Bahá'í youth of India were encouraged to follow 'the example of American Bahá'í young people, so many of whom have entered the field as pioneers during the last ten years, and not only rendered the Cause great services, but prepared themselves, through this experience, for their future tasks as administrators of the Faith.'[13] Many of these American youth had enrolled in universities in South America to be able to settle in those countries. Raḥmat was now using this standard for the rest of the world.

Outside the National Bahá'í Centre, Manila, 1964, with Hand of the Cause Samandarí.

The Philippines had one of the best educational systems, and the government was liberal in issuing visas to students. Raḥmat encouraged the youth of Iran to further their studies in the Philippines. Many sent their papers and applications, and I was volunteered by Raḥmat to process them! The first person to be admitted was Mahshid Ighani. On arrival she was sent by the National Assembly to the mountain town of Baguio, where she enrolled in the university. Her success opened the floodgates. In the years that followed, hundreds of Iranian youth enrolled in universities all over the Philippines. They were instrumental in teaching great numbers of people, and rendered considerable services to the Faith. At the end of their studies many pioneered to other countries, but a good number settled in the Philippines.

As well as encouraging the Iranian youth to pioneer to the Philippines, Raḥmat urged the Filipinos to pioneer and go travel teaching. He hand-picked many of them, assigned them pioneering goals, and helped secure financial support. These young men and women of the Philippines assisted the teaching work in the islands of the Pacific and in Hong Kong, Taiwan, Laos, and in many African countries. Some are still serving in their pioneering posts.

Raḥmat was so confident that the Bahá'ís of the Philippines would respond positively to his suggestions, that he had no qualms about making promises to the Universal House of Justice on their behalf. The following extracts illustrate this point. From a letter of the Universal House of Justice to the National Spiritual Assembly of the Philippines, 2 October 1978:

> There is a great need in the southern zone of Africa for travelling teachers to visit some of the countries of that zone. In consultation with the Hand of the Cause Raḥmat'u'lláh Muhájir, who is currently in the Holy Land, it was decided by the Universal House of Justice to request you to select four teachers who would be willing to spend four to five months visiting the friends . . .

Raḥmat's cable to the National Assembly, 3 October 1978:

> HOUSE JUSTICE SECOND OCTOBER DECIDED PHILIPPINES SEND FOUR TRAVEL TEACHERS LESOTHO, ZAMBIA, BOTSWANA . . . ENCOURAGE . . . ENAYAT SAMIMI FARAMARZ DADGAR PARVANEH SABET TAKE THIS OPPORTUNITY . . .

Cable of the National Assembly to the Universal House of Justice, 11 October 1978:

> YOUR LETTER SECOND OCTOBER NOT RECEIVED STOP IN VIEW HAND MUHJIR'S CABLE . . . ENAYAT SAMIMI FARAMARZ DADGAR AVAILABLE FIVE MONTHS EVENTUAL SETTLEMENT . . .

Raḥmat hạd no doubt that his suggestion would be carried out. The Philippines Bahá'í community was the only one besides India to which Raḥmat felt he belonged. He considered himself one of them, and knew that they loved him and did not mind when he volunteered them for various services. The National Assembly often sent cables and letters to the Universal House of Justice asking his whereabouts, to seek his advice on plans and projects.

Vic writes, 'Sometimes we thought he was using us as guinea pigs to see if a particular plan would work in a given environment. We were happy and proud to have his confidence in our willingness to explore new ways and to give immediate response to his challenge.'

Toni Mantel McCants, an American pioneer who was instrumental in bringing a great number of Filipinos into the Faith and who also served as an Auxiliary Board member, recalls that Raḥmat seemed always to follow a pattern. His cable to the National Spiritual Assembly of the Philippines announcing his arrival a few days hence would result in that body calling the believers to a national teaching conference in Manila. Upon his arrival, Raḥmat would informally gather a few believers together who were available at the time in Manila and discuss his suggestions with them. Toni writes,

> When many Bahá'ís were gathered at the scheduled teaching conference, Dr Muhájir would review the activities and successes of the recent months or years for the whole nation, then map out a detailed plan using the chalk board, ascertain the workers and give assignments to those in the vanguard scattered around the country. In the midst of all this sharing and planning he would take time to meet with the National Assembly and have that body approve his plan, for which they were always very appreciative.
>
> As a member of that National Assembly, it was fascinating to watch this beloved Hand of the Cause in consultation with the institution. He would bring forth a new idea and see where it would go. If there was little response he would bring forth the same thought in a slightly different way. If still not much response he would once again — from a different aspect — present his idea until there was positive reaction. This was a very gentle but effective method that he used. Of course this precious soul was so deeply loved and appreciated by the National

> Assembly as well as by the rank and file of the believers that just about anything he did or said was welcomed with open arms. He was our general in the field and our spiritual leader.

In 1967 Raḥmat proposed that the National Assembly undertake a campaign to proclaim the Faith throughout the country. Addresses of teachers, physicians, judges, engineers and other professionals were collected from different organizations, and Bahá'í pamphlets were systematically mailed to them. Billboards with Bahá'í Writings appeared in many large cities, and advertisements were put in all major newspapers.

This project was so successful that Raḥmat was prompted to propose a Bahá'í correspondence course which could be mailed to all those who responded to the proclamation campaign. We prepared twenty-four lessons, and once every two weeks, hundreds of seekers and Bahá'ís received a lesson which included a questionaire. All the replies were corrected and returned with the next lesson. These courses were translated into the four major dialects, and by 1973, enrolments in the course had increased to 4000 and resulted in many declarations. A slightly modified version of this course was later used in India and several other countries.

In April 1968, Raḥmat was appointed to represent the Universal House of Justice at the national conventions of Taiwan and Laos. The day before he was due to leave the Philippines he was coming out of the Taiwanese embassy after securing a visa when he realized that he had lost his briefcase which contained his passport and other documents. He would have to apply for a new passport which would take many months, as there was no Persian Embassy in Manila.

As a member of the National Assembly, and a delegate, I had to leave that same day for the Philippines Convention, which was being held in Santiago. Raḥmat encouraged me to leave, and calmly assured everyone that there was a reason for this occurrence. We were all positive that no one would return the valuables, but Raḥmat routinely contacted the police. The second day of our Convention he arrived in Santiago. The search for his briefcase had proved futile.

That afternoon, an announcement over the radio requested Raḥmat to collect his briefcase. Raḥmat immediately left for the airport to return to Manila. However, after a few hours he was back at the Convention. He laughingly informed us that it seemed we just could not get rid of him so easily. The door of the small Philippines Airline plane was jammed, and they had to await the arrival of another one from Manila the next day.

Raḥmat told the Convention that 'Abdu'l-Bahá had said that when you try to do something and obstacles appear, it should be taken as the Will of God: you should abandon the project. He remained with us for the rest of the Convention. On return to Manila we went to the radio station and recovered the briefcase. It had been given to a disc jockey by Raḥmat's taxi driver, who did not have much trust in the police. The next morning Raḥmat left for Laos, and there met Mr Payman who had attended the Taiwan Convention on his behalf. All had gone well; though we never found out the wisdom behind this incident.

We left the Philippines in 1969, and, after a short stay in the Holy Land, pioneered to India. Although Raḥmat never again had the opportunity to spend so much time in Manila, he retained a strong link with the friends there.

He participated in the 1970 Convention. The National Assembly reported, 'Inspired by the Hand of the Cause of God Dr R. Muhájir at the National Convention . . . the idea of the University Team Project was approved by the NSA.' This project called for a few people to give six months of their time to concentrate on teaching in the universities all over the Philippines. Volunteers were found among faculty members, teachers and students. This project proved very successful. Hundreds accepted the Faith in the universities, where they started Bahá'í clubs and activities. Within a period of six months, according to the report of the National Assembly, 3100 students in five universities had embraced the Faith.

In August that year, Raḥmat conceived a new project for urban teaching. He felt that the experience of the young people in the universities had prepared them for a similar programme, not only in the universities but in all civic institutions. A team of young people called 'Youth for One World' (Y.O.W.) was appointed by the National Assembly.

The Y.O.W. team in each city visited public officials, newspapers and radio stations, arranged meetings in colleges and high schools and held firesides. As Vic recalls,

> Thousands heard about the Faith, and hundreds enrolled. Dr Muhájir accompanied the team whenever he could, and gave his invaluable guidance and assistance. Very often he sat smiling while a member of the team, shy and trembling, explained the teachings of Bahá'u'lláh to the audience. We now have many active and devoted Bahá'ís in our community who are the fruits of that campaign.

Before visiting Manila again in October for a teaching conference, Raḥmat sent the National Assembly a cable from Africa:

> IMPORTANT GOAL OPEN ALL ISLANDS STOP SUGGEST ARRANGE IMMEDIATE PROJECT INVOLVING HUNDRED BELIEVERS OPENING SCORE ISLANDS AIMING LARGE ENROLMENT LARGE CONSOLIDATION AT LEAST THREE WEEKS EACH ISLAND STOP AIRMAILED DOLLARS TWO THOUSAND STOP DEEPEST LOVE

Fe Samaniego recalls that when Raḥmat arrived in Manila he immediately asked about island teaching:

> We were flabbergasted by the cable and his question. Philippines was all islands and we were teaching in the Philippines! He said, 'Alright, sit down, I'll explain it.' The Island Teaching Programme was thus initiated. The plan was to have the first all-Bahá'í provinces in the two Mindoros and to establish functioning new Assemblies on unopened islands. Apo Island, Polillo Island, and Guimaras Island were the first fruits of that campaign. The $2000 was the gift of an Iranian friend for this project.

The letter of the National Assembly dated 7 October to the Universal House of Justice said,

> The beloved Hand repeatedly emphasized the very great opportunity for teaching in the Islands . . . He told us the story of two young men who were late for an appointment, one said that they should stop and pray while the other one said that they should run and pray. The beloved Hand said that we should be like the latter.

The enthusiasm and determination of the friends prompted us to send you the following cable:

RECENT CONFERENCE CONSULTATION HAND, NSA, FRIENDS DETERMINED IMMEDIATE INCREASE BELIEVERS THROUGHOUT ISLANDS . . .

On 3 November, the Universal House of Justice replied,

We were greatly inspired by your letter of 7 October attaching details of your plans made at the recent Teaching Conference at which you had the bounty of meeting the Hand of the Cause Dr Muhájir . . . We trust that this initial plan for the brief period outlined will meet with such success as to inspire all the dear

With some of the Persian pioneers at the Bahá'í Centre, Manila.

> friends in the Philippines to adopt further plans so that by the end of the Nine Year Plan you will be able to report outstanding gains for the Faith in all areas of the Philippines.

In January 1972 we stopped in Manila on our way back to India from Japan. Iranian youth from all over the country had come there to spend a few days with Raḥmat. Every day we gathered in the Bahá'í Centre, ate together and consulted about the teaching work in the Philippines. The letter of the National Assembly to the Universal House of Justice contains the result of those consultations. 'At the last visit of the Hand of the Cause Dr Muhájir the NSA approved his suggestion to have a Youth Conference for the Far East in Manila . . . It is tentatively scheduled for 2-4 May 1972, one day after the National Convention . . . The plan is to have a major conference in Manila on these dates and then have a 40 day teaching campaign . . .'

On this occasion the Y.O.W. team was reorganized and the campaign of 1970 repeated all over the country. The National Assembly reported,

> Two young believers from Naga City, aided by Auxiliary Board members and travelling teachers, have been instrumental in bringing into the Cause over 800 believers in a few months. In the month of September they enrolled 500 believers, opened five schools to the Cause, as well as 22 towns and 90 new areas. The Faith was spoken about over three local radio stations, and press releases were published in three newspapers. Classroom lectures were given and much literature presented to those who expressed interest. In Pablos City there were very few Bahá'ís when the team of 15 Bahá'í youth [arrived to teach]. On the first visit about 52 became Bahá'ís.

It was also during this trip that three Iranian students sought Raḥmat's advice where they should live. Raḥmat seldom discouraged prospective pioneers. The three young men, Parviz Furughi, Parviz Sadeghi and Faramarz Vujdani had just arrived, and, after consulting their friends had decided to enrol in Mindanao University. There they could be with their friends and serve among the Muslim population of that region. Raḥmat sat with them for hours and suggested many other cities, trying to dissuade them from going to Mindanao. He said that there were enough Bahá'í students in the universities at Mindanao. Other regions needed their services much more.

He finally agreed with them as they were determined to go to Mindanao. On parting with them he again said, 'stay a few weeks in Davao, be with your friends, but try to go elsewhere for your studies.' I was very surprised at this and asked why he insisted on something that they obviously did not want to do. Mindanao needed pioneers, and if they wanted to go there, surely they should. Raḥmat just said that he did not think it was a good idea.

These three wonderful souls — bright, young and totally devoted to the Faith — left for Mindanao the same day that we left Manila. The communication of the Universal House of Justice tells the rest of the story:

> Parviz Sadiqi, Faramarz Vujdani and Parviz Furughi were among a number of Iranian youth who answered the call for pioneers. With eleven others they registered at the Universities in Mindanao with the intention of completing their studies and proclaiming the Faith of Bahá'u'lláh. These three had conceived the plan of making teaching trips to a rural area inhabited by Muslims. When on 31 July the authorities of Mindanao State University were notified that they had left the campus the previous day and had not yet returned, search parties were immediately formed and the assistance of the police and local authorities obtained. After inquiries and search led entirely by President Tamano of Mindanao State University, the bodies of the three young men were found in a shallow grave. They had been shot, grievously mutilated and two had been decapitated. The bodies were removed and given Bahá'í burial in a beautiful plot donated for the purpose . . . The sacrifice made by these youth adds a crown of glory to the wonderful services now being performed by Bahá'í youth throughout the world . . .

Looking at the list of his suggestions and consequent activities in the Philippines, Raḥmat's methodical approach becomes very clear.

Each successful project prompted him to think of another related project. He never left anything unfinished. Those National Assemblies who had close association with him anticipated this, and, at the completion of each campaign, were prepared for another onslaught of activities.

The Nine Year Plan of the Philippines was triumphantly concluded. Raḥmat was with the friends in March 1973 to celebrate their victories, and to assist them in preparing their new plan. The National Assembly described his efforts to the Universal House of Justice: 'Enclosed is an outline of our One Year Teaching Plan and Goals . . . We are deeply grateful that Hand of the Cause of God Dr Muhájir came to the Philippines enlightening us on what this one year Plan that you have requested us to make really means.'

Raḥmat found the time to include Manila in his itinerary and rush to the assistance of the friends of the Philippines whenever they needed him. In March 1974 he was there again and wrote in his diary,

> I arrived in Manila on the 24th. The World Plan had arrived. It surely is going to breathe a new spirit into the communities of the world. I stayed for two days and consulted with the National Assembly. Their Publishing Trust was established. We discussed very important matters. I am sure they will be able to make proper decisions.

He continued to send letters and cables to the National Assembly and encouraged them to try and achieve all their goals one year earlier, so that they could concentrate their efforts in the last year of the Plan on consolidating their achievements. Raḥmat believed that, instead of leaving the achievement of goals to the last months of the Plan, the friends should try to achieve all of them in the first year. This would give time to go over the weak spots and correct mistakes.

In December 1975, he wrote to the Universal House of Justice:

> We had a glorious Teaching Conference in the Philippines. Many friends had come from the province of Luzon. There are many Bahá'í students in Luzon, so it was decided to concentrate most of the effort on that province.

> The government has started to become curious about the tribes, which might make our work more difficult. We formulated extensive plans and many of the youth who are from the tribes and are members of the committees and local Assemblies volunteered to visit their village homes.

The National Assembly reported: 'As a result of the salient points given by the Hand of the Cause to the believers the National Assembly chose 32 key centres where the "family-teaching" concept of Dr Muhájir will be tried. From these 32 localities, 14 regional conferences emerged.'

In his next visit Raḥmat was overjoyed to find Filipino, Iranian and Malaysian pioneers working closely together for the fulfilment of the goals of the Plan. He said, 'There is nothing impossible in this world, everything is possible because of the power of Bahá'u'lláh . . . I believe that you will reach your goals before the end of the Five Year Plan.' His prediction came true.

The Bahá'í community of the Phillipines now possessed a deep reservoir of experienced believers which Raḥmat tapped whenever teachers were needed elsewhere in the world. He sent a cable from Honolulu in March 1977 which read,

> PLEASE CABLE TOKYO IF SOME TRAVEL TEACHERS CAN VISIT KOREA FEW MONTHS STOP REACHING MANILA END MARCH PRAYING TOTAL VICTORY FIVE MONTH PLAN STOP DEEPEST LOVE

The letter of the Universal House of Justice approving this project followed a few days later: Vic Samaniego and others arose for this service.

During this trip Raḥmat suggested that additional tutorial schools be established, and that tribal teaching be increased. He had been away only a few months when the National Assembly implemented his proposals and asked the Universal House of Justice for his presence at their conference. The cable of the Universal House of Justice dated December 1977, lovingly said,

> DELIGHTED ESTABLISHMENT TWO ADDITIONAL TUTORIAL SCHOOLS PLANS TRIBAL CONFERENCE JANUARY PRAYING

SHRINES CONFIRMATION TRIBAL TEACHING PLAN STOP HAND CAUSE MUHAJIR UNABLE ATTEND OWING HIS HEAVY TRAVEL SCHEDULE AFRICA

Raḥmat did get to Manila in July 1978, and wrote in his diary that the Universal House of Justice had sent him a cable, asking him to visit Sikkim, Thailand and Taiwan:

> They have asked that the Iranian youth in the Philippines pioneer to Taiwan. Fortunately the National Assembly was in session. Three of the youth volunteered to go to Taiwan for one week. I phoned Vic Samaniego, who is in Japan, to go to Kuala Lumpur and Taiwan, en route to the Philippines. God willing, if I can get a visa for Taiwan, I will return to Taipei.
>
> I remained in Manila for five days. I was busy from the moment of arrival. The National Assembly drafted a programme for the nine remaining months of the year. They are also going to research the needs for the next plan, which might be for five years. Both of the plans are nearly complete, and there are provisions for great victories in them. The goal is concentration on deepening and expansion.
>
> Marinduque was chosen for this concentration. They hope to teach in five tribes and make the province of Marinduque completely Bahá'í.
>
> We had a conference in Quirino. There were more than 100 participants. They decided to get busy with their teaching work. Establish a local Assembly in each town and village and build another Bahá'í Centre in a few months' time. They are going to bear all the expenses, including those of the teachers who come to that province. Praise be to God. How the influence of the teachings of God transforms the hearts.
>
> It was also decided to approve the proposal of Jack McCants and his wife Toni Mantel to pioneer to the Philippines. They will come for one year and will live in Solano or Santiago. The fund to buy a jeep for them is available so that they can teach in the East of the Philippines all the time. They will arrive on 15 August.
>
> It was also decided that all provinces become self-organizing, self-planning and self-supporting.

It was on this visit that Raḥmat, according to Vic Samaniego, increased his appeals to the friends of the Philippines to help propagate the Faith in other countries:

> He met Walter Maddela en route from the International Convention, and detoured him to the Solomon Islands and to Kiribati. He spurred seven more pioneers on their way to settle in Africa — four Filipinos and three Iranian students. At the same time he started a flood of travel teachers from the Philippines to Asiatic areas to help in their goals.

Raḥmat's last trip to Manila was in April 1979, when he attended the Convention. During the second night of the National Convention he invited the members of the National Assembly, together with the Auxiliary Board members and their assistants, to meet with him and Counsellor Payman in his hotel. He spoke about his teaching experiences and asked the friends to avoid petty jealousies and not to magnify the faults of others: 'Protect the friends from disunity and love each other. Be more prayerful than ever before.' He promised the friends gathered at the Convention that he would return to the Philippines when all their goals were accomplished.

Counsellor Vic Samaniego expressed the effect of Raḥmat's work in that community:

> Dr Muhájir's custom was to plan with the local believers and teachers. Once the plans were in motion he would quietly pick up his bag, take a jeep or a bus and leave for the airport. There we were in the middle of a conference and not able to accompany him. I am sure he knew our feelings of inadequacy, of being deserted, so to speak, but he also knew how tall we stood as we finished the conference alone. We always hoped he would choose one of us to travel with him.
>
> If the mission was to secure the legalization of Bahá'í marriage, he took us to government offices, showed us how to get appointments and how to approach officials with dignity and self-assurance.
>
> He helped us form our National Teaching Committee, call large conferences, and get results from consultation. While

he prodded us to make plans and achieve goals, he at the same time challenged us to dare and do more than we dreamed we could achieve.

Every contact he made was so marked by a complete loving acceptance and such unfailing courtesy and appreciation as to leave an indelible impression on the recipient, and be a lasting example to the Bahá'ís.

He would always sit with the new National Assembly and inspire it with new plans and help set in motion new developments. He urged us to utilize 'family teaching teams', which resulted in teachers being accompanied by their small children. In this way we were able to favourably impress officials who would have been difficult to reach otherwise and who would not have allowed us to teach in their areas without this visual introduction of family unity. In many parts of the Philippines at this later point in time, it is impossible to send any kind of teaching teams except such a family group to visit another family. Now 'family teaching teams' have become all-important.

He initiated teaching of women in their homes and called for regional and local Women's Conferences. He was the first person to put together an instruction book in simple English for teaching children so that it could easily be understood by the native teachers.

In the acquisition of Bahá'í properties, his supreme faith, combined with practicality, provided the momentum needed to accomplish our goals. He encouraged many tribal Bahá'ís to donate Bahá'í Centres, and, in Santiago helped select and finalize the purchase of the Teaching Institute, arranged celebrations in the new property, and immediately donated a gas lamp for the Institute. When transportation of teaching teams became a problem it was Dr Muhájir who found donors for jeeps, which are still used for teaching.

Ten years after his passing, while travelling teachers, accompanied by Zeny Ramirez, one of the early teachers of the Faith, were visiting some remote towns in the Island of Mindanao, they came to a little roadside cafe and stopped for some rest. The owner heard them talking about the Faith, and approached them weeping, and repeatedly saying, 'Bahá'u'lláh, Bahá'u'lláh'. She said she was a Bahá'í, but for the last fifteen years nobody had visited them. She then said, 'Where is Dr. Muhájir? What's happened to him? Why doesn't he visit us any more?' On hearing of his death the whole family went into another bout of weeping. Dr Muhájir had brought them into the Faith and had often visited them. Now they felt bereaved and fatherless.

With his passing to the Abhá Kingdom, the Bahá'ís of the Philippines lost their constant helper, their sincere friend, and many hundreds their spiritual father, who had personally introduced them to the Faith of Bahá'ulláh. His voice still rings in our ears and we long for his unexpected arrival in the Bahá'í Centre to tell us, 'Time is short. Bring the map of the Philippines and tell me about your plans so that I can change them!'

THAILAND

On our way to the Mentawai Islands in 1954, we had stopped in Bangkok for a day and a night. In the ensuing years Raḥmat visited Thailand numerous times, yet he considered his real work there to have begun in 1973.

The friends in Bangkok had been resistant to mass teaching for many years, and insisted on having a strong adimintrative base in Bangkok before contemplating bringing masses into the Faith. Raḥmat wrote in his notes, 'I stayed in Thailand for two nights. I met the friends but it was not very useful. One of them said that they did not need a new plan but needed first to solve their problems. I left them to themselves at 10.30 p.m.'

Raḥmat encouraged the Iranian pioneers to leave Bangkok and settle in the interior, so that they could start teaching the refugees who had fled from the Vietnam War into Thailand. Kamal and Kamelia Ma'aní, Naser and Maliheh J'afari answered his call and left Bangkok. Teaching among the refugees dovetailed into teaching the native people of Thailand.

Kamal had a motorcycle which he used for his travel teaching. Raḥmat would ride with him, and they would trek the dusty and potholed roads of Thailand to meet the Bahá'ís and teach in the villages.

Mr and Mrs Ja'fari lived in Songkhla, 1400 kilometres from Bangkok. Whenever Raḥmat visited Thailand it was for the sole

Dr Muhájir negotiating with Thai Customs in 1974.

With Kamal and Kamelia Ma'aní at airport, 1974.

purpose of seeing them. Their daughter, whom Raḥmat had named Carmel, was two-and-a-half years old. Maliheh recalls that Naser had taught Carmel to address Raḥmat as *Amu Ayadi* — Uncle Hand of the Cause — which made Raḥmat very happy. Maliheh Ja'fari remembers,

> He stayed with us, in our humble dwelling, for three days and three nights. Many friends came to the Feast and he was delighted with them. One day he showed us Gisu's picture and said 'I am not a good father. I left her when she was Carmel's height. Now look at her. And I am still away.' The day he was leaving he asked us to sit with him and said, 'I want to tell you a little about children. Maliheh, you are alright, you are relaxed. Naser, you are too rough with your son. You should look at children as if they are tender flowers. If you are harsh with them they will wilt and spoil. You have to be very gentle. Whenever you forget this put your big hand against his tiny one and remember my words. Write on a big piece of paper *Amu Ayadi* and hang it on the wall. Anytime you are cross with him look at it and remember my words.' His frequent visits to Thailand were the consolation of our hearts at a time when our institutions were in their infancy. Anyone who heard he was in town would rush to his hotel. He would graciously invite everyone to his room and kindly and softly talk to the adults and give sweets to the children. At one time he would lead us on a teaching excursion to Lumpini Park and at another he would let us gather around him, and listen to our complaints and problems.
>
> Once we had a teaching conference in a rose garden, at which Dr Muhájir arrived unannounced. The joy of the friends was unimaginable. On the way to the airport, passing through heavy traffic, in the hot, humid and suffocating weather, we had a glimpse of what he went through every time he visited us. At the airport, even if there was only a little time, he would take the friends to the coffee shop. There he would clear his briefcase, getting ready for the next stop.
>
> The post-Hong Kong conference, held in Port Dickson, Malaysia, in 1977 was another occasion for us to be with him. We travelled by train and car and were 54 hours on the way. I was

With Mrs Boman and Bahá'í friends in Thailand, 1974.

With Naser and Maliheh Ja'fari, Chiang Mai, 1978.

> pregnant with our second child. Three Hands of the Cause, Dr Muhájir, Mr Faizí and Mr Featherstone attended the conference. At recess, Malaysian friends gathered around them and I could not get through. As Dr Muhájir was passing through the crowd, he saw me and invited me to his hotel to have lunch with him and Firaydún Missaghian. We went to his room and he ordered lunch. He was unhappy with the way the conference was going. He expected so much more. His vision was always higher and vaster than the rest of us. He was going to meet with the Board members after lunch to discuss adding more goals.
>
> He knew I was sharing a room with a few friends which had no air conditioning. After lunch he said, smiling, 'God loves his pioneers. While I go to the meeting, you stay here and rest. Enjoy the cool air and the privacy.'

On later trips Raḥmat would only stay in Bangkok for a few hours, then leave for the interior to spend time with the pioneers. Kamelia Ma'aní remembers that on one occasion they heard he had arrived in Bangkok:

> It was the Declaration of the Báb and we had planned celebrations with our local Bahá'ís. The National Assembly also had arranged a lavish feast in Bangkok and we were certain that there was no way that we could have the Hand of the Cause with us. However, we sent an invitation to him. On the day of our celebration Dr Muhájir arrived. He stayed with us for two days, spent time with the friends, gave gifts to our children and chanted prayers for us before leaving. It was the last time that we saw him.

His last trip to Thailand was in August 1978. The Ja'fari family had moved to Chiang Mai, on the border with Laos. Raḥmat went there intending to stay for one night, but remained for four. During those days he visited some villages and gave a talk in the university. Maliheh writes,

> When he was leaving, my sadness was reflected in my face. He smiled and said, 'Maliheh Kh͟ánum don't worry. You are a good

> girl, God loves you.' He went to the airport, but came back, as there was no room on the plane. He said, 'I don't get to stay in my own home for four nights, but I stayed with you for four nights.'
>
> That evening he shared some of the Writings with us. one passage was about tests, and how everything was a test for everything else. He said, 'At first when I read this passage, whatever someone did to me, I said to myself, never mind, he is a test for you. Later I realized that I was a test to others also. I am a bigger test as I am a Hand of the Cause. Everything I do people say, "Look, a Hand of the Cause did that!" I am a test for them.'
>
> He left for Bangkok and we followed him. He met with the National Teaching Committee and advised them to interview the friends to see how they wanted to serve the Faith. When the committee members came out of the room, Dr Muhájir had left for the airport.

In his diary Raḥmat noted:

> On 1 August I went to Chiang Mai and stayed for three days. I spoke in the university and the teacher-training college. They were both wonderful meetings. In Bangkok I met the National Spiritual Assembly and the Counsellors and discussed the teaching work. We formulated three teaching plans for North, South and South-East Thailand. Vic Samaniego stayed on to help them with these plans. In Chiang Mai I had a dream that I was in Rangoon and a Bahá'í teacher gave me a large amount of money and asked me to establish three mass teaching zones. After Thailand I went to Burma and after consultation with the National Assembly we made a few teaching programmes. With the confirmation of Bahá'u'lláh they will pursue those plans.

VIETNAM & CAMBODIA

Vietnam had a vibrant community. Some pioneers had gone there even before the Ten Year Crusade, and, together with the Vietnamese friends, had created a strong Bahá'í Administration.

Raḥmat's first visit was in May 1960, on the occasion of the dedication of the new Bahá'í Centre in Saigon. The American *Bahá'í News* reported,

At the inauguration ceremonies for the Saigon Bahá'í Centre, 1960, with members of various local Assemblies.

Bahá'ís at the inauguration of the Saigon Bahá'í Centre, 1960.

First National Convention, Vietnam, with the Jarai tribe delegates.

Last visit to Vietnam: Saigon, 1974.

> Hand of the Cause Raḥmatu'lláh Muhájir visited Vietnam, May 17-23, and the highlight of his visit was the formal inauguration of the new Ḥaẓíratu'l-Quds which took place on the Anniversary of the Declaration of the Báb before an audience of over 100 believers from Saigon and the nearby Bahá'í communities of Long An, Hiep Phuoc, Nha Be and Phuoc Long.
>
> During the afternoon of May 22, Dr Muhájir advised on the formulation of plans for intensive teaching work as well as the establishment of week-long teaching seminars to be held every month in the new Ḥaẓíratu'l-Quds . . . In Trung Giang, Central Vietnam, Dr Muhájir addressed a gathering of over 200 believers and sympathizers and also visited the Bahá'í communities of Tourne, Quang Ngai and Binh Son as well as the two Bahá'í schools in Nha Be and Phuoc Long. His presence everywhere inspired the friends to reactivate themselves and his invaluable suggestions for organizing the teaching work will, we are sure, by God's Grace, bear abundant fruit in the near future. The Bahá'ís of Saigon are especially grateful for having Hand of the Cause Muhájir for the inauguration of their new Ḥaẓíratu'l-Quds. Our only regret was that his visit was so very short.

In 1964 he represented the Universal House of Justice at the convention held to elect the very first National Spiritual Assembly of the Bahá'ís of Vietnam.

On his frequent visits to Vietnam, Raḥmat participated in many conferences and Summer Schools and attended the meetings of the National Assembly to help them work on the achievement of their goals. Accompanied by the Vietnamese friends, he also made several visits to Bahá'í communities in Cambodia. There were many problems for the growing Bahá'í community and Raḥmat bore much of the duty of solving these. The friends needed support in their efforts to become united. Gradually, after months of constant attention, the problems were surmounted. Eventually the dangers of the war made it impossible for Raḥmat to visit the Bahá'ís in the interior. His last recorded visit was to the National Teaching Conference in 1974.

NORTH-EAST ASIA

HONG KONG

Raḥmat had frequent opportunity to pass through Hong Kong, as it was the link between the countries of the various regions of Asia. The Bahá'í community of Hong Kong was very small, and the only pioneers were Mr Heshmat Azizi and his family. When in Malaysia, Raḥmat encouraged the youth to travel teach in Hong Kong, and, if possible, settle there. He asked Yan Kee Leong and Leong Tat Chee to spend some months there; through their assistance many were attracted to the Faith.

In 1968, he began sending Bahá'ís from the Philippines to teach in Hong Kong. The first person to be chosen for this task was Navidad Cruz. Although a Bahá'í for only two years, Navidad had quickly gained considerable experience in mass teaching, and was not afraid to go to an unknown environment. As usual, Raḥmat urged her not to wait for anything, and sent her off with a small sum of money and a short-term visa. Navidad stayed in Hong Kong for more than a year, and was instrumental in teaching many Chinese people.

Raḥmat travelled by train across Hong Kong, up to Shon Soi at the Chinese border, and showed the friends how they could teach. He told them to go to restaurants and cafes and befriend people to whom they could give the massage. He told them that the Chinese people are hospitable and friendly, and would listen to what we have to say.

In 1967, he decided to find a suitable place for the Bahá'í Centre in Hong Kong. He told me that he had looked at many buildings until he had come to an apartment block which was still under construction. He called the Hong Kong friends and said that they should buy two flats in that building, join them together and use it for their national Centre. The purchase price was about HK$64,000. The friends were astonished. They had no funds with which to buy anything. Raḥmat was not disturbed. With the approval of the Universal House of Justice, the down payment was paid by Mr Azizi, and within a few months the two flats were purchased with the help of the National Assembly of Iran. Those flats still serve as the National Bahá'í Centre, and their value has increased a hundredfold.

A letter of November 1967, from the National Assembly of Iran to the National Assembly of Japan indicates its willingness to comply with Raḥmat's request, '. . . in connection with Hong Kong Ḥaẓíratu'l-Quds . . . please note this NSA has undertaken to extend the help needed for Bahá'í activities in Asia, from all aspects, and would therefore request you to write to the Hand of the Cause of God, Dr Muhájir in this respect . . . '

With the help of travelling teachers and pioneers, five local Spiritual Assemblies were formed in Hong Kong, and the National Assembly established in 1974.

During the time that we lived in Manila, we had to go to Hong Kong annually to renew our visa. Sometimes Raḥmat would go with us. I remember the times when our dear friend Yan Kee was there, and he and Raḥmat would sit together till late at night, discussing the importance of teaching the Chinese in Hong Kong. 'Yankeján,' Raḥmat would say, 'This is the gateway to the mainland of China. How can I make the friends here realize what a great responsibility they have?' Yan Kee would smile and say, 'Dr Muhájir, don't worry, I will talk to them. I will go with them.'

In November 1976, Raḥmat participated in the International Teaching Conference in Hong Kong. This was a magnificent occasion and a great success. Raḥmat was in his element. Kamal Ma'aní, a pioneer in Thailand, who was a member of the organizing committee, recalls that Raḥmat was on the go for hours on end. One morning Raḥmat called Kamal and asked him to have about 20 rooms available in the hotel. 'But Dr Muhájir', Kamal protested, 'there are no vacant rooms at all in the hotel.' Raḥmat could not be bothered with this minor detail. He repeated that he needed the rooms by five p.m. There had to be many transfers from one room to another: the youth were asked to room together, which made 20 rooms available. Raḥmat arranged the rooms himself, moved the beds to the side and asked for extra chairs. Signs were put on the doors assigning each room to one National Spiritual Assembly represented at the Conference. All night long Raḥmat went from room to room, bringing prospective pioneers and teachers to consult with members of the various Assemblies.

Addressing the friends at the 1976 International Bahá'í Conference in Hong Kong.

My father, Hand of the Cause Mr Furútan, who was representing the Universal House of Justice at the Conference, remembers that by the end of each day Raḥmat could hardly stand up.

In his report to the Universal House of Justice Raḥmat said:

> It was a great joy for me to participate in the Hong Kong conference. I will now leave on 2 December for Korea, accompanied by Counsellor Vic Samaniego, David Mockon, the member of the NSA of the Philippines, and Faramarz Ettehadieh, member of the NSA of Austria, who has come for teaching trips to this area. Samaniego and David Mockon will, God willing, remain for the three winter months in Korea and will spend a few weeks in Japan to help in teaching, training the Assistants to the Auxiliary Board members and visiting the

> villages to teach and consolidate the Bahá'ís. I am sure they will be able to carry out all the instructions of the Supreme Body.

His second letter to the Universal House of Justice indicated that their travels had been very successful:

> The few days of our stay in North-East Asia passed very quickly. In Korea, with the bounties of God, I was able to meet the National Assembly and a systematic plan was devised for the election of the local Assemblies in the days of Riḍván. If they carry out these plans they will double the number of their local Assemblies, or at least increase it to 120. They have a four-month plan so that the momentum will continue after the Riḍván period . . . the travels of Vic Samaniego and David Mockon have had great effects in this country. I hope other teachers and pioneers could come to this country from the Philippines.

Raḥmat last visited Hong Kong in 1978.

> *23 July*: We had a wonderful meeting in Hong Kong. I had consultations with the National Assembly and it was decided that they have a conference at the end of December about teaching the Chinese. They will teach for one month and will seek assistance from neighbouring countries. We had a public meeting in the evening. Next day I went to a book store and then to the airport. I called dear Írán and Gisu, talked with them and wished them well for their trip to Germany and France, then left for Bangkok.

JAPAN

The whole region of North-East Asia, consisting of Japan, Korea, Hong Kong and Taiwan, was originally under the jurisdiction of the National Spiritual Assembly of the Bahá'ís of Japan. It had to manage the affairs of the Faith in the other four countries and work towards the formation of their National Assemblies. These were weighty goals, and the Japanese Assembly, despite its fervour, had insufficient manpower to achieve them.

The Faith arrived in Japan in 1909 when two Bahá'í travellers held a public meeting. In 1914 the Hand of the Cause of God Agnes Alexander pioneered to Japan as a youth, at the instruction of 'Abdu'l-Bahá, and gradually the Faith took root. Two years after her arrival, 'Abdu'l-Bahá wrote of her great triumph in the *Tablets of the Divine Plan*: 'Consider ye, that Miss Agnes Alexander, the daughter of the Kingdom, the beloved maid-servant of the Blessed Perfection, traveled alone to Hawaii . . . and now she is gaining spiritual victories in Japan!'[14]

Shoghi Effendi's letters stressed the importance of teaching and pioneering in Japan: 'The Guardian is hopeful that the conditions in Japan may not force many of the pioneers to leave that territory. As you know, he attaches the utmost importance to the teaching work in Japan; he anticipates that the Faith will spread rapidly in that country.'[15]

In 1953 the Katirai, Moghbel and Mumtazi families pioneered to Japan from Iran, and in later years American pioneers settled in various cities.

Raḥmat visited Japan no less than 18 times, the first in March 1961. He tried to familiarize himself with the culture and customs of the people and spent many hours in Japanese libraries, learning as much as he could about that country. His diary reflects his thoughts on his first trip:

> I arrived in Tokyo on the eighth. Mr Katirai and Mr Moghbel were at the airport. As I had changed my route and had arrived from Hong Kong instead of Manila I was two hours late. However, these dear souls had stayed on to see the ceremonies of the arrival of the King of Belgium. Thank God for these ceremonies, otherwise they would have been gone and I would have been left in this city of 10,000,000 inhabitants, and no one, including myself, would have been able to find me!
>
> Today is the ninth and the whole day I have been busy getting visas for Bolivia and Paraguay. I have already been to Pakistan, India, Ceylon, Malaya, Singapore, Indonesia, Vietnam, Philippines, and Hong Kong. It was a very happy time and I gained a lifetime's experience, but alas I was not able to render any service. My hope is in God's assistance.

That same day he met with the National Spiritual Assembly and read them the Guardian's letters to Japan, one of which said:

> Shoghi Effendi feels the time has now come when the Faith will spread rapidly in Japan. the Japanese people have great vision and spirituality, and the difficulties of the last war have prepared many of them for Divine Guidance. He therefore urges each and every one of you to treble your efforts, so that the Cause may grow and develop rapidly.[16]

Raḥmat impressed on the National Assembly the importance of following those instructions closely if they were to be successful. He recorded in his diary that the Bahá'ís currently in Japan only knew English, and had been unable to penetrate the masses. This was a great impediment. He wrote,

> They look only for the educated people and say they do not know how to communicate with the natives of the country. They have very few books in Japanese and they are in need of literature. They suggested that the best way for mass teaching was to send Japanese and non-Japanese together to teach. There is a need for more pioneers and more publicity. The Japanese people are very pure-hearted and intelligent. The friends believe that the spread of the Faith should be gradual, and that we should be very careful about accepting new believers. I think we need local Bahá'í teachers but it is very difficult to find them in Japan.
>
> When I study the letters of the Guardian to Japan I notice how much he has emphasized the teaching of the Ainu people. None of the pioneers or the National Assembly members even knew about them. They were very surprised when they read them and decided to make a new effort. I now understand how important it is to collate and publish these letters, as well as the letters to Africa and other countries. May God assist us in this endeavour.

The National Assembly recalls this visit:

> He spoke to the NSA about mass conversion. This was an entirely new concept to us. He said to accept the villagers when

With the National Spiritual Assembly of Japan and Hand of the Cause Agnes Alexander, 1964.

With the Bahá'ís of Tokyo, 1964.

they enrol, and deepen them later. He said there were many steps to consolidation, and that deepening would go on for years. He spoke about his own experiences with mass conversion in India and Malaysia. At that time he was interested in Hokkaido and wanted to explore the potential for mass teaching there.

Dr Muhjair particularly promoted the teaching work in Korea. He saw it as a possible mass conversion area. After coming to Japan he went to Korea, and, with the help of the pioneers and the native believers, mass teaching started — thousands accepted the Faith.

By January 1963, Raḥmat was more familiar with the opportunities for teaching in Japan, and decided to take the initiative. On his arrival in Tokyo he asked the National Assembly to make a programme for him to travel around the country. The Assembly called Mr Parviz Victory, who was pioneering in Japan with his family, and asked him to accompany Raḥmat to Hokkaido. With his usual concern for saving on expenditure, Raḥmat had booked a twin room in the YMCA. Sapporo, the capital of Hokkaido province, was freezing cold. Mr Victory recalls, 'It was even difficult to breathe. Dr Muhájir, who suffered from bronchitis, did not have proper clothing. I immediately bought a woollen stocking hat for him, and fur-lined boots for both of us so that we could walk in the frozen snow.'

Mr Tehrani, the pioneer in Sapporo, had arranged a small meeting with the native friends, which lasted late into the night. Despite Mr Tehrani's efforts to heat the room, the biting cold would not allow them to sleep. They had to shovel coal into the stove and sit around it. They spent the night reminiscing together about their days in Iran.

The next morning they went to the northernmost spot of Hokkaido Island, the home of the Ainu people, close to Sakhalin. This was Raḥmat's chosen destination. Although some preliminary contact had been made with the Ainu — indeed, one of their chiefs had become a Bahá'í — Raḥmat hoped to fulfil the beloved Guardian's wish that these indigenous people be brought into the Faith in large numbers.

He and his three companions took a room in a small house. The few local Bahá'ís came to see them, and remained with them for some time. Raḥmat wanted to pay his respects to the Ainu chief who was a Bahá'í. Mr Victory recalls,

> Our pleas that he stay in the relatively warm room were to no avail. We knew that it was dangerous for him to go out in the blizzard and freezing cold but he insisted and we did what he wanted. We could not understand the driving force in Dr Muhájir's soul. He did not think of food, sleep, or rest. He was restless and on the go all the time. When there was a plan or a decision about teaching he wanted it to be implemented right away.

Raḥmat's visit to Hokkaido was cut short by a telephone call from the National Assembly. An urgent matter had arisen and he had to leave immediately, but he asked his three companions to remain with the Ainu and continue to teach. An hour before the flight he went to a store and bought a beautiful coat for Gisu, who was then two-years old.

During this trip Raḥmat also visited the island of Honshu. Miss Nabuko Iwakura, who had very recently become a Bahá'í, was appointed his guide by the National Spiritual Assembly. She recalls,

> I had no idea what a 'Hand of the Cause' was. Some older Bahá'ís had warned me that he was very serious and strict and I was afraid and nervous that I could not cope with the work.
>
> The moment I met him I felt better. He was an unassuming, humble, quiet and gentle man. He asked me what we could do on this trip as he did not want to waste a minute. I made some suggestions and we started to work.
>
> We went to Kiushu to meet the pioneers, held firesides for young students and talked to them about Bahá'í education. One of the students was inspired to go to England to study. Dr Muhájir told us to 'Take good care of him, he will become a good Bahá'í.' Mr Higashi later accepted the Faith and is now an active Bahá'í.
>
> When it was time to go to Nagasaki, we asked him if he wanted to go first class, as it was a long journey. He said second class was

just fine for him. All through the journey he only ate some oranges.

Before starting to teach in any place he always asked about topics suitable for the Japanese. I would reply that he was the Hand of the Cause and knew better. But he said being a Hand of the Cause did not mean that he knew the culture of the people. He wanted us to guide him on our manners.

It was very cold and he did not have proper warm clothing, but he never complained. I bought some inexpensive woollen socks which he wore with great delight.

On the train I was busy making schedules and was very concerned for every detail. He said, 'Just relax, we will do our best. It does not matter if everything is not perfect for me. Everything is in the hands of Bahá'u'lláh.' I continued with planning. When the time came to disembark I could not find our tickets. He again said, 'Relax, take your time and look inside your purse again.' I said I had already done that and the tickets were not there. We had to pay for the tickets again. When we left the gate I looked in my purse for something and the tickets were right there. Dr Muhájir just smiled and said, 'You see, I told you they were in your bag. You have no confidence in me.'

He did not want to spend anything on his own comfort, but when we invited reporters he reserved a good room in a big hotel and gave them lunch. He said that as the meeting was for the Faith it should be as dignified as possible. Whenever we visited the homes of the Japanese friends, he always gave me money to buy them gifts.

Once, when flying from one city to another, the weather was very bad. They announced that they were diverting the plane to another city and that passengers could take the train to their original destination. I was agitated and worried that the friends there would be waiting. Dr Muhájir said calmly that I should not worry. I told him that he did not know the Japanese. They would be very upset and I had to find a way to inform them. He smiled and said, 'Alright, we are up in the sky, you do what you like.' He was relaxed and smiling, and I was getting more agitated. But in the end the plane landed on time and at the original destination.

With Mr Teherani, Hokkaido, 1966.

Reading in the Botanical Gardens, Sapporo, 1966.

Many times I saw how relaxed Raḥmat was on planes. The minute we were in our seats he would kick off his shoes and loosen his tie. After saying a prayer, he would sleep till awakened for meals. If he had rested before boarding the plane, then he would take care of his correspondence. Many letters to the Universal House of Justice were written during flights. I once asked him how he could be so relaxed and have no anxiety at all about an accident. He said that his life was in the hands of Bahá'u'lláh. He could not alter his fate, so why worry?

On one occasion, when he was flying from Singapore to Hong Kong, en route to Japan, he had gone to sleep. After some time the plane landed, and he disembarked only to find himself back in Singapore. A sudden typhoon had closed Hong Kong airport, and the plane had returned to Singapore. Raḥmat had been blissfully unaware of turbulence, announcements, or the plane turning back. He told me that the flight attendants could not believe that he had been oblivious to the whole incident.

This relaxed attitude held true for every aspect of his travel. He was always careful that the weight of his suitcase did not exceed the baggage allowance. However, on one trip to Taipei from Tokyo, he had to carry some books for the friends. All his bargaining did not deter the check-in assistant from charging him for excess baggage. So Raḥmat simply cancelled his flight and left an hour later with an American plane with a greater allowance for baggage.

Mr Katirai recalls how he once met Raḥmat in the transit lounge of Hong Kong airport. Mr Katirai was going to Ṭihrán, via India. Raḥmat was going to Japan, but immediately changed his ticket and accompanied Mr Katirai as far as India. One of the reasons that he seldom informed the friends of the times of his arrival was so that he could be free in arranging his schedules. He told me that he was so tired of travelling alone that he appreciated Mr Katirai's company, even if it was for just a few hours.

I was always frightened that, with his flying so often, there was a high risk of a fatal accident. He laughed my worries away, and said he was certain that his death would come when he was seated with the friends, relaxed and laughing.

His guide continues with the story:

In Nagasaki I asked his permission to take his suit with me and iron it for him. He smiled and said, 'It is alright, don't worry. I have everything but time.'

There was a festival in progress, and all the Japanese families were together. I mentioned this to him. He started singing, 'Everybody is home but me.' He then showed Gisu's picture to me and said how much he missed her. While walking, he chanted prayers for some time. I felt very sad for him that he was sacrificing so much, but he never complained.

In one small town I lost the way and stopped to look at a map. Looking up I could not see him. I was very worried that I might have lost him, but I found him in a small roadside Japanese cafe where labourers had their food. He was eating rice and dry fried fish. I asked him if he liked that kind of food. He said, 'Why not? People here eat it.'

In this journey I realized that my fears about his strictness were baseless. He never insulted anyone, and never complained. When he gave a suggestion which was not accepted, he listened carefully to the reasons for the objection. But if it was just ignored without any reason, he again suggested it without blaming anyone. He said Bahá'ís should never give guilty feelings to others.

I accompanied Raḥmat on some of his trips to Japan. Japan is well-known as one of the most expensive countries in the world. Raḥmat, however, managed to travel there as economically as possible. When the Japanese friends or the pioneers wanted to take him to fancy restaurants, he would not allow them to. On one trip, Counsellor Abbas Katirai, a close and dear friend who was Chairman of the National Assembly at the time, invited us to a beautiful hotel restaurant in Osaka. After one look at the menu displayed outside, Raḥmat refused to go in. No amount of persuasion would change his mind. He did not care that Mr Katirai could well afford the prices. We left the hotel and had lunch, consisting of fish-soup and noodles in a small cafe. The next day Mr Katirai did not feel well, and blamed it on the noodle soup. This became a big joke for Raḥmat, who said 'Abbas has had a comfortable life. He needs to travel with me for some time to become tough.'

After 35 years of pioneering in Japan, Mr and Mrs Katirai opened the virgin territory of Sakhalin Islands in 1990, 37 years after the beloved Guardian had designated it a goal of the Ten Year Crusade. The honour of Knights of Bahá'u'lláh was conferred on them by the Universal House of Justice. Counsellor Katirai, who now has to cope with the shortage of food and other difficulties in Sakhalin, remembers that day when he had to eat noodle soup, and says that he often wishes he had travelled with Raḥmat so that he could have toughened up for this pioneer post.

In 1966 two Auxiliary Board members — Mr Ruhollah Momtazi and the first Ainu-Japanese Board member, Mr Kazutomo Umegae — were appointed for North-East Asia. Thus the administration of the Faith took another step forward. Mr Umegae was instrumental in bringing the Faith of Bahá'u'lláh to many members of the Ainu. Mr Momtazi undertook the burden of travelling widely in the region to encourage the friends and help the local Assemblies in their duties.

'Expo '70', an international trade fair, was held in Japan. Months before it opened, Raḥmat was considering how to capitalize on this event. In India, under his guidance, we had produced a small introductory folder which explained the history of the Faith, and the twelve principles, and contained pictures of the Houses of Worship. He took it with him to Japan. Half a million copies were produced and distributed by the youth to the visitors to the exhibition. This was the first time that proclamation on such a large scale had been attempted in Japan. Raḥmat stayed for the duration of these activities, which were extremely successful.

He was back in Japan in October 1970 to review the Nine Year Plan with the National Spiritual Assembly. 'We were way behind in our teaching goals. He gave us some statistics which proved to be true. He said that, on average, you need Bahá'ís in five localities to be sure of establishing one LSA. This is the ratio in the Bahá'í world. He also outlined a correspondence course to be used in Japan.'

The Oceanic Conference was to be held in October 1971 in Sapporo. Raḥmat went to Japan in May to assist with the preparations. The National Assembly noted,

> He wanted to make it possible for all Japanese Bahá'ís to attend the historic conference if they wanted to. He also suggested a theme with some history of the Faith in Japan, ways to teach before and after the conference and to take advantage of the publicity. Of course, he attended the conference and arranged consultation between different groups.

Raḥmat did not agree with the prevailing view that Japan was a very difficult place for mass teaching. He thought that the intelligent and hard-working people of Japan who had brought their country out of the devastation of war to be one of the most advanced in the world, could certainly appreciate the teachings of Bahá'u'lláh. He believed that it was up to the pioneers to find the correct way to communicate these teachings to the Japanese. He urged them to find a way by trial and error.

He copied into his notebooks the Guardian's statements regarding Japan, and read them over and over, trying to glean from them how the Bahá'í activities should be directed.

> The beloved Guardian has said that the future of Japan from every standpoint is very bright indeed. The Faith will spread rapidly in Japan, once the public become acquainted with its universal principles, and its dynamic spirit.

In 1976 he participated in Japan's National Convention and met with the National Assembly. He wrote in his diary,

> I participated in the last hours of the Convention in Japan and the next day met with the National Assembly. Some subjects were approved:
>
> 1. Inviting Hands of the Cause Furútan, Faizí, and Featherstone to visit Japan on their way to other countries.
>
> 2. Arranging teaching teams to travel in at least 30 cities in Japan, and train at least 50 youth to be able to visit different areas, lecture about the Faith and become pillars of teaching in Japan.

North Pacific Oceanic Conference, Sapporo, Japan, 1971.

With Knights of Bahá'u'lláh Mr and Mrs Katirai, Osaka, 1972.

He continued asking individual Bahá'ís to pioneer to Japan and arranged their visas and helped them to settle. In 1976 he asked Javánshír Subḥání, a young student pioneer in the Philippines, to go to Japan. He loaned him $200 and asked him to go there and stay there. Javánshír recalls that only Raḥmat's encouragement and assurances — and his own youth —made him dare to go to the most expensive country in the world without knowing a word of Japanese, and with no means of support. He is now a most effective teacher, fluent in Japanese, with a prosperous business, and has donated thousands of dollars for various Bahá'í projects in Raḥmat's memory, which he considers repayment of the loan plus interest.

On 26 May 1978, while in the Mariana Islands for the election of the first National Assembly, Raḥmat's thoughts were with Japan:

> Through the bounty of Bahá'u'lláh, today the National Assembly of Marianaa Islands will be elected.
>
> I wrote a letter about teaching in Japan, suggesting that the Universal House of Justice direct it in the way 'Abdu'l-Bahá managed teaching in Europe, America and India, and the Guardian managed it in East Africa. If the House of Justice takes teaching in Japan in its own hand, everything will work out . . . I did not send my letter anywhere.
>
> Pioneers should scatter all over Japan. Now they are only settled in the South. They should ask all the Japanese Bahá'ís what should be done for teaching in Japan and then follow their suggestions.
>
> 'Abdu'l-Bahá has said that China and Japan will become enlightened through India. Every three or four months, travelling teachers should be sent to Japan, maybe from the Philippines, to Okinawa, Hokkaido and other minority places. From Canada and America and Australia for other areas of Japan. They should have teaching projects between Philippines and Japan, England and Japan, etc. The same way that they have for India and Malaysia.
>
> Dr Earle should return to Japan, and, in co-operation with the youth and other pioneers, renew the teaching in universities. They should consider Dr Ayman's suggestions seriously and

> teach the prominent people of Japan. Pioneers should go to Japan from all over the world, especially students. I wonder if women can teach better in Japan ?

His last thoughts on Japan were expressed in a letter to the Universal House of Justice:

> I believe that among the Asian countries, Japan has been blessed with great glad tidings and myriad promises by the Centre of the Covenant and the beloved Guardian. The spiritual leadership of this world has been given to this race. These sacred prophecies are not any less than those for Panama.
>
> Now that the Supreme Body's attention is drawn to the rapid progress of the Faith in Japan, and the fulfilment of the prophecies has become the focus of attention by that infallible Body, maybe the establishment of a House of Worship might become the harbinger and the cornerstone of this task. Perhaps this silent teacher could bring in thousands of erudite teachers in the Cause and it could have a new victory and triumph.

KOREA

Korea, in Raḥmat's estimation, was the most fertile land in North-East Asia for teaching the Faith and entry by troops. Since 1963 he had been encouraging pioneers and travelling teachers to go there, and had himself been instrumental in sending several of them. According to the National Assembly of Japan, 'thousands accepted the Faith' in that year. The National Assembly was formed in 1964, and the Korean Bahá'í community became a separate entity from Japan.

Charles Duncan, an American pioneer and Auxiliary Board member, was asked by Raḥmat to go to Korea in mid-1967. In his letter of October 1967, he wrote, 'I have been in Korea for four months and have been trying to be a roving teacher . . . Mr Ki, whom you introduced to the Faith in Kwangju, has been a true teacher. He has brought many people into the Faith, mostly young people in high school and college . . . He is really on fire.'

Once Raḥmat told me about the extreme cold of the winter when he had been there. He said that they sat on the floor hugging the small coal brazier which was the only source of heat, and talked about Bahá'u'lláh. He slept at night wearing all his woollen sweaters and his overcoat and still was chilled to the bone. Yet he was happy that he had met the natives of Korea.

In his effort to help the growth of the Faith in Korea, he wrote to Nahid and Dale Eng in 1973. This letter is a good example of the kind of encouragement — and challenge — which Raḥmat offered so many of the friends:

> I hope that the National Assembly [of Korea] have by now approved your travels, and both of you will, as one person, undertake this most important duty. The one-year plans of Asia are becoming so important that, God willing, they will yield great and unprecedented results for the Faith. In Korea they have decided to teach 5000 people. It is not difficult at all. You and dear Dale can stay in a centre in the East or West and try night and day to teach, first among the students in the cities. Also, go to the villages and bring the people under the banner of the Faith. Korea is so receptive that in a short time a large group will gather around you. There are very good Auxiliary Board members to help you.
>
> You can learn Korean easily in two months' time. The Americans have some new methods through which you will learn Korean very quickly. Make sure to establish yourself in one place in Korea and consolidate one vast region. Three more pioneers are also coming from Malaysia and are going to different areas. God willing, three places in Korea will become strong.
>
> On your way, stay for a few days in Taiwan, encourage the friends and move to Okinawa. I think you can go there with a Japanese visa. Dale has no problem with his American passport. Then go to Fukuoka, which is the southernmost city of Japan. Last year that area had nearly 20 local Assemblies, but they were not deepened. Stay there for at least one month, find the Assemblies; most of them are youth who know very little about the Faith. You will have to teach them anew and also teach new people. Even if you strengthen only five Assemblies you have achieved a lot. Last year they did not have time and the activities were done in a great hurry. You should not do the same. Spend

Travelling north by train from Seoul.

With the friends in Korea to inaugurate new teaching plans, October, 1973.

time with them and talk to them. Even if a few of them understand the Faith correctly they will themselves teach and encourage others. When the work in Japan is concluded proceed to Korea. If possible write a letter immediately to the National Assembly of Korea and consult with them about your visa. If they give you a religious or student visa it is better. Otherwise get a tourist visa and later change it to whatever is necessary.

In North-East Asia, Korea is the only country that has started teaching in the villages, but it has slackened a little. The people are very friendly, serene and intelligent. To teach them is truly exhilarating. It has four seasons and is one of the most active countries in the world. They are all literate. You are very lucky to achieve such a great bounty. I hope that the bounties of Bahá'u'lláh would produce miracles from this wonderful trip of yours and opens doors for you to guide many pure souls.

Write to Mr Katirai directly. He will send you a ticket for Japan Airlines or Air France. Get whatever you need in Manila, Mr Katirai will reimburse it. I mean that you should not wait for anything. The minute you receive the tickets and visas leave. Write the NSA of Japan to send your programme to Taipei. Do not hesitate even for one moment and leave immediately. Time is short. Stay in Taiwan for seven to ten days and move all the time. My love to both of you dear ones.

In his diary Raḥmat noted:

26 February: We are meeting at Dr Kim's room in the hospital. The NSA members and John McHenry are here to discuss the one-year plan. One of the members said that they should not depend on the International Fund for their work, but try to stand on their own feet. He said that the Christians help the church quite willingly, do not work on Sundays and believe that God would reward them on Monday. This member believed that we put too much emphasis on administration, and not enough on spiritual matters.

It was a fruitful meeting and decisions for future activities were made.

> *27 February*: We had a meeting at the Bahá'í Centre and talked about teaching around the country, and especially, in cities. We talked about teaching 5000 people, having 300 teachers, and holding 5 teaching conferences. This night is one of the dearest of my life, as the NSA of Korea has again decided to start mass teaching, and, with the bounties of Bahá'u'lláh, bring 5000 souls under His banner.

> On 5 May I attended the meeting of the National Assembly of Korea, and discussed teaching plans with them. In their last campaign in the villages, 80 to 90 per cent of the inhabitants accepted the Faith . . . It is easy to establish children's classes as the high school students can teach the children. Dr Kim's book is a very useful tool for this purpose. Winter is better than summer, as the children have more time. They should train two teachers in each village, one hundred altogether.

These suggestions were approved by the National Assembly and the Universal House of Justice, which wrote to the National Assembly:

> The Universal House of Justice has received a report from the Hand of the Cause Dr Muhájir following his recent visit to your country . . . The Universal House of Justice was delighted to note that in response to a suggestion of Dr Muhájir, you have drawn up plans to establish the Faith in 30 cities, so that from these 30 cities new Bahá'ís will be instrumental in teaching the Faith in neighbouring communities.

In 1976, Firaydún Misaghian, who was serving as the Counsellor for North-East Asia, was asked by Raḥmat to transfer to Korea. Government restrictions in Laos had greatly curtailed his Bahá'í activities and he had decided to move to Hong Kong. Firaydún recalls,

> Korea was a country outside the jurisdiction of South-East Asia, where I served as a Counsellor. At that point I was not sure what Dr Muhájir meant by mentioning Korea to me. However, I never took any of his suggestions lightly. I gave up the idea of

going to other countries and started to think more about Korea. A few days later Dr Muhájir again mentioned Korea and the wonderful work that I would be able to do in that country. A week later we met in Kuala Lumpur. He talked to me about the Korean culture and their way of life. A month later he came to Bangkok. I was travelling in the north-eastern province of Thailand. He called me to Bangkok and said, 'It is good if you settle in Thailand, but for you to be in Korea is better . . . go for a short visit there and see how things work. I am sure you will like it.' On the following day he told me that he'd had a dream of 'Abdu'l-Bahá. The Master had been standing in front of a world atlas and pointed with His finger to Korea with a strong emphatic gesture. Dr Muhájir told me, 'You should go to the place where you are needed most.' In May 1978 we settled in Korea.

TAIWAN & MACAO

Raḥmat visited Taiwan and Macao on numerous occasions to help the few pioneers and native Bahá'ís in their teaching, and the formation of their respective National Assemblies. The National Assembly of Japan reported, 'Dr Muhájir came to us with problems that needed to be solved in Taiwan — things we were not aware of, although Taiwan was in our area. But he never brought up difficulties without giving concrete advice as to how to deal with them.'

The most important achievement in which Raḥmat assisted the friends in Macao was probably the purchase of their Bahá'í Centre. His diary for February and March 1973 shows how this was done:

> *28 February*: Last night I told Mr Azizi that, if possible, we should go to Macao together. We waited till midnight, but could not find transport. We discussed Macao, and he said that he has bought a house there which could become a gathering centre for the pioneers. I told him, 'what is yours is yours and what is for the Faith is for the Faith.' We have to buy a Bahá'í Centre in Macao, otherwise the Faith will not progress. Mr Azizi, who has spent his life in service to the Faith, agreed whole-heartedly, and we went back to our hotels long after midnight.

At the Bahá'í Centre of Tainan, Taiwan, March, 1964.

In the Botanical Gardens, Taipei, 1964.

3 March: I wrote a letter to the NSA of Japan to decide about a Bahá'í Centre in Macao and collect the funds from Saporo and Mr Azizi, whose wish is to assist this area. I sent it with Philip to Japan. At eight p.m. Mr Katirai called to tell me that the NSA has approved the purchase of the Centre in Macao, and that Mr Azizi should find a place. The money will be sent. Mr Katirai will personally call Mr Azizi in Iran. Mr Azizi informed me that that very morning an agent had contacted him and told him that a very good apartment had come on the market. Relying on Bahá'u'llah, we will leave for Macao tomorrow.

4 March: I am on the boat to Macao.

I stayed in Macao for a few hours. Charles Duncan was there. His neighbour, a Chinese woman, knew Indonesian, and has been a Bahá'í for one year. Both were fasting. I was quite delighted that they are so firm in the Faith.

In Macao they told me that there were thousands of Chinese refugees from Indonesia. Two from Bali and one from Irian Bharat had accepted the Faith. It is obvious that if the Indonesian-speaking Chinese Bahá'ís travel to Macao, in a short while we will have many Bahá'ís among the refugees.

In the evening back in Hong Kong, Mr Azizi told me that the very good apartment in Macao had been sold, but one on the top was available which cost about HK$100,000. I urged him to arrange to purchase it. It depends on the Will of God.

He asked travelling teachers and pioneers to go to Taiwan and Macao, including Yan Kee Leong and Leong Tat Chee, who visited those two regions repeatedly. Many Chinese youth from both Singapore and Malaysia arrived to help Mr and Mrs Suleimani, the devoted servants of Bahá'u'lláh who were the first pioneers to Taiwan, in their teaching efforts. Auxiliary Board member Momtazi frequently went to Taiwan, as well as accompanying Hand of the Cause Samandarí in his travels there.

Mr Suleimani reported: 'It was in 1966 that the National Ḥaẓíratu'l-Quds in the capital city, Taipei, was purchased. After inspecting several constructions Dr Muhájir decided on the one at Hsin Sheng Nah Road.'

In January 1967, in a letter to the National Assembly of North-East Asia, Raḥmat said,

> Bahá'u'lláh willing, this Riḍván the NSA of Taiwan will be formed. This goal is another fruit of the sacrifice of your NSA and the pioneers in that country. Now, after formation of the NSA of Taiwan, your NSA should concentrate on Hong Kong and Macao. We hope their National Assemblies also will be formed in 1969 and 1970, although they are not mentioned in the Nine Year Plan . . .

The first National Assembly of Taiwan was elected in 1967. Raḥmat continued his visits to Taiwan and collaborated in their teaching activities. He arranged for travelling teachers from the Philippines to go to Taiwan, and asked Vic Samaniego to spend several months with the friends there.

During his last visit, Raḥmat advised the friends to keep in mind that, once opportunities to teach the Faith in mainland China arose, the National Spiritual Assembly of Taiwan would play an important role in establishing the Faith there. He reminded them to be diligent in their teaching, since such opportunities may arise sooner than they thought.

Although Taiwan had not begun to make great progress in teaching the masses during Raḥmat's lifetime, the 'Muhájir Teaching Campaign', inaugurated in 1986, brought more than 4000 souls into the Faith. This particular campaign has proved a magnet for international travel teachers, and is still going strong.

Raḥmat described his first visit to the beautiful Bahá'í House of Worship in Sydney as a 'truly spiritual experience'.

Chapter 5

IN THE MIDMOST HEART OF THE OCEAN

Australia, described by the Guardian as that 'far-off continent' had been of special significance to us ever since we left Iran. We had pioneered to the Mentawai Islands to fulfil one of the goals given to the Australian Bahá'í community. In our five years in Indonesia I had regularly sent progress reports to the National Spiritual Assembly of Australia as our 'mother Assembly'. Raḥmat had been notified of this challenging post by Collis Featherstone. Mr Featherstone was elevated to the rank of Hand of the Cause of God at the same time as Raḥmat, and the Bahá'í world was informed of their respective appointments in one and the same cable. This forged another spiritual link between Raḥmat and the Bahá'ís of Australia. Raḥmat had a special attraction towards the aboriginal peoples of both Australia and New Zealand, whom he admired greatly: he often talked about their fine qualities. Our home was festooned with tribal artefacts and gifts, which Raḥmat had brought back from his teaching trips among them.

AUSTRALIA

February 1962 was a turning point for the Bahá'í community of Australia. Their goal for the Ten Year Crusade was to establish 28 local Assemblies, but at the time of Raḥmat's first visit down under, they had only 13. He stayed for just nine days, but he so inspired the friends to arise and teach that they fulfilled their goals within two months.

5 March: It has now been more than a month since I have had time to open this notebook. I am leaving Sydney for Brisbane and these are my last days in Australia.

I arrived on the seventh of February and stayed in the home of John Heller, Mr Featherstone's son-in-law. We had two days of busy programmes, had two teaching meetings, went to see the aborigines, had interviews with two newspapers and a ten-minute talk on the radio. All together, it was a good programme. I then left for Adelaide and stayed with the Featherstones. In the five days and nights we were constantly busy.

Among the wonderful Bahá'ís of this area are Garvey Jorgic, who was in Iran and the Holy Land, and Mr and Mrs Bole. He is an Auxiliary Board member, and a wonderful Bahá'í. The Bahá'ís here are all active and devoted. I visited Renmark and stayed with the Harwood family. They own a fruit farm, and are the only people who spend all their days in teaching the tribes. I stayed with them for eight days and visited all the tribes from Adelaide to Victoria.

Today is the fifth (or sixth?) of April. It is again one month since I have been able to record anything. I am now on board the Pacific Enterprise going to Suva, Fiji. It is not easy to follow the thread of the past month's events.

I went from Renmark to Melbourne and spent three days with the friends. We had many teaching events and discussed teaching the aboriginal people. I then left for Tasmania. I can't even remember what the date was. While there, I met the Bahá'ís of Davenport and Hobart. They had many seekers, and two of the poineers from Tahiti were also there. I was very happy during my stay with them.

I then left for Canberra, the capital of Australia, to get visas for other countries, and after two days left for Sydney. This is the place where Mother and Father Dunn arrived in Australia and started teaching the Faith. That was 42 years before I came to this area. We can now see the fruits of their efforts. Included among the friends who came to greet me at the airport were some who had come to the Faith through those two luminous souls.

> To write about Sydney and its beautiful temple is not possible within the scope of these notes. It was a truly spiritual experience for me. The friends are active and informed about the writings and revolve around the temple, and give all visitors spiritual nourishment. I like to spend hours remembering the wonderful Bahá'ís of Sydney and their temple.
>
> Sydney is the heart of Australia, and the heart of its Bahá'ís shine like bright candles. They all are busy with teaching, and whatever has happened up to now in the Pacific and Australia is the result of the work of these shining hearts. These hearts however have still the power to give more light to this region, and the hope is on them. I am sure that they will render greater services in the future.
>
> I spent three days in Brisbane and again returned to Sydney. I spent some time with dear Peter Khan in the airport and went directly to Oakland.

Some nine years later, in June 1971, Raḥmat returned to Australia, and embarked on a six-week journey around the country at the request of the Universal House of Justice. He travelled across every State, visiting the friends, urging them to take part in mass teaching, and giving radio and newspaper interviews.

The report of the National Assembly in the *Australian Bahá'í Bulletin* of June 1971 gives some idea of Raḥmat's exhausting schedule:

> The Wollongong Bahá'í community had the pleasure once again of a visit by the Hand of the Cause Dr Muhájir to speak at a fireside. It was a joy to see and listen to him speak to us again since his last visit in 1962. He told us about the universal desire for love, peace and unity, which he found expressed by all people he had met on his travels throughout the world, and how the Bahá'í Faith fulfilled this need.
>
> In Tasmania, Dr Muhájir attended and addressed a Bahá'í fireside . . . on Sunday night. On Monday a picture and news paragraph on Dr Muhájir's visit appeared in the *Hobart Mercury* . . . no publicity outlet was left untapped. As a result, a ninety-second film news item appeared on TVT6, plus a five-minute radio broadcast.

A Methodist minister . . . was visited by Dr Muhájir. Interesting exchanges took place. These resulted in the promise by the gentleman to share his pulpit at a Sunday service soon with a Bahá'í speaker. A deepening session on Monday night was held at the Hobart Centre. On Tuesday the Hand of the Cause . . . travelled to Launceston where most of the friends got to meet our visitor, including Greta Lauprtill, the first Tasmanian Bahá'í.

A three-minute interview on radio was broadcast. That night on the way home a visit was made to a person who had indirectly heard of the Faith . . . several years ago. . . . A two-hour fireside resulted, which the Hand declared was the highlight of his day.

Dr Muhájir travelled from Devonport to Burnie after a 15-minute talk on radio 7AD [which was] broadcast live . . . another short three-minute broadcast was taped.

The main event of the afternoon was the presentation of a 'Compendium on Peace and Justice' from Bahá'u'lláh's Writings and also a copy of *Bahá'u'lláh and the New Era* to a newly-appointed magistrate. The magistrate told a local Bahá'í later that he was most impressed by Dr Muhájir, and would be interested to read the material given him.

In Canberra he devoted one morning to the children, many adults also came but were asked to organize a teaching plan. The children loved Dr Muhájir's stories, and the adults struggled with their planning. Teaching the masses was initiated before he left Canberra.

The pace of Raḥmat's work was so hectic and the places he visited so diverse, that the National Assembly had to resort to using cablegrams as a means of keeping in touch with him. Although he had been in Australia for over a month I had not heard from him. I cabled my concern to the National Assembly, but my urgent communications received only routine treatment. A cable sent to him by the National Assembly contained the following messages:

TO: MUHAJIR, ADELAIDE

MESSAGE: FOUR LETTERS SENT SYDNEY STOP ONE MONTH NO NEWS FROM YOU STOP VERY WORRIED STOP PLEASE CABLE

STOP PRAYING SHRINES STOP EVERYONE SENDS LOVE STOP IRAN STOP

REGIONAL GOALS COMMITTEE AT ITS MEETING GAVE THE FOLLOWING INFORMATION:

THE REGIONAL GOALS COMMITTEE WILL BE MEETING WITH DR MUHAJIR AT ELEVEN AM STOP ON SATURDAY NINETEEN AT HEADQUARTERS AND HAVING LUNCH WITH HIM STOP

A FIRESIDE IS TO BE HELD HERE ON MONDAY STOP

A DEEPENING IS TO BE HELD ON TUESDAY STOP

At the end of his six-week visit, he left the National Assembly with several recommendations. Mass conversion had started in Australia and there was great need for simple literature, so he advised use of *The New Garden*. He proposed that youth conferences should be organized for the visits of Hands of the Cause Furútan and Sears, and that Hand of the Cause Faizí should also be invited to visit Australia, after his travels in India. He recommended that further youth conferences should be held in 1972, and that the permission of the Universal House of Justice be sought for the attendance of Amatu'l-Bahá Rúḥíyyih Khánum. To the National Assembly he stressed the importance of each member travelling throughout Australia. His suggestions were, as usual, wide-ranging and challenging, and addressed both local and national needs.

The Melbourne community was in need of a Centre: he was confident that the Persian friends would contribute the necessary funds for its purchase. He advised that the Book Committee should be developed into a Publishing Trust. For teaching in the Bahá'í temple he recommended the following: that all the gardens be landscaped as soon as possible; that benches be put in the gardens for visitors; that the temple be advertised in newspapers, on TV and radio; that teaching teams, preferably of mixed races, be available in the temple at all hours; that different religious communities be approached to participate in the temple services.

Raḥmat returned to Australia in December that same year. The friends were now enthusiastically engaged in winning the goals.

Raḥmat believed that Australia was ready for entry by troops, and, before his arrival, sent the following cable to its NSA:

> SUGGEST COOPERATION COUNSELLORS LAUNCH SPECIAL MASS TEACHING CAMPAIGN TWO MONTHS VICTORIA STATE INVITE MANY BOARD MEMBERS TEACHERS FROM ALL OVER AUSTRALIA NEW ZEALAND REPEAT SAME PLAN LATER IN OTHER STATES STOP HOPE WIN GREAT VICTORIES. VISITING AUSTRALIA SOON STOP DEEPEST LOVE

The National Assembly answered immediately:

> EAGERLY LOOKING FORWARD YOUR ARRIVAL AUSTRALIA STOP DETAILED TEACHING CAMPAIGN BEING ARRANGED VICTORIA. NATIONAL YOUTH CONFERENCE CANBERRA THIRD TO SEVENTH JANUARY STOP SUMMER SCHOOL YERRINBOOL TWENTY-FOURTH DECEMBER TO THIRD JANUARY STOP MOST LOVING WELCOME EXTENDED STOP ANTICIPATE GREAT VICTORIES STOP

Raḥmat's last visit to Australia was to attend the 1974 National Convention. During this trip he visited several centres to prepare the friends for the launch of the Five Year Plan. In Canberra he 'stressed the role of the youth in the Plan', and mentioned the wish of the Universal House of Justice that the 'youth give up specific periods of time and devote that time entirely to working for the Cause.' He said that an 'informal, yet direct approach was the best with indigenous people, and that if one shows love to them they will respond and come to love you. They are so sensitive.'

On 30 May 1974, the National Assembly wrote to him:

> The Universal House of Justice told this National Spiritual Assembly that they had received reports that this was one of the happiest conventions ever held in Australia and we feel that a tribute should be paid to you for enthusing the participants, spurring them on to renewed endeavours.
>
> We are also delighted to advise you that we believe a local Spiritual Assembly of Aborigines is very close to being formed

on Palm Island, which will be the second Aboriginal Assembly in Australia.

The *Australian Bahá'í Bulletin* for May/June 1974 reported:

> At a teaching conference held in conjunction with convention, Dr Muhájir read the Naw-Rúz message of the Universal House of Justice. He then spoke, illustrating his talk with a chart depicting the human body's nervous system and the blood system. He likened the Universal House of Justice and the NSAs and LSAs to the nervous system, and the [International Teaching Centre], Hands of the Cause, Continental Boards of Counsellors and their Auxiliary Boards, to the blood system. Both belong to the same body but provide different functions. 'The red cells are the Board members for Teaching, and the white cells, the Board members for Protection. Both systems must work together, each system assisting the other. The spiritual health of the believers depends upon working and consulting together.' . . . Dr Muhájir spoke of the significance of the erection of the seat of the Universal House of Justice at the World Centre. The spiritual and administrative agencies of the Faith will be linked together forever, for the first time in religious history. The Shrine of the Báb has been called the 'Queen of Carmel'. This building is the 'King'.
>
> Dr Muhájir spoke on the teaching goals all over the world, the protection of the Faith, education, deepening, the significance of having a Publishing Trust in Australia. He said this Five Year Plan is the foundation of many plans to come . . .
>
> In Sydney, Dr Muhájir spoke at the Crest Hotel, Kings Cross. He spoke at length of the completion of the Seat of the Universal House of Justice, and of the buildings that were subsequently to be completed on Mount Carmel, to be known as 'the Arc', at a time that would synchronise with the Lesser Peace.

In a letter sent to Nineteen Day Feasts shortly after Dr Muhájir's visit, the National Assembly communicated to the Australian Bahá'ís,

> We will long have the joy and enthusiasm of 'Melbourne' ringing in our ears, when we had the bounty of the visit of Hand of the

> Cause Muhájir, who so inspired us all. Dr Muhájir expressed his own feelings when on his departure, he said he would leave Australia with just one word — happiness. The spirit which was so abundant at Convention and the teaching Conference must now be diffused throughout the entire community.

As Dr Peter Khan states,

> It is clear that Dr Muhájir's visit had a crucial influence on the achievement of the goals. He provided to the Bahá'ís a clear vision of the ultimate triumph of the Cause and of the great spiritual powers with which it was endowed. He showed them more creative and more flexible approaches to teaching, and gave new emphasis to the importance of reaching the aboriginal minority. Beyond that, his humility and his informality attracted the hearts of the believers and strengthened their motivation to serve the Faith.

Many of the teaching campaigns pursued by the Bahá'ís of Australia in recent years have been launched in Raḥmat's name. These 'Muhájir Teaching Campaigns' have been so called because of the friends' admiration for Raḥmat's teaching successes around the world, and their desire to emulate his methods.

NEW ZEALAND

When Raḥmat first visited New Zealand in 1962, although the National Assembly of New Zealand looked forward to his arrival, the April edition of their *Bahá'í News* reveals that he was something of an unknown quantity to the friends there, and that they were unsure exactly what he could do for them: 'Following so closely on the visit of Miss Jessie Revell, the Assembly feels it should be possible for Dr Muhájir to perform valuable service to our community in following up and widening the opportunities which Miss Revell's visit opened in every community she visited.'

He went to Auckland, Hamilton, Kaitaia, Wellington and Napier during the ten days of his stay. The National Assembly's confidence in Raḥmat's abilities rose dramatically in this short time. The New Zealand *Bahá'í News* reported instances of his teaching successes: 'Dr Muhájir . . . travelled five hours by car [to Kaitaia]. Here in the home of Mr Eprem Te Paa, who first heard of the Cause through HOC [sic] Enoch Olinga, with six Maoris present . . . Dr Muhájir gave a simple and moving account of the message of Bahá'u'lláh . . . following this visit, Mr Te Paa accepted the Faith.'

In Wellington, Raḥmat was involved in a burst of concentrated teaching, which helped bring the Cause to leading figures amongst the Maori people. After radio and press interviews in the afternoon, he spoke in the Maori Meeting House where 40 adults and 30 children heard of the Faith. The next day at the Maori Affairs Department he explained the Bahá'í beliefs for an hour-and-a-half to three Maori officials and their European advisers. He told the Maoris that they should lead the native peoples of the Pacific. One official pointed out that the Maoris were a minority race, but Raḥmat smilingly replied that it was really the white people who were in the minority, as the members of other races far outnumbered them! He spent that afternoon discussing the Faith with Member of Parliament Sir Eurura Tirikatene and his daughter.

He advised the Bahá'ís of New Zealand to, 'use every ounce of energy. All be travelling teachers. Concentrate on teaching, people from the North go to the South and people from the South go to the North. Make people hungry to hear about the Faith, don't be in a hurry to give information until people are hungry. We should be careful about our behaviour.'

His brief diary entry for this visit reveals the happiness he felt while with the friends there:

> I was in New Zealand from the eighth to the eighteenth of March, visited many centres including Wellington, Hastings, and the northern part to meet the Maoris. It was a new and wonderful experience for me and opened a new page in my travels, one which hopefully will not close, but will continue. This was the first time that I had the bounty of visiting the Maoris. I became acquainted with many of their influential members, and saw many others. This is a very spiritual and talented race. One of them named Te Paa, who was Olniga's contact, became a Bahá'í. God willing, he will be a beacon to guide many more to the Faith.

> The beloved 'Alá'í family are scattered throughout this country. They have formed three centres and spend their days in teaching. What a wonderful time we had. The work has just started in New Zealand. We have to think of the results and the future, and not the preliminaries of the work.

Raḥmat returned to New Zealand in 1971. The friends knew him well by now, and thronged to his meetings at Hawke Bay, Christchurch and Nelson. The National Assembly reported that,

> Dr Muhájir emphasized how much was being achieved by mass conversion and urged the friends to use every opportunity of sharing in this phenomenon . . . he stressed the effectiveness of literature in bringing the Faith to the attention of the masses. . . . He cited the example of the little State of Luxemburg, whose National Assembly was planning to distribute 300,000 pamphlets. His urging resulted in New Zealand's publication of 100,000 proclamation pamphlets with paid-reply postcards, to be used in mass teaching.
>
> He talked about the role of non-Bahá'ís in proclaiming the Faith, that they 'achieve publicity for the Faith in areas beyond our control'. He also reminded them of future crises and victories: 'Mass conversion will come. Indigenous people will do mass conversion. The hour will come when many catastrophes will occur. Definitely our prayers will be answered. We should play our part and God will play His. The people are ready, but how much are we using this readiness? There is power in teaching the Faith. We might not know what we are doing, but there is power in talking about the Faith to our friends, to the man in the street.'
>
> He urged the believers to respect local customs in their teaching activities, such as the communal life-style in many of the Pacific Islands. 'Many people will accept the Faith in groups, according to their customs. This is very important to know. The communal system plays a strong role in their lives. Do not teach the Faith individually to those people or you will be separating them from their loved ones, splitting up their closely knit families. Although the task may be onerous, it is preferable to

teach entire groups as this leads to acceptance of the Faith by everyone in the family.' As an example, he cited one village in Fiji, 'all of whose inhabitants had declared their recognition of Bahá'u'lláh after the Suva Oceanic Conference.'

'Do not knock on people's doors. We do not want to disturb their privacy. Teach them outside, when you see them in their gardens. Travel-teach in family groups. Take your wife and children along. People will trust you more.'

Raḥmat wrote to the Universal House of Justice:

> It is now a few days that I am at the service of the friends in New Zealand. With the blessings and confirmation of the Blessed Beauty, a group of dedicated and spiritual youth have arisen to serve the Faith in these islands. They are an example for friends in other communities. The youth of Napier and Hastings are totally united and have no desire but to serve the Faith.
>
> This humble servant was their guest for a day. The attached letter is an indication of their unity and love. I present it to the Supreme Body so that during prayers they could be remembered and prayed for to be assisted and become successful in their efforts to teach the people of New Zealand, especially the Maoris.
>
> This is nothing but Bahá'u'lláh's confirmation, that in these far-off islands so much enthusiasm, love and spirituality has come into existence. It is as if the breezes of blessing and the sweet aroma of bounty has wafted over this sacred land.

The friends in New Zealand were now becoming familiar with Raḥmat's simple, unpretentious and loving manner. At the Invercargill Bahá'í Centre he removed his shoes and sat 'happily on the floor completely relaxed.' At another meeting he suggested that, as the friends who had come were all British, perhaps they'd like to have fish and chips. So they all sat on the floor, eating fish and chips wrapped in newspaper.

The National Spiritual Assembly felt that his 'gift of appearing totally committed to the locality in which he was staying aroused enthusiasm' among the friends. They started teaching campaigns, and volunteered for teaching trips. In Christchurch he asked for a map, and called for pioneers to Kaikaura, 'a town 171 miles to the North. One of the friends immediately volunteered for this task.' Raḥmat chose other towns and cities around Christchurch, 'like spokes from the hub of a wheel', and asked the friends to either pioneer or go travel teaching in them. He advised the friends to visit their goal areas 'every weekend, to frequent cafes and generally become known to the local people, as a prelude to teaching the Cause of God'.

He met with dignitaries and university professors, and was interviewed by local radio and newspapers. In Nelson, he spoke on a radio show entitled 'God in the Twentieth Century', on which he was given equal time with a church minister. This was a phone-in programme, a great opportunity to engender public discussion, which resulted in considerable publicity for the Faith.

Raḥmat 'was brimming with ideas and enthusiasm particularly in relationship to youth teaching. He spoke of how they should collaborate, specially in the field of art and literature. He urged the use of the mass media, and the importance of friendly informality when teaching the Faith in the streets and how this is most easily achieved by taking one's children.' The friends were encouraged to use more examples from nature in their teaching, to make themselves more easily understood. To show what he meant, he likened human beings to lilies in a pond. The roots of the lily, down in the mud, have no idea what lies above the water, or of the beauty of the flower which derives its sustenance through the root. We in this world are like the roots of the lily: we cannot see the beauty of the next world.

At a youth camp in Whangarei, he mixed with the young Bahá'ís and talked to them about the Five Year Plan. Many volunteered to travel teach in the Pacific islands and elsewhere. In Palmerston, at a meeting with new believers and their families, 'his great love for children drew them to him. He sat down, dipped into his bag and brought out a box from which he gave each child an enamelled pin inscribed with the Greatest Name.'

He urged the friends during the course of his journey across New Zealand to pray constantly for the will of God to become manifest. He stressed the importance of preparation through prayer, and then taking action. He often said that the friends were witnessing the unfoldment of the Divine Plan and 'should remember that each plan on its completion becomes the foundation on which succeeding plans will be built.' In urging the friends not to rely on prayers alone to set and achieve their goals he said, 'Remember: all the angels and saints together cannot make a bowl of soup.'

He spoke about the 'importance of the individual and how, as each Bahá'í is a part of 'Abdu'l-Baha's Divine Plan, each believer should have a plan for deepening. He likened the believers to farmers, and said that unless a farmer works there will be no crops to harvest. By their sacrifice the martyrs planted the seeds and now we must work to prepare the season of the harvest.' The friends were asked to 'concentrate their efforts in the cities: teaching plans should be developed by local Assemblies so that Bahá'í urban manpower be harnessed to promote the Cause.' He urged them to hire halls and hold firesides every evening and said, 'nothing must be allowed to defer these meetings, not even the Nineteen Day Feast, which could be celebrated in the daytime or else late in the evening after the fireside had ended.'

On the matter of deepening new Bahá'ís, Raḥmat offered this thought:

> Teaching is a continuous process which goes hand-in-hand with consolidation. Each community should choose its own pattern. Some might decide to teach and deepen on alternate nights, others might prefer to teach for three weeks and then deepen for three weeks. In either event, follow-up is essential and we could do this by compiling albums for people to study or by inviting them to attend a course on the Bahá'í Faith. We might emulate the success of others in their use of the Bible, which is a history of religion, by studying and teaching Bahá'í history.

Raḥmat was very keen that children should be fully involved in Bahá'í activities. 'It is not sufficient for them just to feel their parent's love for the Faith. It is important that they be taken to Feasts and firesides, where they will unknowingly absorb the teachings whilst playing quietly.'

When asked to explain the best method of teaching, he said, 'All methods are the best, we should continue them.'

When his work in New Zealand was over, he reluctantly took his leave of the friends. In his diary he wrote,

> I met with the National Spiritual Assembly and the Youth Committee of New Zealand. The Youth Committee devised a teaching programme for the Pacific. I hope that, with the bounty of God, it will be carried out. I spent five days in New Zealand and went from the northernmost spot to the southernmost town. What a beautiful spirit emanates from the friends. they have enthusiastically announced the Five Year Plan and have shared it joyously.

THE PACIFIC REGION

The archipelagos and isolated islands of the Pacific Ocean held great fascination for Raḥmat. The receptivity of the island people challenged and vitalized his soul. He made at least five lengthy, and sometimes arduous, tours of the Pacific region, during which he visited most of the towns and villages on the islands, often staying for many days to help the local Bahá'ís and the handful of pioneers with their teaching work.

His first visit was in 1962. It took many days on a steamer to get there, and although Raḥmat suffered from acute seasickness accompanied by excruciating headaches, nothing could deter him from undertaking such difficult journeys to meet the friends. After staying for a few days he often had to return with the same steamer, a prospect to which he did not look forward. He was sad that his suggestions about mass teaching were not received with much enthusiasm. He told me that they thought he expected too much of them. 'I wish they would listen to me and take advantage of my experience', he would say. It never occurred to him that not everyone was able to dedicate all the hours of the day and half the night trekking through jungles and barren lands, or crossing shark-infested waters in little boats to teach the Faith.

His notes of this first trip to the Pacific are sketchy:

> I was supposed to leave on the 22nd for Tonga, but as I found a boat ready to leave for Gilbert I took that one. Finding means to travel to Gilbert is so rare that they talk about waiting for

> months, rather than days or weeks, so I took the opportunity. This was an oil tanker which I boarded on the 23rd and arrived in Gilbert on the first of April. I could only stay in Gilbert for three days, I am leaving by the same boat and have to spend another three days travelling, and hope to be in Suva on the ninth of April. I have spent two weeks travelling to be able to have four nights in Gilbert. The first days on the boat were very turbulent, and made me sick. It has now become routine for me. The weather does its own thing and I keep myself busy. These few days on the boat gave me a good opportunity to read *God Passes By*, and be in contact with the days of the Báb, Bahá'u'lláh and the beloved Master.

However, Raḥmat's diary entry for a subsequent visit to the Gilbert Islands, on 29 May 1978, show what remarkable progress the Faith had made:

> In 1962, when I first came to Gilbert, it took me twenty days by boat, and I was only able to meet eight Bahá'ís. This time the situation has completely changed. The friends are at the peak of their activity and spirituality. I was delighted to be with them. There are now 4000 Bahá'ís in these islands.

His later travels across the length and breadth of the huge Pacific region were, thankfully, mostly by plane, which saved him time and rescued him from seasickness. To reach the smaller islands and villages, however, often meant travelling by boat.

There are few details of Raḥmat's subsequent visits in 1964 and 1970. We only know that, during this period, he made trips to New Guinea, the Solomon Islands, the New Hebrides, and Fiji (where, in 1970, he represented the Universal House of Justice in the Convention at which the first National Spiritual Assembly of Fiji was formed). In June 1971 he revisited the New Hebrides and New Guinea, and returned to them in August. In October of that year he toured Melanesia, and in December, Micronesia. Although he did not keep comprehensive records of his travels, itineraries gleaned from his letters to the Holy Land show that he had visited Samoa, the Gilbert and Ellice Islands, Tahiti, Tonga and the Cook Islands in Polynesia; Papua New Guinea, the Solomon Islands, the New Hebrides, New Caledonia and the Loyalty Islands in Melanesia; Truk, Pohnpei, the Marshall Islands, Yap and Palau in Micronesia; and Guam and the Marianas. On each island he would make a point of going to as many of the towns or villages as possible, either to visit the Bahá'ís who were already there, or to open them to the Faith himself.

The main purpose of his December 1971 visit was to take part in the first National Teaching Conference to be held in Micronesia, which he had helped organize. The conference was called to help the friends prepare for the formation of the first National Spiritual Assembly of the North-West Pacific, at Riḍván 1972. The Area Teaching Committee were in something of a quandary over just where to hold the conference so that the greatest number of believers could participate. The friends would have to cross enormous distances, with little available transportation. Raḥmat, as usual, simplified the matter. Why not hold two conferences, one in each of the towns of Sehes Pawe and Kolonia? This was approved with great relief.

Various events were planned, among them a large gathering of the Bahá'ís in Tamuning. At this meeting a new teaching plan was conceived. A teaching trip was organized for the Christmas and New Year holiday period, so that those Bahá'ís who were teachers and government employees could take part.

In Kolonia, Raḥmat stayed at the Cliff Rainbow Hotel, and friends remember how each day began with morning prayers at a long table in the restaurant. Immediately after breakfast, the teaching teams would go to their assigned areas. Each evening they would return to Raḥmat's room, talk about the events of that day, plan for the next day, and pray together before retiring for the night. Counsellor Richard Benson recalls that one of the friends asked Raḥmat what they were to do with inactive believers. Raḥmat answered, 'There are some who serve their purpose and light the path for a time, but later they lose their way and stay behind. We should pray for them.'

The next task was choosing areas for the 16 visiting travelling teachers from Guam. Mr Benson recalls, 'Dr Muhájir engineered it with a master hand. He seemed to be ever conscious of the

On the terrace of the Caravelle Hotel, Saipan, Marianas.

Fourth National Convention of the South Pacific, Suva, Fiji, April 1962.

admonition of 'Abdu'l-Bahá 'Not to rest for a moment . . . disperse . . . and travel'.[1]

Jack McCants, one of the teachers in that group, remembers:

> The Area Teaching Committee had been meeting for months, preparing and planning the event. Dr Muhájir met with the team for breakfast. He told us to eat a big, but inexpensive breakfast, for there was much work to do. Following prayers, he asked for a map, looked at it for quite a time in a very reflective mood, and then asked quietly about a part of the island that had not been mentioned in our proposed plan. It was an area where, only three weeks earlier, a group of Seventh Day Adventists had literally been driven out by the residents. It had never occurred to us to go there. At that time, Pohnpei had almost no roads and all travel was by boat. A completely new plan was made to replace our old plan. That was a test for some, since many hours of consultation and experience in the area was being replaced by a plan made on the spot by someone who had never before set foot on Pohnpei. Our saving grace was that we were happy and obedient. We all set out in boats and arrived in the UH district of Pohnpei around ten a.m. It was just a few days before Christmas. A very large meeting was being held in one of the native buildings, called a *Knas*, which was filled to overflowing. The local head chieftain, who held the title of *Nan-Mar-Kee*, was in charge, surrounded by fellow dignitaries.
>
> Although a great ceremony was in progress, with many huge gifts of food in sight, our presence was announced. A brief consultation was held, after which several members of our team were invited to come forward to sit near the honoured presence of the dignitaries. We were asked to state why we were there and then were permitted to briefly address the entire gathering. Unannounced, in the midst of a special ceremony dear to those people, we had been welcomed and extended the opportunity to speak about our Faith to all present.
>
> Following our return that evening, we met Dr Muhájir to share our experiences. He was pleased, but sorry that we had not left some of our number to follow up on this initiative. As the next day was Sunday, we made a plan to return. Dr Muhájir

instructed us to prepare teaching books with pictures showing all the Holy Places and other such photos that reflected prophecies from the Bible that had been fulfilled in a literal way. He felt that mentioning scriptures that led to endless interpretations was not wise because the islanders had a tendency to think in literal terms. We worked long hours putting together the teaching books and returned the next morning to the area of our earlier welcome. Dr Muhájir went with us on this trip. The long boat ride was difficult for him, but he went more to please us than for any other reason. In his presence we felt assured of victory. Since it was Sunday, we found most of native folk in the small, local church. To our surprise we found that the *Nan-Mar-Kee* was also the local minister. He was very gracious to us and invited us into his church.

Often, in many island areas, the women sit apart from the men. On this day, Dr Muhájir had two Knights of Bahá'u'lláh, Virginia Breaks of the Caroline Islands and Cynthia Olsen of the Marianas, sit with the women and talk to them, while Dr Muhájir, Harlan Lang and I were invited forward with the minister. Dr Muhájir and the minister sat at a table facing the congregation. Two deacons of the church were at the minister's right hand, and Harlan and I were at Dr Muhájir's right hand.

Dr Muhájir began going through the teaching book, explaining, bit-by-bit, the teachings of the Faith and what each photo referred to. The minister then talked to each of the deacons about it before proceeding to the next page. When the deacons asked questions, Dr Muhájir had us explain the point. Whenever the *Nan-Mar-Kee* asked a question, Dr Muhájir answered. At the conclusion the minister and his deacons held a brief consultation, while Dr Muhájir walked to the open window and prayed. The minister then announced that he was giving permission for the Bahá'ís to teach their Faith to all in the area under his jurisdiction.

The next morning our team split up into smaller units to cover more territory. The team I was part of met a young man named Erlinas, who was a schoolteacher in a village in that area. He had heard about the church visit the evening before. News travels fast in those small islands. Erlinas had walked on foot several miles at

> night over the rough trail to speak with the minister of the church. The minister told him that he was convinced that the Bahá'ís were the people promised in the Bible to establish God's Kingdom on earth, and for that reason he had opened his territory to them. Within a week, over 100 new souls accepted the Faith, including Erlinas. Out of respect for the special kindness he had shown them, the *Nan-Mar-Kee* was an honoured guest of the Bahá'ís of Kolonia, Pohnpei, when the new National Spiritual Assembly was formed.
>
> None of this would have happened without Dr Muhájir's guidance and assistance. He knew the habits and thought patterns of island people and knew the value of our message, and so he was able to guide us to victory. He was like a spiritual Geiger counter when it came to ascertaining areas of spiritual receptiveness.

During this visit, Raḥmat met with the Governor in Guam, and was interviewed at least twice on television. These interviews were shown as major features on news programmes. As a result of this great publicity, the public meeting in which he spoke attracted so many visitors that many had to sit on the floor. Although there was a nice rug, Raḥmat advised the friends that the next time they should have enough chairs, so that their guests would not have to sit on the floor. Although he was always concerned about the comfort of others, he had no such thoughts about himself, and often sat on the floor, saying it was more comfortable. On his visit to Tonga he spoke each evening with the friends in their Ḥaẓíratu'l-Quds. Everyone would sit together on the floor to discuss the teaching work.

Raḥmat seldom talked about his personal life, but on this journey one of the pioneers recalls how,

> he would sometimes express his worry about his family and ask for prayers for them. He spoke lovingly of his wife and daughter and how he missed them. He also spoke of the difficulty of living in the Mentawai Islands and how the lack of sanitation, the climate and the rigours of travelling in those islands had affected both his wife's health and his own.

SAMOA

In 1969 Raḥmat visited Western Samoa and met with the local Spiritual Assemblies of Vailele and Matautu. The *Samoa Bahá'í News* reported:

> Many of the friends went to the airport by chartered bus, and he was very happy to see such a large gathering. The meetings with Dr Muhájir were happy and inspiring, and he reminded us that the teachings of Bahá'u'lláh are for the happiness and the good of all people, and that we must bring them to the people of Western Samoa. He encouraged every Bahá'í to study and to play his part in the work of teaching of the Faith. The *Samoa Times* published Dr Muhájir's photograph and an excellent article about him.

When he visited Western Samoa again in December 1971, he was more concerned with mass teaching on the island. It was the Independence Day holiday, and people were gathering in Apia to celebrate. A boat race was taking place and a large crowd had gathered to watch it. Raḥmat believed that Bahá'ís should never miss a teaching opportunity, and where there was a crowd such as this, he just had to go there to give them the message of Bahá'u'lláh.

He got the friends together in one of the Bahá'í homes, divided them into groups and sent them out to teach. He joined one of the groups, and that day many Samoans heard about the Faith for the first time, and were invited to a fireside in the evening. Those friends who had looked forward to a rest during the holiday felt compelled to go teaching instead.

In 1974 Raḥmat returned to Western Samoa. It was in this trip that he was invited to meet the first reigning monarch to accept the Bahá'í Faith. Accompanied by Mr Soheil 'Ala'í, Raḥmat was granted an audience with His Highness Malietoa Tanumafili II of Western Samoa. He told me later that the Malietoa was very gracious, and, after the audience, insisted on accompanying Raḥmat to the gate of the palace and sending the guests home in his own official car. Raḥmat politely requested the sovereign not to take such trouble, but the Malietoa maintained that Raḥmat deserved the highest honour and respect as a Hand of the Cause of God. Raḥmat did not consider this as an honour accorded to him

Arriving in Fiji.

personally, but as one more example of the triumph of the Cause. The acceptance of the faith by the Malietoa and the later construction of the beautiful House of Worship call to mind Bahá'u'lláh's powerful prophecy about His revelation: 'Should they attempt to conceal His light on the continent, He will assuredly rear His head in the midmost heart of the ocean and, raising His voice proclaim: "I am the life giver of the world".'[2]

The only note we find in Raḥmat's diary about this trip says:

> From 23 March to 17 April I visited New Guinea, Solomon, New Hebrides, Fiji, Tonga, Western and Eastern Samoa and New Zealand. In all these places I met with the National Assemblies and hope that soon they will have new projects for the implementation of the Five Year Plan.

FIJI

In the notes of his 1962 trip, Raḥmat recorded very favourable impressions of his first visit to Fiji:

> The beautiful scenery combined with the spiritual beauty of the people gives one a calm and serene spirit. I wish I could embrace all the natives of this area and spend my whole life in service to them.
>
> On Naw-Rúz we had a meeting in one of the friends' homes [in Suva]. Many attended, and there were a few seekers. We started the year 119 with the hope that this new year will bring new bounties for the friends to be able to teach the Faith as widely as possible.

On his 1974 visit, Raḥmat met the National Assembly, and, according to their report, 'gave invaluable guidance on the presentation to the believers of the Five Year Plan goals and on the various stages by which they may be accomplished.'

PAPUA NEW GUINEA

In Papua New Guinea he 'urged the National Assembly to consider purchasing Ḥaẓíratu'l-Quds in the major towns and assisted with the planning of opening many new islands and districts in a visionary far-flung campaign.'

GUAM

In December 1975 he returned to meet the National Spiritual Assembly of the North West Pacific at the request of the Universal House of Justice. In Agana, Guam, a public meeting encouraged many enquirers to attend follow-up firesides, but one of Raḥmat's main concerns was the acquisition of a national Ḥaẓíratu'l-Quds, to be a regional headquarters until the National Spiritual Assembly of the Bahá'ís of the Mariana Islands was established. He went by car with a local Bahá'í, who was a real estate agent, to many locations. While in Agana Heights, he said prayers and pointed down to Agana and said, 'There — somewhere — is a place for the Ḥaẓíratu'l-Quds. If you persevere you will find it.'

One of the friends recalled, 'his mind was so keen, so alert, and he spoke quietly, his ideas were positive, progressive: so much so that sometimes they pressed our imagination.'

His next stop was Saipan, where a public meeting was held for him in the Continental Hotel. He took his theme from a plant at the front of the room: 'The life of a man as an individual is in two parts, the roots and the branches. The roots are our life in this world — difficult; the branches are our life after death, filled with sunshine, leaves, flowers, fruits. The harder this life is, the better the tree.'

The friends had hoped that Raḥmat could meet the students and faculty of the Community College of Micronesia, but as the Christmas vacation had already started, he was unable to do so. However, an interview with him was aired several times over Radio WSZD, and meetings were held with the Bahá'ís. Friends remember him chanting the Prayer of Visitation of 'Abdu'l-Bahá in one of the meetings, while holding the baby daughter of one of the pioneers in his arms.

After a brief visit to Pohnpei, Raḥmat flew to Kwajalein Island and then went by boat to Ebeye. Virginia Breaks reported:

> Ebeye is a barren, overcrowded island where thousands live on an island big enough for about a hundred people. Any visitor to Ebeye must have a sponsor on the island and a special permit to go there. The islanders have few Bahá'í visitors and were very happy to have such a special visitor as Hand of the Cause Dr Muhájir.
>
> The Bahá'í community of Ebeye is devoted to the Faith and active in teaching. Dr Muhájir met with the National Teaching Committee for the Marshalls and the local Assembly of Ebeye. Auxiliary Board member Betro Majmeto arranged for, and interviewed Dr Muhájir on TV, which had just been established on Ebeye.

Raḥmat stayed in Ebeye for two nights. Each night he addressed a public meeting. When the children came in and out of the meeting, Raḥmat stopped the mothers from scolding them and asked that they be allowed to do what they pleased.

The first evening he told the friends that he spoke 'Penglish' — Persian/English — and that they spoke 'Menglish' — Micronesian/

English. This showed the need for a universal language. He talked to the friends about God and His creation, about the symbol of the Greatest Name, about the Universal House of Justice, and answered a question about the concept of sin and Satan in the following manner:

> You have asked me for the Bahá'í teachings about Satan, the devil, evil, sin, etc. In the Bahá'í Faith we believe that God has created everything good. In Buddhism the concept is to remove suffering. Muḥammad taught the unity of God. Moses brought Law. Christianity taught forgiveness of sin. In reality it revealed spirituality to mankind. Christ came to teach that there is a spiritual life beyond the physical life. It was the Christians [rather than Christ] who said that Adam sinned, and that all are sinners because of Adam. Adam was a Prophet of God — a prophet of God has no sin. Adam wanted His age to be the age of maturity — this is the meaning of the eating of the apple. Christians believed that sin belongs to the soul. How could sin come to us from Adam? Our souls are our own, not from Adam. 'Abdu'l-Bahá said that in this world, no one would be punished for the sins of their father. The concept of Christianity is fear of sin, fear of the devil, and then believing in Jesus Christ to be saved. Christians told the people about sin and that all other religions are wrong. When you are a Bahá'í, you will be a real believer in Christ. The foundation of the Bahá'í Faith is neither fear, nor sin. We believe that mankind has been created noble and productive. Humanity was in its infancy, and is now at the threshold of maturity.
>
> Bahá'u'lláh says that, in this day, God is rewarding the goodness of man. Our religion is a religion of hope, of faith and of love. The difference in our belief is that not only is heaven the world of God, but *this* world is also a world of God. Today is more important than tomorrow. All the worlds are circling around this world. Bahá'u'lláh says this world is the most important in the life of man. This life is like the roots of a plant, not its fruit. That is in the future. Your good deeds and good actions will ascend to the Kingdom of God. Under the ground there is no capacity for fruit. The next world is unlimited, and

> you will see the results of your deeds. In this life you act, in the next you reap the harvest. The harder you work, the bigger the tree, the larger the harvest of the fruit. The root cannot see it.
>
> Someone asked 'Abdu'l-Bahá how souls progress toward God in the next world — some are good, some bad. 'Abdu'l-Bahá told him that in the next world, the rich will help the poor, the wise will teach the ignorant. 'Abdu'l-Bahá was asked, who will go to paradise? He said that everyone would. The questioner asked if that included Náṣiri'd-Dín Sháh. the Master said that God could forgive him, if He so desired. The Bahá'í Faith is not based on fear. Bahá'ís have more responsibility than others to be examples, to suffer. Your paradise is here. The next world is in the hands of God. In the Kitáb-i-Aqdas Bahá'u'lláh says, 'Observe My commandments, for the love of My beauty.' In this world, work for unity. Teach sincerely, teach everyone, friends, enemies, look at the need of the person. Do your duty. Leave the rest to God. Work like a watch. Every second missed — you are behind.'

After a short intermission, Raḥmat presented the friends with Bahá'í ringstones which he had brought from Thailand. He then explained the meaning of the Ringstone Symbol. He spoke in detail of the three Kingdoms of creation — the three levels – and that these levels cannot change places: man cannot become a Prophet, and the Prophet cannot become God.

On 20 December 1975, the day he left Micronesia, Raḥmat wrote to the Universal House of Justice:

> I spent eight days in the northern islands of the Pacific . . . In the Marshalls, enthusiasm for teaching is great. The friends are united and spiritual. If in these few months they do their utmost, they'll be able to form nine local Assemblies and have their National Assembly in 1977. They now have a small plan to increase the number of local Assemblies from five to nine. God willing, this will become the basis for future victories. Three of the Assembly members are from this island, which is indicative of their spiritual maturity.
>
> There are at least 20 pioneers in Guam and the Marianas and they have decided to embark on a vast teaching campaign which

> will help form a base for their future activities. In Yap and Palau they have many indigenous believers and can easily form nine local Assemblies. Ponape, which is the seat of the National Assembly, needs strengthening. It now has a few pioneers, a Board member, and some strong and dedicated native believers.

On 29 December, Raḥmat again wrote to the Supreme Body:

> In Hawaii, although my stay was short, I met most of the friends in all five islands and had consultations with the National Assembly about their teaching work and speeding the achievement of their goals. This consultation resulted in a very useful and practical plan.
>
> We also discussed about helping the North Pacific islands. About 30 people are ready to make teaching trips, and also to pioneer to the Pacific islands. There are, among them, many experienced Bahá'ís and many educated youth, some willing to go there for four months, and some to pioneer permanently.
>
> The National Assembly and the pioneering committee of Hawaii are trying their best to send them there as soon as possible. If the Supreme Body sends them a few words of encouragement it will gladden their hearts and speed the process.

The Universal House of Justice, in response to Raḥmat's letter, wrote to the National Assembly of the North West Pacific Islands:

> . . . [Dr Muhájir] was particularly enthusiastic about the condition of the Faith in the Marshall Islands but feels it is also possible to form National Assemblies in Guam and the Mariana Islands and in the West Carolines at Riḍván 1977.
>
> Undoubtedly your National Assembly will vigorously pursue plans for teaching and consolidation in these areas. The Universal House of Justice requests that you regularly report the results of your activities . . .

It took the friends only two months to achieve spectacular results. In February 1976, Counsellor Benson cabled the following report to the Universal House of Justice:

EFFECT MUHÁJIR VISIT — MARIANAS FIVE ENROLMENTS PARTICIPATION ATTENDANT ACTIVITIES SAIPAN STOP DEDEDO SUSTAINED DOOR-TO-DOOR PROCLAMATION PUBLIC MEETING STOP MANY TEACHING OPPORTUNITIES PALAU STOP JEAN GOSS VISIT CONSOLIDATED KOKOK STRENGTHENED NGARDMAO STOP HAWAII TEAM ARRIVES SOON STOP TRUK DOUGLAS TERREL MASAAKI BEGIN TODAY STOP PONAPE SIX ENROLLED ONE LOCALITY ASSEMBLY FORMATION IMMINENT ANOTHER MARSHALLS STOP MAJURO ATOLL AWAKENED MINIMUM FOUR ENROLMENTS STOP SANTO ISLAND ASSEMBLY FORMED STOP TEACHING ACTIVITY MUCH GREATER THROUGHOUT AREA INSPIRED STANDARD BEARER BLESSED VISIT STOP

1978: HIS LAST VISIT

Raḥmat represented the Universal House of Justice at the formation of the National Assemblies of the the Mariana and Caroline Islands. His diary gives a few details of the early part of this visit:

> On May 9 I left the Holy Land to participate in the convention of the Mariana and Caroline Islands . . .
>
> *20 May:* Arrived in Truk [Caroline Islands]. The convention delegates and friends gathered and we had some seekers. We talked about unity and were all very happy. They chose a few villages as goals to teach.
>
> *26 May:* Today, by the grace of God, the NSA of Mariana will be elected.
>
> *27 May:* The National Spiritual Assembly of the Marianas was elected on May 26 at ten p.m. Members include Bahá'ís, both black and white from the Philippines, Truk and Yap. It was a blessed meeting. They made three resolutions: 1. To think maximum. 2. To be self-supporting. 3. To work for entry by troops.
>
> I met the new NSA, attended the Convention and talked about teaching.
>
> I left at two p.m. for Nauru. It took three hours. Nauru is a small island, just 12 miles wide. It has between five and eight

First National Convention of Mariana Islands, 1978.

With children and youth, Apia, Western Samoa, 1978.

With Knight of Bahá'u'lláh, Virginia Breaks, Moen, Truk Islands.

Agana, Guam, 1978.

thousand inhabitants. It is a rich island and a link between all the islands of Hong Kong, Gilbert, Samoa, Australia, Taiwan and Guam.

The Bahá'ís of Guam can help to teach on this island. Also Honiara and Tarawa, which are an hour away.

Today I prayed for a long time that teaching in these islands would accelerate. Maybe the National Teaching Committee under the supervision of the Universal House of Justice can manage this island. Maybe there should be a separate NSA for Nauru.

Virginia Breaks, a Knight of Bahá'u'lláh, recalls Raḥmat's effect on the Convention:

Dr Muhájir felt an urgency to proceed to another destination as soon as possible; so it was that he quietly and gently led us to change the Convention agenda and hold our election during the first session! It seemed he was not in very good health at this time. Perhaps he had a premonition that he had not many more years to serve and he wished to accomplish as much as possible in as brief a time as possible.

Dr Muhájir reiterated his theme, calling upon the friends to take up the work of teaching and deepening with enthusiasm, confidence and consecration — and, he added, 'with a passion for the Faith.'

Another spark was struck with the Convention's adoption of a slogan for all the Bahá'ís in the coming year; 'THINK MAXIMUM'. It was really Dr Muhájir's idea, but it was enthusiastically adopted, and, immediately afterwards . . . one believer withdrew to an adjacent room and came back in a few seconds with the slogan in big print.

After the Convention, Raḥmat travelled to several islands. His diary indicates how happy he became as the teaching work increased and new believers appeared in larger numbers.

29 May: The pioneers and dear indigenous friends came to greet me at Gilbert Island airport. They sang many songs, then we went to town, had a light lunch, and went to the Convention.

They had a meeting for the Ascension of Bahá'u'lláh. More than 100 people had gathered, and all day we discussed teaching and the history of the Faith, and read from the Writings of the Báb.*

After the meeting of the Ascension I dreamt I was with the Guardian and the Greatest Holy Leaf. The Guardian paid great respect to her. The first night I was in Gilbert I dreamt of the Báb.

The NSA is very good. Fortunately Rufo, a member of the NSA of the Philippines, arrived on Wednesday and from the first night started to teach. With the help of Mr Soheil 'Ala'í, they have arranged a six-month plan.

Even though they are a small group, if they concentrate on teaching, most of the towns and islands will become Bahá'í within five years. Now there are nearly 4000 Bahá'ís in these islands.

1 June: We are leaving for Suva. Soheil 'Alá'í is with me. We talked about the teaching possibilities in these islands. If travel teachers from the Philippines and Malaysia come to Samoa and New Guinea, we can do the work of ten years in one. If we can do this, then, as 'Abdu'l-Bahá says, the work of one year can be done in one month.

This can pave the way for teaching plans in the future. We also talked about giving scholarships for the youth from the Pacific to go to the Philippines so that they can learn about methods of teaching and pioneering.

If Nauru can form nine local Assemblies, maybe they can have a National Assembly in 1979 or 1980. This is quite possible if they utilize pioneers from the Philippines.

After meeting the NSA in Suva we went to the mass teaching areas, where in the last year 500 Indians and 500 Fijians have accepted the Faith. It was a wonderful time. We talked constantly about teaching and unity, teaching in the villages. Also, the Writings of the Báb were read.

---

* This was the year in which the Universal House of Justice published *Selections from the Writings of the Báb*, the first comprehensive edition of His Writings in English translation.

In the evening we again met the NSA, and had a public meeting. In all I met the NSA twice, had two public meetings, several meetings in the Institute and a half-hour radio interview. I suggested that they arrange an educational seminar in December, and, with the help of the Counsellors, expand it for the South Pacific.

I sent a cable to the Holy Land. They answered that I should spend three or four weeks in Tonga, Gilbert and Solomon. They also approved my travels in New Guinea and Australia. With God's confirmation I will spend three weeks in Tonga.

7 June, Tonga: I arrived on the fifth, met the NSA and all the dear friends. Last night we had a public meeting, and two people accepted the Faith. Today we will have meetings again. This morning they all memorized prayers and we talked about methods of teaching. We had a public meeting with about 200 people, including a large group of seekers. After a short talk they formed teaching groups, and eight people accepted the Faith. In this town they had six Bahá'ís and now they have fourteen. They will have their local Assembly.

As the teaching work accelerated, Raḥmat's diary entries begin to read like a catalogue of victories.

8 June: In the South of the island we had a very large meeting with more than 100 people. Seventeen accepted the Faith, mostly youth.

9 June: We had a public meeting in the park in front of the police station in Nuku'alofa. Many seekers came, and ten of them accepted the Faith.

We had about 20 groups, all sitting in the park and talking about the Faith. This was a unique meeting in the centre of the town. It is possible to have a similar meeting every Friday.

On Saturday I came to Ha'apai. It has wonderful Bahá'ís. In the evening we had 16 seekers.

11 June: We had a large meeting with 25 present. Three of the youth declared their Faith and the rest were very interested.

Next morning they said another one of them had also accepted the Faith.

13 June: I am in Vava'u. We had a very good meeting and one person accepted the Faith. Tomorrow five people are arriving from Tonga to help in teaching. What a bounty, what a blessing. These young people have arisen with complete dedication and spirituality. I am very happy.

15 June: We had about fourteen seekers in two meetings. Others have been teaching in new areas. I heard that they have four local Assemblies in Tongatapu and each night they have had ten new believers.

16 June: We were at Auxiliary Board member Isi's house. I talked to them about the Writings of the Báb. We had three meetings. They served lunch to everyone. I left at noon for Tongatapu. We had a good meeting in the afternoon, and six people accepted the Faith. On Saturday morning I left for the island of Eua.

In the evening we had a public meeting. 100 came. Today in a garden that they call 'Riḍván' we have a meeting with Bahá'í friends. Up to now, two young men have declared their faith. Tonight we will have a good meeting.

18 June: In the last ten days the number of Bahá'ís has doubled.

19 June: The friends are teaching in one of the eastern towns, and a similar meeting is being held in another one with a group of pioneers.

On the 18th, 16 people accepted the Faith. This weekend more than 40 have come under the banner of Bahá'u'lláh. This is God's bounty. We have to try to have many of the friends participate in teaching.

On 20 and 21 June we had wonderful meetings, and each evening at least five people declared their faith. In one evening the mayor and one priest became Bahá'ís.

22 June: We had a large meeting and at least 15 smaller meetings. All are busy teaching. Today Navidad Mockon arrived from the

Philippines. Two people in Nauru, one in Fiji and one in Guam accepted the Faith. This is happy news. In Nauru the daughter of Willy, who had come to see me, and another lady are now Bahá'ís. The formation of the LSA and the NSA in Nauru is certain.

On the 23rd and 24th we had wonderful meetings. On Friday we went to the park. A group gathered and nine people declared their faith. They decided to have these Friday meetings regularly.

On the 24th, two meetings were held, and, in one of them, eight people accepted the Faith. In this meeting we had a group of children. One of the teachers, while signing the declaration card said, 'I sign this card with my heart and soul.' There is a sense of spirituality here that is seldom seen.

25 June: The NSA is meeting and took some important decisions: to arrange teaching trips for pioneers and travel teachers and to establish a 'Victory Fund', so that they would provide all teaching expenses themselves. The NSA members and others contributed $300 which is enough for at least two months.

They also formed a Publishing Committee to print books which are needed. First *The New Garden* and then others. We made a one-year plan and formed a special committee for the Friday meetings.

We had two meetings and 14 people accepted the Faith. The youth had a whole day conference, and 13 declarations. This is the confirmation of Bahá'u'lláh and the work of the dear friends. It was decided that the youth will continue their Sunday picnics to carry on teaching, and also have some fun.

They will soon cable the Holy Land that they have 300 new believers. Today (Monday) even though all the news from the islands has not yet arrived, the number is already more than 240.

In Samoa we had a good meeting at the temple land and a public meeting in Apia; we had six declarations. Today, all have gone to the surrounding villages, and all are very happy. Maybe, with God's bounty, in Samoa also we can have teaching activities the way they have in Tonga and Fiji.

After visiting the temple site in Tiapapata, Raḥmat met with the National Spiritual Assembly and the National Teaching Committee. He gave a public talk in Lelata at the Teaching Institute. The Teaching Committee reported,

> Much inspiration came from his talks and his remarks that any meeting of Bahá'ís only was a waste of time. He said, 'Always invite non-Bahá'ís so as to teach the Faith. Every night there must be a teaching plan. Make it a simple plan. One night should not pass but that someone is out teaching. Before the Samoan House of Worship is built, there must be thousands of Bahá'ís in Samoa.

The *Nusipepa Bahá'í Samoa* reported,

> During his visit Dr Muhájir talked about his experiences throughout the Pacific area. Even though his visit was very short the friends at least heard about the progress of the Faith in the Tongan Islands. The teaching in those islands was carried out mainly through public meetings. This method of teaching [Dr Muhájir] said enables every individual to participate, and could be done during evenings when everybody is not working and doing family chores. He stressed the importance of teaching the children and indicated that children are to be taught and cared for properly . . . that is the primary duty of parents.

Raḥmat's diary continues:

> I stayed in American Samoa for one night and met the friends. I now hope to leave for Asia. I wrote a detailed letter to the Universal House of Justice about the Plans for North-East and South-East Asia, India and Iran.
>
> *1 July:* Last night a successful meeting was held in Suva [Fiji] and we had three seekers. My prayer is that this month, with God's grace and bounties, I can be of some small service.
>
> It is now three days that I am in Honiara [Solomon Islands] It is their Independence Day soon, and the friends are busy with

preparation for a Bahá'í exhibition. It is a restful time. I am planning to visit all the islands.

4 July: It is Independence Day. The Bahá'í booth attracted numerous young visitors and I talked to many of them. A prominent person, who is going to become the Prime Minister, also visited, and talked to me for a few minutes. The youth are still visiting, and ask many questions.

I stayed in Honiara for a few days and then visited Auki and the North and went to a few villages to see the Bahá'ís. All of the Bahá'í villages had an exceptional spirituality. They decided to teach in 15 nearby villages.

9 July: Today is [commemoration of] the Martyrdom of the Báb. Joseph and a few youth went to the first village and registered 13 new Bahá'ís. From the North we went to Hahui. God willing, Walter Madella will remain in the South and start the teaching work.

The northern part of Talita is very similar to Mentawai. The people still tattoo their bodies, and are kind and gentle. Maybe, with God's confirmation, all these northern inhabitants could come under the banner of Bahá'u'lláh.

10 July: We are in Tawai Hare, which is a beautiful village. All the people are Bahá'ís and they have a Bahá'í school which is now managed by the government. We have to do much work for the education of the children on this island. They are all intelligent and have memorized a few prayers. How fortunate will be the person who could educate them!

I was here a few years ago and the whole village of Lalosi became Bahá'ís. Perhaps I can visit them again.

We had a meeting in the evening and formulated a plan. I hope Malita will achieve great success. It has many experienced youth who were in Honiara and learned the easy method of teaching and giving the message simply. They met many of the youth in South Talita at the exhibition, and became friends with them. God willing, a new day will dawn in the Solomon Islands.

Early on the 11th I came to Auki and stayed for one night. On the 12th I went to Honiara, on the 13th to Port Moresby [Papua New

> Guinea] and today, the 14th, I am on my way to Manila on board PAC.
>
> These few days passed by in meeting the friends. Relying on Bahá'u'lláh, I am returning to Asia once more. The Universal House of Justice has approved this. 'I commit my affairs into His hands.'

On leaving the islands Raḥmat wrote to the Universal House of Justice:

> Thank God the friends are happily teaching and serving the Faith day and night. It needs an able pen to illustrate their dedication and zeal.
>
> In the central island of Tonga, every night at least two large teaching events are held, with 50 to 100 non-Bahá'ís. Last week, on the island of Tonga, every evening on average 15 people have accepted the Faith. Each night at least 50 Bahá'ís have participated in the teaching work. On Fridays, with the approval of the police authorities, they hold meetings in the central park of the city to teach the Faith. Each session they pay $1 to the city for the use of electricity.
>
> Four or five prayers are said and a few friends explain the teachings. Children sing songs and then the friends disperse among the audience and form small groups. Sometimes 15 teaching meetings are held all over the park.
>
> Last Friday was the night of the Nineteen Day Feast. The friends did not want to lose the opportunity of teaching. After the end of the two parts of the Feast they moved the benches from the Ḥaẓírat'ul-Quds to the park and continued the meeting. In the course of that evening they had ten new believers.
>
> The National Assembly has now appointed a special three-member committee to arrange the Friday meetings in the park, to teach and educate the children to sing songs and chant prayers for the crowd. The youth are also being trained to give speeches and memorize the talks of 'Abdu'l-Bahá, so that they can give talks in meetings. The National Assembly also decided to publicize the meetings through the mass media so that it will progress naturally and simply: God forbid it will cause any problems.

In all these meetings they talk only about Bahá'í principles and do not dwell on other religions. This is the reason for their success. Although they have not all accepted the Faith, they are attracted to it and praise the teachings. Some youth have delayed their enrolment pending the approval of their parents, or more study of the teachings. This is indicative of the purity of their hearts and their truthfulness. God willing, one day they will all enter under the banner of the Faith.

Raḥmat's notes list some of the advice and challenging tasks he gave to the friends in the Pacific:

Make your community a model community for the whole world.

Think Maximum.

Always think of mass conversion.

Don't be satisfied with your limitations. The Grace of God has no limitations.

Do not postpone teaching the Faith of God, even for an instant.

Leave your home for teaching. As soon as you move, Bahá'u'lláh will help you.

Don't sit in your homes! Go out! Go to the park and pray.

Teaching is not institutionalized — do it yourselves.

India has a 'one-hour teaching plan'. Every day for one hour or one half-hour, every Bahá'í gives his time for teaching. In one month the membership increased to 150 for every 100 Bahá'ís. One hour a day for 195 people, which is the approximate number of Bahá'ís in Marianas, is the equivalent of 25 full-time Bahá'í teachers.

Raḥmat told them, 'If you are united, wholeheartedly, you will achieve much more. If you are involved in a problem, you will

Public Meeting at the Bahá'í Teaching Institute, Apia, Western Samoa, August 1978.

Attending the first National Convention of the Caroline Islands, May 1978.

become part of the problem. Do not involve yourself. We have institutions, take it to the institutions. Everything should be done to create unity in the community.'

Cynthia Olson reflects on Raḥmat's ability to inspire and give practical advice to the friends to undertake successful teaching work:

> . . . the quality of perceptiveness stands out strongly. He could come into an area or community and immediately sense the strengths, the weaknesses, the needs and the potential of that community. And he programmed himself — and the Bahá'ís — to the accomplishment of goals and victories, based on this perceptive understanding of the respective situations amongst the Bahá'ís and the community in which they lived.
>
> His plan for consecutive days of fireside teaching, rotating from place to place with brief intervals in between the course of each fireside series, was adopted for inauguration in the Mariana Islands, and simultaneously in Guam and in Saipan, in 1980. This was the plan he proposed to the friends in Ecuador which they followed.

One pioneer summarized Raḥmat's influence on the islands of the Pacific by saying that the effect of his visits, so strongly felt now, will continue far into the future both in the acceleration of the international teaching programmes and through the actions of individual Bahá'ís. His visits have undoubtedly bequeathed a rich heritage to the islands of the Pacific.

Raḥmat saw potential for mass teaching throughout Europe.

Chapter 6

MASS TEACHING IS POSSIBLE!

The year 1973 proved to be a turning point in our lives as pioneers. By this time we had been based in India for five years. Raḥmat's long absences had made me responsible for most aspects of our personal lives, and the burden of work which had fallen on my shoulders during the Nine Year Plan had become so great that I was physically and emotionally exhausted. I felt that it would be of no benefit to stay in India any longer. I desperately needed some respite from our long years of pioneering, but at the instruction of the Universal House of Justice, we stayed in India till the conclusion of the Nine Year Plan in 1973, then finally decided to move to Europe. The only country which could both grant us a visa and offer a suitable school for Gisu was the United Kingdom. We enrolled her at the American School in London, which had the same curriculum as the one in New Delhi, and established our residence nearby.

Raḥmat travelled extensively throughout Europe in 1971, '72 and '73, the final years of the Nine Year Plan. Though he had participated in the 1963 World Congress in London, and the Palermo Conference in 1968 commemorating the centenary of Bahá'u'lláh's arrival in the Holy Land, this was to be his most intensive period of association with the Bahá'ís of Europe. He devoted himself to helping the friends win the remaining goals of the Plan. Most of Europe, particularly Germany, was struggling, and the Universal House of Justice had urged Raḥmat to spend as much time on that continent as possible.

Although his travels in Europe were easier than Africa and South America, Raḥmat found them less fulfilling. He lamented that the friends were too conservative, and were frightened by the idea of mass teaching. He was determined to change this, and was preoccupied with exploring ways of accelerating teaching efforts. Pages of his diary overflow with his thoughts on teaching methods for Europe:

> Europe is in need of several teaching plans. One plan could be for teaching at the Bahá'í temple [Frankfurt, Germany]. In the summer, teachers from all over Europe could go to the temple with literature in different languages. It could be advertised in newspapers that a festival to celebrate the unity of religions will be held at the temple to demonstrate how the Bahá'ís have achieved that ambition. There could be many other subjects as well. Each day many people visit the temple and in this manner they could be attracted to the Faith. We might have to consult professional advertisers for this purpose. We can have separate pavilions for each one of the principles of the Faith: unity of religions, unity of mankind, one universal auxiliary language, etc. In each pavilion, information and literature regarding that principle could be distributed to the visitors.
>
> Each teaching project should target a different island, minority or nationality. It is easier to teach the Portuguese in Luxemburg than in their own country. In the same way, all minorities are more approachable. When they are away from their churches and their own environment they seek other communities for friendship and company.
>
> The Latin American Bahá'ís can be very effective in Portugal, Spain, Italy and the Mediterranean islands. American and Canadian friends can teach in England, Scotland and Iceland. Material means are available, it is possible to distribute books and there are many young Europeans who can assist them. Stimulating decisions and good planning are needed. I think this campaign should start from Riḍván 1973 and continue for two years. The West of Germany seems to be weaker than the East, and the North weaker than the South, although many devoted and wealthy Persian Bahá'ís live in the West and the North.

Attending the World Congress, London, 1963.

At the 1968 conference in Palermo with Hands of the Cause, (from left) Faizí, Haney, Olinga, Sears, <u>Kh</u>ádem and Furútan.

It would be easy to start a teaching campaign with a group of teachers travelling all over Europe in a car with books and audio-visual materials. It is possible to have between five and ten teaching units travelling around the country day and night. The local Bahá'ís who are now static can be encouraged by these groups to participate in the activities.

These teaching units could be formed in Dusseldorf and its surroundings, Hamburg, Hanover, Berlin, Essen, Munich, Nuremberg, Stuttgart, and Frankfurt. Each unit should comprise three permanent people with others who could join them for short periods.

I have received a cable from the Universal House of Justice asking me to go to the Scandinavian countries, especially Norway. There is also guidance regarding the summer programme for the youth in Europe . . . I must also concentrate on the teaching work in Germany.

I have come to the conclusion that there must be four youth summer conferences in Europe:

1. Marseilles, which 'Abdu'l-Bahá visited in 1911. This might be the only Mediterranean port blessed by the feet of 'Abdu'l-Bahá. The countries of Portugal, Spain, France, Italy and Belgium can participate. Their plan would be to teach along the coast of Spain, Malta and Corsica.

2. Stuttgart, for communities of Germany, Switzerland, Austria, and Luxemburg; the plan would be to teach in southern Germany.

3. Stockholm, for Scandinavian countries, plus Holland and West Berlin to plan teaching in Lapland, Sweden, Norway and Finland.

4. Edinburgh, in Scotland — which has been blessed by the presence of 'Abdu'l-Bahá — for the communities of Scotland, Ireland, England, Wales and Iceland, and to plan the teaching work in northern Europe and the islands of the North Sea.

On another occasion, while waiting to leave Spain for Germany, Raḥmat reflected on various teaching possibilities.

> I have had a few thoughts about teaching in Europe. We have to start teaching in Germany immediately and not leave it for the summer. There are four things to remember about teaching in Germany: southern Germany, the borders with East Germany, the teaching plan for the temple, and the role it has to play in teaching the minorities of Europe, such as the Turks in Cologne and Munich.
>
> One problem facing the continental youth conferences, which has often been mentioned, is the translation of different languages. This causes delay in the running of the sessions. Although this is a legitimate problem, it is not such an impediment for the youth. They can make each other understand and form friendships. Most of the European youth speak several languages anyway.
>
> Today in Europe enormous amounts are spent to overcome the problem of languages. Young people are sent to other countries to learn new languages. For example, every year 1,000,000 people commute between Germany and France. They spend millions of dollars on this. We have to surmount this language problem, bring the youth together and help them to know each other. These are the people who have to create a new united Bahá'í Europe. These are the people who have to be colleagues. We have to establish their unity now.
>
> One question often asked is whether to teach the migrant minorities. Of course we have to teach them, and as soon as possible. Once they become immersed in materialism, teaching them will become a thousand times more difficult. We should even invite teachers from Turkey to Germany and northern Europe to teach the Turkish minority.
>
> A second question: does the instruction of the beloved Guardian to the pioneers in Africa, telling them to concentrate on teaching the Africans, mean that we should not teach them in Europe? Quite the contrary. The Guardian emphasized teaching the minorities in Europe and America.

The third question is whether to teach the members of various international missions to the United Nations in Geneva. The friends believe that as Switzerland is not a member of the UN and has no representative to the international community, the delegates of other nations should not be approached. The direction of the beloved Guardian is quite the opposite. He said that members of the United Nations should become familiar with the Faith, and, if possible the receptive ones become Bahá'ís.

A fourth question: Most Europeans go as tourists to other countries in Europe. Every year millions of Germans go to Spain and Portugal. As a rule the Bahá'ís shun tourists as they are not from their own country, and so lose the opportunity of teaching them. The Guardian instructed the National Assembly of Iran to befriend the European tourists so that when they return to their own countries they will be helpful to the Bahá'í communities.

Perhaps we can prepare a special pamphlet about the temple and invite tourists to see the temple and have a picnic in the surrounding woods. We can make a jigsaw puzzle with the temple as its theme, and on the back of the box write about the Bahá'í temple and its significance.

We need to have regular conferences in the temple for the youth. They would learn how to teach at the temple, in the South and in Eastern Europe.

We can bring travel teachers from Indonesia to teach in Holland, and from Turkey to teach the Turks in Europe. Teaching minorities might sometimes take precedence over teaching the rest of the population. There has always been emphasis on teaching American Indians in North and South America, and on teaching the Parsis of India in 'Abdu'l-Bahá's time. There is even an instruction from the Guardian that Indian teachers should go to Africa to teach the Indian minority there.

We should at least invite the youth of Turkey to our conferences in Europe.

The Guardian instructed the English Bahá'ís to teach the Indian minorities. Now they should follow those instructions for teaching the Ugandan immigrants to England. Can we have a Continental Youth Committee for Europe?

Teaching Conference, Sicily, Italy.

Raḥmat's efforts and the help and co-operation of the various National Assemblies, together with the visits of the Hands of the Cause of God, were gradually bearing fruit. His joy at the successful teaching being done by the Bahá'ís is reflected in his notes.

> Hand of the Cause Giachery, the Counsellors, seven Auxiliary Board members were present [at the conference in Nice]. We had extensive consultation, and decisions were made to double the number of Bahá'ís in Spain and Italy, to have six regional conferences within the next two years and to publish *Nabil's Narrative* in European languages. It was altogether a fruitful conference. The youth brought a new spirit of joy and service to the gathering. The future of the Faith is in their hands.

Portugal's report was the best of all. They have had 150 new Bahá'ís in the last few months. When Olinga was there they had decided to teach 50 new Bahá'ís but they have had nearly 400! [Counsellor] Anneliese Bopp has gone there to deepen the new Bahá'ís and has arranged a deepening and training programme. In November they organized a five-month teaching programme and now they have more than a hundred new believers. This is a huge success and will encourage other Assemblies. Maybe Spain and Italy will follow in their footsteps.

My mind is occupied with the question of teaching in Europe. For this purpose we must first know what kind of people we are targeting:

1. The majority, such as Germans, French, Italians, etc.

2. The minorities such as Gypsies, Basques, Lapps, etc.

3. The people of the islands such as those to the North of Scotland, West of Portugal, etc.

4. The immigrants, European and non-European, who roam around seeking work.

5. Tourists and visitors who are of two categories: European and non-European.

   a) Tourists within Europe.

   b) Tourists from non-European countries.

   c) Students from abroad.

   d) The young people of Europe.

   e) The Eastern Europeans which need special attention.

   f) Members of international organizations.

These are the people that the institutions in Europe have to keep in mind.

> Europe should be divided into several teaching zones, taking into consideration the languages and other factors. Each zone should have one teaching committee, one Publishing Trust, a youth committee and a minority teaching committee. There should be repeated teaching conferences for each zone.

In 1972, nearly two decades before the doors of Eastern Europe were opened to the Faith, Raḥmat's thoughts were on that region. He was counselling the friends in Europe to start preparing for the day when they could teach there:

> The summer teaching plans for the European youth, particularly the Germans, should concentrate on the borders of Czechoslovakia, Yugoslavia and the Soviet Union, so that the Faith can penetrate into these countries. The youth can thus prepare themselves for the future when it will be possible to teach in these countries and release spiritual powers ready for that day.
>
> Every year 700,000 tourists visit Eastern Europe from Germany, and thousands from Yugoslavia travel to Germany to work. Perhaps a way to Eastern Europe will open very soon. Do we have books and teachers? We have to train our youth now to be ready for that eventuality.
>
> Teaching in Eastern Europe should be emphasized. We should have teaching campaigns to bring about one Bahá'í European community. We must teach each nationality, move around and constantly communicate with others, and, according to the instructions of the Guardian, have special teaching projects for the minorities. I read [Mr Vahdat's] pilgrim notes which contained instructions of the beloved Guardian given during the last years of his life. The Guardian emphasized the importance of pioneering behind the Iron Curtain, especially for the Bahá'ís of Iran, the United States and Germany.

Raḥmat travelled in Europe in the same fashion as he did in the rest of the world, staying at inexpensive hotels, and waiting at airports for many hours. When not eating his customary bread and cheese, he went to inexpensive restaurants. One typical diary entry states 'After the meeting we went to a pizza house and talked about mass teaching in South Germany till one a.m.' Mostly he travelled by train or bus, and when he arrived, there was often no one to meet him, and he would have to find the Bahá'ís himself:

> Went to Nuremberg. No one was at the station, but by coincidence I saw Charles, a Dutch Bahá'í, who helped me find a hotel and who called the Bahá'ís.
>
> Arrived at the airport at 11.00 a.m. Friends came to see me off, but the plane was delayed until 2.30, and I became exhausted.
>
> Arrived in Paris at 4.30 but missed the connection to London. I stayed in a small hotel. Yesterday and today I have been utterly exhausted. I cannot even open my suitcase. I hope to be able to rest for one day in Frankfurt, then meet the National Assembly.
>
> Due to inclement weather it took three hours to reach London, and they had to re-route us to Manchester. From there I left by train for London airport. At the airport a message had been left, telling me to go to Birmingham, so I took a plane and arrived there at 7.30 p.m. Riḍván Moqbel, son of the late Khosrow Moqbel, a most spiritual man who was my teacher in the Friday Bahá'í classes, was waiting for me.

During this hectic period he seldom had time to come home. In July 1973, Gisu and I had arrived in Cologne on our way from India to London. We had not seen Raḥmat for several months and were hoping to spend some time with him. On 22 July he recorded in his diary, 'Spent one night in Cologne with my dear family.' The entry for 23 July said: 'Belgium and Luxemburg'. At the end of July he came back to Cologne to accompany Gisu and me to London, and happily recorded,

> *30 July*: Spent about a week in London with dear Írán and Gisu. We visited the Guardian's Resting Place and had some happy days together.

As usual it was left to me to find a house and settle our family in London.

Appealing for pioneers at a special conference for Persian-speaking friends, London, 1977.

Welcoming prospective pioneers to the stage.

Raḥmat continued to travel around Europe for almost two years, and tried in every way possible to convince the friends that entry by troops was just as possible in Europe as elsewhere.

AUSTRIA

In 1972 he travelled from Switzerland to Austria. On 4 December he wrote,

> I went by bus to Zurich and now am on the way to Vienna by Swiss Air. I can see the beautiful snow-covered mountains. This is my first trip to Austria. I am in need of Bahá'u'lláh's assistance and bounties.
>
> *5 December*: In the evening we had a large gathering of the friends in Vienna. It seems that in the course of the Nine Year Plan they have increased their numbers sevenfold. This might be the most successful Plan in Europe. I spoke to them about the imprisonment and travels of 'Abdu'l-Bahá, the progress of the Faith in other countries, the work of the Universal House of Justice, and the recognition of the Faith by the United Nations. It was an exhilarating evening. I asked a few of the National Assembly members present to act on my suggestion of sending permanent and temporary teachers to Germany so that within these few months they can establish some centres in that country.

A year later, in 1973, he was back in Austria:

> *19 November*: Due to unrest in Athens, flights were cancelled, so I could not go to Eastern Europe and instead came directly to Vienna. I met with the National Assembly and formulated a five-month plan in which ninety-five people will concentrate on the fourteen localities with Local Assemblies during the last months of the year. This plan was made according to the instructions of the Universal House of Justice.
>
> *20 November*: A very good meeting was held with about 40 Bahá'ís. We discussed that the best way to teach involves universal participation and implementing all teaching methods

— direct, indirect, firesides, the distribution of literature, etc. Each person should teach according to his own capacity and inclination.

21 November: I spent the night in Graz. The community is about 20 Bahá'ís. I met with the local Assembly and it was decided that they should have five public meetings and teach twelve people in the remaining five months of the Plan. There are dependable young Iranian Bahá'ís in this city. I hope they can render some service.

He visited Austria again in 1977 to participate in a Summer School. His nephew, Dr Farzin Davachi, remembers how tired Raḥmat was.

He had gone to visit Bahá'í communities and was back very late at night. Very early in the morning he knocked on my door, bringing a breakfast tray, and was surprised that I was still asleep. I insisted that he should listen to my professional advice and take the day off. I took him to the mountains. He loved the scenery and the fresh crisp air. He said it was years since he'd had a day off. . . . It was an enjoyable day. On our return to the hotel a cable from the Universal House of Justice was awaiting him. He immediately packed his bag and asked me to take him to the airport. That was the last time I saw him.

The cable of the Universal House of Justice read:

REAFFIRM GREAT NEED YOUR PRESENCE EUROPEAN SUMMER SCHOOLS COMMUNITIES AUGUST EARLY SEPTEMBER URGE YOU CONSIDER PORTUGAL YOUTH CONFERENCE AUGUST FIVE-SEVEN SCHOOL FOURTEEN-TWENTY, SCHOOLS GREECE AUGUST TWENTY SIX-TWENTY EIGHT ITALY SEPTEMBER THREE-ELEVEN CYPRUS ONE-FOURTEEN EN ROUTE HOLY LAND ARRIVE MID-SEPTEMBER STOP PROCEED IRAN ACTIVATE PROPOSED TRAVELLING TEACHER PROGRAMME STIMULATE VOLUNTEERS . . . SUGGEST REMAIN PERSIA THREE WEEKS ENABLE SUPPORT TEACHING PROVINCES HOME-FRONT PIONEERING STOP THEREAFTER FLY EAST AFRICA ASSIST WORK KENYA TANZANIA

OTHER COUNTRIES REMAINING EACH COMMUNITY LONG ENOUGH PERSONALLY ASSIST FIELD TEACHING ENDEAVOURS TOTAL ABOUT FIVE WEEKS PROCEED WEST AFRICA AS SUGGESTED EARLIER PLANS WILL DETERMINE DETAILS CONSULTATION HOLY LAND DEEPEST LOVE STOP

BELGIUM

Raḥmat made three or four special visits to Belgium, and often passed through en route to other European destinations when travelling from London. Towards the end of 1971 he met with the friends at the national Ḥaẓiratu'l-Quds in Brussels, and encouraged them to adopt bold plans for the expansion of the Bahá'í community, and to arise to teach the Faith.

In 1975 he was able to spend two days at the Summer School in Marcinelle, near Charleroi, together with my father, and returned the following year to attend the summer school in Huy.

In 1977 he attended a special meeting of the European Counsellors and representatives of nearby communities. A new two-year plan was launched to increase the effectiveness of the teaching work and complete the goals of the Five Year Plan. Counsellor Dorothy Ferraby wrote to all the National Assemblies of Europe with this report:

> Last weekend Hand of the Cause Dr Muhájir came to a meeting of the European Counsellors [in Brussels] . . . We have worked out tentative plans for PERMANENT INTER-ASSEMBLY TRAVEL TEACHING TEAMS, which we submit to you, for consultation as quickly as possible . . . The Plan involves teaching team projects in 13 national communities, and several other countries are asked to contribute manpower to help. The visitors from the USA will give added strength to the teams we ourselves form.

His last recorded visit was in 1978 when he spoke at the Ḥaẓiratu'l-Quds in La Rue du Trone in Brussels. Here he met with the National Spiritual Assembly and made an urgent appeal to proclaim the Faith widely and openly to all people of Belgium, whatever their language group or origin.

CYPRUS

In 1973, after a period of four months in Africa and a three-week visit to the Holy Land, Raḥmat was on his way to Europe again.

14 November: I spent three weeks in the Holy Land then came to Cyprus. Many nights I spent in the holy Shrines, and many days with the International Teaching Centre consulting on teaching plans. I met twice with the Universal House of Justice and again we consulted about teaching matters. Thank God everything is moving quickly. In Cyprus, Mustafa Beg and Frances and Eric [Hellicar], British pioneers, were waiting at the airport. The Turkish zone is separated by roadblocks.

I stayed in a hotel in the Turkish sector. A few of us gathered and our meeting lasted until midnight. We went to see a church building which had been converted into a mosque, then we went on up to a hilltop. The weather was heavenly and there wasn't a trace of cloud in the sky. In one of the ancient forts, which is about 500 years old, I chanted the Tablet of Aḥmad and prayed for the future National Spiritual Assembly of Cyprus, which hopefully will be elected soon.

In the afternoon we visited Nicosia, which had been the prison of Azal, and where there is now a group of wonderful dedicated young Turkish Bahá'ís. May Faizí and her family are pioneers there. This small community has a goal to establish six local Assemblies in nearby towns. They now have two Assemblies and each of the friends has volunteered to teach in these towns, hoping to establish a community. After two days, during which I had seen practically the whole island, I left for Athens.

FRANCE

From available records it would appear that Raḥmat visited France on three occasions, to meet with the Bahá'ís and consult with their administrative institutions. In February 1971 he met with a number of local Assemblies, the National Youth Committee, and groups and isolated believers from the Paris and Orleans regions. He assured them all of the confidence of the Universal House of Justice in their ability to fulfil their goals. He also spoke of the complete transformation of those communities which arose to teach, and stressed the importance of paying special attention to each individual, including children. He gave the example of a two-year old in Burma, who was brought to all Bahá'í meetings, and who later became a mass teacher. He warned the Bahá'ís against becoming too rigid in their ways and advised them to try every means possible to spread the teachings of Bahá'u'lláh.

The National Assembly reported, 'The community of France was uplifted by his enthusiam and filled with new energy to teach, reminding us of the example of 'Abdu'l-Bahá in Paris.'

I do not remember a single instance when Raḥmat considered himself a 'guest' at Bahá'í conferences and conventions. Whether he was the representative of the World Centre, or especially invited by the National Assembly concerned, he always arrived earlier to help in the planning and organization of the events. The 1976 International Conference in Paris was no exception. He had started communicating with the organizing committee of that conference months before the event. He was in correspondence with the National Assembly of Iran to try and get maximum participation of the Bahá'ís, especially youth. He hoped that many pioneers would arise at the conference to fill the various international goals. In a letter to the National Assembly of Iran he wrote, 'God willing, the Paris Conference, similar to the conference of Badasht, will become an occasion to reach important decisions and to encourage the friends [of Iran] to greater heights of endeavour and sacrifice.'

In Paris he met with the Conference Committee, urging them to arrange teaching events all over the city. As usual, he expressed his view that simply gathering the Bahá'ís together without any teaching effort would be a waste of time. It would squander the energies of the friends and the resources of the Faith.

In a session devoted to pioneering, Raḥmat talked about the needs of various regions and called for a valiant effort by the participants of the conference. Hundreds volunteered. For the next two days, Raḥmat and members of the Continental Pioneering Committee were busy sorting out résumés and applications. Many of those volunteers are now pioneers around the world.

After his meeting in Brussels with the Board of Counsellors for Europe, Raḥmat visited France to help that community achieve the goals of the Five Year Plan. With his help, the National Assembly adopted the decisions of the Brussels meeting and successfully translated them into swift and positive action. The National Spiritual Assembly resolved to form full-time, inter-Assembly teaching teams, which were directed to Lille and Bordeaux for a period of three months intensive activity. Both cities had lapsed local Spiritual Assemblies and their restoration was identified as priority goals for the Five Year Plan. The NSA also sent one French youth to join the teaching team in Luxemburg in order to support cross-border teaching.The National Assembly wrote to all French believers, asking for their immediate assistance, and stressing the urgency of the hour. Raḥmat's visit generated several further teaching programmes each of which was effectively co-ordinated by the National Spiritual Assembly. One immediate result of these was the re-formation of the Spiritual Assembly of Lille.

The National Spiritual Assembly of France, responding to the announcement of Raḥmat's passing, communicated the deep feelings of the French Bahá'ís in a letter to the Universal House of Justice:

With fellow Hands of the Cause, Featherstone and Khádem, at the Paris International Conference, 1976.

> The Bahá'í community of France greatly admired his courage and intrepid spirit in service to the Cause of Bahá'u'lláh and especially remembers his drive and commitment towards the end of the Five Year Plan in France, and offers our intense prayers for the progress of his soul in the Kingdom of God. We hope that his vision and dynamic spirit will serve as an example and encouragement to each Bahá'í community . . .

In a letter dated October 1991, the National Assembly said, 'His simplicity, his purity of heart and soul touched all the friends who met this great teacher of the Cause. Sadly, his premature death has deprived us all of a great source of inspiration.'

GERMANY

Of all the countries in Europe, Raḥmat's first priority was Germany. Many of its goals of the Nine Year Plan were still to be won, and he frequently broke his trips in other European countries to help the National Assembly of Germany devise plans for their fulfilment. Everywhere he went he met the Bahá'ís, consulted with their local Assemblies and committees, and tried to enthuse them to teach. If even a few enquirers attended public meetings or firesides, he was ecstatic, and considered this a sign of great progress. During his travels in Germany he met several times with the National Assembly and its Publishing Trust, to plan the publication of urgently needed teaching and deepening materials. He was concerned about the lack of Bahá'í literature in European languages:

> Many important Bahá'í books, including *Nabil's Narrative* and the lives of Bahá'u'lláh and 'Abdu'l-Bahá, are not translated into European languages. It was decided that there should be a two-year plan for the translation into German and publication of the Writings. This will be in co-operation with the neigbouring National Assemblies, with tasks given to local Assemblies.

Raḥmat's diary offers a wealth of information about his activities during his months in Germany:

> I arrived on 13 November [1972] in Bitburg. Dr Frank Handel [sic] and his wife brought me there from Langenhain and we had

a good meeting with the friends. On 14 November there was a large meeting in Ludwigshafen in the home of Dr Pezeshkian, and on 15 November in Mainz at Dr Majzoob's. Many non-Bahá'ís attended that meeting, four of them Americans. We talked about the importance of the Divine Plan and its effect in the world, the breadth of the Bahá'í Adminstration and the victories achieved by the Universal House of Justice in the Nine Year Plan. Mr Ardeshir Hezari was there, and spoke about his pilgrimages at the time of 'Abdu'l-Bahá and the Guardian.

Next morning we went to Ulm. On the way I visited the resting place of Dr Grossman to say prayers, and then went to see Mrs Grossman. Dr Grossman's grave is in a superb mountain spot, full of beautiful fir trees and flowers. His parents are also buried there. Mrs Grossman is a true angel and is very sincere, devoted and spiritual. I stayed in a small hotel near the train station in Ulm. Reza and Vafa Rayhani and some others were there.

A few friends gathered in Furth on the 17th, and on the 18th I went to Langenhain by train to meet with the National Assembly. In the afternoon I left for Munich.

We had a very good meeting on the 19th. I talked about the history of the Faith and the teaching methods of Mullá Ḥusayn, who left his home and never returned. I spoke of the progress of the Faith around the world and the importance of mass teaching in the South of Germany. Mr Fazlu'llah Namdar has a Tablet of 'Abdu'l-Bahá in which he emphasizes the necessity of teaching in these areas.

On 20 November there was a large meeting in Stuttgart. I talked about 'Abdu'l-Bahá's journey to the West, His imprisonment, and the Divine Plan. The next day we visited Esslingen, where 'Abdu'l-Bahá had received children in a hotel. They had presented Him with flowers and He had given them chocolates. He had liked this meeting and talked about it when he visited other cities. We said prayers and then went to see the beautiful site of the Summer School.

Next morning we left for Langenhain. On the way we visited a house that 'Abdu'l-Bahá had stayed in. I chanted the Tablet of Visitation.

After meeting with the Publishing Trust, Mrs Kruger, the Secretary of the National Assembly, accompanied me to Marburg, which is a university town. There were many young seekers at the meeting. I met Salvatore, who had accepted the Faith at the home of Artemus Lamb in El Salvador when he was 12 years old.

26 November: Arrived in Hamburg and participated in the meeting of the representatives of the local Assemblies in the house of Maḥmúd Varqá. We discussed teaching methods both for individual Bahá'ís and for the Bahá'í Adminstration.

In the evening we had a large meeting of the friends. I talked to them about travel teaching, and how Bahá'u'lláh's blessing makes everything easy and opens doors.

At six o'clock I went directly to the Bahá'í Centre in Berlin, accompanied by Anneliese Bopp. About 60 of the friends, Persian, German, Turkish, African and American, had gathered to meet us. We talked about the essence of the Bahá'í Adminstration, the importance and grandeur of the Universal House of Justice, the opportunity of each individual to serve in the teaching field and the importance of detachment when teaching — teaching without consideration for personal affiliations and without interfering in other people's way of life. There were many questions. It was a good meeting. One of the most fertile places for teaching in Germany is West Berlin, which has 2,000,000 inhabitants . . . They have great independence of mind and no prejudices. Internationalism is a way of life.

27 November: I went with Dr Jamshid Subhani to see the Berlin Wall and some of the churches. We had tea at the European Centre. I chanted the Tablet of Aḥmad there and we discussed the formulation of a 40-day plan to double the number of Bahá'ís by next Riḍván. So far it has been very easy to teach in Berlin: the friends invite people to their homes and give them the message of Bahá'u'lláh. The results are very encouraging and they have many new believers. Tonight is the Ascension of 'Abdu'l-Bahá. They decided to spend the night in prayers and plan a new teaching programme.

I left by plane for Bremen, arriving there at 5.30. I went directly to Oldenburg, arriving at 7.30. The meeting was at eight. I took a room at Hotel Deus, opposite the train station. There were about ten seekers at the meeting, some very spiritual. A few university students attended and I discussed the teachings with them. Dr Ardeshir Ahmadpur, Mr Riazi and Mr Zabihi were also there. Ardeshir's patients are mostly Turks and he speaks Turkish, so he has a good opportunity to teach them.

I left the meeting early and went back to the hotel, but some stayed on until four in the morning talking about the Faith.

28 November: Arrived in Gelsenkirchen. We had a meeting of nearly 50 people in the evening in the Hotel Martin where I am staying. Ten were German and the rest Persian . . . We talked about the teaching possibilities in Europe and I asked them to have at least 50 more Bahá'ís before next Riḍván. They all believe that it is an impossible task as the people here have no spiritual capacity. I chanted the Tablet of Aḥmad, and prayed that one day some humble spiritual people will be found to arise and conquer the world. Later we went to Dusseldorf, where many had gathered. I told them about the progress of the Faith and how a small seed grows into a large and strong tree. I spoke about the first pioneers of Latin America and how in their own lifetime they had reaped the benefits of their services. We talked about the pioneers in Europe and what the duty of each individual was in service to the Faith. Dear Massoud Berjis translated for me, and the meeting was full of joy and enthusiasm.

Today at 9.55 I will leave for Holland by train. Mr Pezeshkian is with me. He is married to the daughter of Mr Berjis who was martyred in Iran. Pezeshkian has donated all the expenses of the Kilifi teaching institute in Kenya. The institute will start functioning shortly.

After visiting several other European countries, he came back to Germany.

16 December: We had a detailed consultation with the National Assembly and Counsellor Betty Reed regarding the teaching

> plan in Germany. The conclusion was to invite a group from Alaska to come and teach in the North of Germany. Possibly Hamburg can contribute their expenses. Five people from Italy are to be invited to teach in the West. The Berlin community is to establish nine centres in the East, and a group from Iceland will establish 20 centres in the South. Austrian groups are to establish 25 centres in the West. God willing, and with the blessings of Bahá'u'lláh, these groups will hasten to Germany and strengthen this community. It was also decided to have summer conferences in Frankfurt for all the German-speaking people of Europe with three goals in mind: teaching in the South, teaching along the borders of the Iron Curtain countries, and teaching in the temple. We rely on God. His Will be done.

In this period Raḥmat wrote copious notes on the role of the youth in Europe and made suggestions on how to involve them in the teaching work. While in Gottingen, Germany, he wrote to the Universal House of Justice and proposed,

> . . . a programme for the youth of Europe — one for the South of Germany and one for the Mediterranean Islands which could be assisted by the National Assemblies of Italy, Spain and France — and one for the islands around Scotland. All three of these areas have special qualities which make it possible to teach a large group of its people. Another area of importance is northern Europe, which needs the co-operation of various National Assemblies.

In Tubingen, Germany, he wrote,

> I participated in a meeting where six non-Bahá'ís were present. I talked to them about the youth of the world, and told stories about Badí', and how the youth had arisen to serve the Faith in Asia and Europe. It was a wonderful meeting with many enthusiastic and spirited youth. They are very devoted, and hopefully, sooner or later, will make Europe a reflection of heaven.

Mingling with youth in Frankfurt, Germany, 1976.

With Gisu and I at the Frankfurt Temple.

In Bremen he wrote, 'This afternoon the youth went all over the city to teach everyone they could find.'

He encouraged the Bahá'í youth of Europe to assist in the teaching work in Germany, and also asked the Bahá'ís of the United States and Canada to spend their summer vacations in Germany and participate in the teaching activities. These travels proved to be successful, and Germany triumphantly concluded the Nine Year Plan.

While on a train on the way to Graz he wrote,

> Have been up since five a.m. We are passing beautiful ravines. The fir trees are tall and majestic. Snow has covered everywhere but the sun is bright and warm. This is a most stunning country. We have many wonderful Bahá'í youth in Graz, Ruhanis of Najaf-Ábád, Abedian, Assasi, Ferydoon Khadem, Ata Rayhani — these are some of our best Persian Bahá'ís and they are very active. Their main aim is to teach on the border with Yugoslavia. I asked the friends of Graz to assist them so that the youth of Linz, Salzburg and Vienna can help with the work in Germany.

The next day he wrote,

> I woke up very early and left Graz by train for Vienna. In the evening we had a meeting with the youth in the Bahá'í Centre. The youth here are among the best in Europe, whether Austrian or Persian. This is all due to the work of Mr Khadem Missagh whose children have created this enthusiasm among the youth. Many of them volunteered to spend their weekends teaching on the German border. It was agreed to establish five centres in December, ten in January,and another ten in February, so that by Riḍván there will be 25 new centres in Germany. The youth will leave at the end of this week.
>
> I believe there is a teaching conference in England mid-January. I hope to visit the resting place of the beloved Guardian, participate in the conference, and then go to Italy to meet with the Italian National Assembly and be present in their youth conference.
>
> I think that for at least five years there should be a systematic teaching programme for Europe. For example, there could be

> conferences for the youth every August in Frankfurt and every June in Scandinavia. Each year on a certain date we should undertake different activities for different parts of Europe.

After participating in the London conference, Raḥmat noted,

> The conference was wonderful and lasted till past midnight . . . It was most spiritual. Each person spoke very precisely, constantly quoting from the Writings. This was one of the best conferences I have attended. They read and quoted from the Writings so often that one had the feeling that the Central Figures of the Faith were present in our midst. At the end 35 volunteers arose to serve the Faith.
>
> I think about future plans, and believe that the years between 1974 and 1992, the hundredth anniversary of the Ascension of Bahá'u'lláh, should be years of unprecedented activity.
>
> WE SHOULD HAVE A TWENTY-YEAR TEACHING PROGRAMME FOR THE YOUTH. I met with the National Assembly of Switzerland and suggested that they make a programme for the youth to increase their number from 200 to 600, and form 40 youth teaching groups comprising five people.
>
> I had a meeting with the National Assembly of the United Kingdom in London. I suggested they plan for a three-year programme for the youth, give them specific goals and encourage them to serve.
>
> MASS TEACHING IN EUROPE IS POSSIBLE! The youth have remarkable enthusiasm for teaching the Faith, which is a great bounty. Bahá'u'lláh says,
>
>> Blessed is he who in the prime of his youth and the heyday of his life will arise to serve the Cause of the Lord of the beginning and of the end, and adorn his heart with His love. The manifestation of such a grace is greater than the creation of the heavens and of the earth. Blessed are the steadfast and well is it with those who are firm.[1]

Raḥmat's sojourn in Germany was near its end. He had done all he possibly could. When in July 1973, he returned to meet with the National Assembly, his notes reveal some disappointment.

> *22 July*: Returned to Frankfurt and met the National Assembly. Although they had decided to organize a teaching plan for the youth and to announce it at the conference at the end of this month, unfortunately they have not done so.
>
> *27 July*: Participated in the conference in Frankfurt.

He committed his final thoughts regarding the rapid progress of the Faith in Germany to his diary, but did not send them to the National Assembly:

> There is no doubt that there has to be a review in the methods of teaching in Germany. It seems that the friends try to analyse every single point, and insist on their own point of view. It is more or less like the old method of teaching [in Iran] where one always had to give convincing answers. 'Abdu'l-Bahá tells us that as far as possible we should not argue, and should only give glad-tidings to the seekers to exhilarate their soul. This method should be adopted in Germany, and talks should be be confined to the principles of the Faith and quotes from the Writings.
>
> The friends spend most their meetings in questions and answers among themselves, and believe that the seekers benefit from this. However, this creates confusion for those who are hearing about the Faith for the first time, and presents them with difficult questions of which they had not even dreamt. I feel that this form of confrontation with Europeans has created a new method of teaching, which has changed gentle discussion into harsh argument.
>
> There is so much spiritual and material capacity in the world. God should shower down his bounties so that we can employ them in our work.
>
> There is no doubt that Germany should be divided into separate teaching zones, and each zone studied to discover its particular characteristics for teaching the Faith. In Germany it appears that the friends are of three categories. One: those who are willing to contribute large sums of money and then be left alone. Two: those who are rather younger and can help to organize the teaching activities, be members of committees or

help with the correspondence and in the distribution of materials. The third group consists of the youth who can participate in direct teaching: young Germans, Americans, Canadians, Africans, Icelanders, and most of the Persians. If we can have a plan which uses all three groups according to their capacity. We will have miraculous results.

GREECE

Although Raḥmat often passed through Athens en route to other countries, he only ever had the opportunity to spend one evening in the company of the few pioneers to Greece:

> *16 November, Athens*: We had a good meeting. The friends decided to try and teach in their neighbouring villages. Some of the Greek people are interested in the Faith. I believe teaching in Greece IS QUITE POSSIBLE WITHOUT ANY DIFFICULTY! The law states that if 200 people accept the Faith, and a university commission attests that the Bahá'í Faith is a legitimate religion which is not opposed to Christianity, and a church commission approves it, the government will register the Faith. Hence we should find a way to teach in this country so as to increase our numbers. For the moment though, teaching should be done with circumspection until new doors open.

ICELAND

Of his only visit to Iceland, in the summer of 1973, Raḥmat wrote in his diary,

> I arrived in Reykjavik, Iceland. I am staying in a boarding house, and have spoken about the Faith to the proprietors. It is apparent that Iceland has a special spirit, and in future it will become one of the important Bahá'í centres. The next day the friends came to see me and I met with the National Assembly. They devised a two-year plan with the goal of bringing 1200 new believers under the banner of the Faith of Bahá'u'lláh. The next night, about 50 of the friends had gathered and the night after that there was a public meeting in the Asia Hotel. Ten seekers attended the meeting.

He wrote to the Universal House of Justice, 'The friends of Iceland in utmost unity and love firmly believe that they will accomplish their goals of forming all their Assemblies before Riḍván.'

IRELAND

Raḥmat's notes on Ireland were always very optimistic and cheerful. He frequently said that he wished the Bahá'ís of Ireland could travel in Europe to spread their methods of teaching, and to bring their enthusiasm and spirituality to the continent.

Once he told me, 'The Bahá'ís of Ireland are amazing. They are all pioneers. As soon as they declare their Faith in Bahá'u'lláh they are told that they should go pioneering and they do.' In his diary he wrote,

> I have come to Ireland for the first time. We had detailed discussions with the friends about teaching the Faith. They are all in the best of spirits. I stayed at Adib Taherzadeh's home, and the next day we went to Limerick where they have formed a large community in a short span of time. Nearly 80 of them had gathered, mostly youth who are all well deepened in the Faith.
>
> At the meeting with the National Assembly and the Teaching Committee, they formed ten groups of five people each, to go together and teach the Faith. George Townshend was born on this island and predicted great victories for it. I am sure they will succeed. During our discussions I realized that there is a great spirit of pioneering among the friends. Some of them can pioneer to English-speaking countries such as Malta. THERE IS A UNIQUE FEELING OF UNITY AMONG THE FRIENDS IN THIS ISLAND.

After this visit he wrote to the Universal House of Justice:

> Ireland is basking in the sunshine of the Faith. Many firesides were scheduled during my four-day sojourn in that country. We met many seekers, all of whom were attracted to the Cause. These meetings are unique in Europe. If the number of travelling teachers to that country becomes regular and the numbers increase, it is certain that Ireland, God willing, will have mass declarations.

ITALY

In February 1971 a vast teaching programme was devised in consultation with the National Assembly of Italy, to take the Faith to all strata of society. Nine groups were formed to travel to different regions and teach continuously. Raḥmat noted, 'In Italy they have decided to increase the number of Bahá'ís to 5000 before next Riḍván. It is a blessed intention, I wish all in heaven and on earth could rush to their assistance to fulfil this goal.'

Mr Ferydoon Mazloom reported that, 'in one year there were 500 new declarations. This was the very first experience of mass teaching in Italy, and it can be attributed to Dr Muhájir's inspiration.'

In 1977, Raḥmat returned to Italy. He visited the Sicilian town of Catania, where the local Spiritual Assembly reported, 'During Dr Muhájir's visit, there was one declaration. It felt as if the Blessed Beauty had taken us by the hand.'

Raḥmat attended the National Teaching Conference in 1978, and after the reading of the message of the Universal House of Justice, addressed the friends:

> This message of the Universal House of Justice has given a new spirit to Europe. Shoghi Effendi, in one of his letters said that one of the greatest gifts of Bahá'u'lláh to humanity is the House of Justice. When you read the Writings of Bahá'u'lláh you can see how much He loved the House of Justice.
>
> The greatest duty of the House of Justice is to establish the Most Great Peace. Bahá'u'lláh, from the beginning, laid out the structure of this divine institution and even indicated how it would be supported financially. Once He was asked about Ḥuqúqu'lláh, and said that you have to wait for the Universal House of Justice.
>
> In answer to hundreds of questions He said that when the Universal House of Justice decides, you will have the answer. We still do not realize the significance of the Universal House of Justice. It is not an international parliament, but an infallible institution to legislate laws that Bahá'u'lláh has not revealed. Shoghi Effendi said that it is the 'successor' to Bahá'u'lláh and 'Abdu'l-Bahá.

In Palermo, Sicily.

With Hand of the Cause Dr Giachery, Rome 1965.

The Italians have been blessed by having a share in the construction of the beautiful Seat of the House of Justice. Bahá'u'lláh says that arts and sciences will penetrate the world from the West. This edifice is real art.

The Bahá'í world government, The Bahá'í Commonwealth, the World Order of Bahá'u'lláh, are responsible for the maturity and the unity of mankind. In the writings of Shoghi Effendi we find that when the time is right, new doors will open and new blessings will come. When the Universal House of Justice was established, there were 15,000 localities in the world [where Bahá'ís reside], now there are 80,000.

All the success of the Bahá'ís in the world comes from the blessings of Bahá'u'lláh to the House of Justice. Bahá'u'lláh inspires it, and we get the results.

At the time of Shoghi Effendi it was the same way. The blessings of Bahá'u'lláh were with Shoghi Effendi, and through him they were given to the world.

When the House of Justice makes a decision its outcome is assured. I have occasion to work closely with the Universal House of Justice, and I see that through its blessings even a piece of wood achieves great results. The moment it utters a word I see an ocean behind it. I visualize what can happen.

I had a telephone call from India today. They now have 27 teaching projects. I asked how many new Bahá'ís they have, and they said they have stopped counting. All this from a word of the Universal House of Justice. In two years we are going to have miraculous events in India. Impossible to imagine. The world is ablaze with the message of Bahá'u'lláh.

In the *Tablets of the Divine Plan*, 'Abdu'l-Bahá states that if the American Indians are educated they will illumine the world. In Bolivia they wanted 50,000 believers, they have 100,000.

Shoghi Effendi said that the indigenous people are like a reservoir. They will illumine the whole world. I see that this is about to happen.

The Universal House of Justice consults in a special manner. At times they deliberate for six months on one subject. When it has the answer, it is from God.

> We have to sacrifice the most precious thing that we have — TIME. Anything else that we possess does not equal time. Time which passes cannot be recaptured. Can you be younger today than yesterday? So use your time correctly.
>
> Shoghi Effendi used to say that all the youth should have a map of the world in their room, and ask themselves what they can do for a part of the world. So, together with a map of Italy, hang one of the world in your room.
>
> 'Abdu'l-Bahá said that one Bahá'í is like a thousand people — nay, a regiment. When you want to know your number in a meeting, take the highest number and double it. That is your true strength. No one has the capacity to think of the possibilities for the development of the Faith. Whatever we plan can put a limitation on it. The Faith has reached a level for which one cannot have projects. In India we planned for 7000 local Assemblies, now they have 10,000.
>
> The Faith of Bahá'u'lláh proceeds in mysterious ways. It is not calculated. It is not according to a project or a plan. 'Mysterious' means that although you plant a seed, it will not grow according to your wishes, but the way God wants it.
>
> A fireside in your home means many in the future. Present the Faith on the train, on the buses, everywhere. Your steps will continue to eternity. Find the way to take the necessary first step.
>
> Italy, Ireland, Portugal are all ready for entry by troops. With which method? Mysterious. Go out and work.
>
> What formula? Shoghi Effendi said to India that their local enterprise could not cope with the great power released in the world by God. If there is an enormous mass of water and we want to drain it with a straw it will not work. Your plans must be monumental.

Marzio and Vivien Zambalo accompanied Raḥmat on his last trip in 1979, and reported,

> The Hand of the Cause often emphasized the importance of individual firesides in complete confidence that divine assistance will be given, and the importance of frequent contacts with friends in all communities. The exchange of energy among the

> friends dissolves every barrier and transports the heart into a world in which there are no limits. The energy which comes from whoever serves with abnegation and absolute confidence in Bahá'u'lláh is incredible.

John Varney, a pioneer in Italy and member of the teaching team which travelled with Raḥmat, notes:

> From the beginning of his time in Campobasso, Dr Muhájir put himself at the service of the friends and their contacts . . . He recorded an interview for the Bahá'ís which they could use with local radio stations or the newspapers. He talked about the importance of teaching among ethnic minorities and of teaching in the islands — especially the Greek ones. He said that there were few Bahá'ís in Greece, and 400 Greek islands. As Italy is the only country nearby with an appreciable number of Bahá'ís, it is most likely that the teaching in those islands will be the task of the Italian Bahá'ís.

As he did in other European countries, Raḥmat stressed that the time for mass teaching had come. The local Assembly of Catania reported, 'Catania was twice blessed with the visits of the Hand of the Cause Raḥmatu'lláh Muhájir . . . The friends gathered from Catania and surrounding communities. Dr Muhájir shared his vision for entry by troops throughout Italy and presented plans to the assembled friends.'

LUXEMBURG

The National Spiritual Assembly of Luxemburg have records of four visits by Raḥmat to their country, the first being in July 1973, when he met the National Assembly and attended a meeting of 40 friends. He spoke about the *Tablets of the Divine Plan*, and stressed that they were preludes to the plans given by the Guardian. There were to be many more plans and it was imperative for the friends to give importance to each of them and achieve all the goals. He recommended that they study the *Tablets of the Divine Plan* carefully, as it contained all the guidance necessary for teaching and pioneering. He then asked the friends, and particularly the youth, to endeavour to bring at least one per cent of the population of Luxemburg under the banner of the Faith of Bahá'u'lláh. Some years later, while in Bangladesh, he told the Bahá'ís there that the small community of Luxemburg had achieved this feat.

In 1974 he reviewed the Five Year Plan with the National Assembly, and again encouraged them to increase their activities and hasten the achievement of their goals.

In July 1977 the National Assembly reported:

> Dr Muhájir participated at the Luxemburg Summer School in Ansembourg. He had a short consultation with the National Assembly, during which he inspired the National Assembly to launch a two month teaching campaign in seven different goal-towns. Four friends volunteered to participate full-time in this campaign. The campaign led to widespread proclamation of the Faith, good relations with local authorities, the production of a mini exhibition, and valuable experience.

Before leaving the Summer School he told the teaching group, 'You might have many difficulties and disappointments in the group, but it will add a lot to your gaining of experience. So do not lose heart.'

Raḥmat's last visit was in October 1978. He stayed for only a few hours to meet the National Assembly and the friends. He spoke about holding firesides and asked the friends not to be scared of their success. The National Assembly commented,

> All [were amazed] with his ability to arouse and enthuse. Always when meeting him people began a frenzy of activity. These did not always end the way they began, but always led to successful work and happy hearts.
>
> The most striking aspect of his personality seemed to be the speed at which he adapted his plans to a given situation, and his humility when submitting his suggestions to the National Assembly. . . . Each of his visits was a blessing. He always demonstrated a very encouraging nature and stressed the positive points. He was a shining example of Bahá'í life.

THE NETHERLANDS

In the year preceding the start of the Five Year Plan, Raḥmat made a few short visits to the Netherlands, touring several districts to visit the friends, and attending the Dutch Summer School.

Arrived in Utrecht on 30 November. Dr Nusrat Tahzib and Dr Taeed were waiting for me. They took me to an Indonesian restaurant where we had a delicious meal, and spoke with the waiters in Indonesian. The waiter told us that there were about 100,000 Indonesians in Holland, 70,000 having arrived within the last ten years. They are a large minority and we should teach them the Faith. If the Indonesian Bahá'ís — whether indigenous or pioneers — who participate in the election of the Universal House of Justice, spend the summer in Holland they will be able to assist the Dutch Bahá'ís in teaching this minority.

It is quite possible to translate and reprint books in Indonesian in this country. There is a large group of people here from Ambon, Indonesia. If we translate some books for them it would be very beneficial.

I arrived in Groningen at five p.m. In the evening we had a meeting with six seekers who are very familiar with the Faith. I asked each Bahá'í to tell us how he or she had accepted the Faith, and afterwards I spoke about the principles and administration. Many questions were asked and the meeting continued until 11.30. There was a 14-year old boy who had accepted the Faith through his brother, and was now the only Bahá'í in his home town.

1 December: On the way to The Hague I spoke about the Faith to a young man on the train. He became very interested. The Dutch are very nice, simple and hospitable people. Most of them know English. They are very receptive to the Faith. In the evening there was a most wonderful meeting in the Bahá'í Centre. Many people of different nationalities attended. Most of them were young, very active and spiritual. One asked me to tell them about my pilgrimage and the beloved Guardian, so the evening was spent in remembering Shoghi Effendi, and discussing teaching plans. They decided to consult at the Winter School about

> creating a programme of mass teaching in one area of Holland, with many of them concentrating their efforts in that area. We were together until late that night. No one wanted to leave.

Raḥmat and I were able to visit Amsterdam together several times over the years. We would always seek out an Indonesian restaurant and enjoy fragrantly spiced Indonesian food which brought back happy memories of our first pioneering post.

PORTUGAL

Raḥmat believed that Portugal had greater potential for entry by troops than any other country in Europe. Its National Assembly and pioneers were dedicated to mass teaching, and accepted Raḥmat's suggestions quite willingly. He visited that country on more than six occasions. In January 1971, as the final phase of the Nine Year Plan was approaching, the National Assembly held a meeting in Lisbon with most members of the community, where Raḥmat related the victories in other parts of the world:

> In Colombia, two boys, 11 and 13-years old, organized a public meeting at which they presented the concept of progressive revelation with maps and posters. There were 25 seekers, and one of them accepted the Faith. Colombia finished its Nine Year Plan in two years, then they devised another plan and finished that, and now they are in the process of finishing a third plan!
>
> In Malaysia they went to the same village sixty times to get one person to accept the Faith. The next time they had 13, and today they have a large and strong community in that village.
>
> It seems that here Bahá'ís predominantly live in big cities, so their work is not very successful. Go to the provinces and rural areas, There you will find the real population of the world. In Asia when we go teaching we know people are waiting for us. In India some ask, 'Don't you have a message for us?' Others say that they had dreamt that someone was going to visit them and bring them a new message about God. When a prayer is said, people listen. Once, on a visit to a village I told my companions, 'I will stay here under this tree and will say prayers, you go to the village and see what happens.' They went to see the schoolteacher, as the others were in the fields. They came back very

happy. The teacher had accepted the Faith and had gathered 27 people to listen to us.

Once I went to visit the Bahá'ís on an island. On the plane I thought I was going to die, as there was a terrible storm. We finally landed on another island, which wasn't in my programme, and I had to stay there for three days. The island was one of the Mindoro Islands, in the Philippines. The tribes that inhabited that island lived ten miles away. I walked 4 miles until I found a translator named Jose, who got a jeep for me and took me to visit one of the tribes. I spent the night there and spoke to about 50 people about the Faith. Finally the translator said 'I want to be the first Bahá'í on this island'. After that the whole village accepted the Faith. In the Philippines they had many Bahá'ís, but this island wasn't even in their plans. I had not heard its name. 'Abdu'l-Bahá says, do not make plans, just go and let Bahá'u'lláh act.

In Mozambique there is an entirely illiterate village, but all the Bahá'ís chant prayers by heart. It is a warm and united community. In Guatemala, they collected names and addresses and sent them correspondence courses about the Faith. Now 500 people are still studying the Faith, and 515 have become Bahá'ís. They also went to prisons and showed slides. A few prisoners became very interested and gave the names and addresses of their relatives to be contacted by the friends.

During this trip, Raḥmat met with the National Assembly and National Teaching Committee, and suggested that they make activity plans and give individual goals so that each believer is always occupied with work for the Faith; choose areas in the country that are still not open to the Faith so that at least one Bahá'í goes to that area; have border co-operation plans with Spain in Badajoz and Elvas; have a plan of daily prayers by all the believers for the progress of the Faith.

In 1972 he visited Porto and Lisbon, and participated in the National Teaching Conference held in the national Ḥaẓíratu'l-Quds. He worked with the National Teaching Committee and the Auxiliary Board members on a five-month plan for Portugal, which was presented to the conference. The goal was to teach at least 2000

Portrait of Dr Muhájir by Fedros Imani, Portugal.

people. Many of the friends volunteered to go travel teaching, and in the follow-up public meeting there were a few declarations.

Raḥmat was back in Lisbon in 1976, and, with Hand of the Cause Giachery participated in the teaching conference and the Summer School. The *Bahá'í News* reported, 'The guidance and inspiration provided by the Hands of the Cause and the enthusiasm and dedication of the believers, encouraged the National Spiritual Assembly to organize a complementary plan.'

In 1977 the National Assembly announced, 'After the National Convention, the meetings of the National Spiritual Assembly have been exclusively dedicated to the elaboration and development of the Emergency Plan for the Bahá'í Year 134, for which we have been counting on the valuable assistance of the Hand of the Cause Dr Muhájir . . .'

Once, Raḥmat was asked by one of the friends why he was taking notes of the talk of Dr Giachery, although he was a Hand of the Cause himself. He said, 'Dr Giachery is a very deepened Bahá'í and a very special person. I have great respect and admiration for him'.

When a Persian pioneer and very talented musician, Fedross Imani, played the santour at a Bahá'í meeting, Raḥmat told him that he should try to get on television in Lisbon, and, after playing the santour, talk about the Faith. Fedross managed to do this and appeared for 17 minutes on national TV. Half of the programme was dedicated to the Faith, including a rendition of the Hidden Words. This was the first time that the Faith had been proclaimed to a national audience in Portugal. As Fedross recalls, 'This was the fruit of the recommendation of the Hand of the Cause Muhájir. From that day on, we have had many more opportunities for Bahá'í programmes on Portuguese national television.'

Raḥmat's last trip to Portugal was in the summer of 1979. He visited Lisbon and several other communities. He spent a few days in the town of Funchal, on the island of Madeira, to activate its community and help the friends strengthen the local Spiritual Assembly. After a public meeting, he went to visit those Bahá'ís who had not been able to attend the gatherings. The day before he left, all the friends gathered beside an ancient wall on the island and said special prayers for the progress of the Faith in Madeira and Portugal.

SCANDINAVIA

At the request of the Universal House of Justice, Raḥmat visited the countries of Scandinavia in 1972.

Norway: In Oslo I went, with Bahman Tofighian, directly to the Bahá'í Centre to meet with the National Assembly. Some members had come from the northernmost city of Norway. The Secretary was a young man I had met in Malaysia. We discussed their plan and it was decided that a four-member team would spend fifteen days in each of three goal cities, so that, God willing, they will have the necessary numbers to elect the local Assemblies.

19 December: I met a few of the friends in Os, which is a goal town. There are some dedicated youth there. One of them told me that he works at a newspaper stand, and wants to spend most of his time in teaching the Faith. His parents want him to study more and do better at his lessons. He, however, feels that he was not doing any better at his studies before he was a Bahá'í. The youth are eager to serve but their elders prevent their activities.

Sweden: In Uppsala I stayed at the same hotel that I had been in two years ago. It is near the train station. In the evening we had a good meeting at the home of Keivan Nazerian, and I asked the friends to scatter all over town and to give the Message to one and all. They decided to try and teach at least sixty people in the remaining four months of the Plan, and to have a conference for the youth in Umea called the 'Midnight Sun' conference. For two months after the conference they will try to teach everyone they come in contact with. The place they have chosen is a university city, and quite suitable for this purpose.

22 December: One person declared at a meeting at Mr Afsahi's house. The few other seekers were very much interested in the Faith.

23 December: In my meeting with the National Assembly it was decided to plan five teaching programmes in the five goal cities for 20 days. In the evening we had a general meeting for the Bahá'ís and later a fireside.

24 December, Denmark: On arrival in Copenhagen I was told that Mr Faizí was arriving in one hour. It made me very happy, and we waited for his plane.

25 December: Mr Faizí and I had a meeting with the National Assembly, and then went to a public meeting. Many were present and Mr Faizí gave a beautiful talk. He spoke about Christ and Peter. He said that what is needed today is teaching the Faith. If we lose this opportunity we cannot reclaim it for centuries to come. His talk was both beautiful and spiritual. He said that the Bahá'í Faith is progressing with mysterious force.

I told the friends about the effect of prayer, and how the Faith has progressed in Latin America. The Vice-Chairman of the

On the waterfront in Helsinki with Gisu.

> National Assembly announced the details of the 40-day plan and we all consulted about it.
>
> Later I read the history of the martyrs of Ṭabarsí till two a.m. It is a first-hand, day-by-day account written by one of those who took part at Ṭabarsi but it is left unfinished, as the author was unable to write any more.

On 25 and 26 December Raḥmat attended successful meetings and firesides in Denmark. He then went back to Germany. His next visit to Scandinavia was in July 1976, when we attended the International Teaching Conference held in Helsinki, Finland. Before attending the conference, he wrote a letter to the International Teaching Centre in which he said,

> Now after 20 years these two countries, [Finland and France] have been selected through Bahá'u'lláh's grace to be the seat of two large European conferences. I feel it is befitting that a one-year plan on the basis of the instructions of the beloved Guardian should be drawn up in these very two countries. The goal should be to bring the Faith into the heart of the cities, a large number of which are deprived of the message of God. Such a plan will reinforce the victories which are expected from the conferences in those countries.
>
> Now that the army of travelling teachers is about to mobilize, and the International Teaching Centre is in charge to co-ordinate them, I feel it is important that a large number of travelling teachers be invited from Europe, America and Canada to go particularly to Finland this summer. Similarly, a large number may be called from northern Europe and Alaska to go to the places around the North and encourage large participation of friends in various countries.

On arrival in Helsinki, Raḥmat met the National Assembly of Finland. He suggested that this conference be used for wide publicity and teaching activity throughout the country. The youth were assigned to scatter all over Helsinki, and invite whomsoever they met to the public meeting. The conference was reported in the American *Bahá'í News* for August that year:

Dr Muhájir urged the history-making Bahá'ís of the present age to take action, now that the collective maturity of mankind is at stake. 'Whatever we do, whatever we decide, whatever we plan will influence the future. A consciousness that we are the foundation of the future will give us more energy, more hope to build this great edifice of God.'

He urged individual believers to study the Writings more deeply, share them, and teach with Bahá'í literature. Every individual should have his own teaching plan,' Dr Muhájir said, 'Don't sit at home. Movement is an essential part of the progress of the Faith.'

SPAIN

The National Assembly of Spain records at least five visits from Raḥmat between 1971 and 1978. Although the response of the friends to his proposals was not very enthusiastic at first, they gradually warmed to them, and often accompanied him travel teaching. The notes of one of the friends from 1971 say, 'Hand of the Cause Dr Muhájir begged for two youth to spend all their time visiting the villages. He said that now is the time for mass teaching. Alas, no one responded.' In 1976, this same friend recorded a very different response: 'The Hand of the Cause of God spoke of the necessity of teaching and pioneering. About 40 arose to do his bidding. On the next day we all met in the Palacio Hall. It was full. Dr Muhájir talked to the volunteers after the meeting. He was very tired.'

The same friend was present at a meeting for Raḥmat in 1978, and recorded, 'We all had a wonderful Persian meal at the house of Dr Muhájir's sister, Mrs Heshmat Adlparvar. Dr Muhájir looks very well despite his 20 years of constant travel. His eyes are absolutely extraordinary — bright and penetrating. He is 54 and the youngest Hand of the Cause. Many came to meet him and listen to him. In one meeting six contacts came to listen to him.'

Raḥmat had visited Spain in December 1972 after attending the teaching conference in Nice. His diary for that year contains no complaints about the lack of response from the Spanish friends.

> *11 December*: I am on my way to Barcelona. I had a letter from dear Írán, and answered it in the airport and wrote a few words about my health. I spoke to the Counsellors about having six conferences in Europe over two years. They will discuss it at their next meeting. 'Man proposes, God disposes.'
>
> *12 December*: I consulted with the Teaching Committee of Spain in Barcelona. They made a plan to increase the number of the Bahá'ís to 1000 by next Riḍván — they have only 600 now. They also decided that 100 teaching trips will be made and 100 firesides held. They will distribute all their existing pamphlets, about 40,000. It seems that distribution of literature has opened some doors, and about 15 people have become Bahá'ís through the correspondence course.
>
> Last night they held their Nineteen Day Feast, and, as they were busy with their own matters, I went to Terrassa. When I was there two years ago I met nearly a hundred of the friends. They are wonderful Bahá'ís. Last night also was a great occasion for me. The new plan was announced. They continued their Feast and I returned to my hotel, the Regina. This morning I feel much better, and am on my way to Madrid.
>
> I tried to call my family in India in the afternoon but was not successful. In the evening nearly 50 of the friends gathered for a meeting. Many were youth who are very enthusiastic. We discussed the new plan and decided to go to three of the nearby towns.
>
> *13 December*: I feel very well. I wrote a letter to the Universal House of Justice requesting that someone be sent from Latin America to Spain to help in their teaching efforts. Receptivity is great in this country, but there is need of a comprehensive teaching plan to bring the troops under the banner of the Faith.

This plan was approved by the Universal House of Justice, and in July 1973 Raḥmat recorded,

> Dr Habib Rezvani [from Bolivia] was in Madrid. Together we met the National Assembly and it was decided that in addition to

> their three existing projects, they will concentrate on two more areas, Badajoz on the border of Portugal, and also the area surrounding Barcelona. Dear Habib will continue his travels in Spain and Portugal.

With the expert help of Mr Rezvani, and the participation of the youth, many souls were brought under the banner of the Faith.

SWITZERLAND

Raḥmat's first trip to Switzerland was in 1972. Counsellor Agnes Ghaznavi recalls his visit: 'I remember the extraordinary energy that he transmitted and his will to win the goals of the Nine Year Plan. He would step in every time we seemed satisfied with our resolutions.' Raḥmat's diary records,

> *2 December*: I met with the National Assembly and discussed a teaching plan requiring the participation of the National Spiritual Assemblies of Italy, France and Iran. This needs to be presented to the Universal House of Justice for their approval. If at least ten people from those countries, like Heshmat Muayyad, Hasan Afnan, Cyrus 'Alá'í, Ma'súd Khamsí and others come to assist in teaching, the plan will have a great effect. I think the National Assembly should ask all the European communities to send them French-speaking Bahá'ís to assist in their teaching work.

> *3 December*: I am at a large conference in Berne, with more than 150 participants. Hand of the Cause Mühlschlegel and Ursula [his spouse] are also here. It is a most enjoyable occasion. I spoke about 'Abdu'l-Bahá's advice concerning teaching Theosophists, and also about teaching in universities. The enrolment of ten or twenty people in Germany and Portugal is the beginning of mass teaching and entry by troops in Europe. The pattern was the same in Bolivia, Korea and Africa where the first few believers were the harbinger of the masses who entered the Faith.
>
> A few people volunteered to pioneer and promised to start an intensive teaching project. Meetings like this are rare in Europe, and are indicative of the surge of a new spirit in these countries. I

discussed once again with the National Assembly its invitation to Iranian youth to visit Switzerland to travel teach.

Agnes Ghaznavi offers her impressions of Raḥmat during this visit to Switzerland:

I shall always remember the very special, intimate communion Dr Muhájir had while praying. He usually chanted short prayers in Persian, or asked someone to pray in the language of the country. Only once, when we were driving through the interior Cantons of Switzerland, did Dr Muhájir recite the Tablet of Aḥmad whilst in the car. It was very powerful. I firmly believe that great spiritual bounties came from that prayer. The following year, many surprising results came from the teaching in Sarnen, a town very near where he chanted.

To me, Dr Muhájir was a very unusual Persian. He was direct, but always loving, very conscious of time passing swiftly, very dynamic, always directing everything to action. Traditions did not seem to weigh heavily with him, specifically if they were a pretext for not doing the utmost for Bahá'u'lláh's Cause.

The capacities of a physician, I felt, also contributed to his ability to diagnose swiftly the illness of a national community and his eagerness to prescribe global solutions.

Once, on a train to Sion, we shared a compartment with an Italian woman and her child. Dr Muhájir immediately opened the conversation by offering the child some chocolate — later he gave her the whole bar. The woman began telling him about her ill health and liver trouble. Dr Muhájir told her very simply that she should refrain from eating too much fat. He asked the woman all about her daily work and her family. He then told her that he was a Bahá'í, and what it was about. The woman had already heard about the Faith. When she and her child left, happy and beaming, he told me that one must never let an opportunity pass. 'You keep in touch with her,' he said.

In Harbrugg, after a regional gathering, Dr Muhájir watched a group of Salvation Army members singing. He praised several aspects of their work and said, 'They still have to recognize Bahá'u'lláh.' For me, the lesson was in his lack of prejudice

> towards any group of people, even sects, and the possibility that he might learn something from them.
>
> When something was not possible, he did not ever seem to be angry about it. He had an uncommon acquiescence to obstacles when it was clear there was no way to avoid them.

Bijan Ghaznavi also remembers Raḥmat:

> In 1978, we travelled with him to a town called Sion. We had to fetch him from the station, having prepared all the food we needed. Unfortunately, we could not pick him up, as on the way we'd had an accident in the car. This made everything late. Dr Muhájir said many encouraging words to help us overcome the shock of the accident, which had demolished our car. Eventually we went to the town and had a meeting with the friends which was a great success.
>
> In the evening, we had to find our way through the mountains to another part of Switzerland, the Italian region. Unfortunately, we were very late and we were not able to continue on the roads, which were covered with snow. We tried to go on but finally we had to go back and find another way. Dr Muhájir was fascinated with the beauty of the mountains. He made our trip very comfortable, because he had some cheese and other provisions with him. We were impressed by his being so strong and powerful, and at the same time so nice, practical and close to his friends.

As the roads were blocked by landslides, Raḥmat had to cancel his intended visit to the Italian part of Switzerland and instead went to Zug, where Agnes was to give a talk on education. She recalls, 'He let me speak first, and then gave a beautiful talk using four quotations of the Báb on education, and outlining several new discoveries of science on the perception of infants. Afterwards he asked the seekers to speak, and not the Bahá'ís.'

As they had not gone to the Italian region, Bijan promised to visit the area. He recounts,

> We went there together in the spring of 1979. The night we arrived we had to share the same room. I will never forget how

> Dr Muhájir chanted the Tablet of Aḥmad in the morning with his soft and beautiful voice. He told me that he'd just had a very impressive dream, in which several active Bahá'ís of Iran had been executed. This made him very sad, and he was preoccupied by this dream for several hours. This was before the martyrdoms in Iran had started.

Agnes's account concludes with her memories of Raḥmat's visits.

> In 1978, he talked at some length about his mother and sisters, about his time in A<u>dh</u>irbáyján, and his decision to pioneer to Indonesia. I had the impression that his mother had been very important to him, encouraging him on the path of service and love for Bahá'u'lláh.
>
> The next time we saw him, in 1979 he expressed great love for his wife and daughter — and a certain wistfulness at being separated from them so often. He said that he prayed for them every day, and commended them to God.
>
> At one meeting he spoke about the importance of this life in relation to eternal life. He compared this life to the roots of a plant. The roots do not know what the leaves and flowers are like, but still they do their work unendingly, while leaves and flowers and fruits blossom, unfold and develop in the light. His talk was so poignant that very many friends became eager to take the necessary decisions and act.

THE UNITED KINGDOM

Raḥmat's first visit to the United Kingdom was in 1957, on the tragic occasion of Shoghi Effendi's passing. He often stopped briefly in London en route to other destinations, and would always visit the shrine of the beloved Guardian, where he spent many hours in meditation and prayer.

> Today Helen Astani took me to visit the resting place of the beloved Guardian. All the time I was remembering our pilgrimage in his presence. I said many prayers and kissed his precious grave and implored his bounties. We left for the city but I again returned alone to circumambulate his grave, say the Long

> Obligatory Prayer, and pray for Írán and Gisu. I went directly to the airport, and now I am on my way to Tel Aviv.

In 1963, Raḥmat joined with the other Hands of the Cause in celebrating the Most Great Jubilee. This 'King of Festivals' commemorated the centenary of the Declaration of Bahá'u'lláh in the Garden of Riḍván, and the formal assumption of His Prophetic Mission. This first World Congress brought together over 6000 Bahá'ís from all continents and corners of the world, marking the triumphant conclusion of the global Spiritual Crusade launched by the beloved Guardian, who wrote:

> The invisible battalions of the Concourse on High are mustered, in serried ranks, ready to rush their reinforcements to the aid of the vanguard of Bahá'u'lláh's crusaders in the hour of their greatest need, and in anticipation of that Most Great, that Wonderous Jubilee in the joyfulness of which both heaven and earth shall partake.[2]

The purpose of the Crusade, the Guardian had explained, was to establish 'on a world-wide scale, an unassailable administrative foundation for Bahá'u'lláh's Christ-promised Kingdom on earth.'[3] The living proof of those prophetic words were gathered together in jubilation under the roof of London's Royal Albert Hall. Those 'crusaders' — Knights of Bahá'u'lláh, pioneers, teachers and faithful followers — were keenly aware that they were witnessing yet another step in the unfoldment of Bahá'u'lláh's World Order, as they met for the first time the members of the Universal House of Justice, elected just days before on 21 April 1963.

The Hands of the Cause, who had guided the entire Bahá'í World since the tragic loss of the beloved Guardian, with their own self-sacrificial spirit, dedicated that historic gathering to his loving memory and shared their vision of the glorious future of the Cause. Raḥmat spoke on the fourth day of the five-day programme on the 'Enrichment of the World Bahá'í Community and the Enrollment of the Masses'. Sharing the platform that day were several indigenous believers, from countries such as Malaysia, Indonesia, the Philippines, Cameroon, and — to Raḥmat's particular delight

— from the Mentawai Islands. These dear friends spoke with profound emotion of their joyful experiences in teaching the Faith.

From the report of the Congress, published in the fourteenth volume of *The Bahá'í World*, we learn that,

> The Hand of the Cause Raḥmatu'lláh Muhájir expressed delight to have seen 'on this blissful day, the fruits of those who laboured in the teaching field during the Ten Year Crusade.' He said that mass conversion was now inaugurated in 30 countries of the world but that this is just a beginning. We must arise in full confidence that Baha'ullah and the beloved Master will help us as They promised and as They helped those who arose before us. The nations and islands 'yearn for pioneers' and wherever they have gone the pioneers have been greeted with the question 'Why didn't you come earlier to give this Message?' In 1921, he reminded us, Agnes Alexander, Hand of the Cause of God, who was then a young woman, pioneered to Korea and travelled to the Orient where today there are 3000 believers. We must make a beginning. If the result of the labours of approximately 100 friends has been a quarter of a million believers, what will be the result if a vast army of us will arise to pioneer![4]

In the ten years between the World Congress and our settling in London in 1973, Raḥmat visited the United Kingdom several times, though only for short periods. He usually met the National Assembly, and would occasionally attend a conference or Summer School. From 1973 to 1979 our home was in London, so Raḥmat was able to spend more time in the UK. However, I do not recall any special programmes for him during that period. He came to London mostly to rest and recuperate from his exhausting travels elsewhere, though he continued to attend conferences and Summer Schools if they co-incided with his visits.

On 9 July 1973 his diary reads:

> I participated in the meeting for the Martyrdom of the Báb [in Inverness, Scotland]. We were altogether ten, but it was a most spiritual event. The next day was the Summer School.
>
> *31 December 1973*: I spent five weeks in Britain. Met with the National Assembly, which went very lovingly. Visited Carlisle

for one day, made a short trip to the northern isles, and came back to London on 16 December.

I am on my way to the Holy Land. The days in London were truly wonderful. I visited the beloved Guardian's resting place many times and spent time with my beloved Gisu and dear Írán.

1 January 1974: Arrived in Haifa, midnight. Next day, went to the Shrines and said special prayers for Gisu and dear Írán.

Last night in London before moving to the USA.

In 1974, Raḥmat visited Scotland. He addressed a meeting of about 120 Bahá'ís from all over the country at the home of Dr Navai, near Glasgow. Dr Navai had trained in Ṭihrán as a medical doctor, before pioneering with his family to Scotland at the beginning of the

Nine Year Plan. Raḥmat spoke inspiringly about mass teaching in India and other parts of the world. He encouraged the Scottish Bahá'ís to adopt similar goals, to constantly travel and teach all sections of the population. Later he attended a Summer School in the Shetland Islands, the most northerly part of the British Isles. The friends were delighted by his visit, and sent a cable to the Universal House of Justice saying: '. . . BLESSED PRESENCE HAND MUHAJIR FRIENDS AFLAME DESIRE SERVE . . .'

Raḥmat visited Glasgow again in 1978, when friends from throughout central and western Scotland gathered to hear him speak at the home of Dr Riḍván Moqbel. One of the friends who attended remembers; 'His theme was encouragement. Now is the time, mass teaching is possible, here, now, have faith, take the first step, Bahá'u'lláh will do the rest. All the people must hear, must be given the Message. It seemed so simple, but I think that we were afraid of success. His vision was larger than all of ours put together!'

Raḥmat spent a month in London in the summer of 1979. Gisu was graduating from high school and we were preparing to move to America. One last time before our departure we accompanied him to visit the beloved Guardian's Resting Place. The next day we left England for the USA.

Raḥmat was impressed by the maturity and potential of the Bahá'í communities of North America, and believed that they could become an example of 'entry by troops' for the rest of the world.

Chapter 7

TEACHING NEEDS CERTITUDE

Throughout the Bahá'í world, Raḥmat was considered the champion of mass teaching. However, many believed that mass teaching was only possible amongst the indigenous peoples of the developing world. Raḥmat, on the other hand, knew that the teachings of Bahá'u'lláh were for the whole of humanity, irrespective of one's race, culture or homeland.

It is true that masses were entering the Faith in Asia, Africa and South America more rapidly than elsewhere, but Raḥmat felt that this was only because the Bahá'ís of the West did not believe their countrymen capable of accepting spiritual values. He thought that Bahá'í communities needed training in methods of mass teaching before they would be ready to forget their inhibitions and emulate the rest of the world. To prove this point, he often alluded to what the American Bahá'ís were doing to bring the masses into the Faith.

Although he did not visit North America as often as he did other parts of the world, he believed the National Spiritual Assembly of the United States to be the strongest, most malleable, positive and co-operative in the Bahá'í world. Once, after returning from a trip to America, a member of the Indian National Assembly, who was in awe of the highly-educated members of the US Assembly, asked Raḥmat whether he was inhibited in the presence of all those doctors and Ph.D.s. Raḥmat was quite amused. 'Any time I feel scared in their presence,' he said, 'I remind myself that I am a doctor too!' He then went on to explain how the US National Assembly took all his suggestions to heart and tried to implement them in their country, although these plans were almost always concerned with mass teaching.

He said that North America, with its strong Bahá'í Administration and its devoted believers, familiar with pioneering since the days of 'Abdu'l-Bahá, was not only the 'cradle of the Administration', but could become an example of entry by troops for the rest of the world. Many of the pioneers who were having great success in the mass teaching areas of the world were Americans and Canadians. They could easily do the same work in their own country.

HAWAII

Raḥmat's first visits to Hawaii and Los Angeles were in March 1961, spending just one night in each en route to Latin America. He wrote in his notes:

> I enjoyed being with the friends in Honolulu. There were about 40 of them. They had come to the airport and brought *leis* and bouquets of flowers. There were young children, five years to twelve years old, who put *leis* around my neck. I hugged them and kissed them and derived love and spirituality from them. They were such a mixture of different nationalities and races: Chinese, American, Japanese and Brown.
>
> We went directly to the grave of beloved Martha Root and I left all the flowers on the sacred grave of that 'archetype of Bahá'í teachers', and said prayers in all humility. Her headstone was engraved with the statement that she was the first Hand of the Cause of God appointed after the passing of 'Abdu'l-Bahá.
>
> The United States Government is going to establish a major University in Honolulu. I am sure this is the result of the blessings of the soul of beloved Martha Root who is buried there.
>
> In Los Angeles we had a very large meeting in the Bahá'í Centre. All the friends shook my hand and greeted me with love and kindness. There were a few Persian friends among them. They took me to see the city from the top of a hill. It was really beautiful. I remembered 'Abdu'l-Bahá's saying when he saw Frankfurt for the first time. He wept and said it was a pity that it would be levelled to the ground. Los Angeles also appears to be shining and splendid but no one knows its future. I don't know why the people of America have to suffer so much. It must be

because of their materialism. They worship material objects, and they will have to suffer for it.

In 1965 Raḥmat made another visit to Hawaii. This time he travelled to most of the islands, visiting the Filipino Bahá'ís who lived in Mulukai, as well as the leprosy villages. Dr Claud Caver, director of the leprosy centre, recalls that, 'both the patients and staff are understandably distant to visitors as a rule, but the warmth and compassion demonstrated by Dr Muhájir overcame their reticence. He established a warm relationship with all those he met.' When a Bahá'í friend in Mulukai, Monty von Tempsky, died of muscular dystrophy, the Bahá'í ring placed on his finger was a gift from Raḥmat.

He visited Hawaii again in 1971, when he went to all the islands, met with the friends, spoke in large gatherings, attended the Summer Schools, and had meetings with the National Assembly.

His December 1975 trip was scheduled to last three weeks, but the Hawaian National Assembly asked him to assist 'during the immediate months ahead to recruit and train pioneers and thereby stimulate further the work of the International Goals Committee'. They also asked him to 'assist in preparing the reception of these pioneers especially in countries of Africa and Latin America.' In its cable, the National Assembly informed the Universal House of Justice:

OUR SPIRITS UPLIFTED BY VISIT HAND CAUSE MUHAJIR UNITED STATES HIS MEETING OUR ASSEMBLY LAST WEEKEND RESULTING IN AGREEMENT THAT HE WILL ASSIST US WITH NUMBER TEACHING PROJECTS OVER NEXT SEVERAL MONTHS . . . HE HAS ACCEPTED REQUEST ASSIST US RECRUIT TRAIN PIONEERS HERE PREPARE THEIR RECEPTION AT GOALS WITH OBJECT OF FILLING ALL OUR PIONEER ASSIGNMENTS BY NEXT RIDVAN . . . WE FEEL CERTAIN NEW SPARK TEACHING CAN BE IGNITED THROUGHOUT NATIONAL COMMUNITY WITH HIS HELP . . .

The Universal House of Justice cabled Raḥmat directly:

VIEW IMPORTANCE ROLE AMERICAN BAHAI COMMUNITY FULFILMENT GOALS PLAN URGE YOU CONSIDER FIND WAYS

CONTINUE YOUR COOPERATION THAT COMMUNITY INSPIRE ASSIST THEM TEACHING PIONEERING FIELDS

He, of course, was happy to comply with the National Assembly's request, and agreed to stay till the end of April. The National Assembly cabled him:

HAVE INFORMED HOUSE OF JUSTICE YOU ARE EXTENDING YOUR STAY IN UNITED STATES TO ASSIST TEACHING PIONEERING WORK . . . HOUSE OF JUSTICE HAS REPLIED AS FOLLOWS QUOTE DELIGHTED HAND CAUSE MUHAJIRS INTENTION LEND SUPPORT HOME FRONT TEACHING PROJECTS . . . ASSURE DR MUHAJIR YOUR ASSEMBLY LOVING PRAYERS UNQUOTE . . .

THE UNITED STATES

Thus began a period of travel which took Raḥmat to many parts of the North American continent. This resulted in great victories, particularly the influx of masses in the southern United States.

The National Assembly of the USA warmly embraced all Raḥmat's suggestions, and took immediate action to implement them. The most important tasks were recruiting pioneers, teaching the masses in the southern States, and participating in a joint teaching effort with the Alaskan and Canadian National Assemblies, along the Pacific coast from Juneau to Portland. This project, which was to last for three years, was suggested by Raḥmat to the Alaskan National Assembly.

The US National Assembly wrote to him, 'We are impressed with the possibilities of your suggestion that a three year teaching programme be conducted along the Pacific Coast . . . We eagerly look forward to your participation in the planning conference.' It then cabled the National Assemblies concerned:

OUR MEETING WITH HAND CAUSE MUHAJIR LAST WEEKEND PROMPTED US FAVOUR PROPOSAL PROJECT WHICH REQUIRES COLLABORATION ALASKAN CANADIAN UNITED STATES NATIONAL ASSEMBLIES STOP PROJECT INVOLVES THREE YEAR PROGRAM ALONG PACIFIC COAST FROM JUNEAU TO PORTLAND DIRECTED AT MINORITIES PARTICULARLY INDIANS . . . DR

> MUHAJIR HAS ACCEPTED OUR REQUEST HE ATTEND ASSUME SIGNIFICANT ROLE CONFERENCE PROCEEDINGS

Raḥmat travelled to most parts of the United States, creating new plans and activities wherever he went. The United States Teaching Committee reported that,

> The booklet *Design for Victory* was the product of his vision for a teaching plan that could be used by every individual and every Teaching Committee during the first weekend in March 1976. Dr Muhájir travelled everywhere, explaining the teaching plan, consulting on goals, and developing the Border Teaching Program . . . The Border Teaching Program was a joint teaching effort between the United States and Mexico with two sister communities, one on each side of the border, working together. Texas, Arizona, and California were the States involved.

Raḥmat's itinerary included visits to universities and schools, meetings in small towns and large cities. He met dignitaries and officials and was interviewed for the mass media. While in Chicago, he was, according to the National Teaching Committee,

> . . . taking a few moments to relax before meeting his next appointment, one of many he had kept since arriving in the United States. For more than three months he had travelled in almost every State, talking about teaching, consolidation, pioneering and travel teaching. He was impressed by the enthusiasm of the Bahá'ís throughout the country.
>
> 'The American Bahá'ís are lucky', he exclaimed. 'The Faith is safe here, secure. And this is the best time to teach. What we need now is action. Pray and act. Don't keep quiet. Tell someone about Bahá'u'lláh. Even if he does not become a Bahá'í, he will tell someone about the Faith. Perhaps the other person will accept. Be positive. The United States is ready for entry by troops. And the Bahá'ís are ready. Search for all the opportunities. Extend yourself and reach the people. Make yourself into a new pioneer. Be a pioneer in your own home town. We must find the receptive areas and send travelling teachers.

Board of Counsellors and NSA members, USA.

Arriving in the USA, a pensive Dr Muhájir.

With the Board of Counsellors for North America. (Left to right) Florence Maybury, Lloyd Gardner, Edna True, and Hand of the Cause Mr <u>Kh</u>ádem.

'Hundreds of thousands will hear about the Faith and many thousands will accept. I am sure something great [is] to happen. Bahá'ís should always look to the future, but give it time. The problems of humanity have deepened over thousands of years. The healing will take many generations, but we can alleviate the suffering of the world.

[I am] convinced this is a turning point in the history of the Faith in the United States. American Bahá'ís should be conscious of their destiny to advance the cause of Bahá'u'lláh.'

The American friends rose to the occasion and Raḥmat's cry for action and sacrifice. He told them that,

> Now is the time of the harvest. The work of the pioneers around the world in opening new localities, forming local Assemblies, Conventions and National Assemblies, was to put down foundations for one great goal, the spiritual conquest of the hearts. That still remains the goal. We are not at the end of the journey, and must continue.
>
> The aim of our lives should be pioneering and teaching. If you want to know which takes precedence, it is pioneering to the farthest places possible. The farther the better. The sooner the better. This is the time for harvesting the souls of the people. All the efforts of the past hundred years — from the martyrs and Dawn-Breakers to the pioneers and administrators — has made the world ready for the Faith. The people are ready and receptive. Now it all depends on the pioneers and Bahá'ís to reap the harvest.
>
> We plan everything in our lives, why not pioneering? The parents must open a pioneering account for their children to make sure they will go pioneering. No one dies in the place of his birth. That concept is over. You must move, but move in the way that God wants, in the right direction.

The American Bahá'ís rallied round him to fulfil the goals. Eight members of the Spiritual Assembly of Pamona, California, left their city to pioneer. Two thousand Bahá'ís attended the teaching conference in California. They decided to launch teaching programmes in their districts at 88 teaching conferences. A special

Dr Muhájir challenges the American friends to arise at a teaching conference.

Dr Muhájir with a group of American Bahá'í youth.

Taking a stroll with Mr Glenford Mitchell, Secretary of the US National Spiritual Assembly.

project along the Mexican border was to commence with training programmes in the city of Mexicali. The goal of this border teaching plan was to raise local Spiritual Assemblies in Mexicali and Tijuana in Mexico, and El Centro and Chula Vista in California.

In the three months and more of Raḥmat's travels in North America, the Bahá'í institutions worked constantly to support his initiatives. The International Goals Committee reported;

> It was an exciting time for those of us who had the privilege of travelling with him. His wonderful sense of humour lightened even the most difficult and stressful moments. We found ourselves laughing under unexpected circumstances. He would cajole and tease, resurrecting the weak moments of his companions, and, at times, himself. He reminded those of us who were privileged to serve the community by providing information and encouragement that we were fulfilling the promise of sending others in our stead to bring the Faith of Bahá'u'lláh to the whole of mankind. That promise brought solace to our hearts when it would have been easy to be discouraged.

The Southern Teaching Project was the most successful and important of these months. Raḥmat participated in a conference at the Louis Gregory Institute in South Carolina, and toured all the southern States to launch the campaign. The programme called for special projects in South Carolina, North Carolina, Alabama, Florida, Oklahoma, Texas, Maryland, Virginia and Georgia. The goal was to reach all strata of society, using firesides as the foundation of the teaching work. After visiting a Cherokee Indian reservation, Raḥmat travelled to 12 southern cities, working with the various committees, visiting the Bahá'ís, participating in their teaching campaigns and attending firesides.

The southern States were aflame. The prophecy of 'Abdu'l-Bahá was being fulfilled: 'The Hands of the Cause of God must spend all their time in teaching. Ere long will the assistance of the Heavenly Kingdom be manifested beyond all expectation. Then will the words: "thou shall witness the people enter the Religion of God by troops" be fulfilled.'[2]

The *Southern Bahá'í Bulletin* of April 1976 reported, 'Fifty new believers including two families have come into the Faith in South

Carolina due to teaching sparked by the visit of Hand of the Cause of God Dr Raḥmatu'lláh Muhájir in January.' Trudy White, who travelled with him, recalls:

> I drove Dr Muhájir to many of the meetings. In one rural community, as the houses were small, the meeting was held in the backyard of a friend's house. The yard was neat but there were chickens and pigs, and many mosquitoes. Dr Muhájir had a suit on. He removed his coat, and in his spotless white shirt, gathered material to build a fire. After a while the mosquitoes were gone. He then spoke to the crowd, answered many questions and everyone had a wonderful time, and no mosquitoes during the programme.
>
> In another meeting the hostess had been ill for some time, but had decided to host this meeting for Dr Muhájir. She had a beautiful voice and sang spirituals, but some friends had advised her that, as she had become a Bahá'í, she should not sing 'other' religious songs. Although this made her very sad, she accepted the advice. When Dr Muhájir found out that she was a singer, he asked her to sing for him, but she refused. Dr Muhájir finally convinced her that it was alright. She sang 'Amazing Grace' while Dr Muhájir hummed along with that lovely melody. She later promised him never to stop singing, and she never did. He asked one of the friends at the meeting to take her teaching, and let her sing for the people.
>
> At the Louis Gregory Teaching Institute, a crowd of local believers came to hear him. Before they introduced him, he told me these friends were truly like the Dawn-Breakers. He told several stories about the Dawn-Breakers and about his grandfather, who did not know many facts about the Faith, but who had the spirit and recognized the truth, just as that audience had done. It was a wonderful meeting. The happiness in Dr Muhájir's face shone brightly through his eyes and smile.
>
> One day we went to visit the friends at the Cherokee Reservation in North Carolina. Dr Muhájir removed his shoes, and, sitting comfortably, shared stories with the friends. They loved him. He felt a special bond with the Indians and blacks and they responded to him.

> He had a one-track mind, focused on teaching the Cause and his love for all people cannot be forgotten. One lesson I learned from him was to accept and love individuals for what they are. He said ' Take care of them and Bahá'u'lláh will assist you in time of need.'
>
> On one of the trips we were travelling down the street in a black area. He said teach all the people — everyone sitting on the porches, walking, working — everyone should be taught. I wonder what would have happened if we had followed his advice.

Janet Rubenstein recalls,

> He expressed strong views that, as Secretary of the International Goals Committee, it was important for me personally to travel and make the effort to recruit pioneers and travelling teachers. He asked my husband if he had any objection to the trips and the reply was that he never interfered with my serving the Cause. Dr Muhájir then looked at me and said 'So?' My response was that in addition to my husband I also had a 12-year old daughter. He said, 'That's okay, so do I.' I did go and regretted not a minute. My husband and daughter fared well and I have a memory that will not fade.

After Raḥmat's travels in the southern States, the National Spiritual Assembly wrote to him,

> We are immensely grateful for the good fortune which has brought you to America at this time in the Five Year Plan. Many teaching plans have already been adopted which, we feel, will enable the American believers to achieve every goal set before them; some of these plans are already being executed; others, like the Southern Teaching Program, are about to be launched. Your presence among us now and your kind offer of assistance on our homefront in the ways already outlined will undoubtedly aid in releasing the tremendous energies of the friends throughout the country to teach the Cause and win victories which will gratify the supreme House of Justice.

At a special video-taping session in the House of Worship at Wilmette, early in January 1976, one of the questions asked of Raḥmat was, 'How do we prepare ourselves for teaching on a daily basis?' He replied,

> Preparation for teaching is teaching itself. When we want to learn to swim we go into the water and start swimming. Even if you are a newly enrolled Bahá'í, you must teach, and in teaching you will learn more and become better able to teach. You will begin developing the qualities of kindness, of being human, of wanting to understand your fellow man.
>
> The ultimate goal of all institutions is teaching. The Feast is an opportunity for each individual believer to assist in the planning, by giving his ideas in the consultative portion . . . Good planning must be long-term planning.
>
> In mass teaching, when we bring a family into the Faith we have truly opened a locality. It is better to teach families than to concentrate on individuals. If the grandmothers in an area are looked up to by their families, and we teach these grandmothers the Faith, their families will follow. If we teach the children and the grandmothers disapprove, the children may fall away from the Faith. The foundation of any society is the family. Let us think of teaching families. He was asked whether prayer was important for effective teaching. He said that of course it was important, but not unless it was followed by action. 'We must pray, be sincere and act. The bounty of God is hovering between heaven and earth, waiting to shower upon any soul who arises in this way. In every period of your life, you can take action which will attract those bounties.

When asked how we can set about teaching all strata of society, Raḥmat answered,

> There are really two aspects to this question. We must reach all strata of society with the message of Bahá'u'lláh, but we cannot guarantee that all of them will accept the Faith.
>
> Every religion has started with the lowly. These believers disperse through foreign lands, and their children become the

An interview before the cameras.

Planning the campaign.

> professional class and leaders in their respective fields. I teach everybody. I do not know who will accept. But from those who do not accept, Bahá'u'lláh will raise up whatever people he needs to change the future society.

Of the powerful effect on each individual of accepting the Faith, he said, 'The moment a person says, "I am a Bahá'í", he begins to change. The declaration has an effect on him. Similarly when we address an audience, the moment we mention the name of Bahá'u'lláh, we help to change that audience, to attract them to this message.'

He stressed the importance of developing 'consciousness of pioneering' by the American Bahá'ís:

> We must be sure we can do it. We must now make the plans that will permit us to pioneer, if not this year, then whenever it becomes possible. But we must plan toward this goal, not just hope that it will somehow happen.
>
> Waiting to know more of the teachings is not necessary, for we sometimes learn so much that we teach in a complicated way. We should be simple and direct, helping our listeners to learn the fundamental truths, and, if they are literate, to turn themselves to the Writings. It is important to know something of the customs of the area in which we teach, but this can be quickly accomplished if we are sincere and arise to serve Bahá'u'lláh. If we are humble and truthful, the goals will be won.

Raḥmat left the United States jubilant at the success of the friends in rising to achieve their goals. He wrote to the Universal of Justice from Chicago on 12 March 1976:

> While in the US, extensive consultations were held on teaching the Cause, opening new places, proclamation and entry by troops, with the institutions concerned in the various regions and with local Spiritual Assemblies.
>
> God willing, the results of all these consultations, after the approval of the National Spiritual Assembly, will be presented to the Convention. The delegates, who are mostly members of

Regional Teaching Committees and local Spiritual Assemblies, will have further consultation and, God willing, a new fruitful year will dawn to coincide with important international events.

He kept in constant touch with the US National Assembly and pursued the goals agreed upon in their meetings together. The National Assembly responded by informing him of its achievements and acting on his suggestions. A cable sent to him while he was in Helsinki, in July 1977, is an example of this co-operation:

REURCALL TODAY RECRUITMENT TRAVELLING TEACHERS TO EUROPE PROCEEDING STOP TWENTY-SEVEN ALREADY COMMITTED SPEND VARIOUS LENGTHS TIME BETWEEN JULY OCTOBER STOP SOME GOING SEVERAL COUNTRIES STOP

CANADA

Raḥmat was able to visit Canada on several occasions. In 1965 he 'provided a major impulse for the work on the Nine Year Plan, particularly to rapidly increase the number of localities in that country.' Of his visit in 1976, the *Canadian Bahá'í News* reported:

Dr Muhájir spoke so inspiringly and beautifully about the plans for the erection of the building of the Universal House of Justice that many friends were moved to contribute to the building fund. He also spoke of the need for Indian teaching in British Colombia and received an enthusiastic response from the friends in the Vancouver area, where there are close to 30 Indian Reserves within easy reach.

In Toronto, Dr Muhájir addressed a gathering at the Holiday Inn on 16 January. The Hand of the Cause spoke eloquently of the need for Bahá'ís to understand the significance of the times in which they live. He indicated the paramount necessity of a continuing effort by Canadian Bahá'ís to teach the Faith at home as a means of generating Canadian pioneers to serve abroad. He said, in his understanding of the current historical context, that many countries of the world are now ready for a great spiritual harvest, the result of the seed- planting phase and the furrowing of the soil by the earlier pioneers. He warmly encouraged the

World Religion Day celebrations, Halifax, Canada, 1976.

National Teaching Conference, January 1975, Toronto, Canada.

believers who are at present planning to pioneer overseas, to make haste to reach their posts, and promised that in the continents of Africa and South America they will soon witness a new phenomenon called 'Entry by Troops'. In other words, the pioneer of today may be a harvester who can expect to gather a great influx of new believers into the Cause.

In Winnipeg, 22 January, Dr Muhájir spoke at length about Indian teaching with about 90 friends gathered at the North Star Inn, pointing out that the Indians, were a vast resource. He said that we were to teach the older Indians, even though they never gave up drinking. The older ones would introduce the Faith to their families and the families would become deepened in the Teachings if we kept up our teaching. He said that we should be direct with the Indians and present the Message very simply. Do not tell them that you are there to teach them something, they are tired of being taught. Tell them that you have a message to give them and proceed from there.

Dr Muhájir also visited Ottawa, Montreal and Quebec City, and plans to be in Yukon on 17 February.

The response of the friends was very heartening; many rose to fill the overseas goals. The Canadian National Assembly said to Raḥmat, in their letter of February 1976, that the reports received regarding his visits in eastern Canada and Winnipeg had been full of joy, excitement and planned activities: 'We thank you so much for the inspiration and challenge you have given Canada and look forward to meeting you in Seattle.'

HIS FINAL VISIT

Raḥmat's last trip to North America was in 1979. Our daughter Gisu had been admitted to Harvard University, and, as Raḥmat was to travel for a period of two years in Latin America, we decided to move to the United States. We arrived in Massachusetts in August 1979.

At this time, Raḥmat introduced in America his plan of consecutive firesides for 19 or 21 days. He inaugurated this plan in Newton, Massachusetts, and participated in all 19 meetings. The result was more than 30 declarations. After staying in Boston for just one month, he left for the Caribbean and Latin America. He had already met the National Assembly, given talks in various conferences, and was ready for his travels which would again take him to many States. His diary gives some details of this short trip:

12 September 1979: I have begun my journey from Newton to the eastern cities of America. God willing, I will visit the Caribbean and will continue to Latin America.

I am now in Wilmington, Philadelphia. We had a meeting with the friends and spoke to them about firesides for 19 or 21 days and asked them to give some order to their teaching activities.

In Dover, the Capital of Delaware, there are only three Bahá'ís.

13 September: At 7.30 a.m. I had a meeting with the District Teaching Committee. I asked them to have two firesides of 21 days for their two local Assemblies, to have a special plan to bring Persian pioneers to Delaware from Washington DC. To have two teaching campaigns one from 20 October to 12 November, and one from the end of December to mid-January. They should rent a room in the YMCA and systematically teach and have firesides. Perhaps this year they can form a local Assembly in Dover.

The plan was to have a six-month plan to teach 100 families in the South of the State, near Salisbury. The budget required is $3000, of which $1000 will be given by the DTC, and $2000 should be contributed by the local Assemblies and individual Bahá'ís. They will ask for one permanent teacher from South Carolina to help them in this venture.

I left by bus for Salisbury, and arrived at 2.30 in the afternoon. There was a very good gathering in the evening. The friends had gathered from Virginia and had brought their beautiful children, which added to the charm of the meeting. I spoke about the education of children and the way to train them to teach the Faith. There were also two seekers who asked many questions and seemed to be happy. God willing, they will soon be Bahá'ís. I was a guest at the home of George and Sylvia Stroop.

The friends of Georgia have decided to start their mass teaching once more.

14 September: I was interviewed by a very intelligent lady reporter and left for Washington DC. I met the local Assembly and talked to them about doubling the number of their Bahá'ís. They decided to start a 21-day series of firesides.

In the evening we had a huge meeting of the friends. They had gathered from all over the State, and were mostly American. We talked about the continuous firesides. Nearly 20 people offered their homes. It was a most spiritual meeting.

15 September: had a meeting with the DTC and the Iranian Affairs Committee. Participated in the student meeting and asked them to have a methodical teaching plan. The DTC is a vigilant and positive committee. It was decided that they would have a plan to teach 100 families in Frederick, and arrange firesides in that city.

16 September: I met the University Bahá'í Club. It was decided to consult the Teaching Committee to have the month of February 1980 for the teaching of Universities. The DTC to target one of the Universities and send books to all professors.

17 September, Richmond: I stayed at the home of John and Jan Czerniejewski, who were pioneers in Costa Rica. We had a very good meeting. People had come from surrounding neighborhoods. They decided to have continuous firesides.

Jan Czerniejewski recalls that Raḥmat was very cheerful on that visit, and that during the meal he was laughing and joking, almost as if he had received some especially good news. The incident most vivid in Jan's mind is connected to their adopted daughter.

She was a beautiful — but difficult — child and we anguished greatly over her. Early one morning, we heard some chanting in the breakfast room downstairs. We found Dr Muhájir with Andrea on his lap, chanting prayers for her. I cannot describe my feelings. It still moves me to tears. She was so still, not typical of her, concentrating on him and on the beautiful tones. I still feel certain Dr Muhájir is assisting her from the next world.

Raḥmat's diary continues:

18 September: I came to Raleigh very early in the morning. Dr and Mrs Rasekh were at the airport. I met the DTC in the evening. It was decided to have two travelling teachers for six months. In the same meeting a car was given and $1500 was contributed towards the expenses. One person volunteered for six months. They are going to have five continuous firesides.

It was a most unique and spiritual meeting. With the confirmations of Bahá'u'lláh they will achieve all these goals.

The news of dear Olinga's passing was given to me. My grief is so strong that I feel my soul has left me. I think however that his pure soul is in ecstasy in the Abhá Kingdom. He is rid of the toils of this world, and in his blessed name thousands will come to the Faith.

We began the teaching campaign here in his beloved name, so that in North Carolina the teaching of the black Americans could restart.

In all of the United States, especially the southern States, new endeavours should be made to teach the pure souls of the black Americans.

19 September: I visited some of the friends in Greensboro, and in the afternoon there was a good meeting in the university. Nearly 50 people had come from different towns. It was a spiritual meeting. The friends made some decisions for teaching the Faith. As they had no full-time teachers they decided to concentrate for three weeks on cities where they have new pioneers. This will be a source of encouragement for those who have accepted the Faith in the last mass teaching campaign.

I left Greenboro for Charlotte, North Carolina. I met the DTC in the afternoon. They believe there are 6000 Cherokee Indians in this area. They have 400 black Bahá'ís. They decided to have a proper teaching plan for the three groups of people that live in this area [white, black and Indian].

20 September, Colombia, South Carolina: I met the Regional Teaching Committee and discussed how to increase the number of Bahá'ís. I made some suggestions:

1. That South Carolina be chosen as one of the States in the National Assembly's plan for mass teaching.

2. Double the number of the believers.

3. Appoint an education committee to form Bahá'í classes for children.

4. Have three vans to be used for teaching in 21 chosen towns.

5. Contact all strata of society.

6. Appoint two people to be responsible for 21-day continuous firesides.

A considerable number of Bahá'ís gathered in the evening. I spoke about mass teaching and consideration for the indigenous people. I told them about tests which God subjects all of us to, whether communities or individuals.

Seventeen towns pledged to have continuous firesides. At the end of the meeting we spent more than an hour in prayers.

21 September: Permanent teachers and other Bahá'ís gathered in the Institute in the evening. I quoted from the Writings of the Báb and 'Abdu'l-Bahá regarding teaching the masses. I asked each of them to have a plan for teaching. It was decided to begin mass teaching in the neighbouring ten towns. We received news that the work had started in one of the towns.

South Carolina has 7500 Bahá'ís. To double this number is very easy. It is possible to teach 100,000 black Americans within one year. the efforts should be systematic and continuous. They should stop temporary actions. Black Americans are even more receptive to the Faith than Africans. The white Americans are also more receptive than the Europeans.

Bahá'u'lláh's confirmations are needed to create a new zeal and enthusiasm for teaching America. Thousands would embrace the Faith in a short time. They can even ask Bahá'í teachers from South-East Asia, the Philippines and India to help them. This work is quite feasible. Yá Bahá'u'l-Abhá.

22 September: I write these notes in the Louis Gregory Institute. IS IT POSSIBLE TO HAVE A RADIO STATION IN GREGORY INSTITUTE? ITS COST IS ABOUT $30,000 PER YEAR.

Perhaps the National Assembly will approve doubling the number of black American Bahá'ís as a goal for the first two years of the Seven Year Plan. If they do, it will create a new spirit in all the States.

TEACHING IN AMERICA NEEDS CERTITUDE. ALL OTHER MEANS ARE ALREADY THERE.

We had a meeting of about 15 friends at noon. Ten of them were schoolteachers. I suggested they form a Bahá'í Teacher's Club with the aim of teaching all teachers. This could be done all over America: perhaps some activity can be started by these teachers. There are nearly 500 Bahá'í schoolteachers in America. Maybe February will be a good month for teachers and students to give the message of Bahá'u'lláh to their colleagues and fellow students.

I think a goal should be given to all DTCs to teach a certain number of people. They could suggest the number themselves and try to achieve that number. this is especially important for South Carolina.

23 September: This is a blessed day. We had five seekers in Frogmore, and then I went to Hiltonhead and Savannah.

24 September, Savannah, Georgia: They decided to have a three week teaching campaign. I dreamt of 'Abdu'l-Bahá.

25 September, Birmingham, Alabama: We had a very fruitful meeting. The teaching committee has active and dedicated members. They decided to have several firesides, and two of them volunteered for six months of travel teaching. They will need $3500 which they said they could raise themselves. God's Will be done.

26 September, New Orleans and Baton Rouge: The friends chose two areas of Lake Charles and Race Land to concentrate on teaching. They said that they had written the names of 18 spouses who were not Bahá'ís in their prayer books and had prayed for them. They are now all Bahá'ís.

27 September, Memphis: I suggested that the youth start mass teaching among the youth.

28 September, Little Rock, Atlanta: There was a good meeting in the evening. I met the DTC and we chose Merriweather and Henry County to begin mass teaching. Atlanta has 1000 Bahá'ís which they can double within two years. They can also have 25 children's classes.

29 September: I met the National Teaching Committee. They formed a wonderful plan. They are going to have a unity Feast after every two Feasts. The friends not only will be together in harmony and unity, but will consult on the goals of the Seven Year Plan. They decided to double the number of believers in South Carolina, Georgia, and the Spanish-speaking Bahá'ís of California. They will have fireside teaching campaign on 19 days in all the country and will have a plan for women to teach women.

30 September: I had a meeting with the Iranian Bahá'ís. In the next three days I went to Gainsville, Daytona Beach, Longwood, Orlando and Tampa in Florida.

I spoke to the Teaching Committee about teaching on the borders with the Caribbean, which is the instruction of the Universal House of Justice. They can also invite teachers from Haiti and Jamaica to teach in Florida. There are thousands of the natives of those islands in Florida. they can invite teachers from Latin America to teach the Spanish-speaking people of Florida. This in fact would be an exchange of teachers, as they will send teachers from Florida to the Caribbean.

We had a blessed fireside in the evening. There were six seekers. Many of the friends pledged to go travel teaching, nine of them to the Caribbean. There were also contributions to the fund and promises to hold several 19-day firesides.

A simple plan can be devised for mass teaching in the United States:

1. Have experienced people to organize the campaign.

2. Continuous fireside campaign in all cities. Eighteen days of firesides and on the Nineten Day Feast the new believers should participate in deepening.

3. Permanent teachers in each district. One or two to be self-supporting for at least six months.

4. Each district to be responsible for its own plan.

5. Women teach women.

6. Double the number of black American Bahá'ís in two years.

7. Double the number of [believers from] minorities in two years.

8. Teach whole families.

9. Teach in universities through teachers' clubs and student clubs.

The plan in each area should be self-supporting, self-organized and self-planned. Thousands of Bahá'í books are required.

We can easily teach 25,000 in America in two years, if not in one. The newly arrived Iranians are the best asset for teaching in America. Once we have great numbers of Bahá'ís in America the rest of the world could be helped by them. . . . Perhaps there should be a conference of all District Teaching Committees,

Anchorage, Alaska, 1976.

National Teaching Conference, Boston, 1979. Judge Nelson on the left.

Boston, 1979 — his last visit.

national committees and Auxiliary Board members to discuss these points and come to a decision for a plan.

We need a strong Deputization Fund, especially for youth so that we can ask some of them to concentrate solely on teaching for six months of the year.

This is my last night in America. Tomorrow morning, God willing, I will leave for Jamaica.

That night, Raḥmat called me from Florida to ask how we were coping with settling in America. I was sick in bed, and in no mood to reassure him that all was well. I asked him to come back and help me with the new and unfamiliar situation in which I found myself. The next day he was back in Boston. He had to send cables to all countries which were expecting him, postponing his travels. This would be the last ten days that we were to spend together.

He helped me find an apartment in Brookline, which looked over a beautiful lake. Raḥmat liked this place very much, as Brookline had been graced by the visit of 'Abdu'l-Bahá.

He spent these days in our unfurnished apartment meeting the friends and encouraging them to teach. At one such meeting, we all sat on the bare floor, and ate grilled cheese sandwiches which Raḥmat produced from the kitchen.

On 7 October, the Massachusetts Regional Convention was in session. On Raḥmat's suggestion, that State had been added to those already chosen for mass teaching. The National Assembly also announced that from 4 November, 19-day firesides would commence all over the United States.

We spent these few days in Brookline as a family, settling Gisu in her dormitory, buying a few odds and ends for our home, and talking for hours about our future plans. Raḥmat and Gisu decided to spend the summer of 1980 travelling together in Latin America. As Gisu was now living in the dormitory at her college, we decided that from now on, I would accompany Raḥmat on his trips as often as possible.

Looking back, I think that this all-too brief period was one of the happiest times we had. Raḥmat was in high spirits. Although visibly tired, there was no sign of illness. He had a thorough physical examination at a well known diabetes clinic in Boston. The results of all the tests, including blood pressure and heart function, were completely normal. The clinic advised him not to use any medication for his diabetes. In this period, Raḥmat repeatedly said that he'd had a happy life, had done all he could, and had no desire to do anything more.

The revolution in Iran had recently begun, and many of the friends had lost all their possessions. Although pained by this news, he told Gisu and me that we should be thankful we had nothing in the world that anyone could confiscate and cause us grief! At this time the martyrdoms of the Bahá'ís in Iran had not yet taken place, but Raḥmat often said prayers for the protection of the friends there, and believed that the persecutions had only just started.

He left on 15 October. As usual, he did not allow me to accompany him to the airport, saying that he would check in as soon as he got there. I can still see him waving through the open window of the Red Cab, smiling and calling that he would be back before long. Yael Wurmfeld, a member of the International Goals Committee, summarized the effect of Raḥmat's work in the United States thus:

> To this day, friends who had the opportunity to be with him remember his kindness and coaxing, and his assurances that all those who arose would be victorious in their endeavours. The most accurate word to describe his assurances is 'certitude.' He was certain that the goals would be won.
>
> So many took to heart his pleas and his sense of urgency to prepare themselves for future service.
>
> Years after he left this plane of existence, his presence is still felt. The benefits of his visits to the United States are visible in the youth who commit themselves to international service. Most are children of parents who were inspired by Dr Muhájir's enthusiasm, and whose souls were touched by his vision.

THE CARIBBEAN

Raḥmat first visited the Caribbean in 1969, during the closing years of the Nine Year Plan. The National Assembly of Jamaica commented that these visits had resulted 'in an awakening of the Bahá'í community to the challenges of the Nine Year Plan.' In 1974 the National Assembly reported,

Dr Raḥmatu'lláh Muhájir visited Trinidad from 29 September to 7 October 1974. Dr Muhájir paid a courtesy call on the . . . Acting Governor General of Trinidad and Tobago . . . [He] also appeared on 'Community Dateline', a special television interview programme. A reception in Dr Muhájir's honour was held in Couva with many dignitaries and officials present, as well as representatives of the media. Dr Muahjir talked to the gathering on the principles of the Faith, and emphasized that Bahá'ís are obedient to the government of their country.

On 6 October, International Children's Day was celebrated with 50 Bahá'í children and their friends attending. The entire

Guest of Sir A. H. McShine, Governor General of Trinidad and Tobago, 1974.

> program, prepared and conducted by the children themselves, was most spirited and successful. The highlight of the gathering was the presence of Dr Muhájir, whose love for all present was a precious bounty.

The Dominican Republic reported, 'All but one of the goals of the Nine Year Plan were achieved in the last three years of the Plan. The credit for the conception and inspiration of the massive teaching plan must go to Hand of the Cause Raḥmatu'lláh Muhájir, who, in his visit in January 1972 encouraged us to think in terms of mass teaching.'

In the beginning of the Five Year Plan he returned to all the islands of the Caribbean, and again it was reported, 'Through the encouragement of the Hand of the Cause Dr Muhájir, a two-year project was initiated under which intensive teaching was undertaken'.

His next visit to the Caribbean was in 1976. In July of that year the Universal House of Justice cabled him,

> DELIGHTED YOUR PLANS VISIT COUNTRIES CARIBBEAN SOUTH CENTRAL AMERICA . . . URGE PROLONGATION EACH VISIT ACHIEVE MAXIMUM EFFECTIVENESS ARDENTLY PRAYING YOUR ABUNDANT CONFIRMATIONS DEEPEST LOVE STOP

His last sojourn in the Caribbean started on 15 October 1979:

> I arrived in Jamaica from Boston. It is a public holiday and most of the pioneers and the Bahá'ís were at the airport. We all went to the Bahá'í Centre and spent a few hours together.
>
> That night was the Nineteen Day Feast: met the friends. We had extensive discussions about teaching the Faith. The next night the members of the National Assembly and the national committees and other friends decided to start nineteen or nine days of teaching in six large cities. This is in addition to their previous plan of teaching 500 people and forming three local Assemblies.
>
> *17 October*: I arrived in Port au Prince, Haiti. Fortunately, it was again a public holiday. I could meet with many of the friends and

consult with them. With God's help I could get a visa for the Dominican Republic. In the heat I was busy with this work the whole day. I arrived in Santo Domingo about six p.m.

19 October: Today is the Birthday of the Báb. I met the National Assembly and had discussions about the plans of this country. The teaching work in these areas is in need of much assistance.

I then visited Managuez, St Thomas, St Croix, St Thomas and Antigua. The days were all happy ones. I met the National Assembly and we devised plans for the teaching in the islands.

In St Thomas, Raḥmat was greeted over lunch by some of the Bahá'ís. Everyone was talking animatedly around the table, while Raḥmat sat quietly with his head bowed. This went on for some time, when he began to raise his head very slowly, lifted his arms above his head, and slowly brought his fists down on the table. As his fists hit the table he smiled and said, 'Let me tell you a story about 'Abdu'l-Bahá.' This made the conversation turn from triviality to subjects about the Faith.

In St Thomas, that same evening, he spoke at a meeting attended by Bahá'ís and non-Bahá'ís. He was asked to explain briefly the prophecy contained in the tradition uttered by the Prophet Muḥammad that every burden would be cast from the womb at the time of the appearance of the Promised Qá'im. Raḥmat said that this meant that all attributes — good or bad — would become manifest at the time of Bahá'u'lláh. All would become manifest. Then he smiled and said, 'Was that brief enough?'

In St John's, Antigua, he met with nearly 50 Bahá'ís on the night of his arrival, and admonished them to 'Teach, teach, teach. Do not let complaints of others stop you. Keep up your efforts.' At the Technical Teachers College where he was to speak, the headmaster told him that he could have only 15 minutes. Raḥmat said 'Fine'. It started to rain very hard. The rain seemed to stop while he was talking, but during question-and-answer time it started to really pour down.

At the place he was staying, the rain had soaked the room, including the bed and his clothes. Raḥmat did not mind at all. He said that perhaps Bahá'u'lláh was telling him he was carrying too much clothing. So he left some of his clothes in Antigua.

With friends in Antigua, October 1979.

In front of the National Ḥaẓíratu'l-Quds of Barbados, with NSA members, 1974.

Back to school in Trinidad, 1974.

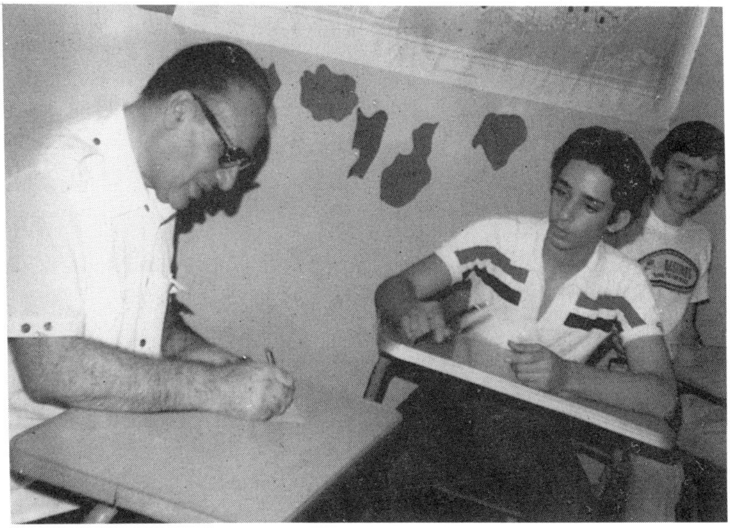

Mayaguez, Puerto Rico, 1979. Countersigning the declaration card of a young Bahá'í, David Kalantar, on his 15th birthday.

In a public meeting later that night, the questions and discussions ran on till late. One of the friends asked Raḥmat if he wouldn't rather say some closing prayers so that they could all go home. He smiled, and said that he had offered prayers in his heart, but nothing should be done to discourage the interest of the souls there, no matter how late the hour. They must be made welcome at all times, and prayers should be said in the heart.

For nearly a month Raḥmat did not write in his diary. He had no time even to jot a few words. On 12 November 1979, he wrote,

> I have not had time to write notes about the last few days. After Barbados I went to St Vincent. It is a beautiful island and has strong and kind inhabitants. The Bahá'ís are united and dedicated. Their future is very bright. They plan to buy a large Ḥaẓiratu'l-Quds. The American and Canadian pioneers know most of the people.
>
> I had an interview on the radio and a talk at the teacher-training school. I stayed for two days and visited some villages. It was the best of times and two blessed days.
>
> I then left for Grenada. On arrival there was a fireside, and the next day I spoke at the Rotary Club and had ten minutes of question and answers. The words of Bahá'u'lláh from the 'Words of Paradise' had a great effect on their hearts.
>
> On the same day there was a radio interview, and the next day I spoke at a girls' school, where nearly 400 were present. The same day I left for Trinidad.
>
> In Trinidad we had a large gathering at the house of Dr Jamalzadeh. Many Bahá'ís and non-Bahá'ís were there. It had a special atmosphere. One of the Bahá'í youth was apprehensive that a new religion might appear!
>
> I met the National Assembly in the evening. They decided to increase the number of Bahá'ís to 6000. They cabled the Universal House of Justice, asking for Nagaratnam from India to come to help them. Their approval also has come.
>
> I went to British Guyana after Trinidad. They have 4500 Bahá'ís, of which 2000 are the youth. If the youth get Bahá'í education they will have a tremendous effect in the whole of the Caribbean.

In consultation with the National Teaching Committee, ten towns were chosen for concentration on teaching. The Teaching committee was very active and progressive.

The *Youth Bulletin* of British Guyana reported,

It is not every day that a Hand of the Cause of God visits Guyana — much more visits with the youth to speak with them separately.

Even though it was on a weekday, more than 75 youth arrived and respectfully awaited the arrival of Dr Muhájir. Dr Muhájir began by saying that people in the world found many things wrong with the youth. He felt, however, that the youth had only one fault: they never believe that they will grow old until it is too late! Youth should go out and teach the Faith to the people . . . [Dr Muhájir] said that everyone was born a Bahá'í, as they are

Port of Spain, Trinidad, television interview, 1979.

born in the age and time of God's universal Manifestation, Bahá'u'lláh. The world has many distractions which lead the people away from God; in teaching we attract their souls back to Him again. Dr Muhájir gave a beautiful account of some of the early Hands of the Cause who were appointed by Bahá'u'lláh; their lives are examples for the youth who want to teach and serve the Faith.

'All are,' he said, 'Hands of His Cause who are humble and serve with humility.'

Raḥmat made his final diary entry for this last journey in the Caribbean islands on 12 November: 'The Birthday of Bahá'u'lláh was celebrated with great splendour. After that I went to Suriname and French Guyana, then left for Brazil.'

Dr Muhájir's visits to South America took him to high mountain villages, remote settlements on desert plains, the heart of the rainforest, and the teeming coastal cities.

Chapter 8

ONLY HEAVEN IS HIGHER

In April 1961 Raḥmat represented the Bahá'í World Centre at the conventions which elected the first National Spiritual Assemblies of Bolivia and Paraguay. He found great joy and new challenges when visiting the countries of South America, especially the mass teaching areas of Bolivia. He prepared himself for this adventure by studying about Central and South America, filling his notes with facts and figures. His diaries contain hand-drawn maps of each country, marked with names of important centres and tribes. Experience had taught him the importance of preparation for teaching in unfamiliar lands. In several places in his notebooks he had copied part of a letter written on behalf of the Guardian dated 11 June 1954:

> The Guardian feels victories can be won in South America the same as they have been won in Africa; and he hopes the friends will redouble their efforts . . . and will show a deeper spirit of consecration and devotion and that the zealous activity of the friends will bring about the quickening of many souls in the Cause of God.

Beneath this extract Raḥmat had written his own entreaty, asking Bahá'u'lláh to enable him to fulfil the Guardian's wishes.

HIS FIRST VISIT

The pages of his diary are filled with personal reminiscences of his South American travels of 1961, and offer an insight into the early struggles of the pioneers and the local Bahá'ís to establish the Faith on that continent. On his way to La Paz in 1961 he wrote:

14 March: I am going to Central and South America and will arrive in La Paz on Naw-Rúz. My journey in Asia is over. My heart and soul is with the wonderful friends. What a spiritual and fertile continent! On arrival in Los Angeles I remembered that I had passed over two oceans and the three continents of Africa, Asia and America. My happiness and gratitude is the size of those oceans and continents. I hope to be able to spend some more time with these wonderful Bahá'ís and help them win great victories for the Cause.

22 March: This is the second day of Naw-Rúz — a beautiful day. We are at the La Paz Bahá'í Centre. Athos has arrived from Oruro and we are consulting about a one-month plan to bring the Faith to the Indians. I've now been here for four days. My soul is full of gratitude for the bounties of Bahá'u'lláh for these blessed days. All the victories here are the result of the beloved Guardian's efforts. He gave his life to guide humanity to the Faith of God.

If we could hold a few teaching conferences, as we did in India, we could achieve great results. This is the Faith of Bahá'u'lláh, it has its own power. Means are not important, the Creator of means is our Helper. In India we first prepared everything and then invited the villagers to be our guests for a few days to study the Faith. Teachers were then sent to visit those villages to teach, enrol and deepen.

Now the 'red race' has entered the arena of service. The fulfilment of the predictions made by the beloved Guardian are now becoming apparent. This is surely the life-giving effect of the Ten Year Crusade and its prime mover is the invincible Will of Bahá'u'lláh.

24 March: On the 22nd we made a programme for our travels, to start on the 23rd from Sucre. At nine a.m. we boarded the train. I have no idea when we are going to reach our destination. All the way we passed through Indian villages. They have mud houses with thatched roofs made of thorns. The people are mostly shepherds, and sheep and llamas are everywhere. Indians are travelling on this train, and, as the third class is full, many are riding on top of the train. Women are wrapped ten times over in cloths on top of their layers of clothing, and over everything they have a large black and red striped shawl.

They are a cordial and kind people, not unlike the Japanese. However they look stronger and healthier.

The train is chugging along, climbing the mountains. We are now at an altitude of 5000 metres. The mountaintops are covered with snow. It is freezing cold, it is impossible to open the window. Bolivia and Tibet are the roofs of the world. How fortunate are the pioneers who can serve in this country.

We have to travel for two days by train, one day by truck, and two days on foot to reach the Bahá'í villages. The pioneers have often covered this road to teach the Faith.

First trip to La Paz, Bolivia, 1961.

The history of the progress of the Faith among the Indians is fascinating. Yvonne Cuellar, who is French, and her husband, a military officer, were the first pioneers and teachers. They established a small boarding house. Before they left, another American pioneer took their place and hung a sign on the door calling the house the 'Bahá'í Academy'. One day, Andreas Jachakollo noticed this sign and asked what it meant. He was the first Bahá'í in that area. He belonged to a group and movement which had started 30 years before. Their teacher and founder, Toribio Mirande, was an Indian who travelled all his life and taught the people not to join any religious groups, not to beg or drink, but just to commune with God in their hearts. He had a few assistants who travelled to many areas. Near the end of his life he advised his followers that others would come from foreign lands to help them. Andreas was one of his helpers. He is the first Indian Bahá'í, and has taught many of Toribio's former followers. The first group became Bahá'ís in 1957. The report of this went to the beloved Guardian, which gladdened his heart.

We are still on the train. All the mountains are covered with snow. I have travelled by train in many countries, but have never seen views as beautiful as these. The train passes the summits of the mountains, they are covered with trees, some black and some green. Every hundred kilometres a small village appears whose inhabitants have gathered to watch the passing train. I hope the day will come when all these beautiful villages will be overflowing with Bahá'ís, and we will have to stop at each station to spend time with them.

The progress of the Faith in South America is of great interest to me. After the arrival of pioneers and the establishment of local Assemblies, the National Assembly of South America was formed in 1951. Its jurisdiction was over ten countries. In 1953 the Guardian instructed that each country should have its own National Assembly, and that the number of local Assemblies should be doubled. The pioneers were astounded that with such small numbers they could elect their National Assemblies. In 1957 the beloved Guardian announced the establishment of two Regional Assemblies, each covering five countries, one for the South and one for the North of South America. This was not included in the Ten Year Crusade. This year, with God's assistance, each country will have its own National Assembly.

26 March: We are in the meeting of the beloved natives; altogether, we are 12 people. One of them, Meliton, said, 'I have been the follower of this religion for 20 years without knowing.' He was a follower of Mirando.

27 March: Today I was supposed to leave for Churumumu, but there is no car and no driver. Everything is in God's hand.

The two days that I have spent with the beloved Indian friends have been great. They told us that in one village, 80, and in another, 400, were awaiting us to hear about the Faith.

I wonder where to go after the conventions. I might go to Asia and the Pacific, or stay here for another two months and work for these dear Indians. I can also go to Africa. I don't know which is preferable. I think if I stay in Bolivia for two months and then leave for the Pacific it is better. God willing, next year I will make a long trip to Africa from North to South, and East to West.

Why should I leave this vast field of service? Where is better than here? The Faith has been in Africa for more than ten years and in Asia for thirty years. It has just reached the Red Indians in the last year-and-a-half. It has still not penetrated deeply.

Yesterday I heard that Ma'súd [Khamsí]'s car had broken down. They were obliged to spend the night in a village where 20 people accepted the Faith. How fertile is this land!

I prayed that God would grant me the privilege of staying here to render some meagre service to these beloved people. If I leave, when can I return? I am afraid my life would be over and I would not be able to help a little to satisfy the thirst of these people.

Yesterday I thought that if Amir Azampanah could come here from Paraguay, he would be very useful. He is young and dedicated. It would be good if we could consult together and spend two months teaching. Athos Costas, Ma'súd, Rocahado (who has ulcers), and Stanislaw (who has rendered great services), and many Bahá'ís are the result of his efforts, are now the only teachers here.

28 March: Yesterday we left for Sucre at one p.m. Until five p.m. the roads were very good, going through beautiful and verdant valleys. Then we arrived at steep mountains, the like of which I had never seen. The road was as narrow as it could possibly be. In most places there were such mud slides that the bus had to come as near to the edge as was possible, stop, reverse and start again.

I have never been on such a scary bus ride. As it reached the steepest point, the bus just slid back towards the deep ravine. A few of us jumped down and put rocks under the rear wheels of the bus so that it could move.

The final 35 kilometres we were in constant fear for our lives. Our driver, however, was very calm and collected, and quite happily told me that the road was not the worst he had seen. I, however, relied on the prayers I had memorized, till we reached the town. A priest told me he had felt exactly like me, and had prayed to Jesus all the way!

We spent the night in a schoolroom in Ikla. I was happy that we had only another 15 kilometres to go. This morning we left at eight a.m. to go to Churumumu. Only one hour has passed. We have reached the river bed at a deep valley. The road is washed out by a flood and we are stuck. The car cannot move in any direction. We are delighted that 15 of the Indian friends have come to greet us and we can spend some hours together.

Seeing this river and the fallen rocks I remembered the dream I had in Africa. I dreamt the beloved Guardian was standing on a huge rock by a river. He was moving the mud and the sand. I understood that he was creating a lake. The place was very similar to this river and these rocks. I believe that these beautiful Indians, so dear to 'Abdu'l-Bahá's heart, are, while moving the rocks, carrying out the beloved Guardian's wishes. In the same dream, the Guardian gave me a large bottle of perfume, a watch and a book. Hopefully the meaning of this part also will become clear to me.

A few nights ago I dreamt I was in the presence of Bahá'u'lláh and 'Abdu'l-Baha. Bahá'u'lláh spoke in the Mazándarání dialect. He read the Tablets to the Kings and asked me, 'How are the friends carrying out my instructions?' I replied, 'On their eyes.'* He smiled and I spent some more time in His presence.

---

* A Persian expression of devotion and obedience.

I am now sitting by this river bed, surrounded by huge mountains. We have only a few kilometres to Churumumu. I wonder how, after only a hundred years, the Faith has reached these far-off corners of the world — the heart of Africa, Asia, the sub-continent of India. In Samgimanda [India] large groups came to the Faith. In Ceylon, in the villages of Malaya, in Solano, Santiago, in the Philippines, in Osaka among the Ainu of Japan, and now in these villages and mountains among these wonderful tribes. They seem to have been Bahá'ís for thousands of years. I have studied the map of the world to see if there is a virgin land left. There are only a few uninhabited islands, and a few very small islands which the Faith has not reached. What grandeur and bounty accompanied the Guardianship. What an influence it had in the world. The history of the world will be repeated thousands of times, but this grandeur, power, influence and creative force will not be seen again.

With the grace of God we arrived in Churumumu at noon. May my life be sacrificed for its inhabitants. Their simplicity, purity and spirituality are reminiscent of the traits of the Dawn-Breakers.

30 March: We left for Ikla. The friends were very kind and bade us goodbye with humility and love. The few days with them were among the best days of my life. If we can find the means to teach and educate their children, they can do what the beloved Guardian foretold 40 years ago and illuminate the world.

The children are healthy and happy, and greet everyone with 'Alláh-u-Abhá'. The first thing we should do is to establish a school and educate them in the Bahá'í spirit.

We arrived in Ikla at 11.00 a.m.. On the way the native friends showed me the utmost love and kindness. On steep uphill roads they held my hand and helped me climb. Sometimes they chanted prayers, and they all removed their hats in reverence. A young man chanted a prayer and they all repeated it. 'Benidiciscka cachun, lugartakh, wasitakh . . . (Blessed is the spot . . .)'.

We walked for 15 kilometres before we arrived in Ikla. We found out that we needed a week to prepare the necessary means

With indigenous believers in Bolivia, 1969.

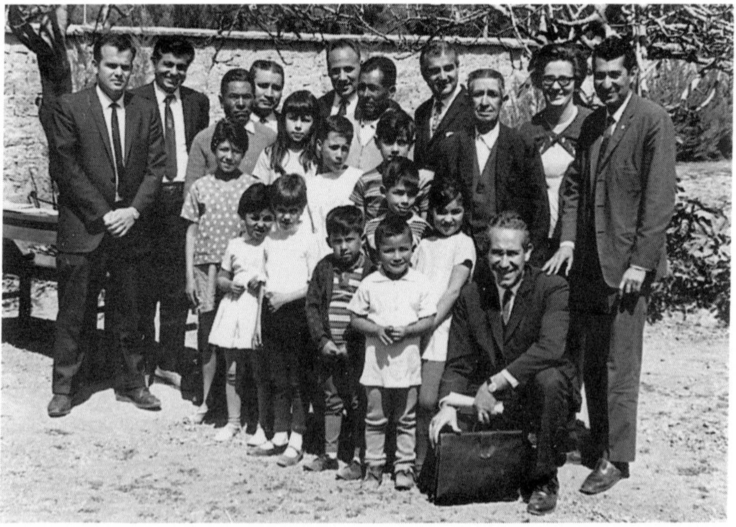

With Counsellors, National Assembly members and a group of happy Bahá'í children in Bolivia, July 1969.

to travel. After a little rest we decided to walk to Pasajamaya, Jatunkasa, and Pukarpampa. Until five p.m. everything went smoothly, but then we had to pass the summit of a mountain. My lungs and legs would not help any more. We had to jump from rock to rock, and pass narrow passages above deep ravines. No end was in sight. Athos and the others helped, and finally this part was over. We reached the top and found that only the sky was higher. Thousands of mountaintops could be seen. The beauty of the scenery, the prayers of the friends and my absolute exhaustion created a special atmosphere for me. The friends removed their hats and prayed.

We finally reached Pasajamaya where four of the friends were getting ready to leave to assist me through the mountain passage and, if necessary, carry me on their backs. What jewels exist in these mountains! They helped us over the final passes and we arrived tired but happy. They guided us to their small hut which they had covered with sheepskins and their clothing so that we could rest on them. The meal consisted of soup and milk.

We spent a happy and comfortable night. This morning we started for our next village, Pukarpampo. It was only a few kilometres away. The friends greeted us, hugged us, fed us and chanted prayers with us.

We talked about their school, which was half-built; they promised to complete it. One man had come from another village 70 kilometres away. He said that their schoolhouse was ready and they wanted a teacher.

At 11.00 a.m. we left for Sucre. We walked for a whole day. At first all my muscles protested and ached, but after a while it became easier. When we reached the road we had some bread, cheese and fruit, rested for a while and again started to walk. I started earlier so as not to hinder the other friends. We arrived at Terabuku at around seven. We fed the helpers and had some tea, and left for Sucre by car. It was only 50 kilometres. I sat on top of the baggage. Moonlight made the valleys and the mountains breathtakingly beautiful. This country is built on mountains. On the way we joked and laughed and had a wonderful time. We arrived at the hotel on 1 April. We left for Cochabamba by plane.

In Cochabamba we met a few of the friends, and the next day dear Athos left for Oruro to continue his travels. I am alone now, and will leave for La Paz tomorrow.

When I remember the serene and smiling faces of the wonderful indigenous Bahá'ís, my heart feels elated and calm. Their hospitality and kindness were unbounded. In one house an old couple and their children were our hosts: it was difficult to part from them. The old man hugged us and said goodbye at least ten times, as if he was parting with his dear children. I wish I had even one per cent of their goodness.

The Faith has now reached 150 localities. Fifty are isolated centres, 35 have more than 9 Bahá'ís, 20 of them have about 50 Bahá'ís. These need Ḥaẓíratu'l-Quds and schools. We need travelling teachers and travelling schools, to travel and stay in each village for a week, to teach the children and help in the building of schools and Bahá'í centres.

On the way I noticed that most of the villagers walking in the road were drunk . . . The Christian missionaries, on introducing Catholicism to these areas, have told these people that Christ was crucified on Friday and resurrected on Sunday. These poor souls consider these two days as days without God, and indulge in drinking to the point that they are drunk until Monday.

On this trip I have dreamt a few times that we had very large gatherings of the Bahá'ís, and that Hands of the Cause Faizí and Kházeh were present. Amatu'l-Bahá participated in one of them. She told me that there was no food. I replied that we had plenty of rice at home, and left to bring it . . . I wonder what the interpretation is? Where am I going to end up after this trip? I feel like a ball that has been tossed in the air and is whirling, not knowing where it will land.

9 April: We left at eight a.m. for Yapayapani by train. We arrived after four hours. The village was holding its annual bazaar. We had to wait until night to see about 20 Bahá'ís and talk a little about teaching and Bahá'í schools.

14 April: We left at five a.m. for Chalipampa. A small clean bus took us to Llallagua. On the way we passed the village of

Huanuni. Ma'súd said that once when they had come to this area in a truck, they heard sounds of gunfire and the truck turned back. The Bahá'ís, however, climbed down and continued on their way. The gunfire had become fiercer, and they thought it prudent to hide in a corner. They walked in the rain till they reached the town gate and the guard gave them shelter in the school. The rebels found the leader of their opponents in the church, dragged him out and shot him. Then they found the Bahá'ís but let them go. These are the conditions under which the friends in this region have to teach the Faith.

We arrived at Llallagua at noon. After a rest we left for Chalipampa. We'd walked for half-an-hour when it started to rain. Large hailstones hit us. The hail was so fierce and the freezing cold so biting that we could not continue any further. I apologized to my companions and told them that I had only walked for two kilometres and was already in such bad shape that I simply could not envisage having the strength to continue. Ma'súd and Carmelo decided to go on and I decided to return.

I was shattered and despondent. I sat there weeping because I could not walk a few kilometres in the path of God. I just sat there in the rain and wept. The weather was getting colder and the rain was worsening. I thought about poor dear Ma'súd, who was walking in these conditions to fulfil my obligations. He can visit them any time. I sent someone to call him back, and for my sake he agreed. Carmelo will go there to tell them why I could not go.

We walked from six a.m. to seven p.m. and accomplished nothing. I have grown old. I have to take my ambitions to the Abhá Kingdom. My only hope is that Bahá'u'lláh will forgive me my sins with a drop from the ocean of His mercy.

When the friends heard that I could not visit them, a hundred of them went to the neighbouring village and Athos and Angelica went to be with them.

15 April: Ma'súd and I left, to return to La Paz early this morning. Ma'súd said that all their teaching trips are either in torrential rain or fierce wind. Often their vehicles break down. Once when their bus had broken down, they had talked to the villagers. On their return trip they found that many of them wanted to become Bahá'ís.

We arrived in La Paz at two p.m., and in the evening had a fireside with two seekers. Last year the Regional Assembly had instructed them to concentrate all their efforts on deepening, and not to teach in new areas. They have gone only to their old centres to deepen them. Only about 400 people have by chance accepted the Faith, and now they have 1400 Bahá'ís. I wish to God they would not stop the wheel of teaching from rolling. Once it has stopped it is very difficult to restart. May God's bounties help us rekindle the fire of service and teaching in our hearts.

16 April: La Paz is 3650 metres above sea level. The oxygen level is 50 per cent and many nights I could not sleep there. I had constant headaches and a dry mouth, just as if I had high blood pressure. The dear pioneers still feel the effect of the altitude, even after being here for more than a year, but nevertheless they are very active and successful. Now there are 1500 Bahá'ís and 150 centres in Bolivia.

I have been with dear Ma'súd and have been busy getting visas for African countries. Ma'súd greatly praises the indigenous people of this country. The first time they had a class in La Paz, a call came from a hospital after the morning session, saying that one of the patients had asked for him. Ma'súd went there but did not recognize the man. The man was very happy to see him, and told him that he wanted to become a Bahá'í before he died. He [recovered and] is now one of the travelling teachers.

They have six Bahá'í schools. I hope to be able to see all of them.

One of the friends told me, 'We live near lake Poopo and there are no people that we can teach'. I suggested that perhaps he could venture a little further.

We started at six a.m. for the city. After an hour's walk, a car came along and took us into town. It was again the bazaar day. The main street was crowded with people, each with something to sell. Many were selling food at small tables set up on the sidewalk. Llamas could be bought for about seven dollars.

People had gathered from miles in each direction. We bought some soup, and had it with some cheese. At two o'clock an old and rickety truck arrived, piled with a cargo of bananas and other goods. Twenty-seven men, women and children were riding on top of the cargo. Ma'súd and I also climbed on top, and tried to hang on to our luggage and our 27 companions.

The winding road was so bumpy, and the valley so steep, that I didn't dare look down. The truck continued in this way until it nearly reached the top, then it suddenly fell into a deep pothole. It practically broke in two. We all jumped down and tried to pull the truck out, but our efforts were no use. Finally we all had to unload the truck and set it on the road. It was loaded again, and everyone jumped on board. By this time it had started to rain. I had reached a point where I simply could not tolerate the ride any more and begged everyone to let me walk. No one paid any attention. I had to crawl to the driver's cabin, bang on it and make him stop. The owner, who was riding beside the driver, gave his seat to me and we started again. It was now twilight and the freezing cold had penetrated our bones. At night the truck stopped in the middle of nowhere. Poor Ma'súd caught a very bad cold and suffered from earache for many days.

We were supposed to walk another 15 kilometres to reach our destination. However, our extreme fatigue and the bitter cold forced us to stop at a little village. We went to an old couple's hut and they gave us their kitchen to stay in. The only light came from the small fire. We had bread and cheese, and some delicious hot soup which Ma'súd prepared. The kitchen was too small for the seven of us. The owners, a family of three, left it for us.

Counsellor Ma'súd Khamsí recalls that, several times during the night, Raḥmat had called out to him to move his feet away from his face. In the morning they realized that the source of disturbance in the night had been *cayu* (guinea pigs), and not poor Ma'súd!

Raḥmat's account continues:

We arrived in Colcokoyo the next morning. The 80 inhabitants of this village are all Bahá'ís. Before our arrival they had cleaned the road so that our path was smooth and easy. The scenery was beautiful, and llamas were grazing around us. We rested on a rock and had some bread and walnuts, then walked another four hours to reach the outskirts of the village. About 16 students of the Bahá'í school and their teacher had come to greet us, and were chanting 'Alláh'u'Abhá' and Bahá'í prayers. They sang a song in praise of the Hands of the Cause, and then we started for the Bahá'í school.

The school was large and clean. It had a few rooms, but only one was being used. It was about seven metres by four metres. In the middle was a U-shaped brick table, with a brick bench around it. The walls were covered with writing and some paintings done by the teacher, who is a young and energetic man. The children, happy and clean, sang Spanish songs that he had taught them. We were then taken to the teacher's house. People had brought food — soups, eggs, boiled potatoes and tea. We were with them for about an hour.

In the afternoon a large group of Bahá'ís gathered. We discussed the importance of teaching, and exchanged ideas. The schoolteacher said that his family of 15, who lived in the next village, wanted to become Bahá'ís. Dear Ma'súd promised to visit them at the end of next month. Some said they were leaving for warmer places for the next four months, and will try to teach everyone on their way. They had delayed the trip until after 21 April and the election of their local Assembly. In the evening we had a deepening on the function of local Assemblies.

Early next morning we started for Oruro. These two villages have 100 Bahá'ís. They had built the school before becoming Bahá'ís, but due to lack of funds had not used it. Now, with the help of the pioneers, the school is functioning. The teacher receives five dollars a month. We asked him to go travel teaching for a month. He said he will bring his brother to replace him and then will go. This shows his dedication to the work.

In the hours that we were walking, we passed more than ten villages which had no Bahá'ís. Perhaps one day, with the blessings of Bahá'u'lláh, all these villagers will become Bahá'í, and their shouts of 'Yá Bahá'u'l-Abhá!' will fill the plains and mountains.

We walked for nearly five hours to reach the road. We had to wait till two p.m. for a car. The road was better than the previous one, but the car had problems and took six hours to cover the sixty kilometres to Challopata.

Ma'súd talked to the driver about the Faith and they became very friendly. Next morning, in the same car, we left for Oruro and arrived there at three p.m.

When we arrived, a loudspeaker was announcing that the previous night a truck had overturned and 14 of those riding on top of the cargo had died. [The identities of] three were unknown, and the people were asked to pray and light a candle for them.

Our beloved pioneers have to travel like this all the time. This is the meaning of sacrifice and placing one's life in the palms of their hands for Bahá'u'lláh. Their only wish is to fulfil the beloved Guardian's instructions.

Bolivia is one of the countries mentioned in the Divine Plan of the Master. His desire was the progress and establishment of the Faith in these countries. Now, after 40 years, His wish has been realized. A large number have accepted the Faith — and this is just the beginning.

The teacher in these villages is Isaac Mamani, who, after an accident, had called Ma'súd and had asked to be registered [as a Bahá'í] immediately. He has enrolled 270 people. This is the readiness that the Master had predicted.

17 April: I spent the whole day in the library, studying the conditions of Bolivia and Brazil. The best place for mass conversion is South America. There are hundreds of tribes with millions of people. Only Bolivia has done something about teaching them.

18 April: Ma'súd and I went to Oruro to help in the election of their local Assemblies. I went to two local Assemblies and then returned to La Paz.

The convention in La Paz was full of spirit. I wept with joy all the time. Three native Indians were elected to the National Assembly. Andreas is Vice-Chairman. Good plans were made for the next year. The first meeting of the Assembly was in my small room, where I had spent so many days in prayer to His threshold.

On the second day of Riḍván, a letter from the Hands arrived. They have agreed that I should go to Asia for three months and then to Africa. Although it will be a much longer route, I will be able to visit the beloved friends in Asia once more.

I left La Paz on the 26th. Ma'súd, Jane, Andreas and Timmy saw me off. My travels in Bolivia lasted 40 days. All of them were spent in prayer and spirituality.

In Paraguay almost all the friends had come to the airport. Meeting them gave me new strength and opened a new chapter in my humble life. I met the pioneers, became friends with them, and will keep them in my heart forever.

My translator in the convention was named Margaret. She is an American pioneer who has a kindergarten. She promised to spend a few days teaching in Alti-Plano.

Allen and his daughter are in Asuncion. Eve Niklin pioneered to South America 21 years ago. She is a wonderful and spiritual lady. Her only thoughts are about the beloved Guardian and the glorious time of his ministry. She loves the Indians, especially those of Peru. She wants to return to Peru, which she considers her home. They have sent her to Incarnacion to establish the local Assembly, and now they have 26 Bahá'ís. Eve should return to Peru.

Mr and Mrs Akhbari and their daughter, and Mr and Mrs Azam Panah and their daughter, are the Persian pioneers. We spent the days before the convention in consultation about teaching. There is great potential in Paraguay. One of the tribes has a population of about 40,000 but all inhabitants have great potential.

I was in Asuncion till 4 May. Teaching plans were formulated. Reggie Sunshine, who has been the teacher of some members of the National Assembly of Bolivia, was also present. He is a pure and wonderful soul.

On 4 May I arrived in Sao Paolo [Brazil]. I am staying at Gharun Ayvazian's house which he bought a month ago. The next day, accompanied by the Meisslers, Mr Shoghi, M. Bartar and a few others, I went to Campinas. A very good and fruitful meeting was held.

The next morning, accompanied by Siranush Khánum Ayvazian and others, I visited San Caitano. All the Bahá'ís were Persians: Mr Abdullah Sahihi, Mr Shafa, Mr Sadeghzadeh, Mr Soltani, Mr Shaikhizadeh and Mr Husain Afnan. In the afternoon we left for Porto Alegre, which is a thousand miles away. The Pustchis, Shayanis, Vahdats and Razi Abbasian and his dear mother were at the airport. We had a beautiful meeting at Ted's house; the Persian friends have truly arisen and scattered in every corner of this country.

On the way back we passed Curitiba and spent some time with the Arjomand and Taherzadeh families. In the afternoon we had a fireside with two seekers. We returned directly to Sao Paolo. We had a very good public meeting at the house of dear Dr Lima and then returned to Gharun's home for another meeting.

The next morning I left for Rio de Janeiro. It took only one hour. We were passing the shore of the Atlantic Ocean, over which the beloved Master, architect of the Divine Plan, had passed. In the airport Cyrus [Munnajem], Jalal [Ighrari] and others were waiting. Seeing them after so many years gave me such joy and such new spirit. I remembered our firm friendship of 20 years ago and became very happy. I stayed at Jalal's house for a few days.

We left for Bahia [Salvador] on 11 of May. I can't describe my happiness. This is that same Bahia which 'Abdu'l-Baha said was named by God's inspiration. God willing, very soon the banner of the Faith will be raised in this land and its teachings will be proclaimed to all the tribes, and the masses will flock under the tabernacle of Bahá'u'lláh's religion. On arrival I had an interview with one of the newspapers.

I am very happy with the trip to Brazil. I met and consulted with nearly all the local Assemblies. I will spend about twelve days in this country. I have already visited Sao Paulo, Campinas, Sao

Caitano, Porto Alegre, Rio de Janeiro, Curitiba and Bahia [Salvador]. Tomorrow I will go to Belo Horizonte.

This country has a very great potential for teaching. It just needs a small spark in one corner to inflame the whole country. I think we can do the following:

1. A two year teaching plan.

2. The goals to include a centre in each State.

3. Divide the country into three zones, and each zone should have seven provinces. One teaching committee for each zone: Porto Alegre, Sao Paulo, Salvador.

4. A plan of teaching for the red Indian and black minorities to vigorously teach in those areas.

5. Amelia Collins gave $500 for mass conversion in this area two years ago. It has not been used. Now it should be used for its rightful purpose.

6. Cyrus [Munnajem] is ready to work for the teaching of the tribes.

7. All activities, thoughts and consultations should be solely concentrated on teaching.

8. Every day each member of the community should read the prayers of 'Abdu'l-Bahá regarding teaching.

14 May: It is early morning and I am leaving Belo Horizonte. I stayed two days in Salvador. Bahia has been so very much praised by 'Abdu'l-Bahá. The beloved Guardian said this city has a very close relationship with the Faith . . . Many of the youth had been given duties to teach in the tribal areas. Among them is Sergio [Couto], who is now 19. During the Guardian's life, at the age of 15, he was given the responsibility of teaching the Indians.

This trip was wonderful. Last night I went to visit a 75-year old man who had a broken leg and could not come to the meetings.

He talked constantly about Bahá'u'lláh and 'Abdu'l-Bahá. He had the Healing Prayer in a bag hung over his bed. I told him that physical infirmity does not matter, what is important is spiritual well-being. He agreed, and said that Jesus said flesh and bones return to dust but the soul remains. He said he prayed daily to leave this earthly plane and reach the Abhá Kingdom . . . Both of us said prayers.

I went to see [others] who had not been able to come to the meetings. I have met all the Bahá'ís of this city. Last night we had a meeting downtown. One of the Bahá'í ladies had invited her neighbours. We had a good fireside and returned home at midnight. This morning Sergio brought me a picture book of the Indian tribes and dedicated it to me in Arabic. He has been studying Arabic for one year and has progressed very nicely. He is on fire with the love of Bahá'u'lláh and has decided to resume teaching among the tribes. He will leave with Anthony [Worley] to teach for one month, and if he can get exemption from military duty, he will remain among the tribal people and continue to teach them.

My stay in Brazil is nearly over. I cannot forget the love and kindness of the friends. I hope to be able to return to this country and teach the indigenous people.

I spent one night in Belo Horizonte and was a guest at dear Cyrus's home. The Abrarpur family were also there. We had some seekers and spent a happy evening. I could not sleep. I wrote letters to the National Assembly of Brazil and to the Holy Land.

I left for Rio de Janeiro very early in the morning. Dr Niva was at the airport. Together we went to the Indonesian Consulate but could not get a visa as neither the Consul nor the Ambassador could be located. I did a little sightseeing.

16 May: I am on the way to Lima. I was Jalal Eghrari's guest for these few days. They showered me with such kindness and hospitality that it exceeded that of my relatives. We are now passing over the mountains of Bolivia. My love and greetings to all the beloved friends of Bolivia.

With Eve Nicklin, 'Mother of Peru', at the Summer School, Lima, 1977.

National Teaching Conference, San Salvador, El Salvador, 1969.

Arrived in Lima at five p.m. Isabel and Josephine were at the airport. Unlike the previous trip, the customs people did not give me problems. I had such a miserable and lonely time on the last trip in Hotel Bolivar, that this time I decided to stay in the Bahá'í Centre. It is a beautiful building in a very good location. They had prepared the best room for me.

We had the Nineteen Day Feast that night. Fatigue and the sudden change of weather did not help my severe cold. I was so ill that I thought I would not be able to tolerate the meeting. Despite my misery I said a few words. I was delighted to see that the local Bahá'ís could manage their meeting so nicely. The meeting was over at 10.30 p.m.

In my room there were many interesting books. I chose *An Appreciation of Shoghi Effendi* [sic]. [My wife] had read all of it to me some years ago. Now I can read English myself. I read half of it until midnight and the rest early next morning. I was ready by eight a.m. Six members of the National Assembly came to the Centre. We reviewed the mass teaching work in detail. They were very happy that Carmelo will come to Peru to teach among the Indians. It was decided to ask the National Assembly of Bolivia to send him as soon as possible. They are also going to invite Eve Niklin to establish her residence in Cuzco.

In the afternoon I studied the letters of the Guardian about South America. Once these are published, the nature of the progress of the Faith in these countries will change. The beloved Guardian says that he feels the progress of the Faith in South America will resemble that of Africa.

In the evening I had a meeting with the Teaching Committee and some other friends.

18 May: It took ten hours to get to Huancayo. The train went to a height of 5000 metres and then plunged down. The scenery is very much like Bolivia. Mr Long greeted me and took me to his house. A few of the Indian Bahá'ís and two seekers were there. It was a warm and happy meeting.

19 May: It is dawn and the birds are chirping. Last night I read the pilgrim notes of some of the friends. I was so tired that I could not read more than half of them. Some were the notes of Hiroyasu Takano, a member of the National Assembly of Japan. I met him in Japan. He noted the Guardian as having said, 'The International House of Justice won't be established without at least 60 National Assemblies. Without that establishment, the true meaning of the Bahá'í Faith won't be realized in the world.'

I stayed one night in Huancayo and left with Mr Long. We went by taxi and travelled for ten hours. It was, however, very pleasant; the scenery was beautiful and the weather was good. We again passed the height of 5000 metres and arrived at midnight in Lima.

22 May: I am leaving Lima. Enrique Sanchez is waiting for me to leave. The next day I arranged my tickets, and in the evening attended a public meeting. We had a meeting with the National Assembly the whole day on Sunday and they made very good decisions. One was that all the National Assembly members will travel around the country to teach and deepen the new believers.

Today is the Declaration of the blessed Báb, a day that started a cycle which will last for 500,000 years . . .

What shall we do for Peru? Eve Niklin and Carmelo will remain here, the National Assembly members will travel, and in each locality they will hold teaching and education classes.

I wrote to Hand of the Cause Khádem [who was responsible for that zone] to send Ma'súd to Peru for a few months, and asked Ma'súd to send Alvarez to the North of Bolivia. In this manner the Bahá'í Faith will spread in Peru from within and without its borders, and, hopefully, great results will be realized.

I arrived in Quito, Ecuador at 12.00 noon. Dorothy, David Becket and Raul Pavon were at the airport. The language of Ecuador is Quechua, and they have different dialects. It has 4,000,000 inhabitants, 50 per cent of whom are Indians. David pioneered here in 1951, and lives in Otavalo. Raul is the first person to have started teaching among the Indians. He is 26 years old and is absolutely dedicated to the Faith. He is a native of Otavalo.

Vagabundo was the first village with Bahá'ís. Raul went to this village, befriended them and started an adult education class for them. Now they have 20 Bahá'ís, all men. Their teaching plan is for David to pioneer to another city and establish a new locality for the Indians. Ferydoon Munajem has left for another town. They have only two native Bahá'ís in Otavalo.

Raul's method for teaching Indians:

1. He establishes a good rapport with the government officials and teachers.

2. He starts an adult education class.

3. He gradually introduces the Faith to them.

4. He helps them in their farming and solves their problems. The Indians are afraid of the white people, but they trust him. He needs three native Bahá'ís to help open new areas.

5. He takes medicines with him and helps them. He stays with them in their huts and visits each village three times a week.

6. He teaches them history and geography. At first they don't show much interest but gradually they like it and when he calls them, 120 gather to listen to him. Everyone calls him 'Senor Bahá'í'. In one village he has 13 new Bahá'ís. In another village, five of the Indians asked to become Bahá'ís but Raul had not accepted them, as they were not well-informed.

The National Assembly has decided to give $25 each to four native Bahá'ís to pioneer to these areas.

I think mass conversion in South America should be closely monitored by the Hands, and should be given priority. Ma'súd Khamsí can travel in Paraguay, Peru and Ecuador, and guide and help them in their tasks. Bolivia should send teachers to other areas. They should have a special teaching plan for tribal areas. The available budgets should be used exclusively for teaching.

25 May: On the way to Colombia. The few days in Ecuador were delightful. I met most of the friends and participated in many meetings. Every minute was busy and useful. On 23 May we gathered at Gale Woolson's home. She is a very dedicated Bahá'í who has been a pioneer in South and Central America for nearly 15 years, and has established the Faith in several countries. She was the first Bahá'í to go to Costa Rica, and now that country has a National Assembly. Her husband was a physician. She is a widow now and works for the Point Four office in Ecuador. She was on pilgrimage in 1956. I read her notes. The Guardian had told the pilgrims that he was contemplating appointing a Hand of the Cause for Central and South America. Olinga and I are volunteering, if he accepts us.

One night [we all] went to Otavalo, which has seven American and two Persian pioneers for a population of only 15,000. Their understanding was that they only had to establish one local Assembly. Last year they stopped teaching and supposedly concentrated on deepening. I do not know how much of the Fund has gone for the establishment of this one local Assembly. There are many things that I do not know and do not understand. When the beloved Guardian has designated the fourth phase of the Ten Year Crusade as the phase for entry by troops for the whole world, how is it that some people do not understand it and use the idea of deepening as a barrier to teaching? We have to rely on Bahá'u'lláh to protect His own Cause and to assist us who are His weak and unknowing flock.

27 May: I am on the way to Panama. I stayed less than 48 hours in Colombia. These hours were more useful than 48 days. Quality is more important than quantity. I met all the National Assembly members . . . I was the guest of Charles [Hornby], an American pioneer, a quiet and dedicated Bahá'í. On the wall of his room he has a map of Iran and two photographs of the beloved Master. I wished the Iranians could be there to see how an American man, in the heart of Colombia in South America, has decorated his room with a map of their country.

The friends told me that, during the Convention, Charles had given his bed to others and slept on the floor in a corner. Early in the morning he would get up to prepare breakfast for the guests. He is a humble and dedicated Bahá'í. May Bahá'u'lláh be with him forever. This morning he gave me three pictures of the tribal people. I took it as a good omen. I hope one day the tribes of the Amazon in this picture will become Bahá'ís.

Last night I consulted with the National Assembly members till very late. Mr Habib Rezvani was with us. I hope he will go to the heart of the jungle which is on the border of four countries — Brazil, Ecuador, Peru and Venezuela. This place is in Colombia, the source of the Amazon river, which is the home of the Indians. The beloved Guardian has given great emphasis to the importance of the Amazon. I wonder if before the end of the Plan the Faith will penetrate that area? I should not even question it. Of course within the next two years all the tribes residing in the jungles will hear about the Faith.

This journey to South America was very short. My hope is to return next year and sing such songs of servitude as to make the Abhá Concourse ecstatic. I have made a commitment to spend at least eight months of the year in South America and four months in Asia. I hope to be able to serve these dear Indians, whom the beloved Guardian has praised so much and loved so much, till the last day of my life.

28 May: Arrived in Panama and was greeted by four members of the National Assembly at the airport. One of them, Allen, is a pioneer in David, and is teaching the Indians. Up to now there is only one Indian Bahá'í, but he is going to other areas.

On my arrival the meeting of the National Assembly was convened and we spent the whole day in the Bahá'í Centre. Details of a plan for mass teaching were consulted upon. In the evening we had a public meeting which many of the friends attended . . . again we had detailed consultations and I went to the hotel at 11.00 p.m. I slept till seven a.m. I have not had a rest like this for a long time.

In the morning Norma Hamilton and Mr Douglas took me to see the Panama Canal and then we left for the airport. I left for Costa Rica at noon and arrived at two p.m.

Panama has a population of more than 1,000,000, 60,000 are Indians who live in nearby areas and are accessible. If a few people like Ma'súd could arise to teach them, great results could be achieved.

29 May: By the bounty of the beloved Guardian I have come to the capital of Costa Rica, San Jose, for the first time. May He assist this insignificant soul to be able to render some service in His path.

A few friends were waiting to greet me. On this trip everywhere I have gone the friends have been at the airport. They resemble so much the Bahá'ís of Iran. Esteban Canales, an Auxiliary Board member, was also there.

In the evening we had a meeting with the National Assembly, the National Teaching Committee, and many of the Bahá'ís, as it was the night of the Ascension of Bahá'u'lláh. The Tablet of Visitation was chanted and the 30 Bahá'ís dispersed at about three a.m. Nine of them stayed on, and the whole night was spent in prayer and meditation.

30 May: I left at nine a.m. for Nicaragua. The number of indigenous Indians in Costa Rica does not exceed 10,000, however the people are all very pure, and mostly live in rural areas. [Costa Rica] has one of the best Bahá'í communities in this area. Its National Assembly has been formed and the Bahá'ís are all active.

I stayed in Nicaragua until 7 June. I went to Bluefields and the village of Wirinkies, where the Damaki tribe lives. Hooper [Dunbar], Ruth [Pringle], Willie and Daniel were with me. It was a very uplifting journey, especially as the terrain reminded me of Mentawai.

I am leaving for El Salvador today. I could not get a visa for Honduras so can only pass by and cannot meet the beloved friends there.

The receptivity of these countries is unbelievable. There are wonderful and sacrificing pioneers; the only thing needed is a good administrator to be able to channel all the energy.

I had a dream that [Hand of the Cause] Featherstone and myself were in the presence of the beloved Guardian. He was

Huehuetenango Conference, Guatemala, 26 March 1965.

With more friends in Guatemala, 1965.

With Mazco Kucel, a Bahá'í from Mexico, 1977.

telling us the importance of teaching 'among the Indians. He pointed to a building, which was the Shrine of Bahá'u'lláh. He said he was building it with rubies. He asked me whether it was 8 or 9 June. I replied it was the eighth. Featherstone asked the Guardian where he was going, and he replied that he was going to cast his ballot in the city elections. I hope the interpretation is that dear Featherstone will come to help in the Central and South American countries and that a Bahá'í temple for the indigenous Indians will be erected in Bolivia.

9 June: I am writing these notes in Guatemala. I spent two days in San Salvador and hope to stay here for a few days. The receptivity in this country resembles that of Bolivia. The population is more than 3,000,000, 50 per cent of whom are Indians of Mayan origin. They are from 21 different tribes. Bahá'u'lláh's bounty is needed so that a few pure souls arise to enlighten the hearts of these people.

Raḥmat's diary of this trip ends here, except for a brief note stating that he left for Mexico and Los Angeles on 19 June. His notes reveal the remarkable pace which he set for his work early in his travels. Only occasionally was he able to snatch a few hours of sleep. He did not note all his suggestions and talks, many of which the pioneers and National Assemblies succesfully put into practice.

Raḥmat enjoyed a warm relationship with the indigenous believers and the pioneers of Latin America, as he did with those of Asia. Many friends from his university years were pioneering in these areas, and he felt he could rely on them to follow his suggestions. He was not afraid to ask for sacrifices from his friends and never thought they would be offended, as he never asked anything that he was not already doing himself. One person in particular was the focus of these requests. I remember many occasions when Raḥmat would be thinking about a specific task for that region and would say, with relief, that he would ask Ma'súd Khamsí to undertake it. Raḥmat's close friendship with Ma'súd continued to the very last moment of his life.

As well as suggesting to his friends the cities in which they should live, and how they could find employment, Raḥmat occasionally arranged marriages for their children. One friend, pioneering with her family in Belo Horizonte, Brazil, told me that on one of his visits, Raḥmat brought a young Brazilian Bahá'í to their home. 'He called my daughter and put her hand in the hand of this young man and told her, "This is your future husband, get to know each other." We immediately agreed, as we were sure Dr Muhájir would not choose the wrong person for our daughter. They eventually married, and are very happy and active in teaching the Faith.'

In the nearly two decades which followed his introduction to Latin America, Raḥmat travelled to that continent seven more times, and visited hundreds of villages to assist in teaching and planning for the progress of the Faith. His travels to every country in the region generated enthusiasm and a new desire for service and dedication in the Bahá'ís. Reports of various National Assemblies show their love for him and their appreciation of his contributions to their work. To write in detail about his activities in each country is beyond the scope of this narrative. However, a few highlights provide a flavour of how Raḥmat worked, and his dedication to the native peoples of South America.

SHARING THE VISION — BOLIVIA

Athos Costas, a close friend and collaborator, accompanied Raḥmat on many of his trips in Latin America. He provides the following account of Raḥmat's work in Bolivia:

> We started mass teaching in 1957. When Dr Muhájir came here in 1961 we already had about 1000 indigenous Bahá'ís. But we were very worried about deepening the new believers, and decided that we should call a halt to the teaching and devote all our time to deepening.
>
> Dr Muhájir told us that we couldn't stop teaching, and actually had us increase our efforts and open new areas. He said that enrolment of new Bahá'ís is like accepting them to a school; they come to learn because they like the school's philosophy and outlook — they like its spirit. They don't come because they know everything already, but because they want to learn.
>
> He asked me, 'What is your purpose in deepening? We all have to go through tests, whether we're learned or not. Do you

Arrival in Bolivia with Hooper Dunbar, 1972.

Visiting the friends of Cochabamba, Bolivia, March 1972.

A special conference given by Dr Muhájir attended by pioneers and native teachers.

Visiting the temple site, Bolivia, 1974.

believe that those who know a lot pass tests easier than those who don't? Now that we have the opportunity we must teach as many of these beautiful and pure-hearted people as we can. We must deepen them slowly, teach them first a few prayers and principles until the community has grown larger and stronger. Then we will have the manpower to do it properly.'

Meditating about these questions I reached my own conclusions. The phrase, 'many are called, but few are chosen' came to mind. I saw how, out of the forty 'educated people' who accepted the Faith in Buenos Aires, only five or six remained. Among our indigenous brothers in Latin America there are chosen spirits. Although mostly illiterate, their spirits illuminate the whole region. Many of them suffered severe opposition, yet they remained steadfast. So we launched an expansion campaign in Bolivia, and doubled the number of Bahá'ís each year. In 1963 we had 6000, which later became 50,000.

I had the privilege of accompanying Dr Muhájir to Argentina, Chile and Bolivia. Though mass teaching was the passion of his life, he was a well-rounded person. He had a deep respect for science and education, which he constantly applied in his speeches. He was an eager reader, and bought many books which filled his suitcase rather than clothes. He stimulated the city Bahá'ís to have firesides immediately following their Nineteen Day Feasts. He insisted that the friends get out and and invite people.

Raul Pavon and I shared his vision, we shared his dream of establishing the first Bahá'í nation among the indigenous people of Ecuador and Bolivia, and we agreed with him that the only solution to our difficulties was to teach and open new communities. He always reminded us that teaching, deepening and consolidation should go hand-in-hand.

INGENUITY, PATIENCE, PERSISTENCE — BRAZIL

Among the pioneers in Brazil were some of Raḥmat's closest friends and their families. He was always delighted to visit that country. Seeing his friends after long years of separation brought tranquillity to his soul.

During his early visits, as reported by the National Assembly, Raḥmat urged for a greater expansion by

> . . . launching great book campaigns to educate both Bahá'ís and the public in general about the glorious message of Bahá'u'lláh. He always spoke in terms of multitudes, and then suggested publishing thousands of books to reach all levels of society. [When] the National Assembly . . . asked, 'But, Dr Muhájir, where will we get so much money for this project? How can we pay for such a huge campaign?' he answered, 'The money will come from the many new, enthusiastic Bahá'ís who will enter the Faith.' So the thousands of books were published and the Bahá'ís entered the Faith.

One of the friends recalls,

> At the start of mass teaching in Brazil, the Hand of the Cause visited Salvador, the central city of the State of Bahia. He was genuinely delighted with what he saw there. Dr Muhájir was especially happy that the Persian Bahá'ís were active participants in this great endeavour.
>
> Mass teaching in those days was progressing like wildfire. In thirteen days we enrolled 270 Bahá'ís. The numbers increased so dramatically that we ran out of registration cards! We were receiving nearly 200 new Bahá'ís every day of that campaign.
>
> One of the new believers was astonished when she first saw a portrait of 'Abdu'l-Bahá. She told us that she'd had a great problem, and for a while had dreamt of Him every single night. When her problem was solved He didn't appear in her dreams again. We found out that the previous owners of her house were Bahá'ís! This was a sign that we were on the right track.
>
> Dr Muhájir, with great happiness, visited these areas. While in the car, on top of a hill overlooking the city, he said, 'For Bahá'u'lláh's sake, do not do anything to jeopardize this mass teaching.' That night, in our rented institute, he spoke only in Persian and said he missed speaking in Persian. Most of the time his talk was about the station of the Universal House of Justice and its grandeur.

When he wanted to leave, there was no seat on the plane. We were all apprehensive. However, Dr Muhájir sat there serenely chanting the Tablet of Aḥmad. Everyone had left when we suddenly heard his name being called. Calmly he said his goodbyes and left us, as if nothing unusual had happened.

In 1974 Raḥmat spent 23 days in Brazil, visiting 15 communities. To spend so many days in one country was a sign that he believed it had great potential, and that he wanted to be of service to the friends for as long as he possibly could. The mass teaching had stagnated, which made him very sad.

His diary records the events of a few days of this journey:

19 October 1974: I arrived at Belem airport at 5.30 a.m. Dear Shafa, Auxiliary Board member, was waiting for me. We bought tickets for Macapa and arrived there together. He lives in Santa Ana, which is 20 kilometres away, and works as an engineer. We arrived in his house and I had a good few restful hours. In the afternoon we went to a nearby village which has about 20 Bahá'ís. This is a farm that was owned by a white person who had left it to be divided among his black labourers. There are about sixty families and about ten Bahá'ís. Macapa has 20 Bahá'ís. We had some discussions and I suggested that on 20 October, which is the day of the birth of the Báb, they should reconvene their Bahá'í children's classes which have been discontinued.

Today is the 20th. We went back to the village. There were about 20 children. We talked and they sang songs and had sweets. I hope Bahá'u'lláh will help them to continue their class. Dolores, who is a Bahá'í and a nurse, is their teacher.

We discussed mass teaching with Mr Shafa. I feel it is possible to start mass conversion in the city of Macapa. It has a population of 60,000. If they purchase a local Bahá'í Centre, which will not cost more than $5000, teach 1000 in two years, distribute 5000 pamphlets and books, and in the months of December to February (which are the school holidays), use the youth for teaching, they will have great results.

An armful of smiles for Dr Muhájir at the inauguration of the new Ḥaẓíratu'l-Quds in Bahia, Brazil, November 1979.

Only Bahá'u'lláh's bounty can help us. Teaching in the North of Brazil will strengthen Guyana also, as there is regular traffic between these countries.

In the two cities of Macapa and Belem the Amazon river flows to the Atlantic. This river by itself is like an ocean. Maybe mass teaching in Macapa can start the teaching in Amazon, which was mentioned by the Guardian in 1953.

I spent a happy and restful time at Mr Shafa's home. He and his dear wife and two beautiful children, Amir and Roshan, live together in harmony and love.

21 October: I am waiting in the airport at Belem. This morning I left Belem at five-thirty a.m. and now have to wait here till four p.m. to catch the plane for Sao Luis. I have time to write and to read.

I arrived at Sao Luis . . . This is the capital of one of the provinces of Brazil. Jeiro Serquera and his wife arrived and took me to the Lord Hotel. A very nice room with a view of the park was reserved for me and they had cleaned it and left flowers and fruit for me. We had dinner together and said many prayers for the progress of mass teaching in that city. We consulted about the North of Brazil and decided that, if possible, Jeiro would transfer to Sao Luis and take on the task of converting 1000 souls.

In the morning we visited an orphanage and talked to the principal and teachers about the Faith for nearly an hour. Then about 50 children sang songs for us and we talked with them. It was a very rewarding morning. Jeiro and his wife became fast friends with the teachers and decided to have future activities. In response to my talk a young man thanked us, and expressed the hope that the whole world would become Bahá'í and follow these teachings.

In the afternoon we visited an old people's home. There were nearly 50 people there. Bahá'í songs were sung and sweets were distributed. I talked to them for a while, they were very happy to see us and asked us to visit them again. We left directly for the airport and came to Teresina. Mrs Surur Mobin who is married to Mr Lin, a Chinese Bahá'í from Indonesia, took me to their home. Their son, Horace, is two-and-a-half years old.

23 October: I was interviewed by the press and radio in the morning. In the afternoon we visited the nearby town of Timun. Twenty people had gathered. Mr Rezvani and his companions have taught these people. There was a public meeting in the afternoon which 150 attended. Most were youth, and it was a very successful meeting. I will leave for Fortaleza on 24 October.

I stayed in Fortaleza for two days. The Rabbani family are the pioneers in that town. Their son Said is very active. Years ago they had hundreds of Bahá'ís. We went to the nearby villages and visited the Bahá'ís in their homes. They have beautiful children who attend Bahá'í classes. We had two large public meetings in [Fortaleza]. They were both very spiritual meetings. The people asked many questions, and many of them expressed their desire for the Faith. I had two interviews on television, once with Leonora [Armstrong, 'the mother of Latin America'] and once by myself. All the newspapers have written about the meetings, and praise the Faith for its teaching of the unity of mankind.

26 October: We are in Natal. There are a few Bahá'ís here. In the morning I had a press interview, and in the afternoon met with the friends. In the evening there was a public meeting at the University Club. The talk went very well and there was great interest.

I stayed in Recife for one night. After meeting the friends we had a fireside with about 15 seekers. The next day we visited the prison, and stayed and talked to the prisoners for a long time. The friends decided to visit the jail every 15 days. Vicente, an English teacher who was my translator, is teaching in this prison. I also had a television interview which was broadcast in the city.

In Joao Pessoa a few friends gathered, and we also had a fireside with about nine non-Bahá'ís. In Maceio there was a small gathering with non-Bahá'ís.

In Aracaju, where Ma'súd Jalálí is the pioneer, there was a large meeting in the university. About 70 prominent people, including the Dean of the press club, university professors, and the vice-president of the university were present. The meeting was truly wonderful. The professors asked many questions, and did not want to leave. This was perhaps one of the best teaching occasions on this whole trip.

In Salvador I met with the friends and had interviews with the press. The next morning we consulted with members of the committees and the Assembly, and went to the villages in the evening. The next day we went all over the city to find a house which could be used as the Bahá'í Centre. In the evening, had a very nice meeting in one of the nearby villages where there is a group of Bahá'ís and a school. Today, Sunday 3 November, I am leaving for Vitoria.

I went to Hotel San Jose in Vitoria, then found the friends and spent two days with them. One night was spent in a suburban village which has a Bahá'í institute and had many seekers. In the teacher-training college there were more than 100 students. I talked about Bahá'í education. We then left for Belo Horizonte.

In the afternoon I had TV and press interviews. In the evening the dear friends, young and old, gathered. The next day there was a majestic conference in the university on the psychology of the elimination of fear. More than 1000 students and faculty members were present, and I spoke about this matter, quoting from the Bahá'í Writings. This was an unprecedented event, and the questions and answers were detailed and continued for a long time. In the evening there was a meeting in the College of Philosophy, and about 70 students and many Bahá'ís gathered. I talked about the unity of mankind. It was a very effective and spiritual meeting.

I left for Rio the next day, and early next morning left for Sao Paulo.

8 November: I received a cable from the Universal House of Justice regarding mass teaching in Brazil:

DELIGHTED TWO YEAR PLAN LARGE SCALE CONVERSION SPECIFIED AREAS PROVISION LITERATURE MERITORIOUS

> ATTENTION CHILDREN YOUTH UNIVERSITIES STOP ASSURE CONSIDERATION POSSIBILITIES PIONEERS TEACHERS LIGHT WORLD NEED URGE YOUR IMMEDIATE CALL ENTIRE HOME COMMUNITY FULLEST SUPPORT PROGRAMME INCLUDING PIONEERS TRAVELLING TEACHERS OFFERING FERVENT PRAYERS DIVINE CONFIRMATIONS WARMEST LOVE SHARE THIS MESSAGE HANDCAUSE MUHAJIR UNIVERSAL HOUSE OF JUSTICE STOP

> With God's bounty we will devise a teaching plan for nine cities in Brazil. My reliance is on Bahá'u'lláh. I consulted with the National Assembly of Brazil about mass teaching in this country. The consensus was to:
>
> 1. To select nine mass teaching areas.
>
> 2. To ask help from the USA and Canada for travelling teachers.
>
> 3. To have a special plan for the education of children.
>
> 4. To activate the Publishing Trust.
>
> 5. To reach all strata of the people, through the mass media.
>
> 6. To have a two-year plan for all pioneers to help in this matter.
>
> 7. The local Assemblies and teaching committees should have freedom to plan and teach in their own provinces.
>
> 8. Habib Rezvani should be asked to come to Brazil to help.

Wherever Raḥmat went, he pointed out the possibilities of expanding the Faith, and urged that the friends have

> . . . large-scale teaching at every social level in preparation for the forthcoming Bahia International Teaching Conference in January 1977. He concentrated especially on the young, active,

> growing, spiritually-conscious community of Belo Horizonte in the State of Minas Gerais. They were already teaching with great success in the schools and universities and bringing in many new Bahá'ís. He challenged the hearts of the young people to a great adventure, suggesting that as many as possible go at once to Bahia to teach with concentration and dedication, and to offer to the International Conference 5000 new Bahá'ís. And it was done.

The National Assembly reported,

> [The project] included publishing vast quantities of books, brochures and pamphlets, the purchase of a local Ḥaẓíratu'l-Quds in Salvador, the concentrated teaching of many children, especially in the Bahia mass teaching area, the rapid expansion of youth activities in the secondary schools and universities, and a concentrated teaching effort in each of the ten most promising communities.

Mass teaching in Brazil was once more a reality. In one discussion Raḥmat begged the friends not to stop it again. He believed that every time teaching stopped, restarting it became more difficult. He advised them,

> When you see that mass teaching is progressing and that the way you have chosen yields results, for the sake of Bahá'u'lláh, do not tamper with it. Do not scatter your teachers to other areas to pursue the same plan. Let the number of Bahá'ís in one location reach the maximum possible, then divert your attention to another. Publicity through radio and television is indeed very useful, but it is not mass teaching. Mass conversion happens through individual, one-on-one teaching. When one whole village has come to the Faith, then go to another one. At the time of 'Abdu'l-Baha, one whole village in Burma became Bahá'í. Then the Faith spread across the country.

He returned to Brazil in April 1976 to participate in the National Convention, and to consult with the National Assembly and Counsellors. A plan was formulated for a great mass teaching project for the entire North-East region of the country. The project placed great emphasis on the winning of families to the Faith, and called for bringing one entire village under the shadow of Bahá'u'lláh. The project generated much enthusiasm at the Convention, was immediately launched and quickly produced rich fruits: the raising of 25 teachers who pledged to devote periods ranging from one to nine months to this work, and who began at once to teach in that same area, successfully enrolling several hundred new believers in this initial undertaking; and spontaneous contributions of cash, Ḥaẓíratu'l-Quds, schools, cars — even a burro [donkey]!

With the challenge in mind presented by Dr Muhájir of finding 1000 new Bahá'ís in Belo Horizonte, a pilot plan was worked out, fired by the urgency provided by the many Bahá'í youth who wished to go out as pioneers without depleting the strength of their community.

These, and many similar stories from around the world, show Raḥmat's flexibility in planning teaching projects for different countries, and the way that he blended ingenuity, patience and persistence. His unique ability was to recognize the potential of each country, and to plan their teaching projects accordingly.

In 1977 he participated, with his beloved friend, Hand of the Cause Enoch Olinga, in the Bahia Conference. Teaching was going on strongly, and these two champions of mass conversion were delighted, praising the friends for their great achievement. Raḥmat's letter to the Universal House of Justice about this event said,

> One of the bounties of this teaching conference was that 5600 were enrolled in the North before the conference. This is unprecedented.
>
> Eighty thousand books and pamphlets were printed as a preliminary to this conference. Funds have been collected and the local Ḥaẓíratu'l-Quds of Bahia has been purchased. Thoughts are now ready for teaching. Everyone now aspires to teach thousands. This is going like wildfire, that has never been witnessed in this continent.

Brazil 1977. Entertaining the troops at the International Conference held in Bahia with Hands of the Cause Paul Haney and Enoch Olinga in attendance.

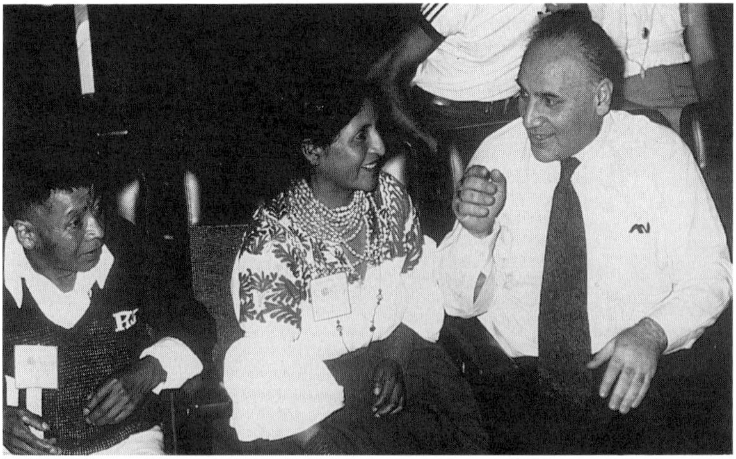

With some of his much loved South American friends at the Bahia conference.

Introducing his close friend and colleague Raul Pavon to the friends assembled at the Bahia conference in 1977.

With Farzin Davatchi in Brazil.

The National Assembly reported,

> In the year following the great International Conference, at the National Convention, which was held in Salvador, Bahia, [Dr Muhájir provided] the spark that fired [the] young people and several more who joined them to leave the Convention and go together to open up the great Amazon region from end to end, and now there are many communities from Belem, at its mouth, to Marco.

Raḥmat's last visit to Brazil was in November 1979. Accompanied by Counsellor Raul Pavon, he visited several areas and, despite his obvious fatigue, sought to rally the friends to undertake mass conversion. Razi Abbasian recounts the events of this journey:

> The Hand of the Cause, accompanied by Counsellor Raul Pavon and Auxiliary Board member Sergio Couto, arrived in Vitoria from Ilheus on 27 November. He went directly to see the Ḥaẓíratu'l-Quds, and then came to our house. As I was a member of the National Teaching Committee and the National Assembly, he immediately started questioning me about the condition of mass teaching in Brazil. He had a very simple dinner and met with the Teaching Committee till late at night.
>
> It was the eve of the Ascension of 'Abdu'l-Baha, and the friends started to arrive for the meeting. He rested for a few minutes and joined the 50 friends who had gathered for the meeting. He talked to them and prayers were said. We had thought that some friends would want to leave early. However, none of them left. He stayed with the friends until the Tablet of Visitation was recited and left to rest at two a.m.
>
> On the 29th, the whole day was spent consulting with the National Teaching Committee, and a plan was devised for mass conversion in ten provinces of Brazil. He had to leave for Belo Horizonte on the 29th. He spent the whole morning of that day with the Teaching Committee. One hour before his departure for the airport he called me and said, 'Razi, come on, you are going to Belo Horizonte with me.' Despite my utter astonishment I immediately packed and we left together.

He said he had about five hours of rest on the first night. The next two nights he complained of severe headaches and pain in the veins of his neck. We all attributed it to his tiredness.

In Belo Horizonte we stayed at Mr Eftekhari's home. He explained to the friends, till late at night, the plans that had been devised by the National Teaching Committee. The next day he was taken to a university where about 30 students had gathered to hear him. He spoke to them about the Faith in a very simple and direct manner, then divided the Bahá'ís into groups and told them to talk to the non-Bahá'ís about all aspects of the teachings. The students were very happy. There were two more meetings in the university on the same day.

That night he was with the friends for several hours, consulting about the teaching activities in that area. I was exhausted and could not keep awake. Dr Muhájir did not show any tiredness and continued till after midnight.

The next day we left for Rio de Janeiro. He had been up since very early in the morning. He said that, on the days he had to travel, he would wake up early and would not be able to rest. He rested for a few hours in Rio and then met with the National Assembly. Detailed plans were formulated and the year 1980 was designated as the year of mass conversion in Brazil.

We left the next day for Sao Paulo and arrived at the Bahá'í Centre before noon. He was with the Bahá'ís till late afternoon. He explained the plan, and funds were donated for teaching trips, many volunteering to give their time.

Raḥmat's diary gives a brief account of these few days in Brazil:

29 November: Belo Horizonte. We had wonderful meetings. The first night at the Bahá'í Centre I talked for four seekers, and also for the Bahá'ís. The next day, about 30 students gathered in the College of Economics and we talked about the solution of the economic problem from the Bahá'í point of view. Then the friends were divided into groups and I talked to them . . . At noon I had an interview with the press and television. At night we met at Mr Eftekhari's house. They planned three consecutive firesides and many of the youth volunteered to go to these meetings. Funds were contributed for the use of a car, and two youths volunteered to work full-time.

1 December: I consulted with the National Assembly in Rio. Raul Pavon and Sergio were also there. We planned:

1. To announce 1980 to be the year of mass teaching.

2. To teach in the cities.

3. To print new pamphlets for the cities, television and radio.

4. To teach in all schools.

5. To have a special fund for teaching.

6. To have full-time travelling teachers. This is very important.

7. To have firesides and book fairs in all the cities.

8. To contact hospitals, old peoples homes, radio and television throughout the country.

9. To strengthen the local Assemblies.

10. To increase the numbers of children's classes to 95 for the whole country.

11. To have a Women's Conference in July 1980.

I had discussions with the National Assembly about all these matters. It is up to them now to approve them. Everything is subject to His might.

In July 1980 the National Assembly reported:

Now, this year, following the visit of our beloved Dr Muhájir in December, both the summer youth projects of January and

February, which have yielded so many victories, and those of the Badí' Project still being pursued in this vacation month of July, were inspired by the dear Hand and are being carried out in his name. [These projects] have sent out more than 100 youths and adults to all corners of Brazil, opening up our last remaining states and expanding the number of localities and deepening the new Bahá'ís everywhere.

New Assemblies are being formed and we can expect that the harvest will, indeed, be great. But the greatest victory from this is the dedication, the love for the Faith and for spreading the Message of Bahá'u'lláh, the confirmations received from the receptivity of those who have been taught and the renewed love and spirit for action, that has been awakened in the whole country. We have so much from our beloved Dr Muhájir to be thankful for.

How can we express our admiration and very deeply felt love for this beautiful, selfless, dedicated and so capable Hand of the Cause of God?

UNIMAGINABLE HEIGHTS — CHILE

Most of Raḥmat's time in Chile was spent in the southern region, where mass teaching was progressing among the Mapuche Indians. He often prayed that no unknown or unexpected reason would cause this activity to stop. He talked to the National Assembly, the pioneers, the teachers — to anyone willing to listen — about this. He stressed that,

> This phenomenon must be extended by means of more support, and its significance must be explained to all the believers. The Faith is undergoing a natural growing process and if we do not hinder it, it will reach unimaginable heights and garner unbelievable triumphs. Mass conversion in the Cautin province is the most significant victory in Chile. It has a very fragile balance. Any negative action or thought, by an individual or an institution, could well disturb this balance and this great opportunity will slip through our fingers, maybe forever. To stop this process for whatever reason will be considered as a crime in the court of Bahá'u'lláh.

With Bahá'í children, Temucu', Chile, 1976.

Annual Counsellors Conference, Valparaiso, Chile, 24–5 December 1974. Seated to the left of Dr Muhájir is Leonora Armstrong, first pioneer to South America.

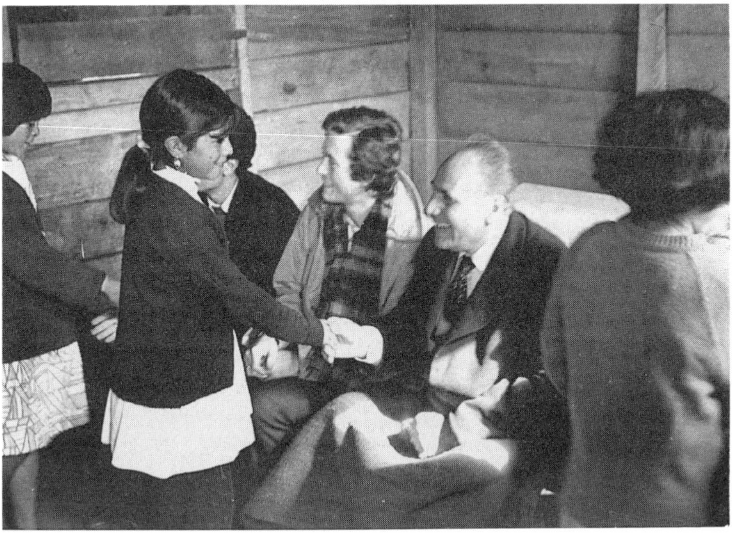

A delighted Dr Muhájir meeting Bahá'í children at the Mapuche Bahá'í Centre, Chile, 1976.

Watching the children perform.

He emphasized, as he had in other countries, that mass conversion has its own dynamic, its own momentum and its own protective power. He believed it only natural that the thousands of souls who were thirsty for the Bahá'í teachings be attracted to the Faith. He asked the friends to teach and educate the Indian people as a group, and enrol them in the Faith. If they did not do this, the Indians

> would lose their traditional identity and togetherness and there will be no lasting results. Masses are like the bees in a beehive. We cannot choose a few bees and expect them to produce honey. If they are all together they will work together, they will organize their own affairs and they will respond to the teachings.

He had to overcome the objections raised by some of the friends to the huge influx of new believers. This problem was not confined to Chile, but was expressed in many communities throughout the Bahá'í world. He told me that the friends thought he was the creator of mass teaching. They did not remember that it was a commandment of Bahá'u'lláh and 'Abdu'l-Baha: it was what the Ten Year Crusade was all about. However, he patiently defended this concept and tried to make the friends less apprehensive.

During one of his visits to Chile, a pioneer challenged Raḥmat to justify the apparent neglect of consolidation amongst those new converts to the Faith who had been brought in by mass teaching. Raḥmat answered,

> Criticism of mass enrolment always seems to revolve around the term 'consolidation'. When faced with a large number of new believers, the Bahá'ís tend to be scared of the great size of the job that they imagine will confront them. They also believe that these new Bahá'ís cannot be 'good' Bahá'ís, because they have accepted the Faith so rapidly. These critics judge the matter without understanding and patience. Mass conversion bears fruit only through the second generation, or in the course of 15 to 20 years. The adults may only understand the basics of the Faith but their children will be presented with all opportunities possible to become well instructed and knowledgable. The real base of the growth of the Faith lies with the children. For this very reason the

> security and health of a mass teaching area depends a great deal on the education programmes for the youth and children.

He visited the Indian communities of Cudico and Cerro Loncoche, where children had gathered for a meeting with him. These children had attended Bahá'í classes, and their happiness, their spirit and their attachment to the teachings left no doubt in the minds of the visitors of their potential, or of their great future in the Faith. Many of the teachers in those areas were themselves children of those who had come to the Faith ten years before as the result of mass teaching. He emphasized this point to the group gathered there and told them,

> Consolidation of new believers in a mass teaching area is not very complicated. A believer is consolidated when a teacher takes him to another community to teach or when he tells him stories about the Faith. By seeing and experiencing the teaching work, a new believer will often become so attracted that he will deepen himself. The image of consolidation being something very complicated often causes the institutions to stop expansion. The community of Cautin has been asked not to open new areas. This is like dousing a fire with ice-water.
>
> Although we must have great impatience with teaching and expansion, we must have patience for consolidation and deepening. It will take many years before we can have administrators and teachers from the new communities.
>
> Is it not better that someone says 'Alláh'u'Abhá' and opens his house for the Bahá'ís and allows us to train his children, than [that someone be] completely ignorant about the Faith?
>
> At all costs, we must avoid criticism and premature judgement. We will see that mass conversion has an unexplainable impulse which rolls over all barriers, preserves and nurtures itself — except when we hinder its growth with our limited vision.

Raḥmat last visited Chile in 1979 and counselled the friends to,

> continue with mass teaching and trust in the power of the Manifestation of God. He said that even when one person

> expresses doubts about the value of mass teaching it will be damaging to the Cause. He asked the National Assembly not to divert the teachers to another area when they find them successful. When the work is progressing in a particular area, every help should be given to sustain it and not to divert the attention by starting it in another place.
>
> In every mass teaching area, travelling teachers are the backbone and very essential. Part-time work is not very effective. In this period of time there should be those who are directly supported by the Fund and are responsible for teaching.
>
> Communities where most of the Bahá'ís are busy in committees suffer in the teaching field. Bahá'ís should give fifty per cent of their time to teaching instead of just ten.

This was his final exhortation to the friends in Chile.

'VILLA RAḤMAT' — COLOMBIA

Even when exhausted by his work and travels, going to Colombia made Raḥmat feel happy and elated. The main reason for his attachment to that Bahá'í community was their methodical expansion and deepening programmes. In addition, his close friend Farzam Arbab, whom he considered his younger brother, lived in Colombia. Dr Arbab gladly accepted all Raḥmat's suggestions and eagerly put them into practice. When these experimental ideas proved successful in Colombia, Raḥmat would carry them with him all around the world and urge the friends to emulate the Colombian Bahá'ís. He told me that pioneering creates lions of servitude in the Bahá'í Faith, one of the examples of which was Farzam Arbab. He said, 'if Farzam had stayed in United States he would be a good professor of physics in some university, would have a comfortable life and would be among the forgotten of the world. Now look what he and Lori are doing. Their names will be associated with the entry by troops in Colombia till eternity.'

Counsellor Arbab, presently serving as a member of the International Teaching Centre, has fond memories of Raḥmat:

> Our family pioneered to Colombia in 1969 and at that time his influence on the Colombian community was already quite

visible. For about a year I heard the members of the National Spiritual Assembly speak with anticipation about the possibility of his next visit. When he finally arrived, he asked us to go directly from the airport to the National Centre, where he immediately entered into consultation with the National Assembly. When we left that consultation, which had lasted till about three in the morning, it was clear to me that no statement I had heard about Dr Muhájir could have ever described the greatness of this unique servant of the Cause of God.

The influence he exerted on our minds and hearts operated on various levels, and simultaneously affected different aspects of our collective thinking and behaviour. He never preached at us, nor did he make strong emotional appeals. It was simply that he constantly moved with amazing speed in the field of service, and his words and example created in us the keenest desire to move along with him. He inspired us, but he did so in action. Before his first visit, I had been told that one of his first questions would be 'What is the plan of action?' Sure enough, he did not even wait for the meeting with National Assembly; on the way to the centre, in the car, he asked the famous question, and we were already in deep consultation by the time we got to the meeting.

We all identify Dr Muhájir with the promotion of mass teaching, and of course, one need only travel to any country with a large number of believers and one will find that he has influenced that community enormously. But I have always felt that to associate him with only one aspect of teaching is to do him an injustice. Having given large-scale teaching its initial impulse in Colombia in the 1960s, his conversations with us were concerned with much broader issues than mass teaching. 'The spiritual conquest of the country' describes the theme of his visits far more adequately. In the Colombian Bahá'í community Dr Muhájir found a united group of believers who had wholeheartedly accepted his vision of taking the Faith to the masses of their people. No one seemed to question the need for continued expansion, and he did not have to spend his energies on each visit to focus the community again on teaching. He was now concerned with helping us gain spiritual forces that had to be utilized if we were to bring millions of people into the Faith. He taught us how to go about elaborating strategies, and how to be alert to new opportunities without losing sight of what we were already doing successfully. The framework within which he discussed these matters with us was our current plan of action, which we freely modified during each one of his visits as we gained more insight into the process of teaching and learned from his wisdom.

We learned from his words, his example, and his unique style of thinking about the growth of the Faith, as he travelled to the towns and villages with us, as he addressed the friends in large and small gatherings, as he consulted with the institutions and the teachers, and as he gave advice to individuals among us. He once heard me say no to someone's suggestion, and told me that he wished I would never say no to anyone for the rest of my life. Look for some positive aspect of everyone's ideas, was his advice, and build on it; that way, you will never again have to say no. Once, he asked Mr Habib Rezvani and me to take him to a village and said that he wished to watch me while I taught. He was not fluent in Spanish, but he listened carefully as I explained the message to a shopkeeper. Afterwards, he sat with me and analyzed how, at certain points in my presentation, I had clearly touched the heart of the seeker, and at which points my words had not had the desired effect.

There was a period of time when some of the friends criticized the National Assembly for demanding too much spiritual discipline from the participants in teaching campaigns and institute courses. The National Assembly decided to relax the conditions and let the friends be more 'normal' in their services to the Faith. When we told him this, he suddenly became very sad. He asked me for a piece of paper and wrote on it, 'The less you expect, the less you achieve.' On the back he wrote, in Persian, three verses of a poem, reportedly a favourite of Mullá Ḥusayn's, on the dangers of seeking comfort and the importance of extreme effort to succeed in our activities. I treasure this small piece of paper and often refer to it to remind myself of the valuable lessons I learned that day.

On another occasion, one of the pioneers complained about his inability to move the native believers to higher levels of service to the Faith. To our surprise, Dr Muhájir told him that he needed to become more generous in order to have success. He then explained that generosity did not refer only to material possessions. One had to be generous in giving other believers, especially the new ones, the opportunity to serve. One had to give room to others so that they would express their opinions and participate in consultation and in plans of action. Without generosity, we would not really share certain privileges of service with others.

Anecdotes are utterly insufficient to illustrate the depth of his influence on the believers and the institutions in Colombia. A whole way of thinking about service to the Faith, a mind-set about the spiritual conquest of the planet, an approach to the analysis of opportunities and problems, and above all, faith: indomitable faith in the efficacy of Bahá'u'lláh's revelation and the power of divine assistance, these were the themes that filled every minute of the short hours that we could spend with him as he visited us once every year or two during a decade that saw the Colombian community grow from a few hundred to about 30,000.

Another close friend and collaborator, Habib Rezvani, who spent many years in pioneering and mass teaching in Colombia and other Latin American countries relates,

[Dr Muhájir's] first visit to Colombia was in 1961. The National Assembly had just been elected and we were all in need of training about mass teaching. One of the friends mentioned that teaching the Indians in Colombia was impossible. There was a directive named 'Concordato' which prohibited the conversion of Indians. He asked who had issued this decree and was told the Pope and the government. He said, 'Do you think the Bahá'ís of Iran, who gave their lives to teach, had the permission of the Iranian clergy? You must go on with your teaching.' Another person mentioned that these Indians were not the ones that 'Abdu'l-Bahá had mentioned. This caused Dr Muhájir a great deal of laughter. He said, 'I promise you, in every country I have been to, the Indians are the same as yours. If these are not the ones that 'Abdu'l-Bahá meant, where are they?' He insisted that this thought should not hinder us from teaching the Indians.

He then asked for our plans and suggested that we choose the three areas of Amazon, Guajira and Choco to spearhead mass teaching. The same night the teachers were also selected. He asked me to go on foot to the Amazon and teach in the name of 'Abdu'l-Bahá.

Step by step, Dr Muhájir guided and trained us. He visited the new believers and praised the pioneers who had taught them reading and writing. One of the pioneers mentioned that the native believers did not truly love Bahá'u'lláh, as they just asked for the first pioneer who had been their teacher. Dr Muhájir was flabbergasted. He was silent for a while and then said, 'The Faith of Bahá'u'lláh is for unity and love among the divers people of the world. If these people still remember the first person who has shown them love, it is not a fault, but shows their purity of heart. As time passes they will come to know and love you too, and through you they will understand the teachings of Bahá'u'lláh.'

We had a policy of not burdening the new native believers with any tasks. Dr Muhájir's method was the reverse. He said that we should guide them on what to do and how to do it, and then leave the responsibility of the work to them.

In Guajira he went with us to look for an institute. Later, when the institute was finished, we called it 'Villa Raḥmat', and brought many natives there for deepening.

Once I talked to him about the hardships in my material life. He said, 'Habib, you know what your problem is? You always think you should have enough money to survive!' He then suggested ways that might help me better our condition of living. He told me not to worry about material things, that Bahá'u'lláh would take care of it. He said, 'Habib, if you were in Iran you would have a car, a house, and some money in the bank. What would be the use of it?'

He always thought about the education of children. He suggested we prepare and print special books for children. This was accomplished in later years and was very much appreciated by other communities of the world.

He not only encouraged the teaching of the Indian natives and in rural areas, he greatly stressed the importance of teaching in the cities and among university students.

From the first minute of his arrival he would ask us about our plans. He then, very gently, would introduce his own ideas, in such a manner that we all thought they were our own. He once said, 'My suggestions for teaching is like making a pot of soup with a little water and a small stone. I bring the water and the stone, and then someone can bring the pot, another one the firewood. While my soup is boiling I will request someone to bring me a little salt and another one to bring a little meat. While all these are cooking I will just mention that if my soup had some vegetables it would taste much better. Someone is sure to provide the vegetables. This way we will all have a delicious soup without anyone having to go to a lot of trouble. My promise to make them a delicious soup out of water and stone will not prove false.'

He said he had once visited a country to help them plan their teaching work. One of the friends told him that his suggestions were impractical, and he was sure that no one would attend the meeting, as they did not like mass teaching. Dr Muhájir asked him if it was at all possible to call just one member of the National Assembly. He arrived, and was asked to call another member. In this way the National Assembly members were gathered and the plan was formulated and implemented.

He always believed that all Bahá'í conferences should have a specific teaching project, otherwise just having the Bahá'ís gather for a conference was a waste of resources. Prior to the dedication of the Panama temple, he suggested that we should teach at least 5000 people in Panama. Three months before the dedication he asked me to go there to help them in this project. On arrival, one of the National Assembly members asked me why I had arrived so early. I told him Dr Muhájir had sent me. He said, 'Oh yes, you are the "follow-up" that he promised. We were sure that he would keep his promises.'

Once we told him that we had decided not to burden the Bahá'ís with a lot of activities and leave them to themselves to decide. Dr Muhájir said, 'On the contrary, the less you expect, the less you achieve. Whenever a country was not very active, the beloved

Guardian would assign them more responsibilities. This would result in the deepening and strengthening of that community.'

Dr Muhájir was never satisfied with small projects. Once, in Colombia, the pioneers planned a project which was thought to be too ambitious. He, however, was very happy about it, and gave us all his help and assistance for its implementation.

On his last trip he laid the foundation stone of the Ruhi Institute. He was very happy about it and believed that the institute would become the 'Ruhi University'.

On his travels in Colombia he always displayed great humility. He would never allow us to attribute any project or suggestion to him. He travelled simply and with great economy. His meals often consisted of bread and cheese. On one occasion he asked me to buy him some grapes, and he had a meal of bread, cheese and grapes while waiting for a plane at Bogota airport.

Once, on our way to Bogota, our plane could not land and was diverted to another city. The next day we had to change planes to go to Bogota. On arrival he asked me where the 'Lost and Found' window was. I was surprised that he had not mentioned that he had lost something. He said that if he had told me that his coat had been left behind I would have made a lot of fuss. We went to the 'Lost and Found' and miraculously the coat was there, and none of his documents or money had been touched.

He very often had dreams which showed him his course of action, and he prayed at length for guidance in his travels. Once we were together in Spain. He said he had dreamt of a close friend who had said to him that as Africa was so close he should go there. He called the Universal House of Justice, and was told that it was indeed necessary for him to go there.

RULES FOR MASS CONVERSION — ECUADOR

When Raḥmat visited Otavalo, Ecuador in 1961, though concerned that so many capable Bahá'ís were concentrating so much effort on only one local Assembly, he offered his suggestions, talked about his experiences, and urged them not to be apprehensive of mass conversion. Helen Hornby provides something of the flavour of Raḥmat's counsels to the friends in Ecuador:

[Dr Muhajr said that] 'Mass conversion has very exact rules and if we make a mistake at the beginning, we may never [overcome] it. One mistake is to help the natives financially — if they expect this they are not pure in heart. Through love and happiness [the pioneers] make the Faith contagious to others.' He mentioned that 120 Bahá'ís came to a conference in Bolivia, many of them walking for four days to get there. Not one cent was spent for their travelling . . . 'Mass conversion is new and we don't have much experience; each country makes a contribution . . .

'Don't say to them that they should not drink, they will pass the word on to others and they will all run from us. Don't tell them anything that is against their customs.' He gave an example by explaining what had happened on the island where he and his wife pioneered earning the titles of Knights of Bahá'u'lláh. 'In the Mentawai Islands the Muslims explained their Faith by saying that they must pray five times a day in Arabic. They [the Mentawais] said, "All right, we will pray but you must translate the prayers into our language." But the Muslims refused. Then the Muslims told them that they must fast for thirty days a year and they replied, "But we eat every hour. How can we fast for thirty days, it would kill us!" Then the Muslims told them that they must be clean and not eat pork, but since pork is the only meat they had, they said, "What do you want to do? Starve us to death?" So they decided they would never want the Muslim Faith. The rules and laws of the Bahá'í Faith should be taught to them after years. We should learn the customs of the people and go along with them — don't fight them . . . We should teach all the people of the village at once and not just a few. It creates a separation between them and other members of the village, if we teach just a few they will not have enough knowledge to teach the others . . .

'There are a few rules for mass conversion. If we observe them we will have great success; if we do not it will be a loss for the Faith. Choose the most backward, isolated and primitive places. The method of teaching and accepting believers in the villages is not the same as in the cities. Teach them first of Bahá'u'lláh and nothing else. If they understand that He is a Messenger of God and love Him, that is enough to accept them as Bahá'ís; they don't need to know Administration or anything else . . . Don't make it too difficult for illiterates, don't be too exacting — the heart may be chilled and interest die out. Their education in the teachings, laws and precepts can be added to as the years go by. Even if they drink, go slowly trying to help them change . . . there is a difference between the civilized and primitive people. We can fool each other but we cannot fool them.

'[The pioneers and teachers] are not creating the capacity in these people, but help them to find their own capacity. Bahá'í teachers are like midwives, we help them to be born spiritually. We as teachers have to have conviction ourselves and faith, then we can inspire it in others . . . When we mention Bahá'u'lláh to someone, a connection is made between that soul and Bahá'u'lláh . . . In the beginning it was difficult for me to know how to teach them . . . In one place . . . the government and the Muslims decided to send 17 people to a village where all had become Bahá'ís, to try and get them to change their religion. They went with the police, government officials, etc. They said to the people, "Why do you listen to this man? He is a foreigner, and you are Indonesian." The villagers said, "No, our religion is Bahá'í, and our government is Bahá'í." We [teachers] don't know how they understand as they do, but it is there — the deep faith and understanding. The officials said, "He means harm to you, and he might kill you." They replied, "No, he doesn't even have a small knife, and you come to our village with police and soldiers with guns . . ."

'In one place, after some villagers had accepted the Faith, I suggested that they start a school. They said, "We will make it tomorrow." I didn't see how they could do that, as they needed wood that had been seasoned, which takes months. But the next morning they began arriving, each one with two planks of wood and with a hundred of them working on it, in two days the school was finished. When I asked where they had got the seasoned wood, they took me and showed me where each man had taken two planks out of his own house and brought them so that they could have the school right away! There was a Catholic priest in this place who had a school with 14 teachers and almost no

> students, while in a short while, the Bahá'ís had five schools and no teachers.
>
> 'In Bolivia, the Indians don't believe in obeying the government. The Bahá'ís [outright] told them they must obey the government and many villagers could not accept the Faith because of this emotional block. Some who accepted the Faith are now doubtful because of this. The mistake of a pioneer can halt the progress of the Cause for years. The Guardian said, bring them into the Faith and through the years teach them . . . do not put obstacles in the way of their coming in. DO NOT PUT OBSTACLES IN THE WAY OF THEIR COMING IN. Do not be rigid — be flexible. The direct method of teaching should be used, not the indirect . . . If it is done indirectly, suspicion is created as to why this is being done and also it is not an effective method for mass conversion. The Faith is like a beautiful girl; don't cover it with veils which have to be taken off one by one until its beauty is discovered.'

Raḥmat's encouraging visits to Ecuador caused a great change in the behaviour of the pioneers, and in the attitude of the National Assembly, which promptly convened a special meeting to study the places in the country best suited to the commencement of mass teaching. Ten provinces with the largest Indian populations were chosen, pioneers assigned and plans formulated. Ecuador was on its way to great victories. In 1961 Ecuador had a handful of indigenous believers. In April 1965, when Raḥmat went there a second time, there were more than 1000 new Bahá'ís.

On this trip he immediately took off for the villages of the North. He visited all the new believers, and assisted in the election of the local Assemblies of Juan Montalvo and San Roque. His joy knew no bounds when the delegates to the National Convention elected two indigenous members to the National Assembly. He had informed the friends that his sole purpose in going to Ecuador was to find ways to fulfil the goals of the Nine Year Plan, 'particularly those of mass teaching.'

In consultation with the National Assembly, the following goals were set: to increase the number of the believers to 5000 by April 1966; to form 60 Local Spiritual Assemblies; to establish a permanent teaching institute in Otavalo where the Indians could come regularly to be deepened. In the Convention he said that the most important task confronting the Bahá'ís of the world at that moment was to pursue mass conversion. He asked the National Assembly to consider purchasing a building to house the teaching institute. The National Assembly approved all his suggestions, and again teaching took a great leap forward. He encouraged the Bahá'í youth in the United States to pioneer to countries where mass teaching was underway. He directed many to Ecuador. Some who took his advice are still pioneers there.

As the years passed, those Bahá'ís who did not think mass conversion a viable teaching method started to change their minds. All were now participating in this wonderfully effective teaching crusade, which was bringing spectacular results. In July 1969 the National Assembly of Ecuador received a cable from the Counsellors of South America saying: HAND MUHAJIR CONVENING CONFERENCE AUXILIARIES REPRESENTATIVES FIVE NSAS QUITO AUGUST EIGHT ELEVEN . . . At the conference, Raḥmat stated that its purpose was 'for the participants to learn something about what is happening in mass conversion in other countries; the expansion of the Cause in indigenous areas, deepening and consolidation, and how to overcome obstacles.'

According to another account,

> . . . the participants found it interesting to observe Dr Muhájir's method of teaching during the week and his approach to accomplishing his wishes. He adroitly outlined the themes which he desired to discuss during the sessions, and, when feasible, he formed workshops. For example, he questioned the participants about the number of Negroes in the country and where they resided. Someone recalled that they used to live in and around Esmeraldas . . . Someone else remembered that there were some in the North of the country around Chota . . . There had been no efforts to contact the Negro minority in the country for a number of years.
>
> After this discussion, Dr Muhájir sent some of the attendants to borrow Ecuadorian history books from libraries and friends. Then he had them look up the minority groups in Ecuador and

> gather all the data possible about them, including where they were located . . . This was accomplished in a few days but no one understood why he wanted so much data nor exactly why he was having them 'go back to school, for what does this have to do with teaching?'

On the last night of the conference, Raḥmat explained that the Universal House of Justice wanted all the minority groups to be found and taught. There were large groups of black people in Ecuador and Peru, and he urged the Assemblies of those countries to devise plans to bring the Faith to them. As a result of this conference the National Assembly of Ecuador chose Esmeraldas for a special concerted teaching project. By December 1969 the pioneers in Esmeraldas, and the friends in other places with a black community, succeeded in bringing more than 1000 new believers under the banner of the Faith. Later, Hand of the Cause Enoch Olinga visited these areas and the friends responded to him with great love and enthusiasm.

Ecuador entered the vanguard of mass conversion. Other Hands of the Cause, including Amatu'l-Bahá Rúḥíyyih Khánum, visited that country and encouraged the friends to attain the goals of the Nine Year Plan one year ahead of time.

Raḥmat's next trip to Ecuador in 1972 was recorded as 'the most important highlight of the last year of the Nine Year Plan'.

> Whenever notice arrived of an impending visit from Dr Muhájir, excitement mounted, teaching projects and activities were reviewed, reports with ready answers were prepared, pioneers and teachers prepared themselves spiritually and mentally for a package of surprises from the much-loved Hand of the Cause who, inevitably, upon his arrival would happily unfold some new breathtaking plan of activity which would stagger the mind and challenge one's mental capacity to cope with it.

During this particular trip, Raḥmat emphasized mass conversion in the big cities. Till this time, effort had been concentrated in rural areas. He now sought to convince the friends that urban populations were ready and able to accept the teachings of Bahá'u'lláh and embrace His Cause.

With the Bahá'ís of Asuncion, Paraguay, December 1979.

Mendoza, Argentina, 12 December 1979.

I recall many meetings in different countries when he brought this matter to the attention of the friends. The reaction was usually one of total astonishment. One National Assembly member called it very 'un-Muhájir-like'! Raḥmat could not understand this kind of reaction. He believed that at the beginning of mass teaching, when many National Assemblies had not yet come into existence, there were not sufficient resources to teach in the urban areas, and pioneers, who were at the forefront of mass teaching, did not have the experience and assurance that mass conversion was possible in cities. He often stressed that the reason mass teaching had progressed only among the primitive and tribal people was not that the more sophisticated and educated people of the world would shun the Faith if presented to them, but that *we* were the ones who needed the experience and the courage. The Faith of Bahá'u'lláh was for the whole of humanity, and, if we hesitated, a golden opportunity would be lost.

He urged the friends not to forget the cities, and told the indigenous Bahá'ís that they were the ones to carry the message of Bahá'u'lláh to the urban dwellers in their regions.

> Dr Muhájir also stressed the need to teach the youth, especially the university students. He was somewhat impatient with the haggling about when the cities and universities could be reached, and observed that the morning had been spent on deciding whether to teach! He suggested a 40-day teaching project in the cities be devised with the goal being to reach professional and university people as well as others who might be interested in the streets and parks. He told the Convention about the initiation of this same type of project in Hong Kong with wonderful success.
>
> The education of children was another subject to which he gave much importance at this time. He asked for as many children's classes as possible, and asked the Esmeraldas pioneers to hold a conference for children later in the year. He told them, 'I hope that you become outstanding in the Bahá'í world for the teaching of children. There should be a book of statistics about the Bahá'í children in the whole country. The mothers must sing their children [to sleep] with Bahá'í songs, thereby educating the mother and the child. The best way to teach . . . is when they are

sleeping. If we sing to the children while they sleep and recite prayers, they will grow in knowledge. 'Abdu'l-Bahá said that if the indigenous people of America become educated in the Faith they will illumine the world. A plan for literacy should [begin] now. You should publish the literacy book that you have or request the ones which have been done in Colombia. This is the time to begin literacy training. With this the Faith will be proclaimed and we will deepen. The Negroes and the Indians should take the Faith to the white people.'

The National Assembly wholeheartedly agreed with all Raḥmat's suggestions. It 'set a goal to open 50 centres in the barrios [around Esmeraldas] with children's classes, deepening classes, weekly public meetings, Nineteen Day Feasts and to enrol 5000 new believers. There were ten children's classes held daily, six days a week, by the audacious, untiring pioneer Nooshin Eskandari. She performed a superhuman job in helping to prepare so many children for their new role as Bahá'í children.

Nooshin recalls that Raḥmat asked her to personally train 1000 children for the conference. Her pleas that such a task was impossible had no effect on him. He advised her never to say 'impossible' when working for the Faith. After the conference she complained to Raḥmat that no one had appreciated her hard work. Raḥmat just pushed her complaints aside and told her that if she had done it for Bahá'u'lláh she should not expect praise from others. He said to her, 'I never get praise from anyone, why should you?' He directed her to other activities and assured her that he would pray for her and that she should be certain that Bahá'u'lláh never forgets anyone's service to His Cause.

The children's conference, held in March 1972 was the first of its kind. It was a resounding success, with almost 1000 children from all over the country taking part.

As a result of Raḥmat's trip 'nearly a hundred children's classes were established throughout the country and a teaching campaign was launched in the city of Santo Domingo de los Colorados; although originally planned for 40 days, because of its success it was continued for two-and-a-half months.' Four hundred and seventy-five new believers embraced the Cause, including nine individuals from the Colorado tribe.'

By this time we had made our home in India, and Raḥmat often brought samples of teaching materials from Latin America. These were often translated into English, published and distributed throughout the world by the Indian Bahá'í Publishing Trust. His habit of choosing the best from each region and exporting it to other parts of the world was typical of him. Just as he encouraged the Latin American friends to copy the methods of Africa and India, he urged Asia and other parts of the world to follow in the footsteps of the friends in Latin America.

In August 1975, the Universal House of Justice informed the National Assembly of Ecuador of Raḥmat's forthcoming trip to their country:

> On this particular journey to Latin America Dr Muhájir hopes to be of service not only through consulting with National Assemblies in their work of the Plan but also by going into the rural areas in support of the teaching and deepening programmes and particularly reaching the Indians, Bush Negroes and other minority groups . . . The two Continental Board of Counsellors in Latin America will assist in the co-ordination of Dr Muhájir's travels and you will be able to consult the Counsellors in making plans or modifications of plans as may be called for in order that the very greatest use may be made of the services of this distinguished Bahá'í teacher and standard-bearer of the Cause.

Raḥmat's years of work in Ecuador were bearing fruit. He, however, wanted to be in the thick of it. He wanted to teach and be with the indigenous people as he had on his first trip to this area. He did not like the sophisticated plans made for him by the National Assemblies. He wanted to go back to the grassroots and leave the television interviews and meetings with Heads of State to others. This did not mean that he thought these things unimportant; simply that he was more interested in teaching, and being with the new believers. However, he did give interviews to national television, radio and the press, bringing great publicity to the Faith, and attracting many new souls.

As early as 1967 he had talked about having Bahá'í radio programmes. He asked several friends with experience in this field to write short pieces which could be used on radio. Like many of his suggestions, the idea of Bahá'í radio programmes — and of a Bahá'í community actually owning a radio station — was greeted with some degree of scepticism and resistance by many of the friends. I was present at one meeting where this subject was discussed, and can well remember our astonishment at his suggestion. This didn't deter Raḥmat. While he could see that we might not have the resources for such a venture at that time, he nevertheless urged us to be prepared for it. A day would come when the resources would be there and we would not be ready. He pursued this matter year after year and suggested it to many National Assemblies around the world, trying to convince them of its importance. Mrs Helen Hornby remembers one such occasion:

> I recall years ago when I was compiling *Lights of Guidance* he told me to get all the books of the Guardian's letters. He started with the earliest editions, looking up quotations on 'radio', and then he told me to use these quotations in my book so that the friends could see how the Guardian advocated the use of radio. I am ashamed to remember that soon I began to think that [they were] too monotonous and I finally decided no one would be interested in them, and did not finish the chore. A year or so later, when we were working so hard to own a radio station he asked me for the quotations which he had told me to compile — he had not found them in the compilation, so he knew I had not done it.
>
> Fortunately, the book had not yet been published, but when it finally went to press in English and Spanish there was a section on radio!

With Raḥmat's assistance, the National Assembly of Ecuador finally agreed to take up this challenge. The possibilities were thoroughly researched. Dean Stephens, an expert on radio communications, arrived in Quito and the result of this research was presented to the Universal House of Justice, which in May 1975 announced to the Bahá'í world, 'The Universal House of Justice has initiated a pilot project in Ecuador for the purchase and operation of a Bahá'í radio station, and at the present time this is the only one for which sufficient funds are available.' Radio Bahá'í Ecuador was born.

During his 1975 trip to Ecuador Raḥmat again sought to encourage the community to use the medium of radio to its full potential. He believed that with this powerful tool, the friends could bring in 10,000 new believers in one year. But he cautioned them that the use of radio by itself would not bring in the multitudes. He told them,

> Two-way communication is necessary . . . In India, in the attempt to help farmers, they discovered that one way communication, radio only, was useless. First they put up loud speakers in the villages, second they printed magazines based on the radio programmes and third they employed special people to go into the field to explain the radio programmes . . . Your aim should be 200,000 [Bahá'ís] . . . you can reach 200,000 with radio, but only if you have other means can you make them Bahá'ís.

The National Assembly decided not to have teachers supported by the Fund. This matter distressed Raḥmat greatly, and he asked them to refer to the instructions of the Guardian and the Universal House of Justice to see that full-time teachers were essential. As he travelled around the world he realized that many Assemblies had dispensed with the concept of Fund-supported travelling teachers. He heartily believed that mass teaching would suffer unless there were individuals who were able to devote all their time to teaching and deepening. Although many National Assemblies wanted to take this advice, lack of money was a great hindrance and in many mass conversion areas the result was a decrease in the teaching momentum which lasted for several years.

In Ecuador he reminded the friends that, 'the 40,000 Bahá'ís had not come through the local Assemblies, but through the work and devotion of the travelling teachers'. He stressed that,

> Decisions attract resources, not the other way around. Plan how to teach and deepen 200,000 people. Conceive the formula, help

> will come. Visualize them. Without vision you will go nowhere. We need to have a large renewal of mass conversion. I believe that every person is receptive and the ways are easy. A lot of prayer, a lot of literature and a lot of person-to-person teaching — and the radio.
>
> Don't look at your own power. Look at the power behind you. The pioneers should know the goals. They should be resourceful and be able to do everything, write articles, print them, organize and accompany some travelling teacher projects. Think that all the responsibility is theirs. They should be in every area, not in one only — high schools, towns, villages. Every Saturday and Sunday they should go somewhere. At midnight they should be writing, at four a.m. saying prayers. This is the way, 24 hours a day. Even when sleeping, dream what to do. If all do this, the work will go fast. Every moment have a new idea for teaching and put it into action.

The National Assembly of Ecuador rose to the occasion and reported to the Universal House of Justice that

> points were considered by the National Assembly in consultation with Dr Muhájir during his visit to Ecuador this month. Under his guidance, the Assembly adopted a new teaching plan aimed at a vast increase in the number of believers during the year, January '75 to January '76. Specifically, 11,000 new enrolments were projected . . .

Raḥmat visited as many villages as possible, and Counsellor Raul Pavon often went with him. The two had become close friends after Raḥmat's first visit in 1961 and Raul understood Raḥmat's vision. Raul himself was a visionary who had started mass conversion in Ecuador, and knew Raḥmat's proposals were feasible. The times they spent together were dear to Raḥmat. On his return from Ecuador he told me in detail about the work Raul was doing, and said how he wished each country had 'a Raul'. He often asked Raul to go to other parts of Latin America to help in mass conversion. Raul and Raḥmat were a team, and worked in perfect harmony.

Ecuador, the final destination. Being welcomed by the friends at Quito airport, 26 December 1979.

At the site of the Esmeraldas Institute, 27 December 1979.

Years of travel and separation from his family were now having a visible effect on Raḥmat, although he continued on the path he had chosen. Mrs Hornby remembers,

> Initially when Dr Muhájir would arrive in Ecuador, he would go to the Bahá'í Centre and talk for about an hour or less with the friends. Then he would accompany us home and he would go to bed and rest for an hour or more and thereafter he would start receiving the friends who wished to consult with him. It was around 1975 and 1976 when I noticed a drastic change in him which I could not understand . . . He told me that he did not wish to rest for there was no time . . . there is too much to do and not much time in which to do it, and I could hear him quietly saying the Greatest Name . . . He put us all to work as usual and he asked my husband and me to go to the South of the United States and help get mass conversion started there again. He made all the arrangements with the National Teaching Committee of the United States . . . I spent three or four months teaching in the South and South-West of the United States.

Raḥmat was more homesick than usual during this trip. Helen Hornby recalls how,

> He often talked about Gisu and wished he could be with his daughter and his wife. One of the pioneers and his wife had a little girl and, when they heard that Dr Muhájir was coming, they waited to name her until he arrived. When the father met him at the airport and asked him for a name. Without hesitation he said, 'Gisu, of course: Gisu.' And what a lovely child she turned out to be!

In April 1976, Raḥmat again visited Quito, the city which was to become his final resting place three years later. He was anxious for the friends to take advantage of their freedom to teach the Faith in that country.

> There is nothing more important in the Bahá'í Faith than consciousness — consciousness of our duties . . . Time will pass,

ages will pass. We should be conscious of opposition. We should be conscious that we are making history, conscious that we are going to change the world — going to change the direction.

We can change the world if we carry the Word of God to the people. Bahá'u'lláh said that His voice is in the world. His wish is here, His ideas, His power. But the people cannot hear. Bahá'u'lláh has a plan, a way to do it. We are the means. Shoghi Effendi said that when we are teaching, even in an inadequate way, Bahá'u'lláh will use this means. If we go out and teach He will speak . . .

When we talk to a person, Bahá'u'lláh inspires that person too. His questions and his change of heart are inspired by Bahá'u'lláh. That is the reason that we must give the other person a chance to speak.

We have the best chance on the planet. We are not the best Bahá'ís, but we have the best channel. Martyrs give their lives. Pioneering, teaching, is martyrdom. We must think: can I find an opportunity this year, can I teach 1000 people? I am sure God will answer.

As a result of this short visit, the National Assembly decided to start a teaching project in the province of Chimborazo, a difficult and sometimes dangerous area. In Raḥmat's diary there is a coloured, hand-drawn map of Ecuador with the date 3 April 1976. The names of the 20 provinces and the number of Bahá'ís are listed under the map and in bold blue ink he wrote, 'Chimborazo has been chosen for mass teaching.' He considered this the quintessence of his efforts in that country.

HIS RESTLESS SOUL

Raḥmat set foot in Ecuador for the last time on 26 December 1979, after a long and tiring journey throughout the Caribbean and Latin America. He had called me from Bolivia three days before, complaining of utter exhaustion. He had been unable to sleep well, and said that it was an effort just getting out of bed. I asked him to remain in La Paz for a few days to rest, and maybe seek some medical help. He agreed to do as I asked. However, his restless soul would not allow it. After three days, during which he had also visited Peru, he was with the friends in Ecuador.

He arrived in Quito, the same smiling and radiant man with whom the friends had become so familiar. No one was aware of anything wrong and, as usual, they planned the kind of schedule they knew he would demand of them.

> A host of friends were at the airport to receive him, including the Counsellors of South America, who were in Ecuador for one of their scheduled meetings. As an expression of love and appreciation, bouquets of red rose buds were presented to him in the name of the national Bahá'í community by two young girls, Najin Mansouri and Elizabeth Wilson Pavon, and by two indigenous believers, Auxiliary Board member Vicenta Anrango and National Assembly member Maria Perugachi . . . Then he presented them all to the two indigenous believers from Otavalo as a token of his love and esteem.
>
> He shook hands and embraced the friends saying 'Alláh'u'Abhá'. When he finished greeting the friends he jokingly said, 'Now I am sure I have said "Alláh'u'Abhá" 95 times for the day.'
>
> His schedule was hectic. He did not pause to rest after arriving as he usually did at this altitude. From the airport he was driven to a television interview . . . [and later to] a radio interview which was very successful. About six p.m. he was taken to the home of [Gretchen] and Kamran Mansuri where the Counsellors were meeting . . . The same night he spoke in Quito to the Bahá'í community, and afterwards had a brief interview with members of the National Spiritual Assembly about his proposed agenda and length of stay in the country. The following day, Thursday, he went to Esmeraldas.
>
> From the airport in Esmeraldas, he went directly to visit the new Bahá'í institute which was being erected and named in honour of the Hand of the Cause of God Enoch Olinga . . . In the afternoon he had three radio broadcasts, gave a fireside in the evening and did a television broadcast that night.
>
> He returned to Quito near midday, Friday 28 December, and continued his busy schedule, meeting in the afternoon with the

> Counsellors, Auxiliary Board members and the National Assembly. A pioneer conference had been called for Monday 31 December. The Hand of the Cause expressed the desire that the meeting be advanced to Saturday, and insisted that the active native teachers be invited as well.

The National Assembly had planned to increase the number of Bahá'ís in the areas which had been thought of as difficult and dangerous. This pleased Raḥmat greatly. Mass conversion had lost its early force; lack of full-time teachers and financial resources had hindered regular visits to mass teaching areas, and contact with many of the early believers had been lost. Raḥmat urged the National Assembly to make a heroic effort to find all the believers and to restart mass teaching and deepening. He also asked them to select a certain number of cities and target them for teaching on a large scale. He suggested: 'Start teaching in a Bahá'í home and invite contacts for firesides, and continue for ten consecutive nights, then rest one or two days. This should be followed by another ten nights of firesides in a different Bahá'í home, rest again for one or two days and start again in another Bahá'í home.' He asked them to continue in this manner for nine months, and thus obtain mass conversion in the cities. He then left the Assembly meeting to join the friends in the Ḥaẓíratu'l-Quds for a public meeting.

The following morning, Saturday 29 December, Raḥmat appeared happy, and did not seem tired at all. The Pioneer Conference opened that morning with prayers in various languages, then the Chairman of the National Assembly invited him to speak. He asked Counsellor Pavon to speak first, teasing him in Spanish during the talk. He spoke a few words, then asked Ma'súd Khamsí to take over. Raḥmat then quietly left the room, with a smile. None of the participants realized that he was unwell, or that this was the last time they would see him alive.

Chapter 9

THE OCEAN OF HIS MERCY

On 22 December 1979 Raḥmat called me from La Paz, Bolivia, and asked about Gisu, and how she was doing in college. He wanted me to call Faramarz Ettehadieh, and ask him to send $30,000 for the Bahá'í radio projects in Latin America. Raḥmat sounded very tired, and casually mentioned that he felt terrible: 'I have pain in my neck and shoulders. I can't sleep at night and I can't drag myself out of bed in the morning.' I asked whether he thought this was because of La Paz's high altitude. 'No', he said, 'it started when I heard about the demolition of the House of the Báb in Shíráz.' He was suffering from severe backache, which he was trying to alleviate by the use of poultices. He also told me that he was worried for Gisu and I, alone in America. My Iranian passport would expire in a few months, and he was certain that the embassy would not renew it. My US visa also had only a few months to run, and he didn't see how I could obtain another.

I tried to reassure him that the National Assembly of the United States would help us in every way possible, and told him that my big mistake was to insist that 'Muhájir' be added to my family name (Furútan) on my passport. Now I was on two blacklists! He seemed to cheer up a bit, and asked what he could bring us from Latin America. 'Bring your usual microscopic gold pins', I replied, 'but this time, bring a magnifying glass too!' We joked and bantered for a few more minutes, and he said he felt much better and would try to rest a while.

By 26 December, he had passed through Peru, gone to Quito, Ecuador, travelled to Esmeraldas by the sea-shore, and back to Quito. In Peru he had asked Jane Khamsí to take him shopping. He told her, 'I want to buy a gold pendant for Gisu and Írán. But first take me somewhere to buy a magnifying glass!'

The last entry in his notebook is for 25 December 1979:

> I arrived in Peru on the 23rd. Today I met with the National Assembly, the Teaching Committee and the Auxiliary Board members. 1980 should be the year of mass conversion in Peru. They should have ten days of firesides, together with proclamation of the Faith in the cities, through exhibitions in the parks and broadcasts on radio.

A few pages are filled with his thoughts about the situation of the Faith in Peru, and with statistics, names of teachers and pioneers. The last words are: TEACHING THE FAITH IS EASY. Three days later, in the midst of a teaching conference, and in the company of his greatly loved indigenous friends, he left this mortal world to join the Concourse on high.

HIS PASSING

On Saturday 29 December, while Gisu and I were planning our afternoon, the simple ring of the phone changed our lives forever. My father was on the line, asking whether we had any news from Raḥmat. I still can feel the strange and dreadful sinking of my heart. I was absolutely certain that something terrible must have happened. I replied that I had talked to Raḥmat just three days before, and asked if he had heard bad news. With some difficulty, my father replied that they had received a telegram that he was not well. I knew that Raḥmat would never allow anyone to cable the House of Justice simply because he was ill. I told my father that I just wanted to know when he had died. He replied, 'two hours ago'.

We were told later that news of Raḥmat's passing had been transmitted to the Universal House of Justice by the Counsellors of Latin America. There was some dilemma over how to inform us. The idea of informing the National Assembly of the United States to send a few emissaries from New York had been discarded as impractical. Amatu'l-Bahá had suggested that the best way would be for us to hear it from a family member, and the best person would be my father. This heavy burden was thus laid on my father's shoulders. He loved Raḥmat as a dear son, and his grief was no less than ours.

We had been in America only a few months. It was a Saturday, and there was no way to get to a bank. I did not have an American driver's licence and would be unable to cash a cheque without a licence or a credit card. The only thing I could do was to call Ramin Abrishamian, the son of an old friend of mine, and ask for help. He was at our door a few minutes later. Hearing the terrible news, he took charge. Gisu and I threw a few clothes into a suitcase, and were ready to leave for the airport.

The Iranian Revolution was in full fury. American hostages were the big issue of the moment. We had no visas for Ecuador. While we were getting ready, Ma'súd Khamsí called from Quito and assured me that there would be no trouble with our entry visa as they had arranged everything. Ramin had booked our seats and purchased tickets by phone, and would go with us to Miami.

Going to the airport, I felt as if I were dead. I could not comprehend what I was doing in a taxi, nor where I was going. It all seemed like a terrible hoax. Only when I looked at Gisu's grief-stricken face could I believe that what we were going through was actually happening.

We arrived, at dawn, in Quito airport, high in the mountains. It was cold, and the altitude made it difficult for us to breathe. The half-light of early morning and the unfamiliar surroundings made it all seem so strange and unreal. Ma'súd and Jane Khamsí, and Rufino (Raḥmat's beloved Indian friend), were waiting on the runway. We were taken directly to the Ḥaẓíratu'l-Quds, where the Bahá'ís were keeping a constant vigil over the closed coffin. Gisu and I were greeted with love and compassion by the indigenous friends, and were able to pray and say goodbye to our beloved in private.

We had to go through the necessary formalities of finding a place of internment, as the Bahá'ís did not own a cemetery, and other arrangements for the funeral. We finally chose 'Parques del Recuerdos', just a few minutes from the city of Quito. The minute we saw it, both Gisu and I were sure that it was the right place for Raḥmat to be buried. The beautiful, uncluttered cemetery is at the foot of a mountain, the lower half of which is veiled with lovely

The local Bahá'ís kept a prayerful vigil around Raḥmat's coffin until our arrival.

Parques del Recuerdos, on a hillside overlooking Quito. Fifteen plots mark Raḥmat's final resting place.

white houses. Tall green trees cover the rest. Small marble stones, with the names of the deceased, and the dates of their birth and death lie over the graves. Pots of flowers are placed at the head of each grave, and the whole area is covered with lush green grass.

We were then taken to the home of Mr Mansuri, and given the same room that Raḥmat had slept in the night before. His open suitcase was in the corner and his books on the bedside table. It was as if he had never left, and was still there with us.

Only then did we discover the circumstances leading to his heart attack. Auxiliary Board member Charles Hornby, and Mrs Helen Hornby, wrote their reports while we were there. These excerpts give a faithful impression of Raḥmat's last days:

> Never one to spare himself, Dr Muhájir's visits were usually crowded with activity, and, if not, he was inclined to be anxious to move on to his next stop. He was not averse to changing his plans or schedule at short notice. He would prolong his visit if opportunities presented themselves, or cut it short if it did not promise to be productive. This last visit to Ecuador was no exception. He was taken directly from the airport, Wednesday 26 December to Channel 8 Television to record an interview. Suspicious that the reporter would be inclined to ask about political conditions in Iran, Dr Muhájir was not comfortable with the situation. As the interview began, the lights went out. When they were restored and the interviewer began again, the power went off a second time, and taping was suspended for 'another day'. Channel 8 lost its chance to be the last to record the Hand of the Cause. He did then, however, have an interview for the national cultural radio.
>
> That night the Quito community held a reception for him. The theme of his talk was 'Unity'.
>
> It fell to Channel 6 of the coastal mass teaching city of Esmeraldas to make a video tape the next night, on which Dr Muhájir, at his own insistence, shared 23 minutes with Auxiliary Board members Jimmy Jensen and Charles Hornby . . . When the Hand arrived in Esmeraldas by plane on Thursday, after a visit to the new Enoch Olinga Institute, he admitted to being very

tired. There was only an hour for him to rest, before a continuous schedule until late at night.

The Hand of the Cause was disappointed that no meeting with the Bahá'ís had been arranged. To resolve conflict of scheduling with the TV interview, the unconventional time of 5.30 p.m. was set for a meeting, and between each of the three radio interviews between 3.30 p.m. and 5.15 p.m. the call was sent out over the airwaves for Bahá'ís and others to convene at the house of the Jensens to meet and hear the Hand of the Cause, so that on arrival at the house some friends had already gathered. Among them was Angel Jara who had considered himself a Bahá'í for ten years but had little contact with the Bahá'ís in recent years. In the interim he had become an outstanding announcer and Master of Ceremonies, having studied and worked with Radio Netherlands in Europe. Dr Muhájir invited him to participate in the television interview, and afterwards removed his necktie to give to Angel in remembrance of the occasion.

Angel got on the air by telephone connection, to invite people to the Bahá'í meeting. Before the evening was out Angel said that he would quit his radio station and collaborate with Radio Bahá'í in Otavalo. Another good prospect for the Faith as a consequence of the visit of the Hand of the Cause was that the owner of Radio Union offered free airtime every Sunday morning to the Bahá'í community.

There must have been 50 people crowded into the Jensen's little house. Dr Muhájir gave a warm loving talk, likening the body of mankind to the human anatomy, relating science and religion in a way that was educational as well as spiritual. Then he turned the meeting over to the Bahá'ís seated with the seekers, as he had been inclined to teach us to do by example for many years. Fifteen were enrolled before the meeting was adjourned for the visit to Channel 6. This was Thursday.

Auxiliary Board member Jimmy Jensen also shared with me his memories of Raḥmat's final hours:

En route from the airport to the Institute, we spoke about the teaching projects of last year around the Colombian border. He was very interested in that area, and said he was going to suggest a teaching project with the National Assemblies of Ecuador and Colombia. We told him that twice a plan had been made in honour of Hand of the Cause Olinga to conquer the northern part of the Province but for various reasons it was never put into practice, and nobody had listened. He said, 'Don't worry, I will listen to you.'

He admired the tranquillity and beauty of the Olinga Institute site, went inside one of the buildings, and said he wanted to chant the Prayer of Visitation of 'Abdu'l-Bahá in Arabic. Before he left, he suggested that we make a plan for Esmeraldas — a two-year plan and divide it into different stages. On Friday morning, all the way to the airport he talked about teaching.

On Saturday morning I sat beside him in the Bahá'í Centre. He told me that night in Esmeraldas that he'd had a dream that the Bahá'í temple of Esmeraldas will be built on our property near the highway. He said, 'Don't sell your land. Bahá'u'lláh will help you, but don't sell that land.' Then he said that he had met last night with the Counsellors and the NSA and they made a plan for nine months to enrol 4000 Bahá'ís in Esmeraldas. 'Follow this plan', he said, 'there are many Iranian pioneers, take them down to Esmeraldas to help with the campaign.'

By noon on Friday 28 December, Raḥmat was back in Quito, had bought a plane ticket to Venezuela, made a reservation for Cali, Colombia for the following Tuesday, and obtained a visa from the Venezuelan Consulate.

At lunch in Cumbaia, a little town where the Board of Counsellors was meeting, Raḥmat asked that a call be placed to the National Spiritual Assembly which was in session in Quito, to request a joint meeting with the Counsellors and the Auxiliary Board members for six p.m. that day, instead of Sunday, as had been planned. This was to be before a programme scheduled to begin at eight p.m.

Raḥmat had cut short his visits in Peru and Bolivia to arrive in time to meet with the Continental Board of Counsellors. At the joint meeting of the Institutions on Friday evening, Raḥmat expressed his opinion that the meeting with the pioneers on

Saturday would bear more fruit if a proper plan could be presented, and he insisted that the active native teachers be invited as well.

Dinner was forgone, the meeting convened, and plans drafted for teaching projects in a number of key cities in the country. He told Counsellor Raul Pavon, 'What would you think if I were to stay several more days. I would like to visit all of the teaching areas.'

The next year, 1980, was to be called 'The Year of Mass Conversion', and the goal was 10,000 new enrolments.

Saturday morning, at about ten a.m., the meeting with pioneers and native teachers was convened. The chairman of the National Assembly introduced Raḥmat and gave him the floor.

Raḥmat had talked for a few minutes in Spanish, then asked Counsellor Raul Pavon to speak. After a while he got up, and, in the words of one eyewitness: 'went out the front door of the Ḥaẓíratu'l-Quds, smiling as if he might have seen someone he wanted to greet.'

Ma'súd Khamsí, his long time friend and true brother, who was with him to the last minute and in whose arms he died, recalls how, after breakfast at the Mansuris' house, Raḥmat chanted the following prayer:

> O my Lord! Thou knowest that the people are encircled with pain and calamities and are environed with hardships and trouble. Every trial doth attack man and every dire adversity doth assail him like unto the assault of a serpent. There is no shelter and asylum for him except under the wing of Thy protection, preservation, guard and custody.
>
> O Thou the Merciful One! O my Lord! Make Thy protection my armour, Thy preservation my shield, humbleness before the door of Thy oneness my guard, and Thy custody and defence my fortress and my abode. Preserve me from the suggestions of self and desire, and guard me from every sickness, trial, difficulty and ordeal.
>
> Verily thou art the Protector, the Guardian, the Preserver, the Sufficer, and verily, Thou art the Merciful of the Most Merciful.[10]
>
> We then all went to the Bahá'í Centre to take part in the meeting of the pioneers. After a short talk Dr Muhájir left the room. The

> meeting continued. Suddenly Helen Hornby entered the room and asked for prayers for the Hand of the Cause. I rushed out and found him lying down on the caretaker's bed on his side with his head supported by his hand. He told me he had sharp pains in his heart and neck, and asked me to rub his neck while he rubbed his heart. I insisted on calling a doctor but he refused, so as not to alarm the friends, and as it was a Saturday we thought it better to take him to a nearby clinic. We walked quietly past the friends who were now gathered in the yard, got into the car, and Charles drove us to the Clinic Americana Adventista.
>
> The doctor asked Raḥmat about his condition and his speciality; he laughed, but did not answer. The doctor was preparing an injection and was rather anxious as he knew he was dealing with an important personage. Raḥmat patted him on the back and said, 'Don't be afraid. Death is nothing to be afraid of.' He himself adjusted the oxygen machine and inhaled some oxygen, which did not seem to help. His pain was becoming more excruciating and we sent for a heart specialist. After a few minutes he turned to me and said, ' Ma'súdján, I am fainting.' He repeated, 'Yá Bahá'u'l-Abha' several times. Those were his last words. He was gone from among us. It was 11.20 a.m., Saturday 29 December, 1979.

Less than an hour had passed from the time Raḥmat took ill till the moment he left this mortal world. It happened so fast that all were stunned by the enormity of the loss to the Bahá'í world. The Counsellors and Bahá'ís accompanied his body as it was taken to the Bahá'í Centre.

By special permit, the legal period within which the burial had to take place was extended to Monday, so that family members and other delegations could arrive. Bahá'ís from Brazil, Bolovia and Peru were able to obtain visas, and came to Quito. Bahá'ís from Colombia travelled all night to be there on Sunday morning.

In consultation with the Counsellors and the National Assembly, we prepared a befitting programme of prayers in Persian, Spanish and English. Charles Hornby recorded the scene:

The funeral service.

The friends walked in silent procession to pay their last respects to their beloved Hand of the Cause.

Amidst the spontaneous grief and desolation of the Bahá'ís, there was beauty and dignity. A profusion of multi-coloured flowers surrounded the casket in the Ḥaẓíratu'l-Quds; a giant red and white heart arrangement in the name of the Universal House of Justice, an exquisite floral blanket from the International Teaching Centre, red roses the full length of the casket from his wife and daughter, arrangements from the Continental Board of Counsellors, National Spiritual Assemblies, pioneers and friends in Ecuador, as well as dozens of several varieties of flowers from many other friends around the world.

There were prayers, some programmed, some spontaneous. Counsellor Khamsí chanted in Arabic the Prayer for the Dead. The cable from the Universal House of Justice was read as a fitting eulogy.

PROFOUNDLY LAMENT UNTIMELY PASSING IN QUITO ECUADOR BELOVED HAND CAUSE RAHMATULLAH MUHAJIR FOLLOWING HEART ATTACK COURSE HIS LATEST SOUTH AMERICAN TOUR STOP UNSTINTED UNRESTRAINED OUTPOURING OF PHYSICAL SPIRITUAL ENERGY BY ONE WHO OFFERED HIS ALL PATH SERVICE HAS NOW CEASED STOP POSTERITY WILL RECORD HIS DEVOTED SERVICES YOUTHFUL YEARS CRADLE FAITH HIS SUBSEQUENT UNIQUE EXPLOITS PIONEERING FIELD SOUTH-EAST ASIA WHERE HE WON ACCOLADE KNIGHTHOOD BAHAULLAH HIS CEASELESS EFFORTS OVER TWO DECADES SINCE HIS APPOINTMENT HAND CAUSE STIMULATING IN MANY LANDS EAST WEST PROCESS ENTRY BY TROOPS STOP FRIENDS ALL CONTINENTS WHO MOURN THIS TRAGIC LOSS NOW SUDDENLY DEPRIVED COLLABORATION ONE WHO ENDEARED HIMSELF TO THEM THROUGH HIS GENTLENESS HIS LUMINOUS PERSONALITY HIS EXEMPLARY UNFLAGGING ZEAL HIS CREATIVE ENTHUSIASTIC APPROACH TO FULFILMENT ASSIGNED GOALS STOP URGE FRIENDS EVERYWHERE HOLD MEMORIAL GATHERINGS BEFITTING HIS HIGH UNIQUE ACHIEVEMENTS STOP MAY HIS RADIANT SOUL ABHA KINGDOM REAP RICH HARVEST HIS DEDICATED SELF SACRIFICING SERVICES CAUSE GOD

> The friends lingered on quietly, with aching hearts full of love for the Hand of the Cause, as though reluctant to leave, and relinquish him to the next world.
>
> When Mrs Muhájir sat down, she and Rufino Gulavisi made a touching sight. This veteran indigenous teacher and Auxiliary Board member, a man so small of stature that his feet did not touch the ground as he sat on a chair beside her, his hand gently on her back, seemed as though he were consoling her in the name of the hundreds of thousands of indigenous believers all over the world whom Dr Muhájir loved so much.

Raḥmat was laid to rest in that exquisite spot, among the wonderful people he so loved, and who returned his love so. Three plots had been purchased at that time, which allowed the grave to be oriented to the East, facing the Qiblih. Directly opposite Raḥmat's grave was a statue of a Christian saint with open arms, eyes turned to heaven. I felt that this was a fitting monument to a disciple of Bahá'u'lláh, who had spent his whole life in obedience to his beloved Guardian, in humility, simplicity and utter abnegation of the material world.

To protect Raḥmat's grave from being trampled by those visiting other parts of the cemetry, I decided to purchase the surrounding twelve plots. It seemed as if this small patch of earth, surrounded by flowers, was all Raḥmat had ever needed of this material realm.

It was decided to continue with the teaching conference immediately after the funeral. One of the Counsellors, while weeping, announced the decision of the Counsellors and the National Assembly to call the conference 'The Muhájir Teaching Conference', and to plan for great victories all over Latin America. The more than 100 friends, who had gathered to mourn his passing, rejoiced in offering their services in his memory.

It was now left to Gisu and me to pack his suitcase and take it back with us. The suitcase contained a few shirts, one suit, a pair of trousers, books, and some other materials. His small black bag contained only his passport, $120, two small boxes containing little gold brooches from Bolivia and one single gold Persian coin. The money was donated to the National Assembly of Ecuador in Raḥmat's name.

His last effort on behalf of the Bahá'ís of Latin America was to seek help for the establishment of Bahá'í radio stations. The requested cheque of $30,000 arrived the day of his funeral. Dr Ettehadieh asked me to send it to the Universal House of Justice in Raḥmat's memory, to be used as he had stipulated.

The last photograph taken of Dr Muhájir, presenting the bouquet given to him to Auxiliary Board member Vicenta Anrango.

WORDS OF LOVE AND SYMPATHY

On our return to Boston, hundreds of letters and cables from every corner of the Bahá'í world were awaiting us. This outpouring of love and sympathy sustained us through the darkest period of our lives, which would otherwise have crushed our spirits under its enormous weight. It is not possible to quote from all those letters which were so gratefully received. I have chosen only a few from Hands of the Cause, from Counsellors, from National and local Spiritual Assemblies, to show how much Raḥmat was remembered with love and affection by his friends around the world.

'He spent his life, from his youth until the last hours, serving the Faith, and bringing the healing message of God to the whole world.'

FROM THE HANDS OF THE CAUSE OF GOD

SHOCKED TERRIBLE LOSS STOP SORROWFUL HEART ACHES SYMPATHY YOU PRECIOUS GISU STOP DEEPEST LOVE RUHIYYIH

OUR HEARTS OVERFLOW WITH GRIEF BUT RESIGNED TO GOD'S WILL STOP PRAYING YOU AND DEAR GISU WILL HELP EACH OTHER BEAR YOUR ANGUISH STOP YOUR CONTINUED SERVICES TO THE CAUSE WILL BRING JOY TO BELOVED RAHMAT'S HEART IN KINGDOM ON HIGH STOP FATHER AND MOTHER

. . . WITH FLAMING HEART HE INITIATED BLAZING TRAIL ALL CONTINENTS ISLANDS WORLD MARKED BY PRIVATIONS, GALLANTRY, PERSEVERANCE, DEDICATION AND DETACHMENT TO WIN MYRIAD SOULS TO GOD'S CAUSE AND LASTING NEARLY THREE DECADES WHICH MAY NEVER BE EQUALLED . . . DR AND MRS UGO GIACHERY

I share with you dear one, and your precious daughter, the grief over the passing of the Hand of the Cause of God Dr Raḥmatu'lláh Muhájir in Quito. He spent his life, from his youth until the last hours, serving the Faith, and bringing the healing message of God to the whole world. His pure soul is now with the Concourse on high.

I am sure that you are resigned to the Will of God: from the depths of my soul I supplicate the Abhá Beauty, that He may grant composure and tolerance to you, his loved ones.

Shu'á'u'lláh 'Alá'í

The light of my eyes, Írán Khánum,

Since hearing the news about Raḥmatján, my heart and soul have been with the two of you. How our hearts and our souls are burning: I cannot imagine what must be happening to you, to hear of the demise of that one who so brightened the meetings of the friends. I wish that I could offer my life for your bleeding heart, and for Gisuján. How she must be suffering, now that God's bounty [literally, 'Raḥmatu'lláh'] is no longer with you.

These days, due to my illness, I am forced to remain at home. When I heard the news, my first thought was with you and Gisuján. But in my agony I could not, and did not want to, write to you. I stayed silent, and suffered the pain of separation and the waves of sorrow. This was no ordinary death, of which we could say, 'May God elevate his soul', and then forget. This was the passing of a pure young soul to the Abhá Kingdom; a young man who suffered a lot, who went to so many places and left such heavenly traces. How many communities he brought to life, how many Bahá'í Centres he built for them, how many schools he established for them. He stirred everyone, and conquered their hearts.

In separation from that beautiful rose, their hearts would burn, until they saw him come to them over the hills and mountains. When they saw Raḥmat coming, what joy they felt. Who could know that his tender heart was in turmoil. They saw his radiant face, but did not know he was a man burning within.

God is my witness, when this horrible news reached us, we were so overwhelmed that I cannot describe it. Our first thoughts were for you and Gisu. How could Gisuján, who was so attached to him and so loved him, accept that she would never see Raḥmat again?

My dear Írán Khánum, my soul goes out to your aching heart. I want to sit in this corner of my room and write, to be able to show a fraction of the pain that I feel in my soul because of Raḥmat's death. 'Faizíján, how are you?' This was the first sentence that he would utter the minute he saw me. We would walk together, and Raḥmat would tell me about the enthusiasm of the friends, and each time he would plan some journey for me. 'Raḥmatján, my heart is not strong enough for me to even walk up a few steps,' I would tell him. How was I to know that his beautiful heart was even weaker than mine, and that he would soon flee to his Beloved?

The only consolation is that he is free from pain, from the burden of sorrow, from the troubles of the needy friends scattered over the deserts and mountains of far-off places. He is under the shelter of the Sadratu'l-Muntahá, and is consorting with the Concourse on high. We console ourselves that he is saying,'I wish every one could know where I am.'

So Írán Khánum, the beloved of my heart, to make Raḥmat happy and confident, we must uproot this extreme pain from our hearts, and must look to that heavenly realm which is his spiritual abode. He will feel content if you are healthy, and if Gisuján is less unhappy.

Since this news has reached me I have not been able to face Mr and Mrs Furútan. I will be unable to console them while I cannot extinguish the fire of my sorrow.

Raḥmat's smiling face, his concentration on teaching never-wavering, and his melodious voice while chanting prayers, attracted all hearts to him. How could he be forgotten? He is always with us, and with you. May God, in his bounty, protect your heart and soul in your far-off abode. I am sure Raḥmat's blessed soul is beside you.

With much love to you and Gisuján,
Faizí

My very precious Gisuján,

I have been ill in bed for six months. Today I felt a little better, and my soul and heart were attracted to Írán Khánum and to you.

The passing of that dearest, most precious, brilliant essence of detachment, Raḥmat, robbed me of my strength, but when I read the Writings of Bahá'u'lláh, I came to understand that after departure, our dear ones are always with us, and are even closer to us forever. This consoled me, and I immediately began to write this humble note.

It is now six months that I have been forced to stay at home. I can't go to the office. There is no more energy in me, and though I suffer because of the departure of dearest Raḥmat, I feel closer to him. Sometimes I hear his warm voice talking to me.

The more you make progress in your studies, and after them, in your services to the Cause, the nearer he will be, and the happier. Ever since they brought this news to me at home, my thoughts, my prayers and my love have all been directed to you and to Írán Khánum. I hope and pray that the sorrow of this event will not become an obstacle to your steady progress in your education. This would sadden our precious Raḥmat. Go on, and you will see that he takes more care of you and Írán Khánum from behind the golden Curtain where he now dwells.

Devotedly,
Faizí

DEEPLY MOURNED HEARTS BLEED SUDDEN PASSING BELOVED HANDCAUSE DR MUHAJIR STOP HELPLESS CONVEY DEEPEST LOVING SYMPATHY YOURSELVES ALL MEMBERS FAMILY STOP OURSELVES NEED MUCH BE CONSOLED STOP MAY BLESSED BEAUTY GRANT YOU ALL OF US PATIENCE STOP JAVIDDUKHT ZIKRULLAH KHADEM

Dearest Írán and Gisu,

The cable we sent you at the time of Raḥmat's passing conveyed the love and the sense of loss we all felt when the so very unexpected news came. We still feel an air of unreality about the loss of the two youngest Hands of the Cause within the space of three months, and undoubtedly the two of you must at times have the same feeling.

Unquestionably Raḥmat's reward in the Abhá Kingdom will be very great, far beyond our bounds to imagine. His life was one of complete devotion and dedication to the Cause, and I am sure that this single-minded dedication is what enabled him to accomplish so much in the path of service to the Faith. His life will indeed be an example for future generations to follow.

The two of you now face a future without him and this is very difficult. Our hearts go out to you in this hour of sorrow and you will continue to be in our thoughts and prayers.

Deepest love to you both,
Paul and Marjorie [Haney]

DEEPLY GRIEVED PASSING DEAREST RAHMATULLAH STOP PLANNING JOIN FRIENDS HAWAII MEMORIAL STOP WARMEST TENDEREST LOVE ALL STOP WILLIAM SEARS

Dear Írán,

Audrey and I send you and your precious Gisu our deepest sympathies in your great loss of your dear husband and father, Raḥmatu'lláh.

We can imagine how he will be missed by his many devoted friends and family members on this earth, but with what joy he will be received by the beloved Guardian and so many other dear ones in the next world.

We send you both our most loving greetings.

John A. Robarts

DISTRESSED NEWS PASSING DEAR RAHMAT STOP HIS ENERGETIC SERVICES ADMIRED . . . COLLIS FEATHERSTONE

My dear spiritual sister,

My heart and soul are immersed in sorrow from hearing the news of the passing of the beloved hand of the Cause of God Dr Muhájir. Ruhaniyyeh and I share in your immense grief and supplicate Bahá'u'lláh to grant you dear ones patience to bear this enormous loss. I pray that the two of you, his loved ones, will have great success in service to the Faith.

'Alí Muḥammad Varqá

FROM THE BAHÁ'Í WORLD CENTRE

MEMBERS OUR BODY HOLY LAND SEND YOU LOVING SYMPATHY TRAGIC LOSS OUR CO-WORKER DISTINGUISHED HANDCAUSE WHOSE GLOBAL SERVICES FAITH HE LOVED SO DEARLY WILL REMAIN HIS IMPERISHABLE MONUMENT STOP HOUSE JUSTICE ARRANGING MEMORIAL MEETING HOLY SHRINES TODAY DEEP-EST LOVE INTERNATIONAL TEACHING CENTRE

My dear Írán,

In a few minutes we shall be gathering in the holy Shrines in remembrance of Raḥmat. I think we are all stunned, as the whole Bahá'í world will be when it hears the news. Louise's and my thoughts turn continually to you and Gisu and our hearts go out to you. It is a terrible loss for you both, and you have already sacrificed so much. There is nothing that one can say that will ease the pain of separation now, but as the years go by I pray that you and Gisu will draw consolation from knowing that your sacrifice in doing without Raḥmat's presence during his travels all these years has enabled him to render to the Cause of God a unique service at a critical period in human history — a service which I am sure has enabled the Faith to advance in country after country at a rate that it could not have attained otherwise, and has helped to place it in a position where it can withstand the attacks that are beginning to be made upon it.

May Bahá'u'lláh comfort and strengthen you both.

With warmest love,
Ian and Louise [Semple]

DEAR RAHMAT TOOK FLIGHT ETERNAL REALM GLORY STOP YOU LOST LIFE COMPANION AND WE LOVING BROTHER STOP HIS INSPIRING LEGEND WILL ALWAYS INSPIRE US AND GENERATIONS TO COME STOP HEARTFELT SYMPATHY LOVE GISU YOURSELF STOP FATHEAZAMS

WITH BROKEN HEARTS OFFER CONDOLENCES TRAGIC LOSS BELOVED RAHMAT HIS RADIANT SOUL CLOSER TO YOU NOW THAN EVER LOVINGLY REMEMBERING YOU SHRINES VIOLETTE ALI NAKHJAVANI

Dear Írán and Gisu,

We must confront the unbelievable, that Raḥmat is no longer with us to galvanize our thinking, to brush away cobwebs of thought, to give us new faith at our powers and capacity to change the world into the Bahá'í rosegarden, and yet, knowing the truth, we have only to promise to regularly call to mind his example, his sweet voice chanting in the Shrine, his impatience with our slowness.

So we grieve with you, but we know too that his meteoric life will be emulated and be a model for numberless persons who will extend his vision, his powers, his great faith.

Our love to you both,
David and Meg [Ruhe]

FROM THE CONTINENTAL BOARDS OF COUNSELLORS

CENTRAL AND EAST AFRICA

DEEPLY STUNNED IMMEASURABLY GRIEVED SUDDEN PASSING BELOVED HAND CAUSE RAHMATULLAH MUHAJIR . . . LOSS TO AFRICA AND MASS TEACHING AREAS WORLD HIS EAGER IMAGINATIVE VISION IRREPLACEABLE STOP CONVEY HEARTFELT SYMPATHY HIS DEAR WIFE DAUGHTER

NORTH-EAST ASIA

WE HAVE NOT LOST OUR BELOVED HAND OF THE CAUSE BUT ALSO LOST OUR SPIRITUAL FATHER WHO GUIDED US DURING ALL PAST THIRTEEN YEARS OF OUR ESTABLISHMENT

CENTRAL AND EAST ASIA

DEEPLY GRIEVED UNTIMELY DEATH HAND CAUSE RAHMATULLAH MUHAJIR STOP CONVEY OUR HEARTFELT CONDOLENCES SUPREME BODY AND BEREAVED FAMILY STOP MAY HIS SOUL PROGRESS ABHA KINGDOM

SOUTH CENTRAL ASIA

IMPOSSIBLE EXPRESS GRIEF ALL INDIAN BAHAIS SHOCKING NEWS SUDDEN PASSING BELOVED DR MUHAJIR STOP HE WAS ESPECIALLY DEAR THIS SUBCONTINENT WHERE HIS LOVING ASSOCIATION FREQUENT VISITS CONSTANTLY INSPIRED

FRIENDS SERVE FAITH THEIR UTMOST CAPACITY STOP WE SHALL SADLY MISS HIS PRESENCE AND ALSO GUIDANCE FROM AFAR

SOUTHERN AFRICA

It is not necessary, we are sure, to express the depth of our sorrow over the passing to the Abhá Kingdom of your beloved husband, father . . . and our loving and inspiring friend . . . The friends in southern Africa, as we are sure all over the world, are grief-stricken by the news. Dr Muhájir has a special place in many hearts and the example of his indefatigable services to the Bahá'í world will remain a model and guiding torch for all to follow for many decades to come.

FROM NATIONAL SPIRITUAL ASSEMBLIES

ARGENTINA

SHOCKED DEATH BELOVED HAND GOD MUHAJIR STOP ARGENTINA BLESSED BY HIS PRESENCE IMPELLED NOW FULFIL HIS PLAN WHICH WILL BEAR HIS NAME STOP PLEASE TRANSMIT DEAR FAMILY OUR GRIEF FOR LOSS SO IRREPARABLE STOP WE ARE PRAYING PROGRESS HIS PRECIOUS SOUL

BAHRAIN

THE PASSING OF THE BELOVED HAND OF THE CAUSE OF GOD DR MUHAJIR WHO WAS A REMNANT OF THE ERA OF THE BELOVED GUARDIAN IMMERSED US IN DEEP SORROW AND GRIEF STOP HIS LOSS AT THIS SENSITIVE TIME WHEN THE WORLD IS IN NEED OF LOVE AND GENTLENESS BROUGHT IMMEASURABLE GRIEF TO THE BAHAI WORLD STOP WE OFFER OUR CONDOLENCES TO YOU AND HOPE THAT ALL OF US CAN BEAR THIS GREAT CALAMITY WITH RESIGNATION STOP WE SUPPLICATE HIS PURE SOUL TO AID US CARRY OUT THE COMMANDS OF THE UNIVERSAL HOUSE OF JUSTICE TO THE BEST OF OUR ABILITIES

BELGIUM

DOULOURESEMENT SURPRIS MORT SOUDAINE DOCEUR MUHAJIR PATAGEONS PEINE PEIONS DIEU VOUS ASSISTER MOMENTS PENIBLES IMPLORONS GRACE DIVINE ACHEMINEMENT AME FIDELE ROYAUME ABHA

BURMA

FILLED WITH DEEPEST SADNESS UNTIMELY PASSING BELOVED HAND CAUSE DR RAHMATULLAH MUHAJIR STOP MANY MEMORIAL GATHERINGS WITH TEARFUL FACES THE SAME AS YOUR FAMILY STOP WITH BROKEN HEARTS . . .

BURUNDI

DEEPLY GRIEVED DISTRESSING NEWS PASSING DEAR HAND CAUSE MUHAJIR FONDLY REMEMBERED HERE FOR HIS EXTREME KINDNESS WISE ADVICE

CANADA

DEEPLY GRIEVED LEARN SUDDEN PASSING BELOVED STANDARD BEARER RAHMATULLAH MUHAJIR WHOSE ASSISTANCE CANADIAN FRIENDS MID-POINT FIVE-YEAR PLAN AND LOVING ENCOURAGEMENT OUR WORK NATIVE PEOPLE CREATED HEART CANADIAN BELIEVERS INTENSE LOVE INSTITUTION HANDS AND ANIMATED ZEAL PURSUE MISSION ENTRUSTED US TABLETS DIVINE PLAN STOP WE SEND TENDEREST SYMPATHY YOUR TRAGIC LOSS AND ASSURE PRAYERS HIS SUPREME FELICITY ALL WORLDS

CHILE

OVERWHELMED PASSING BELOVED HAND MUHAJIR STOP PLEASE SEND OUR CONDOLENCES FAMILY

ECUADOR

Our Assembly and the believers of Ecuador wish to express their warmest condolences to you and your daughter Gisu in regard to the untimely death of the much beloved and respected hand of the Cause of God Dr Muhájir. He will always be with us in mind and spirit.

UNMATCHED SACRIFICIAL SERVICES CONSTANT INSPIRATION LOVING ENCOURAGEMENT CHIEF ARCHITECT MASS TEACHING VICTORIES...

FRANCE

GRIEF STRICKEN SUDDEN PASSING BELOVED HAND CAUSE MUHAJIR ABHA KINGDOM STOP FRENCH COMMUNITY, KNOWING HIS COURAGE, HIS FEARLESSNESS IN SERVICE CAUSE BAHAULLAH IS GRATEFUL HIS INFLUENCE DURING END FIVE YEAR PLAN IN FRANCE STOP FERVENTLY PRAYING PROGRESS HIS SOUL GODS KINGDOM STOP HOPE HIS CREATIVE DEVOTION AND DYNAMIC SERVICE PROVE AN EXAMPLE AND ENCOURAGEMENT FOR EACH BAHAI COMMUNITY

GERMANY

DEEPLY GRIEVED BY NEWS PASSING BELOVED HAND CAUSE RAHMATULLAH MUHAJIR GERMAN BAHAI COMMUNITY BEMOURNS LOSS UNCONQUERABLE HERO FAITH BAHAULLAH

HONG KONG

SHOCKED NEWS DEMISE BELOVED HANDCAUSE DR MUHAJIR STOP MEMORIAL MEETINGS HELD NATIONAL CENTRE MANY ATTENDED STOP CONVEY CONDOLENCES

INDIA

UNABLE EXPRESS SHOCK UNTIMELY PASSING DEAREST DR JAN STOP HE WILL BE SORELY MISSED BY EACH INDIAN BAHAI STOP PLEASE ACCEPT OUR HEARTFELT SINCERE SYMPATHIES YOUR IRREPARABLE LOSS STOP AT THIS JUNCTURE OUR THOUGHTS PRAYERS WITH YOU GISU LOVE ALL NATIONAL ASSEMBLY MEMBERS EVERY COUNSELLOR EACH BAHAI INDIA

DEEPLY GRIEVED NEWS PASSING PRECIOUS HAND CAUSE MUHAJIR EVER REVERED ENSHRINED HEARTS BELIEVERS INDIA UNMATCHED SACRIFICIAL SERVICES CONSTANT INSPIRATION LOVING ENCOURAGEMENT CHIEF ARCHITECT MASS TEACHING VICTORIES . . . DEEPEST SYMPATHY STOP AUXILIARY BOARD MEMBERS

IRAN

DEEPLY GRIEVED PASSING BELOVED DR MUHAJIR KINDLY CONVEY SINCERE CONDOLENCES SYMPATHY

ITALY

UNEXPECTED PASSING BELOVED HAND CAUSE RAHMATULLAH MUHAJIR CREATED DEEP SORROW OUR HEARTS STOP HIS LUMINOUS SOUL SHINES BRIGHTLY IN GALAXY BELOVED CHIEF STEWARDS, HIS SELF-SACRIFICING EXEMPLARY LIFE, HIS ENTHUSIASM SERVING CAUSE, HIS DETERMINATION ACHIEVING GOALS, HIS STIMULATING POWER INSPIRING THE FRIENDS, ARE DEEPLY ENGRAVED HEART EACH SINGLE ITALIAN BAHAI

JAMAICA

WITH SORROWFUL HEARTS SHARING GRIEF IRREPARABLE LOSS BELOVED HAND DR MUHAJIR

JAPAN

SHOCKED LEARNING UNTIMELY PASSING BELOVED HAND CAUSE OF GOD RAHMATULLAH MUHAJIR . . . BAHAIS JAPAN WHO ENJOYED HIS PRESENCE GUIDANCE ENCOURAGEMENT FULFILLING PLANS GOALS IN FOURTEEN TRIPS SINCE NINETEEN-SIXTY-ONE FEEL HIS PASSING A TRAGIC LOSS TO BAHAI WORLD STOP MAY GOD UPLIFT HIS RADIANT SOUL ABHA KINGDOM ASSIST HIS GLOBAL FRIENDS FULFILMENT ASSIGNED GOALS

KENYA

DEEPLY GRIEVED SADDENED SUDDEN PASSING BELOVED HAND CAUSE MUHAJIR STOP PLEASE ACCEPT LOVING CONDOLENCES ON BEHALF KENYA BAHAI COMMUNITY HIS UNTIRING SERVICES AND LOVING CONCERN DEEPLY APPRECIATED ENTIRE COMMUNITY . . . PLEASE CONVEY CONDOLENCES HIS BELOVED FAMILY

KUWAIT

HEARTS GRIEVED HEAVY LOSS SUDDEN PASSING DEARLY LOVED DR MUHAJIR STOP OFFERING PRAYERS AND SUPPLICATING PROGRESS SOUL CONCOURSE ON HIGH

MALAYSIA

ENTIRE BAHAI COMMUNITY PROFOUNDLY SHAKEN UNTIMELY PASSING MOST DEARLY LOVED HAND CAUSE MUHAJIR PERSONAL LOSS INNUMERABLE BELIEVERS MALAYSIA INDESCRIBABLE STOP EXTEND HEARTFELT CONDOLENCE YOU DEAR GISU

PAPUA NEW GUINEA

[We wish to] share with you, his family, our love and appreciation for the help and encouragement Dr Muhájir has been to Papua New Guinea. This was no better evidenced than the sorrow expressed by Bahá'ís living in remote villages throughout Papua New Guinea and by the countless prayers offered from the remote sections of Papua New Guinea for the progress of the soul of our beloved Hand of the Cause.

Our prayer is that countless souls will arise to carry on the vital teaching work in the same spirit as Dr Muhájir. Certainly they can be assured that he will be helping them from the next world.

PHILIPPINES

THE BROKEN HEARTED NATIONAL SPIRITUAL ASSEMBLY IN BEHALF WHOLE PHILIPPINES BAHAI COMMUNITY WISH TO CONVEY TO YOU AND DEAR GISU THE FEELING OF IRREPLACEABLE LOSS MOST PRECIOUS BELOVED DR MUHAJIR STOP HIS GENTLE GUIDING HAND MOULDED PHILIPPINE COMMUNITY TO WHAT IT IS TODAY STOP HIS NAME WILL FOREVER BE ASSOCIATED WITH THE RISE OF THE FAITH IN THESE ISLANDS STOP THIS LOSS WILL SURELY GALVANIZE ALL FRIENDS INTO GREATER SACRIFICIAL EFFORTS IN TEACHING WHICH ALONE CAN BRING JOY TO HIM STOP MAY WE BE GIVEN THE STRENGTH TO LIVE UP TO HIS EXPECTATIONS OF VICTORIES IN THESE ISLANDS STOP OUR LOVE AND PRAYERS ARE ALWAYS WITH YOU AND GISU

SAMOA

. . . Many of his travels were at great personal sacrifice to you and other members of his much loved family, but your example is a challenge to all of us. We want you to know how much we all personally admired him and how grateful we are for the assistance, inspiration and motivation which he gave us when our goals seemed impossible to achieve. He always made it so simple...We will all miss him very greatly, as we know you too will miss him, but because of him, we will never be the same.

SINGAPORE

ENTIRE COMMUNITY PROFOUNDLY SHAKEN NEWS PASSING BELOVED HAND R MUHAJIR STOP AS LOVING FATHER INSPIRED

LED MALAYSIAN COMMUNITY FROM INFANCY TO MATURITY STOP HIS COUNSEL, WISDOM, SENSE URGENCY, SPREAD HEALING WORDS AMONG WAITING MASSES CHERISH HEART EVERY BELIEVER

SOLOMON ISLANDS

DEEPLY DISTRESSED LEARN PASSING HAND CAUSE MUHAJIR STOP REMEMBER UNTIRING SERVICE RENDERED CAUSE HERE AROUND WORLD STOP CIRCULARS SENT ALL COMMUNITIES HOLD MEMORIAL MEETINGS PROGRESS HIS SOUL STOP CONVEY FAMILY DEEP SORROW SUCH LOSS BELOVED ONE

SRI LANKA

DEEPLY SHOCKED BEG AUGUST BODY CONVEY HEARTFELT CONDOLENCES REVERED HAND MUHAJIRS FAMILY OUR COMMUNITY'S GRIEF AT UNTIMELY PASSING VALIANT CHAMPION MASS CONVERSION

SWAZILAND

DEEPLY SHOCKED NEWS PASSING BELOVED HAND CAUSE DR MUHAJIR ACCEPT OUR HEARTFELT SYMPATHY SINCERE PRAYERS HIS PRECIOUS SOUL

SWITZERLAND

. . . His shining example, his deep knowledge of the Faith, his unique experience in teaching in most diverse areas in the world, reaching out to all walks of life, greatly assisted the Swiss Bahá'í community in grasping the need to bring the healing Message of Bahá'u'lláh to every stratum of the swiss population.

The Swiss believers will forever remember the example set by this radiant soul who, by his humility, his staunch determination, his detachment and total dedication has truly filled the high mandate of an 'expounder and protector' of Bahá'u'lláh's glorious Faith.

TANZANIA

DEEPLY GRIEVED LEARN UNTIMELY PASSING BELOVED HAND CAUSE DR RAHMATULLAH MUHAJIR IN QUITO ECUADOR STOP

OUR DEEPEST SYMPATHIES AND CONDOLENCES TO YOU AND MEMBERS FAMILY ENTIRE TANZANIAN BAHAI COMMUNITY JOIN YOU IN THIS HOUR OF DEEPEST GRIEF STOP WE RECALL HIS DEVOTION AND LOVING CARE OUR COMMUNITY PRAYING PROGRESS HIS BELOVED SPIRIT ABHA KINGDOM

TRINIDAD AND TOBAGO

GRIEVED TRAGIC PASSING HOC DR MUHAJIR STOP GRATEFUL FOR LIFE SELFLESS MERITORIOUS SERVICE CAUSE OF GOD AND HIGHER CALLING IN ABHA KINGDOM

TURKEY

GRIEVED PASSING HAND CAUSE RAHMATULLAH MUHAJIR PRAY PROGRESS HIS SOUL

UGANDA

OUR HEARTS CRUSHED WITH GRIEF REMEMBERING HIS TEACHING TRIPS UGANDA AND ASCENSION ANOTHER PILLAR OUR MIDST ONLY THREE MONTHS AGO STOP PLEASE ASSURE HIS FAMILY OUR HEARTFELT CONDOLENCES

UNITED KINGDOM

DEEPLY GRIEVED NEWS UNTIMELY PASSING BELOVED HAND-CAUSE RAHMATULLAH MUHAJIR STOP BESEECH LORD HOSTS ENABLE HIS NOBLE RADIANT SPIRIT CONTINUE INSPIRE BEREAVED CO-WORKERS FIELDS TEACHING ENTRY BY TROOPS

UNITED STATES

WITH SORROWFUL HEAVY HEARTS WE MOURN SUDDEN LOSS DISTINGUISHED ILLUSTRIOUS HAND CAUSE RAHMATULLAH MUHAJIR STOP HIS VAST EXPERIENCE TEACHING PIONEERING FIELDS GENEROUSLY SHARED WITH BAHAI COMMUNITIES THROUGH NORTH AMERICA STOP HIS NUMEROUS AND WELCOME VISITS THIS COMMUNITY CREATED NEW IMPETUS FOR ACHIEVEMENT EXPANSION CONSOLIDATION GOALS STOP ASSURE FAMILY, RELATIVES, FRIENDS PROFOUND LOVING SYMPATHY

FROM LOCAL SPIRITUAL ASSEMBLIES

YAZD, IRAN

This Assembly and all the friends of Yazd, grieve the passing of the beloved Hand of the Cause Dr Muhájir. We still remember the luminous face of that chosen Hand of God who with his talk in the Bahá'í Centre gave the friends such joy.

He achieved such loftiness in the service to the Faith that was the envy of one and all. His passing is an irreparable loss for the Bahá'í world.

This local Assembly, on behalf of all the friends in this region offer our condolences to that distinguished family and pray for the progress of his blessed soul.

BOMBAY, INDIA

CRUSHED HEARTS NUMBED MINDS STILLED TONGUES TEARFUL EYES TURN IN ANGUISH AND PRAYER THRESHOLD BAHAULLAH SEEKING FOR YOU AND PRECIOUS GISU SOLACE STRENGTH SUBMIT DECREE THAT CALLED FROM OUR MIDST BELOVED RAHMATULLAH WHOSE MEMORY SHALL REMAIN EVER GREEN IN INDIA AND BAHAI WORLD WHOSE PRAISES GENERATIONS SHALL SING WHOSE SELFLESS SERVICES GLORIOUS ACHIEVEMENTS ILLUMINED PAGES BAHAI HISTORY CHEERED BLESSED HEART BELOVED GUARDIAN WON ADMIRATION UNIVERSAL HOUSE OF JUSTICE WHOSE EXAMPLE INSPIRATION WILL GALVANIZE ALL CONTINENTS ARISE WIN FRESH VICTORIES BELOVED CAUSE

LOS ANGELES, UNITED STATES

BAHAIS LOS ANGELES COMMUNITY DEEPLY GRIEVED TRAGIC NEWS UNTIMELY PASSING HAND OF CAUSE MUHAJIR STOP EXTEND TO YOU OUR SINCERE SYMPATHY, LOVE, ASSURANCE OUR PRAYERS STOP SERVICES DR MUHAJIR RENDERED TEACHING WORK THIS AREA WILL LONG BE REMEMBERED

THOUSAND OAKS, UNITED STATES

The Bahá'í world has suffered a loss which can only be appreciated when one considers the immense service which Dr Muhájir performed in his lifetime. His devotion to the Cause, the encouragement he gave to so many Bahá'í communities , the seemingly endless energy he expended in carrying out his work, and the uncounted qualities he possessed combined themselves in a unique and mighty warrior of Bahá'u'lláh.

ADANA, TURKEY

WITH PROFOUNDEST SORROW . . . EXPRESS OUR SYMPATHY . . . HIS AFFLICTED FAMILY ON THE BITTER OCCASION OF THE ASCENSION OF BRAVE FAITHFUL SPIRITUAL HERO OF THE TIME BELOVED DR MUHAJIR AT A CRITICAL MOMENT WHEN HE WAS SO MUCH NEEDED

REMEMBERED AROUND THE WORLD

Memorial meetings were held in all Bahá'í temples, in most Bahá'í Centres, and in many local communities.

In their tributes, Raḥmat's friends wrote of his services, of the way he had helped them personally, and how he had made teaching and achieving the goals look so easy.

On the final day of the inauguration of the Bahá'í temple in India, 30 December 1986, a memorial meeting for Raḥmat was held, with 3000 of the friends attending. More than 1500 of these were Indian Bahá'ís, many of whom remembered seeing him in their villages. Amatu'l-Bahá Ruḥíyyih Khánum spoke in his memory:

> In my room in Haifa, in my bedroom, at the foot of my bed, I have a very, very beautiful photograph that I often look at. It's the heads of Muhájir and Enoch Olinga. I think it was taken when they were at a conference in Brazil. And these two heads of these youngest Hands are there, side by side. It's very beautiful. You know, we older Hands, we were so happy that we had these

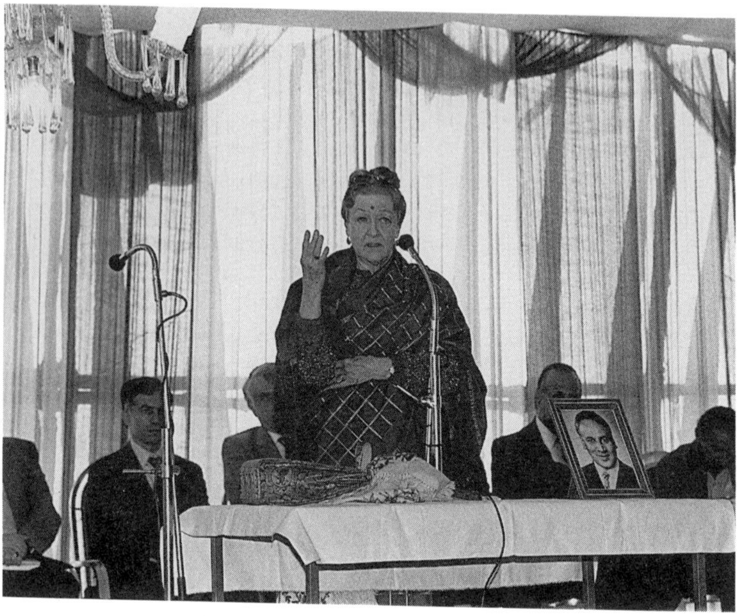

Amatu'l-Bahá Rúḥíyyih Kh̲ánum at the memorial service held in Raḥmat's honour during the Indian temple dedication, December 1986.

young Hands. This is one of the things that is so hard to bear and so hard to understand . . . these were the babies, you see. These were our two young Hands, and we were so happy, and we used to talk about the fact that when we are all dead, the Bahá'ís will have these two young Hands to go on with; they will be with them, they will be able to carry the spirit of the Guardian direcly to the friends for perhaps another whole generation. And then came this horrible shock and news of the murder of Enoch and of the sudden death of Muhájir. This was a tremendous loss to the Bahá'í world.

I think that it's no use mourning for people, friends. We have come here today very fortuitously to remember Raḥmat Muhájir in a country that he served with such devotion, in an age so associated with his pioneering and his services and his travels throughout the world to serve the Cause of God; but we remember him.

Now I think that if we love people like Raḥmat Muhájir — we say, 'What a wonderful man!' We all think he is so wonderful, we love him, we are sitting here, we are remembering him. What use is it? All right, maybe Muhájir is sitting looking at us with that beautiful smile — you know what an irresistable smile he had — and saying, 'Well, look at them all down there: what do they think they are doing? You see I'm perfectly happy; and what do they think they are doing?' Well, I know what he wants. He wants us to serve. He would never be presumptuous enough to say, 'Follow in my footsteps'. He was far too humble a man to say that. But I can say it. What is the use of all these things if we don't *do* what he did! If we don't serve! Enough words, enough platitudes, enough prayers, enough promises, enough postponements! If we *really* love souls like this, why don't we arise and follow in their footsteps?

You remember Bahá'u'lláh says: 'Let deeds, not words, be your adorning.' We've got enough words in the Bahá'í Faith — beautiful words. Words, words, words, words, words! My words: now I'm talking; what's more, so what? What good is that going to do the Cause of God unless I go out of this room and do something bodily, physically, displace myself, inconvenience myself, and do something for His Cause, something to help the Bahá'ís, something to encourage the Bahá'ís, something to bring new people into the Bahá'í Faith? What is it? Just a pretty speech up here, and a very memorable occasion? Is this our concept of religion? I don't think so. Maybe Raḥmat is guiding me to say these words, because I am sure that this is the spirit of Raḥmatu'lláh Muhájir. Work, work, work, work, until you drop dead!

Yan Kee Leong said, in the memorial meeting held in Malaysia,

His sudden passing brought tears of sadness to the Malaysian Bahá'ís. We were fortunate to be guided by Dr Muhájir, by his love, patience and wisdom. He trained and nursed this community to become the most active Bahá'í community, sending pioneers all over the world.

The early administrative order was put right gradually by Dr Muhájir and finally all pitfalls were removed and love and harmony set in.

He was the father of Malaysia. He was a father, an adviser, whose love and encouragement was beyond measure and description. We pray for his guidance always.

Counsellor Chellie Sundram wrote,

Malaysia first went into a state of spiritual lethargy and depression. Indeed the friends were paralysed mentally until it dawned on us that Hand Muhájir would be more versatile from up there than down here.

Hand Muhájir left us for good; and he took with him, as he always did, Malaysia's best pupil of Hand Muhájir, Imbum Chinniah. Only this time the technique for stirring up the Bahá'í communities was different, they are no longer physically present to prod, cajole, enthuse, and chide. This time each Bahá'í, serving in an institutional capacity, Bahá'ís whom the Hand knew individually by name, in one accord, have gone into a frenzy of Bahá'í activity.

Every Bahá'í who knew him, feels that from where he is now he can direct Bahá'í work in many countries and numerous situations at the same time.

Each of us could write books about him — the kindly little things that he did for all pioneers and all those who arose to serve in His Path, the totally unpredictable plans that he gave us for development of the Faith, the exemplary way that he showered love on all that came his way, his complete obedience to the Supreme Body at all times, his incredible ability to tap the divine source for strength and inspiration, his capacity to give love and receive love, all these and more made him a giant of a man and a great pioneer.

Counsellor Shanta Sudram added,

As far as I was concerned, Dr Muhájir did not live on this plane. Only his physical form was here, he was continually in orbit around the earth and he could see the whole world as one country and knew just who could help whom, and how, and when. He just told them, and they went.

He was so tactful. He would inspire the friends with his stories about other countries, and then he would smile his soft loving smile, and say that we in Malaysia could do much more. He would say it in such a sincere tone, and with so much conviction that we really believed we could. Then he would get the friends to give him data on which to base his plans, and he would multiply our figures about ten or twenty times and make us see how easy it was, if only we had faith. His faith just spilled over the friends. His love and his enthusiasm and his vision just opened our eyes and our horizons and we got caught up in his spell.

Then he would meet with the National Assembly and suggest, ever so gently and tactfully, that they draw up a plan. Before he left the country, he would see that the plan was set in motion. His timing was perfect. Each visit was different. He would tell us the same thing, but in a different way. The message was always to TEACH, TEACH, TEACH. Once it would be to teach in the islands, once to nearby areas, once to distant exciting lands, once by road, so the poorest could cycle or go by bus.

At one time he convinced us that the hearts of the villagers were pure and waiting and we should rush to them. On another visit he asked us, 'Where are the largest number of people found? Not scattered in little villages, but crowded in towns. So teach around you in the city and among the white collar people.'

Whatever suggestion he gave us, it was an idea whose time had come. That is how we spread out and out and out, and we have among the Malaysian friends a number of professionals, many teachers and office workers, Chinese, Indians and others, estate labourers who made history in South India, Chinese fishing villagers, schoolchildren, university students, Aslis from the interior. We have in fact a beautiful cross-section of people from all social strata, and all religious and ethnic backgrounds.

Without any doubt it was Dr Muhájir who made Malaysia what she is today.

Raḥmat had planned to be present in the Philippines National Convention in 1980. The National Assembly called that convention the 'Dr Muhájir Teaching Memorial', and cabled the Universal House of Justice:

> ADOPTING THEME 'DR MUHAJIR TEACHING MEMORIAL' ONE HUNDRED AND FIFTY-FIVE FRIENDS INCLUDING THIRTY-ONE DELEGATES BLESSED PRESENCE COUNSELLOR PAYMAN SEVEN AUXILIARY BOARD MEMBERS GATHERED SIXTEENTH NATIONAL CONVENTION . . . DELEGATES PRESENT INCLUDE MEMBER MANGYAN TRIBE WHOSE RADIANT SPIRIT GIVING GLIMPSE NEW WORLD ORDER STOP WITH MEMORIES DEPARTED HANDS PERMEATING CONVENTION URGENCY NAWRUZ MESSAGE PROMPTING NEW MATURITY CONSULTATION PHILIPPINE COMMUNITY DETERMINED ACHIEVE ALL GOALS FIRST TWO YEARS SEVEN YEAR PLAN NEXT NINE MONTHS AND TO ACCEPT ADDITIONAL RESPONSIBILITIES TO HELP FILL VOID TRAGIC LOSS RESOURCES CRADLE FAITH . . .

Neva Gomez Dulay, Chairman of the National Spiritual Assembly of the Philippines , said, 'Are you familiar with a water diviner? One who, with the aid of a stick, can tell if there is water underground? Dr Muhájir was a diviner of souls. He would get a map and point to a place, sure enough that place was where the receptive souls were and mass conversion started.'

Every community in India held meetings in his memory, where they shared their fond recollections. Mrs Boman said,

> The passing of Dr Muhájir was such a shock that for some time we did not believe it. He was a giant among the servants of God. At his passing we felt that the earth was giving way beneath our feet. His passing was a mystery. No one can say anything to add lustre to his great victories and accomplishments. We were all trained by him to move when there was a lull in our activities. All that we can do is to try and follow his guidance and advice. We so much miss him, but we should treasure his memory and be comforted with the knowledge that he is always with us and is praying for us.

Mr Vasudevan, the represetative of the National Spiritual Assembly of India said:

> The ocean of the Indian masses seemed to evoke a response in Dr Muhájir's heart and he longed to open the floodgates for their entry into the Cause of the Lord of Hosts. And how hard he tried!
>
> He felt very close to the National Assembly of India and however frail an instrument we were as a community for God's purpose for the masses, the magic of his presence unfailingly and ever rallied us. When he came, all our problems suddenly appeared petty and we now so much miss him. He had wanted Ḥaẓiratu'l-Quds in Leh in Ladakh in the extreme North, in Kanya Kumari the southernmost end, and in Kalimpong, the gateway to the North-East. God willing, we will achieve all these. He inspired contributions for the continuation of the South and East projects and then one afternoon he flew westwards and on to the Holy Land. Months later, he telephoned from [Bolivia] to ask for sending Nagarathnam to Trinidad for mass teaching. Then he asked 'How many Bahá'ís are there in India now?'
>
> He arranged the Plan and bade us farewell. May his soul in the Kingdom know just how much we love him.

At the memorial meeting held in the Wilmette Bahá'í temple, Judge James Nelson, Chairman of the National Spiritual Assembly of the United States, eulogized Raḥmat thus:

> Perhaps the most famous and effective billboard poster ever created in the United States is one in which 'Uncle Sam', the personification of the American republic, appears alone. He stands, hirsute and resplendent in tri-colour top hat and red, white and blue stripes, and stares, with his right index finger extended and pointing outward from the picture. His eyes make contact with your eyes. His finger follows you at every angle. The caption echoes the image, 'Uncle Sam Wants You!' Every military recruiting office has benefitted from this compelling portrait.

Dedication of Bahá'í Information Centre in Asuncion, Paraguay, in memory of Dr Muhájir, 21 April 1981.

This school in Bollilco, Chile is one of the many educational institutions founded in Raḥmat's name. Member of the Universal House of Justice Mr David Ruhe and Mrs Ruhe in attendance.

But the most effective recruiter the world has ever known was a recruiter for the Army of Bahá'u'lláh. A vibrant man with a charismatic voice, surrounded with the aura of irresistible authority. He was the Hand of the Cause of God, Raḥmatu'lláh Muhájir. Wherever in the world Dr Muhájir would appear, there could be no doubt in the mind of anyone who heard his call, 'Bahá'u'lláh wants YOU!' Bahá'ís everywhere would clear the decks for action at the mere suggestion that 'Dr Muhájir is coming.'

Many an American story of victory in the teaching field starts with, 'When I was with Dr Muhájir . . .'. Countless heroes of the Faith recount the beginning of their service as, 'Dr Muhájir asked me . . .'.

Such inspiration, such dynamism, such motivation are not removed from this world by the end of his physical presence. Indeed, the effect of his life is magnified in the efforts and remembrances of those who seek to emulate the champion. As a Standard Bearer of the Cause, he has taken the banner of Bahá'u'lláh to heights we must stretch to scale. We make that climb assured that from the Kingdom of Abhá he will forevermore spur us on; that we may invoke his name to call new generations to the Army of Light.

Enayat Rawhani, Secretary of the National Spiritual Assembly of the United Kingdom at the time of Raḥmat's passing, wrote the following:

No tongue or pen can adequately describe the lamentable and untimely loss of our dearly loved and greatly admired brother, the Hand of the Cause of God, Dr Raḥmatu'lláh Muhájir. The shining examples of his exemplary devotion have illumined the whole world. It can be truly said that no historian or scholar can as yet adequately trace his blessed footsteps in the path of service to Bahá'u'lláh. Those hearts which he inspired to serve he will continue to inspire. Those feet which he wore out in the path of service have now been transformed into mighty wings which enable his luminous and universal spirit to reach Bahá'u'lláh's loved ones without material fetters. Earth and heaven cannot

> frustrate nor slow down, even for a moment, his amazing urge to teach. In the arena of teaching, he remains the lion-hearted lover that offers his all and spares nothing. At the gate of God's grace his gracious hands offer the key which open the way for the promised entry by troops, the troops whose members owe a debt of eternal gratitude to his favours.

Ola Pawloska expressed the feelings of the Bahá'ís of Zaire:

> Everywhere he went, Dr Muhájir stressed the importance of the education of children. He asked friends to raise goats and chickens to establish a special fund for the education of their children. He also asked them to plant fruit trees around their houses and the Bahá'í Centres, stressing the food value of avocados, papayas, etc.
>
> Dr Muhájir was very practical. Once, when he arrived from London, it was very hot and he wanted to buy canvas shoes. [After a long search] we found a pair that fitted him. But they were *pink*! He did not mind at all and was very happy that he could wiggle his toes in them. He was wearing black trousers, a print shirt and pink shoes.
>
> He gave the impression of someone whose body was on this earth, but his spirit elsewhere. During these trips he had many dreams of the Báb, Bahá'u'lláh and 'Abdu'l-Bahá. It seemed as if he was never alone. His sustenance and strength came from a higher region. He was on this earth but not of it.

Barbara Sims wrote, on behalf of the National Spiritual Assembly of the Bahá'ís of Japan:

> Just to give a chronological account of Dr Muhájir's visits to this area does not begin to convey the impact of that Hand of the Cause. He gave us diferent concepts and ideas, which although sometimes seemingly simple, were basic truths about this area.
>
> He said our efforts must be ceaseless — go on and on. He reminded us that the Japanese are spiritually-minded people, and that we should never forget it and to teach according to their needs. Every time he met with our NSA he had a different kind

of 'theme' to propose. All of these focused on teaching, but on every occasion his approach would be different and offer a new challenge.

For example, he saw that travel-teaching was not as effective as pioneers settling and staying. He encouraged pioneers to come to Japan, scatter around the country and stay forever. With Dr Muhájir's encouragement, the pioneers would become the hub of activity and would produce lasting results. But he consistently emphasized that the Japanese believers must be given their chance for service to the Faith of Bahá'u'lláh, and as the Faith grew in Japan, he turned his loving attention more and more towards encouraging them.

Once, when talking to the National Assembly and Counsellors, he said that we should sacrifice life, prestige, and employment if necessary — but we did not need many to do that, just a few full-time people.

During the years that Dr Muhájir came to Japan, he became very close to some of the pioneers and the early Japanese believers. Sometimes he would give them personal guidance. These friends always took note of his special guidance — he was so perceptive and intuitive that he was almost always right.

Just to be around Dr Muhájir at different times was, in itself, a kind of spiritual education. For example, he was forceful, but extremely kind, and never let go of anyone even though the person was not functioning well as a Bahá'í. He was never critical in a negative way, but would correct the friends in a kindly and loving manner, if need arose. Sometimes Bahá'ís, pioneers especially, were going through hard times, materially and spiritually. He would take time to listen and give advice in his soft way. But his advice would change the lives of those individuals.

Most of his consultations were related to the area of teaching, but he always retained the personal touch, and considered each individual as a unique person. It was the individual effort that accomplished things in the Faith, so the individual was precious to him.

He had great humility, yet had the power to change individuals. By changing individuals, he was able to change vast areas of the Bahá'í world. Whatever we can write about Dr Muhájir is

> inadequate to describe his impact on the progress of the Faith in Japan.

On behalf of the French Bahá'ís, Salim Nounou had written,

> Hand of the Cause of God Dr Muhájir, motivated and inspired by the love and by the blessed words of our well-beloved Guardian — who knew and singled out his unique merits — has removed the words 'impossible' and 'impractical' from the service and propagation of our beloved Faith. Dr Muhájir will always be the example of courage, action, perseverance and dedication for future generations of Bahá'ís especially for the youth in every part of the world.

The final resting place of Dr Raḥmatu'lláh Muhájir, Hand of the Cause of God. This simple headstone is now a place of prayer and pilgrimage for many Bahá'ís who continue to seek inspiration from his spirit and example.

Many communities in different parts of the globe dedicated special teaching projects in Raḥmat's memory, all of which have resulted in great victories for the Faith. The National Spiritual Assemblies of the Philippines and of Malaysia both announced 'Muhájir Teaching Projects' in 1988, which gathered in hundreds of new believers in their urban areas.

Ecuador's *Ano Muhájir* — 'Muhájir Year' — in 1989, resulted in nearly 3000 new believers. At the inaugural conference, attended by friends from 14 Latin and North American countries, the message of the Universal House of Justice inspired the friends to win victories in Raḥmat's memory:

> As our hearts turn to your assemblage, we are moved to recall the remarkable spirit of Dr Muhájir, whose presence is surely felt by all of you gathered on this occasion.
>
> Dr Muhájir was a man of vision, who had an extraordinary ability to recognize the practical needs of the community, but he was also a man of action and his greatest dream was that the masses of humanity would soon awaken to the call of Bahá'u'lláh. He well understood that the greatest gift that Bahá'u'lláh has given us is the privilege to become instruments through which other souls are touched by His healing message. If we offer ourselves in the right manner, if we make selfless efforts, if we arise with love and with courage, then our services and sacrifices will be confirmed and many seeking souls will blossom before our eyes.
>
> Dr Muhájir has left a great legacy and by the grace of God his earthly remains repose in Latin America, in a land and amongst a people that he loved so much. We earnestly pray that the memory of his indomitable spirit will inspire all of those present at this international conference to arise and follow his noble example by offering enthusiastic service during the year-long teaching plan that has been dedicated to his memory.

In Chile, the Muhájir Teaching Project brought thousands into the Faith. In India, to commemorate the tenth anniversary of Raḥmat's passing, a one-year teaching plan was dedicated to his memory. The National Assembly reported that this plan, 'brought a renewed upsurge in our community in the field of mass teaching and mass consolidation. As a result, more than 48,000 have declared their Faith in Bahá'u'lláh, 72 new local Assemblies have been formed, and 83 new localities have been opened to the Faith.'

While he lived, Raḥmat eschewed all accolades. Had he been present to hear such fulsome praise from his friends, he certainly would have been embarrassed. He was not conscious of his sacrifice, and was just doing what he loved to do. He did not believe that he was giving up anything in the path of God. A few days before his passing, he told the friends in Quito that the mantle of 'Hand of the Cause' had been bestowed on him undeservedly by the grace of the beloved Guardian. Knighthood in the service of the Faith had been the result of his obedience to the Guardian, so if he was remembered at all, he would like it to be as a Knight of Bahá'u'lláh.

Chapter 10

TIME IS SHORT

A life of total dedication to the Faith of Bahá'u'lláh thus came to an end. The spirit and power of its example, however, did not. The Universal House of Justice wrote to an individual believer, distressed by Raḥmat's sudden and unexpected death:

> The passing of Hand of the Cause of God Dr Muhájir who spent all his days and nights in diffusing the teachings and strengthing the pillars of the Faith of God, and who was homeless in the Path of Bahá'u'lláh, has truly caused us all sorrow and grief. But these blessed beings, who in their mortal life have attained such servitude and nearness to the threshold of God, after their passing to the eternal realm, are endowed with a much greater power to assist the followers of Bahá'u'lláh.

There are so many stories about Raḥmat that it is impossible to give a complete acount of his life. How can we describe what moved and motivated him to sacrifice all he had to serve the Faith? We can only glimpse his personality, and describe those aspects of his life which might inspire those who would follow in his footsteps.

He started his Bahá'í activities at an early age, but the absolute immersion of his body and soul in the ocean of service to the Faith of Bahá'u'lláh began with his pilgrimage in 1953. The beloved Guardian's comments about the Ten Year Crusade encompassed his thoughts and his heart to such a degree that throughout his life he studied the Ten Year Crusade together with 'Abdu'l-Bahá's Divine Plan, making them the guidelines for all his endeavour.

His desire to carry out the Guardian's wishes burned so fiercely within his soul, that sometimes his friends and colleagues could not understand his single-minded devotion to teaching. Raḥmat was a very talented and capable man. Although his original inclination was to be a physicist and engineer, he chose to study medicine so that he could go pioneering, and became a brilliant physician in the process. His logical mind, if applied to business enterprise, would certainly have brought him great prosperity. However, all his natural business acumen was directed towards investments for the Faith of God. He shunned all the rewards of worldly wealth, position and fame, in pursuit of the goals of the Kingdom.

Raḥmat volunteered for pioneering at the age of 29, and, despite all odds, succeeded in going to one of the most difficult posts of the Plan, and, virtually single handedly, transformed that whole region. He always rushed towards teaching activities, and never waited to be invited. Although, except on two occasions, Raḥmat never bothered the Guardian by writing to him, he spent hours in prayer supplicating Bahá'u'lláh to make him worthy of service in His path. Whenever a word of praise from the beloved Guardian reached him, Raḥmat would be revitalised and exhilarated, but still he would chant the Tablet of Aḥmad, and beg Bahá'u'lláh to make him worthy of the Guardian's trust. He believed that service to Bahá'u'lláh was a privilege which one had to earn through toil and tribulation. He considered service to the Bahá'ís a great bounty, a belief he continually expressed in his frequent letters to the Universal House of Justice:

> This humble servant is unable to express his gratitude to the Universal House of Justice which has given me the opportunity to once more travel to Indonesia, and have the honour of visiting the dear pioneers and the spiritual peoples of that land.
>
> With absolute servitude, I offer my heartfelt gratitude for the bountiful cables of that Sacred Institution. Your constant remembrance of this humble servant in the holy Shrines is a life-giving source for the soul of this worthless servant.
>
> I am immensely grateful to that Sacred Body for its kindness and beseech you to continue your prayers for this journey and also for my family.

I am very happy that I could visit the beloved friends in Turkey and go to Izmir, Adana, Antakia, Ankara and other centres. In each place I met with many seekers and also with the National assembly. I had the same bounty in Switzerland, and Austria.

It was so wonderful that I could spend a few days with the friends of Tonga.

Bahjí, 1957. Raḥmat served temporarily as one of the nine Hands of the Cause who resided in the Holy Land after the passing of Shoghi Effendi.

TRAVELLING FOR THE LOVE OF BAHÁ'U'LLÁH

It would be wrong to think that Raḥmat loved to travel: it was his love for Bahá'u'lláh that made him forgo the comforts of home, and tolerate the heartache of separation from his family. The rigours of constant travel made him physically weak. The same young man who, before leaving for Indonesia, lifted weights and jogged to keep fit, complained at the age of 35 that he was getting old, and could not climb mountains anymore. Yet he continued to follow his life's calling with unwavering determination. There were times when he had to virtually drag himself to the airports or meetings. But drag himself he did. In his diary, he mentions being so worn out that he couldn't even open his suitcase. Sometimes when we arrived at hotel rooms he would just flop into a chair, without the energy to move. Other times he was so tired that he would sleep through even the most severe air turbulence on planes.

I recall one morning in New Delhi, when, after spending only two weeks at home after a long and wearisome journey in Africa, he had to embark on another trip, this time to the Pacific islands and Australia. His suitcase packed, we said our goodbyes and he left for the airport. Fifteen minutes later the doorbell rang. When I opened the door, Raḥmat was leaning against the wall, pale and shaking, with tears in his eyes. 'I cannot face another airport and another flight' he said. It took two weeks of care and rest before he could continue his work.

I don't believe anyone in the Bahá'í world understood just how strenuous Raḥmat's travels were. When they saw him in their own corner of the world, he would be smiling, enthusiastic, full of energy and new ideas. He never complained of tiredness, and sometimes kept going by snatching a few minutes' rest where and when he could — in taxis, buses and airport lounges. Perhaps the friends thought his fatigue was due to a few hours travelling, unaware that his journey had been going on for years rather than hours.

Extracts from the following letters to the Universal House of Justice give us some idea of the nature of his travels:

> If, in future, it is possible to send copies of letters from the Supreme Body to several Latin American countries, this will

ensure that I definitely receive them and so God forbid the instructions of that sacred Body will not be neglected.

I am at the Miami airport awaiting the plane to Belize. The programme of this servant is as follows:

July 14: Belize; *17:* Honduras; *20:* El Salvador; *23:* Nicaragua; *27:* Costa Rica; *31:* Panama.

August 4: Colombia; *14:* Venezuela; *16:* Colombia; *18:* Ecuador; *25:* Peru.

September 1: Bolivia; *15:* Argentina.

My journey in Latin America will end on 1 October, and then I will be free to travel to any other zone.

The major part of my travels in the Pacific Islands will end by 18 July. God willing, I will visit the Marianas, Marshall Islands and Hawaii after the conference in Japan. At most this will last until October. I do not know how to plan my programme after that.

During this trip, God willing, I will visit all the Bahá'í areas in Africa. In the North of Nigeria and in the Kalabar area there are hundreds of thousands of Bahá'ís. I will visit all those areas. I will go to the West of Cameroon and will spend one month in Zaire and will visit three of its major areas, Kisangani, Bukavu and Lumumbashi. I will also go to Kinshasa.

In South Africa I will spend 45 to 50 days visiting Bahá'ís and will journey to the mass teaching areas of Zambia, Botswana, and others and again will return to Tanzania, Kenya and Uganda, and, with God's confirmation, will visit most of their Bahá'í communities.

Raḥmat had to accustom himself to difficult travel conditions all over the world, not just developing countries. In Europe and America for example, delays would sometimes keep him at airports for hours. Once, in Frankfurt, he had to wait 12 hours for fog to clear. He took a shower at the airport facilities, washed his shirt and dried it under the hot-air hand drier. When all the passengers finally boarded the plane, he was the only one who was clean and fresh!

Although he was a seasoned traveller, he never could sleep well the night before a journey. This meant that, often for months at a time, he got very little proper rest. His last itinerary, for his journey through the Caribbean and South America, from October to December 1979, shows the kind of punishing schedule which he followed:

> *Monday 15 October:* Boston to Miami; *Wednesday 17:* Port au Prince; *Thursday 18:* Santo Domingo; *Saturday 20:* Managuez; *Sunday 21:* San Croix; *Tuesday 23:* St Martin; *Wednesday 24:* Antigua; *Friday 26:* Montserrat; *Saturday 27:* Antigua; *Sunday 28:* Guadeloupe; *Monday 29:* Martinique; *Wednesday 31:* St Lucia.
>
> *Friday 2 November:* Barbados; *Sunday 4:* St Vincent; *Tuesday 6:* Grenada; *Thursday 8:* Trinidad; *Monday 12:* Georgetown; *Saturday 17:* Paramaribo; *Tuesday 20:* Belem, Brazil; *Wednesday 21:* Natal; *Thursday 22:* Recife; *Saturday 24:* Salvador; *Tuesday 27:* Victoria; *Thursday 29:* Bello Horizonte.
>
> *Saturday 1 December:* Rio de Janeiro; *Sunday 2:* Sao Paulo; *Monday 3:* Asuncion; *Wednesday 5:* Resistancia; *Friday 7:* Cordoba; *Saturday 8:* Rosario; *Sunday 9*: Buenos Aires; *Monday 10:* Mendoza, Chile; *Tuesday 11:* Santiago; *Friday 14:* La Paz, Bolivia; *Saturday 15-22:* various cities and towns in interior Bolivia; *Sunday 23:* Lima, Peru; *Wednesday 26:* Quito, Ecuador; *Thursday 27:* Esmeraldas; *Friday 28:* Quito.

Raḥmat was always in a hurry. One of his familiar phrases — 'time is short' — changed to 'my time is short' in the last years of his life. There seemed to be a thunderous force in his soul which demolished all physical and emotional obstacles, and impelled him onwards in his chosen mission of teaching the Faith of Bahá'u'lláh to the masses.

NEVER A MOMENT'S REST

Occasionally, against his better judgement, Raḥmat was persuaded to plan for a few days rest and vacation. It never worked out. Once, after Raḥmat had been away for a particularly long time, we decided to take a vacation in Iran. Raḥmat went there from South America and we came from the Philippines to join him. After a few days with our relatives, we left for Bábulsar, a resort by the Caspian Sea. On the first day I decided to buy suntan lotion for Gisu, so we went to a store near the hotel. The owner, of course, just happened to be the Chairman of the local Assembly. He was delighted to see Raḥmat but rather offended that a Hand of the Cause of God had sneaked into his city without informing the LSA. We were told that the regional Summer School happened to be in Bábulsar that week. We were taken there directly. The programmes were put aside so that the friends could benefit from the presence of the Hand of the Cause. Our vacation had come to an abrupt end.

On the way back to our hotel in the afternoon, the Assembly Chairman handed Raḥmat a cable from the Universal House of Justice, stating that an emergency had arisen in an Asian country, and asking Raḥmat to go there as quickly as possible. We left for Ṭihrán the next day, and Raḥmat was off two days later.

On another occasion, after he had been away for months, the Universal House of Justice cabled Raḥmat to return home and take a vacation with his family. Unknown to him the friends in Cameroon had informed the House of Justice that Raḥmat was worn out, and that they feared for his health. I had no knowledge of those instructions until Raḥmat called me. He read me the cable over the phone, and asked whether I would object if he replied that he preferred to continue his travels in Africa, where he was in the middle of a teaching campaign. I readily gave my consent, as I was not aware of the background of that cable. So with my 'full agreement', he stayed in Africa for another four months.

Raḥmat always tried not to burden the friends, and bore their complaints about his tardiness arriving at some destinations with equanimity. He was sure that Bahá'u'lláh knew how difficult it was to make planes, trucks and buses run to schedule, so that the friends did not have to wait on him.

Conclave of the Hands, 1958.

Conclave of the Hands, 1961.

Summer School, Bábulsar, Iran, 1966. Vacations never seemed to work for us, so we gave up trying.

He gradually gave up the practice of informing communities in advance of his arrival, but this in turn created its own difficulties. He would arrive tired after a long journey, and have to find his own transportation into the city. Sometimes there was none. Usually Raḥmat wouldn't know the local language, and it could take him many frustrating hours, often in difficult weather, to find the friends. He would, however, rather bear this extra hardship than impose on the Bahá'ís.

He never thought about his own welfare and never discussed his health. Whenever I fussed over him or worried about the effects of his diabetes, he just laughed it off, and claimed that he had a strong constitution that nothing could erode. Malaria, and the rigours of constant travel, had taken their toll on him, but he never wanted to rest. Whenever a tooth required a lengthy course of treatment, he would simply ask the dentist to extract it. He said that he did not have time to spend on root canals and dental bridges. Our Bahá'í dentist in New York, who zealously wished to work on Raḥmat's teeth, abandoned his quest when he realized that he had only two days to accomplish his task.

Raḥmat relied totally on Bahá'u'lláh to take care of his health — as he did every other aspect of his life. When he found out that he had diabetes he asked me not to tell the friends. He took his medication regularly, but ignored his doctor's advice to rest and avoid stress. He said, 'I told the doctor that tiredness is part of me. I will tend to Bahá'u'lláh's work, and Bahá'u'lláh will tend to my health.'

FATHER AND FAMILY MAN

I have been asked why Raḥmat taxed himself to such limits. No one forced him to do what he did. Many times during the course of our lives together I asked him the same question. Raḥmat's only reply was that each Hand of the Cause had to choose how he or she served the Faith in the way that 'Abdu'l-Bahá had instructed them to do. 'The first duty of the Hands of the Cause of God is to diffuse the Divine fragrance.'[1] Raḥmat had chosen to obey these instructions in this manner, and he was determined to pursue his course, no matter the cost to him and his family.

I have also been asked how we, his family, fared during his long absences, and why he did not consider spending more time with us. It is true that our life was not easy. Gisu, in her early years, would cry for hours while gazing through the window and calling for her father each time he left. Often after these bouts of crying she would suffer a high fever which would last for days. As she grew up and understood what her father was trying to achieve, Gisu bore the grief of separation more calmly, though it was not any easier for her.

Once, in Manila, when Raḥmat had left and we were returning from the airport, one of the friends expressed great astonishment at my sorrow. She said that the Filipino friends believed that Persians had much less feeling than they, and cited the Muhájir family as an example. They had never seen us showing any emotion when we parted from each other. Seeing me shed tears at the airport was a revelation which caused the Filipinos to re-evaluate completely their understanding of the Persians.

These separations were not any easier on Raḥmat. Through all the years of his travels he yearned to be with his family, especially his daughter. Many friends all over the world tell how often he spoke longingly about Gisu and his wish to be with her. He tried to schedule his trips to enable him to be home on her birthday, and on important school events. Friends recall that he hurried through his schedule in Africa and the Pacific so that he could be in London for his daughter's high school graduation. She was the valedictorian, and he proudly told everyone about it.

In Miami, Farzin Davachi, his nephew, had taken him to see the famous musical film *The Sound of Music*. He remembers Raḥmat weeping throughout the movie. On return to the hotel his weeping continued uncontrollably. Suddenly, he told Farzin to help him pack his suitcase and take him to the airport. He was scheduled to go to Canada, but he said he couldn't take any more. He was going home to his family. The next day he was back in New Delhi with Gisu and I, much to our surprise and delight.

Raḥmat loved children, and always wanted them to be free to attend the meetings. He never allowed mothers to take children away or to scold them because they were disruptive. He thought deeply about the education of Bahá'í children all around the world, and wrote guidelines for committees on how to collect materials for

At Manila airport.

With Gisu at the entrance to the Shrine of the Báb, 1963.

this purpose. He said that the Bahá'í children were the future of the Faith, so their Bahá'í upbringing was of the utmost importance.

He was the same way with his own daughter. He never said a cross word to her or punished her. He said that as he saw his daughter so rarely, he would leave that task to her mother! Every time he left her he expressed his love for her and his satisfaction at her conduct. He would hug and kiss her and say, 'I will be back in the blink of an eye!' As the blink sometimes took months, he sent her books and stamps for her collection. Gisu received so many postcards from her father that they now make quite a prized collection. On his return he would bring Gisu a bagful of souvenirs which he would leave in the middle of the room and watch her explore.

Neither did he neglect Gisu's spiritual education. She still has the small cards on which Raḥmat wrote Bahá'í prayers and Hidden Words for her to memorize when she was very young. He sat with her and repeated the verses so often that he learned the English prayers faster than Gisu. She could recite the Long Obligatory Prayer long before she turned fifteen, one verse at a time, using Raḥmat's cards. Before leaving on a journey, Raḥmat would add one verse, and ask her to learn it before he returned.

Raḥmat would always say his own obligatory prayers where Gisu could hear him. He did not mind her talking to him and sitting on his lap. He said that she should realize that her parents performed the same prayers that she was asked to memorize. He would then go to a private room and repeat his prayers. When he was at home we always had sessions of family prayers when Gisu sat with us, said her prayers and listened to her father chanting. Gisu and I continued these sessions until he was back with us. Gradually, prayers became a part of Gisu's life which has remained with her.

In the Holy land, when Gisu was about three years old, Raḥmat would take her to the Shrines, stop at each door of the Shrine of the Báb and ask her to kiss the handle. He then took her to see the cypress trees marking the spot where Bahá'u'lláh pitched His tent on Mount Carmel.

There is a certain jasmine shrub in the northern garden of the Shrine of the Báb, where Raḥmat would take Gisu in the mornings. He would collect the buds that had fallen on the ground and place them in her palm. He told her to remember the sweet fragrance of the jasmine, and to think of that bush as her own. Every time Gisu visits the Holy Land, she goes to that same jasmine tree to collect the flowers fallen on the ground, and offer them at the Shrine of the Báb in her father's memory.

If ever there was real need for Raḥmat to be with us, or with his mother, he would immediately return, no matter how far away he was. He said he was so close to us that if things went wrong there was no need to call him: he would instinctively feel it and come home. While we were living in London, I was hit by a car and badly hurt. I told Gisu that this was the time to test her father's instincts. That same afternoon, Raḥmat called. His first words were 'Is something wrong?' He said he was in a telephone office in some remote corner of an African country. He had suddenly felt depressed and worried, and had insisted to be taken somewhere so that he could contact us.

Once, while visiting the villages in India, I suddenly became gravely ill with a kidney stone. The friends arranged to rush me back to New Delhi, and, without my knowledge, sent a cable to the Universal House of Justice asking them to inform Raḥmat of my illness. When we arrived in Delhi, to my great surprise, Raḥmat was home waiting for us. The message about my illness had not reached him. He said he was giving a talk in a meeting in Kenya when suddenly he felt he had to be home. He went directly to the hotel, packed his suitcase and boarded the first flight to Europe. In Rome he asked for the first plane to New Delhi. As there was no time to transfer his bag he told them to send it later, and caught the first flight out. His bag arrived a week later. He stayed with me until I was fully recovered before leaving on another journey.

He always prayed for his family, and asked others to do the same. Friends recall that on his last visit to Antigua, while at lunch with a large group of Bahá'ís he 'suddenly announced to every one that he had a wife and daughter in Boston. His face was full of joy as he said this. He said that his daughter was attending Harvard University, and took a photograph of her from his wallet. Everyone asked to see it, and commented on her beauty. He bowed his head and said, "She is so young, with so much life ahead of her. Please pray for her. Please pray for my daughter. The only thing I would ask of you is

Bahjí, 1967 with Gisu and Mr Samandarí.

Together in Bahjí, 1975.

that you pray for my daughter."' Raḥmat told me that the whole time that he was away he prayed for us, and every night chanted the Tablet of Aḥmad for our protection.

My love for him also influenced the way we led our lives. I never dreamt of asking Raḥmat to stay home just to take care of Gisu and me. This did not mean that I always submitted cheerfully to all the trials of life. There were many times that I complained and wept, and declared that I could not possibly continue without more help from him. However, when it came to the crunch, I could not ask him to give up his chosen path of service. I too had been brought up to put the interests of the Faith before my own.

Amatu'l-Bahá's words in her beautiful letter of condolence to Gisu and me are the best answer to the question why Raḥmat did what he did and why we, his family, consented to it: 'Would it have been a better life — and above all a better life to make a foundation for an eternal life — for you three to live sedately in some place while Raḥmat was a hospital doctor or a general practitioner being awakened up at night sometimes and usually eating two meals at home? And with all its peculiarities and heartache, was not this a far better life? So much victory, so much undying fame. My own belief is (having had a very blessed and very tragic life) that although God gives us bounties, we pay on the dotted line for what we get.'

Difficult travelling conditions — such as extremes of climate, and unreliable or primitive transport — were not the only problems of Raḥmat's itinerant lifestyle. It was a lonely existence, involving constant struggle agaist the pain of separation from his family and friends. Compounded by fatigue, such emotional tests had to be overcome daily with the help of faith and prayer, so that he could have the strength to face the problems that each community asked him to solve.

DETACHMENT AND GENEROSITY

Raḥmat always exercised strict economy over his travel expenditure. His journeys were planned with the greatest attention to the cost of tickets. He would sit for hours with a travel agent and re-arrange his planned itinerary so that he could include as many places as possible within the permitted mileage. He was so familiar with geography, and so skilled in arranging tickets that no agent was a match for him. A friend remembers Raḥmat spending almost a whole morning trying to reduce the price of a ticket. Finally, when he thought the price had come down enough, he quickly stood up and bade farewell to the agent.

In a letter to the Universal House of Justice he wrote, 'If that sacred Body sends me a cable to apprise me of what it wishes for the remaining months of the year I will try to arrange it so that utmost economy will be made in the purchase of tickets.'

Raḥmat's sense of economy extended to his choice of hotels and meals. He always stayed at the least expensive hotels, and, when not eating his staple of bread and cheese, ate at inexpensive restaurants. Friends in Malaysia remember him eating at a cafeteria which usually catered to the airport workers, as it had good food and was very cheap. Raḥmat often invited them to eat with him at roadside stalls.

A hotel receipt from Kowloon Hotel in Kuala Lumpur for 1972 shows that he had paid the equivalent of US$ 14.56 for three nights, including food and coffee and sweets for his guests. Another friend recalls, 'In Singapore, since the hotel price was high he decided to do something about it. He was finally able to get a 25 per cent discount and then left to have dinner with us at one of the roadside Chinese stalls.'

Despite Raḥmat's frugality during his travels, he was very generous with his personal possessions. He'd had this quality since his early youth. Friends remember him, at the age of 14, giving away his brand new Naw-Rúz coat to a peddler who didn't have one. He gave away his belongings so readily that it almost seemed as if he loathed material wealth. He was not a shabby dresser; in fact he always appeared smart and well groomed. However, he never had more than two suits at any time. Whenever I urged him to buy a new one, he would reply, 'But my suits are perfectly good.' I had to force him to buy new clothes. In our years together I bought him dozens of famous name brand pens, which he promptly gave away. He was always seen with a cheap ballpoint pen. He disposed of so many good watches that we finally gave up buying them for him.

Farzin Davachi, Raḥmat's nephew, remembers that when they were travelling in Zaire, Raḥmat had asked the Bahá'ís to gather for dawn prayers. He woke Farzin while it was still dark, and they went to the small thatched hut which was the village Bahá'í Centre. Though no one was there, Raḥmat was not bothered. He asked Farzin to start the prayers. After a while, getting tired and hungry, Farzin wanted to leave. Raḥmat kept him there and gradually the villagers started to gather. The meeting continued the whole day. Farzin finally asked him what the time was, but his uncle had no watch. Farzin thought that he had finally solved the problem of Raḥmat's early morning vigils: it was because he had no watch. So he offered him his watch. Raḥmat declined, and said, 'When you are here you have to be like these people. Time has no meaning here. Relax. Your problem is that you *have* a watch!' Astonished, Farzin asked, 'But uncle, how do you know how to get to the airports on time?' 'I go very early!' Raḥmat replied.

During the last year of his life, Raḥmat did carry a small inexpensive pocket watch. His conception of the function of a watch was that it should tell the time, not display the name of its manufacturer. When he died, this watch was among his few personal possessions. He gave away so many Bahá'í rings that I finally decided to have my name engraved inside a new one I ordered for him, in the mistaken belief that he would surely not give that one away. Someone in Europe is now in possession of a Bahá'í ring with my name engraved on it!

Raḥmat was a lover of music, especially western classical music, and would spend hours listening to it when he travelled, so we gave him cassette players and tapes to take with him. A friend has related that once, in his hotel, Raḥmat played a tape of his own chants of prayers for him to listen to: 'As it ended, I asked him whether I could have the tape. Dr Muhájir gave the cassette to me. I did not have a tape recorder, and stood there with the tape in my hand. Dr Muhájir laughed, "Are you not going to take my tape recorder as well?" He gave me the tape recorder and said, "I knew this wouldn't last long!"' Another friend relates that, 'When I offered to give him a Malachite necklace for Gisu, he refused and said he had taken one for her on his last trip. He never accepted gifts, as they added to the weight of his luggage. Even when we prepared food for him to take on his trips he would take a small portion and give the rest away.' The little money he had, he gave away freely to whoever was in need, but if someone had given him an amount to be used at his discretion for Bahá'í purposes, Raḥmat was very careful that it went to a genuinely worthy cause.

RELATIONS WITH HANDS OF THE CAUSE

Raḥmat was very much a man of the people, at ease with everyone: young and old, educated and uneducated, rich and poor. He approached people with such disarming friendliness that they immediately warmed to him, and many regarded him as their special friend. His relationship with fellow Hands of the Cause was very special. Raḥmat and Enoch Olinga being the youngest (34 and 33 respectively when appointed), were greatly loved by the older generation of Hands. Aware that he had been denied the guidance of his beloved Shoghi Effendi after his appointment, the other hands treated Raḥmat with special kindness.

Amatu'l-Bahá's relationship with Raḥmat is best expressed in her own words:

> You know how dear Raḥmat was to me since that first conclave, when, after all our deliberations were over, I asked him at the dinner I invited the Hands to, here in the Master's House, to sit by me and tell me about his pioneering in Mentawai and what it was like there. I only knew him by reputation and how much the beloved Guardian admired his services there. He talked about the native people, tattooed and naked in their tropical jungle, and I asked him what he told them, did he tell them to "cover their nakedness"? He said, " No, I did not go there to tell them what to do but to tell them about Bahá'u'lláh." That was when he won my heart completely."
>
> Hand of the Cause Amelia Collins loved Raḥmat as if he were her own son. Whenever he visited the Holy Land during her lifetime, she would invite him to call on her in her room in the House of 'Abdu'l-Bahá. Frail and elderly, and often in great pain, she would sit in her armchair, smile and say, 'Raḥmat'ulláh, tell me about your adventures.' When I brought Gisu to Haifa for the first time, Mrs Collins asked me to take our daughter to her. She put her hand on her head and kissed her.

'She is a lucky child,' she said, 'Her father serves Bahá'u'lláh all the time.' Then she pointed to an envelope on the mantlepiece and said, 'As you see I cannot go to buy a gift for the baby, please buy something for her from me. I will always pray for both of you.'

Hands of the Cause Agnes Alexander and Ṭarázu'lláh Samandarí were both in their early eighties; more than twice Raḥmat's age. Raḥmat cared for them and helped them in any way he could, suggesting programmes of travel for them to the Universal House of Justice. This was not always good news to the two Hands. Once, Mr Samandarí, while laughing told me, 'Raḥmat thinks everyone can climb mountains like him. He is planning a trip for me that is fit for a 20-year old.' However, Raḥmat was not deterred. He took Mr Samandarí's head in his arms and said, 'Samandaríján, you are 20-years old. You have Bahá'u'lláh with you.' They continued to bargain until they reached a mutually acceptable agreement.

Raḥmat loved Mr Samandarí dearly. While the elder Hand was in our home in the Phillipines, Raḥmat served him like an obedient son. When Mr Samandarí took a bath Raḥmat would check on him several times, help him to bathe, dry him, and bring him cold drinks in his room while he rested. In the evenings he would massage Mr Samandarí's legs and back, sometimes for nearly an hour, while they talked about the affairs of the Faith and discussed their plans. Although he had programmes in different parts of the world, he cancelled all of them because Mr Samandarí asked him to be in Manila during his stay.

Raḥmat often joked with Mr Samandarí, to my great distress; but Mr Samandarí enjoyed it. On one occasion he had taken Mr Samandarí to a tailor for a new coat. Unfortunately, the tailor ruined the material, but Raḥmat took the coat and told Mr Samandarí not to worry as he was going to sew it himself. Mr Samandarí took him up on it, and for a few hours our house rocked with laughter as we watched Raḥmat's efforts. The result was a complete disaster, but it lightened Mr Samandarí's heart.

In his numerous letters to Raḥmat, Mr Samandarí called him 'My beloved esteemed Hand of the Cause'. The day before he died he repeatedly asked where Raḥmat was. The next day

With Mr Samandarí in Manila.

With Miss Agnes Alexander.

Raḥmat arrived from Palermo and went directly to the hospital. He sat by the bed and they conversed for some time. Mr Samandarí asked him to chant prayers. Raḥmat was with his beloved Samandarí to the end, and was one of the pall bearers at his funeral.

Miss Alexander called Raḥmat her son, and, though a very strong-minded and independent lady, allowed him to plan her travels and to hold her hand while she walked. She wrote him loving notes and always accepted his suggestions about Japan and Korea, which were her specific areas of service. When she had a fall and broke her hip, Raḥmat asked Ruth Walbridge, an American pioneer to Manila who was a nurse, to transfer her pioneering post to Tokyo in order to take care of Miss Alexander. Ruth agreed, and became Miss Alexander's nurse and constant companion until a few weeks before she departed this world. In the last weeks of her life, before her final voyage to Honolulu, Miss Alexander asked Raḥmat to come and spend some time with her, which he gladly did.

Raḥmat's relationship with my father, Hand of the Cause Mr Furútan, was a close and cordial one which went beyond simply that of son- and father-in-law. On many occasions he urged my father to travel to various regions of the world, and accompanied him in India and North Asia. He treated my father as a senior Hand and always showed special courtesy to him. Their mutual love was apparent to all who saw them together. My father had known Raḥmat as a child, since the days that he was the principal of the Tarbíyyát School in Iran, where Raḥmat was a student. In later years we were neighbours, and Raḥmat brought seekers to my father's firesides. He considered my father his teacher and acted as such towards him.

My father writes,

When Raḥmat was appointed a Hand of the Cause of God, and thus became my spiritual co-worker and colleague, he nevertheless continued to carry on in the same manner as in the days of his youth. It was as if this reverence and dignified behaviour had become a part of his nature. Despite my efforts for him to be informal with me, it never happened.

After the passing of the beloved Guardian, the focal point of the consultations of the Hands of the Cause was the successful completion of the goals of the Ten Year Crusade. Raḥmat's views and suggestions regarding teaching methods and especially mass teaching, which at that time was not so common and widespread, were so simple and practical that they were acceptable to all. I cannot recall a single time when his suggestions regarding teaching indigenous peoples were not unanimously approved.

It is an undeniable fact that he was much loved by the Hands of the Cause of God. His smiling face and joyous countenance were a source of delight for all of us.

On one of my father's visits to India, Raḥmat finally succeeded in persuading him to visit the mass teaching areas in Gwalior. Raḥmat normally bought the cheapest ticket, but on this occasion out of respect for my father, he bought first class tickets and they set off for the train station. Unfortunately it turned out they had been booked on the wrong train. Having brought my father this far, Raḥmat was not about to let him go back. He promised to make my father as comfortable as possible and took him to Gwalior third class.

It was hot, and the soot and dirt of the train did not help my father's mood. They checked into the best hotel, which belonged to the Maharani of Gwalior, where only dignitaries and government official guests were admitted. My father takes up the story:

> The building was truly magnificent and had a large beautiful garden. We checked into two rooms, and finally got ready to sleep. I was woken up very early in the morning by the screeching of the peacocks that roamed the garden. I got up, and feeling very distressed went to Raḥmat's door and woke him. 'I cannot sleep because of the noise of the peacocks', I said. The look on Raḥmat's face is impossible to describe. He looked at me in astonishment and said, 'Jináb-i-Furútan, I have arranged for a place for you in the best hotel. In this region there is no palace more comfortable than this. If it were up to me I would have stayed at the home of the Bomans. I have done this only for you. I do not know what to do about the noise of the peacocks. This

With his father-in-law, Mr Furútan, in Japan.

With his great friend Mr Faizí.

Kindred Spirits. With Olinga in Haifa.

matter is out of my hands, only God can silence them.' We both started laughing.

Hand of the Cause 'Abu'l-Qásim Faizí was one of Raḥmat's closest personal friends. I remember the last time they were together. We had gone to visit the Shrine of Bahá'u'lláh with Mr Faizí and his wife Gloria. In deference to the two Hands, the custodians opened the gate before the usual hour of pilgrimage. Raḥmat helped Mr Faizí up the few steps and held his arm as they stood together at the threshold of Bahá'u'lláh. The four of us were the only ones in the holy Shrine. Mr Faizí said, 'Raḥmatján, chant the Tablet of Visitation for us'. Gloria and I can still recall that occasion quite vividly. The two Hands of the Cause, one frail and weak from a long illness, and one still in the prime of life, standing arm in arm, chanting prayers with tears pouring down their faces.

Raḥmat enjoyed a unique relationship with Hand of the Cause Enoch Olinga. Olinga was only one year his junior, and whenever they were together they engaged in high-spirited competition to see who was the older, and hence should have the last word. They were closer than brothers. From the first moment they met, after the passing of the beloved Guardian, a bond was established which lasted the rest of their lives. 'Enochy', as Raḥmat affectionately called him, was never far from his thoughts. Wherever he travelled he advised National Assemblies to invite Olinga to visit them. During the conclaves of the Hands, they would often sit together, and Raḥmat would urge Olinga to visit different countries. Once, when Olinga was a guest in our house in New Delhi, Raḥmat tried to convince him to accompany him on his trips. They bantered for a while and Olinga's laughter could be heard from far off. He said 'Raḥmat wants to turn me into a gypsy just like himself!'

Raḥmat, however, did not give up. When he visited Quito, Ecuador, and found that there were people of African descent in Esmeraldas, he immediately arranged for Olinga to come to that area. Hundreds accepted the Faith as a result of Olinga's visit. Hand of the Cause Olinga's travels in Asia and India were also largely due to Raḥmat's efforts. He arranged the itinerary, suggested the plans to the Holy Land and urged his friend to undertake the journeys.

When in Africa, Raḥmat would often accompany Olinga to conferences and meetings. During the years when Uganda's political climate kept Olinga at home in Kampala, Raḥmat greatly missed his friend. In 1979 he wanted to visit Olinga despite the danger, but Olinga advised against it. Raḥmat bitterly regretted this missed opportunity to see his friend once more.

News of Olinga's violent and tragic death in September 1979 reached us in Boston. Raḥmat was heartbroken, and said that with Olinga's death something had died within his own soul. After many long prayers he eventually became a little calmer and more resigned. He wrote to the Universal House of Justice:

> The news of the passing of Ḥaḍrat-i-Olinga was so terrible and heart-breaking that it was impossible for me to believe and tolerate. I was so deeply grieved that it has affected my nervous system. I have had severe backache for the past few days.
>
> I then reminded myself that Olinga was a peerless Bahá'í teacher who had achieved incomparable conquests, and now his noble soul was consorting with the Abhá Concourse. The quality of his life surpassed its quantity and he remained steadfast to his last day.
>
> His joyous spirit is a great solace to our hearts, but his passing has brought grief to the souls of the friends. In the South Caribbean, which has progressed in teaching in all areas, a teaching plan was established in Olinga's blessed name, and their aim is to teach thousands of the black people in this land.
>
> In other parts of America also they have made plans in his sacred memory. It is certain that his name will crown thousands of activities and teaching plans in the world.

Raḥmat told me that Olinga had once had a strange dream that he and Raḥmat were standing together, looking down on the earth beneath them. Flames were rising out of every corner, and they could hear screams. Olinga turned to Raḥmat and said it was good that they were not in the carnage, and that they were the ones who had been spared. Raḥmat believed this meant that he would soon join his departed friend in the Abhá Kingdom, and leave behind the toils and troubles of this world. Little did I suspect that this intimation would prove correct so soon.

A FRIEND TO ALL

Raḥmat was gregarious and sociable by nature from the days of his childhood, but the bond which connected him so deeply to so many hearts was born out of his love for Bahá'u'lláh. Because of his love for the Blessed Beauty, he was able to communicate so sincerely with so many different souls, transcending barriers of language, culture and tradition.

He never demanded anything of anyone that he was not prepared to do, or had not already done, himself. If he asked for pioneers he promised that he would go with them until they were settled; he always kept his promise. If he made suggestions for teaching, he showed the friends ways to implement them and often assisted in the work. He would go to the remotest corners of the world to spend a few hours with the pioneers and bring them news. If they needed help he tried to find ways to assist them. A pioneer to Brazil told me that for years after Raḥmat's passing, whenever he saw a man approaching their home he would — just for a moment — want to shout 'Dr Muhájir is here!' They were so used to his visits and so looked forward to them.

His influence on the personal lives of many people around the world is still fondly remembered. He had a unique ability to take interest in personal problems, give advice and propose a solution. Many times he sent young men to pioneer to certain places with the specific purpose of marrying a girl that they had never seen but he thought was suitable for them. To the best of my knowledge all the marriages he arranged in this manner are still solid and successful.

His skills as a physician equipped him with a deep and sincere compassion for people in trouble. Such people felt this, and responded to it. In his Mentawai days he would often sit by the bedside of his patients, chanting the Healing Prayer. Although nobody understood what he was chanting they swore that this made them feel better. He told me that he gave medication and said the Healing Prayer to augment the medicine. He rarely lost a patient.

Many remember his kindness and concern for their lives, whether spiritual or physical. On one occasion an individual who had served the Faith sincerely for many years made an unfortunate mistake which required the removal of his voting rights by the

Universal House of Justice. Raḥmat interceded several times on his behalf. When the old man passed away a few months after his reinstatement, Raḥmat was grateful that the man did not have to face Bahá'u'lláh in shame. In India, one family who owned two very profitable hotels vowed to personally cook for the delegates at every National Convention. They explained to me that a few years ago they had gone bankrupt and were trying to make a living from a little stall. Raḥmat had visited them and eaten at their stall, and said special prayers for the recovery of their business. Now that they were prosperous they felt obliged to Bahá'u'lláh to perform this service.

LOVE AND LAUGHTER

Raḥmat was an unassuming man with a great sense of humour. He eschewed personal recognition and shunned ceremony. He never expected special treatment because of his position as a Hand of the Cause, unless it was for official reasons. Once, at a National Convention in India, when the message of the Universal House of Justice was being read, a passage about the Hands of the Cause and their services to the Faith was so phenomenal that it overwhelmed the audience. Raḥmat was on the podium, following the message from its English text as it was being read in Hindi. I could see his discomfort. He looked at the papers in his hand, looked over the rims of his glasses at the audience and then took off his glasses, pointed to the message, then pointed to himself. This broke the awkward silence. Everyone clapped and laughed: Raḥmat's sense of humour relieved the tension and saved everyone from embarrassment.

A friend in Africa remembers:

> His easy-going manner and simplicity put everyone at ease. Very often he helped in preparation of food for the friends. Once I caught him washing his clothes and begged him to let me do it. When they were rinsed he just hung them on a hanger and said they did not need to be ironed. He had a small suitcase with just the bare necessities. He had only one pair of shoes, which were maroon in colour. One of the pioneers, in his zeal to clean them,

had polished them black as he did not have maroon polish. Dr Muhájir just laughed and joked about the sudden transformation of his shoes.

Water was always cut off in the mornings. Dr Muhájir would get up at midnight and fill buckets and pots and pans so we all could use water the next day.

The friends would just swarm to meet and spend time with him. He joked and laughed and ordered food for them, and was truly a most genial host. When I wanted to offer him the best food on the table he would say, 'You better give it to your American husband, you have waited for him a long time, you don't want him to leave you!' I would translate his jokes and we all had a merry and happy time.

Raḥmat's humility and sense of humour resulted in some amusing incidents. On one occasion he was visiting the Resting Place of the beloved Guardian, during the Fast, in very inclement weather. He was away the whole day and came home long after sunset and told us that he had to help some friends, who were making their pilgrimage, sort out their visas for Israel.

It was only when we received a letter from Hand of the Cause Faizí a few weeks later, that the events of that day came to light. He wrote that a couple had arrived at the Pilgrim House where they were to meet the other pilgrims and the Hands of the Cause. The minute they sat down the husband said,

> Something very unusual happened to us in London. A man wearing an old raincoat approached us at the Guardian's Resting Place, offered us his umbrella and asked if he could chant prayers for us. I asked him what his name was and he said 'Dr Raḥmat'. He then chanted prayers and insisted on taking us to lunch at a small cafe. I became suspicious when he did not have anything himself, not even a cup of tea. He asked us where we were headed and reluctantly I told him we were going to the Holy Land. He asked to see our passports. I looked at my wife and we decided it was better not to refuse. He then said our visas had expired and immediately put us in a taxi and took us to the Israeli embassy. I told my wife that this man could not be a doctor. A

doctor who lived and worked in London would not wear an old raincoat, would not be here in the rain in the middle of the day and would not waste his time with people he did not even know.

He had our passports, so we had no choice but to do what he asked. The man at the embassy told us to return at three o'clock, and this so-called 'Dr Raḥmat' asked me if he could rest in our hotel room for the few hours we had to wait. As he had our passports, again I consented. I pretended to go out for cigarettes and peered through the crack of the door. He was really resting, sitting on a chair, leaning his head against the wall, fast asleep. After an hour I woke him up and asked if he could go out with us and help my wife buy a pair of shoes, but he said that the shoes she had on were fine. He took me to the embassy, gave me our passports and then insisted on taking us to the airport. I told my wife that we had to be very careful and find out what he wanted, but at the airport he just said goodbye and left us. He might have wanted some information which he could not get out of us.

Mr Faizí, keeping his face straight, then asked the gentleman, 'Did this alleged doctor say prayers correctly?' 'Yes,' was the reply. 'He chanted the Tablet of Aḥmad from memory and had a reasonably good voice.' Mr Faizi then asked, 'Have you by any chance heard of Dr Muhájir?' Mr Faizí wrote, 'This hit him like a bolt of lightning. The man removed his hat, hit himself on the head and wept profusely.'

Mr Faizí's envelope contained a letter from the gentleman which read, 'Hand of the Cause of God Dr Muhájir, may my life be a sacrifice for you. Please forgive us for not realizing who you were. I can't bear to think that on top of everything I asked you to come with us to buy shoes for my wife.'

Raḥmat's sense of humour had been my salvation, and had helped me on many instances in our rather unusual and difficult life. I remember on one occasion in our first days of pioneering, when a particularly severe bout of malaria had drained my energy and I was longing for the comforts of home, his jokes kept me going. He would tell me how he, on a trip with his friends in Iran, had kept them waiting in the bus depot for two hours because he had sent his shoes to the cobbler and had no spare ones. He mimicked each of his friends and their rage at having to wait for these old shoes. He would double up with laughter until I would laugh and for a few moments forget my weakness and misery.

THE POWER OF PRAYER

Raḥmat's most outstanding characteristic was his reliance on prayer. It constituted a great part of his daily life. He did not just go through the routine of saying his obligatory prayers and perhaps a few additional prayers. He prayed for hours each day every day throughout his life. He prayed for everything and everybody except himself. He only said prayers on his own behalf to remain steadfast in the Cause. His abnegation was genuine. He truly believed that all were in danger of failing spiritual tests, no matter their title or role in the Cause.

His daily devotions always included the Prayer of Visitation of 'Abdu'l-Bahá. A passage of that tablet is copied in many of his notebooks:

> O Lord my God! Give me Thy grace to serve Thy loved ones, strengthen me in my servitude to Thee, illumine my brow with the light of adoration in Thy court of holiness, and of prayer to Thy Kingdom of grandeur. Help me to be selfless at the heavenly entrance to thy gate, and aid me to be detached from all things within thy hole precincts. Lord! give me to drink from the chalice of selflessness; with its robe clothe me. Make me as dust in the pathway of thy loved ones, and grant that I may offer up my soul for the earth ennobled by the footsteps of Thy chosen ones in thy path, O Lord of Glory in the Highest.[2]

Friends around the world remember the effects of Raḥmat's prayers on behalf of teaching work in their region:

> . . . One day when I was getting him from his hotel in Manila he said that he had just finished saying, 'Say, God sufficeth all things above all things . . . 314 times![3] No wonder he brought so much power when he came for a visit. When he was in Ivory Coast I went to his hotel room to take him to the National Assembly

meeting. I knocked on the door several times and as there was no answer I just entered the room. He was sitting on the floor in a corner of the room, facing the Qiblih. He was so engrossed in his prayers that he did not notice my entrance. He continued chanting for about 45 minutes. I sat quietly listening to him. I have never in my life seen anyone say prayers in this manner. His eyes were closed, and he was imploring Bahá'u'lláh for whatever it was he was asking of Him. His prayers were in Persian and Arabic and all from memory. When he finished praying he realized I was there and apologised for not noticing me.

. . . When we returned to his hotel in Singapore he asked me to say some prayers and he chanted a prayer in Arabic for assistance. All the time he spoke about the Ibon believers in Sarawak and emphasized the Bahá'í education of children. I went to my room around midnight. A few hours later I heard him chanting. I looked in his room, he was sitting on a chair his head resting on the back and he was saying prayers. It was 2.40 a.m. I wanted to understand what was going on in his soul and heart and wished we could take some of the enormous burden of responsibility off his shoulders. That night he did not sleep. He prayed until after dawn, took a short nap and was up again.

. . . In 1979, we were in England visiting the Guardian's Resting Place. My husband and I were alone, when Dr Muhájir entered the precinct around Shoghi Effendi's grave. He stopped at the small gate before entering in close proximity to the grave stone. I could hear Dr Muhájir praying, talking out loud and crying to Shoghi Effendi. He later approached the grave and reverently knelt down, chanting prayers all the while. To those of us who were present, it seemed as if a long, lost friend had been received by his beloved. Dr Muhájir arose and anointed each of us with attar of roses and continued his chanting until we left. I will never forget those images of Dr Muhájir's deep love and respect for Shoghi Effendi.

. . . We had gone to a public meeting, and at ten p.m. a messenger came to tell us Dr Muhájir had been waiting for three hours. He seemed very tired. The next day he said, 'Last night was very strange. Lately very often I feel like this. I started to say a prayer and when I woke up in the morning I was still chanting the same prayer. It seems the whole night I had been saying that prayer.'

Raḥmat's belief in the power of prayer was absolute. Whether for the purchase of a Bahá'í property, teaching of Faith, giving a talk, getting a visa, or the well-being of his family, he prayed, and left his affairs in the Hand of God. When in the Holy Land, Raḥmat would rise at dawn to go to the Shrines. The custodians of the Shrine of Bahá'u'lláh recall seeing him very early in the mornings, before they had started to clean the Shrine, kneeling on the gravel outside the tomb of Bahá'u'lláh, deep in prayer. Often he would refuse to go inside, so as not to disturb their work. Once, before a meeting, he had gone to the Shrine of 'Abdu'l-Bahá. It was getting late, and I worriedly went to look for him. I found him curled in a corner, in his raincoat, fast asleep. I woke him and saw that his eyes were bloodshot with swollen eyelids. He had cried so much that he had become exhausted and had fallen asleep. I never found out what he was so sad about.

AT THE WORLD CENTRE

His visits to the Holy Land and the Shrines always assuaged his extreme fatigue and calmed his soul. His first visit had been as a pilgrim to the holy Shrines, and it was then that he met Shoghi Effendi. In 1957, he made the most difficult trip in his entire life, to go to the Holy Land and not find his beloved there. After this visit, to attend the first conclave of the Hands of the Cause, Raḥmat visited the Holy Land at least once every year in the time before the formation of the Universal House of Justice.

His letters written from London after the funeral of the beloved Guardian and after his participation in the first conclave, though brimming with grief and sorrow, indicated his resolve to humbly offer his soul and physical being to the beloved Guardian. He begged Bahá'u'lláh to assist him to play his part in the completion of the Ten Year Crusade. In his notebook he had copied and underlined these words of Shoghi Effendi, from his message of 4 June 1957:

With pilgrims in Haifa, 1972.

> Divinely appointed Institution of the Hands of the Cause, invested by virtue of the authority conferred by the Testament of the Centre of the Covenant with the twin functions of protecting and propagating the Faith of Bahá'u'lláh, now entering new phase in the process of the unfoldment of its sacred mission. To its newly assured responsibility to assist National Spiritual Assemblies of the Bahá'í world in the specific purpose of effectively prosecuting the World Spiritual Crusade, the primary obligation to watch over and insure protection to the Bahá'í world community in close collaboration with the same National Assemblies is now added.[4]

In the ensuing years, on each trip to the Holy Land, and on each visit to the Shrines, he renewed his pledge and offered his life to the service of the beloved Guardian.

In late 1961 Gisu and I moved to the Holy Land, and Raḥmat's visits became more frequent. During the period between the passing of the Guardian and the election of the Universal House of Justice, if one of the Hands of the Cause based at the World Centre had to be absent for any reason, one of the Hands from overseas would be summoned to take his or her place. From mid-1962 to May 1963 Raḥmat temporarily took the place of my father who had gone to Iran on a mission from the Hands of the Cause in the Holy Land. During these months, Raḥmat assisted in cataloguing the original Persian and Arabic Tablets of Bahá'u'lláh and 'Abdu'l-Bahá. In addition, he participated in the meetings of the Hands, helped receive the pilgrims, and guided them around the Holy Places. Though Raḥmat cherished the hours that he spent in the Shrines in prayer, he impatiently awaited the return of my father so that he could be free to resume his teaching activities around the world.

His collaboration with the Universal House of Justice was always characterized by utter humility and obedience. Often in his diaries he noted that he was seeking permission from the Supreme Body for his trips, and then, that he had been blessed with their consent. He strove to promote and carry out the goals given by the Universal House of Justice with the same endeavour as he did those of the Ten Year Crusade which had been set by the beloved Guardian.

The Research Department of the Universal House of Justice states:

> His letters to the Supreme Body were all written with simplicity and clarity and were full of love and reverence. They always started with an expression of humility and ended with a request for prayers of confirmation. They were bereft of unnecessary Persian compliments and a sense of dedication and willingness for service was conveyed by them.

A few quotations from his letters illustrate this point:

> . . . God willing I will have the bounty of receiving your letters either in Bolivia or another South American country to learn the instructions of that Sacred Body. I beseech you to pray for this worthless servant as always. I will be very grateful. In absolute servitude.

> . . . As this humble servant is leaving for Africa, he is in need of manifold prayers to be able, at this sensitive and momentous time, to encourage the friends and meet the teachers and servants of the Faith, to talk to them about entry by troops which has been prophecies in the Writings and also to be able to render some service. I beseech you for fervent prayers so that I can take a small step in the path of the Almighty in Europe and Africa.

Each time he consulted with the Universal House of Justice he expressed his gratitude for the honour, and his delight for the bounty of that meeting. A year before the end of each plan, Raḥmat was busy thinking about the next one. He noted in minute detail the needs of each Bahá'í community. He also made large charts on which he wrote his suggestions about the plan which he would offer for consideration by the Universal House of Justice. Many of his suggestions were approved by the Supreme Body and were incorporated in the final draft of the Plan.

Extracts from Raḥmat's letters to the Universal House of Justice show his keen interest in the affairs of the Faith throughout the world, and demonstrate the range and far-sightedness of his suggestions:

Up to now in South America we have not had a systematic plan to teach the black race. Most of the friends have rightly been busy with the teaching of the red Indians and with God's confirmation great results have been achieved in South and Central America. It is obvious that if the beloved friends pay equal attention to the black race in these lands, the same results will be achieved.

In Central America, through the guidance of the Supreme Body, special plans have been drafted to teach in the eastern coast of the countries of Belize, Guatemala, Honduras, Nicaragua, Costa Rica and Panama. The inhabitants of those areas are all from the black race. Millions of this race live in Brazil. There is the need for a special plan to teach them and also the inhabitants of the Caribbean Islands who speak French, English and Spanish and their number exceeds 15 million.

Ultimately they could be the ones to raise the banner of peace and tranquillity among the two major races of humanity in the East and the West. One of the important points which needs attention in the future plans is the question of decentralization. The spread of the Faith in each country has reached a point that the teaching and education activities in particular have to be managed regionally. It will entail establishment of a series of regional Bahá'í centres in various districts and formation of regional teaching committees to have periodicals in local languages and have classes managed by local Bahá'ís in each district.

A few subjects have to be considered in Korea. There has been no teaching among women in Korea. Around 80 to 90 per cent of the Bahá'ís are men. We have to have a plan for teaching the women. The teaching of the children in Korea is also neglected. The National Assembly of Korea had submitted a teaching plan a few years with the goal of making the Korean community self-supporting. This should be re-examined.

One of the dependencies of the Universal House of Justice which seems to be very essential is an 'office of international relations'. This office will serve as a foreign office department to establish relationships between the Universal House of Justice and the heads of states and politicians. This work will gradually pave the way for the Most Great Peace.

Official photograph for The Bahá'í World, *taken in Haifa.*

> The expansion of this institution will help establish the new World Order of Bahá'u'lláh, which is presently concerned with the internal affairs of the Faith throughout the world — a system which will have to correct and manage all the affairs of the world. The establishment of such an institution in the Holy Land will create procedures so that in every country influential officials will become familiar with the Faith and develop a close relationship with it. Gradually the principles of the Faith can influence the laws and educational process of each country, even if these influential people do not themselves come under the banner of the Faith of Bahá'u'lláh.
>
> This matter is urgent and of the utmost necessity. Many of the countries of the world have gained their independence in the last 20 years and are in the early stages of their political evolution. Before their laws become solidified and established, the life-giving principles of the Faith — especially in the fields of education, science, women's rights and world peace — can greatly influence them.
>
> The establishment of the Bahá'í International Community, a goal of the Ten Year Crusade, which was to initiate relations with the United Nations, was the preamble to this work. Now these institutions in New York must be administered by the special office in the World Centre and be extended to a great degree.
>
> Another office should be established in Geneva, also administered from the World Centre. These two offices should not limit their contacts to the United Nations, but must keep in touch with all the Heads of State and influential people of the world, to establish the identity of the Universal House of Justice as a source of great power and authority, not only in the spiritual realm but in the field of the world administration.

Raḥmat participated in the four International Conventions between 1963 and 1978. His calls for the teaching of millions were always applauded by the delegates, no matter how exaggerated they seemed to be. In the 1978 International Convention he said:

> I am going to talk about mass conversion. What else do you expect of me? We do not know when the Formative Age will give

In distinguished company, International Convention, 1968.

way to the Golden Age. Shoghi Effendi once said that the efforts of the Bahá'ís would 'Herald the advent of the Golden Age of the Faith of Bahá'u'lláh.' Therefore the Bahá'ís can bring the Golden Age nearer by tireless and effective teaching among the masses of humanity.

This is the time for growing, for gaining numerical strength in the Cause. The time is ripe — it was always ripe for this. The Master said that humanity would enter the Faith in troops. It is not enough that we have one Bahá'í for every 1000 in India, or even one for every 50 in Bolivia. When mass conversion first began in the world, there were no facilities, there was inadequate manpower and resources, yet it was accomplished. Let us have Faith in Bahá'u'lláh; let us go forth and teach. Go back to your own countries and see what you can do about mass conversion.

On one occasion he suggested that five million people be taught within the year following International Convention. The delegates gasped, and the usual applause was not forthcoming. Amatu'l-Bahá Rúḥíyyih Khánum, who was chairing that session, said that when Dr Muhájir asks for 5,000,000, he will be happy with 200,000. Laughter and applause broke the silence, and all was well again.

Raḥmat knew most of the delegates personally, and after each session he talked to them about the teaching work in their respective countries. These meetings were always light-hearted and jovial. Members of the various National Assemblies were with their old friend and this made them happy. They knew that he would soon be with them to help carry out their goals, so they took his suggestions in good heart, and promised to implement them.

While in the Holy Land — as everywhere else — he was always in a hurry to finish his work and leave. Most of the time he stayed at my parents' home, and they often had to cancel their plans for him, as they would get up in the morning and see him packing to leave. He would stay as long as he had to, but not a minute more.

PROTECTION OF THE FAITH

Teaching was Raḥmat's great love, and the aspect of Bahá'í life to which he wholeheartedly devoted himself. However, he also dealt resolutely with duties relating to the protection of the Faith. Often the Universal House of Justice would ask him to go to a particular country to help sort out personal problems affecting the affairs of the Faith. There was, sadly, sometimes disunity among the members of Assemblies. It fell to the Hands of the Cause to resolve these problems through their spirituality and wisdom. On those occasions when the problems could not be overcome by loving consultation, swift action had to be taken to protect the Bahá'ís and the interests and reputation of the Faith.

In the early days of the spread of the Faith in one particular country, disunity and lack of progress of the Faith were like thorns in Raḥmat's flesh. Whenever he had to go there he would pray for hours, imploring guidance. He told me, 'The minute I arrive they gather with their thick folders full of documents against each other and want me to solve their animosities.' He told them that the only way for the believers to overcome their problems was to forget everything and teach. In this way they would all think only of Bahá'u'lláh and forget their disunity. This had no effect on them, as they felt that a Hand of the Cause should be able to deal with their difficulties, which mostly revolved around personalities and finances. His experience of this country showed him how it took just a few stubborn people to hold back the growth of the Faith.

He nevertheless made frequent trips there, as the protection of the Faith demanded it. Once, when Hand of the Cause Samandarí was with us in the Philippines, Raḥmat was again called upon to go to this difficult country. He went to Mr.Samandarí and gently told him, 'Samandaríján, today I have received an invitation to go to [. . .] As it is on your way I want to write to them that they will have the bounty of your visit instead of mine.' Mr Samandarí roared with laughter. He said, 'You young people think you can put something over on this old man? Whenever I am asked to go there by the Universal House of Justice I literally weep. I think they should again have the bounty of your visit this time.' They bargained for a while until Mr Samandarí, out of love for Raḥmat, graciously consented to take the burden on his own shoulders. That country finally overcame its problems. The friends were able at last to concentrate on teaching, and, with the assistance of some new pioneers, a strong community emerged.

As long as the problems did not involve covenant-breaking, Raḥmat would be very compassionate. He advised National Assemblies (who were often too quick in depriving offenders of their voting rights), to show patience and understanding. I remember when the Treasurer of a certain National Assembly got into difficulties over the Fund, the Assembly had decided to remove his voting rights, announce the reason to the community, and take a piece of land (his only possession) to compensate for the missing money. When Raḥmat arrived, he asked them to reconsider. This man had served for many years with devotion, and Raḥmat considered the punishment too severe. He asked the man to voluntarily resign from the National Assembly, arrange the sale of his property, pay what was owed to the Fund, and, with the rest of the money, buy a smaller property in the name of his son, who was then five-years old. This man lived another few years as a good Bahá'í, his reputation intact.

Raḥmat believed that revenge — whether by an institution or an individual — served no purpose. However, if the fundamental laws of the Faith were challenged, he had no qualms at all about an individual being punished. When a new Bahá'í did not want to renounce his membership of a secret society, despite repeated warnings and exhortations by the National Assembly, they had decided to leave the matter be. Raḥmat insisted that they could not do so. The Guardian had specifically directed that membership in that society was not allowed, and no Assembly could decide otherwise.

In his private life, Raḥmat was most forgiving and never complained against another soul, or caused embarrassment to anyone. A gentleman who was very much opposed to Raḥmat's methods of teaching used to write voluminous complaints against him to the Universal House of Justice, with a copy to Raḥmat for good measure. At first Raḥmat would read them and put them aside without any response. In later years the letters became so offensive that I would become ill after reading them. I acted as Raḥmat's unofficial secretary and had to read all his communications, so that I could convey the gist of them to him in my letters or during our telephone conversations. I would not mention those letters when he was away, and when I would tell him about my feelings he would simply say, 'These letters don't mean anything. Next time throw them away unopened.' He believed that the man was entitled to his opinion as much as he himself was.

In all matters, whether related to the Faith or his personal life, Raḥmat strictly avoided confrontation, which he considered a sign of weakness rather than strength. He advised the Assemblies and friends to follow this prudent way also. Those who accepted his advice, saw its effect in creating harmony and unity. Those who did not, had to go through months and sometimes years of conflict for trivial matters which quickly lost their importance, though the disunity they had created lingered on.

Once, a Counsellor who had been very badly treated by one of the Bahá'ís, decided to take his case to Raḥmat for judgment:

I had to take a bus ride of a few hours so that I could meet Dr Muhájir. I used the time while I was travelling to compose my thoughts and prepare a good case to present to the Hand of the Cause. I arrived at his hotel, and he greeted me with loving-kindness and his usual welcoming smile. He suggested that as I was tired and hot, I should take a shower.

After the shower I felt much calmer, and my agitated thoughts were much clearer. Dr Muhájir ordered tea and sandwiches and then sat there and patiently listened to my complaints against this Bahá'í gentleman whom I felt had wronged me. When I finished, he offered me some more tea, smiled and said, 'Yes, what this man has done certainly is terrible, but just think what he would do if he was not a Bahá'í! Leave him to Bahá'u'lláh. Let's make use of the time we have together, and think about some teaching plans for this country.

Raḥmat's last International Convention, Riḍván 1978. With Amoz Gibson, member of the Universal House of Justice, and Hand of the Cause Mr Kh̲ádem.

Raḥmat disliked dwelling on negative matters and would never send a negative report to the Universal House of Justice, as long as the problem stopped short of covenant-breaking. Firaydún Misaghian recounts how when Raḥmat 'read or heard a report that was critical or negative, he became very sad. I had written a lengthy report about a certain country. The first thing that Dr Muhájir said to me was "What kind of a report was that? Didn't you have anything better to write?"' Of course Raḥmat could see the problems with which the friends were struggling, and discussed them with the Universal House of Justice. But he believed that if every matter became the subject of long reports and discussions, then teaching the Faith — the primary objective of the Bahá'ís and of the Administration — would suffer as a result.

A LIFE OF DEDICATION

Raḥmat was a charismatic man who drew a love and response which has rarely been seen among friends. A common comment in the hundreds of letters sent to us after his passing was, 'We did what he asked because of his love.' Raḥmat had chosen his path consciously and freely, and would not listen to those who advised him to slow down. He asked them whether they would give the same advice to the manager of a business concern? 'The business of the Faith is my business' is one of his best remembered phrases. 'People always admire those who work hard at their job, although it is for nothing more than this transient world. Why is it that they think I overdo it?'

He had decided the priorities in his life, and service to the Faith was right at the top. His role model was Shoghi Effendi. He told me that the characteristic of the Guardian which he most desired to emulate was his determination in seeing his tasks through to the end. The Guardian never let obstacles deter him from his plans. He often spoke of the time when the Guardian was building the steps leading up to the Shrine of the Báb. A tree which he was unable to move was in the way, so Guardian simply built the steps around the tree. Raḥmat tried to follow that characteristic, and whenever obstacles arose he never abandoned his plans. Rather, he would try to remove the obstacles, or go round them.

Raḥmat took as his motto the words of 'Abdu'l-Bahá:

> The obligations of the Hands of the Cause of God are to diffuse the Divine Fragrances, to edify the souls of men, to promote learning, to improve the character of all men and to be, at all times and under all conditions, sanctified and detached from earthly things.[5]

He followed the beloved Guardian's exhortations to the best of his ability, up to the very last moment of his life:

> Before the eyes of the warriors enlisting under its banner stretch fields of exploration and consolidation of such vastness as might well dazzle the eyes and strike awe into the heart of any soul less robust than those who have arisen to identify themselves with its Cause. The heights its champions must scale are indeed formidable. The pitfalls that bestrew their path are still numerous. The road leading to ultimate and total victory is tortuous, stony and narrow. Theirs, however, is the emphatic assurance, revealed by the Pen of the Most High — the Prime Mover of the forces unleashed by this world-girdling Crusade — that 'whosoever ariseth to aid our Cause God will render him victorious over ten times ten thousand souls, and, should he wax in his love for Me, him will We cause to triumph over all that is in heaven and all that is on earth.'
>
> Putting on the armour of His love, firmly buckling on the shield of His mighty Covenant, mounted on the steed of steadfastness, holding aloft the lance of the Word of the Lord of Hosts, and with unquestioning reliance on His promises as the best provision for their journey, let them set their faces towards those fields that still remain unexplored and direct their steps to those goals that are as yet unattained, assured that He Who has led them to achieve such triumphs, and to store up such prizes in His Kingdom, will continue to assist them in enriching their spiritual birthright to a degree that no finite mind can imagine or human heart perceive.[6]

Appendix

ITINERARY OF TRAVELS AS HAND OF THE CAUSE OF GOD

This itinerary is based on resources accessible to the author at the time of writing, and does not claim to be exhaustive. Continents and regions appear in the order which they are listed in the text; countries and states are listed alphabetically. Those places which have undergone a change of name are listed as they were known at the time of Dr Muhájir's visit.

1957
INDIAN SUBCONTINENT: India.
CENTRAL ASIA: The Holy Land; Iran.
SOUTH-EAST ASIA: Burma; Indonesia; Laos; Malaysia; Singapore; Thailand.
EUROPE: United Kingdom (London, for the funeral of Shoghi Effendi).

1958
CENTRAL ASIA: The Holy Land.
SOUTH-EAST ASIA: Burma; Laos.

1960
AFRICA: Kenya; Tanzania; Zambia.
INDIAN SUBCONTINENT: India.
CENTRAL ASIA: The Holy Land.
SOUTH-EAST ASIA: Indonesia; Malaysia; Singapore; Thailand; Vietnam.

1961

AFRICA: Uganda (Kampala, for the dedication of the Bahá'í temple).

INDIAN SUBCONTINENT: India.

CENTRAL ASIA: The Holy Land.

SOUTH-EAST ASIA: Laos; Malaysia; Philippines; Singapore.

NORTH-EAST ASIA: Hong Kong; Japan (twice).

NORTH AMERICA: USA (California; Hawaii).

CENTRAL AMERICA: Costa Rica; Mexico; Nicaragua; Panama.

SOUTH AMERICA: Bolivia (represented the Bahá'í World Centre at first National Convention); Brazil; Colombia; Ecuador; Guatemala; Paraguay (represented the Bahá'í World Centre at first National Convention); Peru.

1962

INDIAN SUBCONTINENT: India (twice); East Pakistan.

CENTRAL ASIA: The Holy Land.

SOUTH-EAST ASIA: Malaysia; Philippines; Thailand.

NORTH-EAST ASIA: Hong Kong.

AUSTRALASIA: Australia; New Zealand.

PACIFIC: Fiji; Gilbert Islands; New Hebrides.

1963

INDIAN SUBCONTINENT: India.

CENTRAL ASIA: The Holy Land; Iran.

SOUTH-EAST ASIA: Laos; Malaysia; Philippines; Singapore; Thailand.

NORTH-EAST ASIA: Hong Kong; Japan.

EUROPE: Netherlands; United Kingdom (London, for the first Bahá'í World Congress).

1964

INDIAN SUBCONTINENT: India; Pakistan.

CENTRAL ASIA: Iran.

NORTH-EAST ASIA: Hong Kong; Korea; Macao.

SOUTH-EAST ASIA: Burma; Ceylon; Malaysia; Philippines (represented Universal House of Justice at first National Convention); Singapore; Thailand; Vietnam (represented the Universal House of Justice at first National Convention).

PACIFIC: American Samoa.

1965
INDIAN SUBCONTINENT: India.
SOUTH-EAST ASIA: Laos; Malaysia; Philippines; Singapore.
NORTH-EAST ASIA: Hong Kong; Japan (twice); Korea.
NORTH AMERICA: Canada; USA (Hawaii).
SOUTH AMERICA: Ecuador.

1966
INDIAN SUBCONTINENT: India.
CENTRAL ASIA: Iran.
SOUTH-EAST ASIA: Laos; Malaysia; Philippines; Thailand.
NORTH-EAST ASIA: Hong Kong; Japan; Korea; Macao.

1967
INDIAN SUBCONTINENT: India.
CENTRAL ASIA: Afghanistan; Iran.
SOUTH-EAST ASIA: Laos (represented the Universal House of Justice at first National Convention); Macao; Philippines; Taiwan; Vietnam.
NORTH-EAST ASIA: Hong Kong.

1968
INDIAN SUBCONTINENT: India; Nepal.
CENTRAL ASIA: The Holy Land; Iran.
SOUTH-EAST ASIA: Laos; Philippines.
EUROPE: Italy.

1969
AFRICA: Dahomey; Central African Republic; Congo; Gabon; Gambia; Ghana; Nigeria; Senegal; Togo; Zambia.
INDIAN SUBCONTINENT: India.
CENTRAL ASIA: Iran.
SOUTH-EAST ASIA: Laos; Malaysia; Philippines; Singapore; Taiwan.
NORTH-EAST ASIA: Hong Kong; Japan.

1970

AFRICA: Chad; Central African Republic; Ethiopia; Gabon; Mauritania (represented the Universal House of Justice at international conference); Kenya; Rhodesia; South Africa; Uganda; West Africa.

INDIAN SUBCONTINENT: Ceylon; India; Nepal; Pakistan.

CENTRAL ASIA: Afghanistan; the Holy Land (three times); Iran (twice); Turkey.

SOUTH-EAST ASIA: Indonesia; Philippines; Thailand.

NORTH-EAST ASIA: Hong Kong; Japan (twice); Korea; Taiwan.

AUSTRALASIA: Australia; New Zealand.

PACIFIC: Fiji (represented the Universal House of Justice at first National Convention); New Hebrides; Papua New Guinea; Solomon Islands; Western Samoa.

1971

AFRICA: Central African Republic; Chad; Liberia (represented the Universal House of Justice at Continental Conference, Monrovia).

INDIAN SUBCONTINENT: India; Nepal; Pakistan.

CENTRAL ASIA: The Holy Land.

SOUTH-EAST ASIA: Indonesia; Malaysia; Singapore.

NORTH-EAST ASIA: Japan.

AUSTRALASIA: Australia; New Zealand.

PACIFIC: Caroline Islands; Cook Islands; Gilbert Islands; Loyalty Islands; Mariana Islands; Marshall Islands; New Caledonia; New Hebrides; Papua New Guinea; Solomon Islands; Tahiti; Tonga; Western Samoa.

EUROPE: Belgium; Denmark; Finland; France; Federal Republic of Germany; Italy; Luxemburg; Norway; Portugal; Spain; Sweden; United Kingdom.

NORTH AMERICA: USA (Hawaii).

CENTRAL AMERICA: Costa Rica.

1972

AFRICA: Cameroon; Chad; East Africa; Malagasy (represented the Universal House of Justice at first National Convention);

Réunion (represented Universal House of Justice at first National Convention); southern Africa; West Africa; Zaire.
INDIAN SUBCONTINENT: India.
CENTRAL ASIA: The Holy Land; Iran.
SOUTH-EAST ASIA: Indonesia; Laos; Malaysia; Philippines; Singapore.
NORTH-EAST ASIA: Hong Kong; Japan.
EUROPE: Austria; Denmark; Federal Republic of Germany; Italy; Netherlands; Norway; Portugal; Spain; Sweden; Switzerland; United Kingdom.
NORTH AMERICA: USA (Florida).
CARIBBEAN: Antigua; Dominican Republic; Grenada; Guadeloupe; Haiti; Jamaica; Martinique; Montserrat; Puerto Rico; Trinidad & Tobago; St Croix; St Lucia; St Martin; St Thomas; St Vincent.
CENTRAL AMERICA: Belize; El Salvador; Guatemala; Mexico; Panama.
SOUTH AMERICA: Argentina; Bolivia; Brazil; Chile; Colombia; Ecuador; French Guiana; Guyana.

1973
AFRICA: Botswana; Dahomey; Gambia; Ghana; Ivory Coast; Lesotho; Liberia; Kenya; Nigeria; Réunion; Senegal; South Africa; Togo; Zaire; Zambia.
INDIAN SUBCONTINENT: India.
CENTRAL ASIA: The Holy Land; Iran; Turkey.
SOUTH-EAST ASIA: Laos; Malaysia; Philippines; Singapore; Thailand.
NORTH-EAST ASIA: Japan; Korea.
EUROPE: Austria; Belgium; Cyprus; Finland; Federal Republic of Germany; Greece; Iceland; Ireland; Italy; Luxemburg; Sweden; United Kingdom.

1974
AFRICA: Botswana; Burundi; Cameroon; Dahomey; Ghana; Kenya; Lesotho; Madagascar; Malawi; Mauritania; Mauritius; Nigeria; Réunion; Rwanda; Senegal; Swaziland; Tanzania; Togo; Uganda; Zaire.

CENTRAL ASIA: The Holy Land; Iran (twice); Turkey.
SOUTH-EAST ASIA: Malaysia; Philippines; Vietnam.
NORTH-EAST ASIA: Hong Kong; Japan; Korea.
EUROPE: Belgium; Federal Republic of Germany; Denmark; France; Iceland; Ireland; Luxemburg; Netherlands; Norway; Portugal; Spain; Sweden; United Kingdom.
AUSTRALASIA: Australia; New Zealand.
PACIFIC: Eastern Samoa; Fiji; Gilbert Islands; New Hebrides; Tonga; Papua New Guinea; Solomon Islands; Western Samoa.
NORTH AMERICA: Canada; USA (Alabama, Alaska, California, Florida, Georgia, Illinois, Indianapolis, Louisiana, Michigan, Mississippi, New Mexico, North Carolina, Ohio, South Carolina, Texas, Washington).
CARIBBEAN: Dominican Republic; Jamaica; Trinidad.
SOUTH AMERICA: Argentina; Bolivia; Brazil; French Guiana; Guyana; Suriname.

1975
AFRICA: Cameroon; Ivory Coast; Liberia; Mali; Niger (represented the Universal House of Justice at first National Convention); Nigeria; Togo (represented the Universal House of Justice at first National Convention); Senegal; Togo; Sierra Leone; Upper Volta; Zaire.
INDIAN SUBCONTINENT: Bangladesh; India; Pakistan.
CENTRAL ASIA: The Holy Land; Iran.
SOUTH-EAST ASIA: Burma; Malaysia; Philippines; Thailand.
NORTH-EAST ASIA: Hong Kong; Japan.
PACIFIC: Caroline Islands; Mariana Islands; Marshall Islands; Tonga.
EUROPE: Austria; Belgium; Federal Republic of Germany; Portugal; Spain; United Kingdom.
NORTH AMERICA: Canada; USA (Alaska, Arizona, California, Colorado, Florida, Georgia, Hawaii, Illinois, Michigan, North Carolina, Oregon, South Carolina, Texas, Washington, Wisconsin).
SOUTH AMERICA: Argentina; Bolivia; Brazil; Ecuador; Peru.
CENTRAL AMERICA: El Salvador; Guatemala; Nicaragua; Panama.

1976

AFRICA: Botswana; Cameroon; Gambia; Ghana; Ivory Coast; Kenya; Liberia; Madagascar; Morocco; Nigeria; Togo; Senegal; Sierra Leone; Zaire (twice); Zambia.

CENTRAL ASIA: The Holy Land; Iran; Turkey.

SOUTH-EAST ASIA: Malaysia; Singapore.

NORTH-EAST ASIA: Hong Kong; Japan; Korea.

EUROPE: Belgium; Denmark; Finland; France; Federal Republic of Germany; Norway; Portugal; Spain; Sweden; United Kingdom.

NORTH AMERICA: Canada; USA (South Carolina; Illinois).

SOUTH AMERICA: Argentina; Brazil; Chile; Colombia; Ecuador; Peru.

CENTRAL AMERICA: El Salvador; Mexico; Nicaragua; Panama.

1977

AFRICA: Botswana; Cameroon; Kenya; Lesotho; Madagascar; Malawi; Rhodesia; South Africa; Swaziland; Transkei; Zambia; Zaire.

INDIAN SUBCONTINENT: India.

CENTRAL ASIA: Iran.

SOUTH-EAST ASIA: Malaysia; Philippines; Singapore; Thailand.

NORTH-EAST ASIA: Hong Kong; Japan; Taiwan.

EUROPE: Austria; Belgium; Cyprus; France; Federal Republic of Germany; Greece; Italy; Luxemburg; Portugal; Spain; Switzerland; United Kingdom.

NORTH AMERICA: USA (Hawaii).

SOUTH AMERICA: Bolivia; Brazil; Chile; Colombia; Ecuador; Peru.

CENTRAL AMERICA: Belize; Costa Rica; Mexico; Panama.

1978

AFRICA: Cameroon; Central African Republic; Malawi; Transkei; Zambia.

INDIAN SUBCONTINENT: Bangladesh; India.

CENTRAL ASIA: The Holy Land (three times); Iran; Turkey.

SOUTH-EAST ASIA: Burma; Ceylon; Indonesia; Malaysia; Nepal; Philippines; Thailand.
NORTH-EAST ASIA: Hong Kong; Taiwan.
PACIFIC: Caroline Islands (represented Universal House of Justice at first National Convention); Fiji; Gilbert Islands; Solomon Islands; Mariana Islands (represented Universal House of Justice at first National Convention); Nauru; Samoa; Tonga.
EUROPE: Austria; Belgium; Canary Islands; France; Federal Republic of Germany; Luxemburg; Portugal; Spain; Switzerland; United Kingdom.
NORTH AMERICA: USA (Hawaii).
SOUTH AMERICA: Chile.
CENTRAL AMERICA: Mexico; Panama.

1979

AFRICA: Botswana; Burundi; Cameroon; Dahomey; Gambia; Ghana; Ivory Coast; Kenya; Liberia; Madagascar; Nigeria; Rwanda; Senegal; Sierra Leone; Togo; Zaire.
INDIAN SUBCONTINENT: Bangladesh; India.
CENTRAL ASIA: The Holy Land.
SOUTH-EAST ASIA: Burma; Philippines; Thailand.
NORTH-EAST ASIA:
EUROPE: Federal Republic of Germany; Greece; Ireland; Italy; Portugal; Switzerland; United Kingdom.
NORTH AMERICA: USA (Alabama, Arkansas, Florida, Georgia, Louisiana, Massachusetts, Montana, New York, North Carolina, Pennsylvania, South Carolina, Tennessee, Vermont, Virginia, Washington).
CARIBBEAN: Antigua; Barbados; British Guiana; Dominican Republic; Grenada; Haiti; Jamaica; Puerto Rico, St Croix; St Thomas; St Vincent; Trinidad & Tobago.
CENTRAL AMERICA: Mexico; Nicaragua.
SOUTH AMERICA: Argentina; Bolivia; Brazil; Chile; Ecuador; French Guiana; Paraguay; Peru; Suriname; Uruguay.

NOTES & REFERENCES

p. vii. Bahá'u'lláh, 'A Compilation on the Institution of the Hands of the Cause of God', comp. Research Department of the Universal House of Justice, p. 3. Provisional translation made by a committee in the Holy Land.

CHAPTER 1

1. Mírzá Asadu'lláh Khán-i-Vazír was an influential and famous Bahá'í in Iṣfahán. For many years he was in charge of the province's Office of Financial Affairs. He was imprisoned for his faith, and passed away in Iṣfahán in 1917.
2. These accounts were collected by the author from interviews with Raḥmat's relatives, and include a written account by his cousin, which she recorded from conversations with her mother.
3. 'In the Persian Bayán, Unit 9, chapter 6, the Báb prescribed reciting this prayer 314 times.' (Memorandum from the Research Department to the Universal House of Justice, 28 August 1991).
4. 'Abdu'l-Bahá, *Tablets of the Divine Plan; Revealed by 'Abdu'l-Bahá to the North American Bahá'ís* (Wilmette, Il: Bahá'í Publishing Trust, rev. ed. 1977), p. 39.
5. Shoghi Effendi, from a letter dated 18 July 1953 to the National Spiritual Assembly of the Bahá'ís of the United States, *Citadel of Faith; Messages to America/1947–1957* (Wilmette, Il: Bahá'í Publishing Trust, 1965), p. 120.

CHAPTER 2

1. Shoghi Effendi, from a letter dated April 1957 to the Bahá'ís of the world, *Messages to the Bahá'í World 1950–1957* (Wilmette, Il:

Bahá'í Publishing Trust, 1958), p. 113.
2. Shoghi Effendi, from a letter dated April 1956 to the Bahá'ís of the world. Ibid., pp. 96–7.

CHAPTER 3

1. Shoghi Effendi, from a letter dated April 1957 to the Bahá'ís of the world, *Messages to the Bahá'í World 1950–1957*, p. 111.
2. Cited by Shoghi Effendi in a letter dated February 1953 to the friends gathered at the African Intercontinental Conference. Ibid, p. 136.
3. 'Abdu'l-Bahá, *Will and Testament of 'Abdu'l-Bahá*, trans. Shoghi Effendi, (Wilmette, Il: Bahá'í Publishing Trust, 1944), p. 11.
4. The Báb, *Selection from the Writings of the Báb*, comp. Research Department of the Universal House of Justice, trans. Habib Taherzadeh with the assistance of a Committee at the Bahá'í World Centre (Haifa: Bahá'í World Centre, 1976), p. 39.
5. Shoghi Effendi, from a letter dated April 1957 to the Bahá'ís of the world, *Messages to the Bahá'í World 1950–1957*, p 117.

CHAPTER 4

1. Written on behalf of Shoghi Effendi, from a letter dated 10 March 1936 to the National Spiritual Assembly of the Bahá'ís of India, *Dawn of a New Day; Messages to India 1923–1957* (New Delhi: Bahá'í Publishing Trust, 1970), p. 59.
2. Bahá'u'lláh, *The Seven Valleys*, trans. Marzieh Gail and Ali Kuli Khan (London: Nightingale Books, 1992), p. 77.
3. Shoghi Effendi, from a letter dated 5 June 1947 to the National Spiritual Assembly of the Bahá'ís of the United States and Canada, *Citadel of Faith*, p. 22.
4. Shoghi Effendi, from a letter dated 2 August 1946 to the National Spiritual Assembly of the Bahá'ís of India, *Dawn of A New Day*, p. 117.
5. Written on behalf of Shoghi Effendi, from a letter dated 19 November 1932 to the National Spiritual Assembly of the Bahá'ís of India. Ibid., p. 39.
6. Shoghi Effendi, from a note in his own handwriting appended to a letter written on his behalf, dated 25 May 1946 to an individual

believer, *Letters from the Guardian to Australia and New Zealand 1923–1957* (Sydney: National Spiritual Assembly of the Bahá'ís of Australia, 1970), p. 62.
7. Shoghi Effendi, from a letter dated 18 July 1953 to the National Spiritual Assembly of the Bahá'ís of the United States, *Citadel of Faith*, p. 116.
8. 'Abdu'l-Bahá, *Lights of Guidance; A Bahá'í Reference File*, comp. Helen Hornby (New Delhi: Bahá'í Publishing Trust, rev. ed. 1988), p. 321.
9. Written on behalf of Shoghi Effendi, from a letter dated 8 June 1953 to the National Spiritual Assembly of the Bahá'ís of India, *Dawn of a New Day*, p. 163.
10. Shoghi Effendi, from a letter dated 25 December 1938 'To the beloved of God and the handmaids of the Merciful throughout the United States and Canada, published as *The Advent of Divine Justice* (Wilmette, Il: Bahá'í Publishing Trust, 1984 ed), pp. 45–6.
11. Shoghi Effendi, from a letter dated 28 July 1954 to the Bahá'ís of the United States, *Citadel of Faith*, p. 131.
12. Written on behalf of Shoghi Effendi, from a letter dated 25 August 1926 to an individual believer, *Lights of Guidance*, p. 565.
13. Written on behalf of Shoghi Effendi, from a letter dated 8 April 1946 to the Bahá'í youth of India, *Dawn of a New Day*, p. 184.
14. 'Abdu'l-Bahá, *Tablets of the Divine Plan*, p. 39.
15. Written on behalf of Shoghi Effendi, from a letter dated 20 November 1955 to the National Spiritual Assembly of the Bahá'ís of the United States, *Japan Will Turn Ablaze; Tablets of 'Abdu'l-Bahá, Letters of Shoghi Effendi and Historical Notes About Japan* (Tokyo: Bahá'í Publishing Trust, 1974), pp. 71–2.
16. Written on behalf of Shoghi Effendi, from a letter dated 26 November 1953, to the local Spiritual Assembly of the Bahá'ís of Tokyo. Ibid., p. 78.

CHAPTER 5

1. 'Abdu'l-Bahá, quoted by Shoghi Effendi in a letter dated 24 October 1925 to the members of the National Spiritual Assembly of the Bahá'ís of the United States and Canada, *Bahá'í Administration; Selected Messages 1922–32* (Wilmette, Il: Bahá'í Publishing Trust, rev. ed. 1974), p. 89.

2. Bahá'u'lláh, quoted by Shoghi Effendi in a letter dated 8 February 1934, 'To the beloved of God and the handmaids of the Merciful throughout the West', published as *The Dispensation of Bahá'u'lláh* (London: Bahá'í Publishing Trust, 1981 ed.), p. 18.

CHAPTER 6

1. Bahá'ulláh, quoted in a letter from the Universal House of Justice to the Bahá'ís of the World, Riḍván 1982, *Lights of Guidance*, p. 632.
2. Shoghi Effendi, from a letter dated 23 November 1951 to the National Spiritual Assembly of the Bahá'ís of the United States, *Citadel of Faith*, p. 105.
3. Shoghi Effendi, from a cablegram dated 8 October 1952 to the Bahá'í world, *Messages to the Bahá'í World*, p. 44.
4. Beatrice Ashton, 'The Most Great Jubilee', *The Bahá'í World*, Vol. XIV, pp. 72-3.

CHAPTER 7

1. 'Abdu'l-Bahá, 'A Compilation on the Institution of the Hands of the Cause of God', p. 3. Provisional translation made by a committee in the Holy Land.

CHAPTER 9

1. 'Abdu'l-Bahá, *Bahá'í Prayers; A Selection of Prayers Revealed by Bahá'u'lláh, the Báb, and 'Abdu'l-Bahá*, (Wilmette, Il: Bahá'í Publishing Trust, 1982 ed.), p. 136.

CHAPTER 10

1. 'Abdu'l-Bahá, *Will and Testament*, p. 13.
2. 'Abdu'l-Bahá, *Bahá'í Prayers*, pp. 234–5.
3. See note 3 chapter 1, above.
4. Shoghi Effendi, from a cablegram dated 4 June 1957 to the Bahá'ís of the world, *Messages to the Bahá'í World*, p. 122.
5. 'Abdu'l-Bahá, *Will and Testament*, p. 13.
6. Shoghi Effendi, from a letter dated April 1956 to the Bahá'ís of the world, *Messages to the Bahá'í World*, pp. 101–2.

INDEX

Abbasian, Razi, 540-1
'Abdu'l-Bahá, 4, 9, 108, 256, 500, 529, 551
travels, 404, 419
writings, 169, 280, 652
quoted, 26, 135, 250-1, 336, 376, 465, 580, 626, 648, 663
Abidjan, 110, 115, 120
Accra, 106-7, 118-19
action, 212, 279, 282, 443, 459, 462, 468, 543, 605, 614
Adana, LSA, 603
Adlparvar, Heshmat, 227, 443
administration, 146-7, 154, 252, 365, 456, 556
Afghanistan, 242-4
Africa, 91-166, 247, 251
NSAs, 98, 142, 145
'Akká, 2-5
'Alá'í, Cyrus, 254
'Alá'í, Shu'á'u'lláh, 30, 79, 84, 587
Alaska, 458
Alexander, Agnes, 306-7, 336, 450, 636, 638
All Asia Women's Conference 1977, 221-2
Amata Sinanga, 53, 56, 79
Amatul-Bahá Rúḥíyyih Khánum, 64, 92, 119, 200, 221, 222, 229, 233, 363, 559, 574, 587, 603-5, 632, 635, 658
Arbáb, Farzam, 286, 548-51
Argentina, NSA, 594
Asia, 167-357
Central, 242-56
North-East, 332-57
South-East, 256-332
Astani, Dr and Mrs, 88, 299
Australasia, 359-72
Australia, 359-66
NSA, 362
& New Zealand, 25, 359
Austria, 412-14
Auxiliary Board members, 80, 102, 196, 220, 228, 261, 272, 298, 310, 316, 321, 328, 333, 345, 349, 350, 360, 364, 365, 382, 407, 437, 483, 571, 574, 579, 597
Ayman, Iraj, 251, 252
Azizi, Heshmat, 332, 354, 356

Báb, 2, 14, 256
House in Shíráz, 14, 573
martyrdom, 2, 290
writings quoted, 24, 138, 290
Bábíyyih, 248
Bahá'í Faith, laws, 183, 555
opposition to, 285-91, 569, 592
progress, 235, 285-91
Bahá'í Publishing Trusts, 116, 204, 216-17, 220, 318, 535, 563
Bahá'í radio, 478, 564-5, 573, 585
Bahá'u'lláh, 2, 3-4, 14, 31, 60, 75, 84, 89, 102, 103, 112, 137, 147, 158, 159, 160, 176, 188, 271, 272, 276, 279, 290, 319, 322, 425, 429, 433, 429, 455, 459, 470, 490, 495, 519, 543, 552, 555, 562, 611, 618, 635, 636
message, 44, 243, 250, 280, 367, 379, 420, 468, 543
World Order, 431, 449, 656
writings, 238, 280, 284, 589, 652
quoted, 96, 190, 380, 384, 425
Bahia, 511, 512, 529
International Teaching Conference 1977, 535-6, 537, 540
Bahrain, NSA, 594
Baker, Dorothy, 173
Banání, Músá, 73, 91, 92, 93, 247
Bangkok, 36, 323, 327
Bangladesh, 234-8
Bayzai, Bijan, 260, 261, 263, 265, 270
Belgium, 414
NSA, 595
Benin (Dahomey), 116
Benson, Richard, 374, 385
Berlin, 420
Berne, 445-6
Bhutan, 239
Bolivia, 236, 495, 496-510, 525-8
Boman, Shírín, 188-90, 191, 192, 223, 225, 229, 608
Bombay, 212, 214
Boroumand, Nasrin, 209
Botswana, 106, 157-60
NSA, 106
Brazil, 510-13, 528-43
Breaks, Virginia, 382, 389
Bukavu, 108-9, 114, 139, 140
Burma, 256, 258
NSA, 328, 595
Burundi, NSA, 595

Cambodia, 331
Cameroon, 131-3, 145, 148
NSA, 132
Canada, 458, 471-3
NSA, 595
Canberra, 362
Caribbean, 484-92
Caroline Islands, NSA, 386

Catania, 433
Caver, Claud, 457
Central African Republic, 99-100
Central America, 654
certitude, 290
Chamat 'Abdu'lláh, 46-9, 50, 52, 66, 70, 76
Chee, Leong Tat, 275-6, 332, 356
children, 108-9, 532
  Bahá'í, 11, 138, 371, 530, 628-9
  involved in teaching, 140, 250, 322, 370, 393, 396, 416, 474
Chile, NSA, 595
China, 240, 284, 333, 348, 357
Chinese, teaching among, 292, 332, 335, 356
Christchurch, 370
Christianity, 160, 288, 383, 427
Christians, 362, 370, 383
  teaching, 71, 129, 377-8
cities, teaching in, 169, 313-4, 353, 371, 442, 486, 542, 553, 555, 55, 561, 574, 607
Collins, Amelia, 512, 635-6
Cologne, 191, 410
Colombia, 548-54
Commonwealth countries, 118, 149
consolidation, 123, 139, 140, 155, 162, 165, 180, 182-3, 195, 202, 234, 263, 265, 318, 335, 339, 546-7, 558, 601
consultation, 147, 321, 431
Continental Boards of Counsellors, 113, 228, 229, 245, 255, 328, 536, 558, 563, 571, 574, 579, 581, 593-4
correspondence courses, 112, 204, 312, 345, 437, 444
Costas, Athos, 496, 499, 504, 505, 525, 528
Cruz, Navidad, 332
customs, traditional, 68-9, 183, 368, 555
Cyprus, 415
Czechoslovakia, 409
Czernijewski, Jan, 475-6

Daidahnaw, 256
Daloa, 120
Datu Eloy Epa, 299-300
Davachi, Dr Farzin, 153-6, 157, 413, 627, 633-4
Dawn of a New Day, 200
Dayaram, 172-3, 175, 179
dedication, 265, 392, 396, 439
deepening, 75, 142, 152, 163-4, 192, 263, 264, 268, 280, 298, 320, 339, 371, 389, 408, 418, 428, 519, 525, 528, 543, 547, 548, 558, 571
Denmark, 441-2
detachment, 152, 212, 420
devotion, 11, 279, 422
Diffuncion, 297
Dulay, Neva Gomez, 304, 305, 608
Duncan, Charles, 349
Dunn, Mother & Father, 360

Dusseldorf, 421

Ebeye, 382-3
Ecuador, 517-19, 554-71
  NSA, 595
Edinburgh, 404
Edirne, 244-5
education, 44, 517, 518
  Bahá'í, 104, 134, 138-9, 155, 163, 204-5
  of children, 68, 88-9, 108, 121, 127-8, 129, 133, 156, 165-6, 220, 270, 394, 395, 474, 477, 479, 501, 535, 552, 561, 612, 627
  of girls, 149
  of mothers, 285
  of women, 222, 285
Egypt, 288-9
enthusiasm, 249, 275, 369, 422, 424, 425, 428, 439, 444, 588
entry by troops, 171, 284, 287, 349, 364, 386, 412, 432, 433, 436, 445, 456, 459, 470, 471, 473, 559, 583
Ettehadieh, Faramarz, 150, 573, 585
Europe, 283, 287, 401-52
  Eastern, 406, 409, 412
  NSAs, 407, 422

Faizí, Abu'l-Qásim, 80, 185, 308, 327, 441, 588-90, 642, 646-7
Faizí Institute, 185-6, 224
families, teaching, 140, 147, 162, 319, 322, 468, 474, 475, 480, 537
Fatheazam, Hushmand, 169, 176, 181, 194, 592
Featherstone, Collis, 25, 84, 308, 327, 591
Ferraby, Dorothy, 414
Fiji, 381
Finland, 442
firesides, 11, 153, 202, 278, 371, 381, 399, 413, 432, 444, 465, 473, 474, 475, 476, 477, 479, 480, 493, 542, 571, 574
France, 415-18
  NSA, 597
Frankfurt temple, 402, 406
Fukuoka, 350, 351
Furudi, A. K., 178, 193
Furughi, Parviz, 316-17
Furútan, 'Alí-Akbar, 12, 24, 30, 79, 200, 308, 334, 574, 587, 638-9, 652

Germany (Federal Republic), 93, 94, 148, 401, 402, 405, 418-27
  NSA, 597
Ghana, 118, 119
Ghaznavi, Agnes, 445, 446, 447
Ghaznavi, Bijan, 447
Giachery, Ugo, 407, 439, 587
Gilbert Island, 372-3
Glasgow, 451, 452

God, 3, 64, 71, 100, 146, 154, 158, 159, 250-1, 286, 288, 289-90, 298, 368, 370, 383, 384, 431, 436, 442, 462, 498
Golmuḥammadi, Mr (pioneer to Arabia), 18-19
Gomez, Luisa Mapo, 295, 296, 304-6
Graz, 424
Greece, 427, 433
Grossmann, Herman, 419
Guam, 381-2
Guatemala, 437
Gulavisi, Rufino, 575, 584
Gwalior, 639

Ḥáfizu'lláh Khán, 1, 8-9, 13
Haifa, 191, 195, 300
Hájí-Mírzá-Haydar-'Alí-Iṣfáhaní, 2
Hands of the Cause of God, 96, 135, 200, 250-1, 265, 306, 407, 449, 465, 492, 518, 519, 603-4, 626, 635-43, 658, 663
  conclaves, 83, 91, 650
  for Africa, 91, 95
  for Asia, 80
  resident in the Holy Land, 83, 91, 95, 184, 510, 652
Haney, Paul & Marjorie, 590
Hatami, Parviz, 102
Hawaii, 385, 456-8
Helsinki, International Teaching Conference 1976, 442-3
Hokkaido, 339-40
Holy Land, 169, 218, 256, 313, 401, 656
  Bahá'í shrines, 9, 22, 24, 65, 229, 415, 451, 591, 592, 629-30, 650
Hong Kong, 168, 332-5
  International Teaching Conference 1976, 333-5
  NSA, 597
Honiara, 394-5
Hornby, Charles, 577, 581, 583
Hornby, Helen, 554-7, 564, 568, 577, 581

Iceland, 427-8
Ikot Uba, 127-8
Imám Ḥusayn, 1, 2
Imani, Fedross, 439
immigrants, teaching among, 406, 408
India, 112, 167, 168-233, 237, 238, 345, 401, 410, 436, 444, 608-9
  NSA, 51, 64, 65, 181, 194, 238
indigenous peoples, teaching among, 96, 98, 99, 100, 115, 123, 128, 133, 135, 149, 150, 160, 241, 258, 259, 260, 272, 273, 284, 285, 292, 295, 297-8, 299-300, 302-3, 319, 320, 337, 339-40, 345, 359, 360, 364-5, 367, 369, 406, 431, 465, 466, 471, 473, 476, 477, 496-509, 512, 518, 520, 525, 528, 543, 546-7, 551-2, 553, 555-7, 561, 562, 607, 608, 635
Indonesia, 22, 25, 26, 33-4, 36-89, 91, 92, 93, 167, 169, 237, 271, 272, 282, 293, 299, 359
  opposition to Faith, 84-5, 88, 237
Indore, 172, 185
International Convention, 216, 656-8
International Teaching Centre, 415, 442, 548, 591
Ioas, Leroy, 84
Iran, 1-31, 33-4, 205, 245-56, 308, 359, 413, 484, 551, 577
  persecution, 4, 11, 249, 286
  NSA, 30-1, 163, 165, 171, 200, 216, 220, 303, 332, 333, 406, 416, 597
Ireland, 428
Isfahán, 1, 4, 6, 22, 33, 286, 289
Islám, 84, 288-9
island teaching, 287, 314, 376-8, 402, 404, 408, 422, 433
Iṣmat Khánum, 8, 13-14, 144, 255-6, 448
Italy, 429-33
  NSA, 598
Ivory Coast, 120-1
Iwakura, Nabuko, 340-1, 343-4

J'afari, Maliheh, 323, 324-5, 327-8
Jakarta, 36-7, 69, 80
  Intercontinental Conference 1958, 83-5
  South-East Asian Regional Conference 1957, 79
Jamaica, NSA, 598
Jamal Effendi, 236-7
Japan, 168, 335-49, 350, 612-14
  NSA, 598
Jensen, Jimmy, 578-9

Kampala, temple dedication, 92, 93, 95
Kathmandu, 238-9, 240
Katirai, Abbas, 344-5
Kavivira, 108
Karachi, 34-6
Kbungu, 138
Kenya, 113
  NSA, 598
Kerr, Gordon, 157-60
Khádem, Zikru'lláh, 30, 308, 517, 590
Khamsí, Ma'súd, 499, 505, 506, 507, 509, 517, 518, 524, 571, 575, 580, 583
Khan, Peter, 366
Khuzain, Fuad, 103
Kisangani, 136
Kitáb-i-Aqdas, 18-19
Kivu, 109
Knights of Bahá'u'lláh, 66, 226, 254, 377
Korea, 349-54
Kuala Lumpur, 277
Kuwait, NSA, 598

Laos, 223, 258-70, 353

La Paz, 496, 506, 509-10, 570, 573
Leong, Yan Kee, 263, 272-4, 275, 276, 284, 332, 333, 356, 605-6
Lerche, Charles, 116, 118
literacy training, 15, 68, 562
literature, teaching, 104, 197, 204, 216, 219, 298, 368, 413, 443, 444, 529, 536, 542
translation, 171, 197, 217, 219, 278, 303, 407, 418, 435, 563
London, 144, 150, 256, 283, 401, 448, 630
First Bahá'í World Congress, 79, 300, 401, 449-50
funeral of Shoghi Effendi, 81
Los Angeles, 456
LSA, 602
love, 361, 364, 369
Lubumbashi, 107-8, 134
Luxemburg, 433-4

Ma'aní, Kamelia, 327
Ma'aní, Kamal, 333
Macao, 354, 356, 357
Madagascar, 113
Maddela, Felix, 293
Malaysia, 167, 237, 270-93, 605-7
NSA, 101-2, 598
Malietoa Tanumafili II, 379-80
Mandalay, 258
Manila, 140, 200, 296, 300, 301, 304, 306, 313, 318, 321
Mariana Islands, 381, 348, 386
Marseilles, 414
martyrs, 286-91, 320, 421, 442, 462, 484, 569
Marshall Islands, 384
Mas͟hhad, 249-50
mass conversion (*also* mass declaration), 100, 118, 188, 287, 291, 300, 337, 339, 363, 368, 397, 428, 512, 518, 536, 540, 543, 544, 554-7, 558, 559, 566, 571, 574, 580, 600, 656-7
mass teaching, 75, 99, 103, 106, 120-1, 143, 171-96, 202, 214, 217, 238, 260, 263, 267, 268, 270, 296, 323, 332, 353, 361, 362, 379, 390, 402, 419, 425, 429, 433, 436, 443, 445, 452, 455, 468, 475, 476, 477, 479, 480, 483, 486, 495, 525, 529, 530, 532, 534, 536, 540, 542, 543, 546, 549, 551, 553, 557, 571, 597, 608, 639
materialism, 154, 255, 405
Mazloom, Ferydoon, 429
McCants, Jack, 376-8
McCants, Toni Mantel, 311-12
Mentawai Islands, 25, 27, 30, 39, 40-80, 81, 83, 85, 87-8, 89, 91, 96, 169, 173, 180, 269, 272, 295, 359, 378, 395, 450, 555, 644
Mexico, 459, 465
Mindanao, 316-17
minority groups, teaching, 118-19, 402, 405, 406, 408, 409, 458, 476, 477, 478, 480, 512, 558-9
Mírzá 'Abdu'lláh, 2, 4
Mírzá Assadu'lláh Vazír, 7
Mírzá Fatḥu'lláh, 1, 2, 8, 9, 466
Missaghian, Firaydún, 259, 260-1, 265, 267-8, 353-4, 662
missionaries, 62, 69-72, 504, 556-7
Monrovia, Continental Conference 1971, 100, 154
movement, 103, 279, 280-1, 287, 397, 437, 443
Muarasiberut, 43, 92, 93
Mughrabi, Jan, 99
Muhájir, Gisu, 150, 191, 200, 202, 208, 242-3, 258, 283, 300, 303, 307, 325, 335, 340, 344, 401, 410, 449, 451, 452, 473, 483, 484, 568, 573, 574-5, 584, 589-90, 629-30, 632, 634, 635-6, 652
Muhájir, Írán Furútan, 40, 93-4, 184, 195, 200, 202, 204, 205, 216, 240-1, 267, 300, 303, 307, 309, 362-3, 410, 444, 449, 451, 473, 483, 484, 568, 573, 574-5, 576, 584, 632, 635, 647-8, 652
accompanies Raḥmat on travels, 240-1, 242-3, 244-5, 271, 316, 335, 333, 343, 436
experiences in Mentawai Islands, 45, 48-55, 58-60, 61, 70-3, 74-9
health, 21, 22, 50-1, 58-9, 378, 401, 630
Knight of Bahá'u'lláh, 51, 91
marriage, 19-21
praised by Shoghi Effendi, 65, 74
Muhájir, Raḥmatu'lláh, ancestry, 1-9
before appointment as Hand of Cause:
childhood, 11-13, 410
Director of Summer School, 19
intention to pioneer to Arabia, 21, 22
Knight of Bahá'u'lláh, 51, 91, 583, 616
meets Shoghi Effendi, 22-3, 435
National Pioneering Committee, 17-19
National Youth Committee, 245
pilgrimage, 22-4, 29, 435, 617
Regional Spiritual Assembly, South-East Asia, 79-80
student years, 15, 16
teenage, 13
works in Iṣfahán, 22
chanting, 64, 83, 103, 136, 138, 153, 244, 344, 382, 446, 447, 589
diary extracts, 95, 107, 110, 112-15, 118-19, 120, 121, 123-9, 131, 132-4, 134-6, 137-9, 142-4, 148, 149-50, 173-4, 178-9, 180, 187, 188, 191-2, 217, 218-21, 224, 225, 241, 242, 256, 258, 270, 272, 274-5, 295-6, 318, 328, 335, 336, 337, 346, 352-3, 354, 356, 372-3, 380, 381, 386-9, 389-91, 391-3, 394-6, 402-4, 405-6 407-10, 409, 410, 412-13, 415, 418-21, 421-22, 424-5, 426-7, 428, 435, 436-7,

440-2, 444-5, 448-9, 450-1, 474-5, 476-80, 483, 486-7, 490-91, 496-507, 507-13, 516-21, 524, 530-5, 541-2, 574
example, 590, 592-3, 597, 598, 600, 606, 611, 614
funeral, 583-4, 602
Hand of the Cause of God, 13, 24, 85, 245
appointment, 80, 91, 583, 616
health, 50-1, 66, 151, 189, 229, 237, 282, 372-3, 378, 389, 413, 443, 483-4, 516, 541, 571, 626
interviews, press, 361, 367, 370, 433, 533, 534
radio, 96, 131, 361, 362, 367, 370, 382, 391, 433, 490, 533
television, 96, 110, 118, 361, 378, 382, 485, 533, 534, 577, 578
meets Heads of State, 96
memorials & projects in his name, 165-6, 303, 357, 366
moves to Boston, 452, 473
to London, 144, 217, 401, 410, 450
passing, 417, 574, 581, 604, 617
pioneering, 85, 583
Kalár Dasht, Mázindarán, 13
Manila, Philippines, 140, 167, 195, 300
Mentawai Islands, 25, 29-31, 33, 39-86
New Delhi, India, 202, 313
Pacitan, Indonesia, 85-6
Rezaíyih, Ádhirbayján, 15-16, 448
praised by Shoghi Effendi, 64, 65, 73
qualities, adaptable, 434
calm, 253
charismatic, 611, 662
challenging, 473
compassionate, 306
confident, 34
concentrated, 132
conscientious, 245
courageous, 597, 614
courteous, 322
creative, 583, 597
dedicated, 587, 590, 600, 614
detached, 587, 588, 600
determined, 26, 157, 161, 598, 600
devoted, 590, 597, 601, 603, 611
direct, 446
down to earth, 263
dynamic, 418, 446, 597, 611
encouraging, 465, 471, 486, 595, 597, 598, 599, 603, 606
energetic, 132, 445, 583, 591, 603
enthusiastic, 13, 181, 370, 434, 484, 583, 598, 607,
faith in Bahá'u'lláh, 16, 34, 100, 108, 161, 244, 322, 341, 343, 356, 396, 551, 593, 607, 626
flexible, 174, 302, 537
forceful, 613
forgiving, 660
frugal, 165, 554, 632-3
gallant, 587
generous, 230, 634-5
gentle, 131, 163, 583, 599, 607
humble, 13, 24, 235, 251, 253, 292, 366, 554, 600, 605, 613, 646
informal, 263, 366
ingenious, 537
inspirational, 272, 429, 439, 452, 471, 473, 549, 592, 594, 597, 598, 602, 611
intuitive, 75
kind, 131, 292, 484, 644-5, 595, 613
knowledgeable, 160, 245, 600
lack of prejudice, 446-7
logical, 16
love, 181, 446, 605, 606, 607
for children, 370, 476, 627
for his family, 283, 325, 344, 378, 483, 568, 627-32
for indigenous peoples, 44, 56, 75, 96, 108-9, 155, 160, 235-6, 242, 302, 364, 466, 524
patient, 109, 163, 537, 605
perceptive, 399
persevering, 587, 614
persistent, 537
positive, 292-3, 382, 434
powerful, 263, 593
practical, 322, 399
prayerful, 24, 156, 273, 389, 446, 448
pure, 588, 594
radiant, 592, 598, 600
receptive, 293
relaxed, 343, 369
self-sacrificing, 267, 283, 325, 597, 598, 601, 602
sense of humour, 81, 83, 164, 465, 645-7
sense of urgency, 157, 225, 446, 484, 569, 600, 622
submissive to will of God, 21-2, 84, 94, 119, 134, 151, 174, 224, 270, 313, 320, 356, 370, 391, 447, 479, 650
tactful, 607
tranquil, 34
unpretentious, 369
vibrant, 611
visionary, 418, 429, 433, 452, 484, 593, 607
wise, 595, 600, 605
zealous, 583, 595
service at World Centre, 652
skills as physician, 58-61, 71-2, 79, 86-7, 447, 618, 644
talks, extracts from, 100, 146, 147, 214-6, 279, 280-1, 285-91, 383-4, 429, 431-2, 462, 468, 469, 656-7

tributes to, 418, 583-614
Muḥammad Hashím Kisih-Porkon, 9
Muhlschlegel, Adelbert, 445
Mullá Muḥammad, 1-2, 6
Mullá Muḥammad Baqír, 6
Munje, Mohan & Tuba, 238-40
Muslims, 288-9, 317, 555, 556
Muta'midu'd-Dawlih, 289-90

Nabíl's Narrative, 14, 147, 407, 418
Nadarajan, Silan, 101-2
Na'ím (Bahá'í poet), 243, 244
Nairobi, International Teaching Conference 1976, 123, 145
Nakhjavání, 'Alí & Violette, 592
Nasik, 178-9
Náṣiri'd-Dín Sháh, 284, 290, 384
Navidi, Aziz, 100
Nelson, James, 609, 611
Nepal, 238-42
Netherlands, 61, 435-6
New Delhi, 169, 191, 194, 195, 205, 216, 221, 229, 630
Intercontinental Conferences, 24, 27, 30, 200-1, 248, 268
temple, 222, 229-30
dedication, 230-3, 603
New Garden, 116, 147, 194, 363, 393
Newport, Behin, 107
New Zealand, 366-72
Niamey, 123-4
Nigeria, 116, 124-31, 152-4
Nineteen Day Feast, 157, 371, 396, 468
Norway, 440
Nounou, Salim, 614

Occidental Mindoro, 302, 437
Oldenburg, 421
Olinga, Enoch, 91, 114, 131, 150, 308, 367, 476, 519, 537, 549, 579, 590, 601, 603, 604, 635, 642-3
Olsen, Cynthia, 399
Olyai family, 192-3

Pacific region, 372-99
Pacitan, 85-6, 91, 92
Padang, 40, 81, 88-9
Pakistan, 167, 233-4
Palermo Conference 1968, 401
Panama temple, dedication, 553
Panchgani, New Era School, 233
Papua New Guinea, 381
NSA, 599
Paris, International Conference 1976, 154, 416
Parnian, Shahnaz, 205, 206-8
Pavlowska, Ola, 108-9, 136-7, 156-7, 612
Pavon, Raul, 204, 518, 528, 566, 571, 580
Payman, Khodarahm, 25-6, 36, 37-40, 73, 84, 92, 299, 321
Payman, Rustam, 73
Peru, 516-17
Philippines, 162, 167-8, 237, 293-323, 608
NSA, 599
pioneers (*see also* youth), 17-19, 26-7, 33, 102-3, 104, 106, 129, 133, 142, 220, 247, 270, 282, 296, 299, 302, 320, 323, 332, 336, 340, 348, 349, 384-5, 409, 415, 416, 433, 449, 450, 456, 459, 462, 470, 471, 497, 498, 510, 517, 519, 524, 528, 533, 535, 543, 546, 552, 554, 559, 566, 569, 579-80, 605
Raḥmat advises, 26, 33, 134, 151, 154, 236, 436, 555-6
appeals for, 101, 247, 254, 256, 259, 278, 281, 321, 443, 613
encourages individuals to pioneer, 208, 211, 238-9, 259, 296, 354
supports, 18, 104, 106, 140, 156, 241, 252-5, 259, 268, 321, 606
Plans, 371, 433
Five Year (1974-79), 106, 112, 140, 151, 211, 221, 230, 235, 248, 251, 282, 283, 292, 319, 364, 370, 372, 380, 381, 414, 416, 418, 434, 435, 467, 568, 597
Iranian 45-month (1946-50), 13, 18
Nine Year (1964-73), 101, 154, 196, 216, 260, 277, 278, 299, 304, 316, 318, 345, 357, 401, 412, 418, 419, 42, 436, 445, 452, 471, 557, 559
Seven Year (1979-86), 228-9, 478, 479, 484, 486
Ten Year Crusade (1953-63), 22-3, 24, 27, 29, 39, 66, 73, 91, 171, 188, 196, 218, 272, 291, 299, 345, 359, 449, 450, 496, 498, 546, 617, 639, 652
Pohnpei, 376-8
Port Dickson, 285
Portugal, 436-9
prayer, 37, 104, 279, 370, 371, 377, 397, 436, 437, 441, 446, 459, 468, 490
prisons, teaching in, 304, 305-7, 437
proclamation, 84, 85, 118, 201-2, 277-8, 286, 287, 312, 368, 386, 414, 434, 439, 470, 574
public meetings, 84, 106, 113, 133, 156, 336, 378, 381, 382, 386, 391, 392, 394, 396, 413, 418, 427, 436, 439, 442, 490
Punjab, 208

Quddus, 248
Quirino, 320
Qulám Ḥusayn, 9

Rabbani School, 192-3, 224
refugees, teaching among, 268-70, 323, 356
Réunion, 112-13
Revell, Jessie, 366

Rezvani, Habib, 444-5, 551
Robarts, John, 91, 93, 95, 308, 591
Root, Martha, 293, 456
Rawhani, Enayat, 611-12
Rowhani, Mehri, 6
Rubenstein, Janet, 467
Ruhe, David & Margaret, 593

Sabour, Mr (Secretary, NSA Bangladesh), 235, 237-8
sacrifice, 26, 27, 124, 265, 279, 371, 432, 592, 599, 613
Sadeghi, Parviz, 316-17
Sadru'lláh, 175
Sahba, Fariburz, 229, 230
Saigon, 328, 331
Sakhalin, 345
Samandarí, Ṭarázu'lláh, 84, 89, 265, 306, 307-8, 356, 636, 637, 659
Samaniego, Vicente, 296, 297, 298-9, 300, 301, 308, 311, 314, 319, 320, 321, 328, 335, 357
Samaniego, Fe, 314
Samgimanda, 173, 176-7, 188
Samoa, 379-80, 394
  NSA, 599
Sapporo, 339
  Oceanic Conference 1971, 346
  World Fair, 202
Sears, William, 91, 363, 590
Scandinavia, 425, 440-3
Scotland, 451
Selebi-Pikwe, 106
Semple, Ian & Louise, 592
Seventh Day Adventists, 376
Sháh 'Abdu'l-'Aẓím, 8, 11
Shahjahanpur, 173
Shamshirpur, 178
Sháh, Ramnik, 185, 191, 222, 229, 233
Shetland Islands, 452
Shoghi Effendi, 9, 17, 19, 21, 25, 26, 34, 43, 51, 69, 79, 91, 135, 136, 142, 147, 149, 154, 167, 168, 169, 173, 174, 182, 250, 274, 286, 287, 288, 290, 293, 339, 345, 348, 349, 359, 390, 405, 406, 419, 429, 431, 432, 433, 442, 496, 498, 500, 510, 554, 564, 591, 594, 602, 604, 614, 617, 657, 662
  communications to Raḥmat, 21, 64-5, 74, 80, 618
  passing, 81-3, 169, 235-6, 448, 449, 639
    effect on Raḥmat, 81-2
  messages to Africa, 95, 181, 337
    America, 255
    India, 197-8
    Japan, 337, 346
    South America, 516
  Resting Place, 217, 410, 424, 448, 451, 452, 646-7, 649
  travels in Africa, 95, 115, 133, 135, 136
  writings quoted, 27, 66, 73, 95, 161, 169, 178, 180-1, 187, 197, 252, 253, 255, 280, 308, 336, 337, 449, 495, 652, 663
Shoghipur, 174-5
Shuen, Yin Hong, 292
Siberut Selatan, 43, 80, 87, 88
Sikkim, 225-6, 241-2
Sims, Barbara, 612-13
sincerity, 279, 288, 384
Singapore, 271, 283
  Intercontinental Conference 1958, 85
  NSA, 599-600
Si Pai Pajet, 53, 56, 59, 68, 71, 76
Si Temeh, 49-50
Síyah-Chál, 14, 290
Siyyid Muṣṭafa Rúmí, 236-7, 256
Solomon Islands, 394-5
  NSA, 600
South Africa, 110, 112
South America, 304, 495-571
Spain, 443-5
spirituality, 156, 256, 369, 383-4, 392, 393, 395, 421, 428, 435, 520
Sri Lanka (Ceylon), 167
steadfastness, 27, 271, 425
Stockholm, 404
Stuttgart, 404
Subḥaní, Javánshír, 348
Sudan, 227
Suleimani, Mr & Mrs, 356
Sumatra, 39-40, 43
  Governor, 42, 76, 81
Sundram, Chellie, 606
Sundram, Shanta, 272, 606-7
Suva, Oceanic Conference, 369
Swaziland, 101, 110
  NSA, 600
Sweden, 404
Switzerland, 406, 425, 445-8
Sydney, 360-1
  temple, 363

Ta'eed family, 258, 259
Taiwan, 354, 356-7
Tanzania, 113, 208
  NSA, 600
Tasmania, 360, 361
teaching conferences, 140, 145, 146, 161, 186-7, 188, 228, 271, 280, 281, 301, 311, 314, 315, 318, 335, 365, 366, 409, 424, 425, 429, 437, 439, 443, 462, 496
teaching institutes, 75, 99, 107, 110, 112, 124, 127, 129, 131, 133, 163, 166, 194-5, 202, 220, 233, 303, 322, 391, 394, 421, 558, 577, 579
Te Paa, Eprem, 367
Teherani, Mr (pioneer in Sapporo), 339

tests, 288, 290, 291, 292, 328, 525, 526, 648
Thailand, 323-8
Thousand Oaks, LSA, 603
Tibet, 268
Tihrán, 8, 9, 11, 13, 15, 16, 29, 30, 31, 33, 34, 102, 144, 205, 230, 249, 255
Titikatene, Sir Eurura, 367
Togo, 116-18, 121, 123, 150
Tonga, 391, 396-7
Townshend, George, 428
travel teachers (*see also* youth), 115, 116, 201, 211, 220, 235, 238, 279, 281-2, 310, 321, 335, 336, 348, 356, 357, 390, 393, 402, 405, 406, 414, 439, 422, 442, 444, 471, 480, 490, 535, 548, 565, 613
tribes (*see* indigenous peoples)
Trinidad & Tobago, NSA, 601
Turkey, 244-5, 405, 406
  NSA, 601

Uganda, 92-4, 184
  NSA, 601
United Kingdom, 118, 291, 401, 448-52
  NSA, 601
United Nations, 251, 406, 412, 656
United States, 455-71, 473-84
  NSA, 601
unity, 156, 162, 275, 280, 321, 361, 368-9, 397, 428, 437, 479, 490, 549, 552, 577
Universal House of Justice, 98, 99, 121, 132, 145, 196, 264, 270, 282, 283, 284, 287, 293, 296, 303, 310, 311, 315, 316, 317, 318, 334, 345, 364, 365, 383, 401, 412, 415, 418, 419, 420, 429-31, 445, 449, 452, 457, 467, 479, 529, 563, 564, 566, 574, 583, 585, 602, 606, 615, 617, 650, 652
  approves Raḥmat's proposals, 88, 113, 218, 260, 319, 332, 353, 396, 444
  messages to Raḥmat, 144, 256, 486, 534-5, 623
  Raḥmat consults, 101, 200, 205, 415
  Raḥmat represents, 96, 100, 154, 265, 301, 312, 331
  Raḥmat travels on instruction of, 101, 221, 247, 268, 361, 381, 401, 413, 440, 554, 659
  Raḥmat writes to, 116, 129, 134, 135, 145, 146, 148, 163, 165, 233, 241, 248, 283, 284, 334, 335, 348, 349, 369, 384-5, 394, 396, 422, 428, 444, 470, 618-19, 620-1, 643, 653, 654
  Seat, 230, 365, 373, 386, 431, 471
universities, teaching in, 96, 100, 109, 115, 133, 149, 207, 221, 313, 348, 408, 421, 445, 475, 480, 533-4, 535, 536, 541, 553, 561
USSR, 409

Vajdi, Ṭáhirih, 190-1, 192-3
Varney, John, 433
Varqá, 'Alí-Muḥammad, 251
Varqá, Valí'u'lláh, 30
Vasudevan Mr (member, NSA India), 609
Victory, Parviz, 339, 340
Vietnam, 237, 328, 331
villages, teaching in, 76, 92-3, 96, 103, 108, 127, 145, 147, 149, 155, 156, 157-8, 162, 163, 169, 171-87, 203, 209-11, 212, 218, 219, 222, 224, 235, 237, 269-70, 272, 273, 275, 323, 327, 334-5, 352, 368-9, 390, 395, 427, 436, 496-509, 517-18, 557, 566, 607
Vujdani, Faramarz, 316-17

White, Trudy, 466
Wilmette, temple, 468, 609
women, 214, 221, 322, 349, 479, 480, 542
Wurmfeld, Yael, 484

Yazd, LSA, 30, 602
Yeganegi, Mr (pioneer to India), 222-3
youth, 214, 271, 279, 280, 364, 391, 395, 396, 404, 422, 424, 428, 432, 433, 435, 442, 445, 479, 483, 490, 530, 536, 547, 614
  conferences, 123, 214-6, 225, 280, 316, 363, 404, 405, 406, 407, 409, 413, 416, 425, 440
  enrolment, 104, 397
  pioneers, 145, 149, 205, 235, 250, 271, 273, 308-10, 316-17, 320, 385, 424, 537, 540, 543, 558
  travel teachers 104, 107, 115, 116, 123, 216, 332, 370, 424, 427, 446
  year of service, 15

Zaire, 109, 114-15, 136-7, 144, 154-6, 633-4
Zambalo, Marzio & Vivien, 432-3